Africans and the Industrial Revolution in England

Drawing on classical development theory and recent theoretical advances on the connection between expanding markets and technological develop- ment, this book shows the critical role of expanding Atlantic commerce in the successful completion of England's industrialization process over the period 1650–1850. The contribution of Africans, the central focus of the book, is measured in terms of the role of diasporic Africans in large-scale commodity production in the Americas – of which expanding Atlantic com- merce was a function – at a time when demographic and other socio- economic conditions in the Atlantic basin encouraged small-scale produc- tion by independent populations, largely for subsistence. This is the first detailed study of the role of overseas trade in the Industrial Revolution. It revises inward-looking explanations that have dominated the field in recent decades and shifts the assessment of African contribution away from the debate on profits.

Joseph E. Inikori is Professor of History at the University of Rochester. He was educated in Nigeria and England, and he was formerly Chairman of the History Department at Ahmadu Bello University in Zaria, Nigeria. Professor Inikori's previous books include *Forced Migration* (1982), *The Chaining of a Continent* (1992), and *The Atlantic Slave Trade* (with Stanley Engerman, 1992).

Africans and the Industrial Revolution in England

A Study in International Trade and Economic Development

JOSEPH E. INIKORI
University of Rochester

CAMBRIDGE
UNIVERSITY PRESS

PUBLISHED BY THE PRESS SYNDICATE OF THE UNIVERSITY OF CAMBRIDGE
The Pitt Building, Trumpington Street, Cambridge, United Kingdom

CAMBRIDGE UNIVERSITY PRESS
The Edinburgh Building, Cambridge CB2 2RU, UK
40 West 20th Street, New York, NY 10011-4211, USA
477 Williamstown Road, Port Melbourne, VIC 3207, Australia
Ruiz de Alarcón 13, 28014 Madrid, Spain
Dock House, The Waterfront, Cape Town 8001, South Africa

http://www.cambridge.org

First published 2002

Typeface Sabon 10/12 pt.   *System* QuarkXPress [BTS]

A catalog record for this book is available from the British Library.

Library of Congress Cataloging in Publication data
Inikori, J. E.
Africans and the industrial revolution in England / Joseph E. Inikori.
p. cm.
Includes bibliographical references.
ISBN 0-521-81193-7 – ISBN 0-521-01079-9 (pb.)
1. International trade – History.   2. Industrial revolution – England – History.
3. Slave-trade – Africa – History.   4. Slavery – Economic aspects – England – History.
5. Slavery – Economic aspects – America – History.   6. England – Commerce –
America – History.   7. America – Commerce – England – History.   I. Title.
HF 1379 .I535   2002
382'.44'096–dc21   2001037927

ISBN   0 521 81193 7   hardback
ISBN   0 521 01079 9   paperback

Transferred to digital printing 2004

To the memory of my parents, Adjerharha and Omovie Inikori,
my parents-in-law, Johnny and Elizabeth Adoh,
and my sister-in-law, Mrs. Caroline Enebeli

Contents

Tables

x

Preface

This book is first and foremost about the role of international trade in the process of economic development over the very long run. There have been only two distinct models of successful industrialization processes in the history of the world – a private enterprise, market-based model and a state enterprise, command-based model. England's industrialization was the first of the former model, while the Soviet Union was the first of the latter. The command model entails considerable pains and sacrifices, precisely because structural and technological changes are forced by the state, changes that international trade helps to bring about with less pain. The import of the arguments in this study is that the market-based model of industrialization cannot be successfully completed without an intensive involvement in international trade, particularly for a small country like England. This has been the bitter lesson learned rather late by the countries of the non-Western World, which embarked on industrialization after World War II.

It is argued in this book that the lessons of England's industrialization have been made inaccessible to policy makers because the role of international trade has been discounted in the more recent studies of the Industrial Revolution. Despite the very large volume of literature on the subject, it is hard to understand that this book is the first lengthy study of the role of international trade in the industrialization process in England. That literature, particularly post–World War II scholarship, is dominated overwhelmingly by what may be described as inward-looking explanations. England's industrialization is presented as something so unique that current industrializing nations have nothing to learn from it. One of the objectives of this study is to show that, in fact, England's industrialization process shares important common elements with the ones that have occurred in the non-Western World since World War II: Several centuries of population growth and agricultural production for international trade were the critical factors behind the commercialization of socio-economic life in England from Domesday to the mid-seventeenth century, as it was in several countries of the non-Western World; between 1650 and 1750, the growth of agricultural production for export and entrepôt trade in foreign produce and manufactures helped to create the necessary conditions for industrialization based on import substitution and re-export replacement, similar to the process in many countries in the non-Western World since World War II. The *longue durée* narrative in Chapter 2 is intended partly to provide the needed information for this kind of comparison. It is argued in the study that the successful completion of the industrialization process in England and the failed processes of about the same period in Holland, Italy, and the Yangzi Delta in China, as well as the successful and failed processes of the post–World War II period, can be largely explained in terms of the extent to which they had the opportunity to produce manufactures for export.

The book focuses on the contribution of Africans to the successful completion of the industrialization process in England from the mid-seventeenth to the mid-nineteenth century. The category, Africans, covers continental Africans and diasporic Africans in the Americas. The notion of the Industrial Revolution employed in the study describes the character of the socio-economic changes in England that resulted from the successful completion of the industrialization process; it does not describe how these changes came about nor does it describe how long it took to effect them. The point simply is that these changes were so fundamental and so novel, never before seen anywhere in the world, that they can be described validly as revolutionary. Because they were brought about by developments in industrial production no term can better describe these revolutionary changes than the one popularized over the years – the Industrial Revolution.

Understood this way, what has been studied is the long drawn out process of industrialization in England, with emphasis on the period 1650–1850. We find the idea of a sudden take-off in 1780 or thereabout unhelpful. It is held that the process was not successfully completed before the mid-nineteenth century, when the mechanization of the leading industry, cotton textile, was completed, and the process of transmitting the forces of change from the leading regions to the rest, through the railways, was fully underway. The role of Africans is examined in the study in terms of their contribution to the successful completion of this long drawn out process. The phrase, successful completion, must be stressed. It leaves room for a consideration of the contribution of other factors to the process; it implies analysis involving several factors, without any one of which the outcome in question would not have been produced. The study is clearly conscious of the Chinese proverb that one cannot make a stone lay an egg. Domestic factors have to interact with the forces released by international trade to produce a successful industrialization process based on the private enterprise, market-oriented model. As far as space and coherence permit, this interaction has been noted in the analysis, more so in Chapters 2 and 3. For more details concerning the domestic factors, readers must consult the voluminous literature on that subject. The analytical task in this study is to show that without the critical contribution of international trade the process would not have been successfully completed at the time it was. This is a significant corrective to the closed economy model that has dominated the literature for decades. It is also a significant corrective to the policy choices made by post-war industrializing nations. The assessment of the role of Africans is based, therefore, on their contribution to the growth of England's international trade.

The argument is coherently linked together by a simple structure. The indispensable role of international trade is demonstrated at several levels, in the first instance. Then, step-by-step, the analysis is conducted to show the contribution of Africans to the growth of England's international trade, on which the development of a given element in the equation depended largely. The growth of England's international trade in 1650–1850 is shown as a function of the growth of Atlantic commerce that linked together the main regions of the Atlantic basin. In turn, the growth of Atlantic commerce during the period is explained in terms of the employment of Africans as forced, specialized producers of commodities for Atlantic commerce at a time when the prevailing conditions encouraged small-scale subsistence production by legally free producers.

The main analysis in the study is conducted at three levels. The first is a comparative analysis at the regional level within England. The objective of this analysis is to show the long-run course of development followed by the main regions in England – the southern counties (especially East Anglia and the West Country), the Midlands (especially the West Midlands), and the northern counties (especially Lancashire and the West Riding of Yorkshire) – and to identify the factors that account for the changing relative levels of development over time. This comparative regional analysis of the development process in England from Domesday to the mid-nineteenth century, mostly elaborated in Chapter 2, is an important distiguishing feature of this study. It helps to clarify issues that traditional national analysis cannot accomplish easily and effectively. As shown in the chapters that follow, this is particularly so in matters concerning the role of population, agriculture, and social structures in the successful completion of England's industrialization. The second level of the analysis involves those sectors, including manufacturing and non-manufacturing (shipping and finance), whose development was crucial, directly or indirectly, to the successful completion of the process – the contribution of Africans, through international trade, to the development of these sectors is demonstrated, and, at appropriate points, the sectoral and regional analyses are linked. Finally, the third level is a broad international comparative analysis across time – a broad comparison of England, Italy, Holland, and the Yangzi Delta in China before 1850 and a broad comparison of England's industrialization process and those of the non-Western World since World War II.

The development and diffusion of new technologies is regarded in the study as the critical element in the successful completion of England's industrialization process. The ultimate thrust of the argument in the book is, therefore, to demonstrate the contribution of Africans, through international trade, to the development and diffusion of these technologies. It is argued that the growth of England's international trade interacted with domestic factors – in particular, population growth – to produce rapidly growing mass demand, which created opportunities and pressures that stimulated the development and diffusion of the new technologies. The comparative regional analysis is employed to show the superiority of this trade-based explanation to the supply-side analysis, which dominated the literature for several decades.

The manner in which the central thesis of the study is worked out in the main chapters of the book may be briefly stated. The introductory chapter spells out the problem on which the book is focused and presents a conceptual discussion that informs the arguments developed in subsequent chapters. Chapter 2 provides a descriptive narrative of the development trajectory of the English economy over a very long time period (the *longue durée*). The narrative is deliberately constructed to show the comparative course of development followed by the main regions and the import substitution character of the industrialization process.[1] Both features of the narrative provide critical foundations for comprehending the arguments in subsequent chapters. The historiographical discussion in Chapter 3 attempts to show that the application of inappropriate economic theory is responsible largely for interpretations of the Industrial Revolution that marginalize the role of international trade. Particularly important in this regard is the theoretical treatment of how technology developed historically. Classical economists, especially Adam Smith, conceived technological development as a function of market expansion. Mainstream growth theorists, writing between the 1950s and 1970s, treated technological development as exogenous: something that happened outside the market, outside the economy, and then came to revolutionize the economic process. The failure of this theory to deal satisfactorily with the observed facts of post-war development led to the formulation of a new growth theory from the mid-1980s – the endogenous theory of technological development, which, like Adam Smith's theory, places emphasis on market growth and size. The chapter presents a critical discussion of the literature on the Industrial Revolution in the context of these changing theoretical

---

[1] The concept of import substitution industrialization (ISI) is explained in detail in the introductory chapter.

perspectives, showing the circumstances that occasioned the changes and how they affected interpretations of the Industrial Revolution. Some readers may question why the descriptive narrative in Chapter 2 precedes the literature review in Chapter 3. There are two reasons for this. First, I believe it will help readers who are not specialists in English economic history to have the narrative in Chapter 2 before being confronted with the critical literature review in Chapter 3. Second, the regional and import substitution narrative in Chapter 2 helps to develop the arguments in Chapter 3 more effectively.

Chapter 4 is central to the main thesis of the book. It puts together quantitative evidence with which the magnitude of commodity production for Atlantic commerce in the Americas and the percentage contribution of enslaved Africans and their descendants are measured precisely. The overall annual value of Atlantic commerce from 1501 to 1850, computed in period averages, is also measured precisely. Both computations provide the evidence needed to support the main arguments of the book. Chapters 5 to 9 are based largely on my own archival research. In these chapters, the contribution of continental and diasporic Africans to England's industrialization is assessed, sector by sector, on the basis of evidence from archival research. However, the assessment in these chapters cannot be understood properly without the evidence and analyses presented in the preceding ones. The import of the evidence and arguments in all the chapters is pulled together in Chapter 10, on the basis of which a final pronouncement is made regarding the thesis of the study.

This book covers considerable ground. I am under no illusion that all the issues treated have been resolved conclusively. It is probable that several of the bold statements made in the book are supported inadequately by evidence. Wherever this is the case, I hope the issues raised are sufficiently important to provoke further research that will produce more evidence with which to offer more accurate conclusions. One area in which I particularly invite more work is the computation of the overall annual value of Atlantic commerce from 1501 to 1850. I have made considerable effort to minimize error either way. But, given the nature of the evidence currently available, modification and refinement are to be expected in the years to come. In addition, I have tried hard to treat the literature on the subject comprehensively. I may not have been entirely successful on this, owing to the problem of space and coherence, as well as to limitations of my own knowledge. Need I say no disrespect for any author and his or her arguments is intended in case of omission.

The book incorporates a large proportion of the research and teaching I have done since the late 1960s. It is, therefore, understandable that I owe much debt to people too many to enumerate. My first gratitude must go to Professor Ade Ajayi of the University of Ibadan, who, among other things, encouraged me to move into foreign history at a time when most Nigerian

graduate students concentrated on Nigerian history. The archival research
for the book was all done in England. In the early years the contribution
of the late Arthur H. John of the London School of Economics was invaluable. He generously made available to me his knowledge of the archival
sources, and his letters of introduction were important in accessing records
in private hands, contacts which have remained invaluable since then. Since
we met at Oxford University in 1974, Stanley Engerman has been a very
helpful friend. I benefited from his vast knowledge of the literature, and he
read the entire first draft and provided encouraging comments. The readers
for Cambridge University Press offered the most critical but constructive
review I have ever come across. I thank them and want them to know I
learned much from their comments. I also thank Frank Smith, the execu-
tive editor, for his encouragement. The intellectual support and encouragement I received from friends and colleagues over the years were important
in sustaining the level of interest and energy that went into the research and
writing of the book. Among these I can only mention a few: William Darity,
Jr., Ronald Bailey, Ronald Findlay, Max Hartwell, Seymour Drescher,
Joseph Harris, Karen Fields, the late John Henrik Clarke, Selwyn Carrington, and Colin Palmer. To all these and those I have not mentioned I express
my gratitude. The wide range of sources consulted for the book would have
been impossible to access without the cooperation and help I received from
archivists and staff of private and public institutions across England: the
Public Record Office; British Library; House of Lords Record Office;
Midland Bank record office in London; Lloyd's corporation archives in
London; Liverpool Record Office; Birmingham Reference Library; Barclays
Bank, Heywoods Branch, in Liverpool; Bristol City Archives; University of
Keele Library; National Maritime Museum, Greenwich, London; Lan-
cashire Record Office, Preston; and others. To all of them I express my
appreciation.

The funding for the research and writing came, at different stages, from
the University of Ibadan, Ahmadu Bello University, the British Commonwealth, UNESCO, and the University of Rochester. In particular, the University of Rochester granted two semesters paid leave to allow me time for
the writing.

Ultimately, this book is the product of the collective contribution, in different ways, of every member of my large family: my parents and my
parents-in-law, my wife, Beatrice, and my four children, Josephine, Faith,
Beatus, and Jonah. This book would not have been written without their
love, sacrifice, caring, and understanding. For the past several years my
daughter, Faith, never stopped asking how the book was going. This was
a considerable source of energy. My son, Jonah, handled all the technical
tasks of word processing, particularly the program for compiling the bibliography in alphabetical order. I thank them all and, above all, I thank God
for blessing me with a good and loving family.

Although I have benefited immensely from all the help and advice that I received, I have often been stubborn and held on to my view of the correct thing to say. It is, therefore, fair to say that I am entirely responsible for any shortcoming there may be in the book.

Joseph E. Inikori
Rochester, New York
August 2000

1

Introduction

1.1 THE PROBLEM

IN THE LATE 1930S AND EARLY 1940S the contribution of African people to the economic development of parts of Western Europe featured in the work of four scholars of African descent in the Americas. In a book published in 1938, C. L. R. James made some brief remarks on the link between French industrial progress in the eighteenth century and the French American colony of Saint Domingo, modern Haiti:

In 1789 the French West Indian colony of San Domingo supplied two-thirds of the overseas trade of France and was the greatest individual market for the European slave-trade. It was an integral part of the economic life of the age, the greatest colony of the world, the pride of France, and the envy of every other imperialist nation. The whole structure rested on the labour of half-a-million [African] slaves.[1]

He asserted that virtually all the industries that developed in France in the eighteenth century originated from the production of manufactures for the slave trade in Western Africa or for export to the French American colonies: "The capital from the slave trade fertilized them . . ."[2]

Limited to a few pages, James did not pursue the subject in any detail. That was not the objective of his study. His book was intended to demonstrate that enslaved Africans in the Americas did not accept slavery passively. Confronted with all the instruments of physical and psychological violence at the disposal of the slaveholding class, they employed their mental and physical energy to resist slavery. The book is devoted to a

---

[1] C. L. R. James, *The Black Jacobins: Toussaint L'Ouverture and the San Domingo Revolution* (New York: Vintage Books, Random House, 1963; first published, New York: Dial Press, 1938), p. ix.
[2] *Ibid.*, p. 48.

I

detailed study of the most successful of such resistance – the 1790s revolution in Saint Domingo carried out by enslaved Africans. As James put it:

The revolt is the only successful slave revolt in history, and the odds it had to overcome is evidence of the magnitude of the interests that were involved. The transformation of slaves, trembling in hundreds before a single white man, into a people able to organise themselves and defeat the most powerful European nations of their day, is one of the great epics of revolutionary struggle and achievement. Why and how this happened is the theme of this book.[3]

Earlier in the 1930s a black economist at Howard University, Dr. Abram Harris, conceived an ambitious research project that would demonstrate the role of Africans in the economic development of the Western World (Europe and the United States of America). The project did not take off. The book ultimately published in 1936 focused on a different theme. However, an outline of the early parts of the originally planned work was presented in the first chapter of the published book.[4] In the same year a graduate student at Howard University, Wilson Williams, wrote a Master's dissertation on the role of Africans in the rise of capitalism. Again, the subject was not treated in any detail as the length of the thesis makes clear – 48 typescript pages.[5]

It is, therefore, fair to say that the first elaborate study of the contribution of African people to the economic development of some parts of Western Europe was by Eric Williams. This is contained in his seminal work, *Capitalism and Slavery*, published in 1944.[6] In the preface Williams noted the state of scholarship on the Industrial Revolution as of the early 1940s. He believed that scholarly and popular books had more or less covered adequately the progress of the Industrial Revolution over time, as well as the period preceding it. But scholarship was yet to focus on "the world-wide and interrelated nature of the commerce" of the preceding period, "its direct effect upon the development of the Industrial Revolution, and the heritage which it has left even upon the civilization of today . . ." The contribution of *Capitalism and Slavery* was intended to be located within the latter broad problem area.[7] This contribution centered on the role of African people. "The present study," declared Williams, "is an attempt to place in historical perspective the relationship between early

[3]   *Ibid.*, p. ix.
[4]   Abram L. Harris, *The Negro as Capitalist: A Study of Banking and Business Among American Negroes* (Philadelphia: Published for the American Academy of Political and Social Science by the Rumford Press, 1936), p. ix.
[5]   Wilson E. Williams, "Africa and the Rise of Capitalism" (Master's thesis, Howard University, 1936).
[6]   Eric Williams, *Capitalism and Slavery* (Chapel Hill: University of North Carolina Press, 1944).
[7]   *Ibid.*, p. v.

capitalism as exemplified by Great Britain, and the Negro slave trade, Negro slavery and the general colonial trade of the seventeenth and eighteenth centuries."[8] To ensure that the reader was not misled to expect more than the book offers, it is made clear from the onset that the book "is strictly an economic study of the role of Negro slavery and the slave trade in providing the capital which financed the Industrial Revolution in England and of mature industrial capitalism in destroying the slave system."[9]

Thus Eric Williams's study of African people's contribution to the origin of the Industrial Revolution in England is centered on private profits arising from economic activities connected directly and indirectly with Africans and their descendants. A model constructed on the notion of the triangular trade structures the study coherently. The Atlantic slave trade covers the first two sides of the triangle: British manufactures were sold in Western Africa in exchange for captured Africans for a profit; shipped to the West Indies (the second side of the triangle), the African captives were sold to planters for a second set of profits; enslaved and put to work in the West Indies, the Africans produced a variety of plantation crops – sugar, cotton, indigo, cocoa, etc. – that were shipped to England (the third side of the triangle) and sold in exchange for British manufactures and services yielding a third set of profits. Williams pointed out that the triangular trade,

gave a triple stimulus to British industry. The Negro[e]s were purchased with British manufactures; transported to the plantations, they produced sugar, cotton, indigo, molasses and other tropical products, the processing of which created new industries in England; while the maintenance of the Negroes and their owners on the plantations provided another market for British industry, New England agriculture and the New Foundland fisheries. By 1750 there was hardly a trading or a manufacturing town in England which was not in some way connected with the triangular or direct colonial trade. The profits obtained provided one of the main streams of that accumulation of capital in England which financed the Industrial Revolution.[10]

Eric Williams did not state precisely what range of activities is covered by his notion of profits. From a close and careful reading, it is reasonable to say that the notion of private profits applied in the book implies profits from all activities connected directly and indirectly with Africans and their descendants: profits realized by manufacturers whose goods were exported to Western Africa for the slave trade and to the West Indies; profits realized by the manufacturers who employed raw materials produced by enslaved Africans in the West Indies; profits realized by the planters who employed enslaved Africans to produce plantation products for export; profits realized by traders involved in the buying and selling of Africans, the commodities produced by them in the West Indies, and the

---

[8] *Ibid.*, p. v.   [9] *Ibid.*, p. v.   [10] *Ibid.*, p. 52.

manufactures exchanged at all levels; profits realized by the owners of the ships employed at all levels and by the builders and repairers of those ships; profits realized by financiers; and profits realized from all activities induced by the linkage effects of the triangular trade and the direct colonial trade.

Understood in this broad fashion, the various issues examined by Williams fall into place consistently with the theme of profits specified in the Preface. The discussion of the various manufacturing sectors, the ship-building industry, the growth of population in the port towns trading in slaves and slave-produced West Indian commodities, and in manufacturing centers producing goods for the slave trade and for export to the West Indies – all these fit into the profit theme only when the notion of private profits is understood in the broad sense stated previously. The point that "The British Empire was 'a magnificent superstructure of American commerce and naval power on an African foundation',"[11] quoting Postlethwayt, should also be understood in that sense.

As far as I am aware, there were no noticeable reactions to the brief remarks made on the role of Africans in the development of the Western World before Eric Williams's *Capitalism and Slavery*. That subject became an important academic issue following the publication of the book. The distraction caused by World War II seems to have delayed the reaction of scholars somewhat. But from the 1960s the responses began. Because of Eric Williams's focus on profits, the debate, which he provoked, on the contribution of Africans to the Industrial Revolution in England was centered similarly on the subject of profits.[12] The profits contested were

---

[11] *Ibid.*, p. 52.
[12] K. G. Davies, "Essays in Bibliography and Criticism, XLIV: Empire and Capital," *Economic History Review*, 2nd ser. 13 (1960), 105–10; Roger T. Anstey, "Capitalism and Slavery: A Critique," *Economic History Review*, 2nd ser. 21 (Aug. 1968), 307–20; Roger T. Anstey, "The Volume and Profitability of British Slave Trade, 1761–1807," in *Race and Slavery in the Western Hemisphere: Quantitative Studies*, Stanley L. Engerman and Eugene D. Genovese, eds. (Princeton, New Jersey: Princeton University Press, 1975); Roger T. Anstey, *The Atlantic Slave Trade and British Abolition, 1760–1810* (London: Macmillan, 1975), pp. 38–57; F. E. Hyde, B. B. Parkinson, and S. Marriner, "The Nature and Profitability of the Liverpool Slave Trade," *Economic History Review*, 2d ser. 5, no. 3 (1953), 368–77; Stanley L. Engerman, "The Slave Trade and British Capital Formation in the Eighteenth Century: A Comment on the Williams Thesis," *The Business History Review*, 46 (Winter, 1972), 430–43; David Richardson, "Profits in the Liverpool Slave Trade: The Accounts of William Davenport, 1757–84," in *Liverpool, the African Slave Trade, and Abolition: Essays to Illustrate Current Knowledge and Research*, Roger Anstey and P. E. H. Hair, eds. (Historic Society of Lancashire and Cheshire Occasional Series Vol. 2, 1976), pp. 60–90; David Richardson, "Profitability in the Bristol-Liverpool Slave Trade," *Revue francaise d'histoire d'outre-mer*, 62, nos. 226–227 (1975), 301–08; Stanley L. Engerman, "Comments on Richardson and Boulle and the 'Williams Thesis'," *Revue francaise d'histoire d'outre-mer*, 62, nos. 226–227

almost exclusively those directly connected with the Atlantic slave trade. The questions in the debate were framed in terms of the percentage level of return on the slave traders' investment, the overall magnitude of the profits and of that portion invested in manufacturing industries, and the ratio of the latter to the total amount of capital invested in manufacturing industries in England during the slave-trade era. Apart from about four contributions,[13] profits from the employment of enslaved Africans to produce export commodities in the West Indies were rarely considered, let alone profits from the host of activities mentioned earlier. It is thus fair to say that the voluminous critique of the Williams profits thesis did not incorporate all the elements that could be reasonably included.

Yet, it can still be said that the Williams profits thesis does not fully address the contribution of Africans to the structural transformation of the English economy between 1650 and 1850, which culminated in the Industrial Revolution during the period, even when his notion of profits is understood broadly. In the first place, Williams did not develop the profit argument in sufficient detail. As of the time he wrote, no systematic measurement of the rates of profit in the various activities relevant to his thesis existed, and it would have been practically impossible for him to conduct the research needed for that purpose all by himself if he had wanted to do so. Hence, detailed quantitative analysis could not be deployed to support the profit argument. Apart from the empirical foundation, the logic of the argument is also not worked out systematically in detail. It seems this was a matter of choice. The role of Africans in the Industrial Revolution was really not the central concern of Williams. The main focus of *Capitalism and Slavery*, as the framing of the title makes clear, was the causal relationship between industrial capitalism in England and the abolition of the slave trade and slavery by the British government. In fact, this was the only subject of his Oxford University Ph.D. dissertation, entitled, "The Economic Aspects of the Abolition of the West Indian Slave Trade and Slavery." The contribution of Africans to the Industrial Revolution was

(1975), 331–36; R. W. Fogel and S. L. Engerman, *Time on the Cross: The Economics of American Negro Slavery* (London: Wildwood House, 1974); R. B. Sheridan, "The Wealth of Jamaica in the Eighteenth Century," *Economic History Review*, 2d ser. 18 (Aug. 1965), 292–311; Robert Paul Thomas, "The Sugar Colonies of the Old Empire: Profit or Loss for Great Britain?" *Economic History Review*, 2d ser. 21 (April 1968), 30–45; R. B. Sheridan, "The Wealth of Jamaica in the Eighteenth Century: A Rejoinder," *Economic History Review*, 2d ser. 21 (April 1968), 46–61; J. R. Ward, "The Profitability of Sugar Planting in the British West Indies, 1650–1834," *Economic History Review*, 2d ser. 31 (May, 1978), 197–213; Robert Paul Thomas and Richard Nelson Bean, "The Fishers of Men: The Profits of the Slave Trade," *Journal of Economic History*, 34 (Dec. 1974), 885–914.
[13] Sheridan, "The Wealth of Jamaica"; Thomas, "The Sugar Colonies of the Old Empire"; Ward, "The Profitability of Sugar Planting in the British West Indies"; Fogel and Engerman, *Time on the Cross*.

added later, while he was teaching at Howard University.[14] Of the 12 main chapters of the book, only 2 – Chapters 3 (30 pages) and 5 (10 pages) – are focused directly on that subject; that is, less than one-fifth of the book. Had Williams chosen to focus mainly on the role of Africans he would have framed the title of his book differently, possibly, *Slavery and Capitalism*, and he would have devoted more space to his arguments on the subject.

But even if the profit argument is empirically and logically developed in full, it will still not demonstrate fully the contribution of African people to the Industrial Revolution. Eric Williams's emphasis on profits would seem to have been influenced by the dominant macro-economic analysis of his time, the Keynesian revolution, which treated investment as an autonomous variable related primarily to the availability of investible funds.[15] In a development analysis so conducted profits are a critical element, being the main source of funds for investment. Of course, Keynesian macro-economics was designed not for an industrializing economy in a pre-industrial world, but for a mature industrialized economy operating far below capacity. Where investment is not an autonomous variable, but is, on the contrary, dependent on the availability of market opportunities for productive investment and for the development of new technologies and new forms of organizing production, the issue of profits becomes less important and ceases to occupy center stage. There can be no better example to buttress this point than the problem of the Dutch, who, in the late seventeenth and eighteenth centuries, had an abundance of investible funds but had little market opportunities to invest them productively.[16]

One more point to note – the profit argument in *Capitalism and Slavery* is conducted within a rather narrow geographical context. Apart from occasional references to mainland British America, the argument is limited to the British Caribbean. To demonstrate fully and effectively the contribution of African people to the Industrial Revolution, the geographical context needs to be expanded considerably. The entire Atlantic basin should be the focus of analysis.

The foregoing comments in no way diminish the lasting value of *Capitalism and Slavery*. The main arguments concerning the economic basis of abolition have stood the test of time. In spite of the voluminous criticism

[14] Richard B. Sheridan, "Eric Williams and Capitalism and Slavery: A Biographical and Historiographical Essay," in Barbara L. Solow and Stanley L. Engerman (editors), *British Capitalism and Caribbean Slavery: The Legacy of Eric Williams* (Cambridge: Cambridge University Press, 1987), pp. 318–319.

[15] J. E. Inikori, "Market Structure and the Profits of the British African Trade in the Late Eighteenth Century," *Journal of Economic History*, Vol. XLI, No. 4 (Dec. 1981), p. 745.

[16] See Eric J. Hobsbawm, "The General Crisis of the European Economy in the 17th Century," *Past & Present*, 5 (1954), pp. 33–53; 6 (1954), pp. 44–65.

by scholars since the 1960s, those arguments can still be shown to be basically valid, logically and empirically. There can be no doubt that Eric Williams raised an important academic issue when he drew the attention of scholars to the contribution of African people to the Industrial Revolution in England. His profits thesis is certainly important. The capitalist system cannot function without profits. However, the research of the past five decades, both empirical and theoretical (especially in the area of development theory), now makes it possible to go beyond the consideration of profits in demonstrating the contribution of Africans to the Industrial Revolution.

The present study examines the role of Africans in England's industrialization within the context of international trade and economic development. The Industrial Revolution is studied as the final outcome of a successful industrialization process covering several centuries. This process occurred in a world where an integrated international economy was yet to be fully developed. The task for historical analysis is to show, in part, that an international economy of considerable size did evolve during the period of study. As shown in the chapters that follow, this is a subject that has received much attention in the literature under the familiar theme of the "Commercial Revolution." Yet no elaborately documented effort was made hitherto to measure precisely the overall size of the nucleus of the evolving international economy – the Atlantic World economy – and to show its growth over the 200 years from the mid-seventeenth to the mid-nineteenth century, the critical period for a serious study of the forces that produced the Industrial Revolution.

A logically consistent procedure for assessing the contribution of Africans to the Industrial Revolution, as conceived, would require that first and foremost it be established that international trade was a critical factor in the successful completion of England's industrialization. The latter subject has not received the kind of attention it deserves. There is not a single book-length study of the role of international trade in England's industrialization. Eric Williams was right when he stated, as shown above, that the effect of the "world-wide" commerce of the seventeenth and eighteenth centuries on England's industrialization had not been studied in detail as of the time he wrote. Almost three decades later H. E. S. Fisher repeated the observation that, "surprisingly little detailed examination has been made ... of the actual relationships between trade growth and the general development of the [English] economy ..."[17] Again, almost three decades later, very little has changed. It is fair to say that this study

---

[17] H. E. S. Fisher, *The Portugal Trade: A Study of Anglo-Portuguese Commerce 1700–1770* (London: Methuen, 1971), p. 125. Fisher attempted in Chapter 9 of his book to examine "some of the relationships arising from Anglo-Portuguese trade" (p. 125).

represents the first lengthy examination of the role of international trade in England's industrialization process.

The key issues to deal with in relating international trade to the development process in England may be stated as follows: 1) the influence of international trade on the evolution of interest groups and on changes in their relative strengths and weaknesses over time, and the way all this affected the political process, the character of the state and its agencies, the rules and regulations that evolved, and the enforcement mechanisms fashioned; 2) the influence of the evolving international market on the development and productive utilization of resources; 3) the role of imported manufactures in the development of new consumer tastes and, subsequently, new industries; 4) the role of manufactured re-exports by British merchants in creating overseas markets for manufactures that could later be taken over by British manufacturers; 5) the role of international trade in the provision of vital raw materials for manufacturing industries on advantageous terms; 6) the role of entrepôt trade in manufactures and tropical produce in the growth of service incomes; 7) the role of international trade in the development of shipping and financial institutions; 8) the contribution of the export sector in the general development of division of labor over time and the expansion of the domestic market; 9) the role of expanding overseas sales in creating favorable conditions for the development and adoption of new technologies and new forms of organizing production.

Considerable debate surrounds some of these issues. To be persuasive, arguments need to be founded on detailed empirical evidence, quantitative and qualitative. Comparative analysis at the level of relevant European nations will help to show in a sharp relief the most critical factors in the equation. Even more important in this mode of analysis is a comparative study of the historical experiences of the major regions of England as the national industrialization process progressed over time. By examining the differing paths followed by these regions and the outcome, we gain a much better understanding of the nature of England's industrialization process, thereby making it much easier to identify the factors that were most critical in the successful completion of the process.

Once the role of international trade in England's industrialization has been demonstrated, the main burden of analysis focuses on the extent to which the evolution of the international economy during the period rested on the shoulders of Africans. Africans' contribution centered on the evolution of the Atlantic World economic system. The main thrust of analysis, therefore, has to be on the role of Africans in the growth and development of the Atlantic World economy and of the quantitative and qualitative place of the Atlantic World economy in England's international trade during the period of study. This mode of analysis requires an examination of the role of Africans on the African continent and, more important, those in the Americas, not just British America but all of the Americas. Similarly, all of the Americas and their complex inter-connections with different parts of Europe must constitute the focus of examination when assessing the place of the Atlantic World economy in England's international trade, rather than the focus being limited to British America.

Because of recent trends in the literature, it is pertinent to comment briefly at the onset on the use of the familiar term *Industrial Revolution* in this study. British and other historians influenced by the apparent weak position of the British economy in the current world economic order, relative to the giants – the United States, Japan, and Germany – have tended to underrate in recent times the historical importance of the changes that occurred in England between 1750 and 1850. Emphasis is on how slow the growth of real national income per capita was during the period and on the persistence of traditional forms of technology and organization in manufacturing, measured in terms of national average across all industries. Arising from this, the question is raised whether or not it is appropriate to use the term Industrial Revolution in describing the changes that took place during the period.[18]

The term Industrial Revolution, as it applies to British economic history, means different things to different historians. To illustrate, for Mathias the term refers to the structural change that occurred in England during the period in question; but for Wrigley the term describes a major discontinuity in the rate of economic growth leading to increases in real incomes per capita over time to levels unprecedented in pre-industrial societies.[19] The use of the term in this study is closer to the position of Mathias than that of Wrigley. The term is applied to describe developments in industrial production both at the regional and at the national levels. The use is justified on the ground that the technological and socio-economic changes associated with England's successful industrialization were so great and so radical that it is appropriate to describe the transformation as revolutionary – something no previous society anywhere in the world had experienced – the length of time it took to bring about the changes notwithstanding. This seems also to be roughly the position of Crafts and his collaborators:

We repeat our belief that a key feature of the British industrial revolution was that the trend rate of growth of industrial output increased steadily over several decades, from 0.65 percent prior to the mid-1770s to a peak of 3.7 percent in the mid-1830s.[20]

---

[18] For a recent survey of the literature on the subject, see Rondo Cameron, "The Industrial Revolution: Fact or Fiction?" *Contention*, Vol. 4, No. 1 (Fall 1994), pp. 163–188.

[19] For this view of the positions by Mathias and Wrigley, see N. F. R. Crafts and T. C. Mills, "The industrial revolution as a macroeconomic epoch: an alternative view," *Economic History Review*, XLVII, 4 (1994), p. 771.

[20] *Ibid.*, pp. 771–772.

This rapid growth of industrial output is partly a reflection of the ongoing revolutionary changes in the technology and organization of industrial production. The magnitude of the change is better observed in the key industries and in the key regions that led the process, a phenomenon concealed largely by the construction of national aggregate measurements.

I.2 CONCEPTUAL FRAMEWORK

It is argued in this study that the Industrial Revolution in England was the first successful case of import substitution industrialization (ISI) in history. To explain why the process was successful it will be helpful to employ the conceptual framework of ISI fashioned by several development economists going back to the 1950s. By way of definition, the term *ISI* refers to a process of industrial development propelled by the substitution of domestically produced manufactures for previously imported ones. Early modern writers who employed the term in their analysis of the development process include Albert O. Hirschman[21] and Hollis B. Chenery.[22] It has been suggested that Chenery was the first to apply the term as an analytical and measurable concept.[23] Chenery's problem was to identify the factors that could cause the industrial sectors to grow more rapidly than the rest of the economy during the development process and to measure their relative contributions. These factors he identified as "(1) the substitution of domestic production for imports; (2) growth in final use of industrial products; (3) growth in intermediate demand stemming from (1) and (2)."[24]

The second factor needs some elaboration. Growth in the final use of industrial products may come from one, or a combination, of three sources: a change in the composition of domestic final demand arising from increases in per capita income; a change in the composition of domestic final demand due to a social redistribution of income; or the growth of external demand for manufactures. Increases in per capita income bias demand in favor of manufactured goods. The main explanation for this is Engel's Law, that as the incomes of consumers increase beyond a certain level the proportion spent on food declines, while that on manufactures increases. On the other hand, a redistribution of income in favor of the lower classes shifts demand in favor of manufactured mass consumer goods, while a redistribution in favor of the upper classes concentrates demand on luxury products.

---

[21]   Albert O. Hirschman, *The Strategy of Economic Development* (New Haven: Yale University Press, 1958).

[22]   Hollis B. Chenery, "Patterns of Industrial Growth," *American Economic Review*, Vol. 50 (1960), pp. 624–654.

[23]   Jaleel Ahmad, *Import Substitution, Trade and Development* (Greenwich, CT: JAI, 1978), p. 11.

[24]   Chenery, "Patterns of Industrial Growth," p. 639.

The third factor, the growth of intermediate demand stemming from the first and second factors, depends very much on the size of the domestic market because of the special properties of intermediate and capital goods, as will be shown later in this section. However, a small country with an initially narrow domestic market can expand production for export in import substitution consumer goods industries. This will extend sufficiently the domestic market for intermediate and capital goods to allow the country to produce them efficiently domestically, instead of importing all or most of them.

The foregoing analysis maps out conceptually the factors to look for and measure in explaining disproportionate growth of any or all the industrial sectors. Further development of the ISI concept and its application to the study of historical cases in the more recent past reveal the essential characteristics of this pattern of industrial development. One important characteristic concerns the identifiable stages of ISI. Some analysts have identified two, others three, phases of the process. All analysts identify the first and easy phase with the domestic production of previously imported consumer goods. Analysts such as Stephan Haggard place the production of intermediate goods and consumer durables in a separate phase, the second, and the production of machinery and equipment in another, the third; whereas others such as Bela Balassa place the two in one phase, the second.[25] The sub-division of the process into two or three phases is not particularly important. What is more important is the separation of the easy first stage, the production of consumer goods, from the subsequent extension of production to intermediate and capital goods.

A major difference between the more recent process and that of England should be noted at this point. For the more recent process, domestic production of import substitutes entailed the import of intermediate and capital goods. In the case of England, although some intermediate goods, such as iron, were imported, no capital goods were imported. The suppliers of the imported manufactures being replaced employed traditional techniques dependent on human skills, rather than the application of machines. The problem the English manufacturers had to overcome initially was the perfection of these human skills and the efficient organization of the production process. For this reason, the extension of domestic manufacturing to the production of intermediate and capital goods in England meant the invention and adoption of new technologies, whereas in the more recent process it was a matter of producing substitutes for previously imported

---

[25] Stephan Haggard, *Pathways from the Periphery: The Politics of Growth in the Newly Industrializing Countries* (Ithaca, NY: Cornell University Press, 1990), p. 25; Bela Balassa, *The Process of Industrial Development and Alternative Development Strategies* (Princeton, NJ: Princeton University, Department of Economics, International Finance Section, 1981).

intermediate and capital goods. Although the qualitative difference is significant, the economics of both processes and the factors determining success or failure are basically the same.

During the first and relatively easy phase, the sectors experiencing import substitution grow more rapidly than the rest of the economy. Once domestic production of import substitutes has been sufficiently expanded to the limits of the pre-existing demand, however, the growth rate of output declines to the rate of increase in domestic consumption. At this point, maintaining high industrial growth rates requires moving into either production for export or second-stage import substitution, or both.[26] Another important characteristic of ISI is the state's provision of protection for the import substitution industries through the use of import duties, quotas, or prohibition. Depending on whether protection takes the form of moderate or high import duties or outright prohibition, ISI tends to produce sellers' markets, especially in small countries with relatively narrow domestic markets. This limits competition and gives rise to high production costs, which in turn limit the growth of sales and, therefore, output. This being the case, one may question the wisdom of employing the ISI strategy. The reason is simple. Once the relative advantage of foreign suppliers of imported manufactures is established, it is difficult for inexperienced local producers to emerge and immediately compete successfully without some form of initial protection by the state. This is the infant industry notion of ISI. The analytical task is to identify the conditions and policy choices that make it possible to build competition into the process early enough to avoid the entrenchment of inefficient production structure.

What is more, moving from the first and easy phase of consumer goods production to the later stages in which intermediate and capital goods are produced entails considerable difficulties arising from the peculiar characteristics of intermediate and capital goods. These products tend to be capital-intensive and are subject to significant economies of scale. For efficient production, there has to be a sufficiently large market as costs rise quickly at lower levels of output.[27]

Empirical studies of the more recent cases of ISI offer a helpful opportunity for comparative analysis that points out the critical factors determining success or failure. Haggard and Balassa have examined variations in the application of the ISI strategy of industrial development across countries.[28] Haggard compared the cases of Brazil, Mexico, South Korea, Taiwan, Singapore, and Hong Kong. Starting their process in 1935, Brazil and Mexico followed the domestic production of import substitutes virtu-

[26] Balassa, *The Process of Industrial Development*, p. 7.
[27] *Ibid.*, p. 7.
[28] Haggard, *Pathways from the Periphery*; Balassa, *The Process of Industrial Development*.

ally for the domestic market alone from the easy phase to the production of intermediate and capital goods. Not until the problems associated with this variant of the ISI strategy had become socially and politically critical in the late 1960s did these countries modify their strategy and begin aggressive promotion of manufactured exports. South Korea and Taiwan, on the other hand, began their ISI process in 1945, and as soon as the first and easy phase was completed they pursued aggressive export promotion that encouraged the production of labor-intensive goods for export in the import substitution industries. As sales and output grew rapidly following the combined impact of export and domestic demand, the domestic market for intermediate and capital goods expanded to a point where those goods could be produced domestically on a large scale that permitted economies of scale to be secured. This also made it possible for manufactured exports to be quickly upgraded to include intermediate and capital goods. Singapore and Hong Kong belong to a category described in this study as ISI cum RSI – import substitution industrialization plus re-export substitution industrialization. The process of industrial development in these two countries derived from a preceding entrepôt trade in manufactures. Hence, as Haggard's study shows, ISI moved quickly into the production of manufactured exports as substitutes for manufactured re-exports.

Balassa conducted a broader comparative study in which he divided the ISI countries studied into three categories: those that embarked on aggressive promotion of export production of manufactures after the completion of first-stage ISI (Korea, Singapore, and Taiwan); those that moved into second-stage ISI (production of consumer durables, intermediate goods, and machinery for the domestic market) after completing the first stage but later adopted export promotion policies in the face of difficulties (Brazil, Argentina, Colombia, and Mexico); and those that limited production virtually to the domestic market for a prolonged period of time (India, Chile, and Uruguay). The study shows that the rate of capacity utilization was highest in the first group of countries and increased considerably in the second group after the countries adopted export promotion policies, while it remained low in the third group. Balassa's summary of his findings is instructive:

Manufacturing employment increased by 10 to 12 percent a year in Korea and Taiwan, leading to reductions in unemployment rates. *Pari passu* with the decline in unemployment, real wages increased rapidly as the demand for labor on the part of the manufacturing sector grew faster than the rate at which labor was released by the primary sector. After the 1966 policy reforms, real wages increased also in Brazil. By contrast, real wages declined in India, Chile, and Uruguay. Furthermore, income increments were achieved at a considerably lower cost in terms of investment in countries that consistently followed outward-oriented strategy [export promotion]. . . . The operation of these factors gave rise to a positive correlation between exports and economic growth. The three Far Eastern countries had the highest GNP growth rates throughout the period [1960–73], and the four Latin American countries that undertook policy reforms [adoption of export promotion] considerably improved their growth performance after the reforms were instituted, while India, Chile, and Uruguay remained at the bottom of the growth league.[29]

These comparative studies of the more recent ISI development trajectories may help deepen our understanding of the British process under examination. At appropriate points in a few of the chapters that follow, some direct comparison with the ISI in England is conducted. More generally, the ISI conceptual framework and the comparative empirical studies inform the organization and analysis of the data presented in the study.

An important issue that needs to be addressed in the conceptual framework is the role of culture. Is culture an independent variable in the process of industrialization? How do we conceptualize the role of culture in the economic development process over the long run?

Some decades ago the economic success of the Western World and the economic failures of the rest of the world were both explained in cultural terms. Western culture was presented as conducive to development, whereas culture in the rest of the world was seen as a constraint to development. The one case of success in those decades, Japan, created some explanatory awkwardness, which was taken care of by arguing that Japanese culture contained elements similar, if not identical, to the essential elements in Western culture. It was this cultural similarity, according to the argument, that made it possible for Japan to succeed while the rest of the non-Western World failed. A comparison of Japan and China often provided the empirical details for the argument.

The China-Japan comparison has come under a devastating critique in the past decades. It is argued that culturally pre-capitalist Japan was far more like China than it was like pre-capitalist Western Europe.[30] More recent detailed research now shows that modern economic development in

---

[29] Balassa, *The Process of Industrial Development*, pp. 17, 18. Balassa's findings are consistent with those of other studies: Werner Baer and Andrea Maneschi, "Import Substitution, Stagnation and Structural Change: An Interpretation of the Brazilian Case," *Journal of Developing Areas*, 5 (1971), pp. 177–192; Henry J. Bruton, "The Import Substitution Strategy of Economic Development: A Survey," *Pakistan Development Review*, 10 (1970), pp. 123–146; David Felix, "The Dilemma of Import Substitution – Argentina," in Gustav F. Papanek (ed.), *Development Policy – Theory and Practice* (Cambridge, Mass.: Havard University Press, 1968), pp. 55–91; Anne O. Krueger, *The Benefits and Costs of Import Substitution in India: A Microeconomic Study* (Minneapolis: University of Minnesota Press, 1975); David Morawetz, "Employment Implications of Industrialization in Developing Countries: A Survey," *Economic Journal*, 84 (1974), pp. 491–542.

[30] Frances V. Moulder, *Japan, China, and the modern world economy: Toward a reinterpretation of East Asian development, ca. 1600 to ca. 1918* (Cambridge: Cambridge University Press, 1977).

China up to the mid-eighteenth century compares favorably with the process in Western Europe.[31] The success story of the industrial achievements of the "Asian Tigers" (South Korea, Taiwan, Hong Kong, and Singapore) and the explosive growth of the Chinese economy since the government adopted a more market-oriented strategy have all made it difficult to sustain the cultural explanation.[32] Its application to England's industrialization is now rare, even though its reappearance in future texts may not be ruled out. One area where its application has flourished in recent times is African history, after the critique of Tony Hopkins in the early 1970s.[33] One strand of the current application is that African culture, as expressed in the land laws, prevented the development of private property rights in land during the Atlantic slave-trade era.[34] This argument has no empirical or logical foundation. It was the abundance of land in relation to population and limited opportunity to produce agricultural commodities for market exchange (especially inter-continental market exchange), that delayed the development of private property rights in land in sub-Saharan Africa. When market opportunities emerged in the late nineteenth and twentieth centuries, as population grew and agricultural production for export and for the domestic market expanded no culture or land laws prevented the evolution of private property rights in land in the major African countries.[35]

Historians employing comparative perspective in the study of long-term historical processes now generally agree that culture is not the main engine of history. In her study of the thirteenth-century world trading system centered in the Mediterranean, Abu-Lughod concluded that the collapse of that system and the success of the later system founded in the Atlantic basin

---

[31] Kenneth Pomeranz, *The Great Divergence: Europe, China, and the making of the Modern World Economy* (Princeton, NJ: Princeton University Press, 2000); Xu Dixin and Wu Chengming (eds.), *Chinese Capitalism, 1522–1840* (London: Macmillan; New York: St. Martins, 2000).

[32] In fact, a reverse cultural explanation of the recent Asian successes has been attempted. Confucianism, which was earlier presented as a constraint to Asian development, has been employed to explain the successes. See Hung-chao Tai (ed.), *Confucianism and Economic Development: An Oriental Alternative?* (Washington, D.C.: The Washington Institute Press, 1989).

[33] A. G. Hopkins, *An Economic History of West Africa* (London: Longman, 1973).

[34] John Thornton, *Africa and Africans in the making of the Atlantic World, 1400–1680* (New York: Cambridge University Press, 1992).

[35] Joseph E. Inikori, "Slavery in Africa and the Transatlantic Slave Trade," in Alusine Jalloh and Stephen E. Maizlish (eds.), *The African Diaspora* (College Station: Texas A & M University Press, 1996), pp. 61–62. Some historians explain in cultural terms what should be explained in terms of limited market opportunity. This is where the point by Tony Hopkins, that market principles should be applied in the study of pre-colonial African economic history, is significant. See Hopkins, *An Economic History of West Africa.*

from the sixteenth century by West European powers cannot be explained in cultural terms: No set of religious beliefs or values was needed to succeed in the thirteenth century and no set of religious beliefs or values can explain the successful development of the world trading system and the world economy from the sixteenth century.[36] A similar point was made more elaborately by Johan Goudsblom, Eric Jones, and Stephen Mennell: "We share a suspicion of all forms of mentalistic explanation, where culture, religion, or ideology is seen as the main engine of history."[37]

So, what kind of theoretical construct would more realistically connect culture to the development process? This task was attempted in a preliminary fashion in the 1950s by Arthur Lewis when he asked and answered a series of penetrating questions:

What causes a nation to create institutions which are favourable, rather than those which are inimical to growth? Is a part of the answer to be found in the different valuations which different societies place upon goods and services relatively to their valuation of such non-material satisfactions as leisure, security, equality, good fellowship or religious salvation? . . . What causes people to have one set of beliefs, rather than another set of beliefs, more or less favourable to growth? Are the differences of beliefs and institutions due to differences of race, or of geography or is it just historical accident? . . . How do beliefs and institutions change? Why do they change in ways favourable to or hostile to growth? How does growth itself react upon them? Is growth cumulative, in the sense that once it has begun, beliefs and

---

[36] Janet Abu-Lughod, *Before European Hegemony: The World System A. D. 1250–1350* (New York: Oxford University Press, 1989); Janet Lippman Abu-Lughod, *The World System in the Thirteenth Century: Dead-End or Precursor?* (Washington, D.C.: American Historical Association Essays on Global and Comparative History, 1993).

[37] Stephen Mennell, "Bringing the Very Long Term Back In," in Johan Goudsblom, Eric Jones, and Stephen Mennell, *The Course of Human History: Economic Growth, Social Process, and Civilization* (New York: M. E. Sharpe, 1996), p. 6. They went further to say: "This may come across in what we have written as a hostility toward explanations derived from the work of Max Weber. Whether Weber himself can be blamed for the way his work has been used since his death is questionable. In his defense, it can be said that he was himself reacting against idealistic explanations in the German tradition, as well as against the vulgar 'second International' Marxism of his time. . . . Too often the legacy of his work, especially in the Anglophone academic world, has been to cause sociologists great excitement whenever they spy anything remotely resembling a Protestant ethic, to be too willing – in our opinion – to acquiesce in idealistic, cultural explanations of differences in social development, and too ready to look for unique cultural ingredients in a supposedly unique European track of development" (*Ibid.*, p. 7). See also Andre Gunder Frank, *ReOrient: Global Economy in the Asian Age* (Berkeley: University of California Press, 1998); Jack Goody, *The East in the West* (Cambridge: Cambridge University Press, 1998). For recent opposing views, see David S. Landes, *The Wealth and Poverty of Nations: Why Some are so Rich and Some are so Poor* (New York: W. W. Norton, 1998); David Eltis, *The Rise of African Slavery in the Americas* (Cambridge: Cambridge University Press, 2000).

institutions are inevitably fashioned in such a way as to facilitate further growth; or is it self-arresting, in the dialectical sense that new beliefs and institutions are inevitably created to resist growth, and to slow it down? Are there self-reversing swings over the centuries in human attitudes and institutions, which make the process of growth inevitably cyclical?[38]

His answer to these questions suggests how culture may be realistically connected conceptually to the development process over the very long run:

The continuance of a social institution in a particular form depends upon its convenience, upon belief in its rectitude, and upon force. If growth begins to occur, all these sanctions are eroded. The institution ceases to be convenient, because it stands in the way of opportunities for economic advancement. People then cease to believe in it. Priests, lawyers, economists, and other philosophers, who used to justify it in terms of their various dogmas, begin to reject the old dogmas, and to replace them by new dogmas more appropriate to the changing situation. The balance of political power also alters. For new men are raised up by economic growth into positions of wealth and status; they challenge the old ruling classes; acquire political power slowly or in more revolutionary ways; and throw force behind the new instead of the ancient institutions. . . . In the same way, when growth stops, the situations which suited an expanding economy are no longer appropriate. People cease to believe in them; the priests, the lawyers, the economists and the philosophers turn against them, and the powerful groups who favour the *status quo* are able to enforce changes unfavourable to economic growth.[39]

Douglass North's formal institutional theory[40] demonstrates rigorously and elaborately the kind of connection suggested by Arthur Lewis. The main objective of North's theory is to show how economics, politics, and culture connect and interact in the long-term process of development to determine the way particular economies perform at a given moment. The building blocks for the theory are relative prices, interest groups, institutions (by which is meant rules and regulations that constrain the choices individuals can make, put in two categories, those made by the state and those sanctioned by culture or ideology), and organizations. Relative prices are the cornerstone of the theory, and rules and regulations are the mechanism through which the process of change is transmitted from relative price change. Interest groups and organizations are the agents through whom relative price change brings about changes in rules and regulations. In the long run, cultural or ideological change and the economic consequences are largely a function of relative price change:

[38]   W. Arthur Lewis, *The Theory of Economic Growth* (London: George Allen & Unwin, 1955), pp. 11–12.

[39]   *Ibid.*, p. 143.

[40]   Douglass C. North, *Institutions, Institutional Change and Economic Performance* (Cambridge: Cambridge University Press, 1990).

Effective traditions of hard work, honesty, and integrity simply lower the cost of transaction and make possible complex, productive exchange. Such traditions are always reinforced by ideologies that undergird those attitudes. Where do these attitudes and ideologies come from and how do they change? The subjective perceptions of the actors are not just culturally derived but are continually being modified by experience that is filtered through existing (culturally determined) mental constructs. Therefore, fundamental changes in relative prices will gradually alter norms and ideologies . . .[41]

Douglass North's conceptualization of how economics connects to politics and to culture or ideology in the long-run development process is essentially in accord with the recent historical literature mentioned earlier and the observed facts of current development processes in the non-Western World. The discussion of social structures and institutional factors, and other arguments in this study are in some way informed by the foregoing conceptual discussion of the role of culture. In particular, the *longue durée* perspective in Chapter 2 makes it possible to see the similarities between the English process and those of the more recent past in the non-Western World.

[41] *Ibid.*, p. 138. North realizes that non-economists and some economists may find it mystifying placing such weight on relative prices. But he explains that "relative price changes alter the incentives of individuals in human interaction, and the only other source of such change is a change in tastes" (*Ibid.*, p. 84).

2

The English Economy in
the *Longue Durée*, 1086–1850

STUDIES ATTEMPTING to explain the origin of the Industrial Revolution in England usually go no farther back than the late seventeenth century. There were a few attempts in the 1960s to take the story to the medieval period. A. R. Bridbury tried to demonstrate that the economic growth that led to the First Industrial Revolution can be traced to the late Middle Ages.[1] In 1968 Sidney Pollard and David Crossley made such an attempt.[2] Then in 1969, in a rather provocative paper, Max Hartwell invited historians to take a long-term view of the thousand years of English economic history that preceded the Industrial Revolution, in part, to mitigate the parochialism arising from, "the tendency of each historian to elevate his period, his growth factor, his depression or crisis, to a status of prime importance, either in the history of capitalism or of industrialization..."[3] More recently, in an intellectual effort covering more than 20 years and devoted to the development of an institutional theory of economic history and economic performance, Douglass North has traced the rise of the Western World from the era of the hunters and gatherers to the Industrial Revolution in England. North's central focus is to identify the critical long-term institutional changes that determined the direction of long-term economic change and performance, the central factors responsible for major institutional shifts over long periods of time, and the mechanisms by which

[1] R. Bridbury, *Economic Growth: England in the Later Middle Ages* (London: Allen and Unwin, 1962).
[2] Sidney Pollard and David W. Crossley, *The Wealth of Britain, 1085–1966*, (London: B. T. Batsford, 1968).
[3] R. M. Hartwell, "Economic Growth in England before the Industrial Revolution," in R. M. Hartwell, *The Industrial Revolution and Economic Growth* (London: Methuen, 1971), p. 41, first published in *Journal of Economic History*, Vol. 29 (1969), pp. 13–31.

change was effected.[4] In a somewhat different project aimed at showing that the economies of European countries and of nations created overseas by European migrants have followed a systematic pattern of change over very long time periods, Graeme Snooks has traced the growth path of the English economy from 1086 to the present and beyond. He reports that his study of the English economy over the 1,000-year period reveals three "great waves" of growth lasting between 130 and 300 years each. Snooks uses this study of the English economy over the very long period to demonstrate that modern economists employ neoclassical theory in a way that makes it impossible for them to understand and fashion policy prescriptions that are relevant to real world economies.[5]

These examples of *longue durée* perspective for a study of the Industrial Revolution have not attracted much following. Scholars who consider the Industrial Revolution or related subjects as the primary focus of their research and writing continue to limit themselves to the eighteenth and early nineteenth centuries, with occasional extension to the sixteenth and seventeenth centuries.[6] To have a long-term view of the historical developments within which the Industrial Revolution can be located, causally or otherwise, one must read the work of three broad groups of specialists –

---

[4] See Douglass C. North and Robert P. Thomas, "An Economic Theory of the Growth of the Western World," *Economic History Review*, 2nd series, vol. 22, no. 1 (1970), pp. 1–17; Douglass C. North and Robert P. Thomas, *The Rise of the Western World: A New Economic History* (New York and London: Cambridge University Press, 1973); Douglass C. North, *Structure and Change in Economic History* (New York and London: W. W. Norton, 1981). The theoretical perspective emanating from these publications has been somewhat modified in a more recent work: Douglass C. North, *Institutions, Institutional Change and Economic Performance* (New York: Cambridge University Press, 1990).

[5] Graeme Donald Snooks, *Economics Without Time: A Science Blind to the Forces of Historical Change* (London: Macmillan, 1993); Graeme Donald Snooks, "Great Waves of Economic Change: The Industrial Revolution in Historical Perspective, 1000 to 2000," in Graeme Donald Snooks (ed.), *Was the Industrial Revolution Necessary?* (London and New York: Routledge, 1994), pp. 43–78.

[6] This is exemplified by the more frequently cited books published in the 1980s: Roderick Floud and Donald McCloskey (eds.), *The Economic History of Britain since 1700: Volume I: 1700–1860* (New York: Cambridge University Press, 1981); François Crouzet, *The First Industrialists: The Problem of Origins* (New York: Cambridge University Press, 1985); N. F. R. Crafts, *British Economic Growth during the Industrial Revolution* (Oxford: Clarendon Press, 1985); Joel Mokyr (ed.), *The Economics of the Industrial Revolution* (Totowa, NJ: Rowman and Allenheld, 1985). The publications of the 1990s are following the same pattern. See, for example, Joel Mokyr (ed.), *The British Industrial Revolution: An Economic Perspective* (Boulder, Colorado: Westview Press, 1993), which promises to be a major text for the 1990s. A competing volume is Roderick Floud and Donald McCloskey (eds.), *The Economic History of Britain Since 1700, Volume 1: 1700–1860* (2nd edition, Cambridge: Cambridge University Press, 1994), which continues the period coverage of the first edition mentioned earlier.

medievalists, historians of Tudor and Stuart England, and economic-growth specialists writing on the eighteenth and early nineteenth centuries – with all the confusions arising from studying these periods in isolation one from another. Of course, much can be said in favor of historians limiting themselves to the periods they know best. The risk of making misleading statements when historians wander into periods with which they are not very familiar cannot be overemphasized. But the advantage of using a long-term perspective to identify more accurately the strategic factors in the historical process that produced the Industrial Revolution would appear to outweigh the risk. For this reason the descriptive survey in this chapter follows in some way the lead provided, in particular, by Hartwell and North.

It is not implied by this approach that there was a linear development from Domesday England to the Industrial Revolution. Rather the purpose is to provide the background against which to view the operation of many factors over an extremely long period of time, observing how they operated, their starting and terminal points in time, when they operated as independent variables and when their operation was initially triggered by that of other variables, and taking particular note of the mechanisms by which their operation transmitted structural change. In this way confusion and error may be minimized in attaching a relative weight to the contribution of the factor that forms the focus of this study. Furthermore, to achieve the same purpose, the *longue durée* descriptive survey in the chapter includes a regional dimension.

In their efforts to offer a clearer view of the main factors in the historical process leading to the Industrial Revolution, scholars have attempted in the last two decades or so to provide a comparative perspective through comparative studies of selected national economies in Europe. These studies have been particularly helpful in sharpening our understanding of the issues.[7] Extending the lessons from this to a *longue durée* study of the English economy one finds that a comparative regional perspective produces a similar result. Studies of the Industrial Revolution have typically focused analysis on the national economy in spite of the well-known divergent regional developments and the weak regional linkages of the period. This national focus has helped to conceal from our view some aspects of the historical process that are critical to a proper understanding of the main issues. An examination of the divergent regional developments over the long time period examined in this chapter brings out these aspects sharply to focus and helps to eliminate confusion and minimize error in the identification and analysis of the crucial factors in the historical process in question.

---

[7]   In particular, see the papers in Frederick Krantz and Paul M. Hohenberg (eds.), *Failed Transitions to Modern Industrial Society: Renaissance Italy and Seventeenth Century Holland* (Montreal: Interuniversity Centre for European Studies, 1975).

What is particularly remarkable about the English economy during the long period of this survey is its movement from being a periphery of the more industrially advanced economies of Continental Europe to being the core economy of the whole world. It is the view of this writer that this radical geographical shift in economic power was the product of industrialization, regardless whether or not one agrees that the term Industrial Revolution accurately describes what happened. Hence, the descriptive survey in this chapter, in conformity with the focus of the entire study, lays emphasis on industrial development. At some point the other sectors are examined in their own right, but in general they are viewed, along with the evolution of socio-political institutions, in terms of their contribution to industrial development.

The survey is divided into two main sections, 1086–1660 and 1660–1850, each of which is further divided into sub-sections. The first section combines description with some analysis and discussion to eliminate the necessity for any further detailed treatment of that period in subsequent chapters. The survey in the second section is largely descriptive.

2.1 EVOLUTION OF ECONOMIC AND SOCIO-POLITICAL INSTITUTIONS, 1086–1660

Between the Domesday Inquest and the Restoration there were major changes in economic and socio-political institutions in England that are critical to a proper understanding of the socio-economic processes of the 200 years that followed. There was, among other things, the evolution of market institutions, a gradual shift from the predominance of subsistence production to production largely for market exchange; the development of property rights, in particular, the movement from rights in persons to rights in land, leading to the ending of slavery and serfdom; a change in the structure and organization of production; a change in the regional pattern of production and socio-economic organization; and, particularly important, the evolution of political institutions that were critical to subsequent socio-economic processes. This section focuses on these fundamental changes. Economic growth, that is increases in per capita income over time, is de-emphasized. The latter arises from the fact that, given the kind of economy and society in question, socio-economic change and economic growth may not necessarily go together – major socio-economic changes leading to economic growth in the long run may occur at the same time that income per head declines in the short run. Three periods may be distinguished for the changes examined in the section: 1086–1300, a period of remarkable expansion, followed by a prolonged contraction; 1300–1475; and then further expansion, 1475–1660.

Now what was the nature of economy and society in Domesday England? A central feature of the economy was a general under-utilization of the country's natural resources in the form of fertile soils, woodlands and pastures, and minerals. Relative to Continental Europe, England was a land of much later settlement. Population estimates, with wide margins of uncertainty, indicate a total population of about 2 million in 1086.[8] With a total area of 50,333 square miles,[9] this means an average density for England as a whole of approximately 40 persons per square mile. The total population was, however, unevenly distributed. It was heavily concentrated in the regions of older settlements in the South, particularly East Anglia. A population map of Domesday England shows that only a handful of counties had a density of 15 and above. Most counties had 5 to 10, and all areas of Lancashire included in the Domesday survey had a density of 5 or less.[10] It is understandable why subsistence agriculture was predominant, even though production for market exchange had already made some progress.[11] More will be said on this later.

Although the Norman Conquest strengthened the central administration, for all practical purposes the more or less self-sufficient manor remained the unit of socio-economic, as well as political, organization. The lord's demesne was at the center of production. This is reflected in the social structure. Only 14 percent of the peasant population in rural England was free in 1086. Slaves accounted for 10.5 percent. The rest (75.5 percent) were serfs. The regional distribution of the free peasants and the slaves varied considerably. In fact, about 85 percent of all the free peasants were in 5 counties – Lincolnshire, Norfolk, Suffolk, Nottinghamshire, and Leicestershire – where the proportion of free peasants ranged between 30 and 51 percent. For most counties the proportion was less than 3 percent. The slaves were more widely distributed. Even so, 10 counties in the South of England had about 61 percent of the total, with Devon, Somerset, and

---

[8] The sources contain a wide range of estimates. John Hatcher, *Plague, Population and the English Economy, 1348–1530* (London: Macmillan, 1977), p. 68, gives a range of 1.75 million to 2.25 million, whereas Sally Harvey, after examining the evidence and method employed in the better known estimates, concludes that 2 million is a more reasonable estimate. See Sally Harvey, "Domesday England," in H. E. Hallam (ed.) *The Agrarian History of England and Wales: Volume II, 1042–1350* (Cambridge: Cambridge University Press, 1988), p. 49.

[9] E. A. Wrigley, "The Growth of Population in Eighteenth-century England: A Conundrum Resolved," *Past and Present*, No. 98, February, 1983, p. 121.

[10] Harvey, "Domesday England," p. 47.

[11] S. R. H. Jones, "Transaction Costs, Institutional Change, and the Emergence of a Market Economy in later Anglo-Saxon England," *Economic History Review*, XLVI, 4 (1993), pp. 658–678.

Gloustershire having the largest concentration (in absolute and proportionate terms).[12]

There is very little information on the extent of manufacturing and mining in Domesday England.[13] However, there is an indication that the manufacturing of woollen cloth of some scale existed.[14] With a large number of regions in Europe producing cloth for local consumption and for export at this time, English cloth exports by 1086 must have been on an extremely small scale. Even the great centers of export production in the Middle Ages – the Low Countries and Florence – began their industrial expansion in the eleventh century, with real rapid growth occurring not until the twelfth and thirteenth centuries.[15] The export trade in raw wool must also have been very small at this time, for the major manufacturing regions in Continental Europe were largely self-sufficient in raw material supply.[16] The first important reference to raw wool export from England is dated 1113.[17]

Two contending estimates of the Gross Domestic Product (GDP) of feudal England in 1086 deserve mentioning. Graeme Snooks estimates a GDP of £136,621, with a population of 1.53 million people, which gives a per capita income of 1.8 shillings. Nicholas Mayhew, on the other hand, gives a much higher estimate of £300,000 and a per capita GDP of 2.6 shillings, implying a population of about 2.3 million. Snooks and Mayhew also differ in their views of the social distribution of the GDP. According to Snooks, the ruling elites, with a total population of about 35,500 persons (made up of 5,500 tenants-in-chief and their families and 30,000 under-tenants and their families), being about 2.3 percent of his preferred population of 1.53 million, received 41.7 percent of the GDP; the peasants, with 89.9 percent of the population, had a share of 50.5 percent; and the urban population of 120,000 (7.8 percent of the population) had 7.8 percent. Mayhew believes the lords received only about one-third of the GDP.[18]

[12] H. E. Hallam, "England Before the Norman Conquest," in Hallam (ed.), *Agrarian History*, pp. 10–13.

[13] Lack of information on the subject is indicated by the fact that only one short paragraph is devoted to it by Pollard and Crossley, *The Wealth of Britain*, p. 14. The point is also stressed by Miller that "the history of medieval rural industry in the country as a whole has yet to be adequately studied." Edward Miller, "Introduction: Land and People," in Edward Miller (ed.), *The Agrarian History of England and Wales: Volume III, 1348–1500* (Cambridge: Cambridge University Press, 1991), p. 27.

[14] T. H. Lloyd, *The English Wool Trade in the Middle Ages* (Cambridge: Cambridge University Press, 1977), p. 1.

[15] Eileen Power, *The Wool Trade in English Medieval History: Being the Ford Lectures* (Oxford: Oxford University Press, 1941), pp. 8–9.

[16] Lloyd, *The English Wool Trade*, p. 2.

[17] Ibid., p. 6.

[18] Snooks, *Economics Without Time*, pp. 176–202; John McDonald and G. D. Snooks, *Domesday Economy: A New Approach to Anglo-Norman History* (Oxford:

There is also some disagreement on the extent of production for market exchange. Snooks estimates that the market and subsistence sectors were approximately 40 and 60 percent, respectively, in 1086, with 60 percent of seigneurial production being marketed. However, a detailed study of the gross output of 201 manors sampled within the London region by Bruce Campbell shows that only 45 percent of seigneurial production in 1300 was marketed. According to Campbell, the estimate is biased in favor of the most commercialized manors in the sample, for which reason he believes his figures are "upper-bound estimates." Given Campbell's upper-bound estimates from the unusually commercialized London region and what is known of increasing commercialization from 1086 to 1300, Snooks's estimates would appear to be a considerable exaggeration of the extent of the market sector in 1086. In the light of Campbell's evidence, Snooks's estimate of the market sector of seigneurial production in 1086 for England as a whole may be cut by half to 30 percent. If the population of England in 1086 is put at 2 million, which is more consistent with the most recent review of the evidence by the main authorities, as stated earlier, and the peasants' share of the GDP is raised to two-thirds as Mayhew suggests, then the extent of the market sector in all England in 1086 may have been no more than about 25 percent of the GDP.[19]

The amount of wealth assessed in the counties for the payment of royal taxes enables us to observe the regional distribution of wealth in Domesday England. The ranking of the counties according to the amount of wealth assessed per acre shows that the wealthiest counties in 1086 were all in the areas of older settlement in the south. The top 10 in a descending order of wealth are Oxfordshire, Kent, Berkshire, Essex, Hertfordshire, Middlesex, Dorset, Somerset, Buckinghamshire, and Bedfordshire. The counties up north were at the bottom. There is no ranking for Lancashire and Yorkshire in 1086, but they ranked 34 and 27, respectively, out of 39 counties in 1275.[20]

Between 1086 and 1660 this undeveloped economy of Domesday England underwent a significant transformation. The first phase occurred

Clarendon Press, 1986), pp. 11–36; Nicholas Mayhew, "Modelling medieval monetisation," in Richard H. Britnell and Bruce M. S. Campbell (eds.), *A Commercialising Economy: England 1086 to c.1300* (Manchester: Manchester University Press, 1995), pp. 55–62.

[19] Snooks, *Economics Without Time*, pp. 98–202; Bruce M. S. Campbell, "Measuring the commercialisation of seigneurial agriculture c.1300," in Britnell and Campbell (eds.), *A Commercialising Economy*, pp. 174–193.

[20] E. J. Buckatzsch, "The Geographical Distribution of Wealth in England, 1086–1843: An Experimental Study of Certain Tax Assessments," *Economic History Review*, 2nd series, Vol. III, no. 2 (1950), pp. 186–187. A map showing the geographical distribution of income per household in England in 1086 displays a similar distribution. See Snooks, *Economics Without Time*, p. 195.

between 1086 and 1300. This was a period of prolonged population growth; surplus land and other under-utilized natural resources permitted population to operate as an independent variable and the numbers multiplied. John Hatcher's review of the evidence indicates that the population of England grew by a factor of three between 1086 and the 1290s, increasing from about 2 million to about 6 million during the period.[21]

This expansion of population gave rise to the internal colonization of the vast wilderness that previously separated settled manors. By the early fourteenth century the colonization process and the expansion of cultivated land had been completed in all regions of England.[22] With the phenomenal increase in population densities – from a national average of 40 per square mile in 1086 to about 120 in the 1290s – economy and society in England moved from conditions of scarce labor and surplus natural resources to those of surplus labor and scarce land. The regional distribution of the population continued to be uneven. The areas of older settlement in the southern part of the country remained more densely populated.

The increase in population and the colonization process stimulated the expansion of internal trade and the spread of production for market exchange. The growth of raw wool exports from the late thirteenth century intensified the expansion of market activities. This growth of wool production for export was on such a scale that it touched all aspects of the political economy of England from the later Middle Ages to the Industrial Revolution, the development of the woollen textile industry from the fourteenth century adding a new dimension. The sheep was to medieval and early modern England what crude oil is to contemporary Saudi Arabia.[23]

Annual average exports, by the available evidence, were 9.7 million lbs in 1279–1290, produced by about 5 million sheep. This increased to 14.4 million lbs, produced by 7.6 million sheep, in 1304–11.[24] Although export

---

[21]   Hatcher, *Plague, Population and The English Economy*, p. 68.

[22]   J. A. Tuck, "The Occupation of the Land: The Northern Borders," in Miller (ed.), *Agrarian History*, p. 34.

[23]   Eileen Power made the point succinctly: "The trade which gave England her key position was bound to dominate the domestic scene: her commerce and her politics alike were built upon wool. When her kings got themselves taken prisoner, like Richard I, the ransom was paid – with grumbling – out of wool. When they rushed into war with their neighbours, like the three Edwards, the wars were financed and allies bought – with more grumbling – out of wool. . . . At home honest burgesses climbed upon wool into the ranks of the nobility, only outstripped in their progress there by the dishonest ones, who arrived first, like de la Poles of Hull. The very Lord Chancellor plumped himself down on a wool-sack, and the kingdom might have set on its great seal the motto which a wealthy wool merchant engraved on the windows of his new house: I praise God and ever shall. It is the sheep hath paid for all." Power, *The Wool Trade*, p. 17.

[24]   See Joseph E. Inikori, "Slavery and the Development of Industrial Capitalism in England," *Journal of Interdisciplinary History*, XVII, 4 (1987), fn. 6, p. 777; also

figures are not available, indirect evidence indicates that large-scale production of wool for export dated much further back in the thirteenth century. There were broadly two categories of producers: large-scale demesne producers and small-scale peasant producers. The former reached the peak of their production in the thirteenth century, whereas the latter increased their share of total output as the Middle Ages progressed. Even during the period when the big producers had their largest share of total output in the thirteenth century, it is believed that the peasants produced more than half of the total.[25] This means that thousands of peasants all over the country earned cash on a regular basis, which helped to pull them into active market exchange. As stated above, the extent of the market sector of the English economy was around 25 percent of the GDP in 1086. It is reasonable to suppose that the wool trade, together with the multiplier effects (especially in the area of foodstuffs purchases by wool growers), must have constituted a large proportion of the market sector in the centuries that followed and, so, played a dynamic role in the extension of market activities to the subsistence sector over time. According to Barbara Harvey, the cash economy made remarkable progress in rural England in the twelfth and thirteenth centuries, and by the fourteenth there was an active land market, especially in regions well endowed with pasture.[26]

The growth of markets and the spread of the money economy, together with the availability of cheap labor, following diminishing land-labor ratios, provided a conducive environment for both lords and peasants to accept the commutation of labor dues and renders in kind to money rents. By the fourteenth century this had become the dominant element in the economic relations between lords and peasants. In the judgment of one authority, "It is hard to think of any development in the medieval countryside which was more important than this change . . . [It] revolutionised relations between lords and their tenants and much else beside."[27] These fundamental

---

reprinted in Solow and Engerman (eds.), *British Capitalism and Caribbean Slavery*, fn. 6, p. 85.

[25] Power, *The Wool Trade*, pp. 29–31.

[26] Barbara F. Harvey, "Introduction: the 'crisis' of the early fourteenth century," in Bruce M. S. Campbell (ed.), *Before the Black Death: Studies in the 'crisis' of the early fourteenth century* (Manchester: Manchester University Press, 1991), pp. 12–16.

[27] Harvey, "Introduction," p. 13. North and Thomas believe that with the commutation of labor dues and renders in kind to money rents the classic manor of the tenth century had dissolved by 1200. In their view the classic theory which explains the decline of the manorial system in terms of the rise of the market economy, though now in disrepute, is supported by the logic of their own analysis. See North and Thomas, *The Rise of the Western World*, pp. 35–40. This view recently received a very strong support from Snooks: "Indeed the great transformation from feudalism to mercantile capitalism should be thought of as being caused by the emergence of factor markets" (Snooks, "Great Waves of Economic Change," p. 75). However, Rodney Hilton argues that the commutation of labor dues and renders in kind to

institutional changes were to continue in different forms under a different set of conditions from the late fourteenth to the seventeenth century.

In this second period (1300–1660) the emergence of the yeoman farmers, the development of manufacturing, especially woollen cloth production, and the establishment of parliamentary power in relation to monarchical authority were the major structural changes in the political economy of England. The first one and a half centuries of the period saw a reversal of the population growth of the previous two centuries. The decline reached catastrophic levels during the period of the Black Death, 1347–50. The recurrence of epidemic and infectious diseases caused a prolonged decline that continued to the middle decades of the fifteenth century. By 1450 the population of England had been reduced to less than 2.5 million.[28] Then growth began again in the last quarter of the fifteenth century and continued to the first half of the seventeenth.

The drastic demographic decline had a negative impact on the growth of market activities. Urban populations and the markets they provided for rural products declined. Even the population of London was reduced in the fifteenth century.[29] However, the negative impact of declining

money rents did not end serfdom. He holds that there was plenty of serfdom without labour services in parts of England, and that the institution was not abolished; it simply withered away over time, beginning in the 14th century. See R. H. Hilton, *The Decline of Serfdom in Medieval England* (London: Macmillan, 1969), pp. 29–31. The sources are rather silent on the ending of slavery. It may be reasonably assumed that the change in relative factor prices brought about by population growth and the attendant decline in land-labor ratios made the employment of other forms of labour relatively more economic than slavery. For some discussion of the subject, see M. M. Postan, *The Famulus: The Estate Labourer in the XIIth and XIIIth Centuries*, (*Economic History Review*, Supplement 2, 1954). It should be noted at this juncture that some Marxists will disagree with the points made in this chapter about the role of population growth. In particular, Robert Brenner has argued that class struggle was the central element in the historical process in medieval and early modern Europe, rather than population growth. For Brenner's arguments and reactions to them, see T. H. Aston and C. H. E. Philpin (eds.), *The Brenner Debate: Agrarian Class Structure and Economic Development in Pre-Industrial Europe* (Cambridge: Cambridge University Press, 1985); also Harvey, "Introduction," pp. 16–19. But while class struggle was an important element in the process, it did not operate as an independent variable. Class struggle was provoked by other developments. The classes were formed out of the operation of certain factors, and the outcome of the class struggle at a given moment was determined by the relative bargaining strength of the classes, which was in turn determined by the operating factors at the given moment and preceding institutional changes. Undoubtedly, Douglass North's framework is the most comprehensive on this subject. It treats population growth as the dynamic factor, but incorporates market development, ideology, and class struggle as the mechanisms through which change was effected. For details, see North and Thomas, *The Rise of the Western World*, and North, *Structure and Change*.

[28] Hatcher, *Plague, Population and the English Economy*, p. 69.
[29] Miller, "Introduction," pp. 29–30.

population was mitigated somewhat by the development of the woollen textile industry from the middle of the fourteenth century under government protection.[30]

The woollen textile industry, which existed in the twelfth century, had been severely constricted by the devastating impact of cloth imports from Flanders, which reduced England to an exporter of raw wool and importer of woollen cloth. Cloth manufacturing, therefore, developed in the fourteenth century as an import-substituting industry. English manufacturers struggled to capture the domestic market in the 1330s and 1340s.[31] Thereafter cloth export grew, while raw wool export continued. When the amount of wool employed in producing the quantity of cloth exported and that which replaced imported cloth is added to the quantity of wool exported the indication is that overall wool production in the late fourteenth and fifteenth centuries remained at levels that compared favorably with the peak points of the pre-plague period. Carus-Wilson's estimate put total production at 36,000 sacks per annum between 1353 and 1368.[32] The peak of raw wool exports between 1279 and 1336 was in the years 1304–13, the annual average for the peak period being 39,177 sacks.[33] At this time cloth manufacturing was strictly limited; hence, the export figures represent virtually the total output. Taking account of the years during which exports were less than 30,000 sacks (1279–90, 1297–1304, 1313–29), it can be said that total production was at about the same level in the periods, 1279–1336 and 1353–68.

The evidence shows that wool production continued to depend primarily on the export market in the post-plague period, even as cloth manufacturing for the domestic market grew and replaced imports. Between 1353 and 1368 average annual export of raw wool was 30,966 sacks. During the same period cloth export averaged 9,284.6 cloths.[34] Taking four and one-third cloths to one sack of wool,[35] the cloth export figure comes to 2,144 sacks of wool. Thus the combined quantity of wool involved in cloth and wool exports averaged 33,110 sacks in the years 1353–68. This is 92 percent of the total output estimated for the period by Carus-Wilson, as stated earlier.[36] From the last decades of the fourteenth century through the

---

[30] E. M. Carus-Wilson, "Trends in the export of English woollens in the fourteenth century," *Economic History Review*, 2nd series, Vol. III, no. 2 (1950), pp. 162–179.

[31] *Ibid.*, p. 164.   [32] *Ibid.*, p. 169.

[33] For the figures of raw wool exports from 1279 to 1336, see Inikori, "Slavery and the Development of Industrial Capitalism," fn. 6, p. 777; see also Lloyd, *The English Wool Trade*, pp. 63, 79–80, and 123.

[34] E. M. Carus-Wilson and Olive Coleman, *England's Export Trade, 1275–1547* (Oxford: Clarendon Press, 1963), pp. 47–49 and 75–78.

[35] Peter J. Bowden, *The Wool Trade in Tudor and Stuart England* (London: Macmillan, 1962), p. 37.

[36] Carus-Wilson's estimate may be on the low side; but even so, it is clear that the export market was overwhelmingly dominant.

fifteenth, cloth exports grew as wool exports decreased. Annual average cloth export was 19,249 cloths between 1350 and 1400, and for the whole of the fifteenth century it was over 42,000.[37] Adding raw wool export and wool employed to produce cloth for the domestic market, the indication is that wool production was on a large scale throughout the fifteenth century, and the export market remained dominant.

The fact that wool production from 1350 to 1500 was sustained at about pre-plague levels while population fell to only a fraction of its pre-plague size means that England was producing several times more wool per capita in the century and a half after 1350 than in the preceding two centuries. What is particularly important for the spread of market activities and the commercialization of agriculture is the fact that peasant producers increased their share of the total output considerably after 1350.[38] Thus, on the average, the peasants had significantly more cash to spend after 1350. In general, although the volume of trade may have declined in absolute terms, there is some indication that the proportion of agricultural output marketed increased in the late fourteenth and fifteenth centuries.

These developments, in association with changes in relative factor prices (land and labor), gave rise to some important changes in land use and the social distribution of land, and in lord-peasant relations. Between the Black Death and 1520, there was a general transfer of land from arable to pasture. This may be illustrated with evidence from the West Midlands. In the Avon valley and Feldon, virtually the entire land was devoted to arable farming in 1345–55. But by 1496–1500, 33 percent of the land had been transferred to pasture. In Arden the proportions for pasture are 7 percent in 1345–55 and 38 percent in 1496–1500; and for Gloucestershire the proportion of pasture increased from 2 percent in 1349–54 to 34 percent in 1485–1500.[39] This large-scale extension of pasture in the fifteenth and early sixteenth centuries ultimately made England unique in Europe in terms of the proportion of agricultural land devoted to sheep rearing and livestock farming in general. And this did not escape the attention of European visitors. A Frenchman describing England in the first decade of the seventeenth century wrote:

The face of the countryside bears some resemblance to that of Brittany and Normandy, differing in one thing only from all the other countries of the world, that there is none which uses so much land for pasture as this.[40]

[37] Pollard and Crossley, *The Wealth of Britain*, pp. 71–72.
[38] Power, *The Wool Trade*, pp. 37–40.
[39] C. C. Dyer, "The Occupation of the Land: The West Midlands," in Miller (ed.), *Agrarian History*, pp. 78–79.
[40] Cited by Joan Thirsk, "Introduction," in Joan Thirsk (ed.), *The Agrarian History of England and Wales: Volume IV, 1500–1640* (Cambridge: Cambridge University Press, 1967), p. xxx. As Thirsk shows, this view was also expressed by other European visitors in the sixteenth and seventeenth centuries.

This change in land use had important consequences. It encouraged specialization, and helped to reduce subsistence production and to extend commercial agriculture. In particular, the relative profitability of sheep farming, which required more land per unit of output than arable farming, helped to sustain the value of land at a reasonable level at a time of drastic demographic decline. What is more, rising wool prices stimulated private enclosure for sheep farming.[41] Although this early enclosure movement was not as massive as the outcry against it would seem to indicate, it was an important part of the institutional changes of the period, especially in the Midlands.[42]

An important part of the structural changes of the period was the social redistribution of land and the emergence of the yeoman farmer. The conditions that prevailed between 1086 and 1300 had favored the manorial lords relative to the peasants. In general, both lords and peasants benefited from the commutation of labor dues and renders in kind to money rents. But population pressure, which translated into increased demand for land, led to rising rents, decreasing size of peasant holdings, and a growing landless class among the peasantry. In consequence, there was a significant redistribution of income in favor of the lords.[43] The conditions were reversed between 1350 and 1500, during which the dramatic reduction of the population gave rise to declining rents and relatively rising labor costs.[44]

Under these circumstances the lords generally abandoned direct farming of their lands and the demesnes were leased on commercial rents to tenants. Along with this development, the commutation of labor dues and renders in kind to money rents, which began in the thirteenth century, was further generalized, and other manorial practices less acceptable to the peasants were whittled away. In the words of one authority, "Most landlords by the end of the fifteenth century were primarily rentiers, and most tenants were primarily payers of money rents . . ."[45]

---

[41] Between 1450 and 1489, wool prices rose by 38 percent, while grain prices rose by only 16 percent. See D. C. Coleman, *The Economy of England, 1450–1750* (Oxford: Oxford University Press, 1977), Table 4, p. 35.

[42] Coleman, *The Economy of England*, pp. 35–36 and 175–176.

[43] Cicely Howell, "Stability and Change 1300–1700: The Socio-Economic Context of the Self-Perpetuating Family Farm in England," *Journal of Peasant Studies*, Vol. 2, No. 4 (1975), p. 471; Pollard and Crossley, *The Wealth of Britain*, pp. 38–39.

[44] Miller shows that rents per acre declined in Norfolk from about 10¾ d. in 1376–78 to 9 d. in 1401–10 and then to 6½–8 d. for the rest of the fifteenth century. See Miller, "Introduction," p. 8. On the other hand, Hatcher's evidence shows that wage costs doubled in Westminster and Winchester manors between 1301 and 1450. See Hatcher, *Plague, Population and the English Economy*, p. 49.

[45] Miller, "Introduction," p. 31. There is a general tendency in the literature to explain these developments solely in terms of the drastic reduction of the population. It is often not recognized that the population size which existed in the fifteenth century had existed in earlier centuries without giving rise to such developments. In fact, a

With growing woollen cloth manufacturing, increased wool production by peasant growers, continuing market activities, and the elimination of most of the fettering elements of the manorial system, the stage was set for the more resourceful members of rural England to pull ahead from the crowd. As already mentioned, the leasing of the demesnes made a large amount of land available to tenants between 1320 and 1500. In the course of this period, the more resourceful peasants built up large commercial family holdings to become the celebrated yeoman farmers. To highlight this development the peasant cultivator of the thirteenth century has been compared with the seventeenth-century small farmer. The former had a 12 to 24-acre holding devoted predominantly to subsistence production, while the latter had a 60- to 100-acre family farm devoted primarily to production for market exchange.[46] The transition from one to the other began in the late fourteenth century. The process was quite slow for various reasons. But by the end of the fifteenth century the new class of smallholder commercial farmers was fully established. The price revolution of the sixteenth century, and the large-scale sale of church and Crown lands during the century, brought some changes (especially land purchases by merchants, lawyers, and other members of the urban middle class). On the whole, however, the sixteenth century consolidated the dominant position of the smallholders as commercial farmers.[47] Not until the low agricultural prices of the second half of the seventeenth century was their position threatened.

question that medievalists have failed to pose is why the character of economy and society, after the drastic reduction of population by the fifteenth century, did not simply revert to what it was in the late eleventh century when population size and density were at about the same level. Why was there so much change in the manorial system, a change usually attributed solely to the reduction of the population size? Why did the same population size and density produce different effects in two different periods? The answer to these questions rests with the development of the market and the associated institutional changes of the period 1086–1300, which were outlined earlier in the chapter, changes that were partly due to population growth and the spread of settlements during the period. Economic and political entrepreneurs responded to the conditions created by declining population in the context of a market economy and a general structural environment that did not exist in earlier centuries. This is why the changes of the fifteenth century are treated in the chapter as a continuation of those that were effected in the thirteenth and fourteenth centuries.

[46] Howell, "Stability and Change," pp. 468–469. In Howell's view, the small cultivator of the thirteenth and fourteenth centuries was a peasant, but the smallholder of the seventeenth century was not. And so, the developments of the fourteenth and fifteenth centuries can also be seen in terms of the disappearance of the peasant in England. Howell's study is based on the Midlands.

[47] Howell, "Stability and Change," pp. 471–477; Miller, "Introduction," pp. 13–16, 20–24, and 32; Pollard and Crossley, *The Wealth of Britain*, pp. 69–72; Harvey, "Introduction," p. 23. For a concise summary of these developments, with some statistics, see Coleman, *The Economy of England*, pp. 41–47.

Thus by the seventeenth century English agriculture was fully commercialized. Two groups characterised the new agrarian structure – the family farmers, who were much larger in numbers, and a new class of noncultivating large landholders who invested capital to improve the quality of their lands in order to enhance their profits by attracting more able tenants. These developments were very important for the socio-economic processes of the period 1660–1850.

There is just one more issue to examine briefly to conclude discussion of the socio-economic changes of the late medieval and early modern periods. This concerns the question of what happened to per capita incomes during the prolonged period of dramatic decline of England's population from the fourteenth to the late fifteenth century. The received wisdom has been the view that real income per head increased during the period. Hatcher seems unimpressed by this view of a prosperous age during which families regularly lost young and active members to premature death. But, persuaded by a view with the weight of history and of respected authorities behind it, he could only offer a qualification based on a rather awkward conception of economic well-being.[48]

The received wisdom has now been challenged vigorously by Snooks. Snooks employs the evidence in the Domesday Book and Gregory King's national income estimate, using simulation techniques, to show that real GDP per capita (in 1688 prices) grew from £1.72 in 1086 to £3.30 in 1300, and then declined continuously to £2.02 in 1400, stagnating thereafter up to 1470 before increasing once again to £3.26 in 1510. The 1300 level was surpassed in 1520 when real income per head stood at £3.70.[49] He traces the source of the traditional view that there was an inverse relationship between population and real income per capita to the Brown-Hopkins wage index, which he demonstrates to be based on misleading evidence. Snooks argues to the contrary that there was a positive correlation between population and economic growth during the period in question, and that the dramatic decrease of England's population following the Black Death reduced

---

[48] As he put it, "Finally we must do something to correct an impression given in this account, and in much of the writing on this period, that living standards can be assessed solely in terms of the amount of goods that a man's wage would purchase. In these terms the fifteenth century was truly the golden age of the English labourer. Yet, as we have seen, these high living standards were not due to any decisive advances in techniques or in the structure of the economy, but to the simple fact that there were fewer people to share the resources of the nation. . . . Clearly an age which relies for its prosperity upon large numbers of its members dying at an early age, and suffering the frequent losses of spouses, children, relatives, friends, and colleagues, is somewhat less than golden. Can we wonder that a preoccupation with death and putrefaction is encountered so frequently in the artistic, literary and religious movements of the age?" (Hatcher, *Plague, Population and the English Economy*, p. 73).

[49] Snooks, "Great Waves of Economic Change," pp. 77–78.

drastically the English economy's scale of operation with significant adverse effects on per capita income: "It is just not plausible to argue that a country experiencing a long and savage downswing in population will experience a sustained increase in real per capita income – sustained, according to Brown and Hopkins, for over a century."[50]

One may question whether Snooks's evidence is adequate to bear the weight of his conclusions. However, the logic of the analysis makes better economics than the traditional view, and the critique of the Brown-Hopkins wage index is persuasive. What is more, new evidence produced by research, which shows that real wages in Essex fell by about 24 percent after the Black Death and remained at that level up to the late fifteenth century, appears to support Snooks's position.[51] Also Mayhew's estimates mentioned earlier show a pattern of per capita income growth similar to that of Snooks, though somewhat slower: £2.6 in 1086, £4.2 in 1300, and £10.2 in 1688.[52]

While the commercialization of agriculture, the elimination of the remnants of manorial constraints, and the emergence of new dominant classes in rural England were the major developments in the fifteenth and sixteenth centuries as shown earlier, there were also some changes in the industrial scene. Although England continued to export mainly unfinished cloth – which was finished on the continent and sold back to English consumers – the transformation of England from an exporter of raw wool to an exporter of manufactured cloth was completed in the sixteenth century. What was particularly important for the future of the industry, a new product, the "new draperies," was developed from the middle decades of the sixteenth century. Continental producers had earlier invaded English overseas markets for cloth with this product. By mastering its production, English manufacturers were able to sustain their overall level of export in the early seventeenth century. To illustrate, estimated woollen exports in 1606/14 were as follows: cloth, £1,193,000; new draperies, £347,000. The comparable figures for 1640 are £847,000 for cloth and £605,000 for the new draperies.[53] Thus, while the export of cloth declined, that of the lighter product, the new draperies, almost doubled. This lighter product was to capture new markets in the warmer climates and become the main source

---

[50] Snooks, *Economics Without Time*, p. 263; for details of the argument, see pp. 256–264.

[51] L. R. Poos, *A Rural Society after the Black Death: Essex, 1350–1525* (Cambridge: Cambridge University Press, 1991), pp. 52 and 211, cited by Snooks, "Great Waves of Economic Change," pp. 71–72.

[52] Mayhew, "Modelling medieval monetisation," pp. 71–77. Mayhew presents his estimates in 1086 prices: £0.13 in 1086, £0.21 in 1300, and £0.51 in 1688. To compare with Snooks's estimates, these figures have been converted to 1688 values, using Mayhew's 20-fold increase in prices between 1086 and 1688.

[53] Coleman, *The Economy of England*, p. 64; Bowden, *The Wool Trade*, p. 44.

of export growth in the late seventeenth and eighteenth centuries. The indication is that the woollen industry still sold the bulk of the output overseas. A rough estimate of the annual value of the industry's total output in the 1580s puts it at £1.5 million.[54] This suggests that the exports in 1606/14 stated earlier could not have been less than two-thirds of the total output at the time.

There was also some stirring in other sectors of manufacturing in the late sixteenth and early seventeenth centuries. Joan Thirsk has documented the establishment in England of several manufacturing industries between 1540 and 1630.[55] Apart from the establishment of new industries, output in mining and iron production increased during the period. Pig iron production is estimated to have grown from 5,000 tons a year in the 1550s to about 20,000 tons per annum in the 1630s.[56] Although existing estimates of coal output during the period are of doubtful quality, it is believed nonetheless that coal production increased greatly in the sixteenth and early seventeenth centuries, mainly to meet increased demand for home heating at a time of rapid population growth and urbanization. In the opinion of A. E. Musson, technological improvement in coal mining and use of coal fuel was a major development of the period, with important consequences for subsequent industrial growth.[57]

An important link between the socio-economic changes of the centuries from Domesday England to the Restoration, and the development of industrial production in the 200 years that followed, is the evolution of political institutions in the former period. This political development is characterized by the strengthening of the central administration at the expense of seigneurial authority at the local level and the establishment of effective power sharing between parliament and the monarchy. These institutional changes are described often in the literature as the emergence of the nation-state and the growth of parliamentary power. Central to the process leading to the changes is the need of the central administration for revenue. To stress

---

[54] Sybil M. Jack, *Trade and Industry in Tudor and Stuart England* (London: Allen and Unwin, 1977), pp. 103–104.

[55] As she reports, "I was struck [while indexing a volume on seventeenth-century documents] by the frequency of references to consumer goods like brass, cooking pans, cambric, gold and silver thread, hats, knives, lace, polvadis, ribbons, ruffs, soap, and tape. . . . I recognized some of them as consumer goods which had been roundly condemned in 1547 as foreign fripperies that robbed this kingdom of its bullion. Yet here they were in everyday use in the seventeenth century, and, what is more, being manufactured in England. I decided to pursue their origins. In the end . . . I found a deliberate government policy to foster the native manufacture of consumer goods." (Joan Thirsk, *Economic Policy and Projects: The Development of a Consumer Society in Early Modern England* (Oxford: Clarendon Press, 1978, p. v.)

[56] Jack, *Trade and Industry*, pp. 77–78.

[57] A. E. Musson, *The Growth of British Industry* (New York: Holmes and Meier, 1978), p. 52.

the centrality of this factor, one authority has defined the state as "an organization with a comparative advantage in violence, extending over a geographic area whose boundaries are determined by its power to tax constituents."[58]

The origin of the English state in a conquest situation – the Norman Conquest – had given England a relatively strong central administration at an early stage in comparison with Continental countries, such as France and Spain. In the course of the thirteenth century, the authority of the national government was further extended.[59] The growth of the wool trade in the medieval era gave the Crown a large source of revenue, which was administratively inexpensive to tax but politically difficult to handle. The first export tax on wool, 7 shillings and 6 pence (7s:6d.) per sack, was levied in 1275. By the fourteenth and fifteenth centuries tax on the external trade organized around wool exports had become the main source of revenue for the Crown.[60] But the tax on wool export affected interest groups with considerable political clout – the merchant exporters and the wool growers (made up of large demesne producers and a multitude of small freeholders). Parliament was composed largely of people drawn from these interest groups, especially wool growers. Ultimately parliament won its initial power to check the authority of the monarch out of the fourteenth-century struggle over the wool tax. The compromise that ended the struggle left the king "in possession of a high permanent tax on wool, and parliament was left in possession of the power to control it."[61] The ability of parliament to determine the amount of revenue available to the Crown became the most effective instrument with which parliament influenced the policies of the national government. The Civil War and the Glorious Revolution of 1688 subsequently consolidated the power of Parliament.

The establishment of the power of this representative body, that is Parliament, provided an effective channel for dominant interest groups in England to influence the policies of the national government in both domestic and external matters. To understand the policies of the English government in the seventeenth and eighteenth centuries one must, therefore, study the evolution of interest groups that influenced those policies through Parliament. Robert Brenner's study of London's overseas traders shows how the emergence of a new interest group in overseas trade between

[58] North, *Structure and Change*, p. 21.
[59] North and Thomas, *The Rise of the Western World*, p. 64.
[60] Power, *The Wool Trade*, p. 75; North and Thomas, *The Rise of the Western World*, p. 83.
[61] Power, *The Wool Trade*, p. 85, but see pp. 63–85 for more details on the politics of the wool tax.

1550 and 1653 influenced the direction of England's foreign policy during the period of the Commonwealth.[62] The new group was made up largely of merchants in the trade of the Americas. In the struggle between the Crown and Parliament leading to the Civil War, this group of merchants, because of their socio-economic origin and because Crown policies excluded them from the traditional areas of English overseas trade, joined the landed classes in supporting Parliament. The company merchants, whose monopoly rights depended on the Crown, did the opposite. The merchants in the rapidly growing American trade made a major contribution to the parliamentary cause through their effective mobilization of support among London radical elements, which was financially and militarily crucial for Parliament's ultimate victory. This placed the American traders in a strong position to influence the foreign policy of the Commonwealth administration in a manner consistent with their own commercial interest.

Their influence is clearly discernible in the aggressive and expansionist commercial and colonial policies pursued by the Commonwealth, which left a long-lasting impact on English commerce and economic development. Probably the most important outcome of their influence was the creation of a permanent, well-equipped and highly efficient navy, single-mindedly devoted to the expansion and protection of English commerce. Started in 1649, representatives of the American traders played a major role in the conception and execution of the naval program. They dominated the important committees charged with the implementation of the plan. And most of the naval officers were recruited from among former ship masters in the American trade. The influence of these merchants was also very much behind the laws of the 1650s, aimed at the destruction of Dutch hegemony in the trade of the Americas and the ultimate use of the navy to achieve that purpose militarily.

Several gains made by Parliament were lost after the Restoration, but these were fully reinstituted by the Glorious Revolution of 1688. This development of parliamentary power, and the evolution of socio-economic structures that produced dominant groups whose self-interests were consistent with the growth of English overseas trade and the development of commodity production in England, is pertinent to a proper understanding of the politico-military and economic processes of the late seventeenth and eighteenth centuries. The role of Parliament was particularly important in the relatively more efficient management of English public finance in

---

[62] Robert Brenner, *Merchants and Revolution: Commercial Change, Political Conflict, and London's Overseas Traders, 1550–1653* (Princeton NJ: Princeton University Press, 1993). Much of what follows, up to the next reference, is based on this book.

the eighteenth century as compared with France, especially in the establishment and management of the English national debt.[63]

It is thus reasonable to say that important socio-economic and political changes occurred between Domesday and the middle decades of the seventeen century. No explanation of the growth and development of industrial production, which took place from 1660 to 1850, would be complete without a proper consideration of these changes. To create a helpful context for such a consideration, we need to make a generalized pronouncement on the character and overall level of the socio-economic development of the period and show its regional distribution.

There is a consensus in the literature that the social changes, which occurred in England between 1086 and 1660, created a conducive social environment for the English economy to respond vigorously to growth stimuli. Changes in the social relations of production had eliminated virtually the extraction of economic surplus through extra-economic coercion. The spread of market activities and the drastic reduction of subsistence production increased considerably the capacity of market forces to allocate resources. In particular, the commercialization of agriculture and the establishment of an active land market exposed the relatively large agrarian population to the operation of market forces. On the political side, the development of a representative system of government, with the representatives of the dominant socio-economic groups exercising an effective control over the extraction and utilization of resources by the national government, provided secure protection for the property rights of economic entrepreneurs, and helped to keep in check the phenomenon of rent-seeking by political and bureaucratic office holders.

However, there is some disagreement on the specific character of the agrarian and industrial development, which occurred during the period. It is held in some sections of the literature that England's agriculture had become capitalist by the sixteenth century. Others disagree, arguing that the predominance of free wage labor is the defining element of the capitalist system of production, and that the existing evidence shows that self-employed producers cultivating family farms were still predominant in English agriculture in the first decades of the seventeenth century.[64] It would seem more accurate to characterize England's agriculture in the first half of

---

[63] Brenner, *Merchants and Revolution*, pp. 577–632 and 638–716; Derek Massarella, " 'A World Elsewhere': Aspects of the Overseas Expansionist Mood of the 1650s," in Colin Jones, Malyn Newitt and Stephen Roberts (eds.), *Politics and People in Revolutionary England: Essays in Honour of Ivan Roots* (Oxford: Basil Blackwell, 1986), pp. 141–161; H. R. Trevor-Roper, *Religion, the Reformation and Social Change, and Other Essays* (second edition, London: Macmillan, 1972), pp. 345–391.

[64] For a critical discussion of the literature on the subject, see Joseph E. Inikori, *Slavery and the Rise of Capitalism: The 1993 Elsa Goveia Memorial Lecture* (Mona, Jamaica: The University of the West Indies, 1993), pp. 2–13.

the seventeenth century as a highly market-oriented agriculture dominated by smallholder commercial family farmers.

On the characterization of the industrial development during the period, the views in the literature center on the notion of an industrial revolution in the years 1540–1640, which John Nef propounded several decades ago.[65] This view has now been largely discredited.[66] The new industries encouraged by the government, which Thirsk noted, were not successfully developed. As Musson observes,

> such projects were generally more notable for their exaggerated pretensions, mismanagement, corruption and eventual failure than for their technological innovations . . . , this country [England] long remained heavily dependent on foreign imports of glass, paper, iron, copper, brass, etc., despite protective tariffs.[67]

Coleman expresses a similar view. After examining the industrial development of the 200 years from 1450 to 1650, he warns: "The temptation to resort to hyperbole . . . or to feel oneself present at the unearthing of the roots of modern, materialistic industrial civilisation: such delights must be resisted." And he adds:

> Woollen cloth aside, English exports were still those of a primary producer, with virtually no other manufactured wares in the export list. . . . Nor was it all a matter of supply. English demand for many manufactured wares was limited largely because levels of wealth and income, as of culture, sophistication, and urban achievement, were inferior to those of the great towns of Europe.[68]

Although these views are understandable in the context of Nef's claims, it is still valid to say that some progress was made in the development of mining and manufacturing in England in the late sixteenth and early seventeenth centuries. This industrial progress – amounting to proto-industrialization in the case of the woollen industry – certainly made some contribution to subsequent industrial development in the eighteenth and nineteenth centuries. However, to have a proper sense of the contribution that the socio-economic changes between 1086 and 1660 made to the growth and development of industrial production in the 200 years that

[65] John U. Nef, "The Progress of Technology and the Growth of Large Scale Industry, 1540–1640," *Economic History Review*, original series, V (1934–35); John U. Nef, "A Comparison of Industrial Growth in France and England from 1540 to 1640," *Journal of Political Economy*, XLIV (1936).

[66] See Jack, *Trade and Industry*, pp. 18–26, for a review of the literature; also Musson, *The Growth of British Industry*, pp. 30–53.

[67] Musson, *The Growth of British Industry*, p. 43.

[68] Coleman, *The Economy of England*, p. 88 and pp. 69–70. Robert Brenner disagrees with this view of limited English demand for manufactured wares. He holds that in the first half of the seventeenth century, "a growing English home market was absorbing record imports of commodities of all types." See Brenner, *Merchants and Revolution*, p. 42.

followed, we need to know the regional distribution of the developments in both periods. The distribution in the later period will be examined in the next section of this chapter. Here we examine that of the earlier period.

As noted earlier in the chapter, much of the impetus for change during the period came from population growth and overseas trade. The southern counties, favored by their greater population densities from the very beginning of our period (1086), were the centers of early development. As we have seen, all top 10 counties in the amount of wealth assessed per acre for tax payment at this time were in the south. The tax records of the early sixteenth century show that the most densely populated counties were still in the south,[69] although the population growth of the preceding centuries had filled up much of the wilderness that existed in parts of England in 1086, especially in the northern counties.

The southern counties were also major beneficiaries of the expansion of overseas trade during the period, which was dominated by wool exports, and from the sixteenth century by cloth exports. Outside the south, the Midland counties were also involved in wool exports on a large scale. As England gradually moved from wool exports to cloth exports, the woollen industry developed up to the seventeenth century more or less like an agro-allied industry. Every county produced some quantity of wool. For example, in 1700, 35 counties produced 1,000 packs of wool or more each; 24 produced 2,000 and above; 13 produced 3,000 and more; the largest producers, Lincoln, Kent, Dorset, Northampton, Sussex, and Northumberland, produced 6,000 packs, 5,500 packs, 4,000 packs, 4,000 packs, 4,000 packs and 4,000 packs, respectively.[70] As cloth imports from Continental Europe were reduced, cloth manufacturing developed in the counties based on locally supplied wool. Much of it, in all probability, was at the level of peasant craft for local consumption. Again, in the sixteenth and seventeenth centuries, large-scale cloth production was located in the south, in particular, the West Country and East Anglia.[71] The latter regions supplied the bulk of the cloth exported during the period. They thus developed as the most industrialized parts of England in the late sixteenth and early seventeenth centuries. According to the textile historian, Julian de Lucy Mann:

In 1600 and throughout the previous century the clothiers of Gloucestershire, Wiltshire, and east Somerset had been distinguished from most of their neighbours by the degree of their concentration on unfinished, so-called "white" cloth, mainly for export to Holland and Germany, whence, after being dyed and finished, it was transported all over Europe.[72]

---

[69] Miller, "Introduction," p. 29.
[70] Bowden, *The Wool Trade*, p. 40.
[71] Pollard and Crossley, *The Wealth of Britain*, pp. 101–102.
[72] Julian de Lucy Mann, *The Cloth Industry in the West of England from 1640 to 1880* (Oxford: Clarendon Press, 1971), pp. xii–xiii.

Of East Anglia, Coleman says:

Before the Industrial Revolution, the three counties of Norfolk, Suffolk and Essex had at various times been the scene of important industrial and commercial activity. . . . the widespread woollen industry of Suffolk and northern Essex reached the appex of its considerable importance in the late fifteenth and early sixteenth centuries . . . When the "New Draperies" came to England from the Low Countries, they came first to East Anglia. Norwich added a miscellany of "stuffs" to its traditional worsteds, and Colchester acquired a fame for bayes and sayes. Though these two became the main urban centres for the manufacture and marketing of the new fabrics, many smaller towns and villages, especially along the Essex-Suffolk border were busy with them. . . . The whole area was seemingly in the forefront of advance, prosperous in agriculture as in industry, accepting from the countries across the North Sea new ideas in farming as well as new men and new fabrics in textiles.[73]

Much of the stimulus from the growth of manufacturing in the densely populated and agriculturally rich southern counties of England would appear to have been limited to the south, and to a lesser extent, the West Midlands. The latter supplied wool to the broadcloth regions. But, in general, the industrial centers of the south, located in agriculturally rich areas, supplied the bulk of their own food and raw materials, although the cattle trade from the north may have provided some animal products.[74] In this way, the growth of manufacturing in the south further increased the level of agricultural development in the region as compared with that of the northern counties. It is no surprise that the concentration of wealth in the south further increased over the period. The areas of greatest increase of wealth were in the cloth-producing regions of the southwest (Gloucestershire and Wiltshire) and East Anglia.[75]

Developments in the Midlands over the period under consideration were just good enough to keep the region in the same position as in 1086 in relation to the rest of England. As one historian of the Midlands wrote,

The changes in land use in the East Midland region in the late middle ages, though they have left substantial visible remains, were an adaptation which left the five counties close to the median of wealth in the early sixteenth century, just as they had been in the early fourteenth. The Midland counties indeed show little fluctuation at any time from Domesday onwards.[76]

---

[73]   D. C. Coleman, "Growth and Decay During the Industrial Revolution: The Case of East Anglia," *The Scandinavian Economic History Review*, Vol. X, nos. 1 and 2 (1962), pp. 115–117.

[74]   J. A. Chartres, *Internal Trade in England, 1500–1700* (London: Macmillan, 1977), pp. 13–27.

[75]   Miller, "Introduction," p. 29.

[76]   Edmund King, "The Occupation of the Land: The East Midlands," in Miller (ed.), *Agrarian History*, p. 76.

Because northern England did not share greatly in the developments of the centuries from 1086 to 1660, the northern counties continued to move farther below the southern ones in wealth and socio-economic development during the period. The evidence for Lancashire and Yorkshire shows this clearly. As Edward Miller states,

At the opening of the fourteenth century, even after vigorous expansion in preceding generations, Yorkshire and Lancashire were still relatively poor counties. In terms of the ratio of taxable wealth to acreage, if the four northernmost counties are ignored, only Devon and Cornwall ranked lower than the West Riding; Lancashire and the North Riding were the West Riding's near neighbours in the order; and, while the East Riding came higher in the list, it was still somewhat below the middle point. This relative poverty reflected a terrain and climate which restricted the options open to farmers, so that the natural landscape had been less radically modified here than in many parts of England.[77]

That the stimulus from developments in the south was not seriously felt in the north of England during the period in question is also demonstrated by the author of a detailed social history of Lancashire from 1558 to 1939.[78] His description of mid-Tudor Lancashire shows that the social changes between 1086 and 1550, examined earlier in the chapter, did not reach the county:

Mid-Tudor Lancashire was an obscure, remote, insular and backward corner of England. The population density was low, towns were small and underdeveloped, long-distance trade was very limited in its scope and range, and wide areas of the county were given over to moss and moorland. Local magnates retained considerable autonomy; some still exercised feudal rights of wardship and marriage over their tenants, and labour dues and payment in kind were widespread elements in the relationships between small farmers and their landlords.[79]

As a measure of the gap in wealth and income between Lancashire and the more developed southern counties in the sixteenth century, the tax assessment for 1515 put Lancashire at £3.8 per thousand acres; the comparable figures for Essex, Kent, and metropolitan Middlesex are £102, £100.5, and

---

[77]   After examining the changes of the fourteenth and fifteenth centuries, Miller, again, remarks: "There are indications, therefore, of development as well as of difficulties in the Yorkshire and Lancashire countryside. Even so, both counties at the opening of the sixteenth century ranked even lower in assessed taxable wealth than they had in 1334 and the growth of their taxable capacity was well below the average for the country as a whole. It had been lowest of all in Lancashire, suggesting the limited economic potential of such development of stock farming as there had been, and also the slight progress yet made by the woollen industry of Salfordshire and Blackburnshire." Edward Miller, "The Occupation of the Land: Yorkshire and Lancashire," in Miller (ed.), *Agrarian History,* p. 42.

[78]   John K. Walton, *Lancashire: A Social History, 1558–1939* (Manchester: Manchester University Press, 1987).

[79]   Walton, *Lancashire,* p. 7.

£238.1, respectively. Of the 38 English counties assessed in this year, Lancashire came last, and the county "was to remain so for well over a century."[80]

Thus, although some socio-economic changes occurred in all parts of England between 1086 and 1660, the really fundamental changes were limited to the densely populated, agriculturally rich, and industrially more developed, counties of the south, and, to a lesser extent, those of the Midlands. In particular, Lancashire and Yorkshire were still very backward in socio-economic structure and in the technology and organization of production by the early decades of the seventeenth century. On the whole, the level of industrial development in England in the first decades of the seventeenth century was still considerably lower than that of the major centers of commerce and industry in Continental Europe. But some progress had been made between 1540 and 1660, especially in the West Country and East Anglia.

2.2 GROWTH AND DEVELOPMENT OF INDUSTRIAL PRODUCTION, 1660–1850

The central focus of the survey in this section is the structural transformation of the English economy from the predominance of agriculture to that of industry and the development of the organization and technology of industrial production. But these changes in industry did not occur in isolation from changes in other sectors of the economy – changes in agriculture, in services, and in trade and transport. For this reason, much space is allocated in the section to developments in these sectors. But it must be understood that this is done in order to be able to show in subsequent chapters how changes in these sectors related to the growth and development of industrial production during the period. We start with agriculture.

As was shown in the preceding section, the dominant features of England's agrarian history from 1086 to 1660 were the expansion of production for market exchange at the expense of subsistence production; the freeing of the cultivators from extra-economic coercion; the transfer of the land to small freeholders, copyholders, and tenants; and the emergence of the yeoman farmers and a new class of profit-oriented large landholders. The latter were still a small minority by 1660, as the number of small farmers increased considerably between 1500 and 1650.[81] The 200 years

[80] Walton, *Lancashire*, p. 8.

[81] R. B. Outhwaite, "Progress and Backwardness in English Agriculture, 1500–1650," *Economic History Review*, 2nd ser., XXXIX, 1 (1986), pp. 1–18; E. M. Leonard, "Inclosure of Common Fields in the Seventeenth Century," *Transactions of the Royal Historical Society*, new series, XIX (1905), reprinted in E. M. Carus-Wilson (ed.), *Essays in Economic History*, vol. II (London: E. Arnold, 1962), p. 228; J. H.

that followed witnessed further fundamental changes in the agrarian structure – a reduction of the number of small farmers; the growth and predominance of large landholders, large farms, and large tenant farmers; the
emergence of free wage labor as the dominant form of labor in agriculture;
and the spread of enclosure.

Figures reflecting the over time changes in the agrarian structure are
scarce and of questionable quality. Those generally employed by historians
for the seventeenth century are derived from Gregory King's social statistics for England and Wales in 1688. Peter Lindert has shown that King's
figures exaggerated the size of the agricultural sector in the late seventeenth
century.[82] Accordingly, the King's tables have been revised, first by Lindert
and then by Lindert and Williamson. The latter revision shows that in 1688
there were 227,440 families employed in agriculture in England and Wales,
excluding laborers. Of this total, freeholders (this must mean all small
farmers working farms of 20 to 100 acres employing family labor) numbered 124,058 and farmers (that is, large tenant farmers) counted 103,382.
A similar revision of Joseph Massie's mid-eighteenth-century tables gives a
figure of 140,871 families for freeholders, 134,160 for husbandmen, and
103,977 for farmers, making a total of 379,008 families employed in agriculture in England and Wales in 1759, excluding wage workers. Lindert
and Williamson find Colquhoun's figures generally consistent with local
census and burial data. They, therefore, accept them without revision. For
1801–03, the figures are as follows: freeholders, 160,000 families; farmers,
160,000 families. This gives a total of 320,000 families for 1801–03.[83]
Figures for the rest of the nineteenth century, which are derived from census
data, are generally more reliable. According to the census data of 1831,
there were a total of 961,100 families employed in agriculture in the whole
island of Britain; of whom large tenant farmers, who worked large farm
units rented from large landholders, numbered 144,600, and small farmers
working farms of 20 to 100 acres (mostly owned and partly rented) using
family labor totaled 130,500. In addition, there were 686,000 free wage-
earning families employed by the large tenant farmers.[84] As for changing

---

Habakkuk, "English Landownership, 1680–1740," *Economic History Review*, X
(1939–40), p. 2.

[82] Peter H. Lindert, "English Occupations, 1670–1811," *Journal of Economic History*,
Vol. XL, No. 4 (1980), pp. 706–707.

[83] Lindert, "English Occupations," Table 3, pp. 702–704; Peter H. Lindert and Jeffrey
G. Williamson, "Revising England's Social Tables, 1688–1812," *Explorations in
Economic History*, 19 (1982), pp. 385–408. For a criticism of Lindert's estimates,
which by implication also applies to Lindert and Williamson, see Julian Hoppit,
"Counting the Industrial Revolution," *Economic History Review*, 2nd series,
XLIII, 2 (1990), pp. 177–178.

[84] J. H. Clapham, "The Growth of An Agrarian Proletariat, 1688–1832: A Statistical
Note," *Cambridge Historical Journal*, Vol. I (1923), p. 93.

farm size over time, the average for demesnes, copyholds and leased land in northern England, and in open villages in southern England was 65 acres in 1700, according to estate surveys. Enclosed farms in southern England at this time were larger. By 1800, the average had increased to 150 acres for all types of farms in the south and 100 acres in the north. For the nineteenth century, the data for the 1890s show that there were, in England and Wales, 83,000 holdings of over 100 acres and 129,000 of between 20 and 100 acres; holdings of less than 20 acres made up only 6 percent of the agricultural land in England and Wales at this time.[85]

These figures raise several questions about the nature of England's agrarian structure and its change over time between 1660 and 1850. The capitalist character of English agriculture from the sixteenth century onward is often stressed.[86] The evidence for 1500–1650 referred to earlier shows that self-employed family farmers dominated English agriculture up to the middle of the seventeenth century. The figures just presented indicate that as late as the middle of the eighteenth century, the number of entrepreneur families (379,008) still exceeded that of free wage workers in agriculture.[87] The figures for 1801–03 show that "laboring people in husbandry" numbered 340,000 families against 320,000 entrepreneur families.[88] These figures, therefore, indicate that free wage workers, the defining element of the capitalist system of production, did not become predominant in English agriculture until well into the nineteenth century.[89] Even by then, their dominance was not overwhelming. Chambers and Mingay are certainly right in their view that "The picture sometimes presented of English farming, with a select band of large

[85] Robert Allen, "Agriculture during the industrial revolution," in Floud and McCloskey (eds.), *The Economic History of Britain*, p. 99; G. E. Mingay, *Enclosure and the Small Farmer in the Age of the Industrial Revolution* (London: Macmillan, 1968), p. 14; Patrick O'Brien and Caglar Keyder, *Economic Growth in Britain and France 1780–1914: Two Paths to the Twentieth Century* (London: Allen & Unwin, 1978), p. 127.

[86] Immanuel Wallerstein, *The Modern World System I: Capitalist Agriculture and the Origins of the European World Economy in the Sixteenth Century* (New York: Academic Press, 1974); Robert Brenner, "Agrarian Class Structure and Economic Development in Pre-Industrial Europe," *Past and Present*, No. 70 (1976), pp. 31–75; Robert Brenner, "The Origins of Capitalist Development: A Critique of Neo-Smithian Marxism," *New Left Review*, No. 104 (July-August, 1977), pp. 25–92; Brenner, *Merchants and Revolution*, p. 40.

[87] The social tables analyzed by Lindert and Williamson do not show the number of wage-earning families for each sector. They are lumped together for all sectors, except for 1801–1803. For 1688 wage-earning families in all sectors are put at 284,997, and 240,000 for 1759. Lindert and Williamson, "Revising England's Social Tables," pp. 389 and 397.

[88] Lindert and Williamson, "Revising England's Social Tables," p. 401.

[89] For more detail, see Inikori, *Slavery and the Rise of Capitalism*, pp. 2–13.

capitalist farmers employing a vast army of landless laborers, is patently a false one."[90]

The figures also touch on the old debate about the decline of the small farmer. To the extent that we can rely on the story told by these figures and taking account of the growth of the small family farmers between 1450 and 1650, the indication is that a considerable reduction in the number of the small farmers occurred between 1650 and 1688. Thereafter their numbers increased (from 124,058 families in 1688 to 275,031 in 1759), to be considerably reduced again in the second half of the eighteenth century (down to 160,000 families by 1801–03). Before the census of 1831, the population of small farmers would appear to have been reduced further by about one-third.[91] This would mean that a considerable reduction of the number of small farmers did occur during the era of parliamentary enclosure, 1760–1830, even though a much earlier reduction took place in the second half of the seventeenth century. In this way, the protagonists on both sides of the debate would appear to be half winners and half losers.[92] However, the more recent research holds that the decline of yeoman agriculture from the second half of the eighteenth century was due to factors other than parliamentary enclosure. It is argued that early enclosures and those of the seventeenth century had the effect of enlarging the size of farms and reducing the number of small farmers, particularly the enclosures before the mid-sixteenth century, those of the eighteenth and nineteenth centuries had little effect on landownership.[93]

These structural changes provide the necessary background against which to view the growth of agricultural output during the period under

---

[90] J. D. Chambers and G. E. Mingay, *The Agricultural Revolution, 1750–1880* (London: Batsford, 1966), p. 18.

[91] To arrive at this conclusion, I have assumed that about 20,000 out of the 130,500 families of small farmers in the whole of Britain in 1831 may be assigned to Scotland.

[92] For more detail on the debate, see Mingay, *Enclosure and the Small Farmer*, pp. 9–11, where the extent of the literature and some of the participants are discussed. Basically Karl Marx and his subsequent followers argued that parliamentary enclosure was the mechanism employed by the large landholders to rob the small farmers of their land. Several historians countered with the argument that the small farmers declined largely between 1650 and 1750 owing to the impact of low prices and the land tax.

[93] Robert C. Allen, *Enclosure and the Yeoman: The Agricultural Development of the South Midlands, 1450–1850* (Oxford: Clarendon Press, 1992), pp. 14–15. As Allen put it, "The real collapse of yeoman agriculture occurred in the eighteenth century, in open field villages as well as in enclosed. Many yeomen were freeholders, and they sold their property to great estates. Other yeomen held their land on copyholds for lives or beneficial leases for lives or long terms of years, and they lost their land when large landowners stopped renewing these agreements. These real estate dealings were due to the creation of modern mortgages which increased the propensity of great estates to buy land."

consideration. The more recent literature contains somewhat conflicting estimates. Earlier estimates of output growth by Deane and Cole and by Crafts have been thoroughly reviewed and revised by Jackson.[94] The revised estimates show that output grew considerably between 1660 and 1740, and stagnated during the 50 years from 1740 to 1790. Overall, output grew by 40 percent in the first period, and by 14 percent in the second, being an average of 4.3 percent and 2.7 percent per decade, respectively. Because population stagnated between 1660 and 1740 and grew relatively fast from 1740 to 1790, agricultural output per head increased significantly in the first period, while it declined in the second.[95]

In contrast to Jackson's estimate, Allen shows a much larger growth of output in the second half of the eighteenth century, with an increase of 49 percent between 1750 and 1800 and a further growth of 53 percent between 1800 and 1850.[96] Crafts also shows rapid increases in output for the nineteenth century – 1.18 percent per annum between 1801 and 1831.[97] On the other hand, Gregory Clark argues that the bulk of the agricultural productivity gains in England and Wales before 1850 had been achieved by 1770, so that very little change occurred between 1770 and 1850. He estimates that productivity levels for England as a whole in 1701–30 were 92 percent of their level in 1850.[98] Judging from the whole evidence and analysis, Jackson's estimates for the period 1660–1790 appear to receive more support, even by Allen who thinks that the Crafts's series, as reconstructed by Jackson, "may give a more accurate indication of the rhythm of change."[99] And Clark's conclusion that the bulk of the productivity gains achieved before 1850 had been accomplished by 1730 is consistent with Jackson's estimate.

Although there are disagreements over the specific rate of growth of output in the first half of the nineteenth century, there is a consensus among the authorities that domestic production of agricultural products fell far short of what was needed during the period, and the gap was filled by imports. This was due to the inter-related phenomena of growing industrialization, rising per capita income, and expanding population – the

[94] R. V. Jackson, "Growth and Deceleration in English Agriculture, 1660–1790," *Economic History Review*, 2nd series, XXXVIII, No. 3 (August, 1985), pp. 333–351; Phyllis Deane and W. A. Cole, *British Economic Growth, 1688–1959: Trends and Structure* (Cambridge: Cambridge University Press, 1962), pp. 65, 78; N. F. R. Crafts, "British Economic Growth: 1700–1831: A Review of the Evidence," *Economic History Review*, 2nd series, XXXVI, No. 2 (1983), p. 187.
[95] Jackson, "Growth and Deceleration," pp. 346 and 349.
[96] Allen, "Agriculture during the industrial revolution," Table 5.1, p. 102.
[97] Crafts, *British Economic Growth*, Table 2.10, p. 42.
[98] Gregory Clark, "Agriculture and the Industrial Revolution: 1700–1850," in Mokyr (ed.), *The British Industrial Revolution*, pp. 246–247.
[99] Allen, "Agriculture during the industrial revolution," p. 103.

population of England doubled between 1801 and 1851, increasing from 8.3 million to 16.8 million.[100] Conceptually, the gap has been computed differently by scholars. Crafts calculates that net agricultural imports grew from 16.4 percent of total consumption of agricultural products in 1801 to 22.6 percent in 1841, and 31.8 percent in 1851. Using a broader definition of agricultural products, Clark calculates much larger proportions for imports.[101] On the whole, the available evidence shows that for the entire period 1660–1850, it was only in the years 1660–1740 that the growth of agricultural output exceeded the rate of population growth in England.

The changes in agricultural output outlined in the preceding paragraphs were partly related to the structural developments examined earlier and partly associated with technical and institutional changes.[102] A brief discussion of the contribution of enclosure is pertinent. It is generally agreed that the enclosure movement stretched over several centuries. But historians had believed that more land was enclosed in England in the eighteenth than in any other century.[103] The chronology of English enclosure published in 1983 by Wordie presents a totally different picture. Wordie uses the term enclosure in its legal rather than its physical sense. Thus by enclosed land he means "land held in severalty, falling completely under the power of one owner to do with as he pleased, whether or not he chose to enclose his land in the literal sense with hedges or ditches. Such land was free of all common rights, except possibly for a right of way." On the other hand, open field or common land applies to land "subject to a measure of common rights."[104] Constructed within this context, Wordie's chronology shows the

---

[100] E. A. Wrigley and R. S. Schofield, *The Population History of England, 1541–1871: A Reconstruction* (Cambridge: Cambridge University Press, 1986), p. 129.

[101] Crafts, *British Economic Growth*, Table 6.4, p. 127; Clark, "Agriculture and the Industrial Revolution," pp. 256–257.

[102] For the contribution of the changing structure of farms (small farms versus large farms), see Outhwaite, "Progress and Backwardness," pp. 8–16; G. E. Mingay, "The Land Tax Assessments and the Small Landowner," *Economic History Review*, 2nd series, XVII (1964–65), pp. 381–388; Mingay, *Enclosure and the Small Farmer*, pp. 26–31; Chambers and Mingay, *The Agricultural Revolution*, pp. 54–75. Outhwaite, Mingay, and Chambers treat large farms as intruments for productivity gains. But Allen argues the contrary. He believes that the technical changes of the seventeenth century were accomplished by the yeoman farmers, and, so, characterizes the agrarian developments of 1660–1740 as the yeoman agricultural revolution, to which he attributes the bulk of the agricultural progress in England from 1660–1850. Allen, *Enclosure and the Yeoman*, pp. 18–20.

[103] This view was stated by McCloskey several decades ago. See D. N. McCloskey, "The Economics of Enclosure: A Market Analysis," in W. N. Parker and E. L. Jones (eds.), *European Peasants and Their Markets* (Princeton, NJ: Princeton University Press, 1975), p. 125.

[104] J. R. Wordie, "The Chronology of English Enclosure, 1500–1914," *Economic History Review*, 2nd series, XXXVI, No. 4 (1983), p. 484. See the exchange arising from this paper between Wordie and John Chapman in the same journal, XXXVII, No. 4 (1984), pp. 557–562.

percentage of the total surface area in England enclosed in each specified time period as follows:[105] already enclosed in 1500, 45.0 percent; enclosed 1500–99, 2.0 percent; enclosed 1600–99, 24.0 percent; enclosed 1700–99, 13.0 percent; enclosed 1800–1914, 11.4 percent; Commons remaining in 1914, 4.6 percent.

This would mean that the pre-eminent century for enclosure was the seventeenth and not the eighteenth, although the bulk of enclosures by parliamentary acts occurred between 1760 and 1830. On the available evidence, the indication is that much of the seventeenth-century enclosures took place after 1650.[106] All of this would appear to be consistent with other evidence relating to the second half of the seventeenth century. It is believed that the field cultivation of the new fodder crops, which revolutionized agricultural practice in England, began in the middle decades of the seventeenth century.[107] Research also shows that much of the changes in landholding structure in England occurred before 1780. Evidence from Leicestershire shows that about 75 percent of the land was already owned in units of over 375 acres in 1780. What is more, the evidence shows that parishes enclosed without a parliamentary act, both before and after 1780, uniformly had larger proportions of their lands held in large units. The explanation for this is that to overcome the opposition of small land-holders to enclosure without an act, large landowners intending to enclose had to buy out the former. Thus, to the extent that enclosure contributed to the enlargement of farms, it did so more in the period before 1760 (the beginning of large-scale parliamentary enclosure) than the one after.[108] As was shown in the earlier section of the chapter, the dominant feature of developments in the fifteenth and sixteenth centuries was the transfer of the land to small and yeoman farmers. This being so, the expansion of acreage held in large units must have occurred in the seventeenth century, possibly more so in the second half of the century when enclosure was more rampant.

As to the exact contribution of enclosure to the growth of agricultural output, scholars are reluctant to be specific, even though there is a general agreement that the better defined and more exclusive property rights instituted by enclosure were more conducive to innovation and more cost saving in management than open fields. Dr. Yelling, who probably has done more detailed work on the subject than other scholars, will not specify the

[105] Wordie, "Chronology," Table 7, p. 502. The typographical error in the table pointed out by Wordie in his reply to Chapman is corrected as stated.

[106] Outhwaite, "Progress and Backwardness," p. 4.

[107] Outhwaite, "Progress and Backwardness," p. 4.

[108] J. A. Yelling, *Common Field and Enclosure in England, 1450–1850* (London: Macmillan, 1977), pp. 94–119. Yelling argues that while enclosure, before and after 1780, contributed to the enlargement of landholding units, it did so in conjunction with other factors, especially soil type and market demand.

percentage contribution of enclosure to productivity or output growth over time.[109] However, Wordie is willing to be more specific. He believes that "taking an average of all kinds of land in all kinds of circumstances, the output gains in terms of the cash value of produce may have been anything between 50 percent and 100 percent, once all the technical advantages available to the enclosed farmer had been fully deployed." Based on this, Wordie computes that enclosure contributed between 24 percent and 12 percent to the growth of output in the seventeenth century, and between 13 percent and 6.5 percent in the eighteenth.[110]

Now what about the contribution of technological change? According to Feinstein's figures, gross domestic capital formation in agriculture in Great Britain increased from £2.5 million (1851–60 prices) per annum in 1761–90 to £4.0 million in 1791–1820, £4.5 million in 1821–40, and £6.5 million in 1841–60.[111] But this investment was largely on enclosures, drainage, and farm buildings. The war time labor shortages and high labor costs of 1793 to 1815 did encourage a more widespread adoption of the thresher, which had been introduced in the 1780s.[112] On the whole, however, very little mechanization of agriculture occurred before the later nineteenth century.[113]

Like agriculture, developments in the service sector formed an important part of the overall changes in economy and society, which conditioned the growth and development of industrial production in England between 1660 and 1850. Unlike agriculture, however, the service sector has been little studied. It is, therefore, difficult to display data that show quantitative and qualitative change in all the major sub-sections of the sector over time. If we take a comprehensive view of the composition of the sector, we would say that it is made up of the professions, domestic and personal service,

---

[109] Yelling, *Common Field and Enclosure*, pp. 174–213.

[110] Wordie, "Chronology of English Enclosure," pp. 503–505. See also McCloskey, "The Economics of Enclosure," pp. 158–160. McCloskey computes that in the eighteenth century "a village was roughly 13 percent more productive in an enclosed than in an open state" (p. 160).

[111] C. H. Feinstein, "Capital Accumulation and the Industrial Revolution," in Roderick Floud and Donald McCloskey (eds.), *The Economic History of Britain since 1700: Volume I, 1700–1860* (Cambridge: Cambridge University Press, 1981), p. 133.

[112] G. Hueckel, "Agriculture during industrialization," in Floud and McCloskey (eds.), *Economic History of Britain*, pp. 189–191.

[113] As Chambers and Mingay put it, "Except for an eddy here and there, the 'wave of gadgets' that is said to have swept over England passed it [agriculture] by until well into the nineteenth century. Looked at from this angle, its mode of expansion corresponds rather with that of the domestic industries that could increase production only by reorganization or by an enlargement of the number of productive units working with traditional tools than with the new factory industries." Chambers and Mingay, *Agricultural Revolution*, p. 3.

trade and transport, communication, financial services (including banking and insurance), and government and defense. For some of these, we have a lot of information but for others very little.

Much is known about the growth and development of services connected with overseas trade – merchanting, shipping, insurance, banking, ware-housing, port services, and the defense of sea lanes, markets, and sources of imports.[114] The years 1660–1700 witnessed revolutionary changes in English overseas trade. The combined free on board (f.o.b.) annual value of imports, exports, and re-exports increased from £8.5 million in 1663/69 to £12.3 million in 1699–1701.[115] Even more important was the change in the geographical direction and the commodity composition of English foreign trade during the period. In 1621 northern Europe accounted for 62.4 percent of London imports, and southern Europe accounted for another 31.2 percent, while imports from outside Europe were only 6.4 percent. By 1700, the respective contributions of these three regions were 35.7 percent, 29.7 percent, and 34.7 percent.[116] Because a large proportion of the imports from outside Europe was re-exported to other European countries, and significant portions of manufactured imports from Europe were also re-exported to non-European territories, re-exports became a large proportion of the goods sold abroad by English traders. Up to the early decades of the seventeenth century, woollen textiles of different types overwhelmingly dominated the value of goods sold abroad by England. But by the close of the seventeenth century (1699–1701), re-exports (made up largely of colonial produce from the Americas, and to a lesser extent East Indian calicoes) were 30.9 percent of all exports, and woollens 47.4 percent.[117]

[114]   Much of what follows is based on the work of Ralph Davis: *The Rise of the English Shipping Industry in the Seventeenth and Eighteenth Centuries* (London: Macmillan, 1962); "English Foreign Trade, 1660–1700," *Economic History Review*, 2nd series, VI (1954), and "English Foreign Trade, 1700–1774," *Economic History Review*, 2nd series, XV (1962), both of which are reprinted in W. E. Minchinton (ed.), *The Growth of English Overseas Trade in the Seventeenth and Eighteenth Centuries* (London: Methuen, 1969), pp. 78–98 and pp. 99–120, respectively; *A Commercial Revolution: English Overseas Trade in the Seventeenth and Eighteenth Centuries* (London: Historical Association, 1967); *English Overseas Trade, 1500–1700* (London: Macmillan, 1973); *The Industrial Revolution and British Overseas Trade* (Leicester: Leicester University Press, 1979). Further information comes from A. H. John, "The London Assurance Company and the Marine Insurance Market of the Eighteenth Century," *Economica*, N. S. 25 (May, 1958), pp. 126–141; A. H. John, "Insurance Investment and the London Money Market of the eighteenth century," *Economica*, N. S. 20 (May, 1953), pp. 137–158; and Joseph E. Inikori, "The credit needs of the African trade and the development of the credit economy in England," *Explorations in Economic History*, 27 (1990), pp. 197–231.

[115]   Davis, "English Foreign Trade, 1660–1700," p. 92.

[116]   Davis, *English Overseas Trade, 1500–1700*, p. 55.

[117]   Davis, "English Foreign Trade, 1660–1700," pp. 96 and 97.

This revolutionary change in the character of English overseas trade in the last half of the seventeenth century meant that the amount of mercantile capital employed (in the form of ships, stocks of goods afloat and awaiting sale, extension of credit to colonial producers, marine insurance, etc.) grew much faster than increases in the overall volume of foreign trade. The tonnage of English-owned merchant shipping increased almost three-fold between 1629 and 1686, from 115,000 tons to 340,000 tons.[118] Davis wrote:

> The number and tonnage of ships employed in overseas trade rose more rapidly than its value, and at home a correspondingly greater force of warehousemen, porters and carters was needed to shift the goods. . . . In the seventeenth century the value of trade evidently grew much more rapidly than national income; and resources of capital and labour employed to carry on trade rose faster still.[119]

What all of the foregoing account means is that the demand for and the production of services connected with overseas trade grew rapidly in the second half of the seventeenth century; more rapidly than the growth of the national product, and, in all probability, more rapidly than the growth of output in any other sector of the economy. As will be shown later in this chapter, the export of English domestic manufactures did not increase very much over the 60-year period 1663–1724. This means that the output of services connected with overseas trade grew much faster than the growth of manufactured exports during the period. In fact, it has been pointed out that the development of English entrepôt trade between 1660 and 1701 stimulated considerable investment in commerce that was not matched by industrial investment.[120] Again, it will be shown later in the chapter that although England's entrepôt trade continued to grow, export of English domestic manufactures began to grow faster than increases in the combined value of imports, exports, and re-exports from the second quarter of the eighteenth century onward.

Now what does this tell us about the growth and development of the whole service sector between 1660 and 1850? The distribution of output in the sector between the internal and overseas components in the estimates by Colquhoun for 1811 may be used as a window into the internal component of the sector in 1660–1700. Lindert and Williamson have identified some errors in the Irish and Scottish components of these estimates. But their comments indicate that the trade and transport components may be free of those errors, and the distribution of service sector income between the internal and overseas components may not be seriously affected, if at

[118]   W. E. Minchinton, "Introduction," in Minchinton (ed.), *The Growth of English Overseas Trade*, p. 62.

[119]   Davis, *English Overseas Trade, 1500–1700*, p. 10.

[120]   Davis, "English Foreign Trade, 1660–1700," pp. 93–94.

all.[121] Colquhoun estimated the total amount of income earned by those employed in trade and transport in Britain and Ireland (United Kingdom) in 1811 to be £79,873,748. Included are inland trade and transport (including the incomes of "Innkeepers and Publicans throughout Great Britain and Ireland"), coasting trade and transport, and foreign commerce and shipping (which includes the incomes of underwriters). Of this total, the overseas component amounted to £46,373,748 or 58 percent. Banking income is stated as £3,500,000; income from the professions (clergy, law, medicine, university and school teachers, and miscellaneous) is put at £35,135,355, and government and defense at £34,036,280.[122] The whole service sector, excluding government and defense, thus comes to £115,009,103, out of a total national income of £430,521,372 for the United Kingdom, that is 26.7 percent of the gross national product (GNP). Trade and transport is 69.5 percent of the service sector income (excluding government and defense), and the overseas component is 40 percent. Taking account of the entrepôt nature of English overseas trade between 1660 and 1700 and the rather backward nature of the internal transportation system during the period, as compared with the much greater strength of manufacturing and the more developed state of the internal transportation system by 1811, it is reasonable to suppose that the overseas component of the service sector was overwhelmingly dominant between 1660 and 1700. This will be the more so when Government and defense activities devoted to the protection of sea lanes, markets, and sources of imports are added.

Against this background, the published figures for trade and transport and for the national product may be employed to make some reasonable calculations. In 1700 and 1770, the national product of England and Wales is estimated to be £50.0 million and £80.9 million, respectively. For these years, trade and transport is put at £5.6 million and £17.0 million, respectively, and the corresponding overseas components are £3.4 million and £9.3 million.[123] Based on our reasoning above, we may suppose that trade and transport constituted 75 percent of the service sector income in 1700 and 1770. This would mean a total service sector income of £7.5 million in 1700 and £22.7 million in 1770, that is 15 percent and 28 percent of GNP, respectively. The indication is that the service sector grew faster than the industrial and agricultural sectors between 1660 and 1770, especially between 1660 and 1700 when entrepôt trade predominated. Thereafter the industrial sector increased output more rapidly, possibly up to the middle

---

[121] Lindert and Williamson, "Revising England's Social Tables," pp. 404–405.

[122] Patrick Colquhoun, *Treatise on the Wealth, Power and Resources of the British Empire* (London, 1815), pp. 95, 96, 109.

[123] W. A. Cole, "Factors in demand, 1700–80," in Floud and McCloskey (eds.), *The Economic History of Britain*, Table 3.2, p. 64; Inikori, "Slavery and the Development of Industrial Capitalism," Table 1, p. 780.

decades of the nineteenth century when the service sector began to grow faster again.

Lee is basically right in stressing the importance of the service sector.[124] But the growth and development of the sector, during this period, has to be placed in a proper perspective. Its growth and development between 1660 and 1700, and 1700 to 1770, was critical in creating part of the necessary conditions for the subsequent growth and development of industrial production, particularly the development of financial institutions and the credit economy from the late seventeenth century. But without the vigorous development of industrial production from the late eighteenth to the middle decades of the nineteenth century, the entrepôt trade of the seventeenth and early eighteenth centuries would have simply given rise to a small and weak enclave service sector in the trading centers, especially London. In terms of the transformation of a pre-industrial economy over a long-time period, Mathias is certainly correct in stating that "One cannot set out to increase the national income or expand the economy by increasing the number of clerks and lawyers and dock workers . . ."[125] All the same, the evidence reviewed above supports the view that the initial growth and development of the service sector between 1660 and 1700 was initiated not by the growth of manufacturing but by the expansion of entrepôt overseas trade.

We now come to the growth and development of industrial production between 1660 and 1850, which is viewed in this study as the culmination of all the developments outlined in the preceding sections of this chapter and others that were related more directly to manufacturing to be examined shortly. For purposes of effective organization and clear presentation, a historical model of the industrialization process in England, which flows from the preceding evidence and that soon to be presented, may be stated at the onset. By 1660 the English economy was highly commercialized. Market forces, therefore, played a prominent role in the allocation of resources in the 200 years that followed. In particular, England's rural economy and society were highly responsive to market conditions. But, apart from the products of the woollen textile industry, England remained largely dependent on imported manufactures up to the late seventeenth century. The expansion of manufacturing from the late seventeenth to the early decades of the eighteenth century was, therefore, largely based on import substitution. Domestically produced manufactures replaced manu-

---

[124] C. H. Lee, *The British Economy since 1700: A macroeconomic perspective* (Cambridge: Cambridge University Press, 1986), pp. 98–114. It is hard to see how the service sector could have had a 42.6 percent share of national income in 1700 and 47.7 percent in 1870 as Lee claims (p. 98). What is more, the source cited, Crafts, *British Economic Growth*, Table 3.6, pp. 62 and 63, does not show this.

[125] Peter Mathias, *The First Industrial Nation: An Economic History of Britain 1700–1914* (London: Methuen, 1969), p. 249.

factures imported for the domestic market as well as imported manufactures that were previously re-exported. Developments in agriculture and the growth of entrepôt international trade in the seventeenth and early eighteenth centuries created the necessary conditions for the growth of ISI by helping to provide the markets for manufactured goods at home and abroad, while state policies, fiscal and military, encouraged investment in manufacturing.

However, before the railway age, there was no integrated national market in England for most English producers, specifically because of the nature of inland transportation. For this reason, large-scale production in manufacturing tended to be very much connected with overseas markets. Hence, there were often two broad categories of industrial production, with possible overlap: small and medium scale production aimed largely at local and regional markets, and medium and large scale production aimed largely at overseas markets. Both categories existed in several manufacturing industries, but one or the other was dominant at a given moment in specific regions. Initially, regional concentration of the manufacturing industries was influenced more by the outcome of competition in export than in domestic sales – low cost producers concentrated in a region took overseas markets away from high cost producers located in other regions, but the latter continued to retain their local and regional markets until the railways swept away the de facto protection provided by inland transportation costs.

Much of the initial productivity gains in manufacturing were achieved through changes in organization associated with expanding markets. Further productivity gains came as a result of technological change, which, again, was largely due to expanding markets and increasing scale of production, in the first instance. In turn, the revolutionary changes in technology further expanded the markets overseas and at home, the latter very much connected with the emergence of an integrated national market following the growth of the railways.

This is the model of English industrialization between 1660 and 1850 derived from the available evidence. It is hoped that the model will help in understanding the main thrust of the organization and analysis of the evidence that now follows.

As was shown earlier in this chapter, the growth of manufacturing in the period, 1540–1640, did not carry the development of industrial production, outside the woollen industry, very far. The most remarkable developments in the English economy between 1660 and 1700, again, as outlined above, were the growth of agricultural output and the expansion of entrepôt overseas trade and the associated production of services. Productivity gains resulting from continuing reorganization and the adoption of new techniques provided a significant agricultural surplus as the population of England stagnated. Hence, England achieved net export of grains in the first half of the eighteenth century. As A. H. John pointed out several decades ago, the export of grains made an important contribution to the growth of English domestic exports in the first half of the eighteenth century. The decennial annual average official value of grains exported from England grew from £293,000 in 1700–10 to £938,000 in 1741–50. The main producer of the export surplus was the southeastern region of England, which was also the principal supplier of London's food, the raw materials of the brewing industry, and horse-fodder.[126]

The growth of agricultural productivity between 1660 and 1740 and the expansion of entrepôt overseas trade during the same period helped to raise national income per capita. The additional foreign exchange accruing from the agricultural export surplus and from the export of services in the entrepôt trade also helped to pay for imported manufactures, which ensured that some part of the additional incomes was spent on manufactured goods as consumers' tastes for the imported manufactures developed. The 1697 report of the Board of Trade on the state of the general trade of England offers a window into the developments of the period.

The expansion of imports of manufactures and luxury products apparently gave the government some concern over the balance of trade. The Crown, therefore, commissioned the Board of Trade to examine each branch of trade and advise on corrective measures. In its report drawn up on December 23, 1697, the Board stated that during the period covered by its enquiry, 1670–97, England "imported from some countries goods to a much greater original value than we have exported thither," and that "such trades have occasioned the exportation of coin or bullion, or hindered the importation thereof."[127] Sweden and the southern Baltic, France, and East India were singled out as problem areas. The f.o.b. cost of imports from Sweden and the southern Baltic, during the period, was £205,000 per annum, made up mainly of iron and hemp; and these were carried to a large extent by non-English ships. Import of silks, linens, and wines from France grew from 1670; by the mid-1670s silks and linens imported from France in one year reached £300,000 and £500,700, respectively. On trade with East India, the Board reported:

Our Importations from the year 1670 to Ann. 1688 have amounted upon the sales here to about £1,000,000 per annum as we are informed, of which we suppose [about] one half is usually re-exported; and our exportations in goods for those parts did not exceed £70,000 per annum and in Bullions entered by the Company

126   A. H. John, "English Agricultural Improvement and Grain Exports, 1660–1765," in D. C. Coleman and A. H. John (eds.), *Trade, Government and Economy in Pre-Industrial England: Essays Presented to F. J. Fisher* (London: Weidenfeld and Nicholson, 1976), pp. 52 and 60.

127   Public Record Office (PRO), London, CO. 390/12, A Report Concerning the General Trade of England made by the Board of Trade, December 23, 1697, pp. 133–134 (also 101–102).

from the year 1675 to 1685 about £400,000 per annum. But what was more exported in Bullion for the carrying on of that trade from England and Spain by private traders to those parts, we have no certain information.[128]

The imports from East India were mainly textiles, particularly cotton calicoes, the product of efforts made by the East India Company to popularize the wearing of oriental textiles.[129]

The Board also reported on the state of industrial production in England: Much progress was made between 1670 and 1697 in the manufacture of various types of woollen textiles, but the industry was being threatened by the growth of production in several European countries; domestic production of silks was hampered by the greater acceptability of foreign imports, especially from France; and very little progress had been made in the production of linen textiles, "the stock subscribed for that purpose [having been] diverted by a stock-jobbing trade, and thereby the Corporation disabled to promote it . . ." Very little progress had also been made in the manufacture of paper.[130] In general, the Board recommended tariff measures to promote domestic production of manufactures in England.

The evidence summarized by the Board of Trade is corroborated by other sources. The evidence relating to British trade with Germany between 1736 and 1742 is somewhat representative of the general pattern of English trade with the relatively industrially advanced regions of Europe in the first half of the eighteenth century. The 1697 Board of Trade report just examined showed greater concern about the trade with France than that with Germany, because the latter had an export surplus in favor of England, while the former showed a huge deficit as French economic policies restricted the sale of English woollen textiles and English re-exports in France. Other than that, both Germany and France, as well as the Netherlands, were major sources of manufactured imports into England between 1660 and 1750. The German trade figures for 1736–42 are thus quite instructive. For these seven years, the total value of linens imported into Britain from Germany amounted to £4,311,501, being an annual average of £615,929. Other goods imported totaled £664,514 or £94,931 per annum. The two sets of imports from Germany, during the period, come to £710,860 per annum. On the other hand, British export of non-woollen manufactures to Germany during the same period amounted to only £749,441 or £107,063 per annum. Woollen exports totaled £3,036,539 or £433,791 per annum. Thus even when woollens are included Britain imported from Germany more manufactured goods than the domestic manufactures it exported to that country during the period; removing woollens,

---

[128]   *Ibid.*, pp. 140–141 (also 108–109).
[129]   Beverly Lemire, *Fashions Favourite: The Cotton Trade and the Consumer in Britain, 1660–1800* (Oxford and New York: Oxford University Press, 1991), pp. 12–21.
[130]   Board of Trade Report, 1697, pp. 157–164 (also 125–132).

the figures show that England related to Germany at this time the same way Third World countries relate today to the industrialized countries – huge deficits in manufactured imports. Yet Britain recorded a large surplus in merchandize trade with Germany during the period, amounting to £3,197,611. This was due to re-exports, which totalled £4,387,647 for the whole period, being more in value than woollens and the other manufactures combined.[131]

The more comprehensive figures compiled by Ralph Davis are generally consistent with the pattern revealed by the German evidence. Annual average of manufactured imports into England from all parts of the world for 1699, 1700, and 1701 was £1,844,000, made up largely of linens (49 percent), East Indian calicoes (20 percent), and silks (11 percent). During the same period, non-woollen manufactured exports averaged only £538,000 and woollens £3,045,000.[132]

An important element of English trade outside Europe between 1660 and 1750, which reflected the relative weakness of England's manufacturing industries outside woollen textiles, was the large proportion of re-exports in the value of manufactured exports from England. The trade figures for 1715 to 1726 show this clearly. During this period, manufactured goods totaling £5,264,108 were exported from England to the British "Sugar Colonies in America" (British Caribbean), of which £3,263,397, or 62 percent, were English manufactures, while £2,000,711, or 38 percent, were foreign manufactures re-exported from England.[133] During the same period, manufactured goods totaling £1,652,572 were also exported from England to Africa, of which £737,702, or 45 percent, were English manufactures, and £914,870, or 55 percent, were foreign manufactures re-exported from England.[134] This element in England's trade from 1660 to 1750 meant that the opportunity for import replacement existed not only on the home market but also on markets outside Europe to which English merchants

---

[131]   PRO, T.70/1205/A.7, An Account of the Total Amounts of the Value of All Exports and Imports to and from England and Germany for Seven years ending at Christmas 1742, distinguishing each year and also distinguishing how much by woollen manufactures, how much by other British Manufactures and how much by Foreign Commoditys Re-exported, as also how much by linens and how much by other Foreign Commoditys Imported. Custom House, London, 9 April, 1744.

[132]   Davis, "English Foreign Trade, 1660–1700," p. 96.

[133]   PRO, T.64/273/29, An Account of the Exports to His Majesty's Colonies in America from Christmas 1714 to Christmas 1726, distinguishing how much by Certificate Goods [Re-exports] and how much by English Manufactures. Custom House, London, 4 April, 1732.

[134]   PRO, T.64/273/55, An Account of the Value of the Exports to Africa from Christmas 1714 to Christmas 1726 distinguishing how much by [English] Manufacture and how much by Certificate Goods [Re-exports]. Custom House, London, 4 April, 1732.

re-exported foreign manufactures, especially the British American colonies and Africa.

The evidence available shows that the growth of industrial production in England from the late seventeenth to the early decades of the eighteenth century was due largely to the achievements of British entrepreneurs, aided in several ways by the English government, in taking over these markets previously supplied with foreign manufactures by English traders. To illustrate, in 1751 a Manchester cotton manufacturer, Samuel Touchet, told a House of Commons committee that about 40 years earlier the home market for linen and cotton goods was supplied by foreigners, "which is now supplied by our own manufactures."[135] Similarly, in 1799, Thomas Williams, who completely dominated the copper and brass industries in England in the late eighteenth century, informed a committee of the House of Commons that in the first 20 or 30 years of the eighteenth century most of the copper and brass utensils for culinary and other purposes in England were imported from Hamburg (in Germany) and Holland,

procured from the Manufactories immemorially established at Nuremburg, and various other parts of Germany; even brass pans for the purposes of the dairies of our country could not be procured but of the German make. So late as 1745, 1746, and 1750, copper tea kettles, saucepans, and pots of all sizes, were imported here in large quantities from Hamburgh and Holland; but through the persevering industry, capitals, and enterprizing spirit of our miners and manufacturers, those imports became totally unnecessary, being all made here, and far better than any other country could produce.[136]

The evidence of Samuel Touchet and that of Thomas Williams point to import-replacement industrialization in textiles and metal products, respectively. As the process of ISI progressed in a broad front from the late seventeenth century, the home market was the first to be captured from foreign suppliers. According to Ralph Davis, English industries squeezed most foreign competition out of the domestic market in the early decades of the eighteenth century, but before these infant industries were strong enough to compete with foreign industries in their own countries, their next effort was aimed at capturing the re-export markets in the American colonies and the quasi colony of Ireland.[137] Western Africa followed quickly. The capture of the domestic market, the American and African markets, and the acquisition of markets in southern Europe through diplomatic efforts (especially

---

[135] British Library, London, *House of Commons Reports*, Vol. II, 1738–65, Report of Committee on Chequed and Striped Linens, 26 April, 1751, Evidence of Samuel Touchet, p. 293.

[136] British Library, London, *House of Commons Reports*, Vol. X (1785–1801), Report on Copper Mines and Copper Trade, 7 May, 1799, Evidence of Thomas Williams (a Member of the House of Commons), p. 666.

[137] Davis, *A Commercial Revolution*, p. 18.

Table 2.1. *Growth of Industrial Output*
(percent per year)

	Revised Crafts	Revised Harley	Jackson
1700–60	0.7		
1760–80	1.3		1.3
1780–1801	2.0		2.1
1801–30	2.8		2.9
1770–1815		1.5	
1815–41		3.0	

Sources and Notes: Jackson, "Rates of industrial growth," Table 10, p. 19; Crafts and Harley, "Output Growth," Table 3, p. 712. The figures for Jackson are derived by Crafts and Harley from the decennial figures of Jackson for comparability.

in Portugal and Spain) were critical elements in English industrialization from 1660 to the 1780s.

Quantitative historians and economists attempting to construct a statistical story of the growth and development of industrial production in England continue to debate the figures. The estimates by Deane and Cole,[138] on which scholars had based their arguments, have been challenged and modified by Harley and Crafts.[139] The estimates by Crafts and Harley have themselves been challenged by others.[140]

In response, Crafts and Harley have revised their estimates slightly on the basis of what they have accepted from their critics.[141] These are presented together with Jackson's estimates in Table 2.1. Given the margin of uncertainty surrounding all the estimates, the Crafts-Harley-Jackson figures appear the more soundly grounded, and they tell a broadly similar story, especially Crafts's and Jackson's. Jackson's decennial breakdown shows that overall industrial production grew at 0.3 percent per year in the fourth decade of the eighteenth century, which was less than the rate of popula-

[138] Deane and Cole, *British Economic Growth*.
[139] C. Knick Harley, "British Industrialization Before 1841: Evidence of Slower Growth During the Industrial Revolution," *Journal of Economic History*, Vol. XLII, 2 (1982), pp. 267–289; Crafts, "British Economic Growth."
[140] Julian Hoppit, "Counting the Industrial Revolution," *Economic History Review*, 2nd ser., XLIII, 2 (1990), pp. 173–193; Maxine Berg and Pat Hudson, "Rehabilitating the Industrial Revolution," *Economic History Review*, XLV, 1 (1992), pp. 24–50; R. V. Jackson, "Rates of Industrial Growth during the Industrial Revolution," *Economic History Review*, XLV, 1 (1992), pp. 1–23.
[141] N. F. R. Crafts and Harley, "Output Growth and the British Industrial Revolution: A Restatement of the Crafts-Harley View," *Economic History Review*, XLV, 4 (1992).

Table 2.2. *Changing Structure of Industrial Value Added in Britain (£m. current and percent)*

	1770		1801		1831	
	£m.	%	£m.	%	£m.	%
Cotton	0.6	2.6	9.2	17.0	25.3	22.4
Wool	7.0	30.6	10.1	18.7	15.9	14.1
Linen	1.9	8.3	2.6	4.8	5.0	4.4
Silk	1.0	4.4	2.0	3.7	5.8	5.1
Building	2.4	10.5	9.3	17.2	26.5	23.5
Iron	1.5	6.6	4.0	7.4	7.6	6.7
Copper	0.2	0.9	0.9	1.7	0.8	0.7
Beer	1.3	5.7	2.5	4.6	5.2	4.6
Leather	5.1	22.3	8.4	15.5	9.8	8.7
Soap	0.3	1.3	0.8	1.5	1.2	1.1
Candles	0.5	2.2	1.0	1.8	1.2	1.1
Coal	0.9	4.4	2.7	5.0	7.9	7.0
Paper	0.1	0.4	0.6	1.1	0.8	0.7
	22.9		54.1		113.0	

Sources and Notes: Crafts, *British Economic Growth*, Table 2.3, p. 22. The item, Building, includes investment in dwellings, public building and works, industrial and commercial buildings, railways, roads and bridges, canals and waterways, docks, and harbors, plus half of agricultural investments.

tion growth; hence, industrial output per capita declined by 0.1 percent per year during the period. From 1740 onward, industrial production grew faster than population.[142] Both the estimates by Crafts and by Jackson show a turning point in the growth of industrial output in the decades 1780–1801, in both absolute and per capita terms.

The unequal development of the manufacturing sectors over time produced major changes in the structure of industry during the period being examined. This is shown in Table 2.2. The dominance of the woollen textile industry, for all practical purposes the only major industry in England from the late Middle Ages to the seventeenth century, was whittled down over the eighteenth century. From 30.6 percent of total value added in 1770, its share went down to 14.1 percent in 1831. On the other hand, the share of cotton grew from a mere 2.6 percent in 1770 to 22.4 percent in 1831. The growth of investment in transportation, especially canals and railways, is reflected in the growing share of building, from 10.5 percent in 1770 to

[142] Jackson, "Rates of industrial growth," Table 10, p. 19.

17.2 percent in 1801 and 23.5 percent in 1831. Apart from woollen textile, another major industry that lost ground over the period was leather. Generally speaking, the evidence in Table 2.2 indicates that the the structure of English industry was becoming increasingly characterized by the production of mass consumer products aimed at expanding markets overseas and at home.

These developments are reflected in the trade statistics. From the middle decades of the eighteenth century, the entrepôt nature of English overseas trade began to change. English traders now carried overseas a growing proportion of domestic manufactures. In consequence, as Ralph Davis noted, the wave of commercial expansion of the mid-eighteenth century carried with it the expansion of industrial production at home,[143] in contrast to the growth of commerce in the seventeenth and early eighteenth centuries. A further indication of this transformation of English overseas trade is the change in the relative weights of commerce and manufacturing in the national product. In 1688, commerce, and industry and building, contributed 20.0 percent and 17.6 percent, respectively, to the GNP of England and Wales; in 1759, the respective shares were 21.0 percent and 17.5 percent, and in 1801–03, 19.7 percent and 25.7 percent.[144]

The growth of modern urban industry also wrought a far-reaching transformation of the structure of the whole economy and society of England. Given the conflicting estimates of the annual growth rates for agriculture, industry, and GDP, it is currently impossible to state exact measurements of the over time change of the structure of the economy from 1660 to 1850. Nonetheless, all the estimates show consistently that industry and the urban sectors of the economy grew faster than agriculture during the period. Crafts estimates that agricultural output grew by 0.6 percent per annum in 1700–60, 0.1 percent in 1760–80, 0.8 percent in 1780–1801, and 1.2 percent in 1801–31. On the other hand, Jackson computes that agricultural production increased by 4.3 percent per decade from 1660 to 1740, and 2.7 per decade from 1740 to 1790.[145] When these are compared with Crafts's and Jackson's growth rates of industrial output shown in Table 2.1 above, it is clear that industrial production grew more than twice as fast as agricultural production between 1760 and 1830. If Clark's position as previously stated, that the bulk of productivity gains in agriculture between 1660 and 1850 was achieved before the last quarter of the eighteenth century, is correct, then the gap between growth rates in agriculture and in industry would be much greater still in the decades 1780–1850.

---

[143] Davis, *A Commercial Revolution*, p. 20.
[144] Nick Crafts, "The industrial revolution," in Floud and McCloskey (eds.), *The Economic History of Britain*, 2nd edition, Table 3.2, p. 46.
[145] Crafts, "The industrial revolution," Table 3.3, p. 47; Jackson, "Growth and Deceleration," p. 349.

Table 2.3. *Population of England*
(Selected years)

	Total Population	% In Towns 10,000 Plus
1681	4,930,385	
1686	4,864,762	
1701	5,057,790	13.4
1751	5,772,415	17.5
1801	8,664,490	21.4
1811	9,885,690	25
1841	14,970,372	38
1871	21,500,720	54

Sources and Notes: Roger Schofield, "British population change, 1700–1871," in Floud and McCloskey (eds.), *Economic History of Britain,* 2nd edition, Tables 4.1, 4.5, and 4.6, pp. 64, 88, and 89.The percentages for urban population in 1701, 1751, and 1801 are computed using information in Tables 4.1 and 4.5, pp. 64 and 88.

Even Crafts's apparent conservative estimate of the structural change still shows a major shift in employment away from agriculture to industry between 1700 and 1870. According to Crafts, the percentage of the male labor force employed in agriculture decreased from 61.2 in 1700 to 40.8 in 1800, 28.6 in 1840, and 20.4 in 1870. On the other hand, the percentage of the male labor force employed in industry increased from 18.5 in 1700 to 29.5 in 1800, 47.3 in 1840, and 49.2 in 1870.[146] These figures also indicate that the other non-agricultural sectors – trade and transport, finance, and other services – increased their share of the labor force during the period.

The relatively greater demand of industry for labor and the increasing concentration of industries in the urban centers, away from the countryside, are all reflected in the growth of population and urbanization. This is shown in Table 2.3. The figures show that in the seventy years from 1681 to 1751, the population of England increased by only 17 percent; if John Hatcher's estimates stated previously in this chapter are about right, the population of England in 1751 was still somewhat less than it was in 1300. But in the 100 years that followed, the population more than tripled and

[146] Nicholas F. R. Crafts, "British Industrialization in an International Context," *Journal of Interdisciplinary History,* XIX, 3 (1989), Table 1, p. 417.

Table 2.4. *England's Ten Top Counties in Order of Wealth Assessed for Tax*

Ten Top Counties, 1086 Assessment		Ten Top Counties, 1660 Assessment		Ten Top Counties, 1843 Assessment	
1. Oxfordshire	(15)	1. Middlesex	(1)	1. Middlesex	(1)
2. Kent	(6)	2. Suffolk	(23)	2. Lancashire	(35)
3. Berkshire	(18)	3. Bedfordshire	(26)	3. Surrey	(15)
4. Essex	(19)	4. Kent	(6)	4. Warwickshire	(20)
5. Hertfordshire	(12)	5. Hertfordshire	(12)	5. Staffordshire	(33)
6. Middlesex	(1)	6. Essex	(19)	6. Kent	(4)
7. Dorset	(36)	7. Rutland	(30)	7. Worcestershire	(13)
8. Somerset	(8)	8. Sussex	(22)	8. Somerset	(10)
9. Buckinghamshire	(25)	9. Buckinghamshire	(25)	9. Cheshire	(32)
10. Bedfordshire	(26)	10. Somerset	(8)	10. Leicestershire	(18)

Sources and Notes: Buckatzsch, "Geographical Distribution of Wealth," Table 1, pp. 186, 187. The numbers 1 to 10 represent the ranking of the counties in each assessment; the numbers in parenthesis for 1086 and 1660 are the ranking for 1843, and those of 1843 are for 1660.

became increasingly urban; the proportion living in towns with 10,000 people and over grew from 13.4 percent in 1701 to 54 percent in 1871. Thus, as Crafts and Harley pointed out:

By the second quarter of the nineteenth century, a combination of the rapid growth of the urban based textile industries that exported most of their product and the marked decline in agriculture's share of the labour force produced the first urban industrial economy – a development that was not inherent in the progress of the late seventeenth-century economy.[147]

Now how did the regions of England fare in the development of industrial production between 1660 and 1850? Because the industrial sector grew faster in both employment and income than any other sector during the period, relative distribution of wealth among the regions may be taken as the first approximate measure of their relative performance. Table 2.4 shows the 10 wealthiest counties in England in terms of tax assessment per 1,000 acres in 1086, 1660, and 1843. As was stated earlier in this chapter, the cloth producing areas of East Anglia were among the regions that grew most in wealth between 1086 and 1660. Thus Suffolk, which ranked 18 in wealth assessed for tax in 1301, became the second wealthiest county in the assessment of 1660, second only to Middlesex whose ranking is inflated by the inclusion of the nation's capital city of London. However, by the

[147] Crafts and Harley, "Output Growth and the British Industrial Revolution," p. 705.

assessment of 1843, Suffolk had dropped to 23 in ranking. In fact, of the 10 wealthiest counties in the assessment of 1660, only Middlesex, Kent, and Somerset remained among the 10 wealthiest counties in the assessment of 1843; apart from Hertfordshire and Essex, which ranked 12 and 19, respectively, all the others now ranked between 22 and 30. What is more, 7 of the 10 wealthiest counties in the assessment of 1843 were not among the top 10 in 1086 or in 1660. Another striking feature of the 1843 assessment is the fact that the 10 wealthiest counties were no longer all located south of the line drawn from the Severn estuary to the Wash as had been the case in 1086 and 1660. In fact, 6 of the 10 counties were now located north of that line. Finally, the truly revolutionary change in the regional distribution of wealth revealed by these tax data is the movement of Lancashire from the very bottom in the Middle Ages and at the time of the Restoration to the very top, being second only to Middlesex in 1843.

A study of over-time changes in regional wage differentials in England in the eighteenth and nineteenth centuries presents a similar picture. The logical assumption here is that rapid industrialization increased the demand for labor over and above the expansion of labor supply through natural population increase and migration. In consequence, wages rose over time not only in the industrial sector but in all sectors, including agriculture. And because inter-county labor mobility was not strong enough, wages rose faster in counties experiencing rapid industrialization than they did in those that were not. County wages for agricultural laborers form the basis of the analysis. The evidence shows that in the years 1767–70, all but 2 of the 11 counties with the highest wages in England were in the south, mostly in the southeast – Kent, Middlesex, Surrey, Sussex, Buckinghamshire, Hampshire, Norfolk, Suffolk, and Essex. The two exceptions were in the Midlands: Nottinghamshire and Warwickshire. Lancashire and the West Riding of Yorkshire were among 11 counties with the lowest wages located mostly in northern England. By 1794–95, however, the regional picture of wages had been reversed completely. Only 3 of the 11 counties (counting the West Riding, North Riding, and East Riding of Yorkshire separately for practical reasons) with the highest wages were now in the south – Kent, Surrey, and Sussex. Six of these 11 counties, including the West Riding and Lancashire, were in northern England, with the West Riding having the highest wages. The situation remained basically the same by 1833–45, with only 2 counties in the south, Kent and Middlesex, remaining among 11 counties with the highest wages in England. By this time Lancashire had the third highest wages among the English counties.[148]

---

[148] E. H. Hunt, "Industrialization and Regional Inequality: Wages in Britain, 1760–1914," *Journal of Economic History*, XLVI, 4 (December, 1986), Table 6, pp. 965–966.

The regional picture depicted by the tax and wages data is consistent basically with evidence more directly related to the regional distribution of industrial development during the period under consideration. About four decades ago, D. C. Coleman showed how the counties of East Anglia that had been in the forefront of socio-economic and industrial progress in England for several centuries went through industrial decay in the eighteenth century: "by the middle of the eighteenth century, before the Industrial Revolution had made its mark, much of the region's industrial and commercial life was already in decay."[149] This continued for the rest of the century and into the nineteenth. In the first half of the nineteenth century, the region experienced unemployment, wages fell, and the rate of population growth in the region's three counties (Essex, Suffolk, Norfolk) was consistently lower than the national average.[150] Adjacent to East Anglia in the southeast, the Weald of Kent, Surrey, and Sussex also went through deindustrialization between 1660 and 1850. At the beginning of the seventeenth century, the Weald was a major producer of glass, iron, timber products, and textiles (dyed broadcloth in particular). More than 50 percent of the blast furnaces in England by 1600 were in the Weald. The rapid growth of production of iron and iron products, textiles, glass, and timber products in the sixteenth century made the Weald one of the leading industrial regions of England in the early seventeenth century. But in the course of the seventeenth and eighteenth centuries all these industries declined, leading Brian Short to conclude that the region "provides a clear example of the failed transition from proto-industrialisation to full industrialisation."[151] Several other regions shared the experience of East Anglia and the Weald. Sidney Pollard identified 10 regions in Britain, which were large industrial producers in 1760–90, eight of which were in England – Cornwall, Shropshire, south Staffordshire (the "Black Country"), the uplands of Derbyshire, southern Lancashire, the West Riding of Yorkshire (across the Pennines from Lancashire), the region around the rivers Tyne and Wear, and London. In Pollard's view, "only two clear cases (Lancashire and Yorkshire) and a third slightly doubtful one (the Black Country)" survived as major industrial regions.[152] A similar point was made by D. C. Coleman who identified 12 proto-industrial areas in England in the sixteenth and

---

[149]   D. C. Coleman, "Growth and Decay During the Industrial Revolution: The Case of East Anglia," *The Scandinavian Economic History Review*, Vol. X, Nos. 1 and 2 (1962), p. 117.

[150]   *Ibid.*, pp. 119, 125.

[151]   Brian Short, "The de-industrialisation process: a case study of the Weald, 1600–1850," in Pat Hudson (ed.), *Regions and Industries: A Perspective on the Industrial Revolution in Britain* (Cambridge: Cambridge University Press, 1989), p. 156.

[152]   Sidney Pollard, *Peaceful Conquest: The Industrialization of Europe 1760–1970* (Oxford: Oxford University Press, 1981), pp. 14–20.

seventeenth centuries, of which six failed and only four achieved full industrialization.[153] So much for the failed transitions. Let us now turn to the
successful cases.

The West Midlands, in particular south Staffordshire – the region pop-
ularly known as the "Black Country" because of the thick smoke from its
iron and metallurgical industries which darkened the sky over the region –
was one of the success stories. The counties in the region (West Midlands)
include Warwickshire, Shropshire, Staffordshire, and Worcestershire.[154]
Iron and the production of ironware were its main industries. As was stated
earlier in this chapter, up to the early seventeenth century the iron industry
in England had been concentrated in the southern counties, especially the
Weald. As the southern industry declined from the middle of the seventeenth century, England became more dependent on imported iron. According to Ashton, total output of bar iron in England in 1720 did not exceed
20,000 tons; by the middle of the eighteenth century, production had
decreased further.[155] At the same time England was also largely dependent
on imported ironware.[156]

In addition to the domestic market for iron and iron products, the colonial markets in the British Caribbean and North America expanded rapidly
from 1660, as their populations grew and their production for Atlantic
commerce increased. Large quantities of agricultural implements and iron
nails for plantation needs, but even more for the building of numerous
wooden houses in the mainland colonies, were demanded yearly.[157] Thus,
in the late seventeenth and early eighteenth centuries, English producers had
the opportunity to replace imported iron and iron products both on the
domestic and on the colonial markets.

[153] D. C. Coleman, "Proto-Industrialization: A Concept Too Many," *Economic History
Review*, 36 (1983), pp. 441, 443.
[154] W. H. B. Court, *The Rise of the Midlands Industries, 1600–1838* (Oxford: Oxford
University Press, 1938), p. 2.
[155] Thomas Southcliffe Ashton, *Iron and Steel in the Industrial Revolution* (2nd edition,
Manchester: Manchester University Press, 1951), p. 13.
[156] Court, *The Rise of the Midlands Industries*, p. 160. As Court wrote, "Till the Civil
Wars, England was not a teacher but a learner, and Germans and Italians led the
way in science and invention. The great age of Midland industrial development falls
within the first great century of English science, between 1660 and 1760, as well as
within a period of political peace and active commerce." This view is supported by
Ashton who stated that in the opening years of the eighteenth century the art of
iron casting was far less advanced in England than abroad: "the Dutch in particular, by reason, it was alleged, of superior skill, lower duties, and cheaper labour,
were formidable competitors with the English founders in the home market, especially as regards the sale of iron pots and similar utensils." Ashton, *Iron and Steel*,
pp. 26–27.
[157] Marie B. Rowlands, "Continuity and Change in an industrialising society: the case
of the West Midlands industries," in Hudson (ed.), *Regions and Industries*, p. 115;
Court, *The Rise of the Midlands Industries*, p. 206.

As the southern production centers declined, three regions of England – the northeast, northwest, and the West Midlands – initially became the new centers of production. In the late seventeenth and early eighteenth centuries, the production of iron products was dominant, the iron employed being largely imported. Most producers served local and regional markets but from the seventeenth century through the eighteenth the West Midlands dominated exports to British America and Western Africa. From the 1650s, the British sugar colonies in the Caribbean imported large and increasing quantities of nails, plantation hoes, cane cutters, oxchains, and slave collars from the West Midlands.[158] The demand for nails to build the numerous wooden houses in British North America was also largely met by Midlands producers. South Staffordshire and the northeastern parts of Worcestershire were possibly the largest nail producing region in England for much of the eighteenth century. It was estimated in the late eighteenth century that about 150,000 people were directly or indirectly dependent on the export trade in hardwares, largely in nails. Earlier, it was computed in 1737 that within two miles of Birmingham no less than 9,000 tons of bar iron were used annually by workers employed under a putting-out system of production, the vast majority of whom were engaged in nail making. Other sources estimate that about one-half or more of the total output of nails in England in the late eighteenth century was exported.[159] The Birmingham area of the West Midlands also became the leading exporter of guns, especially to Western Africa.[160] Because the region was involved heavily in export production, its industries benefited immensely from the expansion of metalware exports from 3 percent of total English domestic export of manufactures in 1699–1701 to 9 percent in 1752–54. Consequently, as Marie Rowlands demonstrates,

upswings in national overseas trade, especially marked 1700–15 and 1745–60, were also periods of marked diversification and intensification of industrial activity in the Midlands. Conversely, interruptions to overseas trade were quickly reflected in overstocked warehouses, laying off the workers, and high poor rates in the industrial villages.[161]

As stated earlier, much of the pig and bar iron employed in the production of iron products in England in the late seventeenth and early eighteenth

---

[158]   Rowlands, "Continuity and Change," p. 115.

[159]   Court, *The Rise of Midlands Industries*, pp. 100, 206, 208–209; Ashton, *Iron and Steel*, p. 19.

[160]   J. E. Inikori, "The Import of Firearms into West Africa, 1750–1807: A Quantitative Analysis," *Journal of African History*, XVIII, 3 (1977), pp. 339–368; Alan Birch, *The Economic History of the British Iron and Steel Industry, 1784–1879: Essays in Industrial and Economic History with Special Reference to the Development of Technology* (London: Cass, 1967), pp. 49–51.

[161]   Rowlands, "Continuity and Change," pp. 115–116.

centuries was imported. For example, total production of pig iron in England in 1720 was 17,350 tons,[162] while total supply was 35,800 tons.[163] The imports came mainly from Sweden and Russia. The evidence indicates that initially the growth of domestic production of iron in substitution for imported iron expanded more rapidly in the West Midlands where the production of iron products had been growing fast. The northeast and South Yorkshire were other centers of ironware production. They had coal, limestone, and ore. And two of the three ports through which Swedish and Russian irons were imported into England – Newcastle, Hull, and London – were located there. As Alan Birch noted, "With the adoption of coke-smelting it might have been expected that the iron industry in the north of the country would have expanded. There were at hand the raw materials – ore, coal, and limestone . . ."[164] But it was the West Midlands that took advantage of the protective duties instituted by the British government.[165] This must have been due, partly at least, to the relatively larger and faster growing markets served by producers in the region – markets in the Americas, Western Africa, and at home. Table 2.5 presents the regional distribution of the rapidly growing output of pig iron in England and Wales in the eighteenth century.

As the table shows, in the 68 years between 1720 and 1788, total national output increased by 254.5 percent (from 17,350 tons to 61,500 tons); but in the 18 years between 1788 and 1806 (just a fraction of the first period), output almost quadrupled, increasing from 61,500 tons to 227,200 tons, being an increase of 269.4 percent. As phenomenal as the national increases were, output in the West Midlands grew even faster. In 1720, total output for Shropshire, Staffordshire, and Worcestershire was 4,950 tons, and this was 28.5 percent of the national total. By 1788 output for Shropshire and Staffordshire alone was 31,800 tons, an increase of 542.4 percent, raising the share of the West Midlands in the national output of England and Wales to 51.7 percent. In the next 18 years, production in the West Midlands more than tripled to reach 104,400 tons in 1806. However, the share of the region dropped slightly to 46.0 percent, because of the faster growth of output in South Wales during the period. In 1815,

---

[162] Charles K. Hyde, *Technological Change and the British Iron Industry 1700–1870* (Princeton, NJ.: Princeton University Press, 1977), Table 1.1, p. 12.

[163] Birch, *Economic History of the British Iron and Steel Industry*, p. 18.

[164] *Ibid.*, p. 99.

[165] According to Charles Hyde, "British ironmasters earned profits in spite of their high production costs because the market was highly protected and iron prices were kept artificially high. British import duties and Swedish export duties combined amounted to roughly one-quarter to one-third of the price of Swedish bar iron in Britain. The Swedish government also fostered high iron prices in Britain by deliberately restricting Swedish iron output from the 1720s until the early nineteenth century." Hyde, *Technological Change*, p. 47.

Table 2.5. *Regional Distribution of Pig Iron Production in England and Wales*

	1720		1788		1806	
	Tons	%	Tons	%	Tons	%
The Weald	2,000	11.5	300	0.4	—	—
Forest of Dean	4,250	24.4	4,700	7.6	4,100	1.8
South Wales	1,500	8.6	11,300	18.4	75,600	33.3
N. Wales-Cheshire	2,250	12.9	1,000	1.6	2,100	0.9
Shropshire	2,550	14.6	24,900	40.5	104,400	46.0
Stafford-Worcester	2,400	13.8	6,900	11.2		
S. Yorkshire-Derby	2,400	13.8	9,600	15.6	37,000	16.3
Lancashire-Cumberland	—	—	2,800	4.6	4,000	1.8
	17,350		61,500		227,200	

Sources and Notes: 1720 is from Hyde, *Technological Change*, p. 12; 1806 is derived from Ashton, *Iron and Steel*, p. 98; 1788 is a combination of the former (p. 114) and the latter (p. 98). For 1788 and 1806, Ashton's "South East," "South West," "North West," and "Midlands" are treated in this table as The Weald, Forest of Dean, Lancashire-Cumberland, and Shropshire and Stafford-Worcester, respectively. Parallel evidence for 1788 actually makes it clear that Ashton's "Midlands" represents Shropshire and Staffordshire only.

the region raised its share of the total for England and Wales (370,000 tons) to 47.3 percent, with an output of 175,000 tons. In the years 1788–1815, the fastest growing area in the West Midlands was South Staffordshire (the Black Country). Its output increased from 6,900 tons in 1788 to 125,000 tons in 1815, being 11.2 percent and 33.8 percent of the total for England and Wales in the respective years. During the same period output in Shropshire grew from 24,900 tons (40.5 percent of the national total) to 50,000 tons (13.5 percent).[166]

[166] Hyde, *Technological Change*, Tables 6.6 and 11.1, pp. 114 and 181. Hyde's evidence shows the tendency of the iron industry in the nineteenth century to shift its concentration to regions relatively better endowed with iron ore. Thus, although output continued to grow in the West Midlands (129,000 tons in Shropshire in 1871, 2.4% of the total of 5,467,000 tons for England and Wales in this year, and 726,000 tons for the Black Country, 13.3% of the national total), the northeast had become the leading region by 1871, producing 33.3% (1,823,000 tons) of the total for England and Wales at this time. The northwest (Lancashire and Cumberland), with an output of 857,000 tons in 1871, was now also producing more than the Black Country.

The relatively greater dynamism of the industries in the West Midlands in the seventeenth and eighteenth centuries must have attracted the inventors whose inventions ultimately transformed the iron industry in England and Wales. Abraham Darby, who invented the smelting of iron with mineral fuel, worked at Coalbrookdale in Shropshire. Boulton and Watt also worked in the West Midlands to produce the steam engine, which made the smelting of iron with mineral fuel more efficient. It was in Soho, then a village located between Birmingham and the Black Country, that the Boulton and Watt partnership perfected the manufacture and began the commercial production of steam engines, which soon captured numerous production processes outside the iron industry. It is no surprise that the first engine produced by the partnership was installed in the Black Country.[167] Henry Cort, the inventor of the puddling process, was the only major inventor for the iron industry who did his work outside the West Midlands. It is significant that Cort began his work while he was a Navy agent in London, and his experiments were aimed at producing high quality iron for naval and ordnance purposes.[168] He was thus less concerned with the private sector market. The other major inventors were entrepreneurs actively engaged in the private sector market. Darby was primarily an iron-founder, making iron-cast pots, and his invention came from his efforts to produce pig iron suitable for his own purpose.[169] And, as Court noted, Boulton was "at every stage of his career, both before and after the partnership with Watt, an indefatigable and adventurous, or as some contemporaries thought, crack-brained searcher for markets."[170] The evidence thus suggests that of all the regions of England and Wales with adequate natural resources for the growth and development of iron and ironware production in the seventeenth and eighteenth centuries, access to relatively large and fast growing markets gave the West Midlands, at least in part, some relative advantage.

The other regional success story of industrialization in England between 1660 and 1850 was the West Riding of Yorkshire. This region experienced an explosive growth of industrial production in the eighteenth century. The tax data examined earlier in this chapter did not place the West Riding among the top ten counties in wealth in the 1840s, because the region is lumped together with the North Riding and East Riding under the county of Yorkshire by the available source. In the eighteenth and nineteenth

---

[167] W. K. V. Gale, *The Black Country Iron Industry: A Technical History* (London, 1966), pp. 23–31.

[168] Ashton, *Iron and Steel*, p. 90.

[169] Gale, *The Black Country Iron Industry*, p. 23.

[170] W. H. B. Court, "Industrial Organisation and Economic Progress in the Eighteenth-Century Midlands," *Transactions of the Royal Historical Society*, 4th Series, XXVIII, 1946, p. 99.

centuries, the region contained a wide range of industries: textile industries (woollen, linen, and cotton), iron production, pottery making, lime burning, and lead and coal mining.[171] But by far the largest industry in the region, upon which its industrial fortune depended during the period, was the woollen textile industry. The movement of the industry to this region in the course of the eighteenth century, away from the older regions of production in the West Country and East Anglia, is probably one of the most dramatic examples of acceleration and deceleration in the regional history of industrialization in England between 1660 and 1850.

Phyllis Deane's estimate of the gross value of output of the woollen industry in England and Wales in the eighteenth century provides a national reference point against which to measure the performance of the West Riding industry:[172] 1695, £5.0 million; 1741, £5.1 million; 1772, £10.2 million; 1799, £13.8 million; 1805, £18.5 million. The regional shares at the end of the seventeenth century indicate that the industry was still very much in the south of England and the West Riding was just one of several producing districts. With all the uncertainties of the early regional statistics, Devon's output is valued at £1,350,000; Norfolk £750,000; West Country £900,000; other production centers in the south and areas in the Midlands, roughly £1,000,000. Thus the industries in the south of England had a combined output of probably £3.5 million at this time. With £1 million estimated output for the West Riding, the region's share was about 20 percent.[173] By 1772, however, the value of output in the West Riding had increased to £3,273,701, being about one-third of the total for England and Wales. And between 1772 and 1800 it almost tripled to reach £8.4 million, by which time the West Riding's share of the total for England and Wales had risen to 60 percent.[174] Thus the production of woollen textiles in the West Riding increased by a factor of eight between 1700 and 1800, while production in the rest of England grew by only 40 percent during the same period (from £4 million in 1700 to £5.6 million in 1800).[175]

---

171   R. G. Wilson, "The Supremacy of the Yorkshire Cloth Industry in the Eighteenth Century," in N. B. Hart and K. G. Ponting (eds.), *Textile History and Economic History: Essays in Honour of Miss Julia de Lacy Mann* (Manchester: Manchester University Press, 1973), p. 246.

172   Phyllis Deane, "The Output of the British Woolen Industry in the Eighteenth Century," *Journal of Economic History*, XVII (1957), Table 3, p. 220.

173   Julia de Lacy Mann, *The Cloth Industry in the West of England from 1640 to 1880* (Oxford: Clarendon Press, 1971), pp. 26–36; Wilson, "Supremacy of the Yorkshire Cloth Industry," pp. 226–235; Derek Gregory, *Regional Transformation and Industrial Revolution: A Geography of the Yorkshire Woollen Industry* (Minneapolis: University of Minnesota Press, 1982), pp. 41–44.

174   Deane, "Output of the British Woolen Industry," pp. 215, 220; Wilson, "Supremacy of the Yorkshire Cloth Industry," p. 228.

175   Wilson, "Supremacy of the Yorkshire Cloth Industry," p. 231.

The expansion of production in the West Riding kept pace with the capture of markets in southern Europe from the older regions and the expansion of exports to the Americas. Northwestern Europe was for several centuries the main export market for clothiers in southern England. From the second half of the seventeenth century, competing production in France, Holland, Germany, and Poland took away much of this market. Southern Europe, especially Spain and Portugal, became the growing export market for English woollen textiles in Europe in the eighteenth century. In the course of the century, clothiers in the West Riding captured much of the south-European market from other English producers.[176] At the same time the markets in British America, which absorbed by far the fastest growing volume of English woollen textiles in the eighteenth century, were opened up and dominated by West Riding producers.[177] The achievement of the West Riding in export sales promotion is reflected in the fact that a much greater proportion of the region's total output was exported: It was noted in 1772 by a contemporary who knew the West Riding industry thoroughly for over 30 years that the region exported no less than 72 percent of its total output.[178] The export performance of the West Riding and the growing concentration of the industry in the region account for the increased percentage of the national output exported between the late seventeenth century and the end of the eighteenth, from 40 percent in the former to 67 percent in the latter.[179]

The evidence shows that the loss of the export trade to the West Riding was the principal explanation for the slow growth of the industry in the other regions of England. A case in point, the export success of the West Riding prevented the West Country from sharing adequately in the expansion of cloth exports from the 1760s, especially between 1775 and 1790, and in consequence the latter's export trade became relatively small by 1786.[180] As their export trades declined, the West Country and East Anglia concentrated on production for the domestic market, which continued to grow.[181]

Wilson has attempted to explain the superior performance of the West Riding in export sales. He dismisses the contribution of natural resource endowment: "Clearly, considerations about coal and iron are far less important when applied to the eighteenth century situation. In fact Yorkshire had

[176] Mann, *The Cloth Industry*, pp. xii–xiii, 44–50; Wilson, "Supremacy of the Yorkshire Cloth Industry," pp. 241–244.
[177] Wilson, "Supremacy of the Yorkshire Cloth Industry," pp. 243–245.
[178] *Ibid.*, p. 230 and fn. 15, p. 230.
[179] Deane, "Output of the British Woolen Industry," p. 221.
[180] Mann, *The Cloth Industry*, p. 47.
[181] Wilson, "Supremacy of the Yorkshire Cloth Industry," p. 244; Mann, *The Cloth Industry*, p. 50.

Table 2.6. *Factory Employment in
the Main Woollen Districts*

	1835	1838	1847	1850
Gloucestershire	7,973	5,515	5,308	6,043
Somerset	1,545	2,133	2,180	2,175
Wiltshire	3,080	3,228	3,265	2,877
Lancashire	4,575	4,947	7,971	8,816
Yorkshire	23,636	27,548	38,737	40,611
ENGLAND	46,964	46,928	62,687	62,352

Sources and Notes: Gregory, *Regional Transformation*, Table 2.11, p. 61. Gregory explains that the figures for Somerset and Wiltshire in 1835 cover only part of the counties.

few natural advantages."[182] After considering and rejecting the unique characteristics of the entrepreneurs and of production organization in the West Riding, he settled for variations in sale procedures as the clue to the region's relative performance in export sales. While exports in the other regions of England were controlled by London's general merchants, with very little knowledge about the export markets for woollen textiles, exports from the West Riding were handled by local merchants specializing in the sale of woollen cloth: "Cloth was their life, their sole interest. They had far closer contacts with the clothiers and they knew the trade..." Wilson thus concludes:

The difference between the ways in which the West Riding trade was handled by the active merchants of Leeds, Wakefield (and eventually Halifax) and the exports of every other production area from Norwich down, which were monopolised by non-specialist London traders often working within the restrictions of the trading companies themselves, accounts in good measure for Yorkshire's growing supremacy in the eighteenth century.[183]

From the last decade of the eighteenth century, the West Riding industry began to adopt merchanization and the factory form of production. In the course of the first half of the nineteenth century, the merchanized sector of the woollen textile industry in England was clearly concentrated in the region, as Table 2.6 shows. In 1835, 50.3 percent of all labor employed in that sector were in the West Riding. This increased to 58.7 percent in 1838, 61.8 percent in 1847, and 65.1 percent in 1850.

[182] Wilson, "Supremacy of the Yorkshire Cloth Industry," p. 135.
[183] *Ibid.*, pp. 235–244 for the whole explanation, p. 241 for the quotation.

This regional variation in the pace of mechanization has been explained in two different ways. Mann's argument implies that the more rapid progress of mechanization in the West Riding in the nineteenth century was a function of the rapid rate of expansion of the region's industry in the preceding century, while the slow progress in the West Country and other southern regions was due to the stagnation of their industry in the eighteenth century:

> It was the great increase in demand, especially strong in the early nineties, which induced manufacturers to lay aside their fears and workpeople, or most of them, to acquiesce in the use of spinning machinery. Exports of cloth of all kinds increased from 89,620 pieces in 1786 to 214,489 in 1791; and although they fell in 1792 and were only a little over 133,000 pieces in 1793, this was still a great advance on any year before 1788. By far the larger part, of course, came from Yorkshire, but the West had its share.[184]

On the other hand, Adrian Randall believes that the differing pace of progress was due to differing production organization, which gave rise to differing degrees of labor resistance to mechanization: Labor resistance to machines was greatest in the West Country and this accounts for the slow progress of mechanization and subsequent decline of the industry in that region.[185] Workers' resistance to machines certainly deserves due consideration. However, the evidence showing the correlation between the degree of concentration and the pace of progress in mechanization makes it clear that the critical operating factors were the size of the industry, the extent of the market served, and the pace of growth of both. This point is further strengthened by the evidence showing several decades of market expansion and output growth in the West Riding before the onset of mechanization in the region. What is more, the industry in the south of England went into stagnation or decline for almost a century before machines became important in the woollen textile industry.

Finally, the undisputed, truly dramatic regional success story of industrialization in England between 1660 and 1850 was that of Lancashire. As stated previously, Lancashire was about the poorest and most backward of the English counties at the time of Restoration. It retained much of that honor to the end of the century. As Farnie puts it:

> Until the eighteenth century the society between Ribble and Mersey had maintained a largely self-contained existence upon the fringe of civilization. Cut off from the rest of England by barriers of mountain and marshland, it lay far distant from the great centres of economic activity and from the main channels of commerce. The poverty of a barren frontier region was manifest in the small population, in the

---

[184] Mann, *The Cloth Industry*, p. 135.
[185] Adrian J. Randall, "Work, culture and resistance to machinery in the West of England woollen industry," in Hudson (ed.), *Regions and Industries*, pp. 175–198.

limited supplies of stone and timber for building, and in the staple diet of oatmeal and offal . . .[186]

But, within two or three generations, from the late eighteenth century to the mid-nineteenth, this region that had remained the backwater of England since 1086 "erupted suddenly into a fury of productive power of which its previous history had given but faint promise and of which its later history showed but little trace."[187] There can be no doubt that an industrial revolution occurred in Lancashire between 1780 and 1850, no matter how the term is defined, and that the Industrial Revolution in England was first and foremost a Lancashire phenomenon.

The region had developed some manufacturing in the sixteenth and early seventeenth centuries, mainly woollen and linen textiles.[188] But the first major development that subsequently became very important for the growth of industrial production in the region was the development of Liverpool as a major port in England, with its strong links to the Americas and Western Africa. Initially, the main source of this development was the trade in colonial produce from the Americas (sugar, tobacco, and rum), the trade in African slaves that provided labor for the production of those commodities, and the transportation of salt and coal.[189] Like the national entrepôt trade of England during the same period, treated earlier in this chapter, the growth of Liverpool's overseas trade in the late seventeenth and early eighteenth centuries was not based on local industries. But, as manufacturing developed in Lancashire in the course of the eighteenth century, the markets served overseas by Liverpool and the raw materials from the same regions became central to the growth of the region's industries. Wadsworth and Mann made the point succinctly:

At the present day [1931], Liverpool owes its importance largely to the hive of industry behind it in Lancashire. In the eighteenth century the situation was the reverse. Liverpool was a prosperous and rapidly growing town when large parts of Lancashire were still thinly peopled or barren waste . . . The merchant and shipowner, not the manufacturer, sought and found the outlets for the products of industry; the organisation of industry adapted itself to the demands of expanding commerce.[190]

---

[186]   D. A. Farnie, *The English Cotton Industry and the World Market, 1815–1896* (Oxford: Clarendon Press, 1979), p. 46.

[187]   *Ibid.*, p. 324.

[188]   A. P. Wadsworth and J. de L. Mann, *The Cotton Trade and Industrial Lancashire* (Manchester: Manchester University Press, 1931), pp. 15–16; John K. Walton, "Proto-industrialisation and the first industrial revolution: the case of Lancashire," in Hudson (ed.), *Regions and Industries*, p. 45.

[189]   Walton, *Lancashire*, p. 113; Francis E. Hyde, "The Growth of Liverpool's Trade, 1700–1950," in *Scientific Survey of Merseyside* (Liverpool: Published for the British Association for the Advancement of Science by the University of Liverpool Press, 1953), pp. 148–163.

[190]   Wadsworth and Mann, *The Cotton Trade*, p. 224.

First, the growing trade of Liverpool gave rise to a thriving shipbuilding industry and related manufacturing industries in the port town.[191] But, while these and the earlier woollen and linen industries provided some of the general infrastructures for the industrial revolution in Lancashire, it was a new industry, based entirely on imported raw materials and developed out of the stimulus of an imported product from India – the cotton textile industry – that transformed Lancashire into the first modern industrial society in the world. As mentioned earlier in this chapter, cotton textile production in England had started as a typical import substitution industry in the seventeenth and early eighteenth centuries. Several regions of the country were involved. But increasingly the industry concentrated in Lancashire.[192] By 1787 Lancashire already had close to one-half of the capital value of all cotton mills in Great Britain.[193] In 1820, of the 240,000 estimated handloom weavers in Britain (handloom weaving still remaining overwhelmingly dominant at this time), about 165,000 or 68.8 percent were in Lancashire, about 47,000 or 19.6 percent were in Scotland, and the remainder were in the rest of England. By this time handloom weavers in the cotton textile industry were about 25 percent of the total labor force in Lancashire.[194]

Technological development in the industry was slow. Cotton spinning was mechanized in the last decades of the eighteenth century – first in water-powered factories that were scattered all over the county in search of suitable water sites; then steam power was harnessed to the spinning machines, which freed the spinning factories from dependence on water sites and allowed concentration in urban locations.[195] At about the same time, the finishing process of cotton printing was also mechanized. However, both the spinning and finishing branches of the cotton industry required a relatively small amount of labor. The bulk of the labor employed in the industry was in weaving, which remained largely unmechanized up to the mid-1830s.[196] As weaving was increasingly mechanized from the 1830s, Lancashire led the way. In 1835, of a total of 108,189 powerlooms employed in cotton weaving in the whole of Britain, 61,176 or 56.5 percent

[191]   R. Stewart-Brown, *Liverpool Ships in the Eighteenth Century* (London, 1932), p. 5.

[192]   Wadsworth and Mann, *The Cotton Trade*, pp. 170–177.

[193]   In 1787 the estimated capital value of all cotton mills in Great Britain was £500,000, of which 50 percent was located in Lancashire, Derbyshire, and Nottinghamshire. See Ian Inkster, *Science and technology in history: an approach to industrial development* (New Brunswick, N.J.: Rutgers University Press, 1991), p. 65 and fn. 17, p. 320.

[194]   Geoffrey Timmins, *The Last Shift: The Decline of Handloom Weaving in Nineteenth-Century Lancashire* (Manchester: Manchester University Press, 1993), pp. 25, 26, 37, 39.

[195]   Walton, *Lancashire*, p. 104.

[196]   Timmins, *The Last Shift*, pp. 40, 91, 97, 111.

were in Lancashire, with the rest mostly in Scotland. By 1850, 70.9 percent of all the powerlooms in Britain were employed in Lancashire, 176,947 out of 249,627.[197]

The growth of output in the industry between 1760 and 1871 gives some indication of what was happening in Lancashire at this time. In 1760, the gross value of output in the industry was a mere £600,000. This increased almost tenfold to £5.4 million in 1784–86; by 1798–1800 it had more than doubled again to £11.1 million; thereafter it grew even more rapidly, £30.0 million in 1815–17, £48.6 million in 1851, and £104.9 million in 1871.[198] Because the industry was heavily concentrated in Lancashire, the bulk of this explosive growth of cotton production between the 1780s and 1871 occurred in that county. The backward and forward linkage effects of this expansion gave rise to further increases in industrial production in machine and machine tool industries and clothing. As families in the county responded to the buoyant employment opportunities, the county's population increased phenomenally as the age at marriage fell, the frequency of marriage increased, and birth rates rose sharply. Lancashire's population more than quadrupled between 1664 and 1801 to reach almost 700,000, and by 1851 it was over 2,000,000.[199] The county had the highest birth rate in England between 1740 and 1850, and within it the rapidly industrializing southeast experienced the largest increases. In this way, the industrial revolution in Lancashire created its own labor force, with very little net migration from the rest of England.[200]

The trade statistics show unmistakably that Lancashire's cotton industry was the progeny of overseas trade in all respects. It grew initially on the basis of a domestic market that had been previously created by imported East Indian cotton calicoes. But its rapid expansion from a very small base in 1760 was largely due to the fast growth of exports, from 33.3 percent of the industry's total output in 1760 to 61.3 percent in 1798–1800, 63.7 percent in 1859–61, and 73.7 percent in 1872–74.[201] The growth of exports

---

[197] *Ibid.*, Table 1.1, p. 20.

[198] Joseph E. Inikori, "Slavery and the Revolution in Cotton Textile Production in England," in Joseph E. Inikori and Stanley L. Engerman (eds.), *The Atlantic Slave Trade: Effects on Economies, Societies, and Peoples in Africa, the Americas, and Europe* (Durham and London: Duke University Press, 1992), Table 3, p. 170; Farnie, *The English Cotton Industry*, Table 3, p. 24.

[199] Walton, *Lancashire*, pp. 76–77, 123. The county's population was only 95,000 in 1563 (*Ibid.*, p. 12).

[200] *Ibid.*, pp. 123–124.

[201] Inikori, "Slavery and the Revolution in Cotton Textile Production," Table 3, p. 170; Farnie, *The English Cotton Industry*, Table 2, p. 10. The percentages for 1859–61 and 1872–74 are computed by applying the annual average export figures for these two periods to the output figures for 1861 and 1871, respectively. The point made in this paragraph is consistent with that expressed by Farnie: "The industry had been created in order to supply the markets of Europe with an alternative to Indian

was matched by increases in the import of raw cotton, from 4.2 million pounds (weight) in 1772 to 41.8 million in 1800, and 452 million in 1841.[202]

Some attempts have been made to explain why, of all parts of England that tried to produce a domestic substitute for imported cottons from India, it was Lancashire that forged ahead dramatically to build a whole modern industrial society on the basis of cotton textile production. In some ways it may be tempting to explain the region's success in terms of its natural endowment in coal, water resources, climate, and the like. In this way, Lancashire may fit well into Wrigley's hypothesis on the discontinuity between the organic economy and the inorganic economy in England, a discontinuity occasioned by the use of coal-based energy in the inorganic economy:

Inasmuch as the growth taking place in some sectors of the English economy was contingent upon the use of cheap energy on a large scale and that energy came from coal, it seems prudent to regard such growth not as a structural feature logically comparable to the benefits derived from specialization of function, or from the development of the landlord, tenant farmer and labourer system in agriculture, but as an uncovenanted blessing.[203]

However, Walton has dismissed the role of coal, climate, and religion during the critical period of industrial development in Lancashire between the middle quarters of the eighteenth and the beginning of the nineteenth century. He rests his explanation primarily on the general poverty of the masses in Lancashire induced in turn by the poor agricultural resources of the county:

Explanations involving natural advantages carry little weight at this stage. The presence of accessible coal measures became essential to sustained growth through urbanisation and the steam-powered factory from the end of the eighteenth century . . . More to the point is the nature of economy and society at the beginning of the eighteenth century. . . . the poor quality of much agricultural land, especially in relation to the range of available improvement techniques, helped to push investment in industrial directions. The relationship between poor land, small holdings, subdivided plots and the rise of domestic industry is also highly relevant, of course; but in this respect south-east Lancashire was part of a much wider pattern of development.[204]

calico, to replace England's imports by an indigenous product, and thereby to transform the re-export trade into an export trade in domestic manufactures. In the process of development the industry became increasingly geared to the supply of foreign markets and acquired an export bias which remained without parallel in any other industry, either at home or abroad, and generated an intense export-led boom in the economy." Farnie, *The English Cotton Industry*, p. 81.

[202] Walton, *Lancashire*, p. 104.
[203] E. A. Wrigley, *Continuity, Chance and Change: The Character of the Industrial Revolution in England* (Cambridge: Cambridge University Press, 1988), pp. 114–115.
[204] Walton, *Lancashire*, pp. 66–67.

This more or less places Lancashire in the general context of the literature on proto-industrialization, with emphasis on poor agricultural resources, surplus labor, and mass poverty, all leading to the availability of cheap labor for domestic industry.[205] General poverty in Lancashire meant that industrial expansion must depend heavily on external markets, another important element in the proto-industrialization hypothesis. Ultimately, therefore, Lancashire's success in relation to other regions in England may be seen in the region's ability to exploit its cheap labor and win overseas markets, in comparison with the failure of other English regions to do the same. As Farnie points out: "Ready access to the world's greatest market for cotton manufactures conferred upon Lancashire a unique advantage lacked by the industry elsewhere, whether in Britain or abroad."[206] The availability of cheap labor and the other factors mentioned by Walton become very important in this context. Equally important in this context is the prior development of Liverpool as a major world trading port with its important connections with Western Africa and the Americas.

At this juncture it is pertinent to note some of the essential elements that were common to the three regional success stories of English industrialization between 1660 and 1850, and which marked them apart from other regions in England during the period. First, all three were among the poorer regions of England up to the Restoration (1660): None of them was among the top 10 counties in wealth in 1086 and in 1660; the major developments in agriculture and industry between 1086 and 1660 took place very much outside the three; and, undoubtedly, Lancashire and the West Riding were about the poorest areas of England at the beginning of the seventeenth century. Second, their industrialization during the period was heavily dependent on their ability to win overseas markets relative to competing regions in England. The evidence presented earlier makes it clear enough that the West Midlands dominated overseas sales of English iron and ironware during the period under consideration, although the exact proportions are not known. Similarly, more than half of England's woollen textiles sold overseas during the period came from the West Riding, which exported over 72 percent of its total output. And the proportion of Lancashire's cotton output exported and the county's share of England's export of cotton goods during the same period were even greater. Finally, in the course of their industrialization during the period, all three generated the bulk of their needed labor internally through their own reproduction process. These rapidly industrializing regions did not depend in any significant way on net

---

[205] For a more direct analysis of Lancashire's industrialization in the context of the proto-industrialisation literature, see Walton, "Proto-industrialisation and the first industrial revolution."

[206] Farnie, *The English Cotton Industry*, p. 63.

Table 2.7. *Comparative Decennial Population Growth Rates in
Selected Regions of England*

	Essex	Suffolk	Norfolk	Average of England and Wales	Lancashire	West Riding of Yorkshire	Derbyshire
1801–11	11	11	7	14.5	23	16	15
1811–21	15	15	18	17.5	27	22	15
1821–31	10	9	13	16.0	27	22	11
1831–41	8.6	6.3	5.7	14.5	24.7	18.2	14.7

Source: Coleman, "Growth and Decay," Table 2.2, p. 119. The evidence is from *British Parliamentary Papers 1843*, Vol. XXII, p. 12.

migration from the other regions of England. Against this background, the information presented in Table 2.7 is quite instructive. As the table shows, the rate of population growth in the three counties of East Anglia, which experienced deceleration in industrial production, was consistently lower than the average for England and Wales from 1801 to 1841. During the same period, on the other hand, the rates for Lancashire and the West Riding, particularly the former, were considerably higher than the national average.

Now, if the other regions of England did not contribute much by way of labor supply to the rapidly industrializing regions, did they provide important markets for the latter's industrial products? In other words, was there a nation-wide division of labor in England in the eighteenth and early nineteen centuries? Almost two decades ago, John Langton published a paper that has since been very influential in directing attention to the regional pattern of manufacturing in England in the eighteenth and nineteenth centuries.[207] The descriptive analysis presented shows that in the eighteenth and early nineteenth centuries, the manufacturing regions of England operated largely in isolation from each other; different production systems existed in different regions in the same industries, with very little direct competition among them in the domestic market. This pattern, which originated from the high cost of inland transportation, was further extended and consolidated by the construction of canals, particularly from the late eighteenth century, owing to the regional nature of their construction and operation.

[207] John Langton, "The Industrial Revolution and the Regional Geography of England," *Transactions of the Institute of British Geographers*, New Series, Vol. 9 (1984), pp. 145–167.

As Langton stresses, "one of the most striking peculiarities of English industrialization was that it was based for over a generation upon haulage along a waterway network." Although the canals reduced the cost of transporting goods considerably, those costs rose quickly as more distances were covered. "The vast majority of shipments" along the canals were, therefore, "over short distances or to and from the main coastal ports. . . . It was the realization of the intra-regional nature of the huge benefits that canal transport brought which generated such strongly regionalized pressures for canal construction." For this reason, effective competition in the canal-based economy of England was limited to regions, within which comparative advantage, arising from the combination of local resource endowments, traditional skills, and the nature of the markets served, determined the form and location of production and encouraged intra-regional specialization. In this way, the regional economies became highly differentiated, internally integrated, and very separate from each other.[208]

The separateness of the manufacturing regions was reflected in the regional organization of the industrial labor unions. As H. Pelling pointed out: "The freer movement of men and materials had to wait for the coming of the railways in the 1830s and 1840s, and it was not until thereafter that national unions of particular industries became practicable."[209] It was the construction of a national railway network that ultimately created a truly integrated national economy in England in the nineteenth century: "Raw materials and products for the home market quickly began to flow over long distances and burst through the old regional barriers."[210]

Further evidence on the separateness of the manufacturing regions comes from the political arena. The regional distribution of modern and traditional forms of manufacturing in England in the eighteenth century made it impossible for the manufacturers to present a common national front on the major issues that concerned them in the 1780s:

Command of the overseas markets upon which these industrial regions depended was heavily dependent upon policies pursued by national government. The necessary appositional element in the growth of regional consciousness was provided by the interaction of all the industrial (and agricultural) regions with Parliament in London. It was a threat to overseas markets – or rather a series of them – that set off the intense lobbying from manufacturing interests in the 1780s, and it was in that coming together that the manufacturers of different regions realized the depth of the differences between them.[211]

---

[208] *Ibid.*, pp. 162–163.

[209] H. Pelling, *A History of British Trade Unionism* (London, 1963), p. 4, cited by Langton, "The Industrial Revolution," p. 163.

[210] Langton, "The Industrial Revolution," p. 163.

[211] *Ibid.*, p. 163.

The institution created for the purpose, under the leadership of Midlands manufacturers, was the General Chamber of Manufacturers, which was established in 1785. After some initial successes, the Chamber was destroyed by disagreements along regional lines:

Unanimity shattered when an attempt was made to organize opinion on the proposed commercial treaty with France in 1786 and to put the General Chamber onto a permanent and regular footing. The newer manufactures of cotton, iron and pottery supported the freer trade that the treaty would have encouraged, but deligates from the traditional handicrafts were opposed to it. Based largely in London and the South, they flooded the assembly in the capital in 1787 and passed a petition on behalf of the General Chamber pleading for a postponement of the application of the treaty. The Midlands and Northern deligates were enraged as 'a fatal split . . . more or less on regional lines' developed to cause the collapse of the General Chamber.[212]

The foregoing original findings of Langton were subsequently confirmed by the results of a collective work, *Atlas of Industrializing Britain, 1780–1914*, sponsored by the Economic History Society and the Institute of British Geographers. In their summary of these results, the editors report:

In a more difficult way the related question of regionality is raised: just how self-contained and separate were the various industrial regions? This is clearest in the transport material. The flows of goods along the canals and turnpikes of Lancashire and Yorkshire are clearly greater than flows out of the region, except for the export funnels of Liverpool and the Aire.[213]

According to the editors, the national economic integration that was very evident in the late nineteenth century was the creation of the railways. However, the early fares policies of the railway companies tended to prolong the continued existence of regional economies: "the regional base of many companies meant that pricing policies encouraged intra-regional trade . . ."[214] But, eventually a truly national railway network emerged to produce an integrated national economy in Britain.

---

[212] *Ibid.*, p. 151.
[213] John Langton and R. J. Morris, "Introduction," in John Langton and R. J. Morris (eds.), *Atlas of Industrializing Britain, 1784–1914* (London and New York: Methuen, 1986), p. xxviii. See also the exchange between Derek Gregory and John Langton, *Journal of Historical Geography*, 14, 1 (1988), pp. 50–58, and 14, 2 (1988), pp. 170–176. Both Gregory and Langton agree on the essential issues, including the separateness of the manufacturing regions and their integration into the international economy. Their main point of debate is how best to explain the regional differences. Also in agreement with Langton's findings is Gerard Turnbull, "Canals, coal and regional growth during the industrial revolution," *Economic History Review*, 2nd ser., XL, 4 (1987), pp. 537–560. A more critical view but still basically in agreement is that of Michael Freeman, "The Industrial revolution and the regional geography of England: a comment," *Transactions of the Institute of British Geographers*, New Series, Vol. 9 (1984), pp. 507–512.
[214] Langton and Morris, "Introduction," p. xxix.

All of the foregoing is very much in accord with the evidence concerning the concentration of West Country and East Anglia clothiers on production for the home trade as they lost overseas markets to West Riding producers, which was stated earlier in this chapter. The implication of that evidence is that the rapidly industrializing regions were initially more successful in taking overseas markets from the traditional manufacturers in the south of England than in capturing the latter's local and regional markets at home. Overconcentration on Manchester firms sometimes creates the misleading impression that Lancashire products were the only English cotton textiles sold in England in the eighteenth century.[215] While detailed study of inter-regional product flows may produce more information in the years to come, an attempt to map the geographical spread and density of sales of the products of a Lancashire hand-tool maker (1811–15) and a West Riding linen manufacturer (1791–96) on the domestic market shows concentration of sales within a radius of 50 miles in both cases, but more so for the linen firm; beyond a radius of 100 miles sales diminished to almost zero.[216]

It must not be forgotten that while the rapidly industrializing regions developed modern capitalist industry, traditional manufacturing, some of whose products never even reached the market, persisted in several regions and served a sizable portion of the local markets. Though not directly relevant to this study, some evidence of this type relating to the output and distribution of linen manufactures in Ireland in the late eighteenth century may be cited to illustrate this point. A House of Commons committee report of 1773 shows that in 1770 the total value of linens sold on the market in each county in Ireland was £2,146,800, of which £1,691,787 went for exports, leaving £455,013 of the marketed output for home consumption. But the report adds that a further output worth £378,321 was produced and consumed at home, "and never exposed to sale in Market."[217] Thus, almost one-half (45.4 percent to be precise) of domestically produced linen manufactures consumed in Ireland in 1770 was supplied through subsistence production (produced and consumed directly by the producer). Of course, the English economy in the eighteenth century was more commercialized than the Irish economy. Even so, the extent to which local con-

[215] Beverly Lemire, *Fashion's Favourite: The Cotton Trade And The Consumer in Britain, 1660–1800* (Oxford: Oxford University Press, 1991), pp. 115–160.

[216] Michael J. Freeman, "Introduction," in Derek H. Aldcroft and Michael J. Freeman (eds.), *Transport in the Industrial Revolution* (Manchester: Manchester University Press, 1983), Figure 1, pp. 8–9.

[217] British Library, London, *House of Commons Sessional Papers of the 18th Century, Reports & Papers*, Vol. 25, 1763–74, Report From the Committee Appointed to Enquire into the Present State of the Linen Trade in Great Britain and Ireland, p. 425.

sumption was met by local supply during the period under consideration must not be underrated.

It is now clear that the development of industrial production in England between 1660 and 1850 was first and foremost a regional phenomenon. Three regions – Lancashire, the West Riding of Yorkshire, and the West Midlands, in that order – led the development of modern capitalist industry in England for decades in the eighteenth and early nineteenth centuries. The revolutionary developments in the organization and technology of industrial production in these regions between 1780 and 1850 produced the Industrial Revolution, which transformed the whole economy and society in England irrevocably. Yet these three were among the poorest and most backward regions in England in 1660, judged by the relative amount of wealth and socio-economic structure. This finding raises two fundamental questions. First, why did the agriculturally rich and industrially prosperous south of England, with its highly modernized socio-economic structures in 1660, fail to lead in the full development of modern capitalist industry between 1660 and 1850? And, second, given what we now know of the regional pattern of industrial development from 1660 to 1850, what kind of relationship can we establish between the socio-economic and political developments of the centuries from 1086 to 1660 and the revolutionary developments in industrial production, which occurred at some point in time between 1660 and 1850?

These questions will be explored more fully in the chapters that follow. Here, some preliminary observations will suffice. The evidence previously presented in this chapter makes it clear that the loss of export markets was the principal reason why industrial production in the West Country and East Anglia decelerated in the eighteenth century. On the other hand, as we have seen, the success of the West Riding, Lancashire, and the West Midlands in winning overseas markets was responsible primarily for their explosive expansion of industrial production during the same period. Some of the more convincing explanations for the latter's export success include variations in the organization of export sales and the availability of cheap labour due largely to poor agricultural resources and the proliferation of small property. At some point it appears that the agricultural prosperity of Southern England between 1086 and 1660 was a disadvantage in its industrial development from 1660 to 1850. *A priori*, there are two ways this could have been so. Given an integrated national economy, complementary economies would develop in the regions, with agriculturally prosperous regions specializing in agriculture and the agriculturally poor areas specializing in manufacturing, even if the former were initially more industrially developed. On the other hand, given accessible export markets, and disjointed factor and product markets at home, agriculturally poor regions could take advantage of the willingness of large segments of their populations to accept relatively low wages to capture the bulk of the export markets and outpace the agriculturally rich regions in industrial growth.

The evidence presented in the chapter shows clearly enough that what actually happened approximated to the second of the two logical possibilities. The three leading industrial regions did not initially depend in any significant way on the hitherto more prosperous southern regions for labor or for markets for their industrial products. The bulk of the labor they needed was internally generated through their own demographic reproduction process as their families responded to the buoyant employment opportunities associated with rapidly expanding industrial production. And by far the greater part of manufacturing output sold outside these regions was sold overseas during the period. What then was the relevance of the socio-economic and political development between 1086 and 1660?

From the available evidence it is clear enough that the industrial revolutions that took place in Lancashire, the West Riding, and the West Midlands between 1780 and 1850 were not caused in any direct way by the socio-economic and political developments in England between 1086 and 1660. But that is not to say that the latter were irrelevant to the Industrial Revolution in England. To start, it must be stressed that the overseas markets available to Lancashire, the West Riding, and the West Midlands during the period being examined depended largely on the strength and policies of the British national government. Those strengths and policies ultimately derived from the institutional and socio-economic developments of the centuries from 1086 to 1660 outlined previously in this chapter.[218] What is more, the general socio-economic development that occurred in England, but more so in southern England, between 1086 and 1660 was critical in the rapid transmission of development from the leading regions to the whole country once a national railway network was established in the nineteenth century. Without the development of modern agriculture and the commercialization of socio-economic life in southern England between 1086 and 1660, the industrial developments in the leading regions would

---

[218] The significance of the political role of the national government in the Industrial Revolution is the theme of several papers by Patrick O'Brien: Patrick K. O'Brien, "Political Preconditions for the Industrial Revolution," in Patrick K. O'Brien and Roland Quinault (eds.), *The Industrial Revolution and British Society* (Cambridge: Cambridge University Press, 1993), pp. 124–155; Patrick O'Brien, "Central Government and the Economy, 1688–1815," in Floud and McCloskey (eds.), *Economic History of Britain*, 2nd ed., Vol. 1, pp. 205–241; Patrick O'Brien, Trevor Griffiths, and Philip Hunt, "Political components of the industrial revolution: Parliament and the English cotton textile industry, 1660–1774," *Economic History Review*, XLIV, 3 (1991), pp. 395–423. The role of the central government has also been examined in a number of books, of which the following are but examples: Charles Wilson, *Profit and Power: A Study of England and the Dutch Wars* (London: Martinus Nijhoff, 1978); John Brewer, *The Sinews of Power: War, Money and the English State, 1688–1783* (New York: Alfred A. Knopf, 1989).

have remained a regional, rather than a national, phenomenon for a much longer period.

At this juncture it is important, once again, to place the role of the service sector in southern England, especially London and the home counties, in a proper historical perspective. As stated earlier in the chapter, Lee is right in calling attention to the neglected service sector: But he certainly overstretches his point when he gives the impression that the growth of the service sector in London and the home counties was the root cause of the international dominance of the English economy in the nineteenth century:

For long run prosperity, therefore, the service/consumer economy must be judged to be clearly superior to the industrial export-oriented economy. Thus we should interpret Victorian Britain in terms of the South-East being the most advanced region in the British economy, and making a commensurate contribution to the development of that national economy.[219]

The evidence presented in this chapter shows clearly that south-eastern England declined while the industrializing regions to the north developed rapidly in the eighteenth and early nineteenth centuries. It was after a national railway network established an integrated national economy, with London as its center, that London and the south-east began to grow rapidly on the basis of a service sector dependent on wealth generated largely by industry and the colonies.[220] The British empire was not created by clerks and farmers; it was created by the power of British industry and with the products and technology of British industry. Ultimately, even the service sector of Victorian England itself depended on the technology of the Industrial Revolution – the railways, the steam ship, the telegraph, and so on. Berg and Hudson are basically right in their conclusion:

The metropolitan economy may well have become the major focus of service sector growth and wealth accumulation by the third quarter of the nineteenth century, but in the industrial revolution period itself it is more likely that regional industrial revolutions dictated the course of structural change and colonial expansion.[221]

---

[219] C. H. Lee, "Regional Growth and Structural Change in Victorian Britain," *Economic History Review*, 2nd ser., XXXIV, 3 (1981), p. 452.

[220] As Langton says: "Inexorably, as part of this process of national social and economic integration, London again began to exert the sway over national commerce that it had lost to the canal based regional capitals. With this commercial activity came those whose business it was. The role of London changed from that of an external irritant suffered by all provincial regions to that of a truly national economic and social metropolis to which all regions were more and more closely bound by functionally necessary ties." Langton, "The Industrial Revolution," p. 163.

[221] Maxine Berg and Pat Hudson, "Rehabilitating the industrial revolution," *Economic History Review*, XLV, 1 (1992), pp. 43–44.

To summarize, let us reiterate the main features of English industrialization between 1660 and 1850. It has been stressed in this chapter that the industrialization process in England during the period followed basically the pattern of ISI. To explain why it was successful would, therefore, require an analysis informed by a theoretical framework incorporating critical elements in the conceptual and empirical literature on ISI. The evidence presented in the chapter shows further that the national process of industrialization was led in the first instance by a handful of regions. These leading regions were individually more internally integrated and tied more closely to their overseas markets than they were connected to the other regions in England in the early stages of the process. This pattern of development has serious methodological implications. It raises questions that aggregate national approaches cannot deal with adequately. To illustrate the point, it is often said at the national level that agriculture released labor to industry. But, as we have seen, industrial employment expanded in the north on the basis of locally generated labor supply, while much of the initial agricultural labor was in the South where industrial employment grew very little. Without a national study with a regional focus, facts of this nature get lost in national aggregates. Again, the pattern of development revealed by the evidence presented in this chapter makes it clear that issues such as the role of overseas trade cannot be properly treated on the basis of national aggregate statistics. A more effective and realistic way to conduct the assessment is to examine the relative importance of overseas and domestic markets for the leading regions. These and similar issues are explored more fully in the chapters that follow.

3

A Historiography of the First
Industrial Revolution

THE COURSE AND NATURE of the almost 800-year-long development process in England, which produced the structural and technological transformation controversially referred to as the Industrial Revolution, have been carefully laid out in the preceding chapter. The task now is to show how historians have explained the causes of this major historical event. Since the first systematic study by Arnold Toynbee in the 1880s,[1] economic historians have periodically taken stock of the state of knowledge in the field. One of the earliest such exercise was by T. S. Ashton in 1937, in which we are informed that those who taught economic history before World War I "had but a meagre shelf from which to make up our story of the Industrial Revolution."[2] Between the wars the literature grew quickly. Ashton was, therefore, able to report excitedly, just before World War II, that the problem for students of the Industrial Revolution was "no longer a question of finding raiment to cover intellectual nakedness, but of which many garments to assume."[3] The literature on the subject has grown continuously since then. In 1965, Max Hartwell published the first "reasonably comprehensive and critical survey" of the various attempts by economic historians to explain the causes of the Industrial Revolution.[4] The latter work presents a critical discussion of the different explanations favored

[1] Arnold Toynbee, *Lectures on the Industrial Revolution of the Eighteenth Century in England: Popular Addresses, Notes, and other Fragments* (London: Longmans, 1884).
[2] T. S. Ashton, *The Industrial Revolution: A Study in Bibliography* (London: Published for the Economic History Society by A. & C. Black, 1937), p. 1.
[3] *Ibid.*, p. 1.
[4] R. M. Hartwell, "The Causes of the Industrial Revolution: II An Essay on Process," in R. M. Hartwell, *The Industrial Revolution and Economic Growth* (London: Methuen, 1971), pp. 161–162; R. M. Hartwell, "The Causes of the Industrial Revolution: An Essay in Methodology," *Economic History Review*, Vol. XVIII, no. 1 (1965), pp. 164–182.

by scholars. Since that publication, similar critical surveys of the literature on the causes of the Industrial Revolution have been published, the
most recent and probably the most comprehensive being the one by Joel
Mokyr.[5]

General surveys of the literature on the Industrial Revolution are thus
not wanting. Yet none of the existing surveys contains a systematic and
elaborate study of over time change in the explanations offered by economic
historians and the factors responsible for the change. The nearest to this
kind of study are those focused on over time change in the aspects of the
Industrial Revolution studied and in the perception of the Industrial Revolution held by economic historians. For example, when, in 1959, Max
Hartwell attempted "to give a history of the interpretations of the Industrial Revolution, and to explain them," he limited himself to the changing
view of the Industrial Revolution, at one time as a catastrophic event
that brought all kinds of woes to human society (starting with England)
and at another as the most cherished outcome of the application of human
ingenuity, which brought all the good things of modern civilization, with
England leading the way.[6] More recently, David Cannadine published a
rather provocative history of the writings by economic historians on the
Industrial Revolution from 1880 to 1980, in which he argues that the dominant point of view in each historiographical epoch was a function of the
dominant socio-economic characteristics of the epoch. Again, Cannadine's
article is not focused on changing explanations of the origins of the Industrial Revolution. Rather, it is centered on changing aspects of the Industrial
Revolution studied by different generations of historians and the reasons
for the change: Between the 1880s and 1920s, the dominant theme was
the social consequences of the Industrial Revolution, viewed generally in
negative terms; the negative theme continued in the second generation,
1920s–50s, with a shift of emphasis to socio-economic instability brought
about by the Industrial Revolution – the business cycle, with unstable
employment and income; in the two decades from the 1950s to the 1970s,
the Industrial Revolution was studied as the first example of modern economic growth (sustained per capita income growth) based on the application of scientific principles to economic production; finally, the period since
the 1970s has been characterized by studies attempting to undermine the
idea of an industrial revolution in England between 1750 and 1850 –
emphasis is on the slow pace of technological change and per capita income

[5]   Joel Mokyr, "Introduction: The New Economic History and the Industrial Revolution," in Joel Mokyr (ed.), *The British Industrial Revolution: An Economic Perspective* (Boulder, CO: Westview Press, 1993), pp. 1–131.
[6]   R. M. Hartwell, "Interpretations of the Industrial Revolution in England," *Journal
of Economic History*, Vol. XIX, no. 2 (June, 1959), reprinted in Hartwell, *Industrial
Revolution and Economic Growth*, pp. 81–105.

growth and on the persistence of a small-scale as opposed to factory organization of production.[7]

In contrast to the existing literature surveys, the historiography of the
Industrial Revolution presented in this chapter takes as its point of departure an attempt to explain historically the changing explanations of the
causes of the Industrial Revolution offered by economic historians. Three
historiographical periods are identified – 1880–1945; 1950–85; and the late
1980s to the present. The explanations are divided into two broad groups:
those stressing the role of overseas trade; and others emphasizing the dominance of internally located forces, such as population growth, agricultural
progress, mineral resource endowment, and autonomous technological
change. Over time change in the explanations, therefore, means a change
from the dominance of one of the two groups to the other. It is argued that
explanations centered on overseas trade were dominant in the first period,
1880–1945; there was a change in 1950–85, when domestic forces became
more prominent in the explanations; and the trend emerging since the late
1980s, while its direction is yet to be established firmly, appears to favor
the pre-eminence of explanations centered on international trade. These
changes are explained in terms of two main historical factors; over time
changes in the theories of economic growth fashioned by economists, and
developments in the international ideological environment. This historiographical exercise provides a solid foundation for a deeper understanding
of the contending explanations, which are then critically assessed in considerable detail in the last part of the chapter.

3.1 CHANGING EXPLANATIONS OF THE CAUSES OF THE INDUSTRIAL REVOLUTION

Let it be said from the onset that determining which group of explanations
was dominant in what period is not an easy task. Scholars usually present
wide-ranging and complex explanations. Identifying individual scholars
with particular explanations may sometimes depend on which aspects of
their explanations readers concentrate on. What is more, disagreement
among scholars in the explanations offered extends to all the three periods
identified earlier in the chapter. As early as 1937, T. S. Ashton stated in his

---

[7] David Cannadine, "The Present and the Past in the English Industrial Revolution
1880–1980," *Past and Present*, Number 103 (May, 1984), pp. 131–172. For more
recent similar literature surveys on the Industrial Revolution, see Patrick K. O'Brien,
"Introduction: Modern conceptions of the Industrial Revolution," in Patrick K.
O'Brien and Roland Quinault (eds.), *The Industrial Revolution and British Society*
(Cambridge: Cambridge University Press, 1993), pp. 1–30; Gary Hawke, "Reinter-
pretations of the Industrial Revolution," in O'Brien and Quinault (eds.), *Industrial
Revolution*, pp. 54–78.

bibliographical essay: "It cannot be said that there is general agreement as to the ultimate cause of the Industrial Revolution." The factors regarded by individual scholars as the ultimate cause in the then existing literature, according to Ashton, include inventions, expansion of commerce, capital accumulation, the elimination of corporate regulation (economic freedom), social mobility, and new religious ideas and practices.[8] The problem is compounded by the differing conceptions of the Industrial Revolution held by scholars, which makes it difficult to know what is being explained over which there is disagreement: Is it a sudden upward change in the rate of growth of national income per capita, a phenomenal expansion of the factory system in manufacturing, a major change in industrial technology, or a radical structural transformation of economy and society within a few generations, say, 1750–1850? Each of these may require somewhat different explanations. To eliminate the unnecessary appearance of disagreement in the literature, the discussion here is restricted to studies that view the Industrial Revolution in terms of the major changes in the growth and development of industrial production in England between 1750 and 1850. So focused, the changing explanations that are relevant are those aimed at the absolute growth of industrial output, the changing structure of industrial output and of the economy and society as a whole, and changes in the technology and organization of industrial production. Limited to studies attempting to explain exactly the same historical phenomena, the problem becomes relatively more manageable.

It is pertinent to point out at this juncture that the debate concerning whether or not there was an industrial revolution in England between 1750 and 1850 has now been concluded for all practical purposes. Harley and Crafts, whose research has raised doubts about the occurrence of such a major discontinuity in the economic history of England during the period, now admit that indeed there was:

Our work is seen by some as denying a fundamental transformation of the British economy during the century 1750–1850. This was not, however, the impression we intended to convey and our revisionism needs to be set in a proper perspective. . . . Even though industrial innovations had a more modest impact on economic growth than was previously believed, they did create a genuine industrial revolution reflected in changes in Britain's economic and social structure. By the second quarter of the nineteenth century, a combination of the rapid growth of the urban based textile industries that exported most of their product and the marked decline in agriculture's share of the labour force produced the first urban industrial economy . . .[9]

---

[8]   Ashton, *The Industrial Revolution*, pp. 13–14.
[9]   Crafts and Harley, "Output Growth and the British industrial revolution," pp. 704–705. However, Rondo Cameron continues to attack scholars who support the idea of a British Industrial Revolution. See Rondo Cameron, "The Industrial Revolution: Fact or Fiction?" *Contention*, Vol. 4, No. 1 (Fall, 1994), pp. 163–188.

Crafts and Harley's characterization of the central features of the Industrial Revolution, which call for explanation, agrees essentially with the one adopted in this chapter. Their emphasis is on the rate of industrial growth, technological innovation, and the structural transformation of economy and society between 1750 and 1850, although they are also concerned with the rate of growth of GDP per capita during the period.

As was noted earlier in the chapter, explaining the causes of the Industrial Revolution was not the main focus of the writings on the subject between 1880 and 1945. During the period, economic historians were preoccupied with the social ills of industrial capitalism, particularly its impact on the working class. However, a number of writers did include the historical origins of the Industrial Revolution among other aspects of concern. Now which group of factors stood out prominently in the explanations of these writers during the period? To answer the question, let us examine the writings of the more or less celebrated writers of the period – Arnold Toynbee, William Cunningham, Paul Mantoux, James Gillespie, Harry Barnes, and John Hobson. It should be stressed that the list is not exhaustive. However, their views are sufficiently reflective of the balance of the contending explanations during the period.

It is generally agreed that the first systematic and elaborate study of the Industrial Revolution was by Arnold Toynbee in his lectures and public addresses in the 1880s, which were published in 1884 after his death at the age of 30.[10] Although not very much space was devoted to it, Toynbee offered implicitly what he considered to be the main factors that brought about the major change in England he labeled the Industrial Revolution. Hartwell believes that Toynbee regarded "the change in economic policy, from mercantilism to *laissez faire*," as the main cause of the Industrial Revolution.[11] This is based on a statement in Toynbee's book, Chapter VIII titled, "The Chief Features of the Revolution":

The essence of the Industrial Revolution is the substitution of competition for the medieval regulations which had previously controlled the production and distribution of wealth. On this account it is not only one of the most important facts of English history, but Europe owes to it the growth of two great systems of thought – Economic Science, and its antithesis, Socialism.[12]

It would appear that here Toynbee is talking about the main features of the Industrial Revolution rather than the causes. Taking the whole statement together, what stands out is effect and not cause. An earlier statement in Chapter IV titled, "England in 1760, Manufactures and

[10]   Toynbee, *Industrial Revolution*. See T. S. Ashton's "Introduction to the 1969 Edition."
[11]   Hartwell, *The Industrial Revolution and Economic Growth*, p. 137.
[12]   Toynbee, *Industrial Revolution*, p. 64.

Trade," gives a better sense of what Toynbee saw as the main cause of change:

Yet at the time of which I am speaking [1760], many of the evils which modern Socialists lament were already visible, especially in those industries which produced for the foreign market. Already there were complaints of the competition of men who pushed themselves into the market to take advantage of high prices; already we hear of fluctuations of trade and irregularity of employment. *The old simple conditions of production and exchange were on the eve of disappearance before the all-corroding force of foreign trade.*[13]

It is clear from this passage that Toynbee saw the growth of overseas trade as the principal cause of change, "the all-corroding force" that swept away "the old simple conditions of production and exchange." Toynbee also made it clear that trade with the Americas was responsible primarily for the growth of English foreign trade during the period of the Industrial Revolution. Citing Arthur Young's *Northern Tour* as his source, he pointed out that by 1770, manufacturers in Manchester were virtually dependent on American markets where 75 percent of all their manufactures were sold.

William Cunningham wrote *The Growth of English Industry and Commerce in Modern Times*[14] about the same time that Toynbee delivered his lectures on the Industrial Revolution. Again, he stressed the growth of foreign trade as the principal factor in the Industrial Revolution. Cunningham fully appreciated the importance of invention and technological innovation in the Industrial Revolution. But he saw both activities as a function of the growth of overseas markets for English manufactures and the development of financial institutions, which eased the supply of capital and made it accessible to entrepreneurs. Answering the question why England was first in the invention and application of machines in industrial production, he wrote:

It was not an accident that England took the lead in this matter; the circumstances of the day afforded most favourable conditions for the successful introduction of new appliances. Inventions and discoveries often seem fortuitous; men are apt to regard the new machinery as the outcome of a special and unaccountable burst of inventive genius in the eighteenth century. But we are not forced to be content with such a meagre explanation.[15]

Earlier in his book, Cunningham had argued that England's access to large quantities of gold and silver from Portuguese Brazil and Spanish America made possible the growth of savings by individual English savers:

---

[13] Toynbee, *Industrial Revolution*, pp. 33–34; emphasis added.
[14] William Cunningham, *The Growth of English Industry and Commerce in Modern Times*, 3 Vols. (Cambridge: Cambridge University Press, 1882).
[15] Cunningham, *The Growth of English Industry*, Vol. II, pp. 610–611.

So long as natural economy continued to predominate in rural life, there was difficulty in amassing wealth; corn and other raw produce, cannot be stored indefinitely without loss; the prudent man was prepared to be frugal in the use of his possessions, but he had no facilities for accumulating wealth. When gold and silver came more generally into circulation, it was possible for many people, who had never thought of it before, to lay up a hoard.[16]

The accumulated "hoards" were assembled by the financial institutions and made available to resourceful entrepreneurs striving to take advantage of expanding commerce.[17]

Paul Mantoux, in what is deservedly acclaimed as a classic, and the first authoritative work on the Industrial Revolution in the twentieth century,[18] continued the tradition of Toynbee and Cunningham in identifying the growth of overseas trade as the central factor in the growth and development of industrial production in England in the eighteenth century. He noted the mutual stimulation that usually exists between the growth of industry and commerce, making it difficult to determine where the process started, historically: "Sometimes the advancement of industry, by forcing trade to find new outlets, enlarges and multiplies commercial relations. Sometimes, on the other hand, fresh wants, created by the extension of a commercial market, stimulate industrial enterprise." Mantoux noted that in his day (1906), the first case was the more usual: "Modern industry, driven forward by the internal force of technical progress, urges on trade and credit, which, in the interests of production, have undertaken the conquest of the world." But he argued that this was a new phenomenon associated with the capacity of the modern factory system "to anticipate demand, to modify, or even sometimes to create it," owing to "its extraordinary adaptability and to the rapid and incessant improvements in its technical equipment." Given this capacity, and the revolution in transport and communication, the producer could increase the extent of his market at will to the very limits of the inhabited world. But, Mantoux stressed:

This was not the case with the old industry. Limited by both the slowness of technical improvement, and by the difficulty of communication, production was forcibly confined to the known wants of its habitual market. . . . In those days progress in industry was almost impossible unless it was preceded by some commercial

16 *Ibid.*, pp. 8 and 460–461.
17 Cunningham also implied that technological innovation in the cotton textile industry was induced by competition with East India cottons in overseas markets, the manufacturers having secured "a practical monopoly of the home market," and observed that the industry depended on foreign commerce both for the material used and for access to the markets in which the cloth was sold. *Ibid.*, pp. 624–625.
18 Paul Mantoux, *The Industrial Revolution in the Eighteenth Century: An Outline of the Beginnings of the Modern Factory System in England* (New York: Harper Torchbooks, 1928; original French edition, 1906).

development. . . . Half a century before she became the land of industry *par excellence*, the land of mines, of ironworks and of spinning mills, England was a great commercial country – 'a nation of shopkeepers', as went the famous phrase. The commercial expansion there preceded – and perhaps determined – the changes in industry.[19]

Mantoux also connected the growth of commerce with the Industrial Revolution through the political process in late seventeenth-century England. He saw the Glorious Revolution of 1688 as an important factor in the economic development process in England; while conceding that its origin could not be attributed to the interests of a particular class, he stressed the role played by the merchant class in "these decisive events, which were to have such advantageous consequences for them." Mantoux added:

It was in the Guildhall, the common home of the merchant companies, that the Lords met, after the flight of the King, to summon the Prince of Orange to London. . . . Finally, in order to meet immediate necessities and especially in order to pay the Army, the City lent the Treasury two hundred thousand pounds. It was the token alliance of the new monarchy with the class of merchants and moneyed men.[20]

Across the Atlantic, scholars in the United States and the Caribbean, who wrote during the period under consideration, also stressed the role of overseas trade like their counterparts in Europe. In a work published in 1920, James Gillespie wrote:

The growth of various English industries as a result of world commerce, such as the woolen, silk, cotton and hardware manufactures, mining, shipbuilding and even agriculture, resulted in the employment in England of ever increasing numbers of workmen. Sir Josiah Child estimates that during the second half of the seventeenth century, the plantation colonies alone gave employment to 200,000 persons in England.[21]

Gillespie particularly emphasized the role of overseas trade in the transformation of consumption habits in England and the rest of Western Europe, which created the foundation for the materialist character of Western civilization that was essential for the development of modern industry:

Hitherto civilization and the ideals which had prompted them had come from the East, westward; now an entirely new spirit, that of the New World, was to sweep eastward over the seas and, along with new forces generated from active and regular contact with the Orient, transform and revivify Europe. Its essense was essentially that of materialism, of worldly comforts and interests . . . In the material realm alone what would Europe be today without such creature comforts as potatoes, maize,

---

[19] Mantoux, *The Industrial Revolution*, pp. 93–94, 487–488.

[20] *Ibid.*, pp. 96–97.

[21] James E. Gillespie, *The Influence of Overseas Expansion on England to 1700* (New York: Longmans, 1920), p. 27. Dr. Gillespie taught history at the University of Illinois.

sugar, tea, coffee and chocolate; without cotton cloth; without many such luxuries
as the silks, perfumes and jewels of every-day commerce . . . It takes considerable
imagination to picture England of the pre-discovery period catered to by the ships
of other nations, whose coasts were infested with swarms of pirates, a country
of staid landed gentry moderately rich from the wool sold to the more enterpris-
ing Flemings, a country of industries insignificant in comparison with many other
European nations.[22]

To Gillespie, then, the growth of foreign trade, especially trade with the
Americas, was at the very center of the English development process. The
emphasis on the role of new products and the development of a materialist culture is somewhat similar to the argument more elaborately developed
in the early 1930s by Elizabeth Gilboy in her famous article, "Demand as
a factor in the Industrial Revolution."[23]

Also writing across the Atlantic in the United States, Harry Barnes developed the theme on the importance of changing demand structure for the
development process in Europe, even more than Gilboy did about the
same time, and much more than Gillespie had done earlier. Like Gillespie,
Dr. Barnes attributed the development of the materialist character of
West European culture to the growth of overseas trade with the Americas
and the Orient. "It is to the expansion of Europe," he argued, "that we
must look for a historical force sufficiently powerful and comprehensive to
explain the origins of modern times." Barnes noted that most historians
who preceded him studied the movement of Europeans overseas primarily
in terms of discovery, colonization, and trade with overseas areas. The more
important subject of the impact of the discoveries, colonization, and overseas trade upon economies and societies in Western Europe was neglected
until Robert Shepherd of Columbia University called attention to it in
1919.[24]

---

[22] *Ibid.*, pp. 347–348.

[23] Elizabeth Waterman Gilboy, "Demand as a factor in the Industrial Revolution,"
in Arthur H. Cole, A. L. Dunham, and N. S. B. Gras (eds.), *Facts and Factors in
Economic History: Articles by former Students of Edwin Francis Gay* (Cambridge,
Mass.: Harvard University Press, 1932), pp. 620–639.

[24] Harry Elmer Barnes, *An Economic History of the Western World* (New York:
Harcourt, Brace & Co., 1937), p. 209; William R. Shepherd, "The Expansion of
Europe," *Political Science Quarterly*, Vol. 34, 1919, pp. 43–60. In this paper, William
Shepherd noted: "The 'Renaissance,' the 'Reformation,' the 'French Revolution,'
the 'Industrial Revolution,' 'Nationalism and Democracy,' have been examined,
described and evaluated with reference to the particular period of which they form
a part. But a movement greater than these and contemporaneous with them has been
comparatively ignored. Actually they seem to have been born and bred in Europe
alone, and thus to have communicated their influence to the rest of the world; and
yet, how far were they in reality the product of Europe's ventures beyond its own
frontiers; and if not wholly the product, how far was their inception or development
affected by such ventures oversea and overland in distant portions of the earth? This

The immediate effect of European expansion overseas upon Europe, Barnes explained, was the growth of European and world trade, "narrowly and technically speaking, the Commercial Revolution." This commercial revolution produced a radical cultural change in European taste: "The psychological factor of demand lies at the bottom of all economic activity, and the character of European demand for consumer's goods was transformed during this period."[25] The new products which transformed the consumption habits of all classes in Western Europe, listed by Barnes, include sugar, tea, coffee, tobacco, and a host of Oriental manufactures, including pottery, many types of hardware, glass, upholstered furniture, tapestry, silks, and cottons. The different classes in Europe went through this radical change in consumption habits at different points in time:

By 1600 upper-class life was profoundly affected by the influx of new goods . . . By 1700 the middle classes, particularly in England, Holland, Spain, and Portugal, had generally changed their mode and standards of consumption, but the laboring masses were still living much as they had in the Middle Ages. It was not until the eighteenth century proper that the effects of the expansion of Europe penetrated to the very foundations of European society, stimulating a so-called Industrial Revolution that has altered the conditions of human life more profoundly than any other event in history.[26]

To Barnes, the Industrial Revolution in England was a product of the combined pressure and opportunities emanating from growing overseas demand for English manufactures and the radical transformation of the consumption habits of all classes in England and other parts of Europe. He explained the superiority of England over other European rivals, especially France and Holland, in terms of the greater per capita value of English overseas trade and the growth of manufacturing in England for overseas markets: "England ultimately achieved an enormous economic superiority over France and other competitors (prior to the rise of Germany after 1870) because the future lay with the two lines of activity it was beginning to cultivate: overseas trade and the manufacture of goods demanded abroad."[27]

However, it must not be concluded, on the basis of the foregoing cases, that everyone supported the "Commercial Revolution" thesis during the

---

is a question that has remained substantially without an answer" (p. 47). At the time of writing Dr. Harry Barnes was Lecturer in Economic History at the New School for Social Research, New York.

[25] Barnes, *An Economic History*, pp. 229–230.

[26] *Ibid.*, pp. 231–232, 233, 242–243.

[27] *Ibid.*, p. 233. Comparing English and French trade in the eighteenth century, Barnes showed that total English foreign trade in 1716 was $65 million, while that of France was $43 million; and in 1789, England's foreign trade was $340 million, while that of France in 1787 was $230 million: "This becomes the more significant," Barnes pointed out, "when we realize that the population of France was then more than double that of England" (p. 235).

period under consideration. Certainly, there were some dissenting voices. As early as 1894, John Hobson complained that the role played by foreign commerce in the development of "machine production" in Europe had been blown out of proportion by historians:

The degree of importance which statesmen and economists attached to this foreign commerce as compared with home trade, and the large part it played in the discussion and determination of public conduct, have given it a prominence in written history far beyond its real value.[28]

Significantly, this is an exception that proves the rule. Hobson's complaint that the historians of his day gave to overseas commerce "a prominence in written history far beyond its real value," is probably the best empirical evidence we can get to support the argument in this chapter that explanations stressing the primary role of overseas commerce were dominant in the historiographical period, 1880–1945.

What is more, in the context of the more recent tendencies in the historiography of the Industrial Revolution, even Hobson's own explanations can be seen as stressing the role of overseas trade, although he also developed what could be termed the first example of the "small ratios" argument.[29] Hobson specified five conditions for the development of capitalist industry: the production of investible surplus; the existence of a laboring class deprived of the means of independent employment; development of the technology and organization of industrial production that makes large-scale and mechanized manufacturing profitable; "the existence of large, accessible markets with populations willing and economically able to consume the products of capitalist industry"; and, finally, the existence of "the capitalist spirit, or the desire and the capacity to apply accumulated wealth to profit making by the organization of industrial enterprise."[30] Elaborating, Hobson argued that the slave-based economies of the Americas provided one of the necessary conditions of modern capitalism:

The black population of Africa was, of course, the great reservoir for the new tropical economy of the European colonial system which spread through Central America, Brazil, and the West Indies, taking root later on in North America.... The profits of the European companies embarking in early colonial trade were very

---

[28]   John A. Hobson, *The Evolution of Modern Capitalism: A Study of Machine Production* (London: Allen & Unwin, 1894, revised edition, 1926), p. 31.

[29]   The expression, small ratios argument, originated from Barbara Solow's critique of arguments directed against Eric Williams that the ratio of slave trade profits to British GNP or to total British industrial investment was too small to have produced the kind of effects argued by Eric Williams. See Barbara L. Solow, "Caribbean Slavery and British Growth: The Eric Williams Hypothesis," *Journal of Development Economics*, 17 (1985), pp. 99–115.

[30]   Hobson, *Evolution of Modern Capitalism*, pp. 1–2.

large, for slave economy is not in itself and under all circumstances bad. Merivale clearly points out the main condition of its profitable use. 'When the pressure of population induces the freeman to offer his services, as he does in all old countries, for little more than the natural minimum of wages, those services are very certain to be more productive and less expensive than those of bondsmen. This being the case, it is obvious that the limit of the profitable duration of slavery is attained whenever the population has become so dense that it is cheaper to employ the free labour for hire.' In other words, Western Europe until the nineteenth century did not present the large supply of landless labourers required as one condition of great profitable capitalism. It is for this reason that colonial economy must be regarded as one of the necessary conditions of modern capitalism. Its trade, largely compulsory, was in large measure little other than a system of veiled robbery and was in no sense an equal exchange of commodities. Trading profits were supplemented by the industrial profits representing the 'surplus-value' of slave or forced labour, and by the yield of taxation and plunder.[31]

Like Mantoux who wrote about the same time, Hobson dismissed the chance explanation of inventive activities in time and space:

To those who regard evolution as essentially the product of 'accidental variations,' the inventions of industrial machinery may appear attributable to the 'chance' which assigns to some ages and countries a large crop of inventive geniuses, and denies it to other ages and countries. A more scientific view of history explains the slow growth of mechanical invention by the presence of factors unfavourable to, and the absence of factors favourable to, the application of human intelligence to definite points of mechanical progress.[32]

The unfavorable conditions in medieval Europe mentioned by Hobson include "the vested interests and conservative methods of existing industrial castes and their guild organizations," the small dimensions of markets, the absence of "great 'free' labor market," the restriction of education to classes who regarded with disdain the useful arts and crafts, and the application of the energies of "men of science and intellectual ingenuity"

[31] *Ibid.*, pp. 12–13. In addition, Hobson even attributed the early development of commercial agriculture in England to the impact of overseas trade: "Trade in agricultural produce, bringing an increased use of money into the agricultural economy and stimulating owners and tenants to a more careful and intensive cultivation, so as to earn money rents and profits, was the chief channel of the innovating current. It was the Flemish demand for wool, which, coming upon England in the Tudor age when political and social conditions were favourable, afforded a large profitable use of pasture, leading to the enclosure of great quantities of common lands and wastes, and the formation of large pasture farms under new proprietors ... This foreign market for wool, and the growing market for grain afforded by the increase of London and other centres of population and by a certain sporadic export trade, began that process of converting the small yeoman and cottager into the mere wage-earner which reached its fullest pace in the enclosures at the end of the eighteenth and the beginning of the nineteenth centuries" (*Ibid.*, p. 15).

[32] *Ibid.*, pp. 19–20.

to problems other than those concerning "the humbler paths of detailed mechanical improvement in the useful arts." Of all the unfavorable factors, Hobson stressed that "Difficulties of transport and the slight irregular structure of markets were largely responsible for the retardation of mechanical inventions and capitalistic enterprise in the manufactures." He explained England's leadership in the development of new industrial methods, instead of Holland, in terms of the former's land and population size, the possession of capital, the control of colonies, and the extent of its carrying trade.[33]

But, in a later chapter in the book, Hobson argued that England's overseas trade was very small relative to the home trade. He computed that the official value of England's export trade in 1712 was less than one-sixth of the home trade, noting that "Such an estimate, however, gives an exaggerated impression of the relation of foreign to home trade, because under the latter no account is taken of the large domestic production of goods and services that figure in no statistics." He concluded that in the eighteenth century, England's home trade was "a vast deal greater in value than the whole of the foreign trade."[34]

Taken together, Hobson's position can best be described as an attempt to mellow the dominant explanation of his day, which saw overseas commerce – the Commercial Revolution – as the prime mover in European industrialization, particularly in the case of the first Industrial Revolution. There can be little doubt that in the historiographical epoch from 1880 to 1945, the development of industrial production in England, in terms of the expansion of output and the development of the technology and organization of manufacturing, was explained largely as a function of expanding overseas commerce. Other factors, such as natural resource endowment and socio-political conditions, were usually included. But, ultimately the pride of place was given to the Commercial Revolution.

A new trend in the historiography of the Industrial Revolution began after World War II; by the second half of the 1960s, the change had become clearly visible; and by the 1970s, we can say a new dominant set of explanations of the causes of the Industrial Revolution had been established. The new dominant intellectual opinion, which was to continue up to the 1980s, discounted the importance of overseas trade and shifted emphasis to internal factors, especially those on the side of supply – domestically generated capital supply and the rate of interest; the growth of agricultural productivity and falling agricultural prices; demographic processes (at one time it is economically derived fertility restraint and at another the growth of population); internally derived long-term development of favorable

---

[33]   *Ibid.*, pp. 20–21, 23–24.
[34]   *Ibid.*, pp. 32–34. A graph on page 33 of the book shows the slow growth of England's foreign trade from 1700 to 1800, and an explosive growth from 1830 to 1890.

socio-economic and political structures; the growth of education and scientific knowledge; accidental technological breakthrough and chance endowment of abundant natural resources of coal and metallic ores. Where demand is assigned an important place, it is the domestic market that is stressed, not overseas demand. In the discussions that follow, we propose to present some of the better known works representing the new dominant scholarly tradition. Let it be said, at this point, that unlike the first historiographical period, the dominant explanations of the decades from 1950 to the 1980s were not overwhelmingly dominant. Explanations stressing the principal role of overseas commerce, though stripped of their earlier overbearing presence, remained in serious contention. Later discussions in this section give recognition to their resilience in the literature.

The writings of T. S. Ashton on eighteenth-century English economic history may be taken as a major contribution to the new historiographical trend, which followed World War II. In his book, *The Industrial Revolution, 1760–1830*, published in 1948, emphasis is clearly on the availability of investible funds (capital) as reflected by the rate of interest. He cited approvingly a 1668 statement by Josiah Child that "all countries are at this day richer or poorer in an exact proportion to what they pay, and have usually paid, for the Interest of Money," and declared that "the importance of the lowering of the rate of interest in the half-century before the industrial revolution has never been properly stressed by historians."[35] Throughout the book, supply factors are elaborated. There is no chapter on trade, domestic or overseas. Apart from the introductory chapter, the remaining five chapters are devoted to "The earlier forms of industry," "The technical innovations," "Capital and Labour," " 'Individualism' and 'laissez-faire,' " and "The course of economic change." The expansion of overseas commerce is mentioned not in terms of growing markets for English manufactures and sources of raw material imports, but in terms of ideas – the widening of "men's views of the world." At best, overseas trade is listed as one of the several sources of capital that "made it possible for Britain to reap the harvest of her ingenuity." Ashton summarized the causes of the Industrial Revolution as follows:

The conjuncture of growing supplies of land, labour, and capital made possible the expansion of industry; coal and steam provided the fuel and power for large-scale manufacture; low rates of interest, rising prices, and high expectations of profit offered the incentive. But behind and beyond these material and economic factors lay something more. Trade with foreign parts had widened men's views of the world, and science the conception of the universe: The industrial revolution was also a revolution of ideas.[36]

---

[35]   T. S. Ashton, *The Industrial Revolution, 1760–1830* (London: Oxford University Press, 1948), pp. 10–11.
[36]   Ashton, *The Industrial Revolution*, pp. 21, 94–95.

Ashton's more elaborate work, *An Economic History of England: The Eighteenth Century*, devoted much space to trade: two chapters out of seven, one on internal trade and transport and the other on overseas trade and shipping. But emphasis is still on supply factors and the treatment of trade is mainly descriptive. What is more, while admitting that the expanding industries found their markets largely abroad,[37] he took issue with those who stressed the contribution of the American colonies and that of the Atlantic slave trade:

The rapid development of English industry has been attributed to the exploitation of colonial peoples and to profits wrung from the slave trade. But it was after the Americans had won their independence, and at a time when the West Indian economy was in decline, that the pace quickened.[38]

Closely following Ashton was the work of A. H. John on the role of agricultural productivity. In a paper published in 1961,[39] John argued that the growth of agricultural productivity in England between 1680 and 1750 gave rise to the expansion of the domestic market for all sorts of goods and services. The product of a more intensive use of land, especially in the more populous south of England, the sustained growth of agricultural productivity during the period led to the fall in prices of agricultural products, particularly food, and a change in the terms of trade between agriculture and industry in favor of the latter. The growth of real wages stimulated the expansion of mass demand, and the general growth of middle class incomes shifted the demand curve for middle class consumer goods to the right. As John saw it, the particularly interesting feature of the period, 1680–1750, was "the conjuncture of a sluggish growth of population and of the export trade in English manufactures with a marked rise in agricultural output."[40] Thus John explained the development of the metal-using trades in the West Midlands and the expansion of the textile industries in Lancashire and Yorkshire in terms of home demand.[41] It is conceded that although the export of manufactures during the period was not large, the growth of overseas trade generally, especially re-exports, contributed to the growth of incomes and the expansion of the domestic market. But John concluded:

It is not possible with the evidence available, to distinguish accurately how far it [the expansion of the domestic market] was the result of incomes and investment

---

[37]   T. S. Ashton, *An Economic History of England: The 18th Century* (London: Methuen, 1955), pp. 125–126.

[38]   Ashton, *An Economic History of England*, p. 125.

[39]   A. H. John, "Aspects of English Economic Growth in the First Half of the Eighteenth Century," *Economica*, No. 28 (1961), reprinted in Minchinton (ed.), *The Growth of English Overseas Trade*, pp. 165–183.

[40]   John, "Aspects of English Economic Growth," p. 170.

[41]   *Ibid.*, pp. 174–177.

generated in foreign trade and how far it arose from other factors. But the character as well as the extent, of the expansion, when compared with the growth of overseas commerce between 1700 and 1750, suggest that other powerful forces were at work. In so far as this growth arose from internal factors, they in turn made their contribution to the growth of real capital.[42]

John's argument for the first half of the eighteenth century was extended more forcefully to 1780 by D. E. C. Eversley, who argued that with some variations "the causes operative in the period 1730–50 continued to exercise much influence for the next thirty years, and . . . it is during this period that the most important foundations of the industrial state were laid."[43]

The agricultural argument reached its peak of sophistication in the hands of Deane and Cole, who started their analysis with the important role of overseas trade, almost similar to the "Commercial Revolution" thesis of the preceding historiographical epoch. They assembled and displayed an impressive array of quantitative evidence, showing that English foreign trade and overseas markets for English goods grew much faster than the whole economy and the domestic market in the eighteenth century. For this reason, industries that produced largely for export grew considerably faster than those that produced mainly for the domestic market.[44] But the role of overseas commerce was demoted to a secondary position when Deane and Cole argued, *a priori*, that overseas demand for British goods in the eighteenth century was not determined externally; rather, it was derived from developments within the British economy at the time. The operative factors were population growth and agricultural prosperity in England. The largely deductive argument is that the growth of British domestic exports in the eighteenth century was due mainly to the expansion of exports to the British American colonies. These colonies being "dependent economies," the growth of British domestic export to them depended on the growth of

---

[42]   *Ibid.*, pp. 178–179.

[43]   D. E. C. Eversley, "The Home Market and Economic Growth in England, 1750–1780," in E. L. Jones and G. E. Mingay (eds.), *Land, Labour and Population in the Industrial Revolution: Essays Presented to J. D. Chambers* (London: Edward Arnold, 1967), p. 259. In a footnote, Eversley expressed displeasure with Phyllis Deane's argument stressing the primacy of exports in her book, *The First Industrial Revolution*, "as do most of the Cambridge economists and historians" (p. 211); Phyllis Deane, *The First Industrial Revolution* (Cambridge: Cambridge University Press, 1965). It was particularly fashionable in the 1960s to stress the role of agriculture in the Industrial Revolution. See especially E. L. Jones, "Agriculture and Economic Growth in England 1660–1750: Agricultural Change," *Journal of Economic History*, 25 (1965), pp. 1–18; E. L. Jones, "Agricultural Origins of Industry," *Past and Present*, 40 (1968), pp. 58–71.

[44]   Deane and Cole, *British Economic Growth*, pp. 76, 78, 79. The industries which produced mainly for the home market were beer, leather, candles, and soap. Textiles and metals were largely the export industries.

British demand for imports from them. It was the growth of prosperity for the agricultural community in England after 1743, brought about by the growing demand from an expanding population, that stimulated the growth of imports into Britain from the colonies. In turn, increasing imports from the colonies induced the expansion of their demand for English manufactures that led to the soaring of English domestic exports in the second half of the eighteenth century.[45]

The sophistication and logical coherence of this argument made it very appealing. In consequence, it had considerable influence on subsequent writings on the Industrial Revolution. In fact, it will be hard to find any other single argument in the historiography of the Industrial Revolution that has had as much influence on the views of students of the subject. Among those who extended and popularized it in the 1960s and 1970s were well-known economic historians, such as Max Hartwell, M. W. Flinn, and Robert Brenner, to name but a few. In an influential paper published in 1965, Hartwell wrote:

Most historians of the industrial revolution have attributed greater importance to an increase in overseas trade than to an increase in home demand. However, much of the increased trade came from North America and the West Indies, colonies whose demand for English goods was largely derived from the English demand for colonial goods.[46]

Then in 1966, in a widely circulated book, Flinn stated,

rising demand from the colonies and foreign countries for British products was only made possible by the steady increase in Britain's demand for their products, particularly in view of the compulsory canalization of the greater part of the colonies' exports to British ports. In its turn, of course, the rise in British imports of colonial produce was related to the general growth of the British economy, so that the growth of colonial markets cannot be regarded as a wholly exogenous stimulus to growth.[47]

Even the Marxist historian, Robert Brenner, while querying his fellow Marxists for adopting a Smithian mode of analysis,[48] could not resist the appeal of this explicitly neoclassical argument. His contribution was first made in a seminar whose proceedings were published in 1975. Responding

---

[45] Deane and Cole, *British Economic Growth*, pp. 85, 92.

[46] Hartwell, "The Causes of the Industrial Revolution," in Hartwell (ed.), *The Causes of the Industrial Revolution in England* (London: Methuen, 1967), p. 74. The paper was first published in *Economic History Review*, Vol. XVIII, No. 1, 1965.

[47] M. W. Flinn, *Origins of the Industrial Revolution* (London: Longman, 1966), pp. 61–62.

[48] Robert Brenner, "The Origins of Capitalist Development: A Critique of Neo-Smithian Marxism," *New Left Review*, No. 104 (July–August, 1977), pp. 25–92.

to the arguments of another participant, J. W. Smit, that exports to the Americas were the main factor that explains the differing experiences of Britain and Holland in eighteenth-century industrialization, Brenner said,

the success of England was fundamentally based on the transformation of agriculture and on major increases in agricultural productivity. As Professor Smit commented yesterday, 18th century economic growth in England was heavily dependent on colonial markets. But it may also be argued that these, in turn, depended quite strongly on the ability of the English home market to absorb the colonies' exports.[49]

At some point the agricultural argument merges with another explanation focused on autonomous internal forces in England, that is, the evolution of socio-political structures in the centuries preceding the Industrial Revolution. Most, if not all, writers attempting to present a comprehensive explanation of the Industrial Revolution usually include the development of conducive socio-political institutions as a factor. The issue that warrants discussion, therefore, is the magnitude of the weight attached to this factor. In particular, the discussion here focuses on explanations that give the pride of place to socio-political structures. One example is the argument by W. A. Cole.[50] Excluding the fortuitous gifts of nature, such as natural resource endowment, Cole identified three factors that were central to eighteenth-century economic growth in England, "each of which had been firmly established in the course of the seventeenth century": First, "the development of a social and institutional environment conducive to economic growth, as a result of the economic and social changes of the sixteenth and seventeenth centuries, and . . . the political revolution of the seventeenth"; second, "a more favorable balance between population and other resources, as a result of the relaxation of population pressure shortly before the middle of the seventeenth century;" third, "the radical reorientation and greatly enlarged opportunities for Britain's overseas trade as a result of the foundation of her colonial Empire outside Europe, and the development of an aggressive commercial policy designed to foster the growth of her shipping and com-

---

[49]   Robert Brenner, "England, Eastern Europe, and France: Socio-Historical Versus 'Economic' Interpretation," in Frederick Krantz and Paul M. Hohenberg (eds.), *Failed Transitions to Modern Industrial Society: Renaissance Italy and Seventeenth Century Holland* (Montreal: Interuniversity Centre for European Studies, 1975), pp. 68–70; see pp. 61–63 for Smit's argument, to which Brenner reacted. For a more recent continuation of the Deane and Cole argument, see David Richardson, "The Slave Trade, Sugar, and British Economic Growth, 1748–1776," in Barbara L. Solow and Stanley L. Engerman (eds.), *British Capitalism and Caribbean Slavery: The Legacy of Eric Williams* (Cambridge and New York: Cambridge University Press, 1987), pp. 103–133.

[50]   W. A. Cole, "Eighteenth-Century Economic Growth Revisited," *Explorations in Economic History*, Vol. 10, No. 4 (1973), pp. 327–348.

merce."[51] It is clear in Cole's analysis that the order of the factors presented corresponds to the ranking of their causal importance. This is brought out in his conclusion that "the Industrial Revolution was the natural, if not inevitable, outcome of the conditions established more than a century before."[52]

The agricultural argument and analysis centred on socio-political structure merge more visibly in the works of Marxist writers exemplified by Immanuel Wallerstein and Robert Brenner. Conducting their analysis in totally different ways, both Wallerstein and Brenner see the origin of West European development in the socio-political structure associated with an alleged development of agrarian capitalism in the fifteenth and sixteenth centuries. For Wallerstein, the significance of the supposed agrarian capitalism in the fifteenth and sixteenth centuries lies in the fact that it created the conditions that compelled economic and political entrepreneurs in Western Europe to expand overseas and establish a European world economy, on the basis of which Western Europe subsequently developed industrial capitalism. Hence, for Wallerstein, the proclaimed early agrarian capitalism offered no sufficient condition for the development of industrial capitalism in Western Europe. But, even so, the argument derived from a combination of agricultural development and socio-political structure remains, chronologically at least, central.[53] This is even more so for Brenner in whose analysis the socio-political structure arising from the alleged development of agrarian capitalism of the fifteenth and sixteenth centuries provided adequate conditions for modern economic development in Western Europe. Brenner, therefore, discounts the contribution of the "Commercial Revolution" and overseas trade in general.[54]

The autonomous development of science and technology constitutes another line of argument centered on independent internal forces in England. This is an old argument favored by some historians of science and

---

[51] Cole, "Eighteenth-Century Economic Growth," pp. 346–347.

[52] *Ibid.*, p. 348.

[53] Immanuel Wallerstein, *The Modern World System I: Capitalist Agriculture and the Origins of the European World Economy in the Sixteenth Century* (New York: Academic Press, 1974); "Failed Transitions or Inevitable Decline of the Leader?: The Workings of the Capitalist World-Economy: General Comments," in Krantz and Hohenberg (eds.), *Failed Transitions*, pp. 75–80; *The Modern World System II: Mercantilism and the Consolidation of the European World-Economy, 1600–1750* (New York: Academic Press, 1980); and *The Modern World System III: The Second Era of Great Expansion of the Capitalist World-Economy, 1734–1840s* (New York: Academic Press, 1989).

[54] Robert Brenner, "Agrarian Class Structure and Economic Development in Pre-Industrial Europe," *Past and Present*, No. 70 (1976), pp. 31–75; "The Origins of Capitalist Development" and "The Agrarian Roots of European Capitalism," *Past and Present*, No. 97 (1982), pp. 16–113.

technology.[55] Walt Rostow incorporated it in his controversial take-off hypothesis, in which the expansion of trade and the process of invention and technological innovation are presented as having very little historical connection. He admonished that the income effects of expanded trade must be distinguished from its effects on the process of invention and technological innovation: "The two processes are not identical; income, output, and population can expand without substantial change in technology."[56]

According to Rostow, the new technologies that precipitated the early phase of the first industrial revolution arose from three problems: "how to produce good pig and wrought iron cheaply with coke as the fuel; how to make a reasonably efficient steam engine; and how to spin cotton with machinery."[57] He conceded that the expansion of overseas trade contributed to the creation and solution of the three problems: The import and re-export of Swedish and Russian iron and East Indian cotton textiles created markets leading to import-replacement production of iron and cotton textiles in England; and the commercial revolution also stimulated the growth of real income, population, and urbanization, all of which created a conducive and natural environment for widespread inventive activities and the diffusion of technological innovation.[58] But ultimately Rostow traced the main source of the critical inventions and technological innovations of the English Industrial Revolution to the seventeenth-century scientific revolution and its ramifying social consequences:

Foreign trade played its role in the story of these three critical sectors [iron, coal, and cotton], but, in each case, it was quite a narrow role. The commercial revolution set in motion demands that made it increasingly profitable to solve these problems on the supply side with new technology, but a new mentality was required to yield the corps of inventors and entrepreneurs who actually created the lowered cost curves that define technically the industrial revolution.[59]

This line of reasoning became increasingly fashionable in the 1970s and early 1980s, so much so that even Ralph Davis who had been one of the

---

[55]   A. E. Musson and E. Robinson, *Science and Technology in the Industrial Revolution* (Manchester: Manchester University Press, 1969); A. E. Musson, "Introduction," in A. E. Musson (ed.), *Science, Technology and Economic Growth in the Eighteenth Century* (London: Methuen, 1972), pp. 1–68.

[56]   Walt W. Rostow, *How it all began: Origins of the Modern Economy* (London: Methuen, 1975), p. 126.

[57]   Rostow, *How it all began*, p. 130.

[58]   Rostow, *How it all began*, p. 126–130.

[59]   Rostow, *How it all began*, p. 131. Rostow begins Chapter 4, on science, invention, and innovation, with the statement: "It is the central thesis of this book that the scientific revolution, in all its consequences, is the element in the equation of history that distinguishes early modern Europe from all previous periods of economic expansion" (p. 132).

authoritative proponents of the "Commercial Revolution" thesis in the 1950s and early 1960s was converted to it. Davis had argued in 1962 that

Colonial trade introduced to English industry the quite new possibility of exporting in great quantities manufactures, other than woollen goods, to markets where there was no question of the exchange of manufactures for other manufactures . . . The process of industrialization in England from the second quarter of the eighteenth century was to an important extent a response to colonial demands for nails, axes, firearms, buckets, coaches, clocks, saddles, hankerchiefs, buttons, cordage and a thousand other things.[60]

In another work published the same year, he stated that the opportunities offered for large exports of ironwares and later of cottons "played a vital part in the building of those industries to the point where technical change transformed their momentum of growth." These points were repeated and made even more strongly in a work published in 1967:[61]

The expansion of the American market for iron- and brass-ware was on so great a scale that it must have contributed very significantly to the eighteenth-century development of those industries in England, and so to the process of rationalisation, of division of labour, of search for new machines and new methods which helped so much towards the Industrial Revolution.

Davis turned full circle in 1973 when he wrote:

The innovations in metallurgy made in this period [the first three-quarters of the eighteenth century] were vital to the extension of the Industrial Revolution in the next century; they played no part in instigating it. Expansion of this modest kind could have continued indefinitely . . . had it not been for the appearance of a particular innovation, brought in because of economic necessity but achieving its extraordinary results for reasons that were partly non-economic. This innovation was, of course, the transformation of cotton-spinning technology.[62]

By 1979, Davis's argument on the primacy of autonomous technological development had become more explicit and bolder. It is conceded that overseas exports contributed much to "the modest industrial expansion of the middle decades of the eighteenth century"; but its overall importance is discounted, because this early modest industrial expansion "did not lead to the Industrial Revolution." Strongly affirming his position, he wrote:

---

[60] Ralph Davis, "English Foreign Trade, 1700–1774," *Economic History Review*, 2nd ser. vol. XV, 1962, p. 290.

[61] Ralph Davis, *The Rise of the English Shipping Industry in the Seventeenth and Eighteenth Centuries* (London: Macmillan, 1962), p. 393; Ralph Davis, *A Commercial Revolution, English Overseas Trade in the Seventeenth and Eighteenth Centuries* (London: Historical Association, 1967), p. 20.

[62] Ralph Davis, *The Rise of the Atlantic Economies* (London: Weidenfeld and Nicolson, 1973), p. 311.

I share the view that overseas trade did not have an important *direct* role either in bringing about the Industrial Revolution or in supporting the first stage of its progress. . . . The new growth that took off and violently accelerated in the 1780s arose in a quite different sector of industry, and arose in that particular decade for an entirely new and *direct* reason. The initiative came from the supply side, from technical change in the manufacture of cotton.[63]

The authoritative voice of Ralph Davis, a well-known historian of English overseas trade and shipping, may have spurred several economists in the late 1970s and early 1980s to develop supply arguments with increased boldness. By arguing that the socio-economic developments that occurred in England up to 1780 made little or no contribution to the growth and development of English industrial production that began in the latter date, Davis also seems to have prepared the ground for some fashionable subsequent economists' models of English technological development during the era of the Industrial Revolution. For purposes of maintaining the flow of the narrative and showing the full evolution of their ideas, it is necessary to follow continuously the works of this group of economists to some point in time beyond the limit of the second historiographical period stated earlier in this chapter. It will be shown later in the chapter that even among these hard-line supply economists, there is some evidence of mellowing in the course of the 1990s, as the new operating historiographical forces work themselves out. But clearly the full development of their ideas went beyond the end of the period and they have shown much resistance to the new ideas that began to unfold forcefully from the mid-1980s.

Probably the most persistent of these economists is Joel Mokyr. In 1985, he argued that "Cost-reducing and factor-increasing changes occupy the center of the stage: supply rules supreme." Adding: "The old schoolboy view of the Industrial Revolution as a 'wave of gadgets' may not be far off the mark after all . . ."[64] Then in 1991, he developed a model of technological development, derived from evolutionary biology, to stress the point that the technological innovations that produced the Industrial Revolution in England were all a matter of chance: "The evolution of technological history, just like our biological past, is not one of necessity; things could have gone differently. Among *ex ante* roughly equivalent outcomes there is an element of chance and luck."[65]

---

[63]   Ralph Davis, *The Industrial Revolution and British Overseas Trade* (Leicester: Leicester University Press, 1979), pp. 9–10.

[64]   Joel Mokyr, "Demand vs. Supply in the Industrial Revolution," in Joel Mokyr (ed.), *The Economics of the Industrial Revolution* (Savage, MD: Roman and Littlefield, 1985), pp. 101, 109.

[65]   Joel Mokyr, "Evolutionary Biology, Technological Change and Economic History," *Bulletin of Economic Research*, 43:2 (1991), p. 134.

Under this model, the Industrial Revolution in England is presented as the product of an accidental development of technology in the late eighteenth century. Once England made that technological lucky-dip, the drastic reduction of production costs led to the capture of overseas markets, one after another, until England became the workshop of the world in the nineteenth century. So, as the argument goes, the phenomenal growth of exports in the late eighteenth and nineteenth centuries was the effect, rather than the cause, of the technological innovations of the period. This line of analysis is at the center of an extensive review of the literature on the Industrial Revolution by Mokyr, in which the authority of Ralph Davis is invoked specifically, among others.[66] Although Wrigley's thesis of organic and inorganic economies in England is based on the chance endowment of abundant mineral energy resources, with no specific deployment of the technological lucky-dip argument, ultimately the analysis boils down to the same thing. The chance abundance of mineral energy resources became important only after the technology that required their use was developed. For the whole process to be a matter of chance, the development of the technology must also be accidental. And, like the supply economists, but contrary to Walt Rostow, Wrigley believes that the various stages of the development of the organic economy up to the time of Adam Smith's *Wealth of Nations* (1776) were irrelevant to the development of the inorganic economy from the late eighteenth century.[67]

It is appropriate to end the exposition of the independent internal forces argument with a contribution by Ronald Findlay. This is so, because the role played by J. A. Hobson for the "Commercial Revolution" thesis of the first historiographical period, stated earlier in this chapter, was performed in a different way by Findlay for the autonomous internal forces argument of the second period. In his 1982 paper, he faintly supported the supply side technological argument on the basis of his analysis of British terms of trade movement between 1780 and 1800. But this is qualified so strongly, with much emphasis on the role of overseas trade, that it not only mellowed the uncompromising tone of the "manna from heaven" technological argument, as Findlay characterized it, but virtually amounted to a rejection of the thesis. As he put it:

The analysis of the trade-growth nexus in the formative period of the Industrial Revolution given here seems to imply that the causal arrow runs from growth (in

---

[66] Mokyr, "Introduction: The New Economic History," pp. 1–131; see the quotation from Ralph Davis on pp. 68–69. Readers may find it frustrating to trace Mokyr's quotation in Davis's book, *The Industrial Revolution and British Overseas Trade*. This is because the quotation is taken from several pages (9–10 and 62–63) and only two are stated (62–63).

[67] E. A. Wrigley, *Continuity, Chance and Change: The Character of the Industrial Revolution in England* (Cambridge: Cambridge University Press, 1988).

the form of technological change in the manufacturing sector) to trade rather than in the reverse direction that the literature appears to have emphasised. However, the 'manna from heaven' nature of technical progress as it appears in simple formal models needs to be supplemented with common sense. To begin with imagine that the doubling of efficiency in the manufacturing sector that we arrived at in the previous section took place in a closed economy. . . . Under these circumstances it is difficult to imagine the crucial innovations being diffused as rapidly and pervasively as they were, particularly since the dynamic cotton textile industry was much more export-oriented than any other. . . . Trade and growth, like trade and the flag, are inextricably intertwined in the first take-off.[68]

As noted previously, while explanations of the Industrial Revolution stressing the primacy of independent internal forces in England were on the ascendancy between the late 1940s and early 1980s, some proponents of the "Commercial Revolution" thesis refused to be silenced. The well-known Cambridge economic historian, Phyllis Deane, is one of them. In her book, *The First Industrial Revolution*, first published in 1965, she proclaimed that the commonest way "by which an economy can develop from a pre-industrial to an industrial state is to exploit the opportunities open to it from international trade."[69] She noted the severe constraints on the expansion of trade among the pre-industrial economies of Europe owing to the limited range and similarity of goods produced: "For pre-industrial Europe the obvious way to achieve economic growth was to extend the range of its trading relationships and to open up markets in other continents . . ." Because of its small size, the limited range of its natural resources, and its geographical location, Deane pointed out, Britain had a unique set of incentives to succeed in this general European drive for trading opportunities outside Europe.[70] The success came in the eighteenth century in the form of a world-wide English trading network, built around the British colonies in the Americas, of which the West Indian islands, "administered by a British plantation *elite* on the basis of a slave society, constituted the most valuable and intimate link."[71] For Deane, the importance of the British American colonies derived from the opportunity they offered British merchants to expand their trade with Europe on the basis of tropical products that could not be produced in Europe and yet had developed quickly to become near necessities among a large population of European consumers.[72] Deane's analysis placed technical change at the very center of the industrial

[68] Ronald Findlay, "Trade and Growth in the Industrial Revolution," in Charles P. Kindleberger and Guido di Tella (eds.), *Economics in the Long View: Essays in Honour of W. W. Rostow: Volume I, Models and Methodology* (New York: New York University Press, 1982), pp. 178–188; the quote is from pp. 186–188.

[69] Phyllis Deane, *The First Industrial Revolution* (Cambridge: Cambridge University Press, 1965; 2nd edition, 1979), p. 53.

[70] *Ibid.*, p. 54.   [71] *Ibid.*, p. 55.   [72] *Ibid.*, p. 60.

revolution. But she did not believe that technical change in eighteenth-century England was an accidental development, "a manna from heaven." As she saw it, technical change in eighteenth-century England occurred in a specific socio-economic context:

The eighteenth-century environment was generally favourable to technical change. Over a large part of the century, beginning somewhere before the middle and accelerating in the second half, there seems to have been a tendency for the demand for British manufactures to exceed their supply. The resultant stimulus to technical change was reflected in the wide interest in innovation. Innovation was fashionable, if not yet common, and it was sometimes, though by no means always, highly profitable.[73]

For the leading sector in the technological revolution, the cotton textile industry, Deane argued that, but for rapidly growing overseas exports, the expansion brought about by the new technology would have been halted sooner rather than later:

Prices of cotton yarn fell from 38s. per lb. in 1786 and 1787 to under 10s. in 1800 and 6s.9$^{d.}$ in 1807. Demand proved to be elastic, and as prices fell the amounts sold expanded more than proportionately. Even so, the market would have been readily saturated by the immense capacity of the factory system, had it not been possible to exploit the international contacts which British merchants had been building up for the previous century and to supply a steady succession of new foreign markets.[74]

Earlier, in a joint paper, Deane and Habakkuk had argued that the expansion of overseas exports was the principal factor in the acceleration of growth in British industrial production in the last two decades of the eighteenth century. They explained the explosive growth of British domestic exports during these decades in terms of the wars of the period, which kept away Britain's main European rivals from overseas markets, and the power of the British navy, which kept the sea-lanes secure for British merchants. As they put it,

although British industrialists were confronted by inflation and high taxation during the war period, British merchants drew on sources from which many of their competitors were debarred to supply expanding markets in the old world and the new. This, rather than the lowering of costs in domestic industry, explains the expansion of exports in the war period. Indeed there is little evidence – even in the cotton industry – that there had been a large absolute fall in the price of the final product by the end of the first decade of the nineteenth century. True, the spinning section had enjoyed a spectacular fall in costs and the cost of the raw material had declined sharply, but the weaving and finishing sections were still operating with much of the same techniques as they had used for centuries, and wages were inflated by the wartime labour shortage. It is significant, for example, that the

[73] *Ibid.*, p. 92.   [74] *Ibid.*, p. 92.

declared value of cotton manufactures did not fall below the official value until 1815.[75]

The "Commercial Revolution" thesis was also upheld in the 1960s by the French economic historian, François Crouzet. Writing generally about European economic development in the eighteenth century, he declared:

The eighteenth century can be truly called the Atlantic stage of European economic development. Foreign trade, and especially trade with the Americas, was the most dynamic sector of the whole economy (for instance, French colonial trade increased tenfold between 1716 and 1787), and furthermore the demand from overseas was stimulating the growth of a wide range of industries as well as increased specialization and division of labour. Owing to the superiority of sea transport over land transport, the eighteenth-century European economy was organized around a number of big seaports, the most prosperous being those with the largest share in the growing colonial trade, such as Bordeaux or Nantes; each of these had, not only its own industries, but also its industrial hinterland in the river base of which it was the outlet.[76]

Efforts were also made in the 1970s to present empirical evidence contradicting the argument of Deane and Cole that the growth of English domestic exports in the eighteenth century depended on the independent growth of English demand for imports from the British colonies in the Americas. The evidence presented shows that imports from the British North American colonies retained for consumption in England constituted a small fraction of the goods produced and traded by those colonies between 1701 and 1775, and yet these continental colonies accounted for about 42 percent of the increase in English domestic exports during this period. For the British West Indian islands, it was demonstrated that the growth of their export and import trade in the eighteenth century did not depend on the autonomous growth of incomes in England as implied by Deane and Cole. Initially, sugar production and export by the British Caribbean colonies depended on the taking over of an existing demand in England, previously supplied by Portuguese producers in Brazil. Subsequent

---

[75] Phyllis Deane and H. J. Habbakkuk, "The Take-Off in Britain," in W. W. Rostow (ed.), *The Economics of Take-Off into Sustained Growth: Proceedings of a Conference held by the International Economic Association* (London: Macmillan, 1963), pp. 63–82; see pp. 77–78 for the analysis of the role of international trade, and p. 79 for the quote.

[76] François Crouzet, "Wars, Blockade, and Economic Change in Europe, 1792–1815," *Journal of Economic History*, Vol. XXIV, No. 4, December 1964, p. 568. In a postscript to the 1985 reprint of the article, Crouzet says he may "have somewhat overestimated the role of seaborne trade (and especially colonial trade) in the eighteenth century European economy, and so the impact of its decline during – and after – the wars." François Crouzet, *Britain ascendant: comparative studies in Franco-British economic history* (Cambridge: Cambridge University Press, 1990; translated version of the 1985 French edition by Martin Thom), p. 316.

rapid expansion in the second half of the seventeenth century was due mainly to the success of the English colonies in taking over European markets earlier supplied by Brazilian producers. In due course, cheap British colonial sugar created new demand in England. Before the successful challenge by producers in the French Caribbean some time in the eighteenth century, the market for Caribbean products in England and the rest of Europe had been very much widened by the general changes in taste, consumption pattern, and in income brought about largely by the commercial revolution of the seventeenth and eighteenth centuries. Taking into account the growth of English domestic exports to Portugal and Spain, which depended on their American colonies, and to Western Africa and Asia during the same period, it was concluded that the growth of English domestic exports in the eighteenth century did not depend on the autonomous growth of incomes in England as Deane and Cole had argued.[77] A similar conclusion was reached in 1983 in a paper employing regression analysis by Hatton, Lyons, and Satchell.[78]

The persistence of the "Commercial Revolution" thesis in the 1970s and early 1980s can also be found in the work of Douglass North. In particular, Chapter 12 of his 1981 book, *Structure and Change in Economic History*, tightly linked technical change to improved property rights and market expansion. The defining element of the Industrial Revolution is shown as "an acceleration in the rate of innovation." But the revolution in technological innovation is viewed as an endogenous development whose history is traced to the expansion of markets and the associated improvements in property rights specification.[79] As North expressed it,

economic historians of the Industrial Revolution have concentrated upon technological change as the main dynamic factor of the period. Generally, however, they have failed to ask what caused the rate of technological change to increase during this period: often it would appear that in arguing the causes of technological progress they assume that technological progress was costless or was spontaneously generated. But in sum, an increase in the rate of technological progress will result from either an increase in the size of the market or an increase in the inventor's ability to capture a larger share of the benefits created by his invention. . . . The Industrial Revolution, as I perceive it, was initiated by increasing size of markets,

---

[77] Joseph E. Inikori, "International Trade and the Eighteenth-Century Industrialisation Process in England: An Essay in Criticism," Unpublished Paper Presented at the Institute of Historical Research Seminar, University of London, February 7, 1975. See also Joseph E. Inikori, "The slave trade and the Atlantic economies, 1451–1870," in *The African slave trade from the fifteenth to the nineteenth century* (Paris: UNESCO, 1979), pp. 56–87.

[78] T. J. Hatton, John S. Lyons, and S. E. Satchell, "Eighteenth-Century British Trade: Homespun or Empire Made?" *Explorations in Economic History*, Vol. 20 (1983), pp. 163–182.

[79] North, *Structure and Change*, pp. 158–170.

which resulted in pressures to replace medieval and crown restrictions circum-scribing entrepreneurs with better specified common laws. The growing size of the market also induced changes in organization, away from vertical integration as exemplified in home and handicraft production to specialization.[80]

Finally, in 1982 William Darity, Jr., pioneered econometric modeling of the relationship between African slavery in the Americas and industrialization in Europe. The model was designed to test the validity of the propositions made by three Caribbean historians, two in the 1930s through 1940s, mentioned earlier in Chapter 1, and one in the 1970s. The last one concerns the negative impact of the Atlantic slave trade on African economies, a subject that is outside the confines of the present study. As stated previously, the first two argued that African slavery in the Atlantic world was a critical factor in the development of industrial capitalism in Europe in the eighteenth and early nineteenth centuries. Using a model deliberately constructed to make it difficult for this proposition to be supported, Darity still reached the conclusion that "Even a 'least-likely' test is unable to dismiss their central hypotheses."[81]

It can thus be seen that between the late 1940s and early 1980s, explanations of the Industrial Revolution stressing the role of overseas trade remained visible. However, the resilience of the "Commercial Revolution" thesis during the period notwithstanding, it is fair to say that the period belongs to arguments centered on independent internal forces in England. This was a period, particularly the late 1960s and 1970s, when arguments that centered on the dominant role of agriculture, socio-political structure, or exogenous technical progress were presented with unshakable confidence. Explanations stressing the role of overseas trade were treated at best with polite contempt.[82]

---

[80]   North, *Structure and Change*, pp. 165–167.
[81]   William A. Darity, Jr., "A General Equilibrium Model of the Eighteenth-Century Atlantic Slave Trade: A Least-Likely Test For the Caribbean School," *Research in Economic History*, Vol. 7 (1982), pp. 287–326, p. 320 for the quote. The Caribbean historians referred to are Eric Williams, C. L. R. James, and Walter Rodney.
[82]   In some of the leading departments of economic history in British universities, there were no specialists in eighteenth-century international trade in the 1970s. International trade was never an important focus of the seventeenth and eighteenth-century seminars at the Institute of Historical Research run by F. J. Fisher and A. H. John, respectively, in the late 1960s and 1970s. If you were in the London School of Economics in the 1970s and you told your colleagues in the economic history department that your research was on the impact of international trade on the English economy in the eighteenth century, the polite response would invariably be, "oh, did it have any impact?" It is not a surprise that of the voluminous literature on the Industrial Revolution written in the 1960s and 1970s, there is not a single book-length study of the role of overseas trade, apart from edited volumes containing collections of papers by several authors.

The evidence suggests that the historiography of the Industrial Revolution has moved a full circle, and the role of overseas trade has begun to move to center stage once again. The new trend, which seems to have started in the late 1980s, is still in its early stages. It is difficult, therefore, to write about it with outright certainty. However, the more recent literature clearly indicates that various strands of the "Commercial Revolution" thesis are becoming increasingly fashionable after being relegated to a defensive position for about four decades. What follows is only a selection of some of the recent works representing the new trend.

It is significant that the emerging new trend is very much connected with re-interpretations of the role of the slave-based Atlantic economy in the development of industrial production in England between the middle decades of the seventeenth and the middle decades of the nineteenth century. Between 1979 and 1992, this author published a series of papers re-interpreting the contribution of the Atlantic slave trade and African slavery in the Americas to the transformation of the English economy and society in terms of expanded trading opportunities, shifting emphasis away from the narrow focus on profits from slave trading and slavery.[83] I concede that profits from slave trading and slavery were important for the development process in England and demonstrate that the British slave trade was highly profitable for the larger slave trading firms in the late eighteenth century, but insist:[84]

The emphasis on profits in the explanation of the role of the slave trade and slavery in the British industrial revolution is misplaced. The contribution of the slave trade and slavery to the expansion of world trade between the fifteenth and nineteenth centuries constituted a more important role than that of profits. The interaction between the expansion of world trade and internal factors explains the British industrial revolution better than the availability of investible funds. This is the more so because it is now known that industries provided much of their investment funds themselves, by plowing back profits. In other words, capital investment during the years leading to the industrial revolution was related not so much to the rate of interest on loans (depending on the availability of investible funds) as to the growth

---

[83]   Inikori, "The Slave Trade and the Atlantic Economies;" Joseph E. Inikori, "Market Structure and the Profits of the British African Trade in the Late Eighteenth Century," *Journal of Economic History*, Vol. XLI, No. 4 (Dec. 1981), pp. 745–776; Joseph E. Inikori, "Slavery and the Development of Industrial Capitalism in England," *Journal of Interdisciplinary History*, Vol. XVII, No. 4 (Spring 1987), pp. 771–793; Joseph E. Inikori, "Slavery and the Revolution in Cotton Textile Production in England," *Social Science History*, Vol. XIII, No. 4 (1989), pp. 343–379; Joseph E. Inikori, "The Credit Needs of the African Trade and the Development of the Credit Economy in England," *Explorations in Economic History*, Vol. 27 (1990), pp. 197–231; Joseph E. Inikori, "Slavery and Atlantic Commerce, 1650–1800," *American Economic Review*, Vol. 82, No. 2 (1992), pp. 151–157.

[84]   Inikori, "Market Structure and the Profits of the British African Trade," pp. 745–746.

of demand for manufactured goods, which provided both the opportunity for more industrial investment and the industrial profits to finance it.

An important part of the re-interpretation pertains to the geographical focus of the analysis. In contrast to the Eric Williams debate that limited discussion to the British Caribbean, I argue that African slavery in Spanish America, Brazil, the United States, and the non-British Caribbean all played very important roles in the development process in England as did slavery in the British Caribbean: "The Atlantic region must be seen as a single interdependent economic region within which the major forces operating on the individual economies were significantly dependent upon the operation of the whole system."[85] An array of empirical evidence is marshalled to demonstrate that maritime activities and production for market exchange (as opposed to subsistence production) in the main regions of the United States, from the colonial period to the Civil War, depended on the slave-based economy of the Atlantic as did production for Atlantic commerce in Brazil, a good deal of Spanish America, and all of the Caribbean. Because the bulk of Portuguese and Spanish trade with their European partners during the period depended heavily on slave-generated surpluses in their American colonies, English exports to Spain and, more so, those to Portugal are closely related to African slavery in the Americas.[86] Thus, while my analysis is generally focused on the role of overseas trade, it is argued specifically that the most dynamic part of English overseas trade from 1650 to 1850 was trade with the slave-based economies of the Atlantic.

Several conferences held in the 1980s, leading to the publication of edited volumes in the late 1980s and early 1990s, strongly support and further extend this author's argument.[87] The first one, held in Bellagio, Italy, in 1984, brought together some of the leading specialists in the field. Apart from the consensus that emerged from the papers examining the contribu-

---

[85] Inikori, "Slavery and the Development of Industrial Capitalism in England," p. 771.

[86] See in particular Inikori, "Slavery and Atlantic Commerce," pp. 152–155; Inikori, "Slavery and the Development of Industrial Capitalism in England," pp. 783–792; Joseph E. Inikori, "Africa in World History: The Export Slave Trade and the Emergence of the Atlantic Economic Order," in B. A. Ogot (ed.), *The UNESCO General History of Africa. V. Africa from the Sixteenth to the Eighteenth Century* (Paris and Berkeley, California: Heinemann, UNESCO, and University of California Press, 1992), pp. 74–112, more specifically, pp. 83–93.

[87] See Barbara L. Solow and Stanley L. Engerman (eds.), *British Capitalism and Caribbean Slavery: The Legacy of Eric Williams* (Cambridge: Cambridge University Press, 1987); Barbara L. Solow (ed.), *Slavery and the Rise of the Atlantic System* (Cambridge: Cambridge University Press, 1991); and Joseph E. Inikori and Stanley L. Engerman (eds.), *The Atlantic Slave Trade: Effects on Economies, Societies and Peoples in Africa, the Americas, and Europe* (Durham, NC and London: Duke University Press, 1992).

tion of slavery to the Industrial Revolution in England, there was so much agreement among the participants in the discussion of these papers that one participant could not help reminding the others that they were throwing away the scholarship of more than a decade.[88] The other two conferences were held at Harvard and Rochester, respectively, in 1988. The edited volume from the former, published in 1991, contains papers whose overall thrust shows unmistakably the central role of African slavery in the Americas in the growth of multilateral trade in the Atlantic basin in the seventeenth and eighteenth centuries.[89] In relation to the subject of this chapter, the more directly relevant of these papers is the one by Patrick O'Brien and Stanley Engerman.[90]

O'Brien and Engerman argue strongly in support of the leading role of exports in the industrialization process in England between 1688 and 1802, pointing out the weaknesses in the calculations of the gains from trade by economists, such as Thomas and McCloskey. They show that between 40 and 50 percent of the nonagricultural workforce in England and Wales during the period was employed in production for export.[91] They demonstrate further that increases in overseas sales accounted for much of the increment in manufacturing output in the country during the period:

Between 1700 and 1801 the nonagricultural population of England and Wales increased by 3.14 million people. Over the century, the growth of domestic exports provided enough net revenue (in the form of wages, interest, and profits) to sustain about 70% of the previously mentioned increment at reasonable levels of subsistence. These essentially taxonomic exercises in quantification help illustrate the importance of exports for the development of the British economy over the eighteenth century. They reinforce traditional and contemporary perceptions

---

[88] Broadly speaking, the papers which examined the contribution of slavery to British economic development were written and presented by Barbara L. Solow, Joseph E. Inikori, David Richardson, Selwyn H. H. Carrington, and Richard B. Sheridan. As mentioned earlier in the chapter, Richardson's arguments contain some elements of the British derived trade growth argument of Deane and Cole. But, on the whole, there is a clear consensus among these authors that African slavery in the Americas was a critical factor in British industrialization from the point of view of trading opportunities. For these papers, see Solow and Engerman (eds.), *British Capitalism and Caribbean Slavery*. The participants who discussed these papers included, among others, William A. Darity, Jr., Stanley L. Engerman, Patrick O'Brien, David Eltis, and Herbert S. Klein. It was David Eltis who reminded other participants of the scholarship of more than a decade being thrown away by the consensus in the discussions.

[89] See Solow (ed.), *Slavery and the Rise of the Atlantic System*.

[90] Patrick K. O'Brien and Stanley L. Engerman, "Exports and the growth of the British economy from the Glorious Revolution to the Peace of Amiens," in Solow (ed.), *Slavery and the Rise of the Atlantic System*, pp. 177–209.

[91] O'Brien and Engerman, "Exports and the growth of the British economy from the Glorious Revolution to the Peace of Amiens," in Solow (ed.), *Slavery and the Rise of the Atlantic System*, pp. 177–209.

that the revolution in industry and the growth of employment outside agriculture continued to depend, in large measure, as they had done since Tudor times, on the sales of manufactured goods (particularly textiles) beyond the borders of the kingdom.[92]

In terms of the regional distribution of England's export, O'Brien and Engerman hold that commerce between Britain and the Americas was "effectively responsible for most of the long-run expansion in sales overseas" between 1688 and 1802, and that about 85 percent "of the *increment* to exports sold overseas from 1697 to 1802 was absorbed by colonial or neocolonial markets (such as India and the United States after 1783)."[93] They conclude that "the demand for industrial goods that emanated from productivity growth in agriculture accounted for a far lower proportion of the increment to the sales of industrial output from 1700 to 1800 than exports . . ."[94]

The foregoing argument represents a fundamental movement away from arguments advanced earlier in 1982 by Patrick O'Brien.[95] At that time he had argued that the plantation economies of the southern regions of the United States, the Caribbean, Latin America, Africa, and Asia made no significant contribution to the accelerated rate of economic growth experienced by Western Europe after 1750:[96]

Around 1780–90 when something like 4 percent of Europe's gross national output was exported across national frontiers, perhaps less than 1 percent would have been sold to Africa, Asia, Latin America, the Caribbean, and the southern plantations of the young United States. . . . For particular countries such trade would be more important; especially for smaller maritime powers such as Portugal, Holland, and Britain, where ratios of domestic exports to gross national product probably approached 10 percent by the second half of the eighteenth century; but less than half of these sales overseas consisted of merchandise sold to residents of the periphery.

Continuing, O'Brien quoted Braudel to the effect that food supplies and population size were the critical factors in European development, and concluded:

Such factors, to which I would add improvements to agriculture and technical progress in industry, continued to determine the destiny of Europe throughout the

---

[92]   *Ibid.*, p. 189.   [93]   *Ibid.*, pp. 193 and 200.
[94]   *Ibid.*, p. 208. See Patrick K. O'Brien, "Agriculture and the Home Market for English Industry, 1660–1820," *English Historical Review*, Vol. 91 (1985), pp. 773–800, where it is argued that agriculture made very little contribution to the growth of demand for manufactured goods in England in the eighteenth century.
[95]   Patrick O'Brien, "European Economic Development: The Contribution of the Periphery," *Economic History Review*, 2nd series, Vol. XXXV, No. 1 (1982), pp. 1–18.
[96]   O'Brien, "European Economic Development," pp. 3 and 4.

mercantile era. As long as oceanic trade remained as a tiny proportion of total economic activity it could not propel Europe towards an industrial society.[97]

This change of position between 1982 and 1991 by Patrick O'Brien illustrates the new trend in the historiography of the Industrial Revolution which began in the later 1980s. The trend can be further observed in the last set of conference papers mentioned earlier, the 1988 Rochester conference.

Four of the Rochester conference papers were devoted to the contribution of African slavery in the Americas to the development of industrial capitalism in England, Europe, and the United States. These papers were written and presented by this author, Ralph A. Austen and Woodruff D. Smith, Ronald Bailey, and William Darity, Jr., respectively. All the five authors demonstrated in various ways the critical role of slavery, through the growth of multilateral trade in the Atlantic basin, in the early rise of industrial capitalism in Europe and the United States, but more so in England. The identical position taken by these scholars, which is consistent with that of the Bellagio conference, did not escape the editors of the volume, who asked rhetorically: "Can one interpret this as the emergence of a new trend in the historiography of the Atlantic slave trade? Or is it merely another temporary fluctuation? Only time can tell."[98] What is pertinent to note, Ralph Austen and Woodruff Smith[99] argue the role of slave-produced sugar in the development of consumerist culture in Western Europe, and its contribution to the evolution of industrial capitalism in the region, in a way very similar to the arguments of Gillespie, Gilboy, and Barnes in the 1920s and 1930s, shown earlier in this chapter.

Immanuel Wallerstein's 1989 volume adds to the growth of the new historiographical trend. Criticizing arguments that stress the primacy of the domestic market in England, he writes:

Much has been made by historians of the impact of the British home market. This has always seemed curious to me in two respects. Why would this account for technological advance in an industry which found so large a part of its outlet in foreign trade (and was so dependent on foreign imports, tied in turn to having something to sell in return? And was not the French home market large or larger? Léon gives what seems to me a far more plausible answer to the question why, precisely at this point, there occurred this leap in British productivity. 'Might one not think that the attraction of the [French] home market came to bear with all its force

---

[97] O'Brien, "European Economic Development," p. 18.

[98] Joseph E. Inikori and Stanley L. Engerman, "Introduction: Gainers and Losers in the Atlantic Slave Trade," in Inikori and Engerman (eds.), *The Atlantic Slave Trade*, p. 12.

[99] Ralph A. Austen and Woodruff D. Smith, "Private Tooth Decay as Public Economic Virtue: The Slave-Sugar Triangle, Consumerism, and European Industrialization," in Inikori and Engerman (eds.), *The Atlantic Slave Trade*, pp. 183–203.

against any profound modification of the dynamics of foreign trade?' That is to say, precisely because of profit levels at home, there was less pressure to become competitive abroad – which is why the Treaty of 1786 . . . was so important.[100]

Similarly, Ronald Findlay, whose 1982 paper was discussed earlier in this chapter, has in recent years argued strongly in support of the leading role of overseas trade in the First Industrial Revolution. In a work published in 1990, Findlay declares that there is "little doubt that British growth in the eighteenth century was 'export-led' and that, among exports, manufactured goods to the New World and re-export of colonial produce from the New World led the way."[101] Findlay was also part of a four-man special panel on "The Origins of Uneven Development: The Rise of the West and the Lag of the Rest," during the 1992 meeting of the American Economic Association.[102] Like the three conferences discussed earlier in this chapter, all the three papers of the panel that examined the role of Atlantic commerce in the seventeenth and eighteenth centuries affirmed its critical contribution to industrialization in Western Europe, especially England. Findlay explained the early rise of Western Europe in terms of its political and military capacity to control and dominate the growing intercontinental trade of the seventeenth and eighteenth centuries. Forcefully managed opportunity to trade rather than plunder, he argues, was the critical advantage the West had during the period in question. Central to this growth of intercontinental trading opportunity was African slavery in the Americas: "The slave trade, horrible as it was, was part of a complex intercontinental network of production and trade that stimulated technical progress and investment in Europe and the New World . . ."[103]

The more recent argument of Ronald Findlay is particularly important, because he is one of the two trade theorists whose authority was invoked by Joel Mokyr to support his 1993 argument on the leading role of exogenous technological change: "The role of foreign trade in the British Industrial Revolution is hotly contested. Some of the most prestigious scholars in the field have vehemently denied any essential role for exports." The scholars mentioned are Thomas and McCloskey (1981 publication),

[100] Immanuel Wallerstein, *The Modern World-System III: The Second Era of Great Expansion of the Capitalist World-Economy, 1730–1840s* (San Diego, California: Academic Press, 1989), p. 80.

[101] Ronald Findlay, *The "Triangular Trade" And The Atlantic Economy of the Eighteenth Century: A Simple General-Equilibrium Model* (Princeton, NJ: International Finance Section, Department of Economics, Princeton University, 1990), p. 22.

[102] The others are William Darity, Jr., Amitava Krishna Dutt, and this author. For the four papers, see *American Economic Review*, Vol. 82, No. 2 (1992), pp. 146–167.

[103] Ronald Findlay, "The Roots of Divergence: Western Economic History in Comparative Perspective," *American Economic Review*, Vol. 82, No. 2 (1992), p. 160.

Ralph Davis (1979 publication), and trade theorists, Charles Kindleberger (1964 publication), and Ronald Findlay (1982 publication).[104] With reference to Ronald Findlay, at least, it can be said that Joel Mokyr is yet to observe the new trend in the historiography of the First Industrial Revolution. While it is too early to say with certainty that the new trend will reestablish the dominance of "Commercial Revolution" explanations that characterized the pre-1940s historiographical period, there is clear indication from current evidence that arguments based on autonomous domestic forces have lost mush of their appeal and are now on the defensive, especially those of supply economists derived from exogenous technological innovation.

3.2 FACTORS RESPONSIBLE FOR THE CHANGING EXPLANATIONS

In 1959, as the standard of living debate raged on, Max Hartwell wrote:

Perhaps the most important methodological problem in the writing of history is to discover why different historians, on the basis of the same or similar evidence, often have markedly different interpretations of a particular historical event.[105]

Hartwell's methodological problem appears to be limited to historians writing within the same temporal and geographical location, in which case the differing interpretations may be due to the social origin and disciplinary training of individual historians. When the problem is expanded to include differences in interpretation between historians writing within different temporal and geographical locations, the factors in the explanation take on a more dynamic form. The focus of analysis becomes over time changes in the factors that determine the establishment of dominant interpretations. For economic historians, such factors would include the quantity and quality of empirical evidence; the theoretical framework that informs the interpretation of evidence; and the ideological considerations that, wittingly or unwittingly, impinge on scientific investigations. It is clear that the over time changes in interpretation discussed earlier in the chapter were caused by factors other than changes in the quantity and quality of the empirical evidence on the Industrial Revolution. Certainly, changes in the evidence cannot explain the circular movement of the interpretations. The discussion that follows centers, therefore, on the last two factors.

Over time changes in theoretical perspectives can be viewed as a major factor responsible for the changing explanations of the causes of the Industrial Revolution. Of course, the amount and sophistication of theory employed by economic historians differ considerably. Economic history

---

[104]   Mokyr, "Introduction: The New Economic History," pp. 68–69.
[105]   Hartwell, "Interpretations of the Industrial Revolution," p. 81.

occupies a border territory between history and economics, for which reason its practitioners often come from history and economics, apart from those professionally trained as economic historians (especially in British universities). While the three categories of economic historians employ theory, explicitly or implicitly, to differing degrees, there is little doubt that their writings are influenced in some way, directly or indirectly, by prevailing economic theories. As Arthur Lewis put it:

> Most economic historians explain economic events in terms of the economic theories current at the time of writing (or worse still, current in their undergraduate days when they were learning their economic theory), and a new crop of economic theories is liable to be followed by a new crop of historical articles rewriting history in terms of the new theory.[106]

However, the causal dynamics also move in the other direction: economic theories do also change because of increased knowledge of history or the cumulative effects of observation of contemporary events. Thus in his study of theories of economic growth from the eighteenth century to the 1980s, Rostow reports:

> As I worked forward in this story, I found it increasingly important to relate writers to the particular times in which their views were formed and, sometimes, to the particular narrow interval when they set down a line of argument. The various growth formulations clearly bear the marks of particular passages of economic history intimately observed by their authors.[107]

In relating changes in economic theories to changing explanations of the Industrial Revolution by historians, we, therefore, consider both changes in theory and in the circumstances determining them as combined sources of influence on historians' interpretations. We begin with over time changes in growth theories and the circumstances. These are related subsequently to the changing interpretations.

As is well known, the first set of systematic and elaborate economic theories available to students of the Industrial Revolution was produced by the classical economists, the best known of whom include David Hume, Adam Smith, Thomas Malthus, David Ricardo, John Stuart Mill, and Karl Marx. Two aspects of their ideas are important for our present purpose: the growth theory embodied in their work, and the role of overseas trade in that theory.

The classical economists began their analysis with an economy in a "rude state," that is, an economy in which subsistence agricultural production

---

[106]   W. Arthur Lewis, *The Theory of Economic Growth* (London: George Allen & Unwin, 1955), p. 15.
[107]   W. W. Rostow, *Theorists of Economic Growth from David Hume to the Present, With a Perspective on the Next Century* (New York: Oxford University Press, 1990), p. 7.

was overwhelmingly dominant, for which reason the division of labor, technology, transportation, organization of production and distribution in agriculture and manufacturing, were all at a low level of development. This situation gave rise to a stationary state of income per head at the subsistence level. They then enquired into the factors that would operate over time to move this economy into the path of growth and regularly push income per head above subsistence. The central factor they discovered was capital accumulation arising from increasing division of labor. Growing division of labor was seen as the most powerful force that propelled labor productivity to higher levels in three ways. As Adam Smith put it:

This great increase of the quantity of work, which in consequence of the division of labour, the same number of people are capable of performing, is owing to three different circumstances; first to the increase of dexterity in every particular workman; secondly to the saving of time which is commonly lost in passing from one species of work to another; and lastly, to the invention of a great number of machines which facilitate and abridge labour, and enable one man to do the work of many.[108]

In their growth theory, the classical economists assigned a leading role to trade (foreign and domestic), but more so to overseas trade. We have seen that capital accumulation is the central element in the classical system. But in the system, capital accumulation is dependent on market expansion that produces economies of scale through increases in the division of labor and specialization. Given the kind of economy that formed their point of departure – an economy dominated by subsistence agricultural production – opportunity for sustained large-scale overseas trade was expected to provide the impetus for the expansion of the market sector of the domestic economy, leading to the general commercialization of socio-economic life, which is the basis of growing division of labor and specialization. The classical economists certainly knew British history well. Their expectation of the role of foreign trade fits very well the role of raw wool export in the commercialization of English agriculture.[109]

Three aspects of the writings of the classical economists on international trade may be distinguished: the role of imports in the development of manufacturing; the vent-for-surplus effect of international trade; and the gains

---

[108] Adam Smith, *Wealth of Nations*, Vol. I, p. 9, quoted by Phyllis Deane, *The Evolution of Economic Ideas* (Cambridge: Cambridge University Press, 1978), p. 35.

[109] Rostow makes a similar but more general point: "Smith had the force of expansion in foreign trade primarily in mind as an instrument for moving the economy away from its original rude state. Historically, the commercial revolution of the previous two and one-half centuries was a powerful living reality to Smith's generation"; Rostow, *Theorists of Economic Growth*, pp. 509–510. Malthus and Ricardo were responsible for the development of a more rigorous linkage of the classical system to agriculture.

from international trade through the allocation of resources in accordance with comparative advantage. The role of imports in the development process was elaborated by David Hume. Hume demonstrated that imported manufactures would provide the incentives for agricultural producers to redouble their efforts and be more innovative, and would in the end create the environment for the growth and development of domestic manufacturing. "When a nation abounds in manufactures and mechanic arts," he said, "the proprietors of land, as well as the farmers, study agriculture as a science, and redouble their industry and attention." He added: "Foreign trade, by its imports, furnishes materials for new manufactures ... If we consult history we shall find, that in most nations, foreign trade has preceded any refinement in home manufactures, and given birth to domestic luxury."[110]

The vent-for-surplus element in the classical theory of international trade is generally overlooked by modern economists, who treat Ricardo's comparative advantage as the sole element that characterizes the classical theory. The first modern economist to refer to it was John Williams, who, curiously, still treated Ricardo's comparative advantage as the defining element of the classical theory of international trade.[111] Myint was the first modern economist to treat the vent-for-surplus principle as an integral part of the classical theory of international trade.[112] He traced it to Adam Smith:

---

[110]   E. Rotwein (ed.), *David Hume*, pp. 11–13, quoted by Rostow, *Theorists of Economic Growth*, p. 22. Rostow argues that Hume was influenced by his observation of the impact of imported East Indian cotton textiles on West European economies in the 17th and 18th centuries: "Like all men and, especially, women of his time, Hume was conscious of the quite extraordinary and, ultimately, revolutionary impact on Europe of the expansion, despite inhibitions, of Indian cotton textile imports ... The memorable contemporary description of the impact on French women of Indian calicoes early in the eighteenth century holds generally for Western Europe: 'Fruit défendu, les toiles deviennent la passion toutes les filles d'Eve françaises.' ('Forbidden fruit, cotton cloth became the passion of every French daughter of Eve.').... there could be no more vivid or historically important illustration of Hume's doctrine. Foreign trade did yield an attractive luxury; the demonstration effect set in motion a 'fermentation' in Western Europe (and a profit incentive) that finally resulted in the textile machinery required to manufacture the cotton yarn that European hands were too clumsy to produce by methods long used in India. There is a serious sense in which the British industrial revolution of the late eighteenth century was the first import-substitution takeoff" (p. 22).

[111]   John H. Williams, "The Theory of International Trade Reconsidered," *The Economic Journal*, Vol. XXXIX (June, 1929), pp. 195–209; see pp. 203–205 for a discussion of the vent-for-surplus principle in relation to J. S. Mill's criticism of the principle.

[112]   H. Myint, "The 'Classical Theory' of International Trade and the underdeveloped Countries," *The Economic Journal*, Vol. LXVIII (June, 1958), pp. 317–337, reprinted in Deepak Lal (ed.), *Development Economics*, Vol. III (Aldershot: Edward Elgar, 1992), pp. 29–49.

Between whatever places foreign trade is carried on, they all of them derive two distinct benefits from it. It carries out that surplus part of the produce of their land and labour for which there is no demand among them, and brings back in return for it something else for which there is a demand. It gives a value to their superfluities, by exchanging them for something else, which may satisfy a part of their wants, and increase their enjoyments. By means of it, the narrowness of the home market does not hinder the division of labour in any particular branch of art or manufacture from being carried to the highest perfection. By opening a more extensive market for whatever part of the produce of their labour may exceed the home consumption, it encourages them to improve its productive powers, and to augment its annual produce to the utmost, and thereby to increase the real revenue and wealth of society.[113]

Myint identified two leading ideas in this text by Smith: the idea that overseas trade helps to solve the problem of under-utilization of resources arising from the narrowness of the domestic market by providing overseas outlets for the extra produce of those resources, over and above what the narrow home market could absorb, being the vent-for-surplus theory of international trade; and the idea that international trade helps to broaden the extent of the market, which increases overall productivity of the trading country through improved division of labor, which Myint termed "the 'productivity' theory." Myint then compared the productivity theory with Ricardo's comparative advantage theory:[114]

The 'productivity' doctrine differs from the comparative-costs doctrine in the interpretation of 'specialisation' of international trade. (a) In the comparative costs theory 'specialisation merely means a movement along a static 'production possibility curve' constructed on the given resources and the *given techniques* of the trading country. In contrast, the 'productivity' doctrine looks upon international trade as a dynamic force which, by widening the extent of the market and the scope of the division of labour, raises the skill and dexterity of the workmen, encourages technical innovations, overcomes technical indivisibilities and generally enables the trading country to enjoy increasing returns and economic development. . . . (b) In the comparative costs theory 'specialisation,' conceived as a reallocation of resources, is a completely reversible process. The Adam Smithian process of specialisation, however, involves adapting and reshaping the productive structure of a country to meet the export demand, and is therefore not easily reversible.

John Stuart Mill objected to the Smith's vent-for-surplus principle, arguing instead:

The expression, surplus produce, seems to imply that a country is under some kind of obligation of producing the corn or cloth which it exports; so that the portion which it does not itself consume, if not wanted and consumed elsewhere, would

---

[113] Adam Smith, *Wealth of Nations*, Vol. I, Cannan edition, p. 413, quoted by Myint, "The 'Classical Theory' of International Trade," p. 30.

[114] Myint, "The 'Classical Theory' of International Trade," pp. 30–31.

either be produced in sheer waste, or, if it were not produced the corresponding portion of capital would remain idle, and the mass of productions in the country would be diminished by so much. Either of these suppositions is erroneous. . . . If prevented from exporting this surplus it would cease to produce it, and would no longer import anything, being unable to give an equivalent; but the labour and capital which had been employed in producing with a view to exportation would find employment in producing those desirable objects brought from abroad; or . . . substitutes for them. . . . And capital would just as much be replaced, with the ordinary profit from the returns, as it was when employed in producing for the foreign market.[115]

Mill's argument clearly derived from Ricardo's comparative advantage principle. It is not surprising, therefore, that it shares exactly the same logic with the arguments of modern economists, who are more exposed to Ricardo's theory of international trade (upon which much of neoclassical trade theory itself is based) than to Smith's vent-for-surplus and productivity theory. John Williams's criticism of Mill and the Ricardian theory applies equally to most neoclassical economists' perception of gains from international trade:

It is to be doubted whether Mill today [1929], or indeed the Mill of his later years, the writer of the chapter on the 'Tendency of Profits to a Minimum,' would care to stand by this passage [the one quoted above] in reference to England. . . . What Mill overlooked was the entire absence, under assumptions of predominant foreign trade, of comparable alternatives in purely domestic production . . . He failed to see, indeed, that but for specialisation in world trade such concentration of labour and capital on little land would not be possible. What is more significant, perhaps, he failed to see the relation of international trade to national economic development, spread over time. . . . He failed to see that England's capital and labour were *products* (results) of international trade itself, but for which they would not have existed in any comparable degree.[116]

Addressing Ricardo's comparative advantage principle, which he apparently regarded as representative of the whole classical theory of international trade, Williams declared:

The classical theory assumes as fixed, for purposes of the reasoning, the very things which, in my view, should be the chief objects of study if what we wish to know is the effects and causes of international trade, so broadly regarded that nothing of importance in the facts shall fail to find its place in the analysis. It is the writer's [Williams] view . . . that the relation of international trade to the development of

---

[115]   J. S. Mill, *Principles*, Book III, pp. 579–580, quoted by Williams, "The Theory of International Trade," pp. 203–204. John Williams attributed the expression, "vent for surplus," to J. S. Mill, who used it to describe Adam Smith's foreign trade theory, criticizing the notion as a "surviving relic of the Mercantile Theory" (Williams, "The Theory of International Trade," p. 203).

[116]   Williams, "The Theory of International Trade," pp. 204–205.

new resources and productive forces is a more significant part of the explanation of the present status of nations, of incomes, prices, well-being, than is the cross-section value analysis of the classical economists, with its assumption of given quantums of productive factors, already existent and employed . . .[117]

In general, because of the nature of the issues they addressed, the kind of contemporary economic processes they observed, and their attention to history, the classical economists were long-term development oriented in their theories. They were also less rigorously deductive and more historical in their reasoning. The most deductively rigorous of them all was Ricardo. That Adam Smith's vent-for-surplus and productivity principles of international trade captured the socio-economic reality of the England of their time far more accurately than the more rigorously deductive Ricardo's comparative advantage theory may be a sad comment on overly deductive reasoning in economic analysis.

Yet economic analysis became increasingly abstract and rigorously deductive from the second half of the nineteenth century. In addition, economic theorizing moved away from issues of growth. Apparently believing that the Industrial Revolution had solved for all time the problem of growth which dominated the attention of the classical economists, Marshallian economics could afford to take for granted the growth of the wealth of nations and focus on marginal change and social welfare. Rostow puts it succinctly:

Both orthodox and heterodox economic analysts of the 1870–1914 period . . . more or less silently agreed [that] the analysis of economic growth could be dropped from the agenda. Both groups assumed the existence of an ongoing, viable, expanding economic system. Although the lines between them were not sharp, one group was devoted primarily to refining theoretical knowledge of how it worked, the other to diagnosing and remedying, in more or less radical ways, its inhumanities. But by and large the theory of economic growth was placed by both groups on protracted holiday.[118]

There was very little change in the first four decades of the twentieth century. The most important development of the period was the so-called Keynesian revolution. But Keynes did not address issues of long-term development and socio-economic transformation. His focus was the short-term problem of an advanced industrial economy operating below capacity. Hence, all long-term variables – quantity and skill of labor, technology, production structure, organization, consumers' tastes, and social structure – are held constant.[119] The other major development of the period, preceding Keynes, was Joseph Schumpeter's *The Theory of Economic Development*, first published in 1911. But, unlike the classical economists, whose

[117]   *Ibid*, p. 196.   [118]   Rostow, *Theorists of Economic Growth*, p. 155.
[119]   *Ibid.*, p. 279.

focus was on an economy in a "rude state," the point of departure for Schumpeter's long-term development analysis was, again, an advanced industrial economy.[120]

Thus, between 1880 and the 1940s, classical theory of economic growth provided the only economic ideas that were useful in the historical study of an economy which progressed from a "rude state" to that of mechanized, large-scale industry. To the extent that historians searched for relevant analytic ideas in their production and interpretation of evidence, the available ideas were embodied in classical growth theory. The fact that the classical economists were less rigorously deductive and more historical in their approach made their ideas quite accessible to historians. It is, therefore, fair to conclude that the dominance of the "commercial revolution" interpretation of the Industrial Revolution in the 1880–1950 historiographical period owed something to classical growth theory. A careful examination of the "commercial revolution" arguments presented earlier in the chapter will certainly reveal traces of Adam Smith's vent-for-surplus and productivity principles of gains from overseas trade, as well as David Hume's notion of the role of imports in the development process. In fact, the basic principles concerning import-substitution industrialization can be traced to Hume. It is significant that Ricardo's comparative advantage theory of international trade found little room in the writings of the 1880–1950 period.

Things changed radically between the 1940s and 1970s. First, two world wars and the Great Depression shook the world economy to its very foundation. The collapse of world trade forced both scholars and administrators to lose confidence in the ability of international trade to operate as the propelling force for long-term development. Then there was the anti-colonial movement which ended European colonial rule and led to the establishment of politically independent nations in Asia, Africa, and the Caribbean. The anti-colonial movement generated anti-imperialist ideologies that out-lived colonial rule and were important in the academic debate on the economic costs and benefits of colonial rule. The association of international trade with colonialism added to the pessimism about foreign trade arising from the collapse of the international economy in the early decades of the twentieth century. What is more, the observed lessons of the non-market model of development in the Soviet Union and China in the 1950s and 1960s diminished even further the appeal of the market-oriented development process. These circumstances very much determined the kind of

---

[120] As Rostow argues, "Schumpeter was a rather parochial economist of the advanced industrial world, above all, of post-takeoff Germany, Britain, and the United States. It was logical that his initial insight should lead him, in the end, to speculate on the probable fate of capitalism rather than on the emerging problems of growth and modernization in the developing world." *Ibid.*, pp. 234–235.

growth models that were fashioned, which in turn, together with those circumstances themselves, influenced scholars' interpretation of history during the 1950–1980s historiographical period. These factors are worth examining in some detail, starting with the growth models.

As Arthur Lewis wrote in 1980, with the benefit of hindsight:

The collapse of international trade in the 1930s had seemed irreversible, so much so that Keynes had even declared that we didn't need much of it anyway. So in the 1940s and 1950s we created a whole set of theories which make sense if world trade is stagnant – balanced growth, regional integration, the two-gap model, structural inflation – but which have little relevance in a world where trade is growing at 8 percent per annum. Also many countries, basing their policies on the same assumption, oriented inwards mainly towards import substitution.[121]

Two types of neoclassical growth theory developed during the period. There was formal growth theory, which was adopted by mainstream economics; the other was development-oriented and became a marginal branch of economics called development economics. Formal growth theory focused exclusively on the problems of the advanced industrial economies of the West, while development economics addressed itself to the long-term development problems of the Third World nations.[122] Formal growth theory derived essentially from Keynesian economics and its focus was the cyclical problems of mature industrial economies. It employed basically the same macro-economic variables – savings, investment, and labor – with the accelerator and multiplier principles of Keynes to develop a long-term growth theory from Keynesian static and short-run analysis. From the original Harrod-Domar models to later modifications and refinements, the focus was to construct a mathematical model that connects these variables in a way that could demonstrate a long-run stable growth path.[123] Virtually all the models took demand for granted and had no room for international trade. Technical progress was frequently treated as exogenous, and non-economic factors were not considered.

This general character of formal growth model has attracted considerable criticism even from sympathetic commentators. The most frequently cited critic is K. Berrill, who wrote in 1960:

This article stems from a discontent with current theoretical models of economic growth which have become increasingly elegant while remaining hopelessly unrealistic. . . . These are marked by three features which seem particularly objectionable in that they misread the process of growth and conceal the most important elements

[121] W. Arthur Lewis, "The Slowing Down of the Engine of Growth," *American Economic Review*, LXX (September, 1980), pp. 555–564, reprinted in Lal (ed.), *Development Economics*, Vol. III, pp. 73–74.
[122] Deane, *Evolution of Economic Ideas*, pp. 196–197.
[123] *Ibid.*, pp. 197–204; Rostow, *Theorists of Economic Growth*, pp. 332–349.

in past expansions. The first and fundamental objection is that the models are posed in terms of closed and homogeneous national economies. This means that foreign trade is given very little part to play and that the country is assumed to move forward in one piece so that regional differences are left out of account. The second objectionable feature is that the economy is divided only into two sectors, consumer goods and investment goods. No attempt is made to distinguish the separate roles of agriculture, transport or utilities and least of all the separate roles of particular staple crops or industries. . . . The third drawback in modern growth models, and it is perhaps surprising that it should occur after Keynes, is that demand plays a passive role.[124]

The general view is that formal growth models failed to capture the contemporary reality of even the mature industrial economies in the 1950–1970 period. In particular, those models were incapable of explaining the phenomenal growth of the industrial economies during the period, which was caused by technological innovation and the expansion of international trade. More important for our present purpose, however, formal growth models were totally ill-equipped to deal with the problems of economies in a process of long-term development from a "rude state." Those problems were addressed by growth models constructed by development economists during the same period.

Development economists, concerned with Third World economies that were progressing from a "rude state," saw much similarity between their own objects of study and those that confronted the classical economists. Their growth theories were, therefore, derived from classical theory rather than Keynesian economics as formal growth models did. Their growth models were less formal and often took non-economic factors into consideration. Even so, several of the development economists still failed to overcome the export pessimism of the period. For purposes of illustration, we consider briefly a few of their more representative writings. Arthur Lewis and H. Myint would serve this purpose well.

Arthur Lewis recognized the role of non-economic factors in the development process and allowed for the possibility of change being initiated by non-economic factors. But he did not believe that any set of non-economic factors could prevent development when opportunities for growth are presented.[125] In his more elaborate growth theory published in 1955, Lewis gave much room to international trade, believing as Adam Smith did, that overseas trade would be the main propelling force to move the predominantly subsistence economy from its "rude state" into the path of development:

---

[124]   K. Berrill, "International Trade and the Rate of Economic Growth," *Economic History Review*, 2nd series, Vol. XII, No. 3 (1960), p. 351. See also Rostow, *Theorists of Economic Growth*, pp. 350–351.

[125]   See his statement this volume on p. 17 on the conditions for the continuance and change of social institutions; Lewis, *Theory of Economic Growth*, p. 143.

Accordingly, at low levels of economic activity, production for the foreign market is usually the turning point which sets a country on the road of economic growth. To make an upward movement by producing for the home market is at this stage extremely difficult. . . . At low levels innovation for the home market is unusual. . . . Innovation comes, therefore usually first of all in foreign trade. . . .[126]

But his highly influential paper, "Economic Development with Unlimited Supplies of Labour," published in 1954, and his book, *The Evolution of the International Economic Order*, published in 1978, both minimize the role of foreign trade in the development process.[127] The economy with unlimited supplies of labor is expected to develop on the basis of cheap labor that is transferred from the subsistence sector to the capitalist sector under conditions of autarky – conditions of a closed economy, without international trade. The closed economy assumptions are relaxed only after the expansion of the capitalist sector has absorbed the surplus labor. At this point wages begin to rise, profits fall, and investments decline. The economy then opens up to overcome this predicament by either encouraging the immigration of labor from other labor surplus economies or by exporting capital to such economies to take advantage of their surplus supplies of labor.

The model says nothing about the market where the products of the cheap labor will be sold nor about the incentives that would encourage capitalists to invest their capital in the capitalist sector, given the initial character of the economy and the closed economy assumptions. One would have thought that, given his eloquent statement quoted above, Arthur Lewis would recognize that, short of the Soviet model, sustained export expansion represents the best opportunity for an economy at the stated level of activity to develop through the exploitation of its surplus resource, labor. Somehow, he could not overcome the prevailing export pessimism of the time. As late as 1978, Arthur Lewis still wrote:

[I]nternational trade became an engine of growth in the nineteenth century, but this is not its proper role. The engine of growth should be technological change, with international trade serving as lubricating oil and not as fuel. The gateway to technological change is through agricultural and industrial revolutions, which are mutually dependent.[128]

---

[126] *Ibid.*, pp. 275–276.

[127] W. Arthur Lewis, "Economic Development with Unlimited Supplies of Labour," *Manchester School of Economic and Social Studies*, XXII (May, 1954), pp. 139–191, reprinted in Lal (ed.), *Development Economics*, Vol. I, pp. 117–169; W. Arthur Lewis, *The Evolution of the International Economic Order* (Princeton, NJ: Princeton University Press, 1978).

[128] Lewis, *Evolution of the International Economic Order*, p. 74. In his 1955 book, Arthur Lewis had said: "The fact that an expansion of manufacturing production does not require an expansion of agricultural production if it is backed by a growing export of manufactures is particularly important to those over-populated countries

While Lewis's apparent preoccupation with the export pessimism of the 1950s forced him to construct a closed economy model of growth, H. Myint, as was shown above, appreciated the relevance of Adam Smith's vent-for-surplus and productivity theory of international trade to the conditions of many Third World economies in the nineteenth and early twentieth centuries. Though Myint's model was addressed specifically to economies with surplus land, it can be applied equally to Lewis's economy with surplus labor. In fact, only the introduction of an expanding export market makes Lewis's model realistic.[129]

Thus some variants of the post-war growth models in development economics favored export-led growth. However, such models had little influence on the historiography of the Industrial Revolution between the late 1940s and the early 1980s. The dominant ideas came from mainstream economics and they flowed from formal growth models. This was the more so, because the Industrial Revolution attracted many economists trained in formal growth theory between 1950 and the 1970s. This was the age of cliometrics, counterfactuals, and the "new economic history." As Hughes, to whom the term "new economic history" has been traced,[130] wrote:

Young men who came into economic history from economics in the 1950s and early 1960s to look for the economist's equivalent of 'laws of nature' in the historical record had their primary training in the 'new' and the 'new-old' economics. They seemed to understand little of the methods and motives of the old-time 'fact' men in economic history, and went to work rewriting economic history, revising much of the older interpretation, but also pushing the old-framework aside altogether and producing entirely new information by new methods, statistical techniques and data processing.[131]

which cannot hope to increase their agricultural output for food as rapidly as their demand for food however much they may try. . . . This is very obviously the case with the British economy. The Industrial Revolution was accompanied by an Agricultural Revolution [note the sequence], but home demand soon outstripped the possibilities of agricultural production, and from the end of the Napoleonic War to the outbreak of the American Civil War, what set the pace for the growth of the British economy was the fact that British exports of manufactures were growing by nearly 6 percent per annum, cumulatively" (Lewis, *Theory of Economic Growth*, pp. 278–279).

[129] Other development economists who stressed the positive role of international trade in the development process include Jacob Viner, Gottfried Haberler, and Peter Bauer. For a discussion of the confrontation between export-led and import-substitution models in development economics, see Rostow, *Theorists of Economic Growth*, pp. 422–425, and Hollis Chenery, Sherman Robinson, and Moshe Syrquin, *Industrialization and Growth* (New York: Oxford University Press, 1986).

[130] Lance E. Davis, "'And it will never be literature,' The New Economic History: A Critique," in Ralph L. Andreano (ed.), *The New Economic History: Recent Papers on Methodology* (New York: John Wiley and Sons, 1970), p. 67.

[131] J. R. T. Hughes, "Fact and Theory in Economic History," in Andreano (ed.), *New Economic History*, p. 48.

Economic history in British universities had its share of this development, although to a more limited extent because of the established tradition of economic history as an independent discipline in many British universities. The fact remains, however, that both in the United States and in Britain the economists who moved into the history of the Industrial Revolution were largely responsible for the establishment of a new dominant interpretation between 1950 and the early 1980s. As one would expect from their formal models, most of them discounted the role of overseas trade. They generally treated technological innovation as exogenous and computed gains from international trade in terms of Ricardo's static comparative advantage theory, which enabled them to argue, like Mill, that the resources employed in producing for export between 1650 and 1850 could have been employed to produce for the home market in England without much loss in growth. The influence of their writings, together with the prevailing export pessimism of the time, also persuaded other students of the Industrial Revolution to minimize the role of overseas trade during the 1950–80 historiographical period.

All of this was further reinforced by the mixture of academic and ideological debates on the economic costs and benefits of colonialism, which soon became part and parcel of a raging cold war. Various strands of Marxian theory, including dependency theory, discounted the positive role of international trade in the development process and quite often asserted it was negative, for reasons that were probably connected with the achievements of non-market strategies in the U.S.S.R. and China, and the association of international trade with colonialism, among others. Three aspects of this Marxian scholarship, speaking broadly, are important for our present purpose. There were serious Marxists like Robert Brenner who employed Marxist theory to argue that class struggle arising from agricultural development, rather than overseas trade, was the main factor in English economic development in the seventeenth and eighteenth centuries.[132] Reasoning somewhat similarly, other Marxist scholars argued that international trade under European colonialism distorted the class structure of colonized societies and gave rise to under-development – something that did not happen in Western Europe where class structures are said to have evolved on the basis of internal forces undisturbed by external pressure.[133]

---

[132] See the papers in Aston and Philpin (eds.), *The Brenner Debate*.

[133] See the voluminous literature on dependency theory, of which the following are some of the best known: the first issue of *Latin American Perspectives*, 1, no. 1 (1974), devoted entirely to the subject; so also are the special issues of the same journal, vol. 8, nos. 3 and 4 (1981), entitled, *Dependency and Marxism*; Henry Bernstein (ed.), *Underdevelopment and Development: The Third World Today* (New York: Penguin Books, 1973); André Gunder Frank, *Capitalism and Underdevelopment in Latin America* (New York: Monthly Review Press, 1967); Robert A. Packenham, *The Dependency Movement: Scholarship and Politics in Development Studies*

Finally, other scholars of the period, who included non-Marxists, tried to show that economic development in Western Europe was based on plunder and exploitation of colonized peoples. The best known of the latter group of scholarly publications is Eric Williams, *Capitalism and Slavery*.

These publications did two things: They placed on the heads of Western peoples responsibility for the economic problems of former colonial territories in the Third World; and they questioned the moral basis of Western development. It is no surprise that reaction to them during the 1950–80 historiographical period tended to follow predictable lines – with important exceptions on all sides. Scholars in the West defended Western societies against all the charges, while those in the Third World and the Socialist Bloc strongly supported the said publications. To illustrate, Peter Duignan and L. H. Gann wrote in 1975:

In the colonial period, it is charged, there was growth without development; because of increased population pressure on the land, African living standards remained stationary or rose only slightly. The story of colonialism was, then, the tale of *How Europe underdeveloped Africa*. Our own conclusions are at variance with this interpretation.[134]

In a book published in 1980 after his death, Bill Warren wrote on the same subject:

There is no evidence that any process of underdevelopment has occurred in modern times and particularly in the period since the West made its impact on other continents. The evidence rather supports a contrary thesis: that a process of *development* has been taking place at least since the English industrial revolution, much accelerated in comparison with any earlier period; and that this has been the direct result of the impact of the West . . .[135]

More ideologically explicit, Bauer wrote in 1981:

Acceptance of emphatic routine allegations that the West is responsible for Third World poverty reflects and reinforces Western feelings of guilt. It has enfeebled Western diplomacy, both towards the ideologically much more aggressive Soviet bloc and also towards the Third World. And the West has come to abase itself before countries with negligible resources and no real power. Yet the allegations can be shown to be without foundation. They are readily accepted because the Western public has little first-hand knowledge of the Third World, and because of widespread

(Cambridge, Mass.: Harvard University Press, 1992). See also Walter Rodney, *How Europe Underdeveloped Africa* (London: Bogle-L'Ouverture, 1972; revised edition, Washington: Howard University Press, 1981).

[134] Peter Duignan and L. H. Gann, "Economic Achievements of the Colonizers: An Assessment," in Peter Duignan and L. H. Gann (eds.), *Colonialism in Africa, 1870–1960: Volume IV, The Economics of Colonialism* (Cambridge: Cambridge University Press, 1975), p. 673.

[135] Bill Warren, *Imperialism: Pioneer of Capitalism*, edited by John Sender (London: Verso, 1980), p. 113.

feelings of guilt. The West has never had it so good, and has never felt so bad about it.[136]

The debate on the role of overseas trade in the first Industrial Revolution, especially the slave-based Atlantic commerce, was conducted in the 1950–80 period against the background of this global ideological ferment. This explains why Eric Williams's *Capitalism and Slavery* provoked such a voluminous literature during the period.[137] Without arguing that arguments on either side were consciously ideological, traces of the influence of the international ideological environment of the time, albeit indirect, can be observed in the literature. One or two illustrations will suffice. In 1955 Ashton wrote:

The rapid development of English industry has been attributed to the exploitation of colonial peoples and to profits wrung from the slave trade. But it was after the Americans had won their independence, and at a time when the West Indian economy was in decline, that the pace quickened.[138]

Thirty-eight years later, Joel Mokyr charged quite explicitly that scholars who argue in favor of a positive contribution by the British empire to the process of economic development in England do so because they dislike the Industrial Revolution: "It seems somehow tempting for those who do not have much sympathy for British capitalism to link it with imperialism and slavery." He cites Stanley Engerman, who is reported to have said in 1972: "In this version history becomes a morality play in which one evil (the Industrial Revolution) arises from another, perhaps even greater evil, slavery and imperialism."[139] Thus, just as the association of international trade with colonialism seems to have affected somewhat the attitude of Third World scholars to the role of foreign trade in development during the 1950–80 period, the views of Western scholars concerning the contribution of overseas trade to the Industrial Revolution appear to have also been affected in some way by the charges of exploitation that put into question the moral basis of Western development.

To summarize, effort has been made to show that the dominance of interpretations of the Industrial Revolution centered on autonomous domestic

---

[136]   P. T. Bauer, *Equality, the Third World and Economic Delusion* (London: George Weidenfeld and Nicolson, 1981), p. 66.

[137]   For a survey of the literature, see Richard B. Sheridan, "Eric Williams and *Capitalism and Slavery*: A Bibliographical and Historiographical Essay," in Solow and Engerman (eds.), *British Capitalism and Caribbean Slavery*, pp. 317–345; see also in this same edited volume, Hilary McD. Beckles, " 'The Williams Effect': Eric Williams's *Capitalism and Slavery* and the Growth of West Indian Political Economy" (pp. 303–316), which discusses, *inter alia*, the support for *Capitalism and Slavery* among Caribbean scholars.

[138]   Ashton, *An Economic History of England*, p. 125.

[139]   Mokyr, "Introduction: The New Economic History," p. 75 and footnote 67, p. 75.

forces during the 1950–80 historiographical period was due to a combination of several factors. The collapse of the international economy under the impact of two world wars and the Great Depression led to export pessimism that affected the perceptions of historians and the growth theories constructed by economists. The movement into the study of the Industrial Revolution by a sizable number of economists trained in neoclassical formal growth theory accelerated the momentum of change. And the appeal of the non-market model in the socialist world combined with anti-colonial scholarship to make market-oriented development largely unpopular during the period. While all of these factors made their contributions, individually and collectively, the greatest weight must be attached to the export pessimism associated with the collapse of the international economy and the neoclassical formal growth theory to which it gave birth.

From the 1980s, new forces affecting historians' interpretations of the past, which have been building up over the preceding decades, began to emerge forcefully. As Arthur Lewis stated in the quotation presented earlier, international trade grew cumulatively at about 8 percent per annum between 1950 and 1970. This enabled the industrial nations of the West, operating under favorable terms of trade, to experience a phenomenal rate of growth. Meanwhile, most nations in the Third World implemented ISI policy. These countries fell into three categories: Some started their industrialization process with import-substitution strategy but quickly moved into aggressive export promotion as the limits of the pre-existing domestic market were being reached; others persisted with import-substitution until the difficulties of a limited domestic market forced them into export promotion; and yet others continued with import-substitution in spite of the difficulties. The result is that the first group of countries (the Asian tigers: South Korea, Taiwan, Hong Kong, and Singapore) completed their industrialization successfully and joined the club of industrial nations; the second group began to make more progress after export promotion strategy was adopted (Brazil, Chile, and some other Latin American and Asian countries, in particular, Thailand); finally, the third group, which includes India, made very little progress in their industrialization drive during the period.[140]

Neoclassical formal growth theory constructed in the 1950s and 1960s could explain neither the growth experience of the industrial nations during the period nor the industrialization experience of the Third World nations. As theory diverged increasingly from observed reality, new theories more

---

[140] Balassa, *The Process of Industrial Development*; Hollis Chenery, Sherman Robinson, and Moshe Syrquin, *Industrialization and Growth* (Oxford: Oxford University Press, 1986); Jacques Hersh, *The USA and the Rise of East Asia since 1945: Dilemmas of the Postwar International Political Economy* (London: Macmillan, 1993).

closely related to real world observation began to be fashioned in the mid-1980s. The main difference between the new theories and those of the 1950s and the 1960s is in the treatment of technological change and international trade. As was noted earlier, formal growth theories, to which Harrod-Domar gave birth, paid little attention to international trade and treated technological innovation as exogenous, "a manna from heaven." The new theories regard technological change as an endogenous variable that is affected by market size and trade expansion. For this reason international trade features prominently in the new theories. Summarizing their survey of the new growth literature, to which they themselves have contributed greatly, Gene Grossman and Elhanan Helpman observe:

Many growth theorists raised in the neoclassical, Solovian tradition took techno-logical progress to be an exogenous and fortuitous process. Several common fea-tures distinguish recent efforts to endogenize innovation within general equilibrium models of long-run growth.[141]

And they conclude:

Casual observation and more systematic empirical research suggest that countries that have adopted an outward-oriented development strategy have grown faster and achieved a higher level of economic well-being than those that have chosen a more protectionist trade stance. . . . The approach to modeling endogenous innovation and endogenous human capital formation that has been proposed here may provide a means for improving our understanding of the connection between the interna-tional trade environment including the trade policy regime and long-run growth performance.[142]

Added to the construction of more realistic growth theories, the collapse of the Soviet Union and the adoption of the market system by the former Soviet republics, Eastern Europe, and China have all helped to make the importance of trade in the growth process more generally appreciated. Postwar export pessimism finally seems to have left the scene. Neoclassical formal growth theorists now willingly admit the limitations of their theo-ries and, together with administrators who based their public policies on those theories, regret the mistakes of the preceding decades. It is a

[141]   Gene M. Grossman and Elhanan Helpman, "Trade, Innovation, and Growth," *American Economic Review*, Vol. 80, No. 2 (May, 1990), pp. 86–87.

[142]   *Ibid.*, pp. 90–91. See also Gene M. Grossman and Elhanan Helpman, *Innovation and Growth in the Global Economy* (Cambridge, Mass.: MIT Press, 1991). Paul M. Romer is often cited as one of the originators of the new growth theories. See Paul M. Romer, "Increasing Returns and Long-Run Growth," *Journal of Political Economy*, Vol. 94, No. 5 (1986), pp. 1002–1037. In another paper he states: "The economics profession is undergoing a substantial change in how we think about international trade, development, economic growth and economic geography" (Paul M. Romer, "The Origins of Endogenous Growth," *Journal of Economic Perspec-tives*, Volume 8, Number 1 (1994), p. 19).

combination of all these factors that is forcing the new trend in the historiography of the Industrial Revolution shown earlier in the chapter.

The reaction by Crafts, one of the leading neoclassical formal growth theorists in the field, helps further to make the point. As he puts it:

> Interpretations of the experience of economic growth in Britain during the Industrial Revolution and the later nineteenth century have in recent times been based on the traditional neoclassical growth model and growth accounting. In the last ten years or so, however, economists' theorizing about growth has changed dramatically with the development of endogenous growth models and increased emphasis on the roles of human capital formation and of research and development.[143]

Crafts still holds that some aspects of technological change in the first Industrial Revolution, "macroinventions," were exogenous. However, he believes that some of the new growth theories, especially the Grossman-Helpman type, provide helpful insights for more realistic interpretation of the Industrial Revolution. Further, he admits that the new growth theorists have "found useful ways of formalizing ideas long discussed by economic historians, and the way may now be open for some fruitful interaction between economics and economic history." Crafts specifically suggests that "given the extensive emphasis placed on comparative market size by new growth theory, a substantial effort should be made to find ways to investigate this hypothesis properly."[144] Thus, just as postwar export pessimism and the neoclassical formal growth theory to which it gave rise were principally responsible for inward looking interpretations of the Industrial Revolution in the 1950–1980 period, so also do we conclude that the disappearance of postwar export pessimism and the construction of more realistic growth theories by economists are the main factors driving the new trend in the historiography of the Industrial Revolution.

3.3 ASSESSING THE CONTENDING EXPLANATIONS

We have now seen the over time changes in the historiographical environment that influenced the changing interpretations of the Industrial Revolution between the 1880s and the present. In this last part of the chapter we propose to probe further the merits and demerits of the contending explanations. Emphasis in the preceding discussion was on the relative strengths and weaknesses of the theoretical frameworks that informed the competing explanations. Of course, inappropriate theory usually leads to error in historical analysis. But even where the underlying theoretical perspective is appropriate, a particular historical explanation may still fail to be suffi-

---

[143]   N. F. R. Crafts, "Exogenous or Endogenous Growth? The Industrial Revolution Reconsidered," *Journal of Economic History*, Vol. 55, No. 4 (December, 1995), p. 745.

[144]   Crafts, "Exogenous or Endogenous Growth?" p. 768.

ciently persuasive if relevant evidence is not properly marshaled to present a convincing proof. In the discussion that follows, a clear distinction is drawn between argumentation, assertion, and detailed proof. It is contended that much of the competing and changing explanations of the causes of the Industrial Revolution, examined earlier, contain much assertion and argumentation, and very little detailed historical proof. It is contended further that such proof can be best offered on the basis of recent regional studies whose implications are yet to be fully incorporated into the national studies of the Industrial Revolution. We employ the detailed regional evidence presented in Chapter 2 to confront the competing interpretations discussed earlier and to offer a systematic empirical and logical proof of the leading role of overseas trade in the Industrial Revolution, and the leading position of Atlantic commerce in the overall growth of trade during the period.

Undoubtedly, the determination of the source and course of inventive activities and technological innovation ultimately occupies the commanding height in the competing explanations of the Industrial Revolution. There is a clear consensus in the literature that while changes in the organization of production were important, in the final analysis it was the technological breakthroughs of the late eighteenth and nineteenth centuries that transformed British industry and society irrevocably and turned Britain into the workshop of the world. The most important area of disagreement in the literature is, therefore, how to explain the technological breakthroughs. As we have seen, there are two broad groups of explanation; one is based on autonomous internal forces in England and the other is centered on the impact of overseas trade. The former group contains two opposing views: One presents the technological innovations of the period as fortuitous developments unrelated to markets and trade, the manna-from-heaven view of technical change; while the other sees the changes in technology largely as a function of growing market demand, which was led by growing home consumption as opposed to expanding overseas demand.

Right from the start historians generally rejected the manna-from-heaven view of technical change during the Industrial Revolution. As previously shown, both Cunningham and Hobson, writing in the nineteenth century, anticipated Mokyr's argument based on evolutionary biology and rejected it. In more recent times, Eric Hobsbawn and David Landes, among others, have persistently attacked it.[145]

---

[145]   Eric J. Hobsbawn, "The General Crisis of the European Economy in the 17th Century," *Past & Present*, 5 (1954), pp. 33–53; 6 (1954), pp. 44–65 and *Industry and Empire* (London: Pelican Books, 1969). David S. Landes, *The Unbound Prometheus: Technological Change and Industrial Development in Western Europe from 1750 to the Present* (Cambridge: Cambridge University Press, 1969) and "The Fable of the Dead Horse; or, The Industrial Revolution Revisited," in Mokyr (ed.), *The British Industrial Revolution*, pp. 132–170.

The empirical evidence presented in Chapter 2 makes it hard to believe that technological change during the Industrial Revolution was a matter of chance. As shown, the major inventors were practical men searching for solutions to observed practical problems. For example, Abraham Darby, who invented the smelting of iron with mineral fuel, was an ironfounder making iron-cast pots. His invention resulted from his efforts to produce pig iron suitable for his own use. Also, Henry Cort, the inventor of the puddling process, was a Navy agent in London. His invention came from his efforts to procure high quality iron suitable for naval and ordnance purposes. The history of Boulton and the steam engine shows similar entrepreneurial connection with production and markets. What is more, the influence of the market is strongly indicated by the location of the major inventors' activities in regions where the main industrial sectors requiring the inventions had become comparatively large and were expanding more rapidly relative to other regions in England. Thus the major inventive activities connected with the iron industry were located in the West Midlands, with the exception of Henry Cort's work that was aimed at state demand and, therefore, located in London, the seat of the central government.

The contending arguments on whether trade stimulated technological change or accidental (exogenous) technical change propelled trade expansion can be assessed with the aid of available regional studies as presented in Chapter 2. As we have seen, technological innovation in woollen textile production occurred during the Industrial Revolution, mostly in the West Riding of Yorkshire. This is an important historical development whose implications for the debate on the causes and course of technological innovation during the Industrial Revolution have not been fully explored. We know that the main production centers for the woollen textile industry were for several centuries located in the southern counties in the West Country and East Anglia. It was only in the course of the eighteenth century that the West Riding emerged as the leading region in the production of woollen textiles in England as was shown earlier. The failure of the West Country and East Anglia to initiate technological change in the woollen textile industry, despite their domination of the industry for several centuries, is very pertinent to any assessment of the contending explanations. Even more pertinent are the factors behind the concentration of the industry in the West Riding and the course of output expansion in the region.

As we have seen, woollen textile production in the West Country and East Anglia stagnated in the eighteenth century, while it expanded in the West Riding. It was also shown earlier that the main reason for this differing regional experience was the success of the West Riding in taking export markets in Europe away from the southern counties and in securing rapidly growing markets in the Americas. Again, we saw that the superior export performance of the West Riding was due mainly to its superior export sales practice. The evidence shows clearly enough that several decades of overseas sales expansion and general growth of output and concentration of the industry in the region preceded the growth of technological innovation in woollen textile production in the West Riding. Thus, technological progress in the West Riding and its failure in the West Country and East Anglia can both be explained in market terms. Here we have a clear example of export-led technological progress, which is contrary to the technology-led trade expansion argued by Ralph Davis and Joel Mokyr that was presented earlier in this chapter.

In general, the debate on the relative contribution of domestic demand and overseas markets can also be confronted with the evidence from regional studies. The home market argument is usually conducted at the national level, with agricultural prosperity and population growth as its foundation. The national focus is completed when emphasis is placed on the national integration effects of investments in internal transportation improvements in the eighteenth century. The argument is that eighteenth-century investments in internal transportation improvements led to regional specialization, which widened the domestic market for regions with a competitive edge in particular industrial sectors. As expressed by Rick Szostak in an elaborate work on the subject:

While the role of market widening in the emergence of workshops can be questioned, it is clear that it played a key role in the process of regional specialization. Whereas previously high-cost producers had been able to maintain a hold on local markets due to the heavy expense of importing goods from elsewhere, now it was increasingly possible for low-cost regions to export their produce throughout the kingdom. . . . writers in both the primary and secondary literature attribute particular cases of regions losing or gaining particular industries to peculiar local causes. . . . However, the overriding reason for the concentration of various industries in particular regions during the eighteenth century is the drop in transport costs.[146]

Based on this assumption, Szostak heavily discounts the role of overseas trade and gives the pride of place to internal trade:

By concentrating on the internal transport networks of England and France, this work focuses on internal rather than external trade. I am in agreement with most of the modern literature and at least some contemporary writing in recognizing that it was the internal market that was of primary importance during this period. There had been a certain tendency in the literature to try to attribute a major role in the Industrial Revolution to English foreign trade. This tendency arose partly because international trade leaves better record for the historian rather than internal trade. Moreover, contemporary writers – especially those of mercantilist bent – tended to

---

[146] Rick Szostak, *The Role of Transportation in the Industrial Revolution: A Comparison of England and France* (Montreal & Kingston: McGill-Queen's University Press, 1991), pp. 12–13.

devote more of their energy to discussing foreign trade. Even some industrialists, such as Boulton and Wedgewood, spoke of their need for foreign markets, though they sold the bulk of their output within England. It is now commonly recognized that the links between foreign trade and industrialization are weak.[147]

But on what evidence does Szostak base his claim of the national integration and regional specialization effects of internal transport investments in the eighteenth century? As he admits:

In order to show that the market was widening in the eighteenth century, one would need evidence that particular goods from particular areas were circulated within a particular region in 1700, a larger region in 1750, and even larger region in 1800. Unfortunately, as Hey says about the Sheffield trades, 'The evidence for domestic sales is scrappy.' I have already noted that the greater availability of data on foreign trade has encouraged historians to underestimate the importance of the home market. The same paucity of data makes it extremely difficult to detail the expansion of the geographical market any producer deals with. There is some mention of people establishing relations in areas of the country with which they had not been in contact before. For example, in the cast iron trade, ironfounders ceased to deal with isolated regional markets but sold instead on a national basis. Such evidence, however, is fragmentary.[148]

Thus, by his own admission, Szostak's argument has no real empirical foundation. In fact, the argument is at variance with the evidence produced by regional studies as shown in Chapter 2. In the first place, as the evidence shows, the main effect of internal transportation investments in the eighteenth century was regional rather than national. John Langton's work in the 1980s, which generated further research on the subject, all of which are shown above, makes it clear that canal construction, by far the most important transportation investment during the period, created highly integrated regional economies in England, within which industrial producers operated largely in isolation from those in other regions, while at the same time competing in overseas markets. Again, as shown above, subsequent research, including a collective work sponsored by the Economic History Society and the Institute of British Geographers, all support Langton's main finding. This led to the report of the editors of *Atlas of Industrializing Britain, 1780–1914*, cited: "The flows of goods along the canals and turnpikes of Lancashire and Yorkshire are clearly greater than flows out of the region, *except for the export funnels of Liverpool and the Aire.*"[149] The evidence shows further that it was the nineteenth-century investment in railway construction that eventually destroyed regionalism and created an integrated national economy for the first time in England. Szostak seems to be unaware of these regional studies of the effects of eighteenth-century

---

[147]   Szostak, *The Role of Transportation*, pp. 44–45.
[148]   Szostak, *The Role of Transportation*, p. 98.
[149]   See footnote 213, Chapter 2. Emphasis added.

internal transportation investments, as there is no reference to any of them in his book.

Second, evidence from other regional studies, also presented above, shows that the regions in which revolutionary industrial development occurred in England between 1750 and 1850 were those that were heavily engaged in production for overseas markets – Lancashire, Yorkshire, and the West Midlands – and they sold a vastly greater proportion of their output overseas than they did in other regions in England. The case of the woollen textile industry already mentioned in this chapter shows clearly enough that success in overseas markets was the main factor behind the extraordinary performance of the leading regions in the Industrial Revolution, just as the loss of export markets was largely responsible for industrial stagnation in the West Country and East Anglia. As shown in Chapter 2, the West Riding took over markets in Europe from the West Country and East Anglia but did not displace them in their own regional home markets, which continued to provide outlets for their products. The connection of Lancashire cotton textile to overseas markets was even greater.

Third, evidence from regional studies also shows that the initial effects of population growth was regional rather than national. It is important to note at this point that population growth in England during the Industrial Revolution was a dependent rather than an independent variable. A summary of the evidence from recent research shows that changes in demographic behavior arising from growing employment opportunities in the non-agricultural sector, especially commerce and industry, were principally responsible for sustained population growth during the period.[150] This means that expanding overseas exports by creating more employment contributed to the growth of population and the expansion of the domestic market. This is why, as shown in Chapter 2, population growth in the main export producing and rapidly industrializing regions of the north of England – Lancashire and Yorkshire – was the fastest in the whole country. In this way, the fast growing regions largely created their own labor force through natural increase and did not depend in a significant way on net immigration from other regions in England.

Now if the rapidly industrializing regions of the north of England did not depend in a significant way on the other regions for their labor and for the sale of their products, then the home demand argument based on agricultural prosperity and population growth cannot stand. This is so, because, as shown in Chapter 2, agricultural prosperity during the period occurred in the southern counties where industrial production stagnated. This

[150] See Inikori, "Slavery and the Development of Industrial Capitalism in England," reprinted in Solow and Engerman (eds.), *British Capitalism and Caribbean Slavery*, pp. 89–91.

appears to confirm the argument of Patrick O'Brien, and of O'Brien and Engerman, all stated earlier in this chapter, that the growth of agricultural incomes contributed very little to increments in the purchase of industrial products between 1700 and 1802. This is not to say that the home market did not grow during the period or that its growth did not make an important contribution. What is needed is a proper understanding of the course and significance of the home market expansion.

The import of the evidence presented in Chapter 2 is that the expansion of entrepôt overseas trade and the growth of agricultural productivity between 1660 and 1730, while population stagnated, stimulated the growth of the domestic market for manufactured goods. Much of the increase was initially supplied with imported manufactures. But in due course import substitution industrialization displaced imported manufactures in the domestic market. Many counties in England were involved in the production of import-replacing products, whose sales were generally limited to local regional markets. In this process, regions with limited resources were compelled at an early date to pursue overseas markets aggressively. Aided by the successful imperial and commercial policies of the central government and by their own internal conditions, these regions secured large and growing overseas markets, which enabled them to grow much faster than other regions that continued to produce mainly for their regional domestic markets. The size of the market served and the pace of its growth also ensured that the principal export producing regions would initiate technological innovation, thereby increasing their competitive edge and further expanding their exports. As Maxine Berg and Pat Hudson have noted:

If the increase [in woollen textile production] had been uniform in all regions, it could have been achieved simply by the gradual extension of traditional commercial methods and production functions. But Yorkshire's intensive growth necessarily embodied a revolution in organization patterns, commercial links, credit relationships, the sorts of cloths produced, and production techniques. The external economies achieved when one region took over more than half of the production of an entire sector were also of key importance.[151]

Meanwhile, the lagging regions continued to serve the bulk of their own regional domestic markets, which grew albeit slowly. This means that the latter regions continued to maintain some level of vitality that was important in their ability to adjust quickly and effectively when the railways finally exposed them to direct competition with the leading regions in the nineteenth century.

---

[151]   Maxine Berg and Pat Hudson, "Rehabilitating the industrial revolution," *Economic History Review*, XLV, 1 (1992), p. 38.

A regional approach to the study of the Industrial Revolution thus makes for a better understanding of the relative contribution of overseas trade and the home market. Similarly, comparative regional studies shed considerable light on the Brenner's debate concerning the role of agrarian structure in West European economic development. As mentioned earlier in this chapter, Robert Brenner dismissed the importance of overseas trade in the Industrial Revolution and argued that the class structure produced by the development of capitalist agriculture in England in the fifteenth and sixteenth centuries was the principal cause. The main weakness of this argument, which has been attacked by several writers, is Brenner's presentation of class struggle as the main determinant of development without showing the factors in the historical process that produced the classes and over time changes in their relative strengths and weaknesses, as well as over time changes in the way the members of the classes perceived their self-interests. To show that agrarian class structure was not a sufficient condition for West European development, critics point to the similarity between England's agrarian structure and those of renaissance Italy and seventeenth-century Holland, countries where the agrarian class structures in question developed much earlier than in England without producing an industrial revolution.[152] What has been overlooked in this debate is evidence from regional studies in England that is even more helpful in clarifying the issues.

As shown in Chapter 2, regional studies by the main authorities all show unambiguously that much of the agrarian development in England between 1086 and 1660 was limited to counties in the South of England, that is, counties lying to the south of a line drawn from The Wash to the Severn estuary. It was in these counties of early settlement and population concentration that the combination of demography, foreign trade, and central government activities and policies produced a highly commercialized agrarian system and expanding proto-industrialization, especially the counties of East Anglia. For much of the period, the counties to the north remained agriculturally backward. This was even more so in Lancashire and Yorkshire. As earlier shown, feudal features still characterized the agrarian class structure of mid-Tudor Lancashire: "Local magnates retained considerable autonomy; some still exercised feudal rights of wardship and marriage over their tenants, and labor dues and payment in kind were widespread elements in the relationship between small farmers and their landlords."[153]

Now if Brenner's agrarian class structure were the principal cause of the Industrial Revolution, clearly the leading regions would have been in the South of England. But, as we have seen, it was agriculturally

[152] See Krantz and Hohenberg (eds.), *Failed Transitions to Modern Industrial Society*; Inikori, *Slavery and the Rise of Capitalism*; Hobsbawn, "The General Crisis of the European Economy."

[153] See footnote 79, Chapter 2.

backward Lancashire and Yorkshire that led the way, while East Anglia with its progressive agrarian class structure stagnated. Need we recall Arthur Lewis's point that backward social structures are whittled away over time when opportunities for growth are presented?: "The continuance of a social institution in a particular form depends upon its convenience, upon belief in its rectitude, and upon force. If growth begins to occur, all these sanctions are eroded. . . ."[154] This is not to argue, as Wrigley does, that the socio-economic and political changes between 1086 and 1776 – the organic economy period – were irrelevant to the Industrial Revolution, which created the inorganic economy.[155] As argued in Chapter 2, the long drawn-out institutional changes going back to the late Middle Ages were important in providing the political conditions for the development of the leading regions and in facilitating the quick spread of development from the leading to the lagging regions once the railways created an integrated national economy in the nineteenth century.

It is thus fair to say that in general the arguments and assertions of the proponents of the "Commercial Revolution" thesis are valid. What has been wanting is a detailed empirical and logical proof. What is new in the analysis presented so far is the employment of evidence from regional studies to offer such proof. Evidence from national output statistics and trade figures may help to further strengthen the proof.

Based on national estimates of industrial output, Crafts computed that increases in overseas sales accounted for 58 percent of the increments in British industrial output between 1700 and 1760 and between 1780 and 1800, respectively.[156] This is in general agreement with the result of the "taxonomic exercise" by O'Brien and Engerman stated earlier in this chapter. And they both agree with the evidence of Deane and Cole, also mentioned earlier, which shows that industries producing largely for exports grew much faster than those producing mainly for the home market during the period. The importance of this evidence in the explanation of the Industrial Revolution can only be appreciated fully when it is realized that the faster growth of overseas sales observed at the national level was in fact concentrated in key industrial sectors and in a few strategic regions. As noted earlier, the revolutionary impact of fast growing overseas sales, from the point of view of technological innovation, the reorganization of production, and similar other changes, was considerably greater than the national aggregate statistics indicate because of the sectoral and regional concentration.

One more aspect of the proof being constructed, which is demanded by the central theme of this study, is the geographical location of the main

---

[154]   Lewis, *Theory of Economic Growth*, p. 143; see quote on p. 17 this volume.
[155]   Wrigley, *Continuity, Chance and Change*.
[156]   Crafts, "British Economic Growth," pp. 197–198.

dynamic sector of British overseas trade during the period being examined. This is a relatively easy problem that can be resolved with the use of the available trade statistics. These show that between 1699/1701 and 1772/74, increased sales of English manufactures in Western Africa and the Americas accounted for 71.5 percent of the total increase in overseas sales of English manufactured goods; East India accounted for 11.8 percent; and Europe (including Ireland) accounted for the remaining 16.7 percent. The bulk of the increase in Europe came from southern Europe (mainly Portugal and Spain); sales in northern and northwest Europe actually declined absolutely during the period.[157] For the 20-year period 1784/86–1804/06, increased sales in Western Africa and the Americas accounted for 60 percent of the increases in British manufactures exported; Europe (including Ireland) accounted for 36.8 percent; and the Near East, Asia, and Australia accounted for the remaining 3.2 percent. And for the half century between 1804/06 and 1854/56, Western Africa and the Americas accounted for 29.7 percent, the Near East, Asia, and Australia for 47.9 percent, and Europe 22.4 percent of the increases in British export of manufactured goods overseas.[158] Thus, between 1699 and 1806, the growth of British overseas export of manufactures was virtually dependent on Western Africa and the Americas. The dependence was even greater than the figures indicate, because much of British exports to Portugal and Spain during the period (as is shown in the next chapter) depended on the colonial economies of Portuguese Brazil and Spanish America. In the half century that followed, Western Africa and the Americas continued to be important, but the most dynamic sector of British export trade had become Asia, Australia, and the Middle East, in that order. In Asia, India was particularly important. In the last period, markets outside Europe accounted for 77.6 percent of the increment in the sales of British manufactures overseas.

It is appropriate to end this chapter with a comparison of British import substitution industrialization and the more current experiences of the developing countries. The recently industrialized economies of Asia (often referred to as the Asian Tigers) share much in common with the British Industrial Revolution. Both industrialization processes started with import substitution. But unlike the import substitution strategy of many present day developing countries, the process in England and that of the Asian Tigers quickly moved into export-led growth as the limits of the narrow domestic market approached. What is more, just as the export pessimism and neoclassical formal growth theory of the 1950s and 1960s misdirected economists and historians away from outward-looking to inward-looking explanation of the Industrial Revolution between the 1950s and 1970s, so did the same circumstance prevent mainstream economists from observing

---

[157] Computed from Davis, "English Foreign Trade, 1700–1774," Table on p. 120.
[158] Computed from Davis, *The Industrial Revolution*, Table 38, p. 88.

the explosive export-led industrialization of the Asian Tigers in the 1960s and 1970s. Preoccupied with autonomous internal forces under conditions of autarky, economists saw little chance of growth in open economies, such as South Korea, Taiwan, Hong Kong, and Singapore. They predicted that economies, such as India, Brazil, and Mexico, with their autarkic industrialization processes, had the best chance of successfully completing their industrialization in the 1960s and 1970s: "The world of the 1960s was still convinced that the path to successful development lay with inward-looking import substitution rather than with more outward-looking export expansion."[159] Comparing the two sets of successful ISI processes and contrasting them with the failed processes of today and those of Italy and Holland in the more distant past, may help to bring out more sharply the critical role of overseas trade in the Industrial Revolution.

Recent studies have identified two types of ISI and their critical stages. The first is a process in which autarkic policies are pursued throughout and import substitution is followed to its ultimate end. This case shows four observable phases: 1) a period of primary-product export, usually raw materials or food or both, which helps to create a domestic market for manufactures, initially imported; 2) the production of import-replacing manufactures with the aid of a variety of state policies, the first stage of which is devoted to the production of consumer goods (ISI_1); 3) the extension of import substitution to consumer durables and intermediates (ISI_2); and 4) final extension of import substitution to capital goods (ISI_3). The second type combines autarkic import substitution with aggressive export promotion. The first two phases are exactly the same as in the first type, but in phases (3) and (4), rather than continuing to rely on autonomous internal forces, the expansion of manufactured exports takes the center stage: 3) growth of manufacturing output is led by exports of labor-intensive goods; 4) extension of import substitution to consumer durables, intermediates, and capital goods aimed primarily at export markets and, therefore, upgrading exports.[160]

As shown in Chapter 2, the industrialization process in England followed the second pattern. Of course, being the very first of its kind, it took a considerably long time to complete. In fact, the first major import substitution industry in England, the woollen textile industry, began its unbroken history in the fourteenth century, several centuries before the more broadly based ISI that started in the late seventeenth and early eighteenth centuries. But even so, the pattern fits very well the one described earlier: a long period

---

[159]   George Hicks, "Explaining The Success of the Four Little Dragons: A Survey," in Seiji Naya and Akira Takayama (eds.), *Economic Development in East and Southeast Asia: Essays in Honor of Professor Shinichi Ichimura* (Pasir Panjan, Singapore, and Honolulu, Hawaii: Institute of Southeast Asian Studies and East-West Center, 1990), pp. 21–22.

[160]   Stephan Haggard, *Pathways from the Periphery: The Politics of Growth in the Newly Industrializing Countries* (Ithaca, NY: Cornell University Press, 1990), p. 25.

of raw wool exports and imports of woollen manufactures preceded the establishment of the woollen textile industry in England, and within a few decades the growth of the industry became export-dependent and remained so into the eighteenth century and beyond; similarly, the broadly based ISI of the late seventeenth and early eighteenth centuries was preceded by the growth of primary exports (especially grains) and entrepôt overseas trade, and within a few decades the major import substitution industries (mainly textiles and metal ware) became largely dependent on overseas sales for their growth and development.

Of the more recent experiences of ISI, those of South Korea and Taiwan fit the second pattern previously described, and that of England, very closely. South Korea and Taiwan exported primary products from 1900 to 1945, went through the first stage of import substitution, 1945–64 for South Korea, and 1945–60 for Taiwan. As the limits of the pre-existing domestic market for consumer goods approached at the beginning of the 1960s, rather than move into ISI_2, they expanded the production of labor-intensive consumer goods, which they knew could only be sold overseas.[161] The export-led expansion of consumer goods production that resulted created the proper market size and the competitive incentive for widespread technological innovation in consumer goods production and for the establishment of import substitution industries in consumer durables, intermediates, and capital goods. The latter industrial sectors also became export-dependent as the structure of manufactured exports was transformed over time.

The first type of ISI was followed by India and most Latin American countries, especially Brazil and Mexico. From the sixteenth to the beginning of the twentieth century, Brazil was a major exporter of primary products – sugar in the sixteenth and seventeenth centuries and coffee in the nineteenth. But the devastating social and political consequences of the collapse of the international economy, following the two world wars and the Great Depression, provoked export pessimism in Brazil, leading to a faithful pursuit of autarkic ISI in all its stages from the 1930s. Not until the 1970s did the slow pace of autarkic industrialization compel efforts to promote export expansion. Every one of the developing countries that followed this pattern of industrialization, including India, has come out with a long-term dismal performance. Those that made a bold shift to export promotion, such as Brazil, depending on the timing and the condition of the international economy, have achieved some impressive positive change in their performance in recent years.[162]

Table 3.1 presents a comparative view of the industrialization process in three countries – England, South Korea, and Brazil – that are reasonably

---

[161]   Haggard, *Pathways from the Periphery*, pp. 23–29.
[162]   Bela Balassa, *The Process of Industrial Development and Alternative Development Strategies* (Princeton, NJ: Princeton University, Department of Economics, International Finance Section, 1981), pp. 17–18.

Table 3.1. *Trade and Comparative Performance of Import Substitution Industrialization Strategies* (current price, £ sterling for England, U.S.$ for others)

	England				South Korea				Brazil			
	1700	1760	1801	1851	1960	1970	1980	1990	1960	1970	1980	1990
Population (in millions)	5.1	6.1	8.7	16.7	25.0	32.2	38.1	42.8	72.6	95.8	121.3	150.4
Gross Domestic Product (in millions)	54.4	66.8	198.6	446.6	3,810	8,887	58,250	236,400	24,080	35,546	237,930	414,060
GDP Per Capita	10.7	11	22.8	26.7	152	276	1,529	5,523	332	371	1,962	2,753
Industrial Product (in millions)	10.3	15.5	54.3	179.5	762	2,577	25,882.5	106,380	8,428	13,507	88,034	161,483
Export of Industrial Product (in millions)	3.8	8.3	28.4	67.3	14.4	975.7	15,968.7	62,243.5	142.0	709.9	10,065.5	21,557.7
Percentage of Industrial Product Exported	36.9	53.5	52.3	37.5	1.9	37.9	61.7	58.5	1.7	5.3	11.4	13.3
Industrial Product Per Capita	2	2.5	6.2	10.7	30.5	80	679.3	2,485.5	116.1	141.0	725.8	1,073.7

Sources and notes: For England, the population figures are from Wrigley and Schofield, *Population History*, pp. 208 and 209; the GDP figures are from Crafts, *British Economic Growth*, p. 13 (the 1700 figure is for 1688), except the figure for 1851 taken from Deane and Cole, *British Economic Growth*, p. 166, scaling down the figure for Great Britain by applying the ratio of England's to Britain's income in 1801; the Industrial Product and Industrial Export are from Crafts, *British Economic Growth*, p. 132 (the figures are for Great Britain); Crafts's figures for Gross Industrial Product (GIP) have been reduced to value added, using his ratio of 1.52, for purposes of comparison with the figures for South Korea and Brazil. For South Korea, the population figures are from Andrew Mason and Lee-Jay Cho, "Population Policy," in Lee-Jay Cho and Yoon Hyung Kim (eds.), *Economic Development in the Republic of Korea: A Policy Perspective* (Honolulu, Hawaii: East-West Center, 1991), p. 304, and World Bank, *World Development Report* (New York: Oxford University Press, 1992), p. 219; the figures for GDP, Industrial Product, and Industrial Product Export are computed from World Bank, *World Development Report*, 1982, 1983, 1992, and 1994 (the export figure for 1960 was computed by applying the percentages in the structure of merchandise export (*World Development Report*, 1982, p. 127) to the value of merchandise export taken from David C. Cole and Princeton N. Lyman, *Korean Development: The Interplay of Politics and Economics* (Cambridge, Mass.: Harvard University Press, 1971), p. 134, and that for 1970 is the annual average for 1970–72, computed from Paul W. Kuznets, *Economic Growth and Structure in the Republic of Korea* (New Haven: Yale University Press, 1977), p. 70). For Brazil, the population figures are from Benjamin Keen and Mark Wasserman, *A History of Latin America* (3rd edition, Boston: Houghton Mifflin, 1988), p. 572, and World Bank, *World Development Report*, 1992, p. 219; the figures for Gross Domestic Product (GDP), Industrial Product, and Industrial Product Export are computed from World Bank, *World Development Report*, 1982, 1983, 1992, and 1994 (the export figures for 1960 and 1970 are computed with figures taken from World Development Report, 1994, p. 191, and Victor Bulmer-Thomas, *The Economic History of Latin America Since Independence* (Cambridge: Cambridge University Press, 1994), p. 331). The Industrial Product Exports include manufactures, fuels, minerals, and metals.

representative of the patterns discussed in the preceding paragraphs. Because of the huge differences in prices, the English values are not directly comparable to those of South Korea and Brazil. But the percentages can be compared. As can be seen, a large proportion of the industrial product in England was exported quite early in the process, 36.9 percent, compared with 1.9 percent for South Korea in 1960. This is largely due to the English woollen textile industry whose import substitution development was completed several centuries earlier, as already stated. Other than this, the proportions of the industrial product exported in both countries during comparable periods are quite similar. On the other hand, the contrast with Brazil is very clear. After about 30 years of industrialization, only 1.7 percent of the industrial product in Brazil was exported in 1960, and 10 years later, only 5.3 percent in 1970, as compared with 37.9 percent for South Korea in the same year and 53.5 percent for England in 1760, a roughly comparable stage of industrialization.[163] The proportion of the industrial product exported in Brazil has increased considerably since the 1970s, following the adoption of export promotion. But it still remains very low when compared with South Korea in the same years and with England in comparable years.

The degree and pace of expansion of export production are clearly reflected in the overall growth of industrial output and industrial product per capita, as shown in Table 3.1. The industrial product of Brazil was roughly 11 times that of South Korea in 1960, but by 1990 it was less than two times, and in 1993 the two were almost equal – $164,356 million for Brazil and $142,257 million for South Korea.[164] A more realistic comparison is the industrial product per capita. This is a more accurate measure of the degree of industrialization. As can be seen, that of Brazil was about three times that of South Korea in 1960, but by 1990 South Korea's industrial product per capita was more than twice that of Brazil, and in 1993, it was more than three times – $3,226 for South Korea and $1,050 for Brazil[165] – a complete reversal of positions in just 33 years. All of these are, again, captured by changes in GDP per capita, with South Korea about one-half of Brazil in 1960, and Brazil about one-half of South Korea in 1990 and much less than one-half in 1993 – $7,660 for South Korea and $2,930 for Brazil.[166]

---

[163] Published World Bank figures for Korea and Brazil show gross values for exported manufactures and value added for total industrial product. The English figures in Table 3.1 are presented in the same way to make them comparable. The export percentages will be lower if exports and total industrial product are expressed in the same value.

[164] For the 1993 figures, see World Bank, *World Development Report* (New York: Oxford University Press, 1995), p. 167.

[165] Computed from World Bank, *World Development Report*, 1995, pp. 163 and 167.

[166] *Ibid.*, p. 163.

One major contributory factor in the differing experiences just shown is the extent of utilization of resources, especially labor, but also natural resources in many instances. Sustained expansion of manufactured exports led to very low overall unemployment rates in South Korea, 8.2 percent in 1963, 4.5 in 1970, 5.2 in 1980, and 2.4 in 1991, as compared with Brazil where the unemployment and underemployment rate has been generally over one-third.[167] Yet, Brazil is one of the better cases among the uncompleted industrialization processes of our contemporary times. Taken together with the unsuccessful processes in renaissance Italy and seventeenth-century Holland, what comes out is that sustained expansion of manufactured exports or lack of it could ultimately make the difference between completion and non-completion of the industrialization process. It is significant that the only truly successful cases of industrialization since the 1950s have been export-led. As the proportions of industrial output exported during comparable stages of industrialization show, industrialization in England and in South Korea can both be validly described as export-led. England secured, largely through her naval superiority, a disproportionate share of world trade centered around the rapidly growing commerce of the Atlantic world from the sixteenth to the nineteenth century. Similarly, South Korea and the other Asian Tigers secured, under different circumstances, a disproportionate share of world commerce between the 1960s and 1980s, relative to other developing countries of the time. Aided by the United States and Japan,[168] and compelled by limited natural and abundant human resources, South Korea pursued aggressive export expansion at a time when autarkic industrialization was favored by economists and most developing countries. This enabled South Korea, and also the other Asian Tigers, to capture a relatively large share of world trade, which grew at a rate of 8 percent per annum during the period. Yet, it can be argued that the role of overseas trade in the transformation of the English economy and society was even greater than was the case in South Korea. As shown in Chapter 2, the development process in England was led in an unbroken manner by overseas trade right from medieval times to the nineteenth century, as compared with the rather short period for South Korea and the other Asian Tigers.

[167]   Cho Soon, *The Dynamics of Korean Economic Development* (Washington, DC: Institute of International Economics, 1994), p. 19; Victor Bulmer-Thomas, *The Economic History of Latin America Since Independence* (Cambridge: Cambridge University Press, 1994), p. 312.

[168]   Jacques Hersh, *The USA and the Rise of East Asia since 1945: Dilemmas of the Postwar International Political Economy* (London: Macmillan, 1993), pp. 39–73.

4

Slave-Based Commodity Production and the Growth of Atlantic Commerce

THE EVIDENCE PRESENTED in the two preceding chapters makes it clear enough that the Industrial Revolution in England was the first example of trade-led economic development, and that the sources of trade expansion, or the "Commercial Revolution," which propelled the process to higher grounds in the seventeenth and eighteenth centuries, were located in the Atlantic world. The task in this chapter is to show the factors that made possible the expansion of Atlantic commerce between 1500 and 1850. For this purpose, it is pertinent to examine the state of trade and production in the major regions of the Atlantic world in the middle decades of the fifteenth century before the establishment of regular seaborne contact across the Atlantic. This exercise helps to show the factors which operated to promote or constrain the growth of trade in the major regions of the Atlantic in the centuries preceding the development of multilateral trade across the Atlantic. It is argued that in the centuries or decades preceding the opening up of the Atlantic to regular seaborne commerce, the main constraint to the growth of production and consumption in the individual regions was limited opportunity to trade. In turn, limited opportunity to trade resulted from several factors – the range of resources in each region of the Atlantic; the level of development of the division of labor (local, regional, and international); inland transportation costs; and government trade policies. Each of these is examined briefly to present a context for the analysis of the factors that facilitated the growth of Atlantic commerce between 1500 and 1850. The factors analyzed include the extension of the production and consumption possibility frontier as a result of the integration of the Atlantic world into a quasi common market for production and trade; the widening of the range of resources and products that followed; the income and trade effects of the new products via the vent-for-surplus mechanism; and the income and price effects of specialization and production re-organization. It is demonstrated that, in the final analysis, all of these developments depended on the forced specialization of enslaved Africans and their descendants in large-scale production of commodities for Atlantic commerce in the Americas at a time when demographic, socio-economic and political conditions generally favored small-scale subsistence production by independent, uncoerced producers.

The terms Atlantic World and Atlantic basin are used interchangeably in this study to define a geographical area that includes Western Europe (Italy, Spain, Portugal, France, Switzerland, Austria, Germany, the Netherlands, Belgium, Britain, and Ireland), Western Africa (from Mauritania in the northwest to Namibia in the southwest, comprising the two modern regions of West Africa and West-Central Africa), and the Americas (comprising all the countries of modern Latin America and the Caribbean, the United States of America, and Canada). Modern historians frequently study the economic history of the main regions of the Atlantic world as self-contained and unconnected units. The role of the Americas in the development process in Western Europe – the closest to a study of inter-connected development process – has been debated mainly in terms of the isolated relationship between the individual national economies of the imperial nations of Western Europe and their American colonies.[1] The fact that the Atlantic World developed from the sixteenth century as a quasi common market, with inter-connected linkages to the development process in each national or regional economy in the basin, is not generally realized. The first elaborate study that came closest to this fact was by Ralph Davis. The title of his book, *The Rise of the Atlantic Economies*, gives the impression that the Atlantic basin has been studied as a complex economic unit in a process of development over time. However, that is not the real focus of the book. Davis, whose early works strongly argued the critical role of the British American colonies in the Industrial Revolution, turned full circle in the 1970s and argued, as noted earlier, that "the main influences on European economic development arose within the countries of Europe themselves," which, therefore, freed him from the need to study inter-connections between the economies of the three broad regions of the Atlantic basin.[2] Consequently, *The Rise of the Atlantic Economies* is basically a story of the independent rise of the national or regional economies of the Atlantic World, in which the economies of Western Africa are not even included. The narrative and analysis in this chapter are intended to demonstrate, among other things, the strong linkages that existed between the economies

[1] Williams, *Capitalism and Slavery*; James, *The Black Jacobins*; Davies, "Essays in Bibliography and Criticism"; Anstey, "Capitalism and Slavery"; Engerman, "The Slave Trade and British Capital Formation"; Sheridan, "The Wealth of Jamaica in the Eighteenth Century"; Thomas, "The Sugar Colonies of the Old Empire"; Sheridan, "A Rejoinder."

[2] Davis, *The Rise of the Atlantic Economies*, p. xi.

of the Atlantic basin as slave-based Atlantic commerce expanded in the three and a half centuries from 1500 to 1850.

4.1 TRADE AND PRODUCTION IN THE ATLANTIC BASIN ECONOMIES IN THE FIFTEENTH CENTURY

Before the middle decades of the fifteenth century, the three broad regions of the Atlantic basin – Western Europe, Western Africa, and the Americas – operated in isolation from one another, although there were indirect trade relations between Western Europe and Western Africa through the merchants of the Middle East and North Africa. The Atlantic Ocean was then a relatively quiet sea, the Mediterranean being the main center of seaborne international trade in the world at the time.[3] Also at this time, the Atlantic basin economies were all pre-industrial and pre-capitalist. The vast majority of the populations on both sides of the Atlantic (East and West) were engaged in subsistence agricultural production (that is, the bulk of the agricultural output was consumed directly by the producers and not exchanged on the market). Elaborate craft production, which was largely part of agriculture for all practical purposes, also existed in the economies, making it possible for the basic needs of the people to be met by each of the three broad regional economies. The main elements that set them apart, at this time, were in the area of market and socio-political development; and the driving factors that determined the relative levels of market development were population growth and access to the main currents of international trade centered in the Mediterranean.

Population estimates in the three regions of the Atlantic, with varying degrees of uncertainty, indicate that Western Europe reached relatively high average densities very much earlier than the other regions. The available figures show that as early as 1200, Western Europe already had about 61 million people, increasing to 73 million by 1300. As a result of the general crisis of the fourteenth century, which peaked in mid-century with the Black Death, the numbers went down to 45 million in 1400, before resuming another round of growth, reaching 60 million in 1450 and 78 million in 1550.[4] With a total area of approximately 898,804 square miles,[5] these figures give average population densities for Western Europe of roughly 68 persons per square mile in 1200, 81 in 1300, 67 in 1450, and 87 in 1550.

[3]   Abu-Lughod, *Before European Hegemony*.
[4]   North and Thomas, *The Rise of the Western World*, p. 71.
[5]   Computed from Wrigley, "The Growth of Population in Eighteenth-Century England," p. 121. Wrigley says that the area of England, 50,333 square miles, represents 5.6 percent of the total area of Western Europe, as defined earlier in this chapter. The figure of 898,804 square miles is derived from this statement.

Because the population was not evenly distributed, certain areas had much greater densities than the average. The most densely populated areas were in northern Italy, where Florence had about 200 persons per square mile in mid-century; several great cities of Italy had total populations ranging from 100,000 to 200,000 in the early fourteenth century.[6]

Considerable controversy surrounds estimates of the populations of Western Africa and the Americas in the fifteenth century. Extrapolating backwards from colonial censuses and employing questionable assumptions on the impact of the Atlantic slave trade, John Caldwell estimated the total population of Africa in 1500 to be 47 million.[7] This is an extremely small population for a huge continent with a total area of 11.5 million square miles.[8] If the figure is assigned to West Africa alone, with an area of 2.4 million square miles,[9] the density in 1500 will be approximately 20 persons per square mile; if it is assigned to Central Africa alone, with 3 million square miles,[10] the density is only 16 persons per square mile; assigning it to both regions only, the density is 9 persons per square mile. Yet West Africa and Central Africa constitute less than one-half of the area of the African continent. From what is known of Africa's sociopolitical organization, agriculture, and land-use pattern, the continent's population must have been considerably greater than 47 million in 1500. In fact, before the Black Death reached Egypt, there were about eight million people in that country alone in 1345.[11] Based on various documents, including accounts by Arab travelers, Niane estimated that the total population of Africa in the sixteenth century was about 200 million; the population of the Mali empire in the middle of the fifteenth century is put at between 40 million and 50 million.[12] If Niane's figure for all Africa is assigned to West Africa and Central Africa only, the average density will be 37 persons per square mile.

[6]   North and Thomas, *The Rise of the Western World*, p. 47; Abu-Lughod, *Before European Hegemony*, p. 125.

[7]   John C. Caldwell, "The Social Repercussions of Colonial Rule: Demographic Aspects," in A. Adu Boahen (ed.), *UNESCO General History of Africa, Volume VII, Africa Under Colonial Domination 1880–1935* (Berkeley, California: Heinemann, UNESCO, 1985), p. 483.

[8]   Donald G. Morrison, *Understanding Black Africa: Data and Analysis of Social Change and Nation Building* (New York: Paragon, Irvington, 1989), p. 3.

[9]   Akin Mabogunje, "The Land and Peoples of West Africa," in J. F. Ade Ajayi and Michael Crowder (eds.), *History of West Africa*, Vol. I (London: Longman, 1971), p. 1.

[10] David Birmingham and Phyllis M. Martin (eds.), *History of Central Africa*, Vol. I (London: Longman, 1983), p. viii.

[11] Abu-Lughod, *Before European Hegemony*, p. 238.

[12] D. T. Niane, "Mali and the Second Mandingo expansion" and "Conclusion," both in D. T. Niane (ed.), *UNESCO General History of Africa. IV, Africa from the twelfth to the sixteenth century* (Berkeley: California, Heinemann, UNESCO, 1984), pp. 156 and 684.

Thus, assigning it to Africa as a whole and excluding the areas of desert, that figure does not seem unreasonably large. However, using a modified form of Caldwell's procedure, Patrick Manning estimated the total population of the coastal areas of Western Africa to be 22.7 million in 1850.[13] He stated in a later work that the population of the western coast of Africa in 1700 was about 25 million and that of the Savanna region of sub-Saharan Africa and the Horn was about 20 million.[14] Under Manning's view of the impact of the Atlantic slave trade, the population of the western coast of Africa in the fifteenth century would be about the same as that of 1700, that is, 25 million. Assuming from the reading of Manning that the area of the western coast is one-half of that of West Africa and Central Africa combined, we get an average population density of approximately 9 persons per square mile for Western Africa in the fifteenth century. This seems rather low. We may settle for a figure somewhere between Manning and Niane, but closer to Niane, say, an overall average of 20 persons per square mile (excluding the areas covered by deserts), reaching 40 or more in the more densely populated areas, particularly in West Africa.

Similar disagreements surround the estimates for the Americas. A summary of the literature, in the form of a synthesis, puts the total population of all the Americas in the late fifteenth century at 57.3 million, distributed in percentages as follows: North America 7.7; Mexico 37.3; Central America 9.9; the Caribbean 10.2; the Andes 20.1; Lowland South America 14.8.[15] Whatever one makes of the conflicting figures, the indication is that extremely low population densities characterized the territories of the Americas in the late fifteenth century. In fact, if we relate the above late fifteenth-century figures (about 53 million for Mexico and the rest of Latin America and the Caribbean) to the area of the region, 20.5 million square kilometers,[16] the average density comes to 2.6 persons per square kilometer (about 6.7 per square mile).

The operation of these differing population densities, in conjunction with differences in other factors, such as geography and access to overseas trade, meant that market institutions and socio-political organizations reached differing levels of development in the three broad regions of the Atlantic by the fifteenth century. In Western Europe, continuous growth of population

---

[13]   Patrick Manning, "The Impact of Slave Trade Exports on the Population of the Western Coast of Africa, 1700–1850," in Serge Daget (ed.), *De La Traite à L'Esclavage: Actes du Colloque International sur la traite des Noirs, Nantes 1985*, Vol. II (Paris: Societé Française D' Histoire D'Outre-Mer, 1988), p. 123.

[14]   Patrick Manning, *Slavery and African Life: Occidental, Oriental, and African Slave Trades* (Cambridge: Cambridge University Press, 1990), p. 82.

[15]   James Lockhart and Stuart B. Schwartz, *Early Latin America: A History of Colonial Spanish America and Brazil* (Cambridge: Cambridge University Press, 1983), p. 36.

[16]   World Bank, *World Development Report: Workers in an Integrating World* (New York: Oxford University Press, 1995), p. 163.

before the Black Death led to the movement of population from centers of early settlement to unsettled or lightly settled regions in a process of internal colonization. This population expansion and internal colonization stimulated the growth of local and inter-regional trade, the mechanism of which was the differing resource endowments of the old and new regions of settlement.[17] The Low Countries (the Netherlands and Belgium) and Italy became major centers of manufacturing; so too were several German city-states. Initially, as stated earlier, England specialized in the production of raw materials, especially raw wool, for export to the continent in exchange for manufactures. By the fifteenth century, however, England had become a major producer of woollen textiles, the bulk of which was exported to continental consumers.

In addition to the growing internal trade, Western Europe was also drawn into the international trade of the Mediterranean, led by the merchants of the Italian city-states. Abu-Lughod has described the network of international trade that radiated from the Mediterranean in the first half of the last millennium as a world system. One may object to that characterization on several counts. However, for the purpose of this study, that issue is not important. Suffice it to say that by the standard of the time the international trade based in the Mediterranean world was quite large. Western Europe was drawn into it initially through the Crusades in the twelfth and early thirteenth centuries. The merchants of the Italian city-states became some of its leading traders, making Italy one of the major economic zones of Europe at the time. The other major economic zone of Europe during the period was the Low Countries, whose manufacturing and trading cities constituted important links between other regions of Western Europe and the Mediterranean trading network. The main product of Western Europe in the trade was woollen cloth, which was exchanged for Oriental products, such as spices and silk.[18] Southern England also became an important part of this trade through its export of raw wool to the Low Countries. Through the international trade of the Mediterranean world Western Europe had access to gold imports from Western Africa, which contributed significantly to the amount of money in circulation. The combined force of the international and inter-regional trade led to growing commercialization of socio-economic life in much of Western Europe by the fifteenth century, particularly in Italy, the Netherlands, and England.

In Western Africa, a considerable amount of trade also developed during the same period, especially in West Africa. Geographically based resources were traded between the savanna and forest communities; and the gold trade across the Sahara stimulated a considerable amount of internal trade within West Africa. It is estimated that the trans-Saharan trade to the

---

[17]   North and Thomas, *The Rise of the Western World*; North, *Structure and Change*.
[18]   Abu-Lughod, *Before European Hegemony*, pp. 55–77, 120–125.

Mediterranean world exported from West Africa an annual average of between half and one and a half tons of gold in the 680 years from 800 A. D. to 1490.[19] The extent of market transaction in the economies of West Africa in the early years of their contact with European traders is reflected by the structure of their imports. Ongoing research indicates that the imports in the initial years were overwhelmingly in the form of money, such as cowries. This is an indication of growing market transactions, which needed an expanding medium of exchange. However, the much lower population densities in Western Africa, in addition to problems of physical geography and disadvantageous location in relation to the major center of trade at the time – the Mediterranean – meant that market developments were at a much lower level in the fifteenth century than in Western Europe.[20] In fact, in several areas of West-Central Africa where population densities were generally about 4 persons per square mile by 1400, it has been said that hunting and gathering were still providing about 60 percent of the people's food in the fifteenth century, even though agriculture was already well developed.[21]

Market developments were even at much lower levels still in the Americas. Added to the problem of extremely low population densities were

[19]   Ralph A. Austen, "Marginalization, stagnation, and growth: The Trans-Saharan caravan trade in the era of European expansion, 1500–1900," in James D. Tracy (ed.), *The Rise of Merchant Empires: Long-Distance Trade in the Early Modern World, 1350–1750* (Cambridge: Cambridge University Press, 1990), pp. 318–319. See also D. T. Niane, "Relationships and exchanges among the different regions," in Niane (ed.), *UNESCO General History*, pp. 614–634, and J. Devisse and S. Labib, "Africa in inter-continental relations," in Niane (ed.), *UNESCO General History*, pp. 635–672.

[20]   Abu-Lughod does not include sub-Saharan Africa in the eight circuits making up her thirteenth-century world system. As she explains: "For the same reason that I ignore Spain, Germany, Baltic Russia, Dalmatia, and Africa south of the Sahara in Part I, even though they contributed important resources to the circuit, I reluctantly omit East Africa from Part II. Without any doubt, the coastal zones of current-day Ethiopia, Kenya, Tanzania, and of insular Madagascar were integrated in trade with Egypt, Aden, Basra, Hormuz, and even Gujarat on the Indian subcontinent. Contact among these places was intense. But Africa's geographic reach was relatively limited. African merchants were largely local and African goods seldom made their way to China or Europe. (. . . the Chinese pottery shards that litter the East African coast turn out to be mainly ballast brought in Arab and Gujarat ships)." Abu-Lughod, *Before European Hegemony*, p. 36. Specialists are likely to find much of this objectionable. In fact, one can observe some flaws in the statement. For example, if Chinese and Indian ships came to the East African coast in ballast, as she says, that is no proof that those ships did not carry African products back to China and India as she states. However, one can agree with her that the participation of sub-Saharan Africa in the network of trade radiating from the Mediterranean in the first half of the last millennium was comparatively limited.

[21]   Jan Vansina, *Paths in the Rainforests: Toward A History of Political Tradition in Equatorial Africa* (London: James Currey, 1990), pp. 83, 98, 215.

serious difficulties of physical geography. The major centers of population concentration in Mexico, Central America, and the Andean valleys were separated from each other by high mountains and dense forests. Hence, there was very little contact between these population centers. What is more, isolation from the rest of the world meant that the Americas had no access to the trading opportunities in the Old World that would have given commercial value to the vast natural resources of the region. Given this situation, the economies of the Americas were overwhelmingly dominated by subsistence production in the late fifteenth century. Even in the major centers of population where elaborate state systems developed – the Inca, Aztec, and Maya state systems – redistributive exchange through the state was far more important than market exchange.[22]

Thus a major factor constraining economic development in large areas of the Atlantic basin in the fifteenth century was limited opportunity to trade. Even in Western Europe, where trade had grown most considerably, trading opportunities had become increasingly limited by the sixteenth century. In the first place, inadequate local resources did not permit overall population size to go beyond a certain level, as the crisis of the fourteenth century shows. Secondly, the Mediterranean-based network of international trade, of which Western Europe had been an important part since the twelfth century, began to decline after the Black Death and "by the late fifteenth century, only small parts of it retained their former vigor."[23] Thirdly, the growth of nation-states in the fifteenth and sixteenth centuries, none of which was powerful enough to impose its will on the others, led to an atomistic competition for resources among the states of Western Europe.[24] This further limited trading opportunities within Western Europe as competition among the nation-states tended to encourage the growth of self-sufficiency, each state employing protective measures to stimulate domestic industrial production. Charles Wilson has noted that the policies of economic nationalism pursued by the rising states of Modern Europe, generally known as mercantilism, had their roots in the late Middle Ages:

Nothing was more characteristic of the 'mercantile system' than the attention given by thinkers, administrators, and legislators to reserving supplies of English wool for the use of the English cloth industry. . . . Trade and industrial interests combined with fiscal need to fashion a system of industrial protection – a ban on imported woollen manufactures – with prohibitions on the export of wool. . . . The scarcity of precious metals in the later Middle Ages led one state after another to interfere with their export. . . . The Italians, Hanseatic, and Flemish cities all developed their

---

[22] Arthur Morris, *Latin America: Economic Development and Regional Differentiation* (London: Hutchinson, 1981), p. 55.

[23] Abu-Lughod, *Before European Hegemony*, p. 356.

[24] Nathan Rosenberg and L. E. Birdzell, Jr., *How the West Grew Rich: The Economic Transformation of the Industrial World* (New York: Basic Books, 1986).

own versions of a 'navigation code' restricting their merchants' use of foreign shipping. In Germany the cities regularly carried on a battle against the surrounding countryside for the control of food and industrial raw materials. . . . In France, by contrast, the consciousness of the national implications of economic policy is early and pervasive.[25]

In the course of the sixteenth century these policies were formalized, with their emphasis on the balance of trade. In the seventeenth and eighteenth centuries, they were further extended and consolidated, severely limiting the growth of trade, based on European products, among West European nations. Because of its geographical size and the extent of its human and natural resources, policies aimed at national self-sufficiency were most elaborately developed in France. They reached their highest level of development under Colbert in the seventeenth century. Charles Wilson has traced the development of the English system from 1620 to 1720, while Ralph Davis examined the rise of protection in England from 1689 to 1786.[26] It was these restrictive practices, together with the other factors limiting trading opportunities in Western Europe – in particular, the problem of inland transportation cost in pre-industrial economies – that led to the general crisis of the seventeenth century.[27]

4.2 EXPLORATION, COMMODITY PRODUCTION AND ATLANTIC COMMERCE

In some important sense, it can be argued that the movement of Europeans into the Atlantic, where commodity production offered immense opportunities for trade expansion, was initially triggered by the diminishing extent of the market accessible to European traders and producers. The expansion of trade and the growing commercialization of socio-economic life in Western Europe in the late Middle Ages had given rise to influential merchant classes. As trading opportunities ceased to expand after the Black Death, the interests of the merchant class coincided with the growing needs of the rising states for revenue from trade to provide a major push for trade motivated exploration of the then less known world. This began with the activities of the Portuguese and the Spaniards in nearby Atlantic islands –

---

[25] Charles Wilson, "Trade, Society and the State," in E. E. Rich and C. H. Wilson (eds.), *The Cambridge Economic History of Europe, Volume IV: The Economy of Expanding Europe in the Sixteenth and Seventeenth Centuries* (Cambridge: Cambridge University Press, 1967), pp. 496–497.

[26] Wilson, "Trade, Society and the State," pp. 515–530; Ralph Davis, "The Rise of Protection in England, 1689–1786," *Economic History Review*, XIX, No. 2 (August, 1966), pp. 306–317.

[27] Trevor Aston (ed.), *Crisis in Europe, 1560–1660: Essays from Past and Present* (London: Routledge & Kegan Paul, 1965).

the Azores, Madeira, and the Canary Islands. Islands off the coast of Western Africa – the Cape Verde Islands and Sao Tomé – were added subsequently. It was in these islands that the social and economic structures that would transform the Atlantic into the nucleus of our contemporary world market first took shape.

The main product produced and traded in these islands was sugar. Madeira was the first Atlantic island to develop large-scale sugar production in slave plantations. Island natives from the Canary Islands initially provided the source of slave labor. Subsequently, the supply shifted to the African coast. By the late fifteenth century Madeira had become the largest single supplier of sugar to Europe. The Canary Islands took over the lead in the early decades of the sixteenth century, again on the basis of African slave labor. The third Atlantic island to get into sugar production on a large scale in these early years was Sao Tomé, off the coast of Western Africa. Like Madeira and the Canary Islands, the sugar plantations were worked by African slaves. In the 1550s the island had 60 sugar mills and 2,000 plantation slaves.[28]

Supplying slaves to these island plantations and to estates in Southern Europe and distributing the slave-produced sugar to European consumers were important parts of the developing Atlantic commerce of the fifteenth and sixteenth centuries. However, the most important product, by value, for Atlantic commerce in the fifteenth and early sixteenth centuries was gold. For centuries Western Europe had depended on Muslim traders in North Africa for the gold that came from Africa. It is generally believed that the quest for gold was a major motive in the exploration of Africa by the Portuguese.[29] Existing estimates, with uncertain magnitude of error, suggest that between 1480 and 1720, an annual average of 0.7–1.7 metric tons of gold was exported to Europe from the coast of West Africa.[30] Other

---

[28] Herbert S. Klein, *African Slavery in Latin America and the Caribbean* (Oxford: Oxford University Press, 1986), pp. 18–20; Devisse and Labib, "Africa in inter-continental relations," pp. 645–646.

[29] John W. Blake, *West Africa, the quest for God and Gold, 1454–1578: A Survey of the First Century of White enterprise in West Africa, with particular reference to the achievement of the Portuguese and their rivalries with other European Powers* (London: Curzon Press, 1977; first published 1937); Devisse and Labib, "Africa in inter-continental relations," pp. 648–650.

[30] Austen, "Marginalization, Stagnation, and Growth," pp. 318 and 319. Richard Bean estimated that the average annual value of gold exported by sea from Western Africa between 1500 and 1700 was £200,000, while Ernst van den Boogaart argues that the annual average for the seventeenth century was only 4,250 marks at £32 per mark of gold (that is, £136,000): Richard Bean, "A Note on the Relative Importance of Slaves and Gold in Western African Exports," *Journal of African History*, XV (1974), pp. 351–356; Ernst van den Boogaart, "The Trade between Western Africa and the Atlantic World, 1600–90: Estimates of Trends in Composition and Value," *Journal of African History*, 33 (1992), p. 380.

African products, such as ivory and pepper, added to the volume and value of Atlantic commerce at this time. French, English, and Dutch traders soon joined the Portuguese. They all made efforts to discover products that could be produced in Western Africa for which markets could be found in Europe. The Portuguese endeavored to christianize and develop the Kingdom of Kongo in West-Central Africa "to make it a prosperous trading partner, and a base for future expansion into Africa."[31] All of these efforts were slow to produce results. The arrival of the Spaniards in the Americas in 1492, followed by the Portuguese in 1500, soon changed the pace of development of Atlantic commerce.

The integration of the Americas into the emerging system of production and trade in the Atlantic basin dramatically expanded the production and consumption possibility frontier. With radically differing resource endowments, a wide range of products could be produced in the Americas for which there were no substitutes at all in Western Europe. Even where it was possible to produce substitutes, the abundance and superior quality of the natural resources were such that, other things being equal, production costs for a wide range of possible products would be a small fraction of those in Western Europe. On the other hand, while there was some similarity between the resource endowments of the Americas and those of Western Africa, politically and environmentally, the former were more easily accessible to the Europeans.[32] The establishment of European colonial domination a few decades after 1492 meant that European entrepreneurs had virtually unlimited access to the vast natural resources of the Americas. The exploitation of these vast and varied resources was at the very center of trade expansion in the Atlantic world between the sixteenth and nineteenth centuries.

As was stated earlier, the quest for gold was a major motivation for the explorations of the fifteenth and sixteenth centuries. Within a few years of their arrival in the Americas, the Spaniards found large quantities of gold and silver – first, in the form of accumulations stored over the centuries by the ruling elites in the American societies; and second, in the form of unexploited mines and placers. They also found that the immense forests in different parts of the Americas contained resources that could be exploited for sale in Europe. What is more, they found millions and millions of hectares of rich agricultural land with varied soils and climates that could be employed to produce all sorts of products for export to Europe, much of which was sparsely populated. After trial and error, the Spaniards began

---

[31] David Birmingham, "Central Africa from Cameroun to the Zambezi," in Roland Oliver (ed.), *The Cambridge History of Africa, Volume 3, From c.1050 to c.1600* (Cambridge: Cambridge University Press, 1977), p. 550. For the pepper trade, see A. F. C. Ryder, *Benin and the Europeans 1485–1897* (London: Longman, 1969).

[32] Inikori, "The slave trade and the Atlantic economies," pp. 76–79.

to export a long list of products, the bulk of which were native to the Americas, but a few were introduced from Europe. Probably the most important introduction from Europe was livestock. Pre-European America had very limited domestic animals and these did not include cattle, horses, or pigs. With huge areas of thinly populated suitable lands, livestock introduced by the Europeans multiplied rapidly.[33] This supported hides export in the early centuries. Various woods, plants, and several agricultural products (including sugar, tobacco, and cocoa) were also exported. One source shows a list of 48 products frequently exported to Spain from the Americas in the early decades of Atlantic commerce.[34] Of course, the most important products were precious metals and precious stones.

Data on output and export of silver and gold in Spanish America are incomplete and difficult to interpret. Based on a critical examination of the published literature, Ward Barrett puts estimated total production of silver and gold in the Americas, 1493–1800, at 102,000 metric tons silver and 2,490 metric tons gold.[35] But, citing estimates based on treasure receipts and taxes in Spain, Carla Phillips states that the total value of the silver and gold received in Spain from Spanish America between 1555 and 1600 was 79,000 million maravedis, or £65.3 million (sterling), made up of 24,000 million maravedis (£19.9 million) for the Spanish government and 55,000 million maravedis (£45.5 million) for the merchants and other private individuals. He believes that, by modern standards, the value of pearls,

[33] Carla Rahn Phillips, "The growth and composition of trade in the Iberian empires, 1450–1750," in Tracy (ed.), *The Rise of Merchant Empires*, p. 79.

[34] *Ibid.*, p. 70, fn. 89.

[35] Ward Barrett, "World bullion flows, 1450–1800," in Tracy (ed.), *The Rise of Merchant Empires*, Table 7.1, p. 225. Earl Hamilton's figures for the import of silver and gold into Spain from Spanish America show that between 1503 and 1660 the total was 740,874,946 pesos, or £166,696,870 (sterling), of which £43,695,900 belonged to the Spanish Crown: Earl J. Hamilton, *American Treasure and the Price Revolution in Spain, 1501–1650* (Cambridge, Mass.: Harvard Economic Studies, Vol. 43, 1934), p. 34, taken from John J. Tepaske, "New World Silver, Castile and the Philippines, 1590–1800," in J. F. Richards (ed.), *Precious Metals in the Later Medieval and Early Modern Worlds* (Durham, NC: Carolina Academic Press, 1983), Table 1, p. 441; John J. McCusker, *Money and Exchange in Europe and America, 1600–1775* (Chapel Hill: University of North Carolina Press, 1978), pp. 99–100, where it is shown that one peso of 272 maravedis was 54d (sterling), which is the exchange rate used in converting the peso amount to £ sterling. On the other hand, combining Hamilton's and M. Morineau's figures, Artur Attman presents import figures for 1531–1700, which show a total of 1185 million rix-dollars, or £278.8 million (sterling), £71.1 million of this amount being the imports for 1556–1600: Artur Attman, "Precious Metals and the Balance of Payments in International Trade, 1500–1800," in Wolfram Fischer, R. Marvin McInnis and Jurgen Schneider (eds.), *The Emergence of a World Economy, 1500–1914: Papers of the IX International Congress of Economic History* (Stuttgart: Steiner Verlag Wiesbaden, 1986), pp. 117–118; £1 (sterling) = 4.25 rix-dollars, according to Attman.

emeralds, and other precious stones also imported into Spain from Spanish America during the same period may have equaled or surpassed the value of the precious metals, although the data relating to them are difficult to interpret. On the problem of smuggling, Phillips argues that on the basis of recent research an upward adjustment of the official figures by 10 percent is reasonable.[36] Ward Barrett presents a very extensive review of the literature and explains his preferred estimates in a manner that seems very persuasive. Appendix 4.1 is computed from his preferred figures of bullion exports from the Americas to Europe during the period 1501–1800.

From these figures, total exports of American bullion to Europe in the period 1501–1600 would come to £125,847,200, or approximately £1.3 million per annum; 1601–1700, £280,038,300, or £2.8 million per annum; and 1701–1800, £488,928,000, or £4.9 million per annum. According to S. Sideri,[37] total Brazilian gold export to Portugal in the years 1690 to 1810 amounted to £115 million (sterling). If we assume that £5 million of this amount was for the 10 years 1801–1810, we can subtract £110 million from the eighteenth-century figures, making the rest Spanish American exports, since Brazilian bullion exports were the only non-Spanish American exports up to 1800. This brings down the eighteenth-century total to £378,928,000, or £3.8 million per annum.

As stated earlier, a long list of other products were exported to Spain from Spanish America apart from the precious metals and precious stones. Some of the most important among these were cochineal (a scarlet dye-stuff made of the dried bodies of a specie of insects), cocoa, hides, tobacco, and sugar. About 20 tons of cochineal were exported annually from 1556 to 1560; it rose to 94.9 tons in 1576–80, but fell continuously thereafter to 23.9 tons in 1611–1615; it rose continuously again to 104.5 tons a year in 1717–20, and by 1771–75 it was 360 tons a year. It is estimated that the quantity exported in the sixteenth century amounted to about £103,400 (sterling) a year.[38] Of cocoa, about 19.4 tons a year were exported in 1651–55; the highest quantity exported in the seventeenth century was 245.7 tons a year in 1681–85; the volume increased considerably in the eighteenth century to 1,181.6 tons by 1736–38, and 2,444.2 tons in 1771–75.[39] Hides export ranged from 27,254 (number) to 134,493 a year in the sixteenth century, 6,639 to 86,851 in the seventeenth century,

---

[36]   Phillips, "The growth and composition of trade in the Iberian empires," pp. 84–85. The conversion of maravedis to £ sterling is based on the exchange rate of 272 maravedis (or one peso of 8) to 54d (sterling), as stated in fn. 35 (taken from McCusker, *Money and Exchange*, pp. 99–100). At this exchange rate, £1 (sterling) would be equal to 1,208.9 maravedis.

[37]   S. Sideri, *Trade and Power: Informal Colonialism in Anglo-Portuguese Relations* (Rotterdam: Rotterdam University Press, 1970), pp. 49–50.

[38]   Phillips, "The growth and composition of trade in the Iberian empires," pp. 79–81.

[39]   *Ibid.*, Table 2.6, pp. 92 and 93.

and 3,733 to 186,991 in the first three quarters of the eighteenth century.[40] A few thousand pounds (weight) of tobacco were also exported from Spanish America in the seventeenth century. But the other major product apart from precious metals and stones was sugar. Annual export ranged from 63 tons to 630 tons in the sixteenth century, declined greatly in the seventeenth, and grew in the eighteenth century from 30 tons a year in 1717–20 to 2,747 tons in 1766–70.[41] From the second half of the eighteenth, sugar production in Spanish America was increasingly concentrated in Cuba. In the last quarter of the eighteenth century, sugar production in Cuba grew from 10,000 tons a year in 1775–79 to 24,373 tons in 1795–99. A phenomenal expansion of sugar production occurred in the Spanish Caribbean in the nineteenth century. By 1850–54, Cuban output was 286,950 tons a year and 91,100 tons in Puerto Rico.[42]

The proportion of the non-bullion exports in overall shipments to Spain from all the provinces of Spanish America is difficult to ascertain. Phillips cites a Dutch writer in the early seventeenth century who thought that the combined value of the non-bullion exports from Spanish America exceeded that of gold and silver.[43] For the eighteenth century, Brading's computations show that bullion accounted for 77.6 percent of the total value of shipments from Spanish America registered at Cadiz in the years 1717–78; while figures for 1792, described as the best known year for Spanish commerce, put the total value of imports into Spain from Spanish America at 36.92 million pesos (£8.3 million sterling), of which bullion contributed 21.01 million pesos (£4.7 million), being 56.9 percent, and produce, 15.91 million pesos (£3.6 million), being 43.1 percent.[44] Non-bullion export from the peripheral regions of Spanish America expanded phenomenally from the last decade of the eighteenth century, particularly sugar export from Cuba, which increased from about 3 million pesos (£675,000) a year in the 1790s to over 11 million pesos (£2.5 million) a year in 1815–19.[45]

On the basis of these rough indications of the varying proportions of non-bullion exports in the overall shipments to Spain, it may be reasonable to infer that bullion shipment was about two-thirds of the total value of exports to Spain from the Americas in the sixteenth century, 75 percent in the seventeenth and first three quarters of the eighteenth, and 60 percent in the last quarter of the eighteenth century. Relating this to the figures in

---

[40] *Ibid.*, pp. 70–73.   [41] *Ibid.*, pp. 58–59.

[42] David Watts, *The West Indies: Patterns of Development, Culture and Environmental Change since 1492* (Cambridge: Cambridge University Press, 1987), pp. 287, 485.

[43] Phillips, "The growth and composition of trade in the Iberian empires," p. 79.

[44] D. A. Brading, "Bourbon Spain and its American Empire," in Leslie Bethell (ed.), *The Cambridge History of Latin America, Volume I: Colonial Latin America* (Cambridge: Cambridge University Press, 1984), pp. 416, 418.

[45] Brading, "Bourbon Spain and its American Empire," p. 417.

Appendix 4.1 would mean that the total value of all exports from Spanish America to Spain, annual average per period, is as follows:[46]

Period	£ (sterling)
1501–1525	544,205
1526–1550	1,428,536
1551–1575	2,789,046
1576–1600	2,789,046
1601–1625	2,962,888
1626–1650	3,507,092
1651–1675	3,990,829
1676–1700	4,341,233
1701–1725	4,352,104
1726–1750	4,629,992
1751–1775	5,218,062
1776–1800	7,678,328

For the nineteenth century, figures for the total exports of Spanish America are available for the years 1848–50, 1868–70, and 1888–90. These figures, which are presented as three-year annual averages, are as follows:[47]

	1848–50	1868–70	1888–90
	£000	£000	£000
Cuba	5,409	13,761	18,485
Puerto Rico	1,274	1,319	1,883
Dominican Republic	103	246	664
Rest of Spanish America	17,684	36,601	71,601
	24,470	51,927	92,633

[46] The calculations for 1676–1800 are based on a somewhat arbitrary distribution of the £110 million Brazilian gold export stated earlier: £2.5 million subtracted from the total value of bullion export for 1676–1700; £12.5 million from that of 1701–1725; £30 million from that of 1726–1750; £40 million from that of 1751–1775; and £25 million from that of 1776–1800. The annual average for 1776–1800, £7.7 million, matches rather well the 1792 figure presented earlier (£8.3 million), which is regarded as reliable. This may be seen as some measure of the degree of accuracy to be associated with the estimate.

[47] These figures are tabulated from Victor Bulmer-Thomas, *The Economic History of Latin America Since Independence* (Cambridge: Cambridge University Press, 1994), Table A.1.2, p. 433. The rest of Spanish America includes Argentina, Bolivia, Chile, Colombia, Costa Rica, Ecuador, El Salvador, Guatemala, Honduras, Mexico, Nicaragua, Paraguay, Peru, Uruguay, and Venezuela. Bulmer-Thomas does not show the actual years of his three-year averages. I have assumed that the years stated by him are the last of the three-year periods. The U.S. dollar figures have been converted to pound sterling at the exchange rate of 1:4.8687, pound sterling to the dollar, as computed from Charles P. Kindleberger, *A Financial History of Western Europe* (2nd edition, New York: Oxford University Press, 1993), Table 5, p. 468.

From these figures, it can be seen that Spanish American exports increased by about a factor of three between 1800 and 1850, and in the second half of the century they more or less doubled every 20 years. As the data show, Cuba was the largest export producer among the Spanish American countries up to the last few years of the century when it became second to Argentina. For purposes of comparison, this same set of data shows that the annual value of Brazilian exports for these periods was £7,363,000, £17,228,000, and £28,134,000, respectively.

We now present more details on export production in Portuguese Brazil. The Portuguese had accidentally landed in Brazil in 1500 on their way to India. It so happened that the imaginary line fixed by the 1494 Treaty of Tordesillas between Spain and Portugal placed much of the territory that was later to become Brazil on the Portuguese sphere of the world newly explored by the Europeans. The landing of 1500, therefore, led in successive stages to a Portuguese colony of settlement in Brazil.

Unlike Spanish America, Brazil's contribution to the growth of Atlantic commerce came largely from agriculture. In the first few decades, the tropical forest of Brazil provided the main trading product, brazilwood, from which the country derived its name. But from the fourth decade of the sixteenth century large-scale sugar production in plantations developed to provide the basis of Brazil's Atlantic commerce for much of the sixteenth century, through the seventeenth, thus setting the pattern to be followed by the Caribbean territories from the second half of the seventeenth century. Though declining in relative importance from the eighteenth century, sugar was to remain an important part of Brazil's Atlantic commerce up to the nineteenth century. In the eighteenth and nineteenth centuries, however, the leading products were gold and coffee, respectively. Raw cotton, cocoa, and rubber also became important in the nineteenth century. The contribution of gold and diamonds was rather short lived, being limited largely to the first three quarters of the eighteenth century.

Estimates of the volume and value of Brazil's Atlantic trade exist in several sources. However, the pioneer in the quantification of Brazil's trade, who has been repeatedly cited by historians, is Roberto Simonsen.[48] Simonsen's data have been retabulated by Mircea Buescu,[49] whose figures are largely employed in the discussion that follows.

Buescu's figures show that in 1530 the export of brazilwood (a dyestuff for textile manufacturers) was between £80,000 and £100,000, being about 95 percent of Brazil's total export. By 1570, while brazilwood export still remained at £100,000, sugar export was valued at £270,000, being 71.1

---

[48]   Roberto C. Simonsen, *Historia Economica do Brasil, 1500–1820* (6th edition, Sao Paulo: Companhia Editora Nacional, 1969).

[49]   Mircea Buescu, *Historia Economica do Brasil: Pesquisas e Analises* (Rio de Janeiro: Apec, 1970). I am grateful to my graduate student, Evelyn Jennings, and Professor Charles Carlton of the University of Rochester for their help in translation.

Table 4.1. *Brazilian Export, 1651–1820*
(£000 Sterling)

Period	Annual Average	Period Total
1651–1670	3,250	65,000
1671–1710	2,500	100,000
1711–1760	3,650	182,500
1761–1780	3,900	78,000
1781–1790	3,000	30,000
1791–1810	3,500	70,000
1811–1820	4,000	40,000

Source and note: Buescu, *Historia Economica do Brasil*, p. 213. The first year of each period has been adjusted to reflect the number of years in each period indicated by Buescu's calculation of the period means and totals.

percent of the total value of Brazil's export; in 1600 it was £2.1 million and £3.8 million in 1650, being 90 percent and 95 percent of the total, respectively.[50] Appendix 4.2 shows the annual value of sugar exports during the colonial period. For the whole period, 1536–1822, the total value of Brazilian sugar export comes to £515.3 million.[51] Table 4.1 shows the total annual value of Brazil's export from 1650 to 1820, which includes the value of gold export in the eighteenth century and some other minor products.[52] Buescu computes that the total value of Brazil's export to Portugal during the entire colonial period was £752 million.[53]

For the last decade of the eighteenth century and for parts of the nineteenth, several sources provide data that can be compared with Buescu's figures. José Arruda's data show that Brazil's exports and imports for the period 1796–1807 totaled 140,397.8 contos and 117,025 contos,

[50] Buescu, *Historia Economica do Brasil*, pp. 57, 60.
[51] *Ibid.*, p. 197.
[52] Exports for selected individual years (in £ million sterling) are as follows: 1600, £2.4; 1650, £4.0; 1700, £2.4; 1750, £4.3; 1800, £3.5; 1850, £8.1: *Ibid.*, pp. 167, 199 and 242; gold exports for individual years are stated as follows (p. 199): 1700, £310,000; 1750, £2,035,000; 1800, £855,000. For yearly quantities of gold produced, 1700–1799, see A. J. R. Russell-Wood, "Colonial Brazil: The Gold Cycle, c.1690–1750," in Leslie Bethell (ed.), *The Cambridge History of Latin America, Volume II: Colonial Latin America* (Cambridge: Cambridge University Press, 1984), p. 594.
[53] Buescu, *Historia Economica do Brasil*, p. 197.

respectively.[54] This comes to £39,451,782, or an annual average of £3,287,649, for exports, and £32,884,025, or an annual average of £2,740,335, for imports.[55] For the same period, but with no information for 1798 and 1807, Dauril Alden's data, covering Rio de Janeiro, Bahia, Pernambuco, Maranhao, and Para (99.2 percent of the total), give a total of 115,811 contos for exports and 104,366 for imports.[56] This converts to £32,543,000, or an annual average of £3,254,000, for exports and £29,327,000, or an annual average of £2,932,700, for imports. The two export figures (£3,287,649 and £3,254,000) are reasonably close to Buescu's figure of £3.5 million for 1791–1810, particularly as all the three figures do not cover exactly the same years.

For the 12 years or so following the transfer of the Portuguese royal court to Brazil in 1808 and the opening of Brazilian ports to trade with all nations, data for total Brazilian exports and imports are hard to come by. Alan Manchester's data on direct trade between Brazil and Britain show, for the respective years 1812, 1815, and 1820, £700,000, £829,000, and £1,300,000 for Brazil's exports, and £2,003,253, £1,896,064, and £2,099,396 for imports.[57] For the same years, Arruda's data on Brazil's trade with Portugal show £1,107,660, £2,516,440, and £2,087,000 for Brazil's exports, and £684,330, £2,287,770, and £1,818,440 for imports.[58] The combined exports to Britain and Portugal in the three years thus come to £1,807,660, £3,345,440, and £3,387,000, respectively; and £2,684,330, £4,183,834, and £3,917,836 are the combined imports from them. On the other hand, Frederic Mauro's data on Brazil's overall imports during roughly the same period show £3,125,000 for 1812, £4,444,000 for 1815, £4,213,000 for 1819, and £4,590,000 for 1822.[59] Again, compared with

---

[54] José Jobson de A. Arruda, *O Brasil No Comércio Colonial* (Sao Paulo: Editora Atica, 1980), pp. 313 and 314.

[55] The exchange rate employed is 1:281, contos to pound sterling, computed from McCusker, *Money and Exchange in Europe and America*, p. 107.

[56] Dauril Alden, "Late Colonial Brazil, 1750–1808," in Bethell (ed.), *The Cambridge History of Latin America, Volume II*, Table 13, p. 652. Arruda's evidence shows that the regions included in Alden's table made up 99.2 percent of Brazil's export and 99.3 percent of the imports during the period (Arruda, *op. cit.*, pp. 313 and 314).

[57] Alan K. Manchester, *British Preeminence in Brazil, Its Rise and Decline: A Study in European Expansion* (New York: Octagon Books, 1964), pp. 97–98, footnotes 111–117.

[58] Arruda, *O Brasil No Comercio Colonial*, p. 624. Arruda's figures for 1819 and 1820 are mixed up. The export and import figures are all for 1820 only; there are no figures for 1819 at all.

[59] Frédéric Mauro, "Structure de l'économic interne et marche international dans une epoque de transition: le cas du Bresil, 1750–1850," in Wolfram Fischer, R. Marvin McInnis and Jurgen Schneider (eds.), *The Emergence of a World Economy 1500–1914: Papers of the IX. International Congress of Economic History*, Part I (Stuttgart: Steiner–Verlag–Wiesbaden, 1986), p. 341.

these figures, Buescu's annual average of £4 million for Brazil's exports in the period 1811–20 would seem to be a reasonable figure, considering exports to the United States and other European countries. Thus, to the extent that the foregoing comparative exercise indicates the general level of reliability of the data employed, we may conclude that Buescu's figures are unlikely to greatly exaggerate or understate the volume and value of Brazil's exports for the period they cover.[60]

To Spanish American and Brazilian production, new areas of more rapidly growing export production were added in the seventeenth century. With territories taken away from Spain, countries of northwestern Europe, especially England, France, and Holland, established colonies in the Americas where commodity production for Atlantic commerce developed rapidly from the seventeenth century. The British Caribbean islands were the first major challengers to the predominance of Spanish America and Portuguese Brazil. And the main product with which they did so was sugar, which subsequently spread to the rest of the Caribbean. Ultimately, it was the development of commodity production and trade in British continental America from the seventeenth century that became the dominant force by the nineteenth century.

Because of the great attention paid to trade by Britain, a considerable amount of data on production and trade between the British American colonies and Britain is available. Though containing acknowledged weaknesses, the data are far superior to those available for any other Atlantic empire of the period. Appendix 4.3 shows the value and commodity composition of the exports to Britain for selected years in the seventeenth, eighteenth, and nineteenth centuries.

Throughout the seventeenth and eighteenth centuries, sugar was by far the leading product in value, and the entire export was produced in the British Caribbean. In the eighteenth century, cotton and coffee also came entirely from the British Caribbean. However, by 1804–06, 52.2 percent of the cotton came from the southern states of the United States of America and 47.8 percent from the British Caribbean; from the second quarter of the nineteenth century, virtually the entire export was produced in the former. Coffee continued to be exported almost entirely from the British

---

[60]   For another set of figures for 1822–1891, see Nathaniel H. Leff, *Underdevelopment and Development in Brazil, Vol. 1: Economic Structure and Change, 1822–1947* (London: Allen and Unwin, 1982), p. 80. The main export products for the period were cotton, sugar, coffee, leather, tobacco, cocoa, and rubber. Their percentage contribution to the total value of Brazil's exports in the respective periods, 1821–3 and 1871–3, is as follows: cotton, 25.8 and 16.6; sugar, 23.1 and 12.3; coffee, 18.7 and 50.2; leather, 13.5 and 6.4; tobacco, 3.2 and 3.2; cocoa, 0.6 and 0.8; rubber, 0.0 and 5.3 (*Ibid.* p. 85). Sugar and cotton were produced mainly in Northeastern Brazil, while coffee was produced in the Southeast (mainly Rio de Janeiro and Sao Paulo).

Caribbean. In the eighteenth century, rice and tobacco were also exported from the southern colonies of mainland British America.

The operation of mercantilist policies meant that British America traded largely with Britain. Hence, exports to Britain represent a very large proportion of the total exports of British America. But they do not represent the entire export. British America traded directly with other American territories and also with European nations other than Britain. In addition, the mainland colonies had a considerable amount of trade with the British Caribbean. All of these are not included in Appendix 4.3, which represents, therefore, less than the total value of British American production for Atlantic commerce during the period. Table 4.2 presents the regional distribution of export production in British America from 1663 to 1860. Up to the 1750s, the trade between British America and other American territories, about which some discussion follows later, is not included; the figures are for trade with Britain only. From the late 1760s, the trade of mainland British America is more or less fully covered but that of the British Caribbean with countries other than Britain is still left out, only trade with mainland British America being included in some years.

Table 4.2 shows that in the late 1760s and early 1770s, commodity export production in British America was at least £6.8 million a year, in the 1790s it was £17 million, and £54.8 million in the 1850s. As the table shows, the British Caribbean islands were the leading producers of export commodities in the seventeenth and eighteenth centuries, contributing well over 60 percent of the total for British America in the seventeenth century and over 50 percent in the eighteenth and early decades of the nineteenth century. The Caribbean islands and the southern mainland colonies/states taken together produced well over 80 percent of the total value of British America's export commodities in the seventeenth and eighteenth centuries, and about 79.0 percent in the 1850s.[61]

Data on export production in the French and Dutch American colonies are much more limited as compared with British America. The available data show that sugar production in the French Caribbean in 1683 was 184,000 cwt. (hundredweight), and in the Dutch colony of Surinam it was 49,700 cwt. in 1688.[62] Assuming that continental prices were the same as London wholesale sugar prices in the 1680s,[63] the value of sugar output in the French and Dutch colonies comes to £158,700 and £42,866,

[61] Apart from the sources cited for Caribbean exports in Table 4.2, the following sources also show some figures: Richard B. Sheridan, *Sugar and Slavery: An Economic History of the British West Indies, 1623–1775* (Baltimore: Johns Hopkins University Press, 1973), p. 470; and John J. McCusker and Russell R. Menard, *The Economy of British America, 1607–1789* (Chapel Hill: University of North Carolina Press, 1985), p. 160.

[62] Sheridan, *Sugar and Slavery*, p. 396.

[63] *Ibid.*, p. 397. The London wholesale price stated by Sheridan is 17s.: 3d. per cwt.

Table 4.2. *Regional Distribution of Commodity Export Production in British America, 1663–1860*

| | British Caribbean (£000) | British Mainland America | | Total British America (£000) |
		South (£000)	The Rest (£000)	
1663–69	256	94	71	421
1752–54	1,361	824	499	2,684
1768–72	3,792	1,791.2	1,223.2	6,804.4
1794–96	9,866.8	3,502.4	3,630.8	17,000
1804–06	13,371.4	4,283.5	4,436	22,090.9
1814–16	16,656	4,958	3,089	24,703
1824–26	9,083.6	6,427.9	5,255.9	20,767.4
1834–36	7,946	14,000	5,694	27,640
1854–56	8,709	34,566	11,522	54,797
1858–60		43,440	14,480	

Sources and Notes: Figures for 1663–69 and 1752–54 are computed from Davis, "English Foreign Trade, 1660–1700," p. 96, and Davis, "English Foreign Trade, 1700–74," p. 119; the figures are for exports to Britain only. For 1768–72, the figures are computed from James F. Shepherd and Gary M. Walton, *Shipping, Maritime Trade, and the Economic Development of Colonial North America* (Cambridge: Cambridge University Press, 1972), p. 115; the Caribbean figures are made up of exports to mainland British America, taken from Shepherd and Walton, *op. cit.*, p. 115, and the annual average export to Britain for the period 1766–75, computed from Elizabeth B. Schumpeter, *English Overseas Trade Statistics, 1697–1808* (Oxford: Oxford University Press, 1960), p. 18. For the years 1794–1860, the figures are computed from Davis, *The Industrial Revolution and British Overseas Trade*, pp. 112–125, Timothy Pitkin, *A Statistical View of the Commerce of the United States of America* (New Haven, CT: Durrie and Peck, 1835), pp. 35–36, 50–82, and Douglass C. North, *The Economic Growth of the United States, 1790–1860* (Englewood Cliffs, NJ: Prentice-Hall, 1961), pp. 221, 233, 284; for 1794–1826, the Caribbean figures are for exports to the United States (computed from Pitkin: the 1794–96 figure applied is the average for 1795 and 1796, as there is no figure for 1794, and the figure applied for 1804–06 is for 1804 only, Pitkin simply stating that the figures for 1805, 1806, and 1807 were "nearly the same, as in the three preceding years," p. 212) and exports to Britain (taken from Davis), while the figures for 1834–36 and 1854–56 are for exports to Britain only (a small arithmetical error of £500,000 in Davis's figure for the West Indies in 1854–56 – £8,709,000 instead of Davis's £8,209,000 – is corrected); the regional distribution of the U.S. exports for 1794–96 is based on the percentages for 1804–06, that of 1834–36 is derived from the addition of the total mean value of cotton exports (£12,713,496) and the mean value of other Southern products (sugar, rice, coffee, tobacco, indigo, dyestuffs) exported to Britain only (£947,000), taken from Davis, *op. cit.*, to obtain Southern exports (£13,660,496, rounded to £14,000,000, to take some account of exports to other places), while the distribution of the exports for 1854–56 and 1858–60 is based on the ratio of 75 percent for the South according to Harold U. Faulkner, *American Economic History* (8th edition, New York: Harper & Brothers, 1960), p. 233. Figures for Canada, which are very small for much of the eighteenth century and became large only in the nineteenth century (made up largely of timber exports to Britain) are not included in the table. The exchange rate applied is 1:5 for the eighteenth century and 1:4.8687 for the nineteenth century, pound sterling to United States dollar, as explained in footnote 62 of this chapter.

respectively. As will be shown shortly, export production in the French Caribbean was much less dominated by sugar than was the case in the British Caribbean. Based on this, it may not be unreasonable to assume that overall export production in French America was at least £264,500 a year in the 1680s.[64] The annual value of exports to France from the French Caribbean expanded phenomenally in the eighteenth century. Table 4.3 shows these exports for selected years between 1683 and 1785.[65]

As for the Dutch American colonies, their export production in the seventeenth and eighteenth centuries was quite limited. Dutch American trade had depended heavily on the carrying of products from non-Dutch colonies. Much of that trade was cut off after the 1650s by the restrictions imposed by the imperial countries of Western Europe – England, France, Spain, and Portugal. In the eighteenth century export production in the Dutch colonies was limited virtually to Surinam, with Curaçao concentrating on entrepôt intra-American trade. Data for 1752–54 show that the average annual value of exports from Dutch America to the Netherlands was £470,000.[66] For the period, 1766–76, the average annual value of exports from Surinam to the Netherlands was £619,261.[67] And at the end of the eighteenth century, the total value of Dutch American trade, which apparently includes exports and imports plus carrying charges, insurance, commissions, and merchants' profits – the invisibles are estimated to be about 25 percent of the total – is put at £2,333,000 per annum.[68] Exports alone may have been £875,000, assuming they are 50 percent of what is left after removing the invisibles.

---

[64] This is on the assumption that sugar production was 60 percent of the total value of export production in French America in the 1680s. As is shown later in the chapter, sugar was actually only about 49 percent of total export products in French America in the last quarter of the eighteenth century.

[65] For the two respective years, 1774 and 1785, the commodity composition is as follows: sugar, 48.8% and 48.4%; coffee, 31.2% and 33.2%; cotton, 5.5% and 8.8%; indigo, 13.1% and 8.7%; cacao, 1.3% and 0.9%: Villiers, "The Slave and Colonial Trade in France," p. 214. The author's addition of the values for 1774 is wrong. The total should be 100,093,000 livres and not 100,697,000 livres as stated.

[66] Niels Steensgaard, "The growth and composition of the long-distance trade of England and the Dutch Republic before 1750," in Tracy (ed.), *The Rise of Merchant Empires*, p. 149. The conversion of the pesos to £ sterling is based on McCusker, *Money and Exchange*, p. 311: £1 = 6.03 pesos, the average rate for 1751–1754.

[67] P. C. Emmer, "The Dutch and the making of the second Atlantic system," in Solow (ed.), *Slavery and the Rise of the Atlantic System*, p. 96. The exchange rate applied is the mean for 1766–75, taken from McCusker, *Money and Exchange*, pp. 311–312: £1 = 10.5369 guilders.

[68] Emmer, "The Dutch and the making of the second Atlantic system," p. 89. The exchange rate applied is 1 : 12, pound sterling to Dutch guilders, taken from Jaap R. Bruijn, "Productivity and costs of private and corporate Dutch ship owning in the seventeenth and eighteenth centuries," in Tracy (ed.), *The Rise of Merchant Empires*, p. 189.

Table 4.3. *Average Annual Value of Exports from the French Caribbean to France, 1683–1785*

	(£000 sterling)
1683	264.5
1716–20	564.9
1750–54	2,846.9
1773–77	5,361.8
1785	7,770.6

Sources and Notes: For 1683, see text above; for 1716–85, the figures are computed from Patrick Villiers, "The Slave and Colonial Trade in France just before the Revolution," in Solow (ed.), *Slavery and the Rise of the Atlantic System*, Tables 1, 2, and 3, pp. 211–214. The 1785 figure is computed from figures representing exports recorded only in Bordeaux, Nantes, La Havre, Marseille, La Rochelle, and Dunkerque. Figures for these ports in 1774 and 1775, when compared with the total exports for the same years (Tables 2 and 3, pp. 213 and 214), are 6.8 percent lower than the latter. Villiers's figure of 174,618,000 livres for 1785 has been adjusted upward by 6.8 percent to cover total exports to France. The exchange rates applied for 1716–77 are from McCusker, *Money and Exchange*, pp. 309–312. These are as follows (pound sterling to livres tournois): 1716, 1:15.8730; 1717, 1:15.2091; 1718, 1:19.6292; 1719, 1:25.3700; 1720, 1:43.7158; 1750, 1:22.8426; 1751, 1:23.1362; 1752, 1:22.7273; 1753, 1:22.4299; 1754, 1:22.9080; 1773, 1:24.0964; 1774, 1:23.8332; 1775, 1:23.4528. No rates are available for 1776 and 1777. The rate for 1775 has been applied for both years. The exchange rate applied for 1785 is computed from Public Record Office (PRO, England), C.O. 318/2, folios 290–291, J. Dobson to Mr. J. Stevens, 7 February, 1807, where it is shown that Cuban exports (stated in French money) in 1788 and 1801, 14 million livres and 15.5 million livres, respectively, amounted (in pound sterling) to £583,333: 6s: 8d and £645,833: 6s: 8d, respectively. Both sets of figures give an exchange rate of 1:24, pound sterling to livres tournois.

By the nineteenth century, with the collapse of export production in the main French American colony of St. Domingue, now Haiti, very little export production took place in the Americas outside British America, Spanish America, and Portuguese Brazil. Data for the years, 1848–50, 1868–70, and 1888–90, show that the average annual value of exports from Haiti was £924,000, £1,525,000, and £2,909,600, respectively.[69] For the remaining French Caribbean, 10-year annual average sugar production was 53,000 tons for 1820–29; 54,000 tons for 1830–39; 55,000 tons for 1840–49; 46,000 tons for 1850–59; and 58,000 tons for 1860–69.[70]

The data presented so far in this chapter provide a reasonable basis for measuring the extent and growth of commodity production for export in the Americas from the sixteenth century to the late nineteenth. However, it must be stressed that the data do not cover the entire value of commodities produced for export in the Americas during the period. Restrictions imposed by the imperial European nations on the trade of their American colonies drove a large proportion of the trade of the Americas under-ground beyond the reach of official records. The unrecorded trade was of two types – intra-American trade between the colonies of one European nation and those of another, and the direct trade between the American colonies and European nations other than their mother countries. British America dominated the intra-American trade, while traders from Britain dominated the direct trade with Europe, especially the trade of Spanish America.

It is impossible to estimate the actual magnitude of this trade, but available evidence suggests that it was extensive. The Dutch colony of Curaçao was a major link between British America and the American colonies of other European nations. Mainland British America exported large quantities of provision and the British Caribbean sent sugar and British manufactures, and from Curaçao all of these were distributed to the other European colonies, especially Spanish America, in return for mainly specie, but also some other commodities. A British seaman involved in the trade in the early eighteenth century narrated:

---

[69] See fn. 47 of this chapter, for sources on data and the exchange rate applied.

[70] Applying the average London prices for these periods to the quantities gives the following ten-year average annual values (in £000): 1820–29, £1,590; 1830–39, £2,430; 1840–49, £1,650; 1850–59, £1,288; 1860–69, £1,450: J. R. Ward, *Poverty and Progress in the Caribbean, 1800–1960* (London: Macmillan, 1985), pp. 9 and 27. The average London prices taken from Ward's graph on p. 9 are as follows: 30 shillings (sterling) per cwt. for the 1820s; 45 shillings per cwt. for the 1830s; 30 shillings per cwt. for the 1840s; 28 shillings per cwt. for the 1850s; and 25 shillings per cwt. for the 1860s. The London prices, which certainly included carrying charges, insurance, commissions, and merchants' profits, would considerably inflate the value of sugar exports from the French Caribbean in the nineteenth century. The error may be minimized if these figures are taken to cover all exports from all American territories, excluding British America, Spanish America, Portuguese Brazil, and Haiti.

There is hardly any plantation in America that belongs to Her Majesty Queen Ann but hath a correspondence with Curaçao and not many but what hath raised themselves by it. . . . The Dutch trade with the Spanyards is the greatest they have at that Island, which is the foundation and cause of all the rest. . . . Curaçao hath in one year from their Leeward Trade (as this is called) 5,000,000 pieces of 8 [pesos] . . .[71]

In addition to the Curaçao trade, a much larger direct trade with Spanish America was conducted illegally by British America. Slaves and British manufactures were exported from the British Caribbean in exchange for specie and Spanish American products. The annual value of the entire contraband trade to Spanish America is estimated to be 6 million pesos a year in the first half of the eighteenth century. In addition to this, there was also a large hidden trade with Spanish America conducted by the British under the cover of the asiento contract with the Spanish government, which allowed the British South Sea Company to export slaves to Spanish America. Estimates made from the secret account books of the Company show that the Company's slave ships illegally introduced goods worth £6 million between 1730 and 1739.[72] In return for these illegal goods and for the slaves legally introduced, the Company received specie, whose value is not included in the tables presented earlier in the chapter.

Similar distortions affected the trade of Brazil. The English, the French, the Spaniards, and the Dutch conducted a lively contraband trade in sugar and gold from Brazil. The Dutch had the largest share of the illegal Brazilian trade in the seventeenth century. The Dutch trade was at its peak between 1630 and 1654, when sugar from Brazil (partly under Dutch occupation) was exported direct to Holland.[73] In the eighteenth century, large quantities of gold were also smuggled into England from Brazil. A report of 1799 shows large amounts of gold in dust and bar, together with precious stones, which were carried to British ports.[74] The evidence indicates that British illegal trade with Brazil expanded considerably in the three decades or so preceding the transfer of the Portuguese royal court to Brazil in 1808. The Portuguese colonial minister claimed that in the mid-1780s a dozen English ships a year sailed directly from England to Brazil, where they sold English manufactures in exchange for Brazilian raw materials. And between 1791 and 1800, the number of British ships entering

---

[71]　PRO, CO 388/12 Part II/K.66, Memorial from Mr. Holt relating to the illegal trade carried on between Curaçao, St. Thomas, and the British Plantations, Received 15 December, 1709, Read 11 January, 1710, folios 252–253.

[72]　Desmond C. M. Platt, *Latin America and British Trade, 1806–1914* (London: Adam & Charles Black, 1972), pp. 31–33.

[73]　Frédéric Mauro, "Portugal and Brazil: political and economic structures of empire, 1580–1750," in Bethell (ed.), *Cambridge History of Latin America Volume I*, pp. 458–459.

[74]　Russell-Wood, "Colonial Brazil," pp. 592–593.

Table 4.4. *Annual Value (f.o.b.) of Export Production in the Americas, 1501–1850*

	Spanish America (£000)	Portuguese Brazil (£000)	British America (£000)	French America (£000)	Dutch America (£000)	Total (£000)
1501–50	986	300				1,286
1551–1600	2,789	975				3,764
1601–50	3,235	3,033				6,268
1651–70	3,991	3,250	421	265	43	7,970
1711–60	4,491	3,650	2,684	2,847	470	14,142
1761–80	5,218	3,900	6,804	5,362	619	21,903
1781–1800	7,678	3,250	19,545	7,771	875	39,119
1848–50	24,470	7,363	54,797	2,574		89,204

Sources and Notes: For sources, see text, footnotes, and the preceding tables in this chapter. For Spanish America, the figure for 1711–60 is the annual average for 1701–50. The Brazilian figures up to 1650 are for sugar only, and they begin from 1536, as Appendix 4.2 shows. The British American figure for 1711–60 is the average for 1752–54, and that for 1761–80 is the annual average for 1768–72. The British American figure for 1781–1800 is the combined mean for 1794–96 and 1804–06, while that for 1848–50 is the mean for 1854–56. Canada is not included in the table. The figures for French America are for the French Caribbean only; the 1848–50 figure includes Haiti's exports (£924,100); for the years covered by the other figures, see Table 4.3. For the Dutch American figures, see text.

Rio de Janeiro under the pretext of distress increased from eight to 30 a year.[75]

It must be understood, therefore, that the value of commodities produced for export in the Americas during the period was greater than the data presented in the preceding tables would indicate. How much greater, it is impossible to say. However, it is fair to say that the general order of magnitude suggested by the tables is a reasonable one. Table 4.4 shows a summary of this order of magnitude.

As the summary in the table shows, the f.o.b. value of commodities produced in the Americas for Atlantic commerce was at least £1.3 million per annum in the first half of the sixteenth century, rising to £3.8 million a year in the second half. In the seventeenth century, Brazil produced almost as much export commodities, by value, as all of Spanish America combined; but, as production expanded in the previously peripheral areas of Spanish America, especially sugar production in the Spanish Caribbean (mainly

[75] Alden, "Late Colonial Brazil," pp. 652–653.

Cuba), export production in Spanish America grew much more in the eighteenth and nineteenth centuries than in Brazil. As mentioned earlier in the chapter, treasure made up about 67 percent of the Spanish American figures in the sixteenth century, about 75 percent in 1600–1775, and about 60 percent in the last quarter of the eighteenth century.

The growth of export production in the American colonies of North-West European countries – mainly England and France – raised total production enormously from the middle decades of the seventeenth century. Production in the French Caribbean grew rapidly in the eighteenth century but collapsed following the French Revolution and the slave revolt in Haiti. Ultimately, it was sustained growth of production in British America that propelled total production to new heights in the eighteenth and nineteenth centuries. Between 1760 and 1780, British America produced almost one-third of the total value of export commodities produced in the Americas; in the last two decades of the eighteenth century, the proportion increased to about 50.0 percent; and by the mid-nineteenth century, it had further increased to 61.4 percent.

Now what was the contribution of Africans, forcefully transported to the Americas, to this growth of commodity production for Atlantic commerce in the Americas? As noted at the beginning of this chapter, the integration of the Americas into the Atlantic World, which operated as a quasi common market from the sixteenth century to the nineteenth, considerably extended the production and consumption possibility frontier of the societies in the region through the widening of the range of resources and products that it made available. As will be shown subsequently, because of their cheapness and the potentially high cost of procuring substitutes either in Europe or elsewhere, the American products were in demand everywhere in Europe. The Americas thus presented great possibilities for production and trade following the establishment of regular seaborne contact between the regions of the Atlantic basin. But the scale of production that would maintain unit costs, both in production and in transportation, at levels that would make the American products accessible to the masses in Europe called for a mass of proletarianized producers (producers who are wholly or almost entirely dependent on earnings from working for others), which no market for legally free labor in any region of the Atlantic or elsewhere was as yet able to provide in the quantities and at the prices required. For one thing, population to land ratios and the development of division of labor had not yet reached levels in Europe and Africa that could give rise to a large population of landless people forced into conditions that would encourage them to migrate voluntarily in large numbers to the Americas. On the other hand, because land was abundant in the Americas, legally free migrants from the Old World were unwilling to work for others; rather, they took up land to produce on a small scale for themselves, usually subsistence production in the most part.

Consequently, large-scale production in the Americas depended largely on coerced labor for several centuries. Initially, the indigenous peoples of the Americas were forced to provide such labor. For silver mining and the provisioning of the European colonists, coerced Indian labor was relatively successful in Spanish America.[76] But it was unsuitable in most other areas of production. To make matters worse, the pre-Columbus populations of the Americas were almost totally wiped out a few decades after European colonization. Central Mexico, the most densely populated region of the Americas before the European conquest, provides a good illustration. Its pre-conquest population (about 1519), estimated to be between 18.8 million and 26.3 million, fell to 6.3 million by 1548 and to 1.9 million in 1580. By 1605, it was down to about 1.1 million.[77] This demographic catastrophe was repeated all through the Americas. In the Caribbean islands, in particular, hardly any native population was left by the seventeenth century. With less than half a million Europeans in all of the Americas between 1646 and 1665,[78] the destruction of the Indian populations meant that average population density in the Americas was less than one person per square mile in the seventeenth century. Hence, the production of commodities for Atlantic commerce in the Americas came to rest almost entirely on the shoulders of forced migrants from Africa.

It may be possible, using demographic and some other evidence, to quantify the contribution of African peoples to overall production of commodities for Atlantic commerce in the Americas from the sixteenth to the nineteenth century. As already stated, coerced Indian labor was the main source of labor for silver mining in Spanish America. But even in sixteenth-century silver mining, African labor was not unimportant. As Herbert Klein has noted,

the earliest years of the Atlantic slave trade drew Africans primarily toward Mexico and Peru. Although the relative importance of African slaves was reduced

[76] Lockhart and Schwartz, *Early Latin America*; Bethell (ed.), *Cambridge History of Latin America*, vols. 1–3.

[77] W. Borah and S. F. Cook, "The Aboriginal population of Central Mexico on the eve of Spanish conquest," in Lewis Hanke (ed.), *History of Latin American Civilization: Sources and Interpretation* (2 vols., Vol. 1, London: Methuen, 1967), p. 204. Hoberman's figures are slightly different: a decrease from 25 million in 1519 to about 1.3 million in 1646. See Louisa S. Hoberman, *Mexico's Merchant Elite, 1590–1660: Silver, State, and Society* (Durham, NC and London: Duke University Press, 1991), pp. 6–7. Totally out of line with figures from the more recent research is the figure of 10,035,000 Indians in the Americas in 1650 (of whom 8,395,000 were in mainland Spanish America) taken by Van Bath from an outdated publication (1954). See B. H. Slicher Van Bath, "The absence of white contract labour in Spanish America during the colonial period," in P. C. Emmer (ed.), *Colonialism and Migration: Indentured Labour Before and After Slavery* (Dordrecht: Martinus Nijhoff, 1986), pp. 19–21.

[78] Hoberman, *Mexico's Merchant Elite*, p. 7; McCusker and Menard, *The Economy of British America*, p. 54; Watts, *The West Indies*, p. 236.

within Spanish America in the 16th and 17th centuries, African migrations to these regions were not insignificant and began with the first conquests. Cortez and his various armies held several hundred slaves when they conquered Mexico in the 1520s, while close to 2,000 slaves appeared in the armies of Pizarro and Almargo in their conquest of Peru in the 1530s and in their subsequent civil wars in the 1540s.[79]

In the course of the sixteenth century, Africans and their descendants in the viceroyalty of Peru became increasingly employed outside silver mining. But even as late as 1611, there were still about 6,000 Africans in the silver city of Potosi.[80]

As for the viceroyalty of New Spain (modern Mexico), the available evidence shows that Africans and their descendants provided a large proportion of the labor for silver production in the early years. At this time, large numbers of them worked both above and below ground in the major mines at Zacatecas, Guanajuato, and Pachuco. The mine census of 1570 listed 3,700 African slaves in the mining camps of New Spain, being twice the number of Spaniards, a few hundred less than the Indians, and about 45 percent of the total laboring population. The proportion declined subsequently, but even by the 1590s the number of African slaves in the mining camps still represented about 20 percent of the African and Indian labor force taken together.[81] The African population in New Spain about tripled between 1570 and 1646, growing from 22,600 to 62,400, while that of whites increased from 63,000 to 125,000, and that of *mestizos* (persons of Indian and white ancestry) and *mulattos* (persons of African and white ancestry) rose from 24,793 to 79,396 during the period.[82] If the *mulattos* are added to the African population, the indication is that the population of African peoples and their descendants in New Spain increased more than others between 1570 and 1646.

While sixteenth-century silver production in Spanish America was shared between Indians and Africans, gold production in colonial Spanish America was dominated totally by Africans and their descendants. The bulk of the

---

[79] Klein, *African Slavery in Latin America and the Caribbean*, p. 28.

[80] *Ibid.*, p. 32.

[81] *Ibid.*, pp. 34–35. In northern New Spain, where the silver mines are said to be worked largely by wage laborers, Africans still made up 13.8 percent of the total labor force in 1597. See Peter Bakewell, "Mining in Colonial Spanish America," in Bethell (ed.), *Cambridge History of Latin America*, Vol. II, p. 127.

[82] Hoberman, *Mexico's Merchant Elite*, p. 7. Colin Palmer's figures are much larger. According to him, there were 80,000 African slaves in Mexico in 1645. See Colin A. Palmer, *Slaves of the White God: Blacks in Mexico, 1570–1650* (Cambridge, Mass.: Harvard University Press, 1976), p. 29.

gold was produced in tropical lowlands far removed from Indian populations. The main area of production was modern Colombia, where Spaniards
began employing African slaves to dig gold from Indian graves in the
1530s.[83] As placer mining developed in the Pacific lowlands, where the
pre-conquest sparse Indian population died off very quickly, "large numbers
of Negro slaves were introduced, beginning in the last quarter of the sixteenth century and continuing until the end of the colonial period. Every
mining center of Colombia was, and still is, marked by predominant
Negroid population."[84] The richest placer mines were in the Province of
Novita, which also had the largest concentration of Africans in the Pacific
lowlands.[85]

By combining the share of silver produced by Africans and the value
of gold produced by them, we may be able to offer a rough estimate of
the percentage contribution of Africans to bullion production in colonial
Spanish America. Harry Cross estimates that Colombian gold production
alone was about one-third of the value of silver output in the viceroyalty
of Peru in the seventeenth century.[86] The evidence presented earlier in
the chapter would suggest that the share of Africans in the production
of silver in Spanish America in the sixteenth and seventeenth centuries
together could not have been less than 25 percent. Adding the value of
gold produced by Africans,[87] it should be reasonable to say that
Africans contributed no less than 40 percent of the total value of gold
and silver produced in Spanish America in the sixteenth and seventeenth
centuries.

[83]   Robert C. West, *Colonial Placer Mining in Colombia* (Baton Rouge: Louisiana State
      University Press, 1952), p. 83.
[84]   Robert C. West, *The Pacific Lowlands of Colombia: A Negroid Area of the Ameri-
      can Tropics* (Baton Rouge: Louisiana State University Press, 1957), p. 97. As West
      states in an earlier work: "The inhabitants of the entire Pacific coast, including
      Choco, are chiefly Negro; and the rural lowlands of Antioquia, those of the Cauca
      and the lower Magdalena, and the Patia Basin are populated mainly by Negroes,
      mullatoes, and sambos (mixed Indian-Negro). Even on the high, cold Antioquian
      Batholith there exist small communities of Negroes, descendants of the slave popu-
      lation that once worked the placers of the Rio Chico and Rio Grande near Santa
      Rosa" (West, *Colonial Placer Mining*, p. 90).
[85]   West, *The Pacific Lowlands of Colombia*, p. 98. According to West, in 1778 the
      Province of Novita had 5,692 Africans, while the Province of Citara to the north
      had only 3,316 (p. 98).
[86]   Harry E. Cross, "South American bullion production and export, 1550–1750," in
      Richards (ed.), *Precious Metals*, pp. 410–411. According to Cross, in the 16th, 17th,
      and 18th centuries, Colombian gold production accounted for 18%, 39%, and 25%,
      respectively, of total world production (p. 410).
[87]   The only major gold producing area of Spanish America that was not dominated
      by Africans was Chile. See Bakewell, "Mining in Colonial Spanish America," pp.
      129–130.

To this must be added the contribution of Africans to the production of non-bullion products, such as sugar and other plantation crops which they dominated, particularly in Peru. In 1646 there were about 100,000 enslaved Africans in the viceroyalty of Peru, being between 10 and 15 percent of the total population of the viceroyalty. Of course, their contribution to production for export was several times greater than their proportion of the population, because they were the forced specialists in production for export and for the domestic market. Many of the seventeenth-century Peruvian Africans were employed in plantations in the major sugar and wine producing zones.[88] This continued throughout the rest of the colonial period and even after independence.[89] In the other regions of Spanish America, Africans were similarly employed in plantations to produce cotton, sugar, and other products, especially in the eighteenth century when these activities began their expansion in the Spanish Caribbean, Cuba in particular.[90] The share of these non-bullion products in the total value of Spanish American exports in the colonial period was discussed earlier in this chapter. When the contribution of Africans in their production is combined with the share of bullion production just estimated, the rough indication is that Africans and their descendants produced no less than 40 percent of the total value of Spanish American exports in the sixteenth and seventeenth centuries combined and no less than 50 percent in the eighteenth century.

The difficulty of reconciling some discrepancy in the demographic data creates a measure of uncertainty concerning the margin of error in these estimates. Mainland Spanish America has very limited published data on the population of Africans and their descendants over the colonial period. A source, reported to be based on a census taken by the clergy in 1796, shows that there were 1,219,470 people of African descent in Mexico and Peru, 679,842 in the former and 539,628 in the latter.[91] These are much larger figures than others that are available. For example, Herbert Klein's figures for the late eighteenth century show that there were 271,000 African slaves and 650,000 free colored people in mainland Spanish America. And one even suspects that Klein's "free colored people" may include *mestizos* (persons of white and Indian ancestry), who by this time formed a large proportion of the population of Mexico and Central America.[92] Klein's

---

[88]   Klein, *African Slavery in Latin America and the Caribbean*, pp. 30 and 36.

[89]   Peter Blanchard, *Slavery and Abolition in Early Republican Peru* (Wilmington, DE: Scholarly Resources, 1992), pp. 19–36.

[90]   Phillips, "The growth and composition of trade in the Iberian empires," Tables 2.2, 2.3, and 2.6, pp. 58–63, 66–67, and 92–93.

[91]   See J. E. Inikori, "Measuring the Atlantic Slave Trade: An Assessment of Curtin and Anstey," *Journal of African History*, XVII, 2 (1976), p. 204.

[92]   Klein, *African Slavery in Latin America and the Caribbean*, Tables 1 and 2, pp. 295 and 296; David Eltis, "Free and Coerced Transatlantic Migrations: Some

figures would be consistent with the percentages of export production in Spanish America contributed by Africans earlier estimated. But if the figures from the 1796 census by the clergy are correct, then the contribution of Africans must have been much greater. From the available evidence, it is impossible to reconcile this discrepancy. To be conservative, the lower figures are adopted for our present purpose.

For the other regions of the Americas, combining the data on regional distribution of export production and that on the ethnic composition of the populations of the American sub-regions makes it relatively easy to quantify the contribution of African peoples to the production of commodities for Atlantic commerce in these American sub-regions. In the case of Portuguese Brazil, the northeast and southeast overwhelmingly dominated export production from the sixteenth to the nineteenth century. The main product of the northeast was sugar, which completely dominated Brazilian exports in the sixteenth and seventeenth centuries. Pernambuco and Bahia were the main centers of sugar production in the northeast. The southeast also produced some sugar, mainly in Espirito Santo and Rio de Janeiro.[93] The northeast was also the dominant producer of cotton and tobacco in Brazil. While the northeast completely dominated the production of sugar, cotton, and tobacco, the southeast similarly dominated the production of precious metals (gold and diamonds) in the eighteenth century and coffee in the nineteenth. Gold and diamonds, Brazil's most valuable export products in the eighteenth century, were produced mainly in Minas Gerais, Goias, and Mato Grosso.[94] On the other hand, coffee, the dominant product of the nineteenth century, was produced mainly in Minas Gerais, Rio de Janeiro, and Sao Paulo.[95]

A summary of the export data presented earlier in the chapter shows the following over time percentage contribution of these regionally concentrated products to Brazil's total exports:[96]

Comparisons," *American Historical Review*, Vol. 88, No. 2 (1983), Table 3, p. 278. David Eltis presents a figure of 5,150,000 "Black and Free Colored" people in Spanish America in 1820, a figure which includes mestizos and mulattos, and Eltis believes the African component was "a small fraction" of the total figure.

[93] Lockhart and Schwartz, *Early Latin America*, map 7, p. 203, showing sugar-producing areas in Brazil.

[94] *Ibid.*, pp. 370–373.

[95] Thomas W. Merrick and Douglass H. Graham, *Population and Economic Development in Brazil, 1800 to the Present* (Baltimore: Johns Hopkins University Press, 1979), pp. 64–71; Thomas H. Holloway, "The coffee *colono* of Sao Paulo, Brazil: migration and mobility, 1880–1930," in Kenneth Duncan and Ian Rutledge (eds.), *Land and Labour in Latin America: Essays on the development of agrarian capitalism in the nineteenth and twentieth centuries* (Cambridge: Cambridge University Press, 1977), pp. 301–321.

[96] Merrick and Graham, *Population and Economic Development in Brazil*, p. 12.

Product	1650	1750	1800	1841–50	1891–1900
Sugar	95	47	31	26.7	6.0
Cotton			6	7.5	2.7
Coffee				41.4	64.5
Gold, diamonds, and some minor products	5	53	63	25.4	26.8

This summary, taken along with the main data, shows that in the sixteenth and seventeenth centuries, virtually the entire export of Brazil was produced in the northeast (Pernambuco and Bahia), with some contribution from the south-center (mainly Rio de Janeiro). The share of the northeast declined to about one-half in the eighteenth century and to about one-third in the first half of the nineteenth century. On the other hand, the southeast contributed between one-half and three-fifths of the exports in the eighteenth century, made up largely of gold and diamonds, and about two-thirds in the first half of the nineteenth century, made up largely of coffee.

The ethnic composition of the populations of these export-producing regions is consistent with other evidence, which shows that Brazilian sugar, cotton, tobacco, gold and diamonds, and coffee were produced almost entirely by Africans up to the 1880s. The ethnic composition of the populations of the main Brazilian regions in 1798 and in 1872 is presented in Tables 4.5.A and 4.5.B, respectively. It is clear from these figures that virtually all the commodities exported from the northeast and southeast during the colonial period and up to the 1880s were produced by Africans and their descendants. As the leading export products and producing regions changed over time, so did the regional concentration of the African population. Even in the last quarter of the nineteenth century, when a century and a half of sustained population growth, capitalist development, and large-scale proletarianization (formation of propertyless workers totally dependent on wage labor) in Europe provided a large pool of voluntary migrants to the Americas, coffee producers in southeastern Brazil still depended on African slave labor.[97]

---

[97]   As Merrick and Graham put it, "at the same time the total national stock of slaves declined, from 1,715,000 slaves in 1864 to 1,240,806 slaves in 1883, there was an interregional and intraprovincial concentration of the remaining slave population into the major coffee municipalities of the provinces of Minas Gerais, Rio de Janeiro, and Sao Paulo. From 1874 to 1883, there was an actual increase from 317,147 to 350,085 slaves in their coffee municipalities. Thus, the national decline of the slave population up to 1883 did not compromise the absolute growth of slave manpower in the coffee areas of the Southeast (especially Sao Paulo). . . . These findings help explain the lack of interest on the part of coffee slave owners in importing European manpower for the coffee plantations prior to the mid-1880s. Only after abolitionist pressures increased, in 1883, did these coffee municipalities begin to experience a net

Table 4.5.A. *Ethnic Composition of the Populations in
the Main Regions of Brazil, 1798*

Region	Population (Number)	Africans %	Europeans %	Indians %	Africans (Number)
Amazon and far north:					
Para	123,500	20.0	57	20	24,700
Maranhao	123,500	63.3	31.0	5.0	78,176
Piaui	81,250	54.6	21.8	23.6	44,363
Northeast:					
Pernambuco	617,500	68.2	28.5	3.2	421,135
Bahia	386,750	78.6	19.8	1.5	303,986
Southeast and Interior:					
Minas Gerais	640,250	74.6	23.6	1.8	477,627
Rio de Janeiro	393,250	64.3	33.6	2.0	252,860
Sao Paulo	243,750	37.8	50.8	2.6	92,138
Goias	81,250	82.4	12.5	5.2	66,950
Mato Grosso	42,250	80.4	15.8	3.8	33,969
Rio Grande do Sul	58,500	26.5	40.4	34.0	15,503
Other Regions	458,250	39.0	40.0	21.0	178,593
Total for Brazil	3,250,000	61.2	31.1	7.8	1,988,000

Sources and Notes: The overall population of Brazil in 1798 (3,250,000) and its
ethnic distribution (Africans, 1,988,000, Europeans, 1,010,000, Indians, 252,000)
are taken from Merrick and Graham, *Population and Economic Development in
Brazil*, Table III.2, p. 29. The preference for Merrick and Graham's figures is based
on their persuasive review of the different estimates of Brazil's population at this
time (pp. 26–30), including that of Dauril Alden, "The Population of Brazil in the
Late Eighteenth Century: A Preliminary Study," *Hispanic American Historical
Review*, 43 (May, 1963), pp. 173–205. However, because Merrick and Graham's
figures for 1798 are not regionally distributed, Alden's regional percentages have
been applied to distribute them regionally. For these percentages, see Alden, "Late
Colonial Brazil," Table 2, p. 604 and Table 4, p. 607. Percentages may not add to
exactly 100 because of rounding.

It is, therefore, reasonable to infer, on the existing body of evidence, that
Brazil's exports shown in Table 4.4 were produced almost 100 percent by
Africans. The viceroy of Brazil captured the historical reality of colonial
Brazil when he wrote to the King of Portugal in 1739 that "without Negroes

decline in their slave-based manpower. And it was only after 1883 that plantation
owners in Sao Paulo seriously began to consider mobilizing provincial support and
resources to attract labor from abroad" (*Ibid.*, p. 68).

Table 4.5.B. *Ethnic Composition of the Populations in
the Main Regions of Brazil, 1872*

Region	Population (Number)	Africans %	Europeans %	Indians %	Africans (Number)
Northeast:					
Maranhao	359,040	68.1	28.8	3.1	244,506
Ceara	721,686	55.4	37.3	7.3	399,814
Pernambuco	841,539	64.0	34.6	1.4	538,585
Alagoas	384,009	72.7	25.5	1.8	253,003
Bahia	1,359,616	72.3	24.0	3.7	983,002
Southeast:					
Minas Gerais	2,039,735	57.6	40.7	1.7	1,174,887
Rio de Janeiro	782,724	48.8	38.8	2.4	381,969
Sao Paulo	837,354	43.5	51.8	4.7	364,249
Rio Grande do Sul	434,813	34.7	59.4	5.9	150,880
All of Brazil	9,930,478	58.0	38.1	4.0	5,756,238

Source and Note: Merrick and Graham, *Population and Economic Development in Brazil*, Table IV.8.A, p. 70. The African percentages are the sum of columns (2) and (3) of Merrick and Graham's table (that is, combining the percentages for mulattos and blacks); the number of Africans is computed by applying the combined percentage of mulattos and blacks to the total population of each region; the percentage for Indians is the residual after adding the African (mulatto and black) and European percentages. The figures for all of Brazil are greater than the regional figures taken together, because not all Brazilian regions are included. The overall ethnic figures are 3,787,289 Europeans, 5,756,238 Africans, and 386,955 Indians.

there can be neither gold, nor sugar, nor tobacco."[98] For all practical purposes, particularly in export production and demography, Brazil was an African country up to at least 1872, with 61.2 percent African population in 1798, and 58.0 percent in 1872.[99] Yet the contribution of the Africans to export production was even greater than the demographic proportions, because Africans were the forced specialists in export production.

As stated earlier in the chapter, excluding British America, Spanish America, and Portuguese Brazil, export production in the rest of the Americas from the seventeenth century to the middle decades of the nineteenth was virtually limited to the Caribbean. The demographic evidence for these

---

[98] The Viceroy of Brazil to the King of Portugal, 20 September, 1739, in Pierre Verger, *Trade Relations between the Bight of Benin and Bahia from the 17th to 19th Century* (Translation by Evelyn Crawford; Ibadan: University of Ibadan Press, 1976), p. 141.

[99] Merrick and Graham, *Population and Economic Development in Brazil*, p. 29.

territories makes it clear that the plantations that produced the export commodities were worked entirely by Africans. In 1665, before large-scale export production developed, the French Caribbean islands had 11,061 Europeans and 10,280 Africans. With a massive import of enslaved Africans to work the expanding export-producing plantations, the three French Caribbean islands of Martinique, Guadeloupe, and St. Dominigue (now Haiti) had in 1789–91 a combined population of 54,986 Europeans and 686,319 Africans, the latter being 92.6 percent of the total population. With the independence of Haiti in the 1790s, what was left of the French Caribbean islands had in 1833 a combined population of 19,288 Europeans and 219,678 Africans, the latter constituting 91.9 percent of the total.[100] From this evidence, we conclude that export production in French America shown in Table 4.4 was produced 100 percent by Africans. This conclusion should also apply to the limited production in Dutch America shown in the table, because the demographic data are similar.[101]

Before we move on to British America, some further analysis of the Spanish American data is necessary. The earlier discussion of the data did not include the nineteenth century. By this time the employment of Africans to produce plantation crops for export in Spanish America was largely in the Spanish Caribbean – Cuba, Puerto Rico, and the present Dominican Republic – which had become more like Brazil and British America than the rest of Spanish America. Although the European population was proportionately larger than in Brazil, production for Atlantic commerce was still almost entirely by Africans. In fact, the Spanish Caribbean evidence supports very strongly the view that for several centuries European migrants were more interested in small scale independent production, largely for subsistence, than in working for others in plantations. For this reason, the Spanish Caribbean, with their large European populations, remained marginal in export production until the large-scale importation of enslaved Africans from the late eighteenth century. A contemporary European observer, who wrote in 1807 that Cuba had, in 1788, 170,000 Europeans and 30,000 Africans, stated:

Cuba is very fertile, and the lands are universally considered as being equal to the best parts of St. Domingo, nevertheless although it is 700 miles in Length and 70 miles in Breadth its produce in 1788 was little more than that of Barbados which is only 24 miles long and 14 broad. The population of Barbados at that period was 17,000 whites and 62,000 negroes . . . and to the small number of negroes and the imperfection of their negro code must the scanty produce of that fine Island be attributed.[102]

[100] Watts, *The West Indies*, pp. 236 and 320.
[101] *Ibid.*, p. 236.
[102] PRO, C.O. 318/2, folios 290–291, J. Dobson to Mr. J. Stevens, 7 February, 1807, cited in Inikori, *Slavery and the Rise of Capitalism*, p. 22.

Following the massive importation of Africans from the late eighteenth century, the Spanish Caribbean had a total population of 552,135 Africans in 1833, and in 1860–61 Cuba and Puerto Rico alone had a combined African population of 885,821.[103] With the large African population, Cuba and Puerto Rico produced 36.5 percent of the total Caribbean output of sugar in the 1830s, and 69 percent in the 1860s.[104] Based on the evidence, we conclude that the export figures for Cuba, Puerto Rico, and the Dominican Republic, presented earlier for 1848–50, 1868–70, and 1888–90, were produced almost entirely by Africans. These figures represent 27.7 percent, 29.5 percent, and 22.7 percent of the figures for all Spanish America in the respective periods. It is impossible to determine the percentage of African contribution to the figures for the rest of Spanish America during these years, although there is clear evidence that the contribution remained significant in several republics, particularly Colombia, Venezuela, and Peru. We may do no better than conclude that the contribution of Africans to export production in all Spanish America taken together could not have been less than one-third of the total figures for 1848–50 and 1868–70.

We now come to British America. Like the rest of the Caribbean islands, export production in the British Caribbean, from the seventeenth to the nineteenth century, was entirely by Africans. As export production expanded in those islands from the mid-seventeenth century, the African share of the total population increased from 42 percent in 1660 to 91.1 percent in 1780, and 93.8 percent in 1833.[105] In mainland British America, the production of plantation crops (tobacco, rice, indigo, cotton, and sugar) for export was also by Africans. These were produced in the southern colonies (later southern states of the U.S.A.). Other exports of mainland British America during the colonial period were foodstuffs, draught animals, lumber, fish, and wooden ships. Foodstuffs were produced in family farms by Europeans in the middle colonies and exported mainly to the Caribbean slave plantations. The other exports were produced by Europeans in the New England colonies.

The plantation crops of the South dominated the domestic exports of mainland British America in the colonial period, and even more so after independence, with the phenomenal expansion of cotton production and the growth of sugar production in Louisiana. In 1768–72, exports from the upper South (Maryland and Virginia) were 41 percent of the total; 91.3 percent of the Maryland and Virginia exports during the period was made

---

[103] Watts, *The West Indies*, p. 236; Klein, *African Slavery in Latin America and the Caribbean*, p. 297. In 1833 there were 593,362 Europeans in the Spanish Caribbean (Watts, *The West Indies*, p. 236).

[104] Ward, *Poverty and Progress in the Caribbean*, p. 27.

[105] McCusker and Menard, *The Economy of British America*, p. 222; Watts, *The West Indies*, p. 236.

up of tobacco and rice. During the same period, exports from the lower South (North Carolina, South Carolina, and Georgia) were 22 percent of the total, and these were made up largely of rice and indigo (75.6 percent).[106] Thus, the southern colonies produced 63 percent of the total domestic exports of mainland British America in 1768–72. By 1815, cotton alone was 38.1 percent of total U.S. domestic export, 53.4 percent in 1850, and 60.7 percent in 1860.[107] Adding rice, tobacco, and sugar, approximately 75 percent of U. S. domestic exports were produced in the southern slave states in 1860.[108]

Table 4.6.A shows the growth of the African population in British America from the seventeenth to the nineteenth century. As the table shows, the African population was concentrated in the export commodity producing regions of the Caribbean and southern mainland British America. As the African populations of these regions grew over time, so did their production of export commodities increase. This point is brought out more clearly in Table 4.6.B, which shows the export producing regions of southern mainland British America in more detail for selected years. In particular, the table shows the positive correlation between the regional pattern of the growth of the African population up to 1860 and the spread of cotton production from the old to the new South of British mainland America. Thus, the African population in Alabama grew from 119,100 in 1830 to 440,000 in 1860; that of Mississippi, from 66,200 to 437,000 during the same period; and that of Texas, from 58,000 in 1850 to 183,000 in 1860. These were the years when cotton production expanded in these and other states of the new south.[109]

The enslaved Africans in the South were held by a few plantation owners, estimated to be 384,000 in number in 1860; about 1,815,000 of the Africans were employed in cotton plantations in 1850, and about 180,000 were in Louisiana sugar plantations, producing 280,000 hogsheads of sugar in 1860.[110] Like the Europeans in Cuba in the late eighteenth century, the population of whites in the slave states produced mainly for themselves and for the local market. As Harold Faulkner wrote several decades ago:

Although the economic life of the South was dominated by the commercial crops already described, other crops were raised, chiefly for home consumption. In

[106] Walton and Shepherd, *The Economic Rise of Early America*, Table 22, p. 196; McCusker and Menard, *The Economy of British America*, pp. 130 and 174.
[107] North, *Economic Growth of the United States*, pp. 221, 233, and 284. For exports of U.S. domestically produced goods and foreign goods (shown separately), 1790–1817, see also Eli F. Heckscher, *The Continental System: An Economic Interpretation* (Oxford: Clarendon, 1922), pp. 103 and 146.
[108] Faulkner, *American Economic History*, p. 233.
[109] Faulkner, *American Economic History*, pp. 202–203.
[110] *Ibid.*, pp. 204, 314, and 316.

Table 4.6.A. *Africans and Europeans in British America, 1650–1860*
(in thousands)

| | British Caribbean | | Mainland British America | | | | Total |
| | | | South | | The Rest | | |
	Africans	Europeans	Africans	Europeans	Africans	Europeans	Africans
1650	15	44	0.3	12.4	0.9	26.3	1.2
1660	34	47	0.9	25.0	1.2	37.4	2.1
1670	52	44	2.7	42.3	1.2	58.2	3.9
1680	76	42	4.7	61.8	2.0	81.4	6.7
1690	98	37	9.1	77.9	3.5	118.4	12.6
1700	115	33	15.8	98.8	5.4	140.6	21.2
1710	148	30	29.0	120.1	8.8	175.9	37.8
1720	176	35	45.4	152.8	14.8	259.2	60.2
1730	221	37	79.2	205.4	17.8	346.5	97.0
1740	250	34	134.2	270.3	25.0	485.3	159.2
1750	295	35	210.4	309.6	31.7	624.7	242.1
1760	365	41	284.1	432.0	41.7	835.8	325.8
1770	434	45	406.8	587.6	50.3	1,086.7	457.1
1780	489	48	512.4	779.8	56.8	1,378.9	569.2
1790			673.2	1,193.2	84.0	1,979.0	757.2
1800	835.5[a]	64.8[a]	906.0	1,660.5	97.8	2,645.9	1,003.8
1810	824.8	64.0	1,254.8	2,137.3	123.0	3,724.7	1,377.8
1820	789.4[a]	61.2[a]	1,635.8	2,754.7	135.8	5,112.1	1,771.6
1830	788.0	55.7	2,162.4	3,575.6	166.3	6,961.8	2,328.7
1840			2,848.5	4,543.4	24.5	9,652.4	2,873.0
1850	796.4	34.1	3,608.5	6,113.3	29.5	13,439.8	3,638.0
1860	962.5	41.1	4,401.5	7,946.1	39.5	18,976.4	4,441.0

Sources and Notes: a. These figures are computed by applying Higman's 1810 percentages for the slave, freedman, and European populations to his slave population figures for 1807 and 1820, respectively. All the figures for 1650–1780 are compiled from McCusker and Menard, *The Economy of British America*, Table 5.1, p. 103, Table 6.4, p. 136, Table 7.2, p. 154, and Table 8.1, p. 172; those for the Caribbean in 1800–30 are from Barry W. Higman, *Slave Populations of the British Caribbean, 1807–34* (Baltimore: Johns Hopkins University Press, 1984), Table 4.2, p. 77, and Table S1.2, p. 417; the African and European populations for the Caribbean in 1850 and 1860 are computed as explained in the sources and notes to Table 4.6.B. The figures for mainland America, 1790–1830, are derived from Pitkin, *A Statistical View*, pp. 586–595, and *The South in the Building of the Nation*, Vol. V (Richmond, Virginia: The Southern Historical Publication Society, 1909), pp. 111–112, footnote, and those for 1840–60 are from the latter source only. Where there is an overlap between McCusker and Menard's figures and those of *The South*, the former are higher: 159,200 Africans in 1740 for the former, and 140,000 for the latter; McCusker and Menard's figures show 325,800 Africans in 1760, and for 1776 (16 years later), *The South* shows a figure of only 300,000. For 1840–60, where there are no comparable figures, the African population shown for *The Rest* of Mainland British America, taken from *The South*, is clearly understated, as the figures for the preceding years suggest. The European population in the southern states for the years 1810–1860 are taken from *The South*, p. 607, footnote; the southern european figures are subtracted from the United States European total in Faulkner, *American Economic History*, p. 286, to obtain the European figures for *The Rest* of Mainland British America. For 1790, 1800, and 1810, Pitkin's figures for "all other free persons except Indians not taxed" are taken to mean free Africans.

Table 4.6.B. *Africans in the British Caribbean and the Southern Slave Colonies/States of Mainland British America (in thousands)*

	1740		1780		1830		1850		1860	
	Africans	Total	Africans	Total	Africans	Total	Africans	Total	Africans	Total
Caribbean	250	284	489	537	788	843.7	796.4	922.8	962.5	1,115.3
Maryland		116.1		248	168.2	486.9	240	635	255	762
Virginia	84*	180.4	303.6*	538	517.1	1,211.4	580	1,422	607	1,596
North Carolina		51.8		270.1	265.1	738.0	343	869	391	993
South Carolina		54.2		180	323.3	581.2	403	669	421	704
Georgia	50.2**	2.0	208.8**	56.1	220.0	516.8	387		468	
Alabama					119.1	309.5	347	771.7	440	964.2
Mississippi					66.2	136.6	310	606.6	437	791.3
Louisiana					120.3	215.5	279	517.8	368	708.0
Tennessee					146.2	681.9	251	1,003	290	1,110
Kentucky					170.1	687.9	230	982	246	1,156
Missouri					25.7	140.5	92.5		121.5	
Arkansas					4.7	30.4	47	209.9	111	435.5
Florida					16.3	34.7	41	87.4	63	140.4
Texas							58		183	

* These figures are for both Maryland and Virginia.

** These figures are for North Carolina, South Carolina, and Georgia. Maryland's figures for 1830 and later years include the District of Columbia.

Sources: Except where stated otherwise, the sources are the same as those for Table 4.6.A. Total population figures for 1850 and 1860 (mainland slave states) are from North, *Economic Growth of the United States*, p. 129, and D. V. Glass and D. E. C. Eversley (eds.), *Population in History: Essays in Historical Demography* (London: Edward Arnold, 1965), p. 664. Total population figures for the Caribbean in 1850 and 1860 are compiled from Brian R. Mitchell, *International Historical Statistics: The Americas, 1750–1988* (2nd edition, New York: Stockton, 1993), pp. 1–7; the 1850 figures do not include British Honduras, St. Kitts, Nevis, and Anguilla; the figures are for 1851 and 1861, except Jamaica's 1850 figure, which is for 1844, Dominica's figure for 1850, also for 1844, and the figures for the Virgin Islands in both years are for 1841 (the figures for 1841 and 1871 being the same, 6,700). Figures for the Caribbean African population in 1850 and 1860 are computed by applying the ratio of 86.3% (for 1880) computed from Stanley L. Engerman and Barry W. Higman, "The Demographic Structure of the Caribbean Slave Societies in the eighteenth and nineteenth centuries," in Franklin W. Knight (ed.), *General History of the Caribbean, Vol. III*, Table 1: Africans, 86.3%; Asians, 10%; Europeans, 3.7%.

addition to the usual garden vegetables, cereals were produced in 1859 as follows: Indian corn, 433,067,000 bushels; wheat, 49,158,000 bushels; oats, 32,163,000 bushels; rye, 4,070,000; and barley and buckwheat in small amounts. The southern soil was more adaptable to corn than the other cereals, and it served as the chief food for the slaves. The crop, however, was barely half that raised in the five states north of the Ohio and was not adequate for southern needs. These crops, nevertheless, occupied the attention of a majority of the small farmers, who far surpassed the plantation owners in number.[111]

This point has been further elaborated in the more recent literature, which seeks to demonstrate the dual nature of the economy of the Antebellum South: large-scale export-oriented plantation agriculture worked by Africans and small-scale family-based agriculture by the much larger European population, producing food mainly for the immediate consumption of their families but selling some surplus corn to the plantation owners to feed their slave labor force.[112] As expressed by Rothstein:

In every census count from 1810 to 1860, about forty-five percent of the population in the lower South were slaves. A large proportion of the white population – about two-thirds in 1860 – did not own slaves, and substantial numbers of these whites scratched a bare living from the land in a manner little different from the 'self-sufficiency' (that delightful euphemism for rural poverty) of farmers in the backward areas of the world today. . . . Difficult as it is to draw a sharp line between 'poor whites' and 'yeoman farmers,' both qualitative evidence and the spotty, rough calculations made thus far seem to indicate that the bulk of nonslaveholding whites were only marginally concerned with production for the market.[113]

Based on the foregoing evidence, we assign the southern exports fully to African workers. Of course, there was a small amount of non-plantation products in the southern exports. However, this should be more than made up by the contribution of Africans to export production outside the southern slave states.

On the basis of the foregoing assessment of the share of export commodities produced by Africans in Spanish America, Portuguese Brazil, British America, French America, and Dutch America, we can now present the overall share of export commodities produced by Africans in the Americas from the sixteenth to the nineteenth century. This is shown in Table 4.7. As the table shows, in the sixteenth century export production in the Americas was shared almost equally between Africans and the Indian population, which was relatively large at the time, especially in Spanish America where export production was dominated by silver and gold. But,

---

[111] *Ibid.*, p. 205.
[112] Morton Rothstein, "The Antebellum South as a Dual Economy: A Tentative Hypothesis," in Eugene D. Genovese (ed.), *The Slave Economies: Volume II, Slavery in the International Economy* (New York: John Wiley, 1973), pp. 157–170.
[113] Rothstein, "The Antebellum South as a Dual Economy," pp. 160–161.

Table 4.7. *Share of Export Commodities Produced by Africans in the Americas, 1501–1850*

Period	Average Annual Value of Export Commodities Produced in the Americas (£000)	Share Produced by Africans	
		Value (£000)	%
1501–50	1,286	694.4	54.0
1551–1600	3,764	2,090.6	55.5
1601–50	6,268	4,327	69.0
1651–70	7,970	5,504.4	69.1
1711–60	14,142	11,397.5	80.6
1761–80	21,903	18,073.2	82.5
1781–1800	39,119	31,247	79.9
1848–50	89,204	61,368.7	68.8

Sources and Notes: As stated in the text, the share of exports produced by Africans in Spanish America is 40% in the sixteenth and seventeenth centuries, 50% in the eighteenth, and one-third in 1848–50. For British America, Caribbean and Southern (mainland) exports in Table 4.2 are taken together for African share. For more explanation, see text; for sources, see Table 4.4.

as the Indian population declined (as shown earlier in the chapter), and plantation agriculture and gold mining became overwhelmingly dominant, the labor force in export production in the Americas became almost entirely African. Hence, the share of export commodities produced by Africans in the Americas increased to 69 percent in the seventeenth century, over 80 percent in the eighteenth, and 69 percent again in the first half of the nineteenth century. In matters of export production for Atlantic commerce, the Americas were indeed an extension of Africa in 1650–1850. This was the more so for British America, Brazil, and all territories in the Caribbean.

As the Americas increased their production of commodities for Atlantic commerce, so did their import of goods and services from Europe and slaves from Africa expand, giving rise to a phenomenal growth of the total volume of Atlantic commerce (merchandise export and re-export plus import plus invisible exports and imports) from the sixteenth to the nineteenth century. On the evidence currently available, it is impossible to show exactly the over time total value of Atlantic commerce during this period. Allowing for the possibility of under-estimate discussed earlier, it is reasonable to say that the figures for export production in the Americas presented above may not be very far from the truth. But evidence for a similar computation of the aggregate value of re-exports, imports, and invisible exports and imports is yet to be produced in sufficient quantity and spread by research. However, a careful and imaginative use of the evidence that is available should produce a tentative estimate, about which we can have some confidence.

First, we examine the evidence on imports and re-exports. For British America, a considerable amount of evidence exists on imports from Britain and on British American re-exports, especially mainland British America's re-exports from 1790 to 1860. The evidence shows a very large re-export trade by mainland British America, exceeding the value of domestic exports in some years, particularly during the period of the French Revolutionary and Napoleonic Wars (1793–1815). In the period 1790–1833, United States domestic exports averaged $42,914,000, per annum, while re-exports averaged $22,162,000.[114] For this period, the re-exports were slightly more than one-half of the domestic exports and about one-third of all exports. Similar data do not exist for British Caribbean re-exports. But bullion exports from these islands to Britain offer a reasonable reflection of their re-exports to Spanish America, paid for mainly in bullion. Between 1748 and 1765, bullion totaling £2,948,420 was sent to the Bank of England from the West Indies, the bulk of it coming from Jamaica.[115] This amounts to an average of £163,801 per annum. The evidence indicates that the volume of the re-export trade with Spanish America was considerably greater in the last quarter of the eighteenth century.

For the other American territories, especially Spanish America and Brazil, data on imports are rather limited and virtually non-existent for re-exports. To establish the annual value of their exports plus imports, we have to examine the balance of their merchandise trade with their respective European mother countries for years in which the evidence is available. For Brazil, total exports to Portugal in 1809–19 exceeded imports from Portugal by 10.6 percent.[116] Spanish America also recorded regular surpluses in its merchandise trade with Spain in the colonial period. The figures for 1792, regarded by the authorities as the best year for Spanish American trade data, may be taken for illustration. In this year, Spanish American exports to Spain exceeded imports from Spain by 41.8 percent.[117] Similar large surpluses were recorded in the merchandise trade of the Caribbean islands with their European mother countries.[118] Mainland British America was the only region in the Americas whose imports con-

---

[114]   Computed from Heckscher, *The Continental System*, pp. 103 and 146, and Pitkin, *A Statistical View*, pp. 35 and 36.

[115]   Sheridan, *Sugar and Slavery*, p. 506.

[116]   Computed from Mauro, "Structure De L'Économie Interne et Marche International," p. 342.

[117]   Brading, "Bourbon Spain and Its American Empire," p. 418.

[118]   For the French Caribbean, see Villiers, "The Slave and Colonial Trade in France," pp. 211 and 213.

siderably exceeded the domestic exports in value from the colonial period to the first half of the nineteenth century.

However, when the value of slave imports from Africa is added to that of merchandise imports from the European mother countries, the surplus in merchandise trade is significantly reduced and the deficit for mainland British America increases. For example, the average annual (f.o.b.) value of British Caribbean exports to Britain in 1772–74 is £3,039,000 and that of British exports to the islands (f.o.b.) is £1,341,000. When the value of slaves imported from Africa is added, the islands' imports increase to £1,981,000, and exports to Britain exceed merchandise and slave imports by 34.8 percent, instead of a surplus of 55.9 percent without slave imports.[119] For territories like Brazil, which imported very large numbers of slaves, the merchandise surplus may have been virtually wiped out by the cost of slave imports.

It is, therefore, reasonable to assume that when the total cost of slaves imported yearly into the Americas from Africa is added to the large deficit of mainland British America's merchandise imports and domestic exports, overall commodity exports of the Americas presented in Table 4.4 above should be about equal to their imports. For the avoidance of doubt, it may be helpful to know the extent to which British mainland America's merchandise imports exceeded domestically produced export commodities. As stated earlier, U.S. domestic exports averaged $42,914,000 a year in 1790–1833. During the same period, merchandise imports averaged $77,782,000[120] a year, being a deficit of $34,868,000, or about £7 million, a year on the average. Of course, the deficit was smaller in the colonial period. But there can be little doubt that the mainland British American deficit, together with the value of slave imports into the Americas, should be about equal to the export surpluses of the Caribbean, Brazil, and mainland Spanish America. As for re-exports, with very little information available on the re-export trade of most American regions, the known value of mainland British American re-exports may be taken to represent re-exports in Atlantic commerce. This comes to an annual average of $18,118,500, or £3,623,700, in 1790–1800, and $8,701,333, or £1,787,198, in 1848–50.[121]

To complete the estimate of the total yearly value of Atlantic commerce in the period under consideration, we examine next the evidence on Atlantic commerce in business service – shipping, marine insurance, commissions, interests on merchants' loans, and merchants' profits. The most

[119]   The figures used in the calculation are taken from Sheridan, *Sugar and Slavery*, pp. 470, 500, 501.
[120]   Computed from North, *Economic Growth of the United States*, pp. 228 and 234.
[121]   Computed from North, *Economic Growth of the United States*, pp. 221, 233, 284.

comprehensive evidence available centers on U.S. balance of payments calculations.[122] For this reason, the evidence is often presented in the form of net U.S. earnings from trade in services, without adequate information on the earnings of U.S. trading partners. This makes it difficult to calculate the overall value of Atlantic commerce in services. For example, the estimate by Shepherd and Walton shows that mainland British America's earnings from trade in services averaged £832,200 a year in 1768–72.[123] This is very helpful, but without knowing Britain's earnings in its service trade with British North America it is impossible to compute the ratio of services to merchandise trade between Britain and its mainland American colonies, particularly because Britain dominated the much larger trans-Atlantic part of the colonial trade.[124]

For periods during which the United States shipped the bulk of its imports and exports, the problem is less serious. In 1801–19, part of which was the peak of the French Revolutionary Wars and the Continental System, the U.S. captured a very large share of Atlantic commerce in services. United States shipping earnings alone averaged $30,057,894 per annum during the period, while domestic exports averaged $41,811,473.[125] If the domestic exports are doubled as a proxy for merchandise exports plus imports (in line with the procedure established above), the shipping earnings are 35.9 percent of the total. Adding marine insurance, merchants' profits and the other services will raise the proportion significantly.[126] This would appear

---

[122]   Douglass C. North, "The United States Balance of Payments, 1790–1860," in *Trends in the American Economy in the Nineteenth Century: Studies in Income and Wealth, Volume Twenty-Four, By the Conference on Research in Income and Wealth* (Princeton, NJ: Princeton University Press, 1960), pp. 573–627. For estimates of British balance of payments, see Elise S. Brezis, "Foreign Capital Flows in the century of Britain's industrial revolution: new estimates, controlled conjectures," *Economic History Review*, XLVIII, 1 (1995), pp. 46–67; R. C. Nash, "The balance of payments and foreign capital flows in eighteenth-century England: a comment," *Economic History Review*, L, 1 (1997), pp. 110–128; Elise S. Brezis, "Did foreign capital flows finance the industrial revolution? A reply," *Economic History Review*, L, 1 (1997), pp. 129–132.

[123]   Shepherd and Walton, *Shipping, Maritime Trade, and the Economic Development of Colonial North America*, pp. 128, 134.

[124]   McCusker and Menard, *The Economy of British America*, p. 189. As the authors say: "The one major trade in which the colonists had traditionally taken little part, largely because it had been successfully dominated by British merchants, was the transatlantic carrying trade between the colonies and the metropolis" (p. 189).

[125]   The shipping earnings are computed from North, "United States balance of payments," p. 595, and the domestic exports, from Heckscher, *The Continental System*, p. 103, and Pitkin, *A Statistical View*, p. 35.

[126]   For United States trade with Spanish America during this period, Esteban's estimate shows that the combined value of marine insurance and mercantile profits was 63.2 percent of shipping earnings ($1,640,800 annual average shipping earnings and $1,036,300 annual average for marine insurance and mercantile profits). See Javier

consistent with other evidence on the service component of the British and Dutch Caribbean Atlantic commerce, allowing for wartime increases in service costs. For the British Caribbean, Sheridan's estimate shows that service costs associated with commodity exports to Britain averaged £1,286,000 a year in 1772–74, and for imports from Britain it was £370,100.[127] If the value of exports to Britain (£3,187,000) is doubled, following the procedure explained earlier, the service costs come to 26.0 percent of the total. This ratio is almost exactly the same as the one computed for the export and import trade of Dutch Surinam in 1766–76 (25.5 percent) by P. C. Emmer.[128] This peacetime ratio of 26 percent may be taken as a long-term average for the entire period of the study.

With this service ratio and the procedure earlier established, the over time total value of Atlantic commerce during the period has been computed and it is presented in Table 4.8. The estimate should be treated with caution. With more research further refinement is possible. But it may be valid to say that the reader is unlikely to be seriously misled, one way or the other, by these figures in terms of the magnitude of Atlantic commerce during the period.

4.3 AMERICAN PRODUCTS AND INTRA-EUROPEAN TRADE

In a volume examining the rise of merchant empires in the early modern world, the point is made that, "Because much of the increase in trade within Europe [between 1350 and 1750] was related to overseas colonies and markets, it is difficult to separate long-distance and intra-European trade."[129] This point is very much in agreement with the growing evidence produced by research and it is logically consistent with the earlier preliminary examination (Section 4.1 above) of factors constraining the growth of

Cuenca Esteban, "The United States balance of payments with Spanish America and the Philippine Islands, 1790–1819: Estimates and Analysis of Principal Components," in Jacques A. Barbier and Allan J. Kuethe (eds.), *The North American Role in the Spanish Imperial Economy, 1760–1819* (Manchester: Manchester University Press, 1984), pp. 44–45.

[127]   Sheridan, *Sugar and Slavery*, pp. 470, 500–501. To arrive at the service cost on imports, the official value of exports from Britain to the British Caribbean is subtracted from the c. i. f. value of imports estimated by Sheridan. Imports from Ireland are not included in the service cost on imports, but exports to Ireland are included in the service costs on exports; service costs on imports from Ireland could not be computed, because imports from Ireland are not included in the official export figures.

[128]   See Emmer, "The Dutch and the Making of the Second Atlantic System," p. 96: Surinam's exports of cash crops, 6,525,091 Dutch guilders, imports of European goods, 1,337,513 (making a total of 7,862,604 for exports and imports), and 2,001,401 for service costs.

[129]   Phillips, "The growth and composition of trade in the Iberian empires," p. 100.

Table 4.8. *Total Annual Average Value of
Atlantic Commerce (exports plus re-exports
plus imports plus services), 1501–1850*

Period	Annual Average (£000)
1501–50	3,241
1551–1600	9,485
1601–50	15,795
1651–70	20,084
1711–60	35,638
1761–80	57,696
1781–1800	105,546
1848–50	231,046

Sources and Notes: See Table 4.4 and text for sources.
As explained in the text, the figures in Table 4.4 have
been multiplied by 2 to obtain the value of merchandise
exports plus imports, and the annual average value
of United States re-exports for 1790–1800 and for
1848–50 (shown in the text) is added to the figures for
1781–1800 and 1848–50, respectively. Next, each
period's figure is increased by 26 percent to take account
of business services. Since the procedure adopted (as
explained in the text) incorporates the value of slaves
from Africa in the imports of the Americas, only the
value of the direct import and export trade between
Western Africa and Europe should be included in the
table. This has been done for the three periods from
1761 to 1850. For the two periods, 1761–80 and
1781–1800, an annual average of £2.5 million each
is added (£2,245,000, Western African imports from
Europe, c. i. f., and £252,000, European imports from
Western Africa, c. i. f.); and for 1848–50, £4 million
is added (£2.5 million, Western African imports from
Europe, c. i. f., and £1.5 million, European imports
from Western Africa, c. i. f.): These are all computed
from J. E. Inikori, "West Africa's Seaborne Trade,
1750–1850: Volume, Structure and Implications," in
G. Liesegang, H. Pasch and A. Jones (eds.), *Figuring
African Trade* (Berlin: Dietrich Reimer Verlag, 1986),
pp. 52–54, 57–58, 59, 62–63. For an earlier estimate of
the value of Atlantic commerce and the contribution of
Africans, see Inikori, "Slavery and Atlantic Commerce,"
pp. 151–157. The figures estimated are slightly different mainly because the periods are somewhat different.

trade in the economies of the Atlantic basin in the fifteenth century. To reiterate the latter point, the gradual extension of the market sector of West European economies in the early centuries of the last millennium – stimulated by population growth, internal colonization (intra-European migration), and international trade centered in the Mediterranean – was affected adversely in the fourteenth century by the crisis of feudalism, the Black Death, and the stagnation of Mediterranean-based international trade. From the fifteenth century onward, intra-European trade faced another constraining factor – the policy of economic nationalism pursued by the rising nation-states of Western Europe, later known as mercantilism. Viewing international trade as a zero sum game, in theory and practice, West European governments erected protective barriers through which only goods considered essential (for various reasons) but could not be produced at home (largely because of natural resource endowment) could penetrate. The American products, which were natural resource based (precious metals and tropical products), belonged to the latter category.

As the imperial nations of Western Europe integrated their American colonies into their mercantilist arrangement, the American products by law had to go to the respective European mother countries – Spain, Portugal, England, France, and Holland – through which other European countries received them as re-exports. European products from non-mother countries going to the American colonies also had to go through the same mother countries as re-exports. In this way, through direct and indirect stimulation, intra-European trade expanded at rates that were a multiple of the rate of growth of Atlantic commerce itself, and the Americas became a major factor in the commercialization of socio-economic life in Western Europe between 1500 and 1800. The empirical evidence supporting the foregoing general statement is presented in the next several pages.

In temporal sequence, it is logical to begin with precious metals from Spanish America. It is well known that the silver and gold shipped yearly from Spanish America to Spain, both in respect of the Spanish government and private owners, moved quickly out of Spain to the rest of Europe to finance the government's expensive imperial ambitions and a large amount of imports for consumption in Spain and for re-export to Spanish America. This re-export of Spanish American bullion to the rest of Europe stimulated the growth of trade in Europe in several ways: by expanding the physical quantity of a reliable medium of exchange, it contributed immensely in extending the frontier of production for market exchange at the expense of subsistence production in Western Europe; by making possible the growth of imports from the rest of Europe into Spain, it stimulated the growth of intra-European trade and further expansion of the market sector via the multiplier and division of labor mechanisms; and, what is more, by providing a means of payment for Asian products that helped to create mass consumer markets in Europe, it stimulated indirectly the growth of intra-European trade in Asian re-exports. The evidence relating to each of these may now be summarized.

As has been pointed out:

> In the European economy, silver was the basis of a coinage which, at this early stage, was not yet backed by paper money or a very complete system of credit. Issuing coins, mostly silver or copper, was the main way of expanding the circulating medium, so American silver was far more important than the mere quantity shipped to Spain might suggest.[130]

It is this role of the Spanish American bullion that provoked a lively debate several decades ago. Applying the quantity theory of money, economic historians explained that the distribution of Spanish American bullion in Europe raised the quantity of money in circulation much faster than the expansion of output of goods and services, thereby precipitating the general rise in prices known in European history as the price revolution of the sixteenth century. It is argued further that, because prices rose faster than wages, the rate of profits went up, the investment ratio increased, and the spread of capitalism in Europe was stimulated.[131]

The debate on the subject involved the mobilization of data on population, agriculture, manufacturing, and the over time flow of bullion from Spanish America to Spain and the rest of Europe. One popular counterargument is that food prices rose faster than the prices of manufactured goods, suggesting the pressure of population on food supply, it is argued, meaning that population growth was a more important contributory factor than American bullion. Whatever judgment one reaches on the debate, there can be little doubt that the data generated demonstrate that the circulation of Spanish American bullion in Western Europe was a major factor in the transformation of the region's economies from the dominance of subsistence production to the preponderance of the market sector.

Concerning imports from Western European countries into Spain, information is relatively plentiful. The main sources of these imports were France, England, Holland, and the German states. France was the leading source of manufactured imports into Spain during the period. It is no surprise that Spain was the main market for French exports in Europe in the eighteenth century. French exports to Spain grew from £2.0 million (44.7 million livres tournois) in 1730, when they were 45 percent of total French exports to Europe and the Levant, to £3.3 million (76.4 million livres tournois) in 1765, when they were 32 percent, before declining

---

[130]   Murdo J. Macleod, "Spain and America: The Atlantic Trade, 1492–1720," in Bethell (ed.), *The Cambridge History of Latin America*, Vol. I, p. 366.

[131]   E. J. Hamilton, "American Treasure and the Rise of Capitalism," *Economica*, 9 (November, 1929), pp. 338–357; J. D. Gould, "The Price Revolution Reconsidered," *Economic History Review*, 2nd series, 17 (December, 1964), pp. 249–266.

slightly to £3.1 million (71.7 million livres tournois) in 1776.[132] Since the figures for total exports to Europe and the Levant include large quantities of colonial produce exported largely to Northern Europe,[133] the exports to Spain, which were mostly manufactured goods, must have constituted a very large proportion of French manufactured exports sold in Europe. Adding imports from the other countries mentioned earlier, it can be seen that Spain at this time was an important center of trade in European manufactures. These were paid for largely in American bullion.

A large proportion of these manufactures were re-exported to Spanish America, Spanish industry having been weakened by a combination of state policy and the economics of easy revenue from mineral wealth. It has been estimated that in 1689 of 27,000 *toneladas* of merchandise shipped legally from Spain to Spanish America, only 1,500 was produced in Spain, being 5.6 percent of the total: "The bulk of exports from Cadiz consisted of manufactured goods shipped in from France, England and Holland."[134] In the early eighteenth century, Zabala, a Spanish economist, stated that the total value of foreign goods exported yearly from Seville to Spanish America was between £3.1 million and £4.2 million, approximately.[135] Even with the vigorous pursuit of industrialization policy by the Bourbon rulers in Spain in the latter half of the eighteenth century, large quantities of foreign European manufactures continued to be shipped from Spain to Spanish America. As late as 1792, almost one-half (48.1 percent) of goods shipped from Spain to Spanish America were foreign. Yet, this in fact is a considerable understatement, as it is believed that a large proportion of the so-called Spanish goods were foreign products fraudulently relabeled Spanish:[136]

Insofar as the bulk of registered exports, measured by value, consisted of textiles, it follows from what we know of Spanish industry that the overwhelming proportion of these goods came from abroad. Indeed, even Catalan cottons and Valencia

---

[132]   Paul Butel, "France, the Antilles, and Europe in the seventeenth and eighteenth centuries: renewals of foreign trade," in Tracy (ed.), *The Rise of Merchant Empires*, Table 4.2, p. 163. It is not explicitly stated that the figures in the table are export figures; this became clear only after comparing them with those published by Villiers, "The slave and colonial trade in France," pp. 211, 213. The exchange rates applied are from McCusker, *Money and Exchange*, pp. 310–312.

[133]   Hans C. Johansen, "How to pay for Baltic products?" in Fischer, McInnis, and Schneider (eds.), *The Emergence of a World Economy*, pp. 127–140.

[134]   Brading, "Bourbon Spain and Its American Empire," p. 410.

[135]   Jean O. McLachlan, *Trade and Peace with Old Spain, 1667–1750: A Study of the Influence of Commerce on Anglo-Spanish Diplomacy in the First Half of the Eighteenth Century* (Cambridge: Cambridge University Press, 1940), p. 12. The amounts stated in Spanish dollars (15,000,000 and 20,000,000) have been converted to pound sterling at the rate of a Spanish dollar to 4s.2d. as stated by McLachlan (p. 11).

[136]   Brading, "Bourbon Spain and Its American Empire," pp. 415–416, 418.

silks were not exempt from the charge of being French goods bearing a Spanish stamp.

Finally, Spanish American bullion was also the principal means of payment for Asian products imported in large quantities into Western Europe in the seventeenth and eighteenth centuries. The main importers at this time were the English and Dutch companies trading to Asia. Their combined annual sales of Asian products in Europe grew from about £1 million (4.7 million pesos) in 1661–70 to about £3 million (13,558,200 pesos) in 1741–50. In 1752–54, the English company's annual re-export of Indian cotton calicoes alone to northwestern Europe was £434,000.[137] But while European demand for Asian products grew during the period, Asian consumers found few European goods that were of sufficient value. One product that was in large demand in the major Asian regions, especially India and China, was precious metals (silver and gold). With huge deficits in their merchandise trade, the European merchants shipped annually large quantities of bullion (particularly silver) to Asia, without which very little imports would have reached Europe from Asia at this time. One estimate shows that the annual average export of bullion from Europe to Asia by the English and Dutch companies rose from 19 tonnes in 1626–50 to 74 tonnes in 1776–80.[138] Thus, in an important sense, intra-European trade in Asian re-exports in the seventeenth and eighteenth centuries was partly a function of American products.

Evidence produced by research also shows unmistakably that Portugal's trade in Europe during the period depended very largely on American products from Brazil. From the late sixteenth century to the early decades of the seventeenth, Portuguese Brazil was the main source of sugar for Europe. As Caribbean sugar took much of the European market from Brazilian producers from the late seventeenth century onward, Brazil supplied other products – gold, cotton, rice, tobacco, coffee, cocoa – which combined with sugar to make Brazil the main source of Portugal's exports to other European countries. The available trade figures are for 1796–1806. Like Spain, Portugal made a vigorous effort to encourage the growth of domestic production in the latter half of the eighteenth century. This resulted in the export of more domestic products from Portugal. Even so, goods produced in Portugal still formed a small proportion of the total value of goods exported from Portugal to Europe between 1796 and 1806:[139]

---

[137] Niels Steensgaard, "The growth and composition of the long-distance trade of England and the Dutch Republic before 1750," in Tracy (ed.), *The Rise of Merchant Empires*, pp. 112 and 128. The exchange rate applied is 1 peso to £0.225 sterling (or 1 peso to 54d.), taken from McCusker, *Money and Exchange*, pp. 98–100.

[138] Barrett, "World Bullion Flows," p. 251.

[139] Computed from Arruda, *O Brasil No Comércio Colonial*, p. 299. Exports to the United States and Barbary are included, but these together make up less than 1 percent of the total. This is why they are not mentioned.

Percentage of All Exports from Portugal to Europe Produced:

	In Portugal	In Brazil
1796	24.4	61.7
1797	30.2	57.4
1798	31.4	59.0
1799	27.6	57.7
1800	19.7	68.5
1801	28.6	60.1
1802	24.8	67.9
1803	33.6	55.0
1804	22.9	62.5
1805	26.5	61.3
1806	26.1	62.4

Throughout the period Brazilian products made up about 60 percent of all exports from Portugal to the rest of Europe, while goods produced in Portugal were about one-quarter. The rest came from Asia, Portuguese Atlantic islands, and other places. Hamburg, Germany, was the leading recipient of the exports, taking 29.1 percent of the total during the whole period, England came next with 24.0 percent, Italy with 20.0 percent, France 16.0 percent, Holland 3.7 percent, with the rest going to a host of minor importers.[140]

Exports from Portugal to Brazil were also dominated by foreign products, mostly English manufactures. As Merrick and Graham put it:

To counter Spanish influence and secure British protection for its Atlantic trade, Portugal conceded a commercial monopoly to English manufactures in her territories, at the same time agreeing not to establish her own competing industries. As a result, much of the gold mined in Brazil in the eighteenth century ended up as payment to English merchants.[141]

Between 1796 and 1807, 35 percent of total imports into Portugal from Europe, the United States, and Barbary came from England, 11.6 percent from Russia, 10.2 percent from Hamburg, 8.2 percent from Italy, 6.2 percent from Holland, 6.1 percent from France, and the rest from the United States, Barbary, and other European countries.[142]

It can thus be seen that through Spain and Portugal the products and demands of the Spanish American and Brazilian economies were firmly integrated into the trading and production circuit of the economies of Europe, including even faraway Russia. In other words, the trade of Spain and Portugal with other European countries between the sixteenth and the

---

[140]   *Ibid.*, p. 316.
[141]   Merrick and Graham, *Population and Economic Development in Brazil*, p. 12.
[142]   Arruda, *O Brasil No Comércio Colonial*, p. 315.

early nineteenth centuries was really Spanish American and Brazilian trade for all practical purposes.

Similarly, the intra-European trade of the other major colonial powers in the Americas and the leading trading nations of Europe at the time – England, France, and Holland – was very much influenced by the products and demands of the Americas. In the sixteenth and early seventeenth centuries, England had imported American plantation products from Spain and Portugal. In the early seventeenth century, the annual value of tobacco imported into England from Spain was £200,000.[143] But in the course of the seventeenth century, the British American colonies extended and improved upon the Spanish and Portuguese model of plantation agriculture dependent on coerced African labor. As the scale of production grew and improved efficiency in the trans-Atlantic slave trade provided a regular flow of African slave labor cheaply, production cost fell and competition passed the benefits to consumers in Europe in the form of falling prices. The drastic reduction of the prices of these plantation products, especially tobacco and sugar, transformed them from luxuries for the rich to consumer products for all classes in Europe, thereby creating a mass market. As Ralph Davis put it,

vast new sources of demand were being opened up in England and Europe – demand created by sudden cheapness when these English plantation goods brought a collapse in prices which introduced the middle classes and the poor to novel habits of consumption. . . . Tobacco was a luxury at the end of the sixteenth century. . . . Before 1619 twenty to forty shillings a lb was being paid for tobacco in England; in the 1670s it retailed for a shilling or less. . . . there was a rapid expansion of production in the plantations which by 1630 had driven the plantation price down to less than a penny a pound. . . .[144]

Sugar prices came down in the same manner. The high sixteenth-century prices had fallen to about 1s.3d. per lb by the 1630s. Despite an increase in the customs duties, they fell further to about 7d. in the 1680s.[145] With these prices, British America secured the domestic market in England and took over much of the markets in Europe from the Spaniards and the Portuguese.

The latter development is reflected in the contribution of re-exports to the growth of English exports to northwest Europe (Germany, Holland, Flanders and France) and northern Europe (Norway, Denmark, and the Baltic) in the seventeenth and eighteenth centuries. Between 1699–1701 and 1772–74, English domestic exports to northwest and northern Europe declined in absolute terms from £2,114,000 a year to £1,769,000. During

---

[143]   Gary M. Walton and James F. Shepherd, *The economic rise of early America* (Cambridge: Cambridge University Press, 1979), p. 38.

[144]   Davis, "English Foreign Trade, 1660–1700," p. 80.

[145]   *Ibid.*, footnote 6, pp. 81–82. See also Davis, *A Commercial Revolution*, p. 10.

the same period, re-exports grew from £1,243,000 to £3,223,000, which helped to increase total exports from £3,357,000 to £4,992,000, an increase of 48.7 percent instead of a 16.3 percent decrease that would have occurred without re-exports.[146] Colonial produce from British America made up 44.7 percent of the re-exports in 1699–1701 and 67.8 percent in 1772–74. The rest were mainly Asian textiles. Initially, the main colonial products were tobacco and sugar, but as French colonial sugar took over markets on the continent, British Caribbean coffee and mainland British American rice became important additions to tobacco.[147] These products were exported largely to the trading cities of the Low Countries and Germany, from where they were distributed to other places on the continent, especially the Baltic. In this way, the American products provided export surpluses that partly helped to pay for English import of strategic raw materials from the Baltic.[148] Thus, while Brazilian and Spanish American products helped to increase trade between England and southern Europe (Spain and Portugal), plantation products from British America made possible the growth of English trade with northwest and northern Europe in the seventeenth and eighteenth centuries.

As already hinted, the production of export commodities in plantations worked by Africans expanded explosively in the French Caribbean from the early eighteenth century in response to the vigorous efforts of the French minister, Colbert.[149] Sugar, cotton, coffee, and other products were produced and exported to France on a very large scale. By 1711–60, as Table 4.4 shows, the French Caribbean were exporting as much produce as all of British America put together. It was from the last two decades of the eighteenth century, and more so in the first half of the nineteenth, that British America completely outdistanced French America in export commodity production. But for several decades preceding the French Revolution of 1789, the re-export of French American produce was responsible for much of the growth of French exports to other European countries, especially northern and northwest Europe.[150] Direct exports were made from France to the major German trading cities for redistribution to other parts of Europe. However, the Dutch, having been forcefully pushed out of trans-Atlantic trade with Europe by England and France, took consolation in buying from France and distributing the French colonial products in Europe, especially in the Baltic. By the middle of the eighteenth century,

---

[146]   Computed from Davis, "English Foreign Tade, 1700–1774," p. 120.
[147]   *Ibid.*, p. 120.
[148]   Johansen, "How to pay for Baltic products?," pp. 127–140.
[149]   Butel, "France, the Antilles, and Europe in the seventeenth and eighteenth centuries," p. 162.
[150]   Villiers, "The slave and colonial trade in France," pp. 210–214; Butel, "France, the Antilles, and Europe in the seventeenth and eighteenth centuries," pp. 159–164.

more than half of French exports to Holland were made up of re-exports from the French Caribbean.[151] Thus, in a way somewhat similar to England, the expansion of French trade with southern Europe (Spain and Portugal) from the sixteenth century to the Revolution depended heavily on the Iberian American colonies, while the growth of French exports to north-west and northern Europe was sustained by plantation products from French America. Clearly, François Crouzet was right when he described what happened in the eighteenth century before the French Revolution as the Americanization of the economies of Western Europe. His later "post scriptum" disclaimer would, therefore, appear to be unnecessary.[152]

4.4 ATLANTIC COMMERCE AND BRITISH OVERSEAS TRADE, 1650–1850

To conclude the chapter, it is appropriate to make some general observations concerning the place of the Americas in the growth of British overseas trade between the mid-seventeenth and mid-nineteenth centuries. The evidence presented in the chapter is summarized to show that the American economies, centered around plantation agriculture and mining worked by coerced labor, were the most dynamic in the Atlantic basin during the period. The summary is also intended to show that mercantilist policies of the European colonial powers notwithstanding, the Atlantic basin functioned as a quasi common market within which the participating economies went through a process of interconnected change, though unequal in magnitude and different in character. For reasons more or less made clear by the summary, British trade was a major beneficiary of the process.

It is clear from the evidence presented in the chapter that the economies of the Atlantic basin were strongly linked together through the specialized, large-scale operation of the plantation and mining economies of the Americas from the sixteenth to the nineteenth century. On both sides of the Atlantic, the plantation and mining economies of the Americas were by far the most extensive market-oriented sectors of the Atlantic economies at the time. Surrounding these highly specialized and commercialized sectors were huge areas of subsistence and semi-subsistence production on both sides of the Atlantic. The existence of extensive subsistence and semi-subsistence production sectors meant the existence of extensive surplus resources in the form of unemployed and under-employed natural and human resources. The expansion of the plantation and mining economies of the Americas,

---

[151] Butel, "France, the Antilles, and Europe in the seventeenth and eighteenth centuries," pp. 159–160.

[152] Crouzet, "Wars, Blockade, and Economic Change in Europe," pp. 568, 569; Crouzet, *Britain Ascendant*, pp. 316–317.

acting through the domestic market sectors of the Atlantic economies (as just observed in the West European economies), pulled subsistence producers to the market across the Atlantic. The growth of the market sectors and the reduction of subsistence production brought unemployed natural resources into production and provided opportunities for increased utilization of labor time. Every movement of producers from subsistence to market production offered market opportunities, through specialization and division of labor, for other subsistence producers to do the same and the vent-for-surplus process was extended and intensified, raising incomes per head and further stimulating the growth of trade, domestic and international, across the Atlantic basin.

The effects of the plantation and mining economies of the Americas on the expansion of market production was probably more immediate and more far reaching in the Americas themselves, where extensive surplus natural resources encouraged subsistence production and rapid population growth (by natural increase and migration). The literature on the development process in British America shows how the market opportunities provided by the specialization of the plantation and mining economies of the Americas stimulated the growth of market production in mainland British America. Plantation agriculture developed in the British Caribbean and the Southern colonies of mainland British America. But by supplying provision to the plantation and mining economies of the Americas, British and non-British, the family farmers of the middle mainland British American colonies were pulled into market production. What is even more important, lacking the natural resources for large-scale plantation agriculture, the New England colonies took advantage of the market for mercantile services provided by the plantation and mining economies to engage in maritime trade and shipping on a large scale, giving vent to the abundant forest resources for shipbuilding and the deep natural harbors in the region. Just as the middle colonies exported provisions to British and non-British America, New England (and also some of the middle colonies to a lesser degree) exported mercantile services to all the plantation and mining economies of the Americas. These maritime activities and the shipbuilding industry linked to them stimulated the growth of the domestic market and an industrial infrastructure in the region, all of which pulled subsistence producers into market production. As Walton and Shepherd elaborate:

Despite extensive experiments with all varieties of crops New England failed to produce any crop with extensive overseas demand. Rocky soils and an inhospitable climate permitted production only for subsistence and local trade.... Nevertheless, New England was a major trading area.... In fact the most valuable export from New England was shipping services, and in the late colonial period these services, in combination with the shipping services of the middle colonies, were more important than any of the commodity exports except for tobacco.... This development of a resident commercial sector contrasted sharply with the economies south of

Pennsylvania, and even more sharply with the limited commercial development in Spanish America.[153]

The commodity and service exports of New England and the middle colonies went mainly to the Caribbean. For example, in 1768–72 the value of commodities exported to Great Britain and Ireland was only 18 percent of New England's total exports and 23 percent for the middle colonies, while exports to the Caribbean constituted 64 percent and 44 percent, respectively. Caribbean's share of service exports, estimated for the period at £820,000 per annum (larger than the export value of any single colonial commodity at the time) was even much greater as it was only in the intra-American trade that the shipowners of New England and the middle colonies had a significant comparative cost advantage over the metropolitan British shippers.[154]

These developments in northern mainland British America, dependent on trading opportunities provided by the plantation and mining economies of the Americas as they did, created an important development zone with the capacity to suck incomes from the plantation and mining zones, and with social structures and an income distribution pattern that gave rise to mass consumption of manufactured goods. Because of colonial arrangements and cultural attachment, the incomes gathered in the hands of producers and consumers in northern mainland British America were spent on imports from Britain. To illustrate, while exporting very little to Great Britain and Ireland in 1768–72 as shown earlier, New England and the middle colonies took 66 percent and 76 percent of their imports, respectively, from Great Britain and Ireland during the period.[155] This was a unique phenomenon in the Atlantic basin. No other European power was similarly situated during the period.

These dynamic developments in northeastern continental British America kept pace with the growth of the plantation and mining economies of the Americas. The explosive growth of cotton exports from the southern slave states and service exports from the northeastern states of the United States in 1790–1860, shown earlier in this chapter, powerfully stimulated the expansion of commercial food production and migration into the western region of the United States.[156] Though less pronounced, similar extension of market production and the growth of domestic markets in the rest of the Americas[157] also stimulated the growth of shipping and trade in northeast-

---

[153] Walton and Shepherd, *The Economic Rise of Early America*, pp. 46–47.
[154] *Ibid.*, pp. 80, 90–94, 99–101.
[155] *Ibid.*, p. 82.
[156] North, *Economic Growth of the United States*. Criticism of North's well-structured analysis has produced only minor modifications. By combining southern cotton exports and northeastern services and manufacturing, much of the ground for the criticism disappears.
[157] See Hoberman, *Mexico's Merchant Elite*, for the effects of silver and gold production on market production and domestic trade in New Spain (Modern Mexico).

ern United States. And through its trade with the United States and its direct and indirect trade with non-British America, England's overseas trade had a multiple stimulus from the continuing dynamism of the plantation and mining economies of the Americas in the late eighteenth and first half of the nineteenth century.

It is important at this juncture to note that in general the economies of the Americas, with their abundant natural resources, were more dynamic than the Old World economies during the period under consideration. The best evidence for this is population and the opening up of new settlements. As stated earlier in this chapter, the demographic catastrophe of the sixteenth century had reduced the Indian population of New Spain (Mexico) to 1.3 million by 1646. Adding Africans, Europeans, and mixed populations, New Spain had a total population of 1,566,796 in 1646.[158] The population began to grow rapidly in the eighteenth century, reaching 2.6 million in 1742 and 6.1 million in 1810.[159] Due to similar growth in the other provinces, the total population of Spanish America in 1800 was 14.5 million, much larger than the 10.5 million people in Spain at this time.[160] This population growth led to the expansion of settlements and market production in the previously peripheral regions of mainland Spanish America, such as Venezuela and the Argentine Pampas.[161]

Brazil registered similar population growth and expansion of settlements from the Atlantic seaboard into the interior. In 1600 the settled area of Brazil was only 28,800 square kilometers, with a total population of 100,000. By 1700 the settled area was 110,700 square kilometers and 350,000 people. Over the eighteenth century, the settled area almost tripled to 324,000 square kilometers, while the population grew almost tenfold to 3,300,000, in 1800. Fifty years later, the population of Brazil more than doubled to 7,234,000 in 1850.[162] All of this made the Brazilian economy and society more dynamic than the metropolitan economy and society in Portugal during the period.

Population growth and the expansion of settlement were even more explosive still in British America. In 1650 the total population of the British American colonies was only 114,000. This increased almost fourfold to 412,000 in 1700. In the next 70 years it grew by almost a factor of seven to 2,762,000 in 1770, more than doubled in the next three decades to about 6.2 million in 1800, and by 1850 it had quadrupled to 24 million.[163] During the same period (1651–1851), the population of England increased from

---

[158]   *Ibid.*, p. 7.
[159]   Bakewell, "Mining in Colonial Spanish America," p. 146.
[160]   Brading, "Bourbon Spain and Its American Empire," p. 427.
[161]   *Ibid.*, pp. 423–424.
[162]   Buescu, *Historia Economica Do Brasil*, pp. 168, 200, 242.
[163]   McCusker and Menard, *The Economy of British America*, p. 54, for 1650–1770; for 1800 and 1850, see Table 4.6.A, above.

5.2 million to 16.7 million.[164] The indication is that, with abundant natural resources and a rapidly growing population, per capita incomes for free whites in British America were significantly greater and the GNP grew much faster than in Britain.[165] As McCusker and Menard put it:

The total product of the continental colonies advanced at an annual rate of roughly 3.5 percent over the 120 years following 1650, a truly remarkable performance by any standard. Just how remarkable it was is suggested by a contrast with Great Britain: there, the gross national product grew at a rate of something less than 0.5 percent per year during the same period.[166]

Through the operation of the plantation and mining zones of the Americas the dynamism of the American economies was communicated from one American region to another through trade, though unequally. As we have seen, through the trade of the European colonial powers with their American colonies and with other countries in Europe, the dynamism of the American economies was also communicated to the economies of Western Europe, giving them a new lease on life, although, again, unequally. The great advantage which England had, partly by accident, but largely by its military superiority, was the nature and size of her American colonies and advantageous treaties signed with Portugal and Spain at different points during the period. For this reason, Brazil and, to a lesser extent, Spanish America were, for purposes of British Atlantic commerce, part of British America. Viewed this way, it becomes clear that the place of the Americas in the growth of British commerce in the period under consideration is much greater than hitherto thought. Mercantilism did not prevent the development of a single system of international economic relations in the Atlantic basin, it only ensured that the country which succeeded in combining commerce with military might will reap most of the benefits.

[164] Wrigley and Schofield, *The Population History of England*, pp. 208–209.
[165] McCusker and Menard, *The Economy of British America*, pp. 51–57.
[166] *Ibid.*, p. 57. McCusker and Menard's estimate shows that between 1770 and 1775 the average net worth of free Europeans in British America was £33 in New England, £51 in the middle Continental colonies, £132 in the Upper and Lower South of the Continental colonies, and £1,200 in Jamaica (p. 61); per capita GNP of the 13 mainland colonies in 1774 is put at £160.8 ($804, 1980 prices), p. 57.

5

Britain and the Supply of African Slave Labor to the Americas

WE HAVE SEEN IN THE PRECEDING CHAPTERS that the development process in England between 1650 and 1850 was strongly linked not just to British America but to all of the Americas. The supply of African slave labor – the central element in the development and operation of the Atlantic system during the period – constituted one of the linkages. The Portuguese had been buying and selling Africans for more than 100 years before the first known English attempt by John Hawkins to enter the trans-Atlantic slave trade in the 1560s. Even at this point, the effort could not be sustained as the Spaniards and Portuguese strove to defend their monopoly of the more lucrative areas of Atlantic commerce. But, just as through war and diplomacy, British America came to dominate commodity production for Atlantic commerce from the eighteenth century, so did British traders in England and in the Americas come to dominate Atlantic commerce, including the supply of African slave labor to all the Americas. In this chapter we attempt to show the dimensions of the trans-Atlantic slave trade conducted by traders resident in England and, to a lesser extent, by those resident in British America. By showing the distribution of the British slave trade between British and non-British America, the evidence in the chapter is intended to reinforce the main argument of this study that the English economy during the period in question was linked significantly to activities in both British and non-British America. The measurement of the magnitude of the British slave trade itself provides some part of the evidence for determining the extent of the pressure and opportunities provided by the Atlantic system for the development of British resources and institutions. For the same purpose, the chapter includes a detailed discussion of the hazards regularly confronted by the traders. While the latter issue has a direct bearing on the various debates on the volume of the British slave trade, its main importance for this study is the opportunity that the risks of the trade offered for the development of financial institutions in

England, particularly marine insurance, a subject treated in more detail in Chapter 7.

It should be noted from the onset that while effort to establish reasonably reliable figures for the magnitude of the Atlantic slave trade is an important scholarly endeavor in its own right – that effort needs to go on – the continuing disagreement over the specific numbers to assign to the volume of the British trade is of little relevance to the central issue of this study. As we have already seen in the preceding chapter, there is enough evidence with which to measure the contribution of forcefully transported Africans and their descendants to the production of commodities in the Americas for Atlantic commerce during our period. Because the slave trade had unique characteristics that were important for the development of British resources and institutions, as already mentioned, it is important to have some knowledge of the magnitude of the British-carried trade within a certain range. For this and other issues mentioned earlier, the areas of agreement among the main researchers on the subject are more than adequate.

5.1 THE EARLY BRITISH SLAVE TRADE

There are very limited currently known archival sources on the basis of which the volume of the early slave trade conducted by British traders (resident both in Britain and in the Americas) up to 1700 can be estimated. The sources show that English traders traded yearly to West Africa from 1553 to 1632, the first chartered English company trading to Western Africa having been granted a monopoly charter by Queen Elizabeth in 1558.[1] The Portuguese sources used by Walter Rodney indicate that English traders conducted a flourishing business in the Gambia River and Sierra Leone in the late sixteenth and early seventeenth centuries. As Rodney notes, English trade to West Africa was given some legality in the 1580s by the encouragement offered by the Portuguese Prince, Antonio Crato, who took refuge at the English court. By the 1630s, the English and the Dutch had several trading factories in Sierra Leone, and between them they employed 10 to 12 ships a year. According to the Portuguese sources, private traders consistently violated the monopoly rights of the chartered company, as evidenced by the private London firm, Wood and Company, which, as of

---

[1] Joseph E. Inikori, "The Volume of the British Slave Trade, 1655–1807," *Cahiers d'Études africaines*, 128, XXXII (4), (1992), p. 645; M. Oppenheim (ed.), *The Naval Tracts of Sir William Monson*, 5 vols., (Navy Records Society, 1902–1914), vol. IV, pp. 407–408, cited by John C. Appleby, "A Guinea Venture, c. 1657: A Note on the Early English Slave Trade," *The Mariner's Mirror*, Vol. 79, No. 1 (February, 1993), p. 84.

1648, had been trading in the Sherbro for about 25 years.[2] There is also evidence that suggests that Scotland was involved in West African trade in the 1630s, for in 1636 there was a company in Scotland trading to West Africa called the Guiny Companie of Scotland, one of whose ships was seized by a Portuguese governor in that year.[3]

It is not clear how much slave trading was involved in these early British trading activities in West Africa. The best known early British slave trading ventures are those of John Hawkins in 1562, 1564, and 1567, which were more of slave raids than trade. The early companies seem to have placed emphasis on products, such as gold, redwood, ivory, and pepper. The ship of the Guiny Companie of Scotland seized by the Portuguese governor in 1636 was carrying mostly gold worth £10,000.[4] However, there are clear indications that these early English trading activities in West Africa, particularly those of the early seventeenth century, also involved slave trading. For example, while the Company of Adventurers of London trading to Gynney and Bynney, chartered in 1618 by James I, never mentioned slaving as one of its concerns, during the Anglo-French war of 1627–29 the company reported a loss of £20,000 when its ship, the *Benediction*, was captured in Senegal with a cargo of slaves by French privateers in June 1629.[5] The company's involvement in slave trading appears to have increased from the 1630s; in the 1640s its slaving activities in the Slave Coast area were being reported by the Dutch.[6]

Even more important in these early years of the British slave trade were the private traders, usually called interlopers because they traded in West Africa contrary to the monopoly rights of the chartered companies. At no time during the seventeenth century did the chartered companies succeed in preventing private traders from entering the trade: "The evidence . . . suggests that this was an open and competitive trade, despite the Guinea Company's monopoly in West Africa, and that it continued to be so even after the renewal of the monopoly in 1651."[7] It will be shown later that this remained the case up to the final disappearance of the last monopoly company in the eighteenth century. The private traders were more fully committed to the slave trade in the early years of British African trade. London merchants were particularly active. The Dutch sources show

[2] Walter Rodney, *A History of the Upper Guinea Coast, 1545–1800* (Oxford: Clarendon Press, 1970), pp. 124–138.

[3] Inikori, "The Volume of the British Slave Trade," p. 676.

[4] *Ibid.*, fn. 54, p. 676; Appleby, "A Guinea Venture," p. 84; R. Porter, "The Crispe Family and the African Trade in the Seventeenth Century," *Journal of African History*, IX, No. 1 (1968), pp. 57–71.

[5] Porter, "The Crispe Family," pp. 60–61.

[6] Larry Gragg, " 'To Procure Negroes': The English Slave Trade to Barbados, 1627–60," *Slavery and Abolition*, Vol. 16, No. 1 (April, 1995), p. 67.

[7] Appleby, "A Guinea Venture," p. 85.

considerable activity from the 1640s. But without much evidence for the preceding decades it is impossible to say how the post-Civil War activities compare with those of earlier decades. According to the Dutch governor in El Mina (on the Gold Coast), between February 1645 and January 1647, 19 English ships bought slaves on the coast. On the basis of these Dutch sources, it is further computed that at least 84 English ships traded for slaves on the Gold Coast between 1652 and 1657.[8]

In addition to the London private slave traders, planters and merchants in British America also developed an active direct trade in slaves with West Africa in the first half of the seventeenth century. It is suggested that New England's slave trading activities started in 1644 with a venture reported in John Winthrop's *Journal*; in 1645 further evidence shows a three-man venture in the *Rainbow*, Captain James Smith, master; and in 1649, a Barbados planter, John Parris, went to Massachusetts to help organize four slaving ventures within twelve months.[9]

While we can be sure that the British had become active slave traders at least from the 1620s, the foregoing evidence does not provide a firm basis for quantifying the volume of the trade before the second half of the seventeenth century. The market for slaves in British America in the early seventeenth century, especially the Barbados market, has been used as a measure of the extent of British slave trading during the period. The question is whether the Dutch or the British supplied the bulk of the slaves demanded by British America at this time.[10] The more current view suggests that although the Dutch were greater slave traders than the British in the first half of the seventeenth century, Brazil rather than British America was the main market for the Dutch trade.[11] It has thus been argued that British traders possibly transported all the slaves imported into the British Caribbean from the mid-1640s.[12] That being the case, the African population in Barbados in the seventeenth century may give some indication of the magnitude of the early British slave trade. In 1660 this was 27,000;[13]

---

[8] Robert Porter, "European Activity on the Gold Coast, 1620–1667" (Ph.D. thesis, University of South Africa, 1974), p. 223, cited by Gragg, " 'To Procure Negroes,' " fn. 32, p. 79; also *Ibid.*, pp. 68–69. See also Robin Law, "The Slave Trade in Seventeenth-Century Allada: A Revision," *African Economic History*, 22 (1994), pp. 68–69, 71, fn. 45, p. 87.

[9] Gragg, " 'To Procure Negroes,' " pp. 72–73.

[10] Ernst van den Boogaart and Pieter C. Emmer, "The Dutch Participation in the Atlantic Slave Trade, 1596–1650," in Henry A. Gemery and Jan S. Hogendorn (eds.), *The Uncommon Market: Essays on the Economic History of the Transatlantic Slave Trade* (New York: Academic Press, 1979); Johannes M. Postma, *The Dutch in the Atlantic Slave Trade, 1600–1815* (Cambridge: Cambridge University Press, 1990).

[11] Gragg, " 'To Procure Negroes,' " pp. 67–69.

[12] Boogaart and Emmer, "Dutch Participation," p. 371.

[13] McCusker and Menard, *The Economy of British America*, p. 153.

it grew to 32,473 in 1676, 42,000 in 1696, and 41,970 in 1712.[14] The total population of Africans in the British Caribbean in 1665 is put at 36,123.[15] In spite of the known import of 41,769 slaves into Barbados between June 24, 1698 and 1712,[16] the island's slave population in 1712 was 30 less than it was in 1696. This is consistent with the evidence of the governor in 1708 that "it annually required 3,640 [slave imports] or about 7 percent [of the slave population] to keep up the stock,"[17] because deaths considerably exceeded births in the Caribbean slave populations. It may, therefore, have taken a total import of over 100,000 slaves between the early seventeenth century and 1660 to produce the slave population of 27,000 in Barbados in 1660 and 36,123 in the British Caribbean as a whole in 1665. This would mean an export figure of over 120,000, assuming 20 percent mortality rate during the Atlantic crossing.[18] Taking account of the contribution by the Dutch traders, it may be reasonable to conclude that the early British slave trade up to the beginning of 1662 may not have transported less than 100,000 slaves from Africa.[19]

The second part of the early British slave trade ran from 1662 to 1671, a 10-year period during which both company and private traders had become fully committed to the transportation of slaves to the Americas as their primary trading concern. The Company of Royal Adventurers Trading to Africa, which held monopoly rights over British African trade during the period, devoted its main attention to the slave trade and treated the trade in African products as a supplement. The extant records of the company make it possible to have a clearer view of the British slave trade in this period than in the previous decades. The known journals and ledgers of the

[14] PRO, CO 318/12, p. 115, An Account of the Number of White Inhabitants, Free Negroes and Slaves in Barbadoes.
[15] Watts, *The West Indies*, Table 6.1, p. 236.
[16] PRO, CO 390/12, p. 223; CO 33/15, folios 9–14. 34,583 were imported between June 24, 1698 and December 1707, and 7,186 imported between March 25, 1708 and 1712.
[17] PRO, CO 318/2, p. 115; CO 390/12, pp. 224–225.
[18] The mortality rate in the trade of the Royal African Company of England in the second half of the seventeenth century was 23.7 percent on the average. See Inikori, "The Volume of the British Slave Trade," p. 677.
[19] David Eltis's estimate of slave imports into Barbados from 1662–1695 (about 106,000) implies that it took over 127,000 slaves exported from Africa to Barbados (using 20 percent middle passage mortality rate) to increase the slave population of Barbados from 27,000 in 1660 to 42,000 in 1696, an increase of about 15,000. See David Eltis, "The Volume and African Origins of the British Slave Trade before 1714," *Cahiers d'Études africaines*, 138–139, XXXV (2–3), 1995, Table I, p. 618. It should be noted that the Caribbean slave population figures, which were derived from the tax rolls by the officials, significantly understate the actual numbers. For example, in 1748 the governor of Barbados stated that the real number of African slaves in the island in that year was 68,000 instead of the 47,025 derived from the tax roll. See CO 318/2, p. 116.

company contain information on some of its vessels that transported slaves to the Americas during the period: 10 in 1662 (all in September); 26 in 1663; 36 in 1664; 16 in 1665; 13 in 1666.[20] It will be unwise to treat these figures as representing all the shipping employed by the company to transport slaves from Africa in these years, because we do not have all the records of the company. In 1667 the company stated that it had imported into British America, 6,000 slaves each year since it started operation in 1662. Although George Zook thought this was an exaggeration,[21] available evidence relating to goods carried to the African coast by the company's known vessels suggests otherwise. For example, of the 26 ships for 1663, mentioned earlier, the cargoes carried to the African coast by 12 vessels are known and these amount to a total of £52,900. Similarly, the cargoes carried by 12 of the 36 vessels for 1664 are known and they add up to £40,009.[22]

Using some other evidence from the company's records, along with the evidence on goods shipped to the African coast, some general view of the volume of slave shipment from Africa by the company during the period can be shown. In 1662, the company's ship, *Blackmore*, traded in West Africa and the details of the venture are available.[23] The f.o.b. (free on board) cost of the ship's cargo in England was £866:14s:11d. With this cargo, 217 slaves were purchased in Calabar at a total coastal cost of £1,304:12s:6d; 81 elephant teeth (ivory), weighing 2,019.5 lbs, were bought at a coastal cost of £126:4s:4d; 33 ounces and 10 ackies of gold costing £117:14s:0d; gifts to the king of Calabar and his family, £34:8s:3d; goods sold at Princes and unsold goods, £65:17s:2d. The total coastal value of the ship's goods, £1,614:16s:3d, represents a mark-up of 86 percent to take account of freight, insurance, and other charges, plus merchants' profits. The gifts to the king and his family, which come to 2.4 percent of the total, may be treated as customs duty. The combined value of the African products (ivory and gold) comes to 15.1 percent of the total, and that of the slaves is 80.8 percent. While we cannot rely too heavily on the evidence from one venture, it should at least provide a general picture of the company's trade on the coast in the 10-year period.

We can thus apply the mark-up of 86 percent to the known cargoes of 1663 and 1664. The f.o.b. value of the goods (the prime cost of the goods in England) employed in purchasing the 217 slaves in 1662 comes to £3.24

[20] PRO, T70/309, T70/599, and T70/600 Part I. As George Zook noted in 1919, "The records kept by the factors in the island [Barbados] have nearly all disappeared." See George F. Zook, "The Company of Royal Adventurers of England Trading into Africa, 1660–1672," *Journal of Negro History*, Vol. IV, No. 1 (January, 1919), p. 217.

[21] Zook, "The Company of Royal Adventurers," p. 217.

[22] PRO, T70/599.

[23] PRO, T70/309, "Journal, Company of Royal Adventurers Trading to Africa, Commencing 26 September, 1662."

per slave, which appears consistent with the average of £3 sterling per head for the period 1676–79 computed from the Board of Trade records by the Committee of Council in 1789.[24] The problem is to determine the proportion of the goods shipped to Africa by the company that went for the purchase of slaves. This is unclear from the available company's records. Even if the company was still buying large quantities of African products in addition to its commitment to the shipment of slaves, the evidence on goods shipped and on slave prices indicates that a six-year average of 6,000 slaves landed in the Americas from 1662 to 1667, as claimed by the company, was not an exaggeration.

As mentioned earlier, private traders, who traded proportionately more in slaves than the companies did, remained very active during the period, the monopoly rights of the Royal Adventurers notwithstanding. One of the reasons for the failure of the company mentioned in the sources is competition with private traders.[25] In fact, when the company came under pressure by the planters in British America in 1667, to appease them it had to grant licenses to the private British traders, who thus dominated the trade from 1668 to 1671.[26] Unlike the trade of the company, however, there is no evidence with which an estimate can be made. It may be reasonable to assume that over the 10-year period the private traders shipped as many slaves as the company, which would mean a period average of no less than 10,000 slaves shipped from Africa per year and a period total of 100,000. This is simply an indication of the order of magnitude.

An alternative way of measuring the volume of slave shipment by the British traders in this 10-year period is by employing the official statistics of export and import trade between England and Africa. These official statistics are available at the beginning and at the end of the period, 1662–63 and 1668–69. Assuming that the difference between the value of exports to and imports from Africa was equal to the value of goods employed in buying slaves, and using the mean slave price derived from the records of the Company of Royal Adventurers stated earlier, gives total slave exports of 14,464 in 1662–63 and 15,465 in 1668–69.[27] This

---

[24] House of Lords Record Office, *Parliamentary Papers, Accounts & Papers*, Vol. XXVI, No. 646a, 1789, Report of the Lords of the Committee of Council, Part IV, No. 25: The Chronological Prices of Negroes. It should be noted that slave prices on the African coast fell over the first half of the seventeenth century, but began to rise from the late 1670s. See Law, "Slave Trade in Seventeenth-Century Allada," pp. 78–79.

[25] Inikori, "The Volume of the British Slave Trade," p. 646.

[26] Gragg, "'To Procure Negroes,'" p. 77.

[27] In 1662–63, the exports were £56,766:5s:0d and imports, £15,886:13s:0d; and in 1668–69, the comparable figures are £54,402:14s:0d and £7,646:7s:0d. Both the export and import figures are, in all likelihood, understatements, but the differences should cancel out to minimize error. For the details of the computation, see Inikori, "The Volume of the British Slave Trade," pp. 677–679.

indicates that the 10-year average of 10,000 shipments per year earlier adopted, though possibly on the low side, is reasonable.

The last part of the early British slave trade is the period 1672–1700, during much of which the last of the chartered companies, the Royal African Company, held monopoly rights. As already mentioned, the trade remained open and competitive in spite of the Royal African Company's monopoly rights. The volume of British slave shipment during the period was, therefore, made up of shipments by the company and by the private traders, including trade originating both in Britain and in British America. The company's shipments were estimated over four decades ago by K. G. Davies in his classic work on the history of the company.[28] Davies computed that the company delivered a total of 74,529 slaves in the British Caribbean between 1673 and 1700. An examination of sources that were not available to Davies shows that he underestimated the volume of the company's trade in these years. For example, he states that in 1673 and 1674, the company delivered a total of 220 and 1,945 slaves, respectively.[29] But in July 1676, the company itself stated:

This Compa[ny] hath been setled [sic] little above four years; in the two first whereof Navigation was obstructed by the Dutch Warr, and the general Imbargos laid on all ships; Yet we were not wanting in our applications to his Ma.ᵗʸ who thereupon graciously permitted us to send forth seven ships, to carry soldiers, ammunition, provisions etc to preserve the forts and factories in Guiny, whence they proceeded, with Negros, to the several plantations and four of them to the Barbados. The third year [1674], when the warr was ended y company . . . sent out fifteen ships to the Coast of Africa and thence ordered six of them to the Island of Barbados with about two thousand Negros, which their Factors disposed of, at several rates . . .[30]

The numbers stated by the company imply an average shipment of 333 slaves per company ship. This would mean that the seven ships of 1672–73 shipped from Africa 2,331 slaves, and the 15 ships of 1674 carried 4,995.

Again, for the period 1680–88, Davies estimated a total delivery of 37,675 slaves in the Americas by the company. During the same period, documents in both the Colonial Office and Treasury series show a total shipment from Africa of 60,783 slaves by the company, of which 21,521 were landed in Barbados, 18,801 in Jamaica, and 6,073 in the Leeward

[28]   K. G. Davies, *The Royal African Company* (London: Longmans, 1857), Appendix IIIA, p. 363.

[29]   *Ibid.*, p. 363.

[30]   PRO, CO 268/1, "Reply of the Royal African Company to charges by the Council and Assembly of Barbados, Received by the Committee of Trade and Plantations on 16 July, 1676." Davies's figures show a delivery of 1,066 slaves in Barbados in 1674, about half of the figure stated by the company itself, and 879 for the other colonies. And yet 9 out of 15 ships were expected to deliver their slaves in the other colonies.

Islands, making a total delivery of 46,395.[31] The latter figure is about 23 percent higher than that of Davies. It should be noted that Davies is aware that his figures understate the actual volume of the company's trade in these years. In fact, he suggests that about 10,000 more deliveries should be added to the total for the period 1672–1711.[32] The foregoing evidence suggests that at a minimum an upward adjustment of 20 percent should be made for the years 1672–1700. This raises Davies's delivery figures to 73,863 for 1672–90, and 19,299 for 1691–1700, making a total of 93,162 for the whole period 1672–1700. The company's Atlantic crossing mortality is indicated by the shipment of 60,783 and the delivery of 46,395 in 1680–88. This means a ratio of 0.763, delivery to shipment. Applying this ratio to the delivery figures gives export figures of 96,806 for 1672–90 and 25,294 for 1691–1700.

As already mentioned, the other component of British slave shipment between 1672 and 1700 is the trade conducted by the private traders, about which very limited information is available because of its clandestine nature. Indirect evidence provided by the Royal African Company and the Board of Trade, and some other pieces of evidence, do provide a sufficient body of information on the basis of which a reasonable order of magnitude can be established for the private traders. It should be noted that the company that immediately preceded the Royal African Company, the Company of Royal Adventurers, after waging a losing battle with the private traders, conferred legality on what they had been doing illegally by granting them licenses in 1667. For this reason, as noted earlier, the British slave trade was dominated completely by private traders in the five years preceding the establishment of the Royal African Company in 1672. The company's testimony shows that the dominance of the private traders continued even after the establishment of the new monopoly company. In a petition written in January 1676, the company stated:

Your Ma.[tie] was graciously pleased, by several Orders of Council, vitz on the 20th December 1672 and 4th September 1674, to Order y stopping of such ships as were then going out till such time as the Masters had given security not to proceed to any of the limits of Yo.[r] Pet.[rs] charter. Since which time, May it please Your Ma.[tie] those Loose Traders [private traders] have been more cautious by entring at the Custom House the Goods they intend for that Trade for some other places . . .[33]

The company's observation shows that for the private traders it was business as usual, monopoly charter or not. Even after the orders of the Crown all that happened was the concealment of the intended place of trade

---

[31] PRO, T70/175; CO 388/10/H.108.
[32] Davies, *The Royal African Company*, p. 299.
[33] PRO, CO 268/1, fol. 66, "Petition of the Royal African Company, Read in Council, 26 January, 1676."

by false declaration in the Custom House. The inherent under-recording of the volume of the British slave trade arising from this practice has been frequently discussed in the literature.[34] Some evidence published recently indicates the magnitude of the under-recording involved.[35] The evidence shows that between 1713 and 1725, ships which traded on the African coast but cleared out in the Custom House fraudulently to Madeira carried goods totalling £708,224. This comes to 42.3 percent of the total value of exports to Africa (£1,675,052) recorded in the Customs Ledgers during the same period.[36] And Madeira is just one of several places used for this purpose.

It is important to state the context of the Madeira evidence. Due to concerted pressure from the planters in British America and from the private traders, Parliament enacted a law allowing private traders to trade legally to Africa, with effect from June 24, 1698. All such private traders were made by the law to pay to the Royal African Company 10 percent of the value of goods they exported to Africa. This regulation was experimental and it was to last for 13 years. When the period expired, the private traders fought to extend it but failed. It was not until March 26, 1726, that the separate traders finally won, when Parliament declared the trade completely open to all British nationals, without any charges other than normal customs duties. The monopoly rights of the Royal African Company were, therefore, in effect, between 1672 and 1698, and between July 1711 and 1726.[37] The fraudulent clearance to Madeira, for which we have clear evidence, was thus one of the ways the private traders concealed their violation of the company's monopoly rights. For the years 1672–98, there are no similar customs records that could yield the kind of evidence presented earlier. However, the evidence thus far presented in this chapter is enough to believe that the practice existed for much of the seventeenth century whenever there was a monopoly company.

In addition to their operation from ports in Britain, the private traders conducted extensive slave trading from ports in British America. In March 1675, it was noted in Whitehall that contrary to royal proclamations against private slave trading from British America, "there are several ships that have arrived at Barbados from those parts of Africa with Negroes and

[34]   Joseph E. Inikori, *The Chaining of a Continent: Export Demand for Captives and the History of Africa South of the Sahara, 1450–1870* (UNESCO Project Published by the Institute of Social and Economic Research, University of the West Indies, Mona, Jamaica, 1992), pp. 7–9; Inikori, "The Volume of the British Slave Trade," pp. 645–650.

[35]   David Richardson, "Cape Verde, Madeira and Britain's Trade to Africa, 1698–1740," *Journal of Imperial and Commonwealth History*, Vol. 22, No. 1 (1994), pp. 1–15.

[36]   Richardson, "Cape Verde, Madeira," Table 3, p. 12.

[37]   Inikori, "The Volume of the British Slave Trade," pp. 646–647.

other goods; and several others are now on the said coasts, all of which are set out by private traders . . ."[38] In May 1677, the company itself petitioned the Crown that contrary to its royal charter of monopoly, "several of your Matie's^ subjects, in contempt thereof, doe frequently use that Trade as well from England as from your Matie's^ Foreign Plantations . . ."[39]

A number of factors facilitated illegal private slave trading in British America. One of these was the existence in the British Caribbean of many remote places where vessels could fit out and discharge their cargo undetected. As the company put it:

Yo.^r^ pet.^rs^ have notice that several Interlopers do still go out to trade upon the Coast of Guiney which will, the most of them, go to Your Ma.^tys^ Plantations in America . . . But in regard those plantations have many remote ports, and the owners of such ships, goods and Negros (conscious of their own guilt) do clandestinely land them in some of the said remote ports, whereby they avoid the punishment that ought to be laid upon them.[40]

The other factor was the role of the colonial officials in British America. The evidence shows that the officers of the Crown in the colonies did not only corruptly collude with the private traders but were in fact part owners of illegal slave trading ventures. To illustrate, there was an incident in 1675, when the company's officers in Barbados seized 80 slaves imported from Africa by a vessel belonging to private traders. As these officers narrated, they were beaten up and the slaves forcefully taken away from them, without the colonial officials doing anything to protect them or prosecute the offenders. Expressing their helplessness, the company's officers concluded:

From hence you may conclude what probability there is for us to hinder interlopers coming hither, when if they are discovered, we are beaten and wounded; and the offenders come off better than the sufferers, and little discountenanced in what they doe. We do not think fit to prosecute an action for the recovery of the Eighty Negros [who] were seized and violently taken away from us . . . being assured a jury will find against us: For possibly it will not be easy for us to make such proof as will satisfy a Barbados Jury that they came from within the limits of your charter; or if such proof could be made, yet considering the Baron of the Exchequer and some of his assistants (who are the same with the Baron etc.) are concerned in Interlopers, it will be noe easy matter for us to obtain a verdict against Interlopers, especially since it is a Maxim with many in this Country, That the King cannot grant any such Charter, as yours is, to exclude the rest of his subjects

---

[38] PRO, CO 268/1, fols. 29–31, "Order in Council for a letter to be sent to the Governor of Barbados, Whitehall, March 1st, 1675."

[39] PRO, CO 268/1, fol. 69, "Petition of the Royal African Company to the King of England, Read in Council, 4 May, 1677."

[40] PRO, CO 268/1, fols. 117–118, "Petition of the Royal African Company, Presented to the King, 18 October, 1686."

from trading where they please, without it were ratify'd by Act of Parliament in England.[41]

And yet another factor was the collusion of the company's own officers on the African coast with the private traders. These officers seized every opportunity to make money for themselves at the company's expense. They traded privately on their own, in which activity they found collaboration with interlopers privately rewarding. The assistance offered by several of the company's senior officers on the coast made it relatively easy for the private traders to do business within the limits of the company's charter without serious obstruction. For example, in November 1675, the company's agent in Barbados reported:

The Dutch have 3 or 4 ships on y Coast that compa[ny] being restablisht . . . those ships endeavor to take the Interloper that lately came thither, which in all probability they had done if Mr. Archer your factor at Wiamba [sic] had not given him soe quick a dispatch . . . This Archer furnished the Interloper with one hundred and odd Negroes, as we are informed, and is reported to be a general assister of Interlopers, and a dealer with them of which we hold ourselves bound to acquaint the Compa[ny], we being so many ways assured it is truth . . .[42]

It is thus clear enough that the private traders conducted an extensive slave trading between 1672 and 1700, both from England and from British America, the monopoly rights of the Royal African Company notwithstanding. The problem is how to translate what the evidence says into specific numbers. It may be possible to do so by combining the foregoing evidence with some other roughly quantifiable information. In February 1708, the British Board of Trade stated that,

From the establishment of the Royal African Company (by Charter) in 1672 to the year 1680, that Trade [the slave trade] was greatly neglected, & heavy complaints were made from several of the plantations of their not being sufficiently supplyed with negroes, which complaints encouraged many private adventurers to enter into the said Trade, by which means it was considerably advanced . . .[43]

---

[41]   PRO, CO 268/1, fols. 34–36, Royal African Company's agent in Barbados to the Royal African Company in London, Barbados, 26 November, 1675. Evidence about this kind of attitude to colonial laws abounds in other sources relating to other British American colonies. See, in particular, PRO, CO 388/12 Part II/K.66, "Memorial from Mr. Holt relating to the illegal trade carried on between Curaçao, St. Thomas, and the British Plantations, Received, 15 December, 1709, and Read, 11 January, 1710." This document details the corrupt practices of the colonial officials and their direct participation in illegal trade.

[42]   PRO, CO 268/1, fols. 36–37, Royal African Company's agent in Barbados to the Royal African Company in London, 26 November, 1675.

[43]   PRO, BT 6/17, "Board of Trade's Comments on the Petition of the Royal African Company, 3 February, 1707/8" [date should read 1708].

Then in January 1709, in a "General State of the Trade to Africa" presented to the British House of Commons, the Board further stated: "Several private ships with their cargoes were seized . . . on the coast of Africa and in the Plantation for trading contrary to the Company's charter whereby such private trade was in a manner crushed. But upon the late Revolution [1688], it revived again and was carried on for some years to a much greater degree than formerly."[44]

The other piece of roughly quantifiable evidence relates to the known volume of the private traders' business in the very first year of legal trading after Parliament declared the trade open to all British nationals with effect from June 24, 1698. In this very first year, 1698/99, the private traders cleared out to the African coast from London alone 36 ships as compared with 15 by the company.[45] When private trade from Bristol and Liverpool is added, as also the extensive private trade from British America, the indication is that in this very first year of partial free trade, the ratio of private trade to company trade was over four to one. This relative volume of private trade in the first year of partial open trade could not have been a sudden growth, taking into account the complex and specialized nature of the slave trade. It certainly reflects the pre-existing volume of private trade which had gone on underground for years.

All the foregoing evidence taken together suggests strongly that at the very least the volume of private trade should be equal to that of the company in the period 1672–90, and for the last decade of the century, it should be twice that of the company. Following from this, total British empire slave exports from Africa in the years 1672–90, and 1691–1700, come to 193,612 and 75,882, respectively, bringing the total for both periods to 269,494. Adding the figure for the years 1662–71 gives an export figure of 369,494 for the entire period, 1662–1700. This brings the volume of the entire early British slave trade, from John Hawkins up to 1700, to 469,494.

5.2 SLAVE TRADE ORIGINATING FROM BRITISH AMERICA IN THE EIGHTEENTH AND NINETEENTH CENTURIES

The slave trade of the British empire in the eighteenth and nineteenth centuries was conducted and recorded in three distinct components: trade originating from and recorded in ports in England, by far the largest; trade originating from and recorded in ports in mainland British America, second

---

[44] PRO, CO 390/12, fols. 140–247, "General State of the Trade to Africa Presented to the House of Commons by the Council of Trade, 27 January, 1708/9" [date should read 1709], fol. 142 (p. 174).

[45] PRO, CO 390/12, fols. 181–193. See also PRO, CO 388/11.

in volume; and trade originating from and recorded in ports in the British Caribbean, which was small relative to the first two and has been least studied. The next section of the chapter is devoted to the much larger trade. In this section, we examine the two components of the trade that originated from British America. The distinction is based entirely on the ports from which the vessels cleared out to the African coast to purchase and transport slaves to the Americas. This distinction is very important, because, as will be shown later, shipping clearance records are the closest to complete data available for the estimate of the volume of the British slave trade, and information about vessels clearing out to the African coast from one port cannot be found recorded in another port.

The trade originating from the British Caribbean may be taken first. Because of the focus on the port of outward clearance to Africa, the slave trade that originated from the British Caribbean during the period in question was in four categories. The first category was conducted with ships belonging to traders resident in England. These vessels usually cleared out to the African coast from ports in England in the first instance. Thereafter, they made one or more repeated voyages between the Caribbean and the African coast, transporting slaves, without touching ports in England, before once again returning to their home ports in England. Sometimes the vessels in this category cleared out to the Americas from ports in England, and from the Americas they went to the African coast to transport slaves to the Caribbean. The second category was conducted with ships belonging to British Caribbean islands but hired by traders in England to transport rum to the African coast and slaves back to the Caribbean. The third category, a rather limited trade, was conducted with vessels belonging to ports in British North America. These vessels cleared out to the African coast from British Caribbean islands and returned there with slaves. These must not be confused with ships which cleared out to the African coast directly from ports in mainland British America. Only the latter are counted as part of the mainland trade. The fourth category, which was the largest in volume during the first half of the eighteenth century, was conducted with ships belonging to the British Caribbean islands, and the slaves transported belonged to traders or planters resident in the British Caribbean.

By the very nature of this portion of the British slave trade, the only official source of information about the clearance of the ships to the African coast for the specific voyages in question is the one officially recorded in the British Caribbean. Unfortunately, the colonial customs records were poorly produced and irregularly transmitted to the Custom House in London. Thomas Irving, the meticulous Inspector General of the Exports and Imports of Great Britain and the British Colonies in the late eighteenth century, frequently complained of the poor quality of the records transmitted from the colonies. In May 1789, he specifically stated that,

The Account of the Number of Negroes imported into, and exported from, the several Ports in the Island of Jamaica cannot be carried further back than the Commencement of the Year 1773, the Original Returns from the West Indies prior to that Time being very imperfect: And even, in some Instances, in the Period for which the present Account is made up, some of the Quarterly Accounts for the small Ports are wanting; but as the Trade of these ports was very inconsiderable, it is probable few Negroes were either imported or exported into or from them during that Time. The Accounts for the Year 1788 have not been all received as yet from the West Indies.[46]

Again, in May 1792, while transmitting to the British House of Commons an account of ships transporting slaves from Africa to the British Caribbean in 1789, 1790, and 1791, Thomas Irving commented: "The above Account is made up in the best Manner which the very imperfect Returns from the West Indies enabled the Inspector General to prepare it."[47] Apart from the weaknesses highlighted by Thomas Irving, the extant records from the West Indies, the Naval Officers Lists, contain many gaps, which make it impossible to produce a comprehensive and accurate list of ships that cleared out to the African coast from the British Caribbean in the eighteenth century. However, a careful combination of all the available sources can provide a basis for a reasonable estimate.

The private records of the Royal African Company of England are very helpful in indicating the volume of the company's slave trade that originated from the Caribbean. A summary reference to some of these will suffice. Early in the eighteenth century, the governor of the company, Sir Dalby Thomas, who was resident on the Gold Coast, recommended to the company that "3 or 4 ships a year to go to Ireland and Barbados to fit up with Rum would be proper by which would be supplyed cheap with provisions and with Tallow & that part of the Irish cargo might be sold at Barbados to purchase Rum."[48]

The company's trade conducted via the Caribbean-African-Caribbean route was generally referred to by the company's officers as the "rum trade," rum being virtually the only product brought to the African coast by the vessels on this route. The evidence indicates that Barbados, Antigua, and Jamaica were the main centers for this branch of the company's trade. The company had factors in these islands who managed the trade on its

[46] HLRO, *Parliamentary Papers Vol. 82, Accounts and Papers*, Vol. XXIV, No. 622, 1789, An Account of the Number of Negroes Imported into, and exported from the Island of Jamaica . . . Signed by Thomas Irving, Inspector General of the Imports and Exports of Great Britain and the British Colonies, Custom House, London, May 12th, 1789.

[47] British Library, *House of Commons Sessional Papers of the 18th Century, Reports & Papers*, Vol. LXXXII, 1791 & 1792, p. 303.

[48] PRO, (Treasury Papers) T 70/5, fol. 10, Sir Dalby Thomas to Royal African Company, Cape Coast Castle, 2, 4, & 6 March, 1705/6 [to read 1706].

behalf – hiring local vessels, purchasing rum in the islands, and generally fitting out the hired ships and the company's vessels making repeated voyages between Africa and the Caribbean. In 1707, the company employed at least five vessels on this route, four from Antigua and one from Barbados.[49]

Sir Dalby Thomas complained frequently that the company's vessels sent from the West Indies were too small for the number of slaves they were intended to carry: "The *Grand Content* sloop arrived from Antegua [sic], is too small to take in 170 Negroes . . . ;" "your *Flying Fame* from Antigua was arrived & was not fit to carry the Negroes she went for . . ." He recommended to the company that proper directives should "be given to the factors in the West Indies for what ships they send."[50] The company's officer's on the coast also complained that the goods sent from England were not enough in quantity to buy all the slaves required for the company's ships from England and those from the Caribbean, and also to buy gold on the coast. In fact, among seven factors thought by the officers to be responsible for the company's poor performance, the "rum trade" was listed sixth:[51] 1) great mortality of slaves bought on the Gold Coast; 2) lowering of goods and raising of slave prices due to competition with 10 percent men; 3) hired ships prejudicial; 4) charges of the coast very great; 5) company traded for too many slaves in proportion to the goods sent, which caused the gold trade to be neglected; 6) the rum trade drains the coast of goods by which gold is purchased; and 7) the Natives by custom send their slaves to the English and their gold to the Dutch.

Thus, the company's private records indicate that the slave trade originating from the Caribbean was an important part, by volume, of the Royal African Company's trade in the early eighteenth century.

Evidence presented to the British Board of Trade by the private traders and by the Royal African Company during their struggle over the company's monopoly rights in the first decade of the eighteenth century also sheds some light on the volume of the slave trade that originated from the British Caribbean. In a document sent to the Board of Trade in January 1708, the private traders stated that "between midsummer 1698 and December 1707," 14 vessels were cleared out each year from the British "plantations" to the African coast to transport slaves, being a total of 133 vessels, out of which 128 belonged to the private traders and 5 belonged

---

[49]   PRO, T 70/5, fols. 32–43. These vessels are mentioned in the letters of the officers on the coast. The indication is that the company employed more ships on this route at this time.

[50]   PRO, T 70/5, fols. 19 and 32, Sir Dalby Thomas's letters of 5 October, 1706, and 25 April, 1707.

[51]   PRO, T 70/5, fol. 38, James Blaney to Royal African Company, Cape Coast Castle, 3 August, 1706.

to the Royal African Company.[52] The private traders indicated in their statement that they were not sure of the exact number of ships cleared from the "plantations" during the period: "supposed to have been dispatcht from the plantations," as they put it. Other sources indicate that the private traders may have understated the actual numbers. Evidence submitted to the Board of Trade by the governor of Barbados during the same period shows: "That since the 9th of December 1698, 111 vessels have been fitted out from that Island for the Coast of Africa, 18 whereof were for the Company's Account [Royal African Company], & 93 on Account of the Separate Traders."[53] Thus, the Royal African Company cleared out 18 vessels from Barbados alone during the period, as opposed to 5 from all the British colonies as stated by the private traders. In fact, another source shows that between 1703 and 1709, the Royal African Company dispatched 31 vessels from the West Indies to West Africa.[54] The figure of 111 vessels for Barbados alone also shows that the 133 vessels stated for all the colonies by the private traders is a significant understatement.

Taking the preceding figures along with those of the Naval Officers Lists for Antigua, Jamaica, and Barbados, which appear to be tolerably good for the early years of the eighteenth century, we can produce a reasonable estimate of the volume of the British slave trade originating from the British Caribbean in the first quarter of the eighteenth century. The Naval Lists show the names of the vessels, the ports to which they belonged, the dates of clearance, the dates of entry, and sometimes the number of slaves imported. The counting is based virtually on clearance evidence. On a few occasions, however, because of the gaps in the sources, when a Caribbean vessel entered its home port from Africa without evidence of a previous clearance for more than one year, such a vessel was counted on the basis of the entry information, since the round trip, Caribbean to Africa to Caribbean, invariably took less than a year. For Barbados, the evidence covers two distinct periods: December 1699 to December 1707, and March 25, 1708 to March 25, 1726. The evidence for the latter period relates only to vessels belonging to Barbados; their names and the number of slaves imported into Barbados by each vessel are all shown.

Counting as indicated, these sources show that between October 19, 1705 and September 19, 1719 (14 years), 21 vessels traded from Antigua to the African coast; 11 from Jamaica, 1712 to 1715 (landing a total of 2,509 slaves); 145 vessels from Barbados, December 1699 to December

[52] PRO, CO 388/11/I.8, "Answer of Divers Separate Traders to Africa to the queries sent them 15 December, 1707, with a Supplement thereto, Received and Read 2 January 1707/8" [to read 1708].

[53] PRO, CO 390/12, fol. 193 (or 225, both shown on the same page).

[54] P. Kup, *A History of Sierra Leone, 1400–1787* (Cambridge: Cambridge University Press, 1961), p. 70, cited by Rodney, *Upper Guinea Coast*, p. 179.

1707; and 87 vessels belonging to Barbados landed a total of 10,750 slaves in Barbados between March 25, 1708 and March 25, 1726.[55] Thus, in the first quarter of the eighteenth century, we have some tolerably good information for Antigua for 14 years, Jamaica for four years, and Barbados for virtually all the years. For the three islands, the total comes to 264 vessels, of which the more or less complete information for Barbados accounts for 232. It should be noted that our Barbados figure of 145 vessels for 1699–1707 from the Naval Officers List is some 34 vessels more than the figure stated by the governor of the island for the same period, which was mentioned earlier.

From the second quarter of the century onwards, the information available to us becomes increasingly unsatisfactory. The evidence indicates a decline in the trade originating from the British Caribbean in the late eighteenth century. This is revealed by the clearances from the British West Indies to the African coast contained in some of the parliamentary papers of the period:[56] For the 14 years, 1783–96, 7 vessels were cleared out each year in 1786 and 1788, with a total of 1,342 tons, an average of 78.94 tons per vessel; 5 each year in 1783, 1785, 1789, 1791, and 1792, with a total of 2,156 tons, an average of 86.24 tons; 4 each year in 1784, 1790, and 1794, with a total of 1391 tons, an average of 115.94 tons; 3 each year in 1787 and 1795, with a total of 695 tons, an average of 115.83 tons; and 1 vessel in 1796, measuring 88 tons.

It seems also that by the late eighteenth century, the slave trade originating from the British Caribbean belonged virtually to traders resident in England. Thus, a committee of the Jamaican House of Assembly stated in 1788:

It seems not to be understood in Great Britain that the inhabitants of the West-India Islands have no concern in the ships trading to Africa. The African trade is purely a British trade, trade carried on by British subjects, residing in Great Britain, on capitals of their own – the connection and intercourse between the planters of this island, and the merchants of Great Britain trading to Africa, extend no further than the mere purchase of what British Acts of Parliament have declared to be legal objects of purchase.[57]

[55]   For Antigua, see PRO, CO 157/1; Jamaica, PRO, CO 142/14 Part 1; Barbados, PRO, CO 33/13, 14, 16 Parts 1 & 2, and PRO, T 64/48, for 1699–1707, and PRO, CO 33/15 for 1708–1726.

[56]   HLRO, House of Lords Main Paper, 31 May 1793; PRO, CO 318/1, fols. 159–164; HLRO, House of Lords Main Paper, 21 June, 1799. As will be shown later in the chapter, the parliamentary papers generally understate the volume of the trade. In fact, the sources stated here show conflicting information that is characteristic of the parliamentary papers. PRO, CO 318/1 shows that no vessels were cleared to the African coast from the British West Indies in 1789, while House of Lords Main Paper, 31 May 1793, shows 5 vessels measuring 482 tons for the same year.

[57]   PRO, CO 137/88, "Report of the Committee of the House of Assembly of Jamaica on the Slave Trade; First Report, presented, 16 October, 1788" (printed).

But earlier in 1711, the planters of Jamaica had petitioned the British Board of Trade saying, among other things: "That many of your petitioners (sending for their woollen & other manufactures from England) have fitted & sent vessels from here to the Coast of Africa to furnish their own plantations with Negroes for their use & Service."[58]

It would appear, however, that by the middle of the eighteenth century the trade originating from the British Caribbean was still considerable. This is indicated by evidence on the trade of the Gambia River in the 1750s. Between July 27, and November 17, 1755, a list of ships in the said river, "sailed and ready to sail," shows four vessels belonging to Antigua, four belonging to Barbados, and one belonging to St. Kitts.[59] And between December 25, 1755 and December 24, 1756, seven Caribbean vessels are listed, four belonging to Antigua and three belonging to St. Croix.[60]

Now, what can we make of the evidence presented in terms of the volume of the British slave trade originating from the British Caribbean? The evidence does not cover all the islands, nor does it cover adequately all the years for the islands about which some evidence is available. However, the evidence can certainly sustain a conservative generalization. Combining the evidence on the first quarter of the eighteenth century with that of the mid-century, and the mid-century evidence with that of the late eighteenth century, we are able to say that the long-term mean for the first half of the century cannot be less than 10 vessels a year, and that for the second half cannot be less than 5 vessels per annum. This means that the total for 1700–50 is at least 510 vessels and that for 1751–1807, 285 vessels, at the minimum.

As to the mean number of slaves imported per vessel, this can be computed from the import data presented earlier in the paper. As stated above, 11 Jamaican vessels and 87 Barbados vessels imported a total of 13,259 slaves in the early decades of the eighteenth century. This gives a mean of 135 slaves per vessel. At a 20-percent middle-passage mortality rate, the mean export per vessel is 169 slaves. This can be used for the first half. In the second half of the century, although the vessels on the route became larger on the average, parliamentary regulations in the late eighteenth

---

[58]   PRO, CO 388/14 Part I/M.5, "Petition of Jamaican Planters enclosed in a letter from Mr. Harris to Commissioners of Trade, dated 4 January 1710/11" [this should read 1711].

[59]   PRO, T 70/1523, "Detached Papers of the Company of Merchants Trading to Africa."

[60]   PRO, T 70/1525, "Detached Papers of the Company of Merchants Trading to Africa." It should be noted that the trade of the Gambia River at this time constituted a very small fraction of the British slave trade from Western Africa. The relatively large number of Caribbean vessels in the Gambia River at this time is, therefore, an indication that the trade originating from the British Caribbean was still substantial in the middle decades of the eighteenth century.

century may have had some adverse effects on loading. To be consistent with the conservative generalization already applied to the number of vessels, we reduce the export loading arbitrarily to 140 slaves per vessel and the import figure to 130 for the whole period, 1751–1807. These calculations lead to the conservative conclusion that the British slave trade originating from the British Caribbean transported from Africa at least 126,000 slaves and landed at least 106,000 between 1700 and 1807.

Unlike the trade originating from the British Caribbean, that of mainland British America has been the focus of several studies. A reasonable estimate of its volume may be based on a discussion of these studies. In their 1974 publication, Fogel and Engerman revised previous estimates of slave imports into the United States between 1760 and 1810: 1760–70, 62,668; 1770–80, 14,902; 1780–90, 55,750; 1790–1800, 79,041; 1800–10, 156,335.[61] These figures were derived from the United States slave population figures, with the assumption of a 2 percent per annum natural rate of increase. The share of the imports carried by U.S. slave traders was, however, not stated.

In 1975, Roger Anstey carried out a detailed study of the available primary and secondary sources, quantitative and qualitative, relating to slaves shipped from Africa to all the Americas by North American traders. The incomplete nature of the clearance lists is stressed:

American port clearance lists throughout the period are mostly available only as mediated through newspapers. They are incomplete at all times, and increasingly so from the nineties onwards as Federal and State legislation against participation in the slave trade began to induce concealment of the true purpose of a slaving voyage.[62]

To make up for the gaps, Anstey employed a variety of quantitative and qualitative evidence to make estimates where clearance evidence does not exist or is inadequate. For the last two decades, 1791–1810, the revised import figures by Fogel and Engerman, mentioned earlier, were employed along with other data. Based on this exercise, Anstey produced an estimated total export figure of 294,900 for the whole period, 1761–1810: 1761–70, 40,300; 1771–80, 35,900; 1781–90, 17,800; 1791–1810, 200,940.[63]

---

[61]   Robert W. Fogel and Stanley L. Engerman, *Time on the cross: The economics of American Negro Slavery* (Boston: Little, Brown and Company, 1974), p. 25. The figures for 1620–1860 are shown in a graph. The precise numbers stated here were communicated by Stanley Engerman to Roger Anstey, who included them in his article, "The Volume of the North American Slave-Carrying Trade from Africa, 1761–1810," *Revue française D'Histoire D'Outre-Mer*, LXII, Nos. 226–227 (1975), fn. 75, p. 63.

[62]   Anstey, "North American Slave-Carrying Trade," p. 48.

[63]   *Ibid.*, pp. 64–65.

The other major study of the North American slave trade is by Jay Coughtry, who conducted an extensive archival study of the Rhode Island slave trade. Unlike Roger Anstey, however, Coughtry made no allowance for incomplete data. His method was based on counting only the ships whose trade was clearly documented and could be verified. As he expressed it himself:

To ascertain the total number of trans-Atlantic slaving voyages undertaken by Rhode Islanders during the eighteenth century, I checked every available scrap of evidence, and tabulated only positively indentified [identified] slaving voyages. . . . None of these figures contain projections or estimates of any sort. They are authenticated slaving voyages, each of which can be verified by at least one, and in many cases, by several primary sources.[64]

Having counted the total number of slaving voyages in this manner, "actual slave cargo totals were manipulated and combined" to estimate the mean number of slaves carried on Rhode Island vessels. Based on this method, Coughtry produced a total count of 106,544 slaves shipped from Africa by Rhode Island ships between 1709 and 1807. He then adds that this figure represents 60 to 90 percent of the total North American trade in African slaves during the same period.[65]

The problem with Coughtry's method – and similar ones to be discussed later – is that it gives the reader unfamiliar with the gaps and other weaknesses in the documented shipping clearances a misleading sense of accuracy derived from the appearance of "thorough" archival research. With so much gap in the sources and with the widespread problem of conscious under-representation of actual slave trading in the sources, no amount of thoroughness in searching for "every available scrap of evidence" can produce what was not recorded in the first instance, or what was recorded but has been destroyed by one mishap or another and, therefore, no longer exists. Based on the kind of evidence students of the Atlantic slave trade have to work with, the kind of method employed by Coughtry of necessity leads to a gross understatement of the volume of the trade. What is rather methodologically curious is the claim that the Rhode Island figures represent 60 to 90 percent of the total volume of the North American slave trade. Since Coughtry's "authenticated slaving voyages" relate only to Rhode Island, how can they be used to produce a percentage of what is not known?

Coughtry's figures form the basis of David Richardson's "new estimate" of the North American trans-Atlantic slave trade. Richardson presents no new evidence. He accepts Coughtry's figures for the years 1709–80, and

[64]   Jay Coughtry, *The Notorious Triangle: Rhode Island and the African Slave Trade, 1700–1807* (Philadelphia: Temple University Press, 1981), p. 25.
[65]   *Ibid.*, pp. 25–28.

employs Herbert Klein's figures of slaves shipped from Africa to Cuba by United States vessels to adjust upward the figures for 1780–1807, on the basis of which he produced a total export figure of 208,000 for the entire period of the North American slave trade.[66] Richardson criticizes Fogel and Engerman's figures based on demography as exaggeration. This criticism is extended to Anstey's figures for 1790–1810, but Richardson offers no explanation at all for the huge difference between his figure of 58,000 for the years 1760–89 and Anstey's figure of 94,000 for the same period (1761–90). What is more, if the method employed by Coughtry produced an error of the magnitude shown by Richardson for the period 1780–1807, on what basis can one believe that the same does not apply to the years 1709–80? Clearly, the estimate by Coughtry is a good example of the problem arising from missing data.

Richardson certainly made some valid points when he raised issues concerning problems in the use of demographic data to estimate slave imports.[67] But his reliance on Coughtry's figures makes his estimate inferior to that of Anstey for the reasons already stated. In fact, contrary to Richardson's argument, an examination of the United States slave population data suggests that earlier import estimates derived from them may be too low by a considerable margin. In their 1995 article, Antonio McDaniel and Carlos Grushka question the received wisdom that African slaves in the antebellum United States lived longer than those in the Caribbean and Latin America.[68] After reviewing the U.S. census data and slave trade evidence, and applying the techniques of mathematical demography, they conclude:

The central proposition of the history of enslaved Africans in the Americas is that they survived longer in the United States than in the Caribbean. However, the Caribbean estimates of mortality generally fall within the lower and higher bounds of our estimates for the United States. . . . Our results suggest that current historiography of the robustness of enslaved Africans in the United States reflects more the optimistic assumptions underlying past research than the efforts of slaveholders in the United States to preserve the health of their slaves.[69]

If this revision can be sustained, it will lead to a substantial upward adjustment of the existing estimates of slave imports into the United States: If mortality rates among enslaved Africans in the United States were not radically different from those in the Caribbean, then it must have taken

---

[66]   David Richardson, "Slave Exports from West and West-Central Africa: New Estimates of Volume and Distribution," *Journal of African History*, 30 (1989), pp. 5–9.

[67]   *Ibid.*, pp. 6–7.

[68]   Antonio McDaniel and Carlos Grushka, "Did Africans Live Longer in the Antebellum United States? The Sensitivity of Mortality Estimates of Enslaved Africans," *Historical Methods*, Vol. 28, No. 2 (Spring, 1995), pp. 97–105.

[69]   *Ibid.*, p. 104.

much larger imports to produce the antebellum slave populations than was previously thought. This will raise the slave trade global figures considerably, and so, too, North American shipments.

The overall evidence thus indicates that none of the more recent estimates of the volume of the slave trade that originated from mainland British America in the eighteenth and nineteenth centuries is without some weakness. But from the foregoing review of the evidence used and the method employed, there can be no doubt that Anstey's has a superior grounding in quantitative historical scholarship. Everything considered, it should be safe to conclude that North American slave traders could not have shipped less than 300,000 slaves from Africa during the whole of the eighteenth and nineteenth centuries. This brings the total export for the trade originating from British America in this period to 426,000.

5.3 TRADE ORIGINATING FROM ENGLAND, 1701–1807

For the trade originating from ports in England during the period 1701–1807, a large amount of information is available. But there are so many pitfalls in the sources that they must be used with the utmost caution.[70] For purposes of isolating issues that need some clarification, the whole period is sub-divided into four: 1701–49; 1750–76; 1777–89; 1790–1807. A summary of the estimates is shown in Table 5.1. The estimate for the whole period comes to 10,967 ships, which exported a total of 3,319,756 slaves from Africa and landed in the Americas 2,931,012. For the four distinguished components of the estimate, the respective figures are as follows: 1701–49, 3,442 ships and 1,039,607 slaves exported; 1750–76, 3,516 ships and 947,276 slaves exported; 1777–89, 1,206 ships and 454,260 slaves exported; 1790–1807, 2,803 ships and 878,613 slaves exported.

For the first period, 1701–49, the shipping figures are as stated by the sources, with the very small number of non-slave ships that are occasionally stated left out. For the second period, 1750–76, the entries for Liverpool show a total of 51 ships cleared out to Africa that were not involved in the slave trade. These are taken out of the Liverpool total. For the other ports in England, the total clearance to Africa was reduced by five percent to take account of non-slave ships. The validity of this five percent non-slave ship ratio, which is consistently applied for the two remaining components (1777–89 and 1790–1807), is discussed below.

As for the measurement of the mean slave loading per unit of shipping, we have used the time series of slave imports into Jamaica, 1702–75, for

---

[70]   Some of the pitfalls are discussed below. For more details see Inikori, "The Volume of the British Slave Trade," pp. 645–650.

Table 5.1. *Estimate of the Number of Slaves Transported by*
Ships Clearing from Ports in England, 1701–1807

Years	Ships	Slaves Imported	Slaves Exported
1701–09	492	118,572	148,215
1710–19	525	133,875	167,344
1720–29	874	215,573	247,785
1730–39	913	213,646	267,058
1740–49	638	179,916	209,205
1750–59	978	220,050	255,872
1760–69	1,451	352,593	409,992
1770–76	1,087	253,271	281,412
1777–89	1,206	408,834	454,260
1790–1800	1,715	534,394	562,520
1801–07	1,088	300,288	316,093
1701–1807	10,967	2,931,012	3,319,756

Sources and Notes: Ships cleared from ports in England – *1701–1709*, PRO, CO
388/11/I.8, CO 388/12 Part II, CO 388/13/L.86, House of Lords Record Office,
Parliamentary Papers Vol. 84 of the General Collection, Accounts and Papers, vol.
XXVI, No. 646a, 1789; *1710–24*, PRO, CO 388/18 Part 1/0.19, CO 388/25/S77,
CO 390/7/1, CO 390/5, CO 390/8. The Bristol figures for this period (1710–24)
are from the port books as compiled by David Richardson, *Bristol, Africa and the
eighteenth-century slave trade to America*, vol. 1 (Bristol Record Society, Bristol,
1986). The Liverpool figures for 1712–23 are also from the port books as compiled
by David Richardson, "The Eighteenth-Century British Slave Trade," 186–187. The
figures for 1724–29 are estimates based on the value of exports from England to
Africa as shown in BT 6/241, using slave prices in House of Lords, *Parliamentary
Papers, vol. 84, Accounts and Papers*, Vol. XXVI, No. 646a, part IV, No. 25, 1789.
The details of the computation are discussed further below. *1730–1776*, PRO, T
70/1205/A.11, T64/276A/273, T 70/1205/A.18, BT 6/7, BT 6/3, British Library,
London, *Parliamentary Papers, Accounts and Papers*, vol. 82, 1789, No. 633,
p. 49 (for Liverpool, 1751–1776), House of Lords, *Parliamentary Papers, Vol. 84,
Accounts and Papers*, vol. XXVI, 1789, No. 646a, part IV; *1777–1807*, PRO, Cust.
17/5–29. For mean slave loading per ship, see Appendix 5.1.

the first two components, 1701–49 and 1750–76. For the third component,
1777–89, we have employed slave imports into Jamaica, Barbados, St.
Christopher, and Dominica, as shown in the Naval Officers Shipping List.
The export data provided by the House of Lords List (order date, July 28,
1800) have been used, along with imports into Cuba, to compute the mean
for 1790–1800. Finally, the mean for 1801–07 is based on imports into
Jamaica, Barbados, and Dominica, as shown in the Naval Officers Shipping

List, and imports into Cuba. All these sources provided a total of 2,846 cargoes employed to compute the mean number of slaves transported per unit of shipping, 1,190 cargoes for 1701–49 and 1,656 cargoes for 1750–1807. The total number of cargoes employed for these calculations constitutes approximately 26 percent of the 10,967 cargoes estimated for the entire period. The detailed breakdown is shown in Appendix 5.1, where the sources and the difficulties associated with them are also discussed.

The procedure adopted regarding two problems in the computations needs to be elaborated. The first problem concerns the inclusion of the slave trade conducted from ports in England in the late eighteenth century by a foreign firm; the second relates to the level of allowance to be made for ships which cleared out to Africa from ports in England and returned directly with African products without carrying slaves to the Americas.

The information we have about the slave trade conducted from ports in England by a foreign firm comes from the report of the Privy Council committee, appointed by the British crown in 1788 to investigate the state of the African trade.[71] The committee was informed that a year or so preceding the investigation, the Asiatic or Philippine Company of Spain appointed an agent in England, Mr. Testati, to fit out slave ships from ports in England. The ships were to fly English flags, wholly fitted and supplied with cargoes in England, manned entirely by English officers and crew, to sail directly from ports in England to the African coast, from where to carry slaves to Spanish mainland America, and then return to England. These vessels, therefore, operated as English ships, but the trade they conducted from England was owned by a Spanish company. The Philippine Company of Spain was not a slave trading company. Its business was in the East India trade. But, like all European companies trading to East India at this time, it needed a lot of bullion, which it found difficult to procure. The slave trade from England to South America was intended to be a means of procuring American bullion to be kept ready at Buenos Aires for the company to pick up on its way to East India. Possibly with the hope of taking over full management of the slave trading branch at some point, three or four Spaniards, "Men of Some Consideration," were put on board each of the ships to under-study the English officers.

This is the only foreign company mentioned in the sources as trading to Africa from England for slaves. Other firms with contracts to supply slaves to Spanish America, such as Baker & Dawson or John Dawson, were large-scale slave trading firms owned by British nationals. The extent of slave trading conducted from England on behalf of the Philippine Company is not known. On the other hand, it is not clear if British slave traders used the operations of the Philippine Company in England to gain access to the

[71]   House of Lords Record Office, London, *Parliamentary Papers, vol. 84, Accounts and Papers*, Volume XXVI, 1789, No. 646a, Part VI.

Spanish American slave markets or to evade the British laws regulating the carrying of slaves in British ships from 1789 to 1807. What is important to note, the recording of ships in the customs ledgers did not distinguish between British ownership and foreign ownership. The distinction was between British built and foreign built ships. For example, the customs ledgers show that in 1796, 138 "British built" ships and 11 "foreign built" ships cleared outward from England to Africa.[72] It is not clear whether the Register General's Office applied the term to foreign owned ships or it means exactly what it says. However, subsequent summaries of shipping data compiled from the customs records appear to present the original entry of "foreign built" ships as simply "foreign" ships.

For our present purpose, however, all these confusions are really not important. Whether what the sources show as foreign ships were actually owned by British or foreign firms, for as long as those ships operated from English ports as the sources describe, conceptually their business formed part of British overseas trade to be recorded and treated as such. Were we to remove today the international business of foreign companies in each nation of the world from the international trade statistics of such nations, export and import business owned by American, European and Japanese companies in the Third World will disappear from the volume of world trade. The same thing will happen to the international business conducted by companies owned by the nationals of the developed nations in each other's country. By the time this is over, the volume of world trade and shipping would have been substantially reduced. This is why modern statisticians recording and analyzing international trade do not follow the principle of ownership. The principle employed is the place of origin of international business.

Practically speaking, if we have to base our estimates of the volume of the slave trade on ship clearance data, then removing some ships clearing outwards from ports in England on the basis of ownership will remove those ships from our estimates altogether. This is the more so, because there was no independent slave trading from ports in Spain at this time. Hence, there can be no estimate based on clearances from Spain that could include any of these ships, if that were ever possible.

As for the few non-slave-carrying ships among the vessels cleared outward to Africa from ports in England during the period, determining the level of allowance to make for them has been made difficult by the confusion created by the customs officers in England. In recording English ships trading to Africa from England, they did not distinguish between vessels employed in shipping slaves to the Americas (the bulk of the ships) and the small number that returned directly to England with African products without transporting slaves across the Atlantic. And there is clear evidence

[72]   PRO, Cust. 17/18, Imports.

that the vessels transporting African products to England – via the Americas and directly from Africa – were mixed up in their recording: Some of the vessels bringing to England African products they had carried along with slaves to the Americas being recorded along with their products as coming from Africa, while others are entered as coming from the Americas. When, in May 1806, Parliament requested information on both sets of vessels, the Register General of Shipping, Mr. T. E. Willoughby, stated:

> It not having been customary to distinguish such vessels as were intended to make voyages to Africa and the West Indies, from such as were merely intended to go to Africa and back, the Number of the former has been ascertained, by deducting from the total Number cleared, such as returned direct from Africa to England, and assuming that the rest were destined for Africa and the West Indies.[73]

In fact, the customs records cannot be used to make the distinctions made by Willoughby. What he regarded as vessels returning to England "direct from Africa" actually included slave ships bringing African products to England via the Americas. This may be demonstrated. Between 1787 and 1793, the customs ledgers show a total of 1,125 ships, measuring 187,530 tons, cleared out to Africa from England, and a total of 447 ships, measuring 67,267 tons entered from Africa.[74] Using the data as Willoughby did would mean that about 40 percent of the ships and 36 percent of the tonnage cleared out to Africa in these seven years were employed in the bilateral direct product trade between England and Africa. It is well known that the slave ships carried a large proportion of the African products to England through the Americas. Sydenham Teast of Bristol, the best known specialized trader in African products in the late eighteenth century, told the Privy Council Committee in 1788 that the most valuable product imported into England from Africa was ivory, and that "About half the quantity of ivory now imported, is imported in slave ships, but it could not be imported in any other way to profit, for there is no demand for the bulky articles, which must make up the cargo."[75] A ship's captain in the specialized trade in African products, Thomas Dean, also informed the committee that the specialized trade in African products "is much hurt by the slave ships purchasing these articles which we go solely to bring home."[76] Adding the products brought by the slave ships to what the customs records imply as direct shipment from Africa would mean that the product trade at this

[73]   *House of Lords Papers, Accounts & Papers*, 1806, VII, no. 199. An account of the number of ships, their tonnage and men, which cleared from England for Africa and the West Indies, in the last ten years, distinguishing each year.
[74]   PRO, Cust. 17/10–15.
[75]   PRO, BT 6/9, folios 374–378.
[76]   PRO, BT 6/11, Evidence of Thomas Dean, 24 January, 1789.

time was much greater in volume than the slave trade. This is the direct opposite of what the overwhelming body of evidence points to. It is clear, therefore, that the vessels entered as returning direct from Africa included slave vessels bringing African products through the Americas.

The confusion of the Register General's office about vessels in the slave trade and those in the bilateral product trade between Africa and England in the late eighteenth century is further exemplified by parliamentary lists showing several vessels as being employed in the slave trade and, at the same time, as not employed in the slave trade. This kind of confusion exists in two parliamentary papers relating to 10 Bristol vessels that traded to Africa between 1789 and 1793. Interestingly, both lists are signed by the same person, the Assistant Register General of Shipping, one dated 14 May, 1792, and the other, 22 March, 1794.[77] In the parliamentary paper of 1792, the five Bristol ships, *Alfred*, *Royal Charlotte*, *Mary* (101 tons), *King George*, and *Mary* (41 tons) are listed as vessels employed in the slave trade in 1789. But the House of Lords Main Paper of 24 March, 1794, lists the same vessels as "not in the slave trade" for the same year, 1789. Within the Lords paper itself, some vessels are listed as "in the slave trade" one year and in another year as "not in the slave trade."

Further comparison of the parliamentary papers shows more confusion. The House of Lords Main Paper of 28 July, 1800, contains a long list of slave ships, which cleared out to Africa from Liverpool, Bristol, and London between 1791 and 1797, that failed to submit their log books and surgeon's journals at the completion of their voyage, as required by law. An examination of this list in respect of Bristol reveals 11 vessels listed in other parliamentary papers as not in the slave trade between 1791 and 1797.[78] Of these 11 vessels, two are of particular interest. These are the *St. Patrick*, 32 tons, and the *Gibson*, 26 tons, both listed in the House of Lords Paper of 24 March, 1794, as not in the slave trade in 1791. Both vessels happened to belong to the Bristol slave trading firm of James Rogers & Co. The firm's private papers show that both vessels were tenders to larger slave ships of

---

[77] For the sources and details on the issue, see Inikori, "The Volume of the British Slave Trade," Table V, p. 662. In the two documents, the name of the Assistant Register General of Shipping is spelled somewhat differently in four places: J. Dalley; J. Dally; J. Dalby; and J. Dalby. The first carries the date, May 14, 1792, and the remaining three all carry the date, March 22, 1794. There is no doubt that the same person is involved and the differences are just typographical errors.

[78] House of Lords Main Paper, Order date, 28 July, 1800; British Library, London, *Parliamentary Papers, Accounts & Papers*, 1806, Vol. XIII, pp. 21–22; House of Lords Main Paper, Order date, 24 March, 1794. These vessels are *St. Patrick*, 32 tons (1791), *Gibson*, 26 tons (1791), *Swallow*, 12 tons (1791), *Lioness*, 213 tons (1791), *Dragon*, 45 tons (1792), *Experiment*, 10 tons (1792), *Young Crescent*, 15 tons (1792), *Flora*, 44 tons (1795), *Mohawk*, 284 tons (1795), *James*, 18 tons (1795), and *Peggy*, 53 tons (1796).

the firm. It was not uncommon for slave ships to have tenders, smaller vessels, which could be used to get into the inland rivers of Africa. The tenders were very often the first vessels to be dispatched from the coast to the Americas, while the larger ship completed its cargo. Sometimes the smaller vessel made repeated trips between Africa and the Americas, often returning to Africa with cargoes of rum and tobacco. In April, 1791, Captain William Roper of the ship, *Crescent*, wrote to James Rogers from Isles De Los about the *St. Patrick*:

> I will be much obliged if you will leave orders at Barbados for the schooner *James* to sell at some of the Windward islands as her cargo is small, so as she may return to me in Africa if occasion requires. . . . If Captain Walker will let me have the *St. Patrick*, I don't know whether I may not have it in my power to send the ship off early, or keep the *Princess* which comes with the Rum, which will ease my expences greatly in this country.[79]

The House of Lords Paper of March 24, 1794, also lists as not in the slave trade several other vessels of James Rogers & Co. that were tenders to their larger slave ships: the *Anamaboe Packet,* tender to the ship, *Jupiter* in 1790; the *Nimble,* tender to the ship, *Sarah* in 1789.[80] These wrong listings are all clear indications of the difficulties the Office of the Register General of Shipping had in distinguishing between vessels employed in the slave trade and those employed in the bilateral product trade, which developed from the late eighteenth century.

We have tried to overcome the difficulty by employing the value of goods exported to and imported from Africa to measure the relative magnitude of the bilateral (direct) product trade between England and Africa during the period. Since it was the goods exported from England to Africa that paid for both slaves and African products, the proportion of the exports expended in purchasing the African products should indicate the share of shipping space devoted to them. The computation shows that in the decades, 1701–40, the sterling f.o.b. cost of goods exchanged on the African coast for African products imported into England, direct and via the Americas, was between 9.2 percent and 14.1 percent of the total value f.o.b. of exports from England to Western Africa; for the six decades and seven years, 1741–1807, it was between 5 and 9.2 percent.[81] The highest proportion of export goods expended on the purchase of African products was 14.1 percent in the 1730s. In general, the proportion of export goods so expended was highest in the first four decades of the eighteenth century.

---

[79]   PRO, C. 107/5, Captain William Roper to James Rogers, Ship *Crescent*, Isles De Los, 13 April, 1791.

[80]   PRO, C. 107/11.

[81]   For the sources and the details of the calculation, see Inikori, "The Volume of the British Slave Trade," Table VI, p. 665.

Thereafter, the proportion declined, being generally lower in the last quarter of the century.

When it comes to the employment of shipping, however, the story is different. Although a larger proportion of the goods exported to Africa was exchanged for African products in the early decades of the eighteenth century, those African products were almost invariably carried to England in slave ships, and sometimes even by British naval ships. The business of one of the large-scale slave trading firms in London in the 1730s and 1740s may be used to illustrate. The firm of Thomas Hall & Co. of London, while exporting about 1,000 slaves a year at this time, probably had about 30 to 40 percent of its returns from the proceeds of African products and re-exported Brazilian gold brought to England by the firm. And these products were carried either by slave ships or by British naval ships, which frequented the African coast during the period. Thus, the firm's manager on the coast, Captain George Hamilton, reported in 1738 that he had shipped on board Her Majesty's Ship (HMS), *Centurion*, Capt. Anson, 30 tons of ivory and 2,540 oz of gold dust and expected another officer of the firm, Mr. More, to add more to the shipment. He added, "We deal largely in tobacco, which brings the gold, we hope soon to fall into a method to procure that commodity directly from the Braziel.ˢ [Brazilians] ourselves which must be kept very secret."[82] In April 1741, Hamilton, again, reported shipping on board HMS *Chatham* 1,100 oz gold dust and about 12 tons of ivory. He expected Mr. More to ship on board the same vessel about 2,500 oz gold dust and 3 tons of ivory.[83] The *Diamond* and the *Greenwhich* were other naval ships used in shipping products from Africa to England by the firm. The firm's slave ships regularly carried gold, ivory, and other products along with the slaves. In 1740, the *Sarah* was reported having on board 180 Gold Coast slaves, 400 oz gold dust, and 3,165 lbs of ivory, with Mr. More expected to add more to the gold and ivory. In the same year, another ship of the firm commanded by Captain Clove Talbot shipped from the Gold Coast 291 slaves, 990 oz of gold dust, and 31,785 lbs of ivory, with Mr. More expected to make up the ships cargo of 440 slaves and add 2,000 oz of gold dust, "at least."[84]

---

[82]   PRO, C.103/130, Captain George Hamilton to Thomas Hall, 10 January, 1738. The gold being exported from West Africa at this time was brought largely from Brazil by Brazilian traders, which explains the reference to the Brazilians.

[83]   *Ibid.*, Hamilton to Hall, 16 April, 1741.

[84]   *Ibid.*, Hamilton to Hall 16 August, 1740, and 27 August, 1740. Both the slaves and the products to be carried by the ship commanded by Captain Talbot were expected to "make good £17,000 sterling." The firm's captains also reported the slave vessels of other British slave traders carrying considerable quantities of products along with the slaves. For example, the *Berkly Gally* of Bristol was reported shipping 401 slaves to Barbados in 1735, along with 40 tons of barwood (C. 103/130, James Pearce to Hall, Bath, 31 January, 1735).

There is thus a clear indication in the sources that the limited quantities of African products and re-exported Brazilian gold imported into England in the first half of the eighteenth century were carried virtually by slave vessels and naval ships. The Royal African Company occasionally sent one or two vessels directly from Africa to England with African products and these have been picked up in the estimates presented above. The private traders were wholly committed to the slave trade in the first half of the eighteenth century, as mentioned earlier, the volume of the product trade at this time being too small for specialization. Specialization in bilateral trade between England and Africa was a new development in the late eighteenth century. This view is supported by the testimony of the Bristol ivory and wood trader, Sydenham Teast, who told the Privy Council Committee in 1788 that "The trade [the specialized bilateral product trade] has not been tried more than five years and a half."[85] Thus, while a larger proportion of goods exported to Africa was expended on non-slave exchanges in the first than in the second half of the eighteenth century, it was not until the late eighteenth century that a small group of ships was employed in carrying African products only. But even then, as stated earlier in the chapter, the slave ships continued to carry a large proportion of those products.

Now, as shown above, in the period 1751–1807 the proportion of export goods expended on the purchase of African products varied between 9.9 percent and 5 percent. In the last quarter of the century, the highest proportion was 7.3 percent. Since the evidence shows clearly enough that a large proportion of the products was transported by slave ships, being around one-half, as the sources indicate, our 5 percent allowance actually overstates the relative magnitude of the non-slave-carrying shipping during much of the last 58 years of the trade to which it is applied.[86] There is no reason to believe that the proportion of shipping employed was greater than the proportion of export goods expended. In fact, there is clear evidence that, apart from the slave ships, British naval ships continued to carry some of the African products to England in the second half of the eighteenth century and early nineteenth. In July 1806, Captain G. Wenman of the slave ship, *Bedford*, was instructed by the owners:

[85] PRO, BT 6/9, p. 378, Evidence of Sydenham Teast.
[86] Adding the indirect imports via the Americas discovered by Marion Johnson makes little difference: 1751–60, 11.2%; 1761–70, 5.9%; 1771–80, 7.6%; 1781–90, 7.2%; 1791–1800, 5.5%; 1801–1807, 7.2%. Since the non-slave ships carried no more than one-half of the African products, the proportions shipped by them, even with Johnson's discovery, would be, for the respective decades, 5.6%, 2.9%, 3.8%, 3.6%, 2.8%, 3.6%. For Johnson's data, see Marion Johnson, *Anglo-African Trade in the Eighteenth Century: English Statistics on African Trade 1699–1808*, Edited by J. Thomas Lindblad and Robert Ross (Leiden: Intercontinenta No. 15, Centre for the History of European Expansion, 1990), Table 4, pp. 64–66.

You will take care to send home (being carefully packed up in a Box sealed over the nails & Iron hooped) such Gold Dust as you may purchase, barter for or receive; also all the Ivory you may purchase or barter for, by the first Ship of War bound from the Coast of Africa to England direct or with leave to call at the West Indies . . . bearing in mind that we have effected Insurance say £2,000 on ship or ships of War as before described . . .[87]

Between 1808 and 1815, 17 naval ships brought from Africa to Portsmouth, England, gold valued at £255,088:5s.[88] Our 5 percent allowance can, therefore, be shown on the basis of the evidence to be more than adequate.

Coming to the impact of institutional change on the import data mentioned earlier, the evidence shows clear incentives for ships transporting slaves to British America to understate the numbers carried from Africa in order to avoid the heavy fines stipulated by the regulations of 1789 and after. For example, in 1802 the *Princess Royal*, measuring 400 tons, had 386 slaves on board at one time, being 28 more than she was permitted to carry, for which a fine of £30 per head was paid, that is, £840. One or two other cases are also mentioned by the source.[89] Those familiar with customs fraud would know that heavy fines are associated with large-scale evasion, and only those who do not know how to "play ball," or those for whom luck runs out once in a while, pay the heavy fines. In any case, the very fact that someone was willing to carry more slaves than the law allowed, in the face of the heavy fines, is itself an indication that it was possible to do so profitably. That is, it was possible to secure the cooperation of customs officials at a cost that still brought a profit from the sale of the extra slaves.

On the other hand, the evidence shows that British ships carrying slaves to non-British America were not bound by these regulations. The House of Lords Main Paper of July 28, 1800, which most students of the subject have used and referred to, indicates that ships carrying slaves to non-British America were not expected to submit their log books showing the number of slaves they carried, as required by law. This source also shows that failure to submit the log books by any slave ship was never punished. Hence, a very large number of the slave ships never submitted their log books and surgeons' journals on the completion of their voyages. The source in question shows that between 1791 and 1797, a total of 561 slave ships that cleared out to Africa from England did not submit these documents on the

---

[87]   PRO, C. 114/158, Ship *Bedford*, Third Voyage, 1st July, 1806, Supplementary Instructions to Capt. Wenman.

[88]   British Library, State Paper Room, *Reports, Committees*, 1816, VII.2: Report from the Select Committee on Papers Relating to the African Forts, Evidence of Simon Cock, Esq., 12 June, 1816, p. 10.

[89]   British Libray, London, *Parliamentary Papers, Accounts and Papers*, 1806, vol. XIII.

completion of their voyages: 414 from Liverpool; 74 from Bristol; and 73 from London. The compiling officer added a note:

It does not appear that the owners of the preceding ships have in any instances assigned reasons for not having delivered in the Documents required by law, on the termination of their respective voyages, and therefore the particular causes are not known. It may however have happened that some of the vessels were captured or lost and that *others may have traded to Foreign Islands where no British officers reside to whom the Journals could be delivered or before whom the Affidavids of the Masters & Surgeons could be made.* Others may have completed their voyages but have omitted to deliver in their documents.[90]

This statement shows that British ships carrying slaves to non-British territories were not obliged and were not expected to follow the letters of the laws regulating the carrying of slaves in British ships. It also shows that other ships could avoid submitting their log books and surgeons' journals showing how many slaves were taken on board in Africa without being punished. The latter left much room for fraud.

That the vessels carrying slaves to non-British America loaded much greater numbers per ship is revealed by the data on British ships carrying slaves to Cuba between the 1790s and 1804. Export data for ships transporting slaves to British territories in the 1790s yield 324 slaves exported per ship, while the data for those carrying slaves to Cuba, when converted to export data at 5 percent middle passage mortality rate, yield 397 per ship. Thus, British ships carrying slaves to British territories in the 1790s carried 22.5 percent less slaves per ship than those transporting slaves to Cuba. For the period, 1801–07, a similar pattern is shown. Data for ships that sold their slaves in British America produce a mean of 274 slaves imported per ship, while the mean for British ships that sold their slaves in Cuba during the same period imported 287 per ship. The difference for the last period is much lower, 5 percent, but it is still important.[91]

5.4 DISTRIBUTION OF THE BRITISH-CARRIED SLAVES IN THE AMERICAS

From the estimates made in Sections 5.1, 5.2, and 5.3 in this chapter, the entire British empire slave trade, from John Hawkins to the early nineteenth century, comes to a total export from Africa of 4,215,250 people. A large part of this total was transported to non-British America, in particular Spanish America but also the French Caribbean. Quite early in the seventeenth century, the British traders in Britain and in British America took

---

[90]   House of Lords Record Office, London, House of Lords Main Paper, Order date, 28 July, 1800. Emphasis added.

[91]   For the sources, see Appendix 5.1, below.

full control of the supply of African slave labor to British America. But, while supplying the British American markets, they also extended their supply very early to the Spanish American market, where slave prices were higher than in British America at all times. As the British trade expanded the proportion of it aimed at the non-British American markets increased. The supply to the latter markets followed two channels: One was direct shipment from Africa to some non-British American colony, and the other was re-shipment from British American colonies. Sometimes the shipments were by contract and, therefore, legal; at other times the shipments were illegal and, therefore, clandestine, the latter being mostly the case. Because of the largely illegal nature of the trade, its full volume is difficult to ascertain. However, some effort is made here to indicate its general magnitude and direction.

Before the British Caribbean colonies were established in the seventeenth century, the early British slave trade was illegal and it carried unknown number of slaves (including those by John Hawkins) to non-British America. While the British colony of Barbados became the main focus of British slave shipment in the first half of the seventeenth century, clandestine shipment to Spanish America went on at the same time. Chance evidence shows four British ships which carried slaves directly from Africa to mainland Spanish America in 1647, three of which belonged to a syndicate managed by Samuel Vassal and carried over 450 slaves.[92] No doubt the private traders continued the illegal trade throughout the rest of the seventeenth century. For the eighteenth century more information on shipments from the British Caribbean is available.

Colin Palmer has estimated that the South Sea Company, which held the *asiento* contract to supply Spanish America with slaves between 1713 and 1739, shipped a total of 74,760 to those colonies during the period, purchased mostly in the British Caribbean. He refers to an extensive illegal shipments by private traders, including shipments even by British naval ships, from Africa as well as from British America (before and during the South Sea Company's contract), but no effort is made to estimate the actual numbers involved.[93]

Official records in Jamaica show that from September 22, 1702 to 1772, 460,310 slaves were imported into Jamaica from Africa, of whom 132,074

---

[92]   John C. Appleby, "English Settlement in the Lesser Antilles during War and Peace, 1603–1660," in Robert L. Paquette and Stanley L. Engerman (eds.), *The Lesser Antilles in the Age of European Expansion* (Gainesville, Florida: University Press of Florida, 1996), p. 98. As Palmer put it: "From the days of Queen Elizabeth I the English had delighted in defying the Spanish imperial system by encouraging a fairly extensive contraband trade in slaves and other commodities with the Spanish colonies" (Colin A. Palmer, *Human Cargoes: The British Slave Trade to Spanish America, 1700–1739* (Urbana: University of Illinois Press, 1981), p. 83).

[93]   Palmer, *Human Cargoes.* pp. 83–88, 110–111.

were re-exported.[94] For the period 1773–87, 141,775 were imported from Africa and 25,859 are stated as re-exported to "Foreign West Indies" (presumably French and Spanish), and 3,780 are said to have been re-exported to "All other Parts."[95] It is unclear whether the latter included parts of British America or just mainland non-British America. The re-exports of 1702–72 are not geographically distributed. In all likelihood they went largely to Spanish America. In fact, some of the shipments by the South Sea Company in 1714–39, mentioned earlier, may be included. For the years 1789, 1790, and 1791, the information covers all the British Caribbean colonies. For these three years a total of 75,053 slaves were imported into the British Caribbean colonies from Africa, of whom 29,109 were re-exported, the re-export being an average of 9,703 per year.[96] More than half of the imports went to Jamaica (39,255), but most of the re-exports were made from Grenada (12,945), followed by Dominica (6,146), and Jamaica (6,915).

None of the sources mentioned so far says anything about the direct British slave trade from Africa to non-British America. A printed summary of the evidence taken by a Parliamentary committee in 1788 provides a clearer picture of the dimensions of the British traders' supply of African slave labor to non-British America. The summary shows that the total number of slaves "annually carried from the Coast of Africa, in British vessels," was about 38,000 in the 1780s. Of this number, a yearly average (four-year average, 1784–87, as specified) of 22,500 was carried to the British Caribbean, out of which an average of 17,500 was retained and the rest re-exported.[97] Taking these figures together, the implication is that

---

[94]　PRO, CO 137/38, "Jamaica: Negroes Imported from Africa, into the said Island and Duty on them, and Exported from the said Island, and Drawback on them, yearly from 22nd September 1702 to 1775." There is a three-year overlap between this series and the one from 1773 to 1787. The figures are slightly different. To eliminate the overlap, this series is taken from 1702 to 1772.

[95]　House of Lords Records Office, *Parliamentary Papers, Vol. 82, Accounts & Papers*, Vol. XXIV, 1789, No. 622, "An Account of the Number of Negroes imported into, and exported from, the Island of Jamaica: Also, An Account of the Number Annually retained in the Island, as far back as the same can be made up." Signed by Thomas Irving, Inspector General of Imports and Exports, Custom House, London, May 12, 1789.

[96]　British Library, *House of Commons Sessional Papers of the 18th Century, Reports & Papers*, Vol. 82, 1791 & 1792, p. 315: "An Account of the Number of Slaves which have been imported from Africa into the British West India Islands, between the 5th January 1789 and the 5th January 1792, distinguishing each year; and of the Number retained in the British West India Islands, and the Number re-exported thence to the Settlements of Foreign Powers." Signed by Thomas Irving, Inspector General's Office, Custom House, London, 10 May 1792.

[97]　House of Lords Records Office, *Parliamentary Papers, Vol. 82, Accounts & Papers*, Vol. XXIV, 1789, No. 626: Summary of Evidence taken by the Committee.

the British traders supplied about 20,500 Africans annually to non-British America in the 1780s, being approximately 54 percent of the entire British slave trade originating from England at the time. The direct British shipment from Africa to non-British America comes to 15,500 yearly, or about 41 percent of the total. The recorded imports into the British Caribbean in the three years 1789, 1790, and 1791, presented earlier, come to an annual average of 25,018, which compares well with the average of 22,500 for 1784–87, stated by the parliamentary committee's summary being examined. This is an indication that the evidence of the parliamentary committee is reliable, even though the re-export figures appear relatively smaller than those for 1789–91.

Further evidence, mostly qualitative but also quantitative, helps to confirm the general magnitude of the trade to non-British America, especially the direct shipments from Africa to the foreign colonies. Bristol delegates to the enquiry of 1788 testified that between 1787 and 1788, eight British ships measuring 1,990 tons were involved in shipping slaves, on behalf of Spanish and French subjects, to Spanish and French America; six others carrying 2,400 slaves obtained French colors in France to benefit from the French bounties on slaves shipped to French America. In addition to these, other British traders shipped slaves directly from Africa to Spanish America under special contracts. John Dawson of Liverpool had a contract to supply a minimum of 3,000 and a maximum of 7,000 a year in the 1780s. Another Liverpool firm, Tarleton and Company, had a contract for similar numbers and together they are stated as purchasing nearly 80 percent of the slaves sold in Bonny and New Calabar at the time.[98]

Parliament took much interest in this branch of the British slave trade in the early 1790s. It asked a three-man group, made up of Miles, Anderson, and Bailey, to investigate the slave trade conducted by British traders "on account of the French & Spaniards." Reporting their findings, they wrote:

In complyance with the wish expressed by your Lordships, we have made every possible enquiry the time would permit into the nature and extent of the slave trade carried on of late by British adventurers and on British account, through the medium of resident merchants in France, to Africa and the French West India Islands, and by British adventurers avowedly on Spanish account for slaves, direct to Africa & the Spanish settlements on the Southern Continent of America, both of which objects we find to be considerable in the Ports of London, Bristol and Liverpool. In regard to the latter we conceive that your Lordships may easily get every necessary information from merchants who are now fitting out several vessels in this City, but tho we cannot discover anything in the proceedings of the Adventurers in the former branch of Commerce, in the smallest degree repugnant to the Laws or Injurious to the Interests of this Country, yet we cannot help joining these Gentlemen in seeing

[98] Inikori, "Measuring the Atlantic Slave Trade," pp. 208–209.

the Propriety and security of declining any Public investigation of the Subject, or reducing such information as they can give to the form of Evidence on your Lordships Journals, for tho they would think themselves perfectly secure in committing the whole Facts to your Lordships knowledge, yet the least Public mention of them would we conceive endanger the safety of the French Merchant who cloaks the property of ships and cargoes from the moment they enter the Ports of France untill the Remittance is made for the Slaves from the West Indies, and by that means ultimately prove injurious to the British Merchant; at any rate it would deprive the British Adventurer of the vast advantage of the Bounty on Tonnage given to vessels apparently French who carry on this Trade and of the Collonial gratuity paid by the French Island Treasurers on the delivery of the Slaves. The outward cargoes we are well informed are chiefly made up in this Country, except in the article of Brandy, which they get on better terms in France. The Remittance must, from the nature of the Business, be all made through France and for the most part in Cotton, which valuable raw material the British Adventurer can at his pleasure order to this Market from France. Notwithstanding that we are well convinced of the great advantages to the individuals immediately engaged and to the Country at large by this circuitous Commerce, yet we are fully persuaded that it would be infinitely more beneficial . . . if the trade was conducted as formerly, through the medium of the British West India Islands, for the supply of both the French and Spanish settlements with slaves . . .[99]

Roger Anstey's evidence indicates that British slave traders were also using the Dutch as a cover in shipping slaves to non-British America in the late eighteenth century. Anstey discovered among Dutch vessels, captured by the British Navy in 1803, 44 ships with English names, "the names of their masters have a distinctly Anglo-Saxon ring and they near unfailingly were allowed to take bail at Liverpool, or Bristol." According to him:

Collation with lists of British vessels clearing for the slave trade from British ports reveals that a number of these "Dutch" prizes had cleared as British vessels participating in the slave trade, often three or four weeks before capture. On the other hand, between four and six of the prizes appear probably not to have cleared as British slavers even though their appearance on clearance lists before or after indicates that they were British slavers.[100]

Anstey was compelled to ask "the extent of the iceberg of which these cases were perhaps the tip."[101] To all of these must be added shipments by the Spanish firm trading from ports in England mentioned earlier in the chapter.

The foregoing evidence is consistent with the dimensions of the British slave trade to non-British America implied in the petitions sent to

[99] House of Lords Record Office, House of Lords Main Paper – "1794 Undated: Certificates of Slaves, etc." The document quoted was put in a file among other documents. The whole file bears the above reference.

[100] Roger Anstey, *The Atlantic Slave Trade and British Abolition, 1760–1810* (London: Macmillan, 1975), fn. 31, pp. 11–12.

[101] *Ibid.*

Parliament in the early 1790s, when it attempted to abolish this branch of the British slave trade. Among those who petitioned was John Dawson of Liverpool, easily the largest supplier of African slave labor to non-British America in the late eighteenth century. He referred to the proposal before parliament, "That from and after the 1st of May 1793, it shall not be lawful to carry any African Negro from the Coast of Africa to any of the Dominions of any Foreign Power in any ship owned or navigated by British subjects," and stated that his capital invested in the trade, worth £509,000, would be adversely affected if the bill became law.[102] Up to 1794 the bill was still being debated; "the merchants and traders" of the town of Liverpool petitioned against the bill, arguing,

the supply of Negro Labourers to the Foreign Colonies in the West Indies and America has always been one of the Branches of the African trade the most beneficial to this country, the Merchandize employed mostly British manufacture, the Navigation British, and the returns generally in hard specie. . . .

They computed the total capital invested in the African trade by Liverpool merchants to be £1,920,000, of which "at least two-thirds has been employed in that particular branch of the trade, the abolition of which is intended by the present bill."[103] A similar petition from the manufacturers of the town of Manchester informed parliament:

The British trade to Africa is carried on with merchandize composed chiefly of the Manufactures of this country, and the petitioners have embarked very large sums of money in the manufacture of goods calculated solely for that particular trade, and unfit for any other. If the Bill for the abolition of the trade carried on for supplying Foreign Territories with slaves be passed into a Law, it will affect an immediate abolition of two-thirds of the said trade . . .[104]

The evidence thus indicates strongly that from the late eighteenth to the end of the legal trade in the early nineteenth century, the direct trade to non-British America was the main driving force for the British slave trade originating from England. Because of its covert nature its full magnitude may never be known. But those in a position to know thought it was about two-thirds of the total. Adding re-exports from the British Caribbean would

---

[102]   British Library, *House of Commons Journal*, Vol. XLVII, January 31, 1792 to November 15, 1792, April 27, 1792, pp. 742–743, Petition of John Dawson.

[103]   British Library, *House of Commons Journal*, Vol. XLIX, Jan. 21, 1794 to Nov. 25, 1794, February 25, 1794, p. 236: A Petition of the Merchants and Traders of the Town of Liverpool against the Bill for abolishing the supply of slaves to foreign colonies by British Merchants.

[104]   *Ibid*, March 7, 1794, p. 304: A Petition of the Manufacturers of the Town of Manchester. The bill was passed in the House of Commons in March, 1794. Wilberforce was asked to carry it to the House of Lords. Later petitions against a similar bill, as late as 1806, suggest that the bill did not become law. See *House of Commons Journal*, Vol. LXI, January 21, 1806 to October 9, 1806, pp. 210–226.

raise the proportion further. It should be noted also that the clandestine nature of the trade, shown by the evidence, suggests that much of it may not have been included in the overall volume estimates made above in the chapter. Finally, it is important to add that non-British America was also a major driving force for the British North American slave trade in the last decades of the legal trade. Anstey's estimate, discussed earlier in the chapter, shows a total U.S. export from Africa of 200,940 in 1791–1810, of which 80,632 went to Spanish and French America.[105] Britain and British America were, therefore, central to the supply of African slave labor to all of the Americas in the eighteenth and early nineteenth centuries.

5.5 THE PERILS OF THE BRITISH SLAVE TRADE

Several factors contributed to make the European slave trade to Africa extraordinarily hazardous for the traders' capital, and for the lives of the seamen employed and the human beings traded and transported as commodities. These perils confronted by the merchants affected the way the trade was conducted in various ways. The one that is directly relevant to the subject of this chapter concerns the loss or redirection of ships and their "cargoes," and the implication for the estimated volume of the trade. For purposes of clear understanding, the main causes determining the nature and dimensions of the perils and the implications for the estimates made in the preceding sections of the chapter are examined in this section. Other issues relating to these hazards that are relevant to the study are taken up in subsequent chapters.[106]

Information covering 1,053 vessels lost by their owners between 1689 and 1807 constitutes the basis for identifying the main causal factors. The information is displayed and analyzed in two tables. Of the 1,053 vessels, 679, or 64.5 percent of the total, were taken by the enemy in wartime; 188, or 17.9 percent, were wrecked at sea outside the African coast; and 186, or 17.7 percent, were lost as a result of slave insurrection, conflict with coastal Africans, and wrecks on the African coast. Thus, war was by far the greatest hazard faced by the traders. This was particularly so, because struggle over the control of overseas trade was a major factor in these wars.[107] In fact, competition in international trade in Western Europe of the seventeenth and eighteenth centuries was, for all practical purposes, hardly

---

[105]   Anstey, "North American Slave-Carrying Trade," p. 64.

[106]   For more details, see Joseph E. Inikori, "Measuring the unmeasured hazards of the Atlantic slave trade: documents relating to the British trade," *Revue Française D'Histoire D'Outre-Mer*, 83, No. 312 (1996), pp. 53–92.

[107]   C. Wilson, *Profit and Power: A Study of England and the Dutch Wars* (London and New York: Longmans Green, 1957).

distinguishable from war. When wars actually broke out, the governments did not hesitate in granting licences (letters-of-marque) to private individuals to prey on enemy merchant ships. This became a lucrative business for those with adequate resources to properly arm private ships for privateering. Many of the larger British slave traders, especially those in Liverpool, combined slave trading and privateering in wartime.[108] Because the Atlantic slave trade was conducted triangularly across the entire Atlantic – North and South, East and West – and requiring relatively long permanent stationing of ship and cargo in Africa and the Americas, it was unusually vulnerable to privateer attacks.

Between 1688 and 1807, England was involved in seven major wars that affected the Atlantic slave trade.[109] Earlier in the seventeenth century, there were the Anglo-Dutch Wars.[110] But, of all these wars, the French Revolutionary and Napoleonic Wars, 1793–1815, had by far the greatest impact. Over one-third of the 679 vessels mentioned earlier (248 in all) were taken between 1793 and 1807.[111] These wartime captures constituted a major headache for the traders and for the marine insurance underwriters who provided cover for the trade. But, in terms of the lives of the seamen employed and the people traded and transported as commodities (the slaves), the adverse effect was relatively less. Privateering was a profit-oriented business. The privateers had to preserve their captured property to make a profit from the sale. Of course, some lives and property were destroyed in the fighting that preceded capture. And, on occasion, some privateers behaved irrationally, as was reported in the *Lloyd's List* of June 23, 1747:

The *Ogden*, Tristram, of Leverpool [sic], from Africa for Jamaica, with 370 Negroes, was taken off the East-End of that Island by a Spanish Privateer. The Spaniards were so Irritated at their gallant Defence, that, on boarding, they killed Whites and Blacks without Distinction: Soon after the *Ogden* sunk, and only 1 Man, 5 Boys, and 3 Negroes were saved.[112]

---

[108]   G. Williams, *History of the Liverpool Privateers and Letters of Marque, with an account of the Liverpool Slave Trade* (London, 1897).

[109]   S. Dowell, *A History of Taxation and Taxes in England, from the Earliest Times to the Present Day*, 2 Volumes, vol. 2 (London: Frank Cass, 1965; first published by Longmans Green in 1884). Among these were the war in Ireland and against France, 1688–1697; War of Spanish Succession, 1739–48; Seven Years' War, 1756–1763; War of American Independence, 1776–83; French Revolutionary and Napoleonic Wars, 1793–1815.

[110]   Wilson, *Profit and Power*.

[111]   See Table 5.2 below.

[112]   *Lloyd's List*, National Maritime Museum, Greenwich, London, report of Tuesday, 23 June, 1747, No. 1208. The *Lloyd's List* is the main source of information on the 1,053 vessels mentioned earlier. For the history of the *Lloyd's List*, see Inikori, "Unmeasured Hazards," pp. 55–58.

A somewhat similar emotional outburst by privateers was reported in February, 1760:

A store ship from Cape Coast, with about 130 slaves, whose crew consisted of 23 men, fell in with two or three French Privateers, whom he fought for two Days, but was at last taken; and in Return for such a bold Defence, the crew were cut and wounded in a most barbarous manner.[113]

In general, however, irrational behavior by the privateers was rare. The cost of fitting out a ship for privateering was quite high. To recover the cost and make a profit, the privateers had to properly manage their captured property.

Though relatively less frequent, the most destructive of ships and lives of seamen and slaves were wrecks at sea, slave insurrections, and conflicts with coastal Africans. The wrecks were an important part of the risks of the Atlantic slave trade. The perils of the vast ocean separating Africa from the Americas and the annual hurricanes of the Caribbean took their toll. In Africa, the ship captains had to contend with sand bars, limited natural harbors, and tropical thunderstorms. As Alfred Crosby observes with some exaggeration: "The worst large expanse of ocean in the world for thunderstorms lies off the coast of Africa from the Senegal River to the Congo River."[114] For the wooden vessels to spend several months anchored in open waters, with few natural harbors, during the period of trade in Africa, then several weeks of Atlantic crossing, and several weeks more in New World ports (with the possibility of being caught by the annual hurricanes), before spending yet more weeks from the Americas to England, several wrecks have to be expected annually.

The extant issues of *Lloyd's List* for 1741–1807 show a total of 188 vessels that were wrecked at sea outside Africa. The rather imprecise phrase, "lost on the coast of Africa," makes it difficult to say how many wrecks in Africa were reported by the same issues. In some cases, additional information makes it clear that reference is to a loss by wreck. But there are 61 instances in which it is unclear whether loss is by wreck or some other cause.[115] If we assume that all 61 cases were wrecks (which may not be altogether correct), then there were 107 wrecks in Africa reported by the extant issues for the period. This makes a total of 295 wrecks reported by the available issues for the period, as compared with 451 losses due to wartime enemy action during the same period. Of the 188 wrecks outside Africa, 72 occurred between England and Africa, 88 during the Atlantic crossing and in New World ports, and 28 on the way to England from the

---

[113] *Lloyd's List*, report of Friday, 29 February, 1760.
[114] A. W. Crosby, *Ecological Imperialism: The Biological Expansion of Europe, 900–1900* (Cambridge: Cambridge University Press, 1986), pp. 114–115.
[115] See Inikori, "Unmeasured Hazards," Table 2, pp. 64–74.

Americas. In all likelihood, many wrecks on the last route have not been picked up because of the difficulty of distinguishing between the slave ships and other vessels reported wrecked on this route by *Lloyd's List*. The evidence indicates that sand bars and limited natural harbors on the African coast may have been mainly responsible for the wrecks in Africa. Thunderstorms are rarely mentioned, contrary to what Crosby's description would lead one to expect.

Of the 186 vessels lost on the African coast, 79 were related primarily to slave insurrection and conflict with coastal Africans. Of all cases of wreck connected with slave insurrection, only three occurred during the Atlantic crossing. All others took place on the African coast, very often just before or at the point of departure of the ships from the African shores. The sight of the African shores may have given the slaves the assurance that they could escape to freedom if they succeeded in overpowering the crew. In fact, one such incident was reported in 1773, involving the *Industry*, a London slave ship.[116] Four days after leaving Gambia for Carolina, the slaves succeeded in killing all the crew but two, took the ship to Sierra Leone, where they ran her ashore and made their escape. There is also some indication that during such uprisings on the coast, the slaves may have received some assistance from ordinary free Africans in the coastal societies. This is suggested by the report relating to the ship *Nancy*, Captain Williams, of Liverpool, in 1769.[117] As the report shows, the gunshots fired by the crew, while the insurrection was in progress on the shores of New Calabar, attracted the attention of the town's people. They went to the ship in their canoes, boarded and took out the slaves. The ship was set adrift after removing ivory and other goods.

It is not clear whether the latter incident was simply an act of robbery, taking advantage of the uprising, or a show of solidarity with unfortunate fellow human beings. Whatever the case, this incident does bring to mind the attitude of ordinary free Africans in the coastal societies to the trade in human beings conducted regularly on such a vast scale before their very eyes. One is referring here to free Africans who were not traders, not soldiers, not government functionaries of any sort, and who could not afford to employ slaves in any form. It is not unreasonable to expect such people to dislike the trade and the maltreatment of the export captives they daily observed. Whenever they calculated that the risk to their own lives was not very great, some of these people may have assisted the slaves in their insurrections on the African coast. This is speculative. The attitude of this segment of the coastal populations to the Atlantic slave trade is a neglected subject, which deserves some attention. However, the possibility of such assistance, real or imagined, may have been a factor in the greater frequency of insurrections on the coast than in the middle passage.

[116]   Inikori, "Unmeasured Hazards," Table 2, p. 69.   [117]   *Ibid.*, Table 2, p. 67.

More generally, the evidence suggests a degree of hostility by coastal Africans to the European slave traders much greater than what is usually acknowledged in the literature. Consistently, when the reports employ the term "Negroes," reference is to the export slaves, while the term "Natives" meant coastal free Africans.[118] This makes it possible to distinguish between incidents involving the export captives primarily and those initiated by the coastal Africans. The latter show a considerable degree of hostility. Even when the vessels were involved in normal wrecks on the coast, the surviving crew were, more often than not, humiliated and brutally treated. A case in point is the ship *Matthew*, a tender to the *Sawrey*, in 1766.[119] The vessel was wrecked on the Gold Coast. All the crew survived, but they were "stripped naked by the inhabitants." In another incident involving the *Ann*, Captain Irving, of Liverpool, in 1789, the ship's cargo was plundered and the "crew made slaves."[120]

The incidents described in the *Lloyd's List* reports may not represent the dominant attitude of the coastal populations to the European slave traders. All the same, they do indicate a level of hostility not adequately reflected in the literature. Part of the explanation may be the attitude of the ordinary coastal Africans mentioned earlier. Quite often, however, the hostility was ingrained by the intemperate behavior and sharp business practices of the European traders on the African coast. A few cases may be taken to illustrate.

In the early nineteenth century, there was a disagreement between a British trader and an African merchant prince in Cape Coast town, on the Gold Coast (now coastal Ghana), over the quality of gold sold. The African merchant agreed to take the gold back and return the goods he received in payment. But this did not satisfy the British trader. The African trader was seized and locked up, with no regard to the fact that he was a chief in the town. This provoked a crisis in the town, to which the British company's officials on the coast responded by burning the entire town. In its report of this incident in October 1803, the Governor and Council of the British company on the Gold Coast wrote:

We are extremely sorry that the licentious conduct of the Cape Coast people should be such as to compel us to commence Hostilities against them, but their great insolence was not to be borne longer, and required a curb, in consequence of which, we have destroyed their Town by fire. . . . The loss of the natives is not known; but from what we can learn, many must have been killed and wounded.[121]

The matter was subsequently investigated by Captain W. Brown of HMS *Rodney*. In his report, dated January 2, 1804, he condemned the action of

---

[118]   *Ibid.*, Table 2, pp. 64–74.   [119]   *Ibid.*, Table 2, p. 66.   [120]   *Ibid.*, Table 2, p. 71.
[121]   PRO, T 70/1580, Governor and Council on the Gold Coast to the African Company Committee in London, Cape Coast Castle, 31 October, 1803.

the British company's officials in no uncertain terms, and held them totally responsible for the disruption of peace on the Gold Coast.[122]

Earlier in the late eighteenth century, Duke Ephraim of Old Calabar wrote several times to the Bristol slave trading firm of James Rogers & Co., complaining that the firm's ship, *Jupiter*, carried off his free citizens to the Americas.[123] The extent of the conflict provoked by this and similar incidents in the area was referred to indirectly by a Mr. J. P. Degravers, M. P. He wrote to Rogers & Co.:

I have now finished the History of the Kingdom of Haifock, Commonly called *Old Calabar* . . . I have not mentioned the transactions of your ship masters, nor those of others, leading to the ideas which a copy of my journal have naturally raised within you; the barbarians would most undoubtedly have been productive of another argument to abolish the slave trade, which obviously is clearly demonstrated humane in the actual state of that part of Africa.[124]

Similar incidents were reported by *Lloyd's List*. For example, the issue of April 23, 1773, carried a report from Cape Coast Castle, dated December 12, 1772:

A sloop about 60 tons, and which by all accounts must be a Pirate, has considerably hurt the Trade for Gold at Assinee and Basam, having carried off several of the free Blacks from those places and killed several others, so that no English Boats can go to those places, which is a great hurt to the Trade at Annamaboe.[125]

---

[122]　PRO, T 70/1581, Report of Captain W. Brown of His Majesty's ship *Rodney*, 2 January, 1804. Earlier in the seventeenth century, another town on the Gold Coast was razed to the ground by the officers of the Company of Royal Adventurers Trading to Africa. See Makepeace, "English Traders on the Guinea Coast," p. 250.

[123]　PRO, C. 107/12, Duke Ephraim to James Rogers & L. Roach, Old Calabar, 16 October, 1789, and 17 November, 1789.

[124]　PRO, C. 107/7 Part I, J. P. Degravers M. P. to James Rogers & Co., Bath, 7 October, 1791. I have searched in vain for the book on Old Calabar mentioned in the letter. Earlier in 1768, the captains of five Liverpool and Bristol slave ships trading in Old Calabar, taking advantage of a quarrel between the leaders of New Town and Old Town, arranged with the leaders of New Town and treacherously brought those of Old Town to their ships in the pretext of trying to settle the quarrel. As soon as the latter got there, they were massacred by the captains and their men; others were seized and shipped to the Caribbean, including two brothers of the king of Old Town. The king himself managed to escape with several gun wounds. The king's brothers got to England, after being sent to North America; with the help of James Jones of Bristol, who traded heavily in Old Calabar, the king's brothers were finally returned to Old Calabar, after about five or six years, in the 1770s. This treacherous act of the Liverpool and Bristol slave ship captains caused a war between New Town and Old Town, which lasted for about three years, the captives taken being sold to the European traders. See House of Lords Record Office, *Parliamentary Papers, Volume 84 of the General Collection, Accounts and Papers*, Vol. XXVI, 1789, No. 646a, Part I: Evidence of Captain Hall.

[125]　*Lloyd's List*, report of Friday, 23 April, 1773, No. 426.

Also the report relating to the *Ave Maria*, Captain DuBlays, in 1770, refers to an incident "occasioned by some of the crew endeavoring to defraud the natives."[126] Again, it can be argued that these and similar incidents were not typical of the relationship between coastal Africans and the European traders of the period. Nevertheless, they must have contributed to the deep-rooted hostility of the coastal African populations to the European slave traders, which flared up from time to time in different parts of the coast during the period, as reflected in the *Lloyd's List* reports.

The evidence displayed on the loss of ships and cargo has important implications for the estimates of the volume of the British slave trade made in the preceding sections of this chapter. As stated above, the evidence shows 1,053 vessels that were lost by their owners to privateers, wrecks at sea, and other causes between 1689 and 1807. For the period, 1701–1807, the number comes down to 969. The latter figure is 8.8 percent of the 10,967 ships produced for the trade originating from England during the same period in the preceding sections of this chapter. It should be noted that the evidence does not cover all the years of the period.[127] Although there are indications of double counting in the report of losses,[128] it may be reasonable to add about 200 vessels to the figure to make up for missing reports. This brings the total for the period to 1169, or 10.7 percent of the total number of ships estimated earlier for the period.

Now, how does this relate to the estimated volume of British slave exports from Africa by ships clearing from England during the period in question? In the first place, it should be noted that the reports in *Lloyd's List* do not regularly distinguish between slave and non-slave ships, although this is done occasionally. The losses reported, which are displayed in the tables in this chapter, therefore, include slave ships and non-slave ships, as well as vessels trading from the Americas, and a few even from continental Europe. On this account, the calculations made above exaggerate the proportion of slave ships cleared out from England that were lost during the period. More important, however, is the extent to which the vessels lost had loaded their cargo of slaves before they were captured or lost.

The latter problem would have been easy to resolve had the sources regularly stated the content of every vessel at the time of capture or loss. *Lloyd's List*, our main source, shows this for a few ships. For most ships, however, this vital information is not given. Even ships in the Atlantic crossing are frequently reported as captured or lost on their way from Africa to the Americas, without stating specifically that they had slaves on board and

---

[126] Inikori, "Unmeasured Hazards," Table 2, p. 67.
[127] See the discussion of the sources in Inikori, "Unmeasured Hazards," pp. 55–58.
[128] *Ibid.*, see Table 2, *Note*, p. 74.

the number. Based on the available evidence, I have attempted to solve the problem in two stages.

It is clear enough that vessels captured or lost outward, that is, between England and Africa, had not yet bought any slaves before the incident. It is also clear enough that ships captured or lost during the Atlantic crossing[129] or homeward (that is, from the Americas to England) already had their full cargo of slaves before the incident. The only area of uncertainty is captures or losses that occurred on the African coast. The evidence relating to the point of capture or loss, in terms of these four geographical locations, is very good and permits the grouping of the 1,053 vessels mentioned above accordingly.[130] A summary of the information relating to these vessels, together with the location of their capture or loss, is presented in Table 5.2.

As Table 5.2 shows, between 1701 and 1807, 169 of the vessels lost were captured or lost outward, 353 on the African coast, 293 on their way to the Americas, and 96 homeward. Thus, of the 911 ships of the period, whose geographical points of capture or loss are known, we know for certain that 389 had their full cargo of slaves before the incident occurred, while 169 had no slaves at all on board at the time. The problem now is to determine the proportion of their full cargo of slaves already purchased by the 353 vessels captured or lost on the coast of Africa before their capture or loss occurred. This cannot be computed directly from the reports. But it can be done if we know the average length of time the vessels were on the African coast before their capture or loss, and also the average length of time it took to purchase a full cargo of slaves during the period. The detailed information we have for the 10 years, 1796–1805, a critical period for the study (as stated above), permits the computation of these lengths of time. From the computations it has been estimated that, in terms of slaving capacity lost, 25 percent of the 353 vessels captured or lost on the African coast between 1701 and 1807 should be regarded as having purchased no slaves at all before the incident occurred, and the remaining 75 percent as having already had their full cargo of slaves before the incident. This gives 88 and 265 vessels, respectively. Thus, of the 911 vessels stated above, the equivalent of 654 ships in slaving capacity completed slave purchases, while 257 made no purchases at all. If these ratios are applied to the 58 vessels, whose geographical point of loss is not stated, and the 200 vessels added for missing reports, we have the equivalent of 330 vessels in slaving

---

[129]   This route is described in the tables of this chapter as "Africa to Americas." It includes vessels captured or lost after their arrival in the Americas, but before their departure to England.

[130]   Of the 1053 vessels, only 58 ships lost by the private traders between 1708 and 1711 cannot be grouped according to the geographical points of capture or loss.

Table 5.2. *Number of British Vessels in the African Trade Lost in Peace and Wartime, 1689–1807*

Year	Outward	African Coast	Africa to Americas	Homeward	Unspecified	Total
			Where Lost			
1689	—	—	3	6	—	9
1690	—	—	—	3	—	3
1691	—	—	1	5	—	6
1692	—	—	—	9	—	9
1693	—	—	—	7	—	7
1694	—	—	1	16	—	17
1695	—	2	2	6	—	10
1696	1	—	1	9	—	11
1697	1	—	—	4	—	5
1698	—	1	—	4	—	5
1699	1	1	—	—	—	2
1701	1	1	—	1	—	3
1702	1	—	4	2	—	7
1703	1	7	5	2	—	15
1704	5	2	4	10	—	21
1705	4	—	2	9	—	15
1706	3	—	—	13	—	16
1707	—	1	—	2	—	3
1708	—	—	—	8	22	30
1709	—	—	—	—	14	14
1710	—	—	—	—	17	17
1711	—	—	—	—	3	3
1741	2	1	—	—	—	3
1744	1	1	8	—	—	10
1747	4	1	10	—	—	15
1748	1	—	7	—	—	8
1749	1	1	2	—	—	4
1750	—	5	2	—	—	7
1751	2	3	—	—	—	5
1752	1	1	1	1	—	4
1753	—	1	—	1	—	2
1755	—	2	—	—	—	2
1757	4	12	17	—	—	33
1758	4	3	9	—	—	16
1760	2	4	8	1	—	15
1761	5	5	11	2	—	23
1762	9	20	7	3	—	39
1763	5	4	4	1	—	14
1764	4	2	1	1	—	8
1765	—	5	—	—	—	5
1766	1	6	3	—	—	10
1767	1	7	1	3	—	12
1768	—	4	2	—	—	6
1769	—	4	1	1	—	6
1770	3	6	2	2	—	13

Table 5.2 *(cont.)*

Year	Outward	African Coast	Africa to Americas	Homeward	Unspecified	Total
			Where Lost			
1771	1	9	—	2	—	12
1772	1	2	1	1	—	5
1773	3	5	1	—	—	9
1774	—	8	4	1	—	13
1775	1	6	4	1	—	12
1776	1	5	8	—	—	14
1777	1	2	18	1	—	22
1779	2	1	—	1	—	4
1780	—	1	—	—	—	1
1781	2	—	2	2	—	6
1782	3	2	7	3	—	15
1783	3	6	3	1	—	13
1784	—	1	2	2	—	5
1785	—	4	1	—	—	5
1786	1	3	—	1	—	5
1787	2	4	2	—	1	9
1788	1	5	—	1	—	7
1789	—	4	3	—	—	7
1790	2	2	—	—	—	4
1791	2	3	4	—	—	9
1792	—	5	1	—	—	6
1793	2	6	9	—	—	17
1794	18	3	2	2	—	25
1795	3	40	7	—	—	50
1796	3	5	12	2	—	22
1797	11	14	13	2	—	40
1798	7	12	4	2	—	25
1799	7	5	5	1	—	18
1800	3	20	7	4	—	34
1801	6	7	10	—	—	23
1802	2	4	5	—	1	12
1803	2	1	7	1	—	11
1804	6	8	15	1	—	30
1805	5	13	11	1	—	30
1806	2	23	8	—	—	33
1807	1	5	6	—	—	12
1689–1807	172	357	301	165	58	1,053
1698–1807	170	355	293	100	58	976

Sources and Notes: Public Record Office, Kew Gardens, London: (Treasury Papers) T 70/175, An Account of the Royal African Company's Losses Commencing Anno 1689; (Colonial Office Papers), C.O.388/15Part1/M.157, An Account of Separate Traders' Ships Lost between Michaelmas 1707 and 1711 (for the 56 vessels of 1708–11). *Lloyd's List*, National Maritime Museum, Greenwich, London. The unspecified 56 vessels for the years, 1708–11, are for the private traders; all other vessels (172 in all) for the years, 1689–1708, are for the Royal African Company.

capacity wiped out by captures and other losses in the whole period, 1701–1807. This is approximately 3 percent of the total figure of 10,967 vessels for the period, stated above. As pointed out earlier, if allowance is made for non-slave ships, and the vessels belonging to ports in the Americas and continental Europe included in the Lloyd's reports, the proportion may go down to about 2 percent. Small as it appears, it is still important in volume estimates to recognize this depressant factor.

Incidentally, a comparison of the shipping data in the *Parliamentary Papers* with the *Lloyd's List* reports confirms the limitations of the former that have been stressed in the literature.[131] Of the total number of 245 ships reported to be captured or lost between 1796 and 1805, 80, that is, 33 percent, could not be found on the rather detailed clearance lists for the period, among the Parliamentary papers. These vessels are shown in Appendix 5.2. The implication of this finding is similar to that of the 1803 Dutch prizes discovered by Roger Anstey.[132] Let's assume, for the sake of argument, that non-slave ships, together with vessels belonging to ports in the Americas and continental Europe, account for about one-half of the vessels in Appendix 5.2. This rather generous allowance still leaves about 16 percent of the vessels reported captured or lost between 1796 and 1805 unaccounted for in the parliamentary clearance lists. It is reasonable to conclude that the parliamentary clearance lists understate the magnitude of British slave ships at least in the same proportion (over 16 percent) that they underrepresent the ships reported captured or lost by *Lloyd's List* between 1796 and 1805. Hence, even after allowance has been made for lost slaving capacity due to wartime captures and other causes, the fact still remains that existing estimates of the volume of slaves transported from Africa by British traders (including the estimate in this chapter) are minimum estimates with a significant room for upward adjustment, although the exact proportion may be difficult to determine.

As to the implication of the evidence presented in the chapter for the rate of mortality among the slaves purchased by the British traders in Africa, no exact measurement can be made. It is clear from the evidence that privateering accounted for a very large proportion of the losses reported. Although these were clear losses to the traders who owned the ships and slaves captured by privateers, as far as slave imports into the Americas were concerned, there was no loss of imports, except to the extent that a few

[131]   Roger Anstey, "The Volume and Profitability of the British Slave Trade, 1761–1807," in Stanley L. Engerman and E. D. Genovese (eds.), *Race and Slavery in the Western Hemisphere: Quantitative Studies* (Princeton, NJ: Princeton University Press, 1975), pp. 3–31; Inikori, "Measuring the Atlantic Slave Trade"; Inikori, "Volume of the British Slave Trade."

[132]   Anstey, *The Atlantic Slave Trade*, pp. 11–12, fn. 31. See also Inikori, "Volume of the British Slave Trade," pp. 659–660, fn. 20.

slaves may have been killed in the process. All that happened was a change of destination in the Americas.

Yet the evidence shows that many slaves died in the wrecks at sea and in various incidents on the African coast, which are not captured by existing measurements of slave mortality. These existing measurements are derived exclusively from ships that actually arrived in the Americas. Hence, no account is taken of mortality relating to those ships that never arrived at all. Unfortunately, the reports in *Lloyd's List* do not provide adequate evidence for exact measurements. Quite often the number of slaves killed in these incidents is not stated. However, given that these cases constituted a rather small proportion of the shipping employed, as shown above, they may have added altogether no more than one or two percentage points to the overall mortality rate. So, again, taking account of the probable magnitude of the understatement of the volume of the trade by the extant records, existing import estimates still leave a significant room for upward adjustment, although to a relatively lower degree than the export estimates.

6

The Atlantic Slave Economy and
English Shipping

THE RATHER LIMITED MODERN LITERATURE on English shipping is somewhat ambivalent on its importance in the development process leading to the Industrial Revolution. One of the best known authorities on the subject, Ralph Davis, thought its effects on the process "cannot easily be disentangled from those of trade," and concluded: "The shipping industry was an important part of the English economy, both before and after the decisive decades of the Industrial Revolution, but it cannot be said to have made a contribution of a special character to the transition."[1] Robert Craig, another leading authority, viewing the relationship apparently from a different consideration, is more optimistic: "There can be little doubt," he says, "that the capital invested in shipping represented one of the most important forms of fixed . . . capital in Britain in the period of industrialization."[2] The ambiguity in the literature probably arises from a consideration of shipping in isolation from the shipbuilding industry. Of course, conceptually the separation makes good sectoral sense, for shipping is a service industry, while shipbuilding produces a physical product and, therefore, belongs to manufacturing. However, for purposes of a more accurate assessment of the contribution of the shipping trade to the industrialization process, under the conditions of the mercantilist world of 1650–1850, it makes more practical sense to take the shipping and shipbuilding trades together. This makes it possible to examine the role of the shipping trade in terms of the employment and income it generated (together with the multiplier effects) and the foreign exchange it provided, which paid for vital imports, as well as the more direct contribution to industrialization by the shipbuilding industry (tightly linked to the shipping trade by mercantilist regulations) in terms of employment and income (and the multiplier

---

[1] Davis, *English Shipping Industry*, p. 393.
[2] Craig, "Capital Formation in Shipping," p. 131.

effects), and in terms of the backward linkage effects on other industries – iron, copper, ropery, wood production, etc.[3] Viewed this way, the quantitative and qualitative importance of the combined role of the shipping and shipbuilding trades in the industrialization process under consideration becomes more obvious and less ambiguous.

The main focus of this chapter is to show that the shipping needs of the Atlantic slave economy were central to the growth and development of British shipping and the shipbuilding industry between 1650 and 1850. To connect this to the central theme of this study, we first examine the growth of the English merchant marine and the shipbuilding industry over the period and show their combined contribution to the industrialization process, then proceed to demonstrate the relative contribution of the Atlantic slave economy to the progress of these two closely related trades.

6.1 GROWTH OF THE ENGLISH MERCHANT MARINE AND THE SHIPBUILDING INDUSTRY

Because of its insular location, Britain experienced repeated invasions by sea from the European Continent. In response to these invasions Britain developed quite early a naval force to defend the nation's territorial integrity. Ironically, the Danes, who were the most frequent invaders, helped to create (during the years of their rule in England, 1016–42) the foundation upon which the British Navy was subsequently built. At the beginning of Danish rule in 1016, the navy had only 40 ships; by the time of the last Danish king the strength of the navy had almost doubled to 72 ships.[4] For the next several centuries slow and steady progress was sustained until the time of the Tudor kings (1485–1603), especially the Elizabethan period, when the pace quickened to produce the formidable naval force that defeated the Spanish Armada in 1588. By the latter date England had established herself as the leading naval power in Europe.[5]

While by necessity England devoted resources to the development of a naval force quite early, England's foreign trade remained in the hands of alien traders and the nation's exports and imports were carried largely by foreign shipping for centuries. Before the late sixteenth century, English import and export trade was dominated by Italians and by traders from German cities, whose interests were strongly protected by their association, the Hanseatic League. These alien traders used their international

---

[3] Curiously enough, as far as I am aware, there is no book-length work on the English shipbuilding industry of the period 1650–1850, similar to that of Davis on the shipping industry.

[4] Henry C. Hunter, *How England Got its Merchant Marine, 1066–1776* (New York: National Council of American Shipbuilders, 1935), pp. 3–7.

[5] Davis, *English Shipping Industry*, p. 2.

connections and their formidable financial resources (sometimes even military resources also) to secure commercial privileges from the English kings, who depended heavily on foreign trade for their revenue.[6] The favors granted to the foreign merchants added to the difficulties of the native English traders struggling to secure a share of their nation's foreign trade. The monopoly of England's import and export trade by alien traders created the conditions for their domination of the shipping of England's imports and exports. Hence, in the late sixteenth century England was far behind the leading maritime nations of Europe in the development of a carrying trade.

In 1603, Walter Raleigh painted a dismal picture of England's carrying trade in comparison with that of Holland: in the trade with the Baltic there were 3,000 Dutch ships to 100 English; in that with France, Spain, Portugal, and Italy there were 2,000 Dutch ships to zero English; in the Russian trade, there were 30 Dutch ships to 3 English. Thus, according to Raleigh, in these areas of the carrying trade there were a total of 5,030 Dutch ships to 103 English at this time.[7] There may be some exaggeration of the extent of Dutch leadership over England as stated by Sir Walter Raleigh. However, it is broadly consistent with the view expressed by Ralph Davis:

In 1560 England ranked low among the maritime states; though her navy was a real force, her merchant fleet was by European standards an insignificant one. It stood far behind that of the Dutch ... far behind the combined tonnage of Spain and Portugal; behind Hamburg and perhaps even the declining Hanse city of Lubeck; probably behind France; behind Venice or even Ragusa and Genoa. A meager coastal traffic, a fishery of moderate scale, a trickle of carrying traffic with the Low Countries, Spain, Portugal, France and the Baltic; this was the maritime basis which Elizabeth I inherited.[8]

By the seventeenth century, Dutch pre-eminence in the carrying trade of Europe was well established. With possible exaggeration, the Dutch were said to possess four-fifths of all the ships employed in seaborne commerce; for every one English ship trading to Barbados there were ten Dutch. But between 1650 and 1750, the positions were completely reversed, as the commercial supremacy of England was firmly established by the latter date.[9] England now carried not only her own goods but also those of other

---

[6] Hunter, *Merchant Marine*, pp. 8–12. According to Hunter, revenues from the customs were sometimes more than half of the total royal revenue (p. 8). The Hanseatic League is probably the most powerful commercial organization that ever existed in Western Europe. At one time there were more than 70 German towns in the association; it made war on its own account as well as on behalf of clients; it held a monopoly in the supply of naval stores through its domination of the Baltic trade; and with its financial and military resources, it "held the balance of power in Europe" (*Ibid.*, pp. 11–12).

[7] *Ibid.*, pp. 338–343.

[8] Davis, *English Shipping Industry*, p. 2.

[9] Clive Day, *A History of Commerce* (New York: Longmans, 4th ed., 1938; first published, 1907), pp. 194–223.

nations. Customs shipping clearance and entry figures provide the basis for measuring the changing proportion of English exports and imports carried by English ships between 1663 and 1857. This is shown in Table 6.1.

In the period 1663–69, as the table shows, English shipping carried about 67 percent of English total exports. But between 1700 and 1791, the proportion was less than 80 percent only in 1782, when it was 72.7 percent. There are more gaps in the evidence for imports. However, what is presented in the table makes it clear enough that English shipping also carried the bulk of English imports in the eighteenth century, generally 80 percent and above. The proportions decreased in the course of the nineteenth century. But in the fifth decade of the century British shipping still carried on the average over two-thirds of the combined exports and imports of the United Kingdom. What is important to note, the figures in the table do not include the overseas cross-country British carrying trade which could not

Table 6.1. *Quantity and Percentage of England's Exports and Imports Carried by English Ships, 1663–1857*

	Exports			Imports		
	Total (000tons)	By English Ships (000tons)	(%)	Total (000tons)	By English Ships (000tons)	(%)
1663–69	142	95	66.9			
1686	361	331	91.7	446	399	85.6
1688	285	190	66.7			
1692–94	162	82	50.6	189	83	43.9
1696–97	210	118	56.2			
1700–02	318	274	86.2			
1709–10	301	244	81.1			
1711–15	405	371	91.6			
1718	445	428	96.2	369	354	95.9
1751	694	648	93.4	480	421	87.7
1758	526	427	81.2	413	283	68.5
1765	758	690	91.0	693	568	82.0
1772	888	815	91.8	780	652	83.6
1779	720	581	80.7	710	482	67.9
1782	761	553	72.7			
1783	954	796	83.4	997	703	70.5
1784	959	846	88.2	1,068	869	81.4
1785	1,055	952	90.2	1,077	888	82.5
1786	1,264	1,078	85.3	1,104	926	83.9
1788	1,356	1,234	91.0	1,345	1,130	84.0
1790	1,405	1,261	89.8	1,475	1,211	82.1
1791	1,511	1,333	88.2	1,503	1,200	79.8

Table 6.1 *(cont.)*

	Exports Plus Imports		
	Total (000 tons)	By English Ships (000 tons)	(%)
1841	8,951	7,109	79.4
1842	9,127	6,670	73.1
1843	9,825	7,181	73.1
1844	10,347	7,500	72.5
1845	12,077	8,546	70.8
1846	12,416	8,688	70.0
1847	14,279	9,712	68.0
1848	13,307	9,290	69.8
1849	14,004	9,670	69.1
1850	14,505	9,443	65.1
1851	15,980	9,821	61.5
1852	16,130	9,986	61.9
1853	18,390	10,268	55.8
1854	18,669	10,745	57.6
1855	18,489	10,920	59.1
1856	21,589	12,946	60.0
1857	23,179	13,694	59.1

Sources and Notes: 1663–1669 and 1688, Hunter, *Merchant Marine*, p. 334; 1686 and 1692–1779, Davis, *English Shipping Industry*, p. 26; 1782–91, Customs 17/7-13 (PRO); 1841, John Armstrong & Philip S. Bagwell, "Coastal Shipping," in Aldcroft and Freeman (eds.), *Transport in the Industrial Revolution*, Table 18, p. 153 (figure is for the leading 10 ports in England only); 1842–57, W. S. Lindsay, *History of Merchant Shipping and Ancient Commerce*, 4 vols., vol. 3 (London: Samson Low, Marston, Low and Searle, 1876), p. 376. Figures for 1663–1791 and 1841 are for England; those for 1842–57 are for the UK. Figures for periods of two years and above are annual averages. It is assumed that shipping statistics correspond roughly to those of cargo.

be recorded by the British customs, because it was conducted between regions overseas without touching ports in Britain. For example, as will be shown later in the chapter, the figures in the table do not include the carrying of slaves from Africa to the Americas by English shipping, a quantitatively important part of the British carrying trade in the eighteenth century. Thus, in the seventeenth and eighteenth centuries, a "revolution" in English carrying trade accompanied the better known commercial revolution.

This revolution in English carrying trade created the conditions for the growth of English-owned merchant shipping in the seventeenth and eighteenth centuries. Table 6.2 shows the growth of the English merchant

Table 6.2. *English-Owned Merchant Shipping and English-Owned Merchant Shipping Employed in Foreign Trade, 1560–1857*

	All English-Owned Merchant Vessels		Shipping Employed in Foreign Trade	
	No. of Vessels	Tons (000)	No. of Vessels	Tons (000)
1560		50		
1572		50		
1582		67		
1629		115		
1663		200		126
1686		340		190
1771–73		581		375
1783			2,320	325
1784			2,765	426
1785			3,061	464
1786			3,133	495
1788	9,375	1,055		
1790	9,603	1,040		
1791	9,974	1,075		
1792	10,633	1,187	4,300	710
1793	10,779	1,205		
1794	10,956	1,221		
1795	10,827	1,208		
1796	10,961	1,241		
1797	11,044	1,253		
1798	11,274	1,287		
1799	11,499	1,337		
1800	12,206	1,467		
1801	12,759	1,543		
1802	13,464	1,643		
1803	14,029	1,710		
1804	14,604	1,784		
1805	14,790	1,799		
1806	14,877	1,787		
1807	15,087	1,797		
1814	19,585	2,329		
1836	20,388	2,350	7,133	1,737
1849	18,221	3,096	7,653	2,233
1850	17,892	3,137	7,989	2,302
1851	18,184	3,361	8,165	2,493
1852	17,819	3,381	8,133	2,531
1853	18,206	3,730	8,856	2,873
1854	17,407	3,729	8,024	2,870
1855	17,828	3,990	8,603	3,130
1856	19,270	4,156	9,057	3,279
1857	19,328	4,211	8,682	3,260

Notes to Table 6.2 *(cont.)*

Sources and Notes: 1560–1773 and 1788, Davis, *English Shipping Industry*, pp. 1, 15, 17, 27, 33, and 405 (Davis thought that the tonnage of English-owned vessels in 1640 was about 150,000 and 200,000 in 1660; the latter figure is entered for 1663); 1783–1807, Customs 17/7–29. The number and tonnage of shipping employed in foreign trade in 1792 has been computed by applying Ralph Davis's calculation of the number of voyages per ship per year (one voyage being equal to one clearance plus one entrance) in each area of English trade in the 17th and 18th centuries to Ernest Fayle's figures of entrances and clearances: C. Ernest Fayle, "The Employment of British Shipping," in C. Northcote Parkinson (ed.), *The Trade Winds: A Study of British Overseas Trade during the French Wars 1793–1815* (London: Allen and Unwin, 1948), p. 73. Ralph Davis did not compute the number of voyages per year for the ships in the slave trade; an average of one voyage in two years has been applied to Fayle's clearance figure of 250 ships (more is said about this below). Figures for British owned ships in 1814 are also from Fayle (*op. cit.*, p. 83). The figures for shipping employed in foreign trade in 1836 are for the United Kingdom and are computed by applying Davis's number of voyages per ship per year to G. R. Porter's clearances and entrances: G. R. Porter, *The Progress of the Nation, in the Various Social and Economical Relations, from the Beginning of the Nineteenth Century to the Present Time*, 3 vols., vol. 2 (London: Charles Knight, 1838), pp. 177 and 178; ships trading to the Western Coast of Africa in 1836 are assumed to have made one voyage in a year. The figure for all UK-owned ships in 1836 is taken from B. R. Mitchell, *Abstract of British Historical Statistics* (Cambridge: Cambridge University Press, 1962), p. 217. The figures for 1849–57 are for the United Kingdom and are calculated from Lindsay, *Merchant Shipping*, vol. 3, p. 378; the figures for vessels "employed partly in the home trade and partly in the foreign trade" have been split in halves and one-half added to the figures for vessels in foreign trade.

marine from 1560 to 1857. In 1560 the total tonnage of English-owned merchant shipping was a mere 50,000. For the next three decades very little progress was made. Rapid expansion began in the second half of the seventeenth century, and by 1686 the total figure was 340,000 tons, of which 190,000 tons (or 55.9 percent) were employed in foreign trade. In the course of the eighteenth century, the tonnage of English-owned (British-owned 1792–1814, and U.K.-owned 1836–57) shipping would appear to have increased by a factor of three; over the period of about 300 years between 1560 and 1857, the expansion was almost a hundredfold.

This growth of the English Merchant Marine was due largely to the phenomenal expansion of English shipping in foreign trade. Before 1640, coastal shipping and fisheries provided the basis for the limited growth which occurred. But from 1660 very little change took place in the tonnage of shipping employed in the home trade. As Ralph Davis stated, "At the Restoration [1660], coastal shipping and fisheries probably occupied well over half the total tonnage of English shipping; in the next 30 years they made little progress. The great expansion during this period took place among vessels for foreign trade."[10]

There are gaps in the quantitative evidence with which to compare the tonnage of English shipping employed in the home and foreign trade. The evidence in Table 6.2 shows that in 1686, 55.9 percent of all English-owned merchant shipping tonnage was employed in foreign trade. By 1771–73, the proportion was 64.5 percent. The proportion for 1792 was somewhat lower, 59.8 percent. The available evidence shows that in the nineteenth century the proportion was generally above 70 percent – 73.9 percent in 1836, 73.4 percent in 1850, and 77.4 percent in 1857. It is important to note that much of the shipping employed in the home trade actually depended on foreign trade – the carrying of domestic exports to the ports; the shipping of imports from the ports to various inland markets; the transportation of domestic raw materials for the production of export products.

The growth of the British shipping industry contributed significantly to the general growth of employment and income in the modern sector of the English economy in the period 1650–1850. In a motion made in the House of Commons in 1848, during the battle to abolish the Navigation Acts, Mr. Herries, who was for many years before 1828 the Chancellor of the Exchequer, was reported to have stated that the total tonnage of the merchant marine belonging to the United Kingdom and her colonies at the time

... amounted to 3,900,000 tons; the number of sailors employed in our mercantile marine, to 230,000; and the capital embarked in shipping, to little less than [£]40,000,000; while the trades immediately connected therewith, or subservient to the shipping interest, employed a capital of from [£]16,000,000 to [£]17,000,000. In this way there was between [£]50,000,000 and [£]60,000,000 of property which would be immediately affected by the proposed change. In this branch of national industry about 50,000 artisans, whose wages amounted to [£]5,000,000 a year, were employed; while the cost of victualling the ships he estimated at [£]9,000,000, and the freights the mercantile marine earned per annum at nearly [£]30,000,000.[11]

These mid-nineteenth-century estimates made by Mr. Herries may be compared with those made in 1812 by Patrick Colquhoun, who estimated, on the average for the two years 1810 and 1811, that there were 20,000

---

[10]   Davis, *English Shipping Industry*, p. 16.

[11]   Lindsay, *Merchant Shipping*, Vol. 3, pp. 195–196. Lindsay stated in a footnote (fn 1, p. 196): "All these figures may now [1875] be at least doubled, except the number of men, as the improvements in mechanical contrivances have materially reduced manual labour since the repeal of the Navigation Laws."

people employed on board of vessels in the coasting trade, whose earnings in wages and provisions amounted to £1 million a year, while 200,000 were employed by shipping engaged in foreign trade, earning in wages and provision £14 million a year, making a total employment of 220,000 and a total income of £15 million a year. Colquhoun further estimated the annual average freight earnings of the vessels employed in foreign trade in 1810 and 1811 to be approximately £25 million, of which £4 million was the profit of the shipowners. Yearly incomes in ship and boat building and repairing, "including the labour of shipwrights, boat-builders, mast and oar-makers, block-makers, rope-makers, sail-makers, riggers, etc. after deducting for the raw materials," are put at £2 million, £1 million each for the merchant marine and the British navy. When the value of raw materials employed – timber, iron, copper, hemp, tar and other raw materials – is included the total comes to £4 million, split equally between merchant shipping and the navy.[12] Considering the magnitude of increase in the size of the British merchant marine between the early and mid-nineteenth century, the estimates by Herries and Colquhoun, where they are comparable, would seem to be reasonably consistent.

For the period 1790–1807, Customs 17 contains the tonnage of ships belonging to England on September 30, each year, and the number of seamen employed. This is shown in Table 6.3. The figures indicate a slowly growing efficiency in the employment of labor in the shipping industry, from 13.5 tons per man in 1790 to 15 in 1807. Herries's figures of 230,000 seamen and 3,900,000 tons, mentioned earlier, would mean 17.0 tons per man in the mid-nineteenth century. Again, this appears consistent with the trend in Table 6.3, further confirming the general reliability of the estimates by Herries and Colquhoun. Thus, allowing for the colonies, Ireland, and Scotland in Herries's figures, the implication of the foregoing evidence is that employment, and by implication income also, in the shipping industry of England more than doubled between 1790 and 1850.[13]

This growth of employment and income must have contributed significantly to the growth of the domestic market for English manufactures during the period. However, a more direct and quantitatively more

---

[12] Patrick Colquhoun, *Treatise on the Wealth, Power and Resources of the British Empire* (2nd edition, London, 1815), pp. 94–95. See the estimates of shipping earnings by Brezis, "Foreign capital flows"; Nash, "The balance of payments"; Brezis, "Did foreign capital flows finance the industrial revolution?" The estimates by Brezis and Nash are incomplete and are, therefore, not comparable with the ones presented here.

[13] Colquhoun's figures for 1810, 1811, and 1812 show that employment figures for Great Britain were about 86 percent of the total for Great Britain, Ireland, and the colonies. I have guessed that figures for Scotland could not have been more than 10 percent of the total, leaving England with about three-quarters of Herries's figure of 230,000. For Colquhoun's figures, see Colquhoun, *Treatise*, p. 101.

Table 6.3. *Tonnage of English Merchant*
Shipping and Number of Seamen Employed,
1790–1807

	Tons (000)	Seamen Employed	Tons per Man
1790	1,040	77,090	13.5
1791	1,075	86,897	12.4
1792	1,187	87,718	13.5
1793	1,205		
1794	1,221	87,248	14.0
1795	1,208	84,950	14.2
1796	1,241	88,635	14.0
1797	1,253	91,551	13.7
1798	1,287	95,360	13.5
1799	1,337	99,309	13.5
1800	1,467	105,147	14.0
1801	1,543	109,604	14.1
1802	1,643	113,671	14.5
1803	1,710	115,274	14.8
1804	1,784	115,365	15.5
1805	1,799	117,668	15.3
1806	1,787	118,089	15.1
1807	1,797	119,631	15.0

Source: Customs 17/12–29.

important contribution to the growth of manufacturing was in shipbuild-ing, fitting and repairing already alluded to in the figures presented earlier. As already mentioned, the shipbuilding industry deserves a book-length work that is yet to be written. It is, therefore, not possible to present here much detail on the subject. What follows is a summary of the available evidence.

Table 6.4 shows the tonnage and value of newly built and registered ships in England from 1787 to 1807. Apart from the years 1800–03, this period appears to be a trough, following the shipbuilding boom of 1781–84, which peaked in 1783, referred to by Craig.[14] The downward trend would seem to have continued through 1787 to 1795, before rising again from 1796 to 1803, with a peak in 1800. Not having firm data for the years before 1787, the extent of the boom that preceded the trough is unclear. For the years that followed we have good evidence. The data published by Mitchell for

[14] Craig, "Capital Formation in Shipping," p. 140.

Table 6.4. *Tonnage and Value of Ships Newly Built and Registered in England, 1787–1807*

	London		Outports		All England	
	Tons	Value (£000)	Tons	Value (£000)	Tons	Value (£000)
1787	16,999	306	60,997	915	77,996	1,221
1788	8,534	154	52,064	781	60,598	935
1789	8,280	149	40,828	612	49,108	761
1790	9,743	175	39,727	596	49,470	771
1791	6,673	127	42,068	673	48,741	800
1792	11,003	209	45,041	721	56,044	930
1793	4,086	78	51,753	828	55,839	906
1794	1,971	37	45,382	726	47,353	763
1795	7,122	135	49,824	797	56,946	932
1796	22,313	424	52,957	847	75,270	1,271
1797	20,342	386	49,083	785	69,425	1,171
1798	6,763	128	61,192	979	67,955	1,107
1799	4,830	92	67,883	1,086	72,713	1,178
1800	19,993	380	81,785	1,309	101,778	1,689
1801	5,843	129	86,157	1,723	92,000	1,852
1802	15,129	333	75,474	1,509	90,603	1,842
1803	15,994	352	79,135	1,583	95,129	1,935
1804	5,987	132	61,132	1,223	67,119	1,355
1805	6,694	147	54,443	1,089	61,137	1,236
1806	3,113	68	47,316	946	50,429	1,014
1807	2,876	63	46,409	928	49,285	991

Sources and Notes: Tonnage of ships built and registered in London and all England is taken from Customs 17/12–29; tonnage for the outports is computed by subtracting the London figures from those for all England. The prices applied to the tonnage figures are based on the evidence discussed by Craig, "Capital Formation in Shipping," pp. 141–145; for London, the prices per ton applied are £18 for 1787–90, £19 for 1791–1800, and £22 for 1801–07. For the outports during the respective periods, the prices are £15, £16, and £20. These prices are for the hull as well as the cost of fitting out the ship ready to sail. The latter cost depended very much on the particular area of trade in which the ship was going to be employed. In general, the fitting cost was much greater for ships intended for the long distance trades than for those in the coasting and other short distance trades. On the average, however, the fitting cost per ton was about equal to the cost of the hull per ton. More is said on this below. The estimate here may be compared with that of Deane and Cole, who put the annual average value of ships built and registered in the United Kingdom in 1795–1804 at £2.0 million. The average for England alone in the same period in this Table is £1,433,200. The two figures are very close. See Deane and Cole, *British Economic Growth*, Table 62, p. 234.

the first half of the nineteenth century shows that for Great Britain the highest tonnage figure for the years 1808–36 was just over a hundred thousand; thereafter a boom occurred between 1837 and 1840, with a growth of tonnage for the United Kingdom from 131,200 in 1837 to 211,300 in 1840. It then fell over time to 133,700 in 1850.[15] The figures in Table 6.4 may thus represent a low point in the shipbuilding industry in England between 1781 and 1850.

Even so, the values in the table indicate a significant contribution to manufacturing activities by the shipbuilding industry. This is the more so when the yearly cost of repairing and fitting out the existing stock of shipping is added to the value of new ships built each year. According to Stewart-Brown, a contemporary writer estimated in 1792 that the shipowners made a yearly profit of 18 percent on the capital employed. Based on the existing stock of shipping in England and Scotland in 1792, totaling 1,365,000 tons, this contemporary writer computed a total profit of £2,063,880, out of which £1,375,920 was reckoned to have been spent on keeping the stock in service for the year, being 12 percentage points out of the 18 percent profit.[16] This gives an annual cost of repairs for the hull and outfit of £1.008 per ton. With due caution on the margin of error to be expected in this kind of estimate, it may be safe to apply this as a general rate for the period 1780–1850. The result for 1788–1807 is presented in Table 6.5.

As the table shows, maintenance cost for the existing stock was greater in most years than the value of new ships added to the stock each year. For the whole period the value of new ships built in England and added to the stock averaged £1.194 million per annum, while the cost of keeping the existing stock in service averaged £1.413 million. Taking the two together, the average is £2.607 million per year for the period. For the last eight years, 1800–07, the average is over £3 million. Taking into account that value added in manufacturing and building in England and Scotland together (including Wales, of course) amounted to £22.9 million in 1770 and £54.1 million in 1801 (both at current prices),[17] these shipping figures for England alone represent a significant amount of manufacturing activities centered around the shipyards in England.

It is important to note that the growth of the shipbuilding industry in England in the seventeenth and eighteenth centuries was not proportionate to the expansion of the English merchant marine during the same period because of a large import of vessels from the British American colonies

[15]   Mitchell, *British Historical Statistics*, pp. 220–221.
[16]   R. Stewart-Brown, *Liverpool Ships in the Eighteenth Century* (London: University of Liverpool Press, 1932), p. 42.
[17]   Crafts, *British Economic Growth*, p. 22.

Table 6.5. *Annual Cost of New Ships Registered and Maintenance Cost of Existing English Shipping, 1788–1807*

	Cost of New Ships (£000)	Cost of Repairs for Existing Stock (£000)	Total Cost (£000)
1788	935	1,063	1,998
1790	771	1,048	1,819
1791	800	1,084	1,884
1792	930	1,196	2,126
1793	906	1,215	2,121
1794	763	1,231	1,994
1795	932	1,218	2,150
1796	1,271	1,251	2,522
1797	1,171	1,263	2,434
1798	1,107	1,297	2,404
1799	1,178	1,348	2,526
1800	1,689	1,479	3,168
1801	1,852	1,555	3,407
1802	1,842	1,656	3,498
1803	1,935	1,724	3,659
1804	1,355	1,798	3,153
1805	1,236	1,813	3,049
1806	1,014	1,801	2,815
1807	991	1,811	2,802

Sources and Notes: For the cost of new ships, see Table 6.4. The annual cost of repairs is computed by applying the general rate of £1.008 per ton (explained in the text above) to the tonnage of English-owned merchant vessels in Table 6.2. The total cost column is the sum of the other two columns. Because the existing stock of shipping in each year would include the new ships registered in the year, some element of double counting may be involved in the calculations. However, this should be offset by the much higher outfit cost for prizes taken in wartime and converted to English ships, which the rate applied does not seem to include. For the high outfit cost for prizes, see the comment by Craig, "Capital Formation in Shipping," pp. 136–137.

and the appropriation of wartime prizes. Ralph Davis has shown that the proportion of American-built ships in the English merchant marine increased from one-sixth in 1730 to one-quarter in 1760, and to nearly one-third in the 1770s.[18] This is confirmed by analysis of the data in the *Lloyd's Register* of 1776, which shows that almost 40 percent of the British tonnage

[18]   Davis, *English Shipping Industry*, p. 68.

listed was American-built; foreign-built and colonial-built tonnage together exceeded the amount of tonnage built in Britain.[19]

Apart from the figure of 50,000 artisans earning £5 million a year stated by Herries in 1848, mentioned earlier in the chapter, no national figures of employment in the shipbuilding industry are currently available. Stewart-Brown's figures published several decades ago are for only seven districts and include only shipwrights (with their apprentices) and caulkers. For these seven districts in 1804, there were 2,583 shipwrights, 1,800 apprentices, and 399 caulkers, making a total of 4,782.[20] The 1776 *Lloyd's Register*, mentioned earlier, shows a total of 57 shipbuilding sites in England and Wales (five for Wales and 52 for England).[21] Of the 490,963 tons analyzed for England and Wales, 2.8 percent were built in Wales, and the rest in England; the main building sites in England were in the northeast (40.2 percent of the total), River Thames (19.3 percent), and the northwest (14.0 percent).[22] This regional distribution agrees with Ralph Davis's observation based on the 1787 registration figures.[23]

Taking into account the amount of labor employed to produce materials, such as timber, iron, copper, ropes, sails, and so forth, for the shipbuilding industry, activities in the shipyards in the 57 sites mentioned earlier must have supported manufacturing employment much larger than the 50,000 estimated by Herries for the mid-nineteenth century. The evidence presented earlier in the chapter suggests a significant growth in manufacturing employment connected with shipbuilding (directly and indirectly) after the elimination of American competition, reaching a peak in 1783; further growth occurred in the first half of the nineteenth century. On the whole, the evidence presented thus far would appear adequate to support the generalization that the shipping and shipbuilding trades made significant contributions to the expansion of employment and income in the modern sectors of the English economy between 1650 and 1850, more so in the last three-quarter century from 1775 to 1850. This factor needs to

---

[19] Joseph A. Goldenberg, "An Analysis of Shipbuilding Sites in *Lloyd's Register* of 1776," *The Mariner's Mirror*, Vol. 59, No. 4 (November 1973), p. 422. By the Navigation Laws, ships built in the American colonies were entitled to the privileges of British-built ships if owned by British citizens (which included people in British America). After the independence of the United States in 1783, vessels built in the United States ceased to qualify for the privileges of the Navigation Laws and English shipbuilders were glad to be freed from the American competition (*Ibid.*, p. 422).

[20] Stewart-Brown, *Liverpool Ships*, p. 34. The seven districts are Bristol, Chester, Hull, Liverpool, London and River Thames, North Shields and vicinity, and Whitby.

[21] Goldenberg, "Shipbuilding Sites," pp. 424–431.

[22] *Ibid.*, p. 424.

[23] As Davis put it, "when the registration of ships began in 1787, the north-east coast from Newcastle down to Hull was by far the largest seat of the shipbuilding industry, and had obviously been so for a very long time." See Davis, *English Shipping Industry*, p. 62.

be taken into consideration when discussing the growth of industries, such as iron and copper. More details on the subject are presented in the section that follows, as the contribution of the Atlantic slave economy to the growth and development of the shipping and shipbuilding trades in England is examined.

6.2 CONTRIBUTION OF THE ATLANTIC SLAVE ECONOMY

For the rest of the chapter, focus is on the role of Atlantic commerce. The transportation of African slave labor to the Americas, the shipping of slave-produced American products across the Atlantic to England, and the re-export of these products to other European countries were the main driving force behind the growth of the English shipping and shipbuilding trades in the seventeenth and eighteenth centuries. This was made possible by the successful use of the British navy to expand British colonial territories in the Americas at the expense of rivals and the successful employment of the same naval power to protect and secure the carrying trade of British America for English shipowners. In this regard, the victory over the Spanish Armada in 1588, the defeat of the Dutch, the French, and the Spaniards in the seventeenth and eighteenth centuries, and the taking over of their American colonial territories were critical events. These events, coupled with the construction of the Navigation Laws from the mid-seventeenth century to keep away all rivals (especially the Dutch) from British American trade, were the main mechanisms through which the conditions were created for the growth and development of the English shipping and shipbuilding trades. Once British naval power had incorporated large areas of the New World into British America, the Navigation Laws performed two important functions: 1) They ensured that, by law, only British-owned ships manned by British citizens could carry the products of British America across the Atlantic, to Britain alone in the first instance, and later, by way of re-export, from Britain to the rest of Europe. The European goods exchanged for these American products and for English domestic exports were also similarly shipped to Britain or in ships belonging to the European countries of origin; in the same way, that portion of the imports from Europe destined for British America could be shipped, along with English domestic products, only in British-owned ships manned by British citizens. And, 2) in order to encourage the growth of the shipbuilding industry in England, the privileges created by the Navigation Laws were made accessible only to British owned ships built in Britain or in the British colonies, with the exception of wartime prizes converted to British ownership.[24] In

---

[24] For more details on the Navigation Laws, see Hunter, *Merchant Marine*, pp. 119–149.

Table 6.6. *Regional Distribution of English-Owned Ships Employed in Foreign Trade (in 000 tons)*

Geographical Region	1663	1686	1771–73	1792	1836
Northern Europe	13	28	74		
Nearby Europe and British Isles	39	41	92		
Southern Europe and Mediterranean	30	39	27		
Americas and West Indies	36	70	153		
East India	8	12	29		
British Isles				53	15
Northern Europe				194	244
Southern Europe and Mediterranean				60	115
The Whale Fisheries				36	28
Africa (except Mediterranean Africa)				101	67
West Indies (British and Foreign)				139	229
British North America				40	530
United States of America				43	98
Brazil					44
Rest of Latin America (Mainland)					24
East India				45	344
Total	126	190	375	711	1,738

Sources and Notes: For the sources and method of computation, see Table 6.2. Because of rounding to the nearest thousand, the total figures for 1792 and 1836 in this table are slightly higher than those for the same years in Table 6.2. For the years 1663, 1686, and 1771–73, the region, Americas and West Indies, includes Western Africa. The composition of the geographical regions for 1792 and 1836 is somewhat different from that for the other years; hence, the separate arrangement.

this way, the growth of the British carrying trade and that of the English shipping and shipbuilding trades were tied directly to the growth of production and trade in British America.

Table 6.6 shows the regional distribution of English-owned ships employed in foreign trade. From this table it can be seen that the tonnage of English-owned shipping employed in the trade with Western Africa and the Americas increased from 28.6 percent of all English shipping employed in foreign trade in 1663 to 36.8 percent in 1686, 40.8 percent in 1771–73, 45.4 percent in 1792, and 57.1 percent in 1836. Between 1663 and 1686, increase in the shipping employed in the trade with Western Africa and the Americas accounted for 53 percent of the overall increment; between 1686 and 1836, it accounted for approximately 60 percent. During the same period, the share of English-owned shipping employed in the trade with

Europe and the Mediterranean declined from 65 percent in 1663 to 21.5 percent in 1836. Yet a significant part of the English carrying trade with Europe was dependent on the re-export of produce from the Americas. As Ralph Davis has shown, the share of re-exports in all exports from England rose from 22.0 percent in 1663/69 to 30.9 percent in 1699–1701, and 37.1 percent in 1772–74.[25] Among the re-exports, the articles of great bulk in relation to their price – sugar, tobacco, rice, coffee, dyestuffs, etc. – were from the Americas. It should be noted further that much of the English carrying trade with the Baltic region, an important part of the trade with Europe, was dependent on the shipment of timber and other materials needed in the shipbuilding industry, whose growth, as we have seen, was a function of the expanding trade with Western Africa and the Americas. As Davis put it:

> To a significant extent . . . the English shipping industry was pulling itself up by its own boot-straps. A ship built entirely of foreign materials – foreign timber, iron, pitch and tar, hemp – would call for the transport services of as many as two or three ships of its own size to carry the materials, and the annual extent of repairs and replacement was substantial. . . . Of course much of the material used in ship-building . . . was in fact home produced . . . yet it is worth underlining the fact that the expansion of English shipping engaged in the Northern trades, which in this period [seventeenth and eighteenth centuries] contributed so much to the overall growth of the shipping industry, was to an important extent due to the demands of the industry itself.[26]

That the growth of production and trade in the slave-based economies of the Americas was the dominant factor in the rise of the English shipping and shipbuilding trades in the period 1650–1850 may be further demonstrated by examining the peculiar shipping needs of the trade with Western Africa and the Americas, which the figures in Table 6.6 do not reveal. As already stated, with the exception of timber and iron from the Baltic, the most bulky products transported by English shipping in the seventeenth and eighteenth centuries were from the Americas and Western Africa – sugar, rice, tobacco, and cotton from the Americas, and several types of wood (cam-wood, redwood, ebony, timber) and palm produce from Western Africa. In addition, the transportation of forced migrant labor from Western Africa presented a unique shipping need not at all captured by the published data on British shipping. Added to the characteristics of what was transported are elements such as distance, pattern of employment of shipping, exposure to the elements and the ravages of tropical waters for wooden vessels, and, what is more important, a much greater exposure to

[25] Davis, "English Foreign Trade, 1660–1700," p. 92; Davis, "English Foreign Trade, 1700–1774," p. 109.
[26] Davis, *English Shipping Industry*, pp. 19–20.

enemy attack and capture during the frequent commercial wars of the period. These peculiarities of the Atlantic carrying trade meant that the vessels employed had a rather short average life span, which called for frequent replacement with new ones, and a high cost of repairs and outfit. All of these elements are clearly shown by the evidence on the Western African trade. It should be noted that the discussion that follows contains some elements unique to the Western African trade. However, English trade with Western Africa and the Americas shared several common shipping characteristics during the period of study.

The actual volume of English shipping employed in the Western African trade in the seventeenth and eighteenth centuries and the yearly demand made by that trade for new ships and for repairs and outfit are little known, because no detailed studies exist. What is presented here may, in some way, help to fill the gap. A remarkable element in the trade was the integration of trading and shipowning as a single business. The monopoly companies which controlled the trade in the early years had employed chartered ships to transport their goods. But the private traders, who took over the trade from the late seventeenth century, started a trend that became generalized in the eighteenth century: Instead of hiring ships to transport their goods, the merchants bought their own vessels to ship their own goods. In this way, the cost of goods shipped, the purchase cost of the ship, the cost of outfit and repairs, seamen's wages and provision, and insurance costs were all combined in a single venture. Some of the factors responsible for this development are shown in the evidence presented to a House of Commons committee in 1788 by John Tarleton, one of the largest Liverpool merchants in the African trade at this time. He told the committee that vessels were seldom hired to transport slaves from Western Africa to the Americas. Tarleton explained that when ships were chartered to carry slaves across the Atlantic,

there are two separate and distinct interests, the shipowner and the merchant who sent out the adventure. The shipowner's profits are certain . . . but the adventurer runs every risk of advance price of the purchase of Negroes, mortality and low average in the West Indies, against which he has no mode of security; but when the risks are both held together, they mutually assist each other.[27]

The degree of risk involved in the African trade and other possible elements not mentioned by Tarleton thus gave rise to the integration of shipowning and trading in England's trade with Western Africa in the late

---

[27]   PRO, BT.6/7, Evidence of John Tarleton before a House of Commons Committee in 1788. It has been said that the coastal coal trade and the Western African trade were the only branches of trade in England in the eighteenth century in which "shipping and trading intertwined in a single common venture": Davis, *English Shipping Industry*, p. 91.

seventeenth and eighteenth centuries. This integration led to the growth of a specialised class of vessels regularly employed in the African trade. These vessels, built purposely to meet the peculiar needs of the African trade, were generally referred to as Guineamen, the term Guinea being applied to the whole stretch of the Atlantic coast of Africa from Senegambia to Angola. Because the length of time it took to cross the Atlantic was critical to the health of the forced migrants being transported from Africa, and so to the profitability of the enterprise, the ships were specially built for quick sailing and were equipped with special conveniences adapted to the lodging of slaves. This is borne out by the consistent testimony of the ship captains and merchants in the trade. A few of these will suffice. Captain William Sherwood, a very experienced shipmaster in the African trade in the employ of John Dawson of Liverpool, told members of the Assembly of Jamaica in December 1789 that he considered the construction of ships more material than the tonnage for the health of the slaves.[28] Earlier in March 1788, James Penny, a prominent Guinea merchant in Liverpool, had told a committee of the Privy Council in London that[29]:

Our ships at Liverpool are built on purpose for this trade [the African trade], and are accommodated with airports and gratings, for the purpose of keeping the slaves cool – great improvements have been made at Liverpool, within these 20 years, in the construction of these ships – the space between the Decks is sufficiently large to contain [large numbers of slaves], and is planed very smooth and painted; we are also provided with windsails, and most of the ships have ventilators.

James Penny added, with some sense of humor, that as a proof of these improvements, "I have shown to the principal people of the country the accommodations on board my ship, and they have held up their hands, and said, the slaves here will sleep better than the gentlemen do on shore."

Because the ships were built purposely for the trade, they remained in it for the whole of their life span. The first owners employed them in the trade year after year and sold them to other merchants in the trade if they decided to quit. Occasionally some secondhand vessels were bought and made into Guineamen. But the cost of doing so was often close to the cost of building a new vessel. The special characteristics of the Guineamen created both advantages and disadvantages for the owners when the African trade was seriously disrupted by war as was the case during the War of American Independence (1776–83). As early as August 1775, a Guinea merchant in Liverpool wrote to a correspondent, "I am sorry to say that most of our

---

[28] PRO, C.O. 137/88, Assembly of Jamaica, Report on the Slave Trade, Session beginning 20 Oct. 1789.

[29] PRO, BT 6/9, Minutes of Evidence taken by a Committee of the Privy Council appointed by the king to enquire into the slave trade. Evidence of James Penny, 8 March, 1788, pp. 340 and 346.

Guineamen is [sic] layed by as they come in owing to the American disturbances . . ."[30] This kind of complaint was to be heard in all English ports in the trade with Western Africa during the period of the war. However, there were two alternative employments in wartime for which the Guineamen were well suited: government service as transports and privateering (preying on enemy merchant ships). Being fast sailing ships and usually well armed, Guineamen found employment with the government as transport in wartime. Thus, a Bristol merchant reported in November 1776, "indeed all the Guineamen belonging to this port [Bristol] are in government service as transports."[31] The same qualities also made privateering a profitable area of temporary employment for Guineamen in times of war. As the historian of Liverpool privateers tells us:

Those vessels that could not be profitably employed in the slave trade were easily converted into privateers, and so great was the energy displayed in their equipment, that, between the end of August, 1778, and April, 1779 no less than 120 private ships of war were fitted out.[32]

The operation of the Guineamen as a specialized class of ships continuously employed in the African trade makes it practicable to follow their pattern of employment, measure their volume and frequency of replacement over time, and assess the demand that their building, outfit, and repairs made on the shipyards in England during the period of study. Apart from the frequency of replacement, and outfit and repair costs induced by the characteristics of the African trade, regulating laws enacted by the British government in the late eighteenth century also compelled changes in the physical structure of the Guineamen – changes that called for more work in the shipyards. These laws, together with the growing volume of the trade, distances covered, the pattern of employment of shipping, the ravages of tropical waters for wooden vessels, exposure to the elements, slave rebellions, and other hazards of Atlantic commerce determined the level of demand made by the trade for new ships, type of outfit, and the extent and frequency of repairs. For a proper understanding of subsequent calculations, these elements need some elaboration.

The series of regulating laws that forced changes in the construction of the Guineamen began in the 1780s. The first was the law of 1788, which stipulated that from August 1, 1788, no vessel clearing out from Great

[30]   380 Tuo. 2/4, Tuohy Papers, Liverpool Record Office, David Tuohy to Ryan, Liverpool, 12 August, 1775.

[31]   PRO, T.70/1534, John Cockburn to a trader on the African coast, Bristol, 30 November, 1776.

[32]   Gomer Williams, *History of the Liverpool Privateers and Letters of Marque with an account of the Liverpool Slave Trade* (London, 1897), p. 183. The total tonnage of these private ships of war was 30,787, carrying altogether 1,986 guns and 8,754 men.

Britain was to carry slaves from Africa in greater numbers than five for every three tons if the vessel did not exceed 201 tons. All vessels exceeding this size were to carry one slave per ton after the first 201 tons. Vessels were to be deemed of the tonnage described in their certificates of registry. Masters of vessels, before they could land any slaves in British America, were to declare upon oath, before the officer of the Customs, the burden of the vessel, produce the certificate of the registry and give an exact account of the number of slaves on board; masters landing slaves fraudulently were to forfeit £500 for every such offense. No vessel was to be allowed to carry slaves unless it had entered for that purpose at clearing out, and unless the surgeon gave bond to keep a journal of the number of the slaves during the voyage. This journal should be delivered to the officer at the first British port of arrival. No vessel was to be cleared out for purposes of carrying slaves that had not a surgeon to her, who had passed his examination at Surgeons Hall.[33]

This act continued in force in all its essentials, with a few additions and amendments to the minor articles, until 1797 when a far-reaching addition was made to it by an act passed in that year. This was titled, "An Act for regulating the height between decks of vessels entered outwards for the purpose of carrying slaves from the Coast of Africa (19 July, 1797)."[34] The act stipulated that no vessels should clear out from Great Britain for the purpose of carrying slaves from the coast of Africa, in which the space between the decks allotted for the reception of slaves "shall not be, in every part through the whole length and breadth thereof, of the full and complete perpendicular height of four feet one inch at least, measuring from the upper surface of the lower deck to the under surface of the upper deck." In vessels having only one deck, a floor or false deck to be fixed in the hold for the reception of the slaves was to be taken as the lower deck for the purposes of this act. Vessels clearing out were to obtain a certificate from H. M. Customs at the port of clearance showing that the vessel conformed to the necessary restrictions, which certificate was to be produced to the collector or other proper officer of the customs at every port in British America before any slaves could be landed.

Within two years another act was passed styled, "An Act for better regulating the manner of carrying slaves, in British vessels, from the Coast of Africa (12 July 1799)."[35] This act stated that the height between decks should be five feet instead of four feet one inch required by the 1797 Act. No vessel was to clear out for the purpose of carrying slaves from the coast of Africa until a proper officer of the customs at the port of clearance had measured it and certified in writing the height between decks, and the

---

[33] British Library, London, 28 Geo. 3 Cap. 54, Public General Acts.
[34] British Library, London, 37 Geo. 3 Cap. 118, Public General Acts.
[35] British Library, London, 39 Geo. 3 Cap. 80, Public General Acts.

extreme length and breadth, in feet and inches, of the lower deck of the vessel. The product of the length and breadth was to be considered the "true superficial contents of the said deck"; the said contents being divided by eight, the quotient in whole numbers was to express the maximum number of slaves the vessel was permitted to carry. The certificate obtained after this measurement had to be produced to the proper officer of the customs at every port in British America before any slaves could be landed. Vessels were to have painted on their stern the words, "allowed to carry slaves," and the number they were permitted to carry. No cargo of slaves, of whatever dimensions the vessel, could exceed 400. If any penalty imposed on masters was not paid within 14 days their vessels could be seized and sold. From August 1, 1799, only Liverpool, London, and Bristol were to be permitted to clear out vessels for the slave trade.

As shown in Chapter 5, these regulations were not completely effective, because some of the traders found ways to successfully evade them. One easy way to do so was to expand the direct trade to non-British America, especially the Spanish and French Caribbean, where the regulations could not be enforced. However, the evidence indicates that the regulations did induce a significant amount of modifications in the physical characteristics of the Guineamen as traders doing business in British America could not totally ignore the laws. For example, during the debate in the House of Commons to amend the 1797 Act and raise the height between decks from four feet and one inch to five feet a merchant, who had been in the African trade for 18 years, complained that[36]:

If the ships were to be heightened, many of them will be excluded, the alterations being very expensive – vessels already raised to four feet one inch are generally incapable of service, and are not profitably to be employed in any other trade.

This alteration, he added, would exclude a large proportion of small vessels the heightening of which rendered their navigation dangerous by making them top heavy: "Since passing the Act of 1797 I can speak particularly to one vessel (my own) which was thrown off the trade, and I sold her on account of the expence of alteration." Ultimately such arguments did not deter Parliament from enacting the 1799 Act, which raised the height between decks to five feet, among other things.

Changes in the average tonnage of vessels cleared out to Africa from England appear to support the claim made by the merchant cited above. Between 1750 and 1780, the average tonnage changed very little, from 103.6 in 1750–60 to 111.9 in 1771–80. The phenomenal expansion of the African trade which followed the termination of the American War of Independence seems to have carried with it a significant change in the

---

[36]   British Library, London, *British Parliamentary Papers, Accounts & Papers 1798–99*, Vol. 106 No. 966, Evidence of James Rigby, p. 2.

size of ships employed, the average tonnage increasing by 23.5 percent between 1771–80 (111.9 tons average) and 1781–86 (138.2 tons average). The further increase of the average tonnage to 166.5 in 1787–90 may not be real; in all likelihood it was due to the more accurate measurement of shipping tonnage brought about by the registration act of 1786.[37] Between 1787–90 and 1791–97, very little change occurred, an increase in average tonnage from 166.5 to 180.1 tons, being only 8.2 percent. But in the three years that followed the 1797 Act, 1798–1800, the average tonnage jumped by 25.6 percent to 226.2 tons. This figure remained unchanged in 1801–07, suggesting that the 1799 Act effected little change in the size of the ships.[38]

As can be seen from the foregoing discussion, the effects of the regulating laws came at the tail-end of the eighteenth century. The other elements that determined the number and tonnage of shipping employed in the African trade and the cost of their outfit and maintenance operated more or less persistently throughout the period of study. The pattern of employment of the ships was one such element.

Between 1650 and 1807, the transportation of slaves from Western Africa across the Atlantic to the Americas was the main employment for the Guineamen, although a few ships carried African products directly to England from Africa. The vessels that shipped slaves to the Americas were employed by the traders in very complicated ways dictated by the complexities of the slave trade. We are used to the descriptive notion of the triangular trade – ships carried manufactured goods from England to Western Africa; these goods were exchanged for captives, who were then transported across the Atlantic to the Americas; to complete the triangle, the same ships carried slave-produced American products to England. In reality things were very different and far more complex. Because detailed information on the complicated pattern of employment will help us understand why the actual volume of shipping employed was much greater than the annual clearance figures – number and tonnage of ships cleared out annually from England to Western Africa as compared with the total number and tonnage of ships employed in the African trade at a given moment – it is pertinent to lay out much of the available evidence.

To start with, the movement of the ships from England to Western Africa was not always direct. The trade was basically by barter – slaves were paid for directly with goods, not money. Sellers in Western Africa demanded to

---

[37] It is generally believed that before the registration act of 1786 the tonnage of vessels was fraudulently understated to the customs officers by the traders. See Robert Norris, *A Short Account of the African Slave Trade* (London, 1789), footnote, p. 28; Craig, "Capital Formation in Shipping," p. 134.

[38] For the detailed figures showing the number of ships and their tonnage, as well as the sources, see Table 6.12 below.

be paid with an assortment of goods that met their consumption and investment needs. This meant that the British traders had to carry to Western
Africa a well-selected assortment of goods in the right proportions and
quality, in accord with the prevailing taste of the time. But before England
became the "workshop of the world" in the nineteenth century, most of the
goods needed for the trade had to be procured from outside England. Sometimes these goods were brought to England by other British traders, from
whom the Guinea merchants bought them – the English East India
Company did considerable business importing and selling East Indian
cotton textiles to the Guinea merchants in England. But quite often the
traders found it necessary to send their Guineamen to Continental Europe
to complete their assortment of goods before continuing their journey
to the African coast. Holland was a frequent stopping point, where
Continental products, especially German linens and hardware, and Asian
textiles were picked up. There were other stopping places in Europe. The
information on these movements is plentiful, and it can be used to show
some order of magnitude, but it is not exactly quantifiable.

The extant private records of a London merchant firm, Thomas Hall &
Co., which was extensively involved in the African trade in the first half of
the eighteenth century provide suggestive information.[39] The firm shipped
about 1,000 slaves a year from Western Africa to British America, Spanish
America, and Brazil. In addition, it bought large quantities of African products – ivory, gold, wood, etc. – which were carried to England in British
naval vessels or via the Americas in slave ships. The firm had an agent in
Rotterdam (in Holland), Jacob Senserf & Co., responsible for purchasing
goods in Holland for the ships to pick up on their way to Africa. There
was another agent in Buenos Aires in charge of the firm's business in South
America.

Evidence from the extant papers of the firm indicates that the ships, as
a matter of course, went to Holland to complete their assortment of goods
before proceeding to Western Africa. The firm's ship, *Argyle*, Captain
Hamilton, master, was sent to Western Africa in 1732 with a total cargo of
goods worth £2,854:10s., of which goods valued at £2070 were put on
board in Holland by Senserf & Son.[40] In a letter of March 18, 1732, Senserf
& Son informed Thomas Hall: "As to the East India Goods fit for a Guinea
cargo we find in general the goods of our Company better than yours in
England . . ." Another letter of March 21, 1732, mentions three ships of
Thomas Hall & Co. that were going to pick up their cargo in Holland: the
Princes Emelia, *Mermaid*, and *Judith*. The total amount of goods shipped

---

[39]   The private papers of Thomas Hall & Co. are in the Public Record Office, London,
among the Chancery Masters Exhibits. Those that are particularly relevant here are
C.103/130, C.103/131, C.103/132, C.103/133.

[40]   C.103/132, Senserf & Son to Thomas Hall, Rotterdam, 19 February, 1732.

from Rotterdam by these ships was £8,276:1s.[41] In October 1735, Thomas Hall was informed by his partner, James Pearce, how English ships did business in Holland:

All the ships which go to Holland & Guinea take on board at least 1/4 part of their India goods in London so that if they should have more goods than would purchase their number of slaves these goods so taken in in London may be reserved to the last on the coast & returned (if there should be an overplus) on the ship and may either [be] sold publicly in the West Indies or brought home & lodged in the Custom house for another voyage, whereas the Dutch goods returned on the ship makes not only the goods, but ship and cargo liable to a forfeiture, as well in our plantations as in England.[42]

A year earlier James Pearce had expressed disappointment with one of his ship-masters, Captain Pinkethman, who had made a very successful voyage, sending to England from Buenos Aires 432,000 pesos of eight, "exclusive of your own [Thomas Hall's] and the Company's," but carried with him homeward "a large parcell of Remains of his English and Dutch Guinea cargoe without giving the particulars of either." Pinkethman was to be advised to throw the goods overboard before the ship "comes above the hope":

This silly fellow I am sure might have sold these things at Buenos Aires at least have bought his full compliment of slaves on the coast for as I am told he sold many brass pans and guns at Bayres. These India goods would have made a proper assortment to have bought more slaves.[43]

Information on the insurance of the firm's ships and goods shows the circuitous movement of the vessels. To illustrate, in July 1735 the firm's vessel, *Hiscox*, Captain John Butler, Master, was insured for £2,000 at 14.7 percent. The route covered by the insurance was described as follows: "at and from London to Holland and at and from thence to any ports and places where and whatsoever in Africa and at and from thence to Buenos Ayres and at and from thence back to London."[44] Again, in September 1736 Captain George Hamilton wrote to Thomas Hall:

We have insured this day at the Royal Exchange Insurance in Mr. Lascelle's and Captain Pinnell's names on the ship *Argyle* twenty thousand pounds [£20,000] that is ship and cargo to Rotterdam, & from thence to Annamaboe on the coast of Africa; ten thousand pounds at two and a half per cent; and from Rotterdam cargo

[41] *Ibid.*, Senserf & Son to Thomas Hall, Rotterdam, 18 March, 1732, 21 March, 1732, and 27 May, 1732.

[42] C.103/130, James Pearce to Thomas Hall, Bristol, 15 October, 1735.

[43] C.103/130, James Pearce to Thomas Hall, London, 11 October, 1734.

[44] C.103/130, Policy of Insurance on the *Hiscox*, Captain John Butler, Master, 8 July 1735.

only, to the above mentioned Port; ten thousand pounds more at two per cent in case of a loss.[45]

The firm's agent in Holland, Senserf & Son, frequently expressed the difficulty encountered in getting insurance cover from Buenos Aires to London:

Our Insurance Company & no private Insurers care to insure on the ships from Buenos Aires to London. They would do it from hence to Guinea to Buenos Aires, but not further. We would advise you to make this Insurance in London where they know the Capt., the ship, & the concerned.[46]

The firm's records also show that Ireland was another stopping place for some of the vessels, quite often to pick up provision before proceeding to Africa. Thus Captain Hamilton reported in December 1738: "Our sloop, *Expedition*, Capt. Geo. Cload, has found his way at last to Annamaboa" after eight months' passage from Ireland.[47]

Even in the third quarter of the eighteenth century, when more goods for the African trade became increasingly available in England – both from local production and from imports – the records of an underwriter still show a large percentage for vessels which did not follow the direct route of England to Western Africa. Out of about 140 known voyages given coverage down to Western Africa between July 1759 and December 1772, 33 did not follow the direct route, being 23.6 percent of the total. Appendix 6.1 shows the names of these vessels, the masters, the owners, and the routes taken to Western Africa.

William Braund, who insured these vessels, was an underwriter based in London. Many of the owners, such as Oswald & Co. and Samuel Touchet, were also well-known Guinea merchants in London. A couple of the ships were probably part of those operating under special arrangement between the British owners in England and agents in Europe, as discussed in Chapter 5, or they were actually owned by traders on the Continent but insured in England. Whatever the case, Appendix 6.1 clearly shows the circuitous movement of the British Guineamen, reaching the African coast through all directions – Continental Europe, the Americas, Ireland, and even India. The need to go to the Continent for part of the assortment of goods appears to have continued to the late eighteenth century, as correspondence from the Continent shows:

---

[45]   C.103/130, George Hamilton to Thomas Hall, London, 1 September, 1736. It is clear from this letter that more goods were taken on board in Rotterdam than in London – the value of goods taken on board in Rotterdam was at least £10,000, while the value of the ship and the goods taken on board in London amounted to about £10,000.

[46]   C.103/133, Senserf & Son to Thomas Hall, Rotterdam, 15 July, 1735.

[47]   C.103/130, Captain Hamilton to Thomas Hall, Ship *Argyle*, Annamaboe, 24 December, 1738.

Considerable business is done from hence to Africa by vessels coming from England & loading here. We have been much in this line from your place and annexed you will find prices of commodities for that trade. . . . The London and Liverpool people find their interest in this market, in the African way & we shall be glad should you find any of our articles answer which we should imagine do very well.[48]

As shown in Chapter 5 of this study, the regulations mentioned earlier and the efforts of continental governments to expand the supply of African slave labor to their American colonies increased immensely the movement of British slave ships from England to Western Africa via Continental ports in the late eighteenth and early nineteenth centuries. These new elements combined with the need for additional goods to make the Continental ports important components of the British slave trade up to at least 1807.

The other important aspect of the pattern of employment of the Guineamen is the way they operated on the African coast. This took a number of forms. There were those ships which cleared out regularly from England to Western Africa, going through the poly-angular or triangular routes and back to England to refit and start another round. These are the ones whose average duration of voyage is often estimated. In general they were in two categories – the "capital ships" and the "tenders." It was a general practice for the Guinea firms to own at least two vessels, one a large ship (the capital ship) and the other a smaller vessel (the tender), which sailed in company with the larger vessel as an auxiliary.[49] Both the capital ship and her tender or tenders (as some capital ships had more than one) went out as a single venture, but the vessels were entered separately in the Customs books when clearing out. Sometimes the capital ship cleared out first, the tender or tenders going later to meet her on the coast. As soon as the number of slaves bought was sufficient to load the tender, this was done and the tender was dispatched to the Americas. If there were more than one tender to a capital ship, they were dispatched in turn, while the capital ship remained behind to collect her own cargo of slaves when all the tenders had been dispatched. Sometimes the tenders crossed the Atlantic repeatedly, while the capital ship remained on the Guinea coast. To illustrate, in May 1789 Captain Walker, the master of a capital ship, wrote to his employers from the African coast:

I have finished my purchase and it amounts to upwards of 260 Negroes. I should have sent off the *Fly* but could not get slaves sufficient. She sailed from this place April the 29 with 45 Negroes, and as we have considerable more slaves, than both vessels can carry, I have ordered her back to me again, and as soon as she returns

---

[48] C.107/7 Part I, John Kirkpatrick & Co. to James Rogers & Co., Ostend, 21 March, 1792.

[49] These must not be confused with the long boats or pinnaces which every Guineaman had to carry (some had more than one). The boats or pinnaces were used for going into the creeks and small rivers to trade.

I will dispatch her immediately with her full number, for Jamaica again. She returns in ballast. I really believe I shall not be off the coast before September or October, as Mr. Cleveland has got a deal of engagements on his hands before it comes to my turn. But so long as we get paid by September and no mortality we must make a great voyage . . .[50]

In July 1789 Captain Walker asked his employers: "Be pleased to pay to Messrs. Thos. & Wm. Salman & Co. the sum of one hundred and ninety pounds currency with which they supplied your Schooner the *Fly* to refit her to the Coast of Africa . . . which it was agreed they should deduct out of the first payment of the net proceed of the *Fly*'s cargo of slaves sold by them."[51]

Evidence abounds in the private records of this Bristol merchant firm showing this pattern of employment. Besides, the masters letters give a general picture of this manner of employment among the vessels of other merchants as well. Thus, in October 1787, Captain Richard Rogers wrote to his employers from Africa: "the last Tender that sailed lay along side her ship 9 months, came after 500 and carried off but 300 slaves."[52] He wrote again in March 1788 announcing the arrival of the *Juba* (one of his employers' ships); he reported that the *Juba* could not be sent off to the Americas with a cargo of slaves immediately and added, "but there has not been one Tender in this river that has sailed in less than 5 months – which I hope will not be the case with *Juba*."[53] In his letter of April 1788, he expressed the,

Hope to leave this [place] if no vessels come out to me, in October after purchasing 500 slaves for ship besides Tender. Should a vessel come [I] hope to sail in November with near 600 slaves but shall dispatch the small vessel, I hope, in a few days.[54]

As an indication of the length of time the capital ships remained on the coast, the following information contained in the Captain's letter of November 1787 may be noted:

Ships now lying in the River: Ship *President*, Hughes, arrived 6 months, sails 4 months 500 slaves. *Ellis*, Ford, been here 16 months, sent off 400 slaves, sails about 5 months 450 slaves. *Langdale*, Fatern, sent off a Tender 300 slaves, has been here 16 months, very few slaves on board. Ship *Iris*, Potter, Tender sales in 1 month & expects to sail with 600 in 8 months. *Gascaigne*, Cumberbath, sends off his Tender in 2 months, expects to leave this [place] 8 months 600 slaves.[55]

[50] C.107/14, Capt. Walker to James Rogers, Africa, 14 May, 1789. Mr. Cleveland mentioned in the letter was a European merchant resident on the African coast.
[51] C.107/6, Captain Walker to James Rogers, Africa, July 1789.
[52] C.107/12, Capt. Richard Rogers to James Rogers, Ship *Pearl*, Old Callabar, 29 October, 1787.
[53] C.107/12, Same to Same, Ship *Pearl*, Old Callabar, 26 March, 1788.
[54] C.107/12, Same to Same, April 1788.
[55] C.107/12, Same to Same, 10 November, 1787.

In this particular voyage, Captain Richard Rogers's capital ship herself, the *Pearl*, remained on the African coast from October 4, 1787, to about October 1788 (as the vessel arrived Barbados on November 30, 1788). That such a protracted stay in the tropical waters of Western Africa was highly destructive to wooden vessels is evidenced by the history of the *Pearl*. In July 1788 Captain Rogers had informed his employers: "The *Pearl* when arrived will want a Great outfit am afraid."[56] On his way home to England from the Americas in April 1789, the *Pearl* proved so unsound that he had to go to St. Kitts for repairs, for which he paid £541.27.[57] The ship did not arrive at Old Calabar in the next voyage until March 27, 1790. This probably meant a long stay in the graving dock. In the whole of the ship's life it cleared out from England to the African coast five times: 1783, 1785, 1787, 1790, and 1792. In the first year the outset was £3,617:9s:10d.[58] In the last year, outfit alone amounted to £3,260:17s:10d, exclusive of the value of the ship's hull put at £1,500.[59] The ship could not complete the last voyage as it was condemned in Antigua as unfit to proceed to Bristol. This may serve to indicate the life of a capital ship.

Another class of Guineamen was made up of vessels that made periodic clearances from ports in England, staying in Western Africa for a number of years and returning to England to refit and clear out again to Western Africa for another round if fit to do so. These were known as "Floating Factories." The best documented example of this is presented in some detail. This is the "Floating Factory" adventure of Thomas Hall and Company of London in the 1730s, mentioned earlier in the chapter. During the period of its operation the firm had about eight ships permanently stationed at different parts of Western Africa. Each vessel was commanded by an officer, but they were all under the management of Captain George Hamilton, who commanded the ship *Argyle*. A number of small vessels assisted the stationed ships in collecting slaves and products from all parts of Western Africa. As the stationed ships became worm-eaten, they were sent back to England for repairs, being replaced by others sent down from England. Planks, sheathing boards, and other materials were sent down from England to effect minor repairs on the African coast. Periodically, vessels were sent from England to ship off the slaves and products collected by the stationed ships. Captain Hamilton frequently complained about the delay in getting their small vessels. Thus he wrote in February 1739:

We are under great difficulties for want of our small vessels and no account of them. Our being disappointed in those craft, which ought to have been with us 8 or 10

[56] C.107/12, Same to Same, Ship *Pearl*, Old Callabar, 20 July, 1788.
[57] C.107/12, Same to Same, St. Kitts, 14 April, 1789.
[58] C.107/13. It is unclear whether this amount includes the value of the ship's hull.
[59] C.107/59.

months past, give me leave to say, has been the loss of thousands of pounds to the concerned.[60]

In the context of the main focus of this chapter, the more pertinent of Hamilton's complaints concerned the way their vessels were fitted. Because it reveals some of the special outfit needs of Guineamen, it is important to quote at some length the letter of October 1738 to Richard Pinnell, one of the members of the floating factory syndicate:

In regard to the fitting of our vessels that are sent out to us, there are several of them badly put out of hand; Example the *Mary*, Fox, is in so very poor a condition; sending her abroad without having her whole sheathed, that she is entirely ruined; am afraid [she] will not be capable to proceed home . . . it's very certain if due care were taken in the fitting out of our vessels, to have them well corked and well sheathed and the said sheathing well nailed on before that it is filled and then well burnt and the whole is sheathed with 1&1/4 or 1½ inch Board, then they would last as long again on the coast; but the Builders have a notion anything will serve the coast of Guinea. Our ships at times have valuable cargoes on board and ought to be well fitted . . . If we can spare the *Polly* in the Spring [we] will send her home or else she will be ruined with the worm.[61]

Evidence from the private records of Thomas Hall & Co. is thus helpful in showing this pattern of employment of the Guineamen and the problems associated with it. What proportion of the ships employed in the trade operated in this manner is difficult to say. However, other evidence suggests that the floating factory operation of Thomas Hall & Co. was not an isolated practice but rather something that was quite general throughout the eighteenth century. On this score, it is pertinent to note that in the petition of John Dawson of Liverpool, easily the largest slave trader in Europe in the late eighteenth century, there is this item: "Value of warehouses, Floating Factories, and Factories and Goods contained therein £70,000."[62]

One more example of the floating factory form of employment of the Guineamen will suffice to establish the point. This is the case of the ship *Hercules*, whose principal owner was Miles Barber of Swithins Lane, London. In April 1786 the ship sailed from Gravesend for Western Africa, commanded by Arthur Bold. She had as a tender a schooner, the *Marcus*, Robert Cleet being the Chief Mate and his son, James Cleet, the ship's carpenter. Previous to February 25, 1787, 1,000 slaves had been bought and shipped to the Americas by two French vessels and a third French

---

[60] C.103/130, George Hamilton to Thomas Hall, Annamaboe, 9 February, 1739.
[61] C.103/130, George Hamilton to Richard Pinnell, 22 October, 1738.
[62] British Library, *House of Commons Journal*, Vol. XLVII, 27 April, 1792, Petition of John Dawson, pp. 742–743. The occasion of this petition was a bill in Parliament to abolish the carrying of slaves to foreign colonies in British ships. John Dawson was the most prominent English merchant engaged in the supply of slaves to foreign European colonies.

vessel was on the coast to ship off more. In a letter to his wife Robert Cleet wrote:

Our time I find is to be three years. The most of our people is gone and dead and what is not gone the first man of war they will go . . . I can't think of staying 3 years on the coast not for all the gains that may arise from the *Hercules*.[63]

He wrote again in February 1787 informing his wife that his son, James, was preparing to go back to England with the first man-of-war that arrived,

which I cannot blame him for, as all the crew is a going and then I hope I shan't remain long after, as I have given Captain Bold timely notice to provide one in my place. Mr. Meson is left us and indeed most of all that came from London is gone and dead together only a few left, and it is dam'd hard to lay here soaking off our souls out for a French King. [We have] now purchased 1 thousand slaves since we have been here, sent two French vessels off and a third arrived that there is no end to this voyage.[64]

As it turned out, the ships supposed to be French vessels were in fact English Guineamen operating under French colors which enabled them to transport slaves to the French Caribbean. A letter from William Woodville of Liverpool to James Rogers of Bristol, both large slave traders, shows that the former was the owner of the so-called French ships.[65] As in this particular case, the owners of some of the vessels employed in this manner were shipping slaves to non-British colonies in the Americas.

Again, there was a large number of vessels, mostly small, permanently employed on the Western African coast by resident British merchants and agents. The amount of English private investment on the Guinea coast in the eighteenth century has not been studied in detail. The evidence suggests there were a good number of English private establishments on the Guinea coast in the eighteenth century involved in one form of trading or another. Probably the largest of these private trading posts or factories (as they were often called) was Factory Point, belonging to Messrs. John and Thomas Hodgson, Guinea merchants in Liverpool, at the Isles de Los. There is an oil painting of "A S.W. view" of this factory contained in a ship's journal in the National Maritime Museum, Greenwich.[66] This gives the impression that the establishment was a fairly large one. In 1790 there were said to be

---

[63] PRO, C.O.267/21, Robert Cleet to his wife, Annamaboe Road, Africa, 20 January, 1786. The correct date should read, 20 January, 1787, for the ship left England in April 1786. The date of the letter may be due to the use of the Julian Calendar in which the new year began on 25 March, or it was an error.

[64] C.O.267/21, Same to Same, Annamaboe Road, Africa, 25 February, 1787.

[65] C.107/13, Woodville Senior to Rogers, Liverpool, 4 February, 1790.

[66] LOG/M/21 MS53/035, Journal of a voyage from London to Africa on board the *Sandown* by Samuel Gamble, Commander, 1793–94, National Maritime Museum, Greenwich.

41 vessels (sloops, schooners, and boats) employed on the coast by this factory. Two vessels are mentioned as carrying goods to the Guinea coast on freight for the factory.[67]

There were other important private English establishments. John Anderson and Alexander Anderson, London Guinea merchants, stated in 1798 that they owned "large Factories" in Bance Island and in the neighborhood in "River Sierra Leone." An invasion of American and French subjects in 1794 had, they said, caused them to lose property on the island worth £20,000 sterling, which they "have since replaced and laid out the amount of such property so destroyed, and have, at a great risk and labor, and at an immense expense, established a great trade at the said Island."[68] In April 1799 Robert Seller, merchant in Liverpool, disclosed that he and his brother, John Seller, had "a very valuable Factory" on the "River Riopungas," where his brother, John Seller, resided. They had another establishment on the "River Rionoones," near the Isles de Los, with several vessels used in trading to several parts of the Guinea coast.[69] There was yet another private establishment, which seems to have been a very large one, belonging to John Dawson of Liverpool (mentioned earlier) and managed by a Mr. Clemison. In April 1790 a letter from Cape Coast informed James Rogers of Bristol that "Mr. Clemison, agent for Messrs. John Dawson & Co. of Liverpool is dead and I imagine there will be no one to take charge of that business so as to conduct it with any spirit." The establishment survived the death of Mr. Clemison, for in March 1799 John Dawson said he owned property in the vicinity of Sierra Leone valued at £30,000 and upwards.[70]

The foregoing claims concerning private English establishments on the African coast are confirmed by a description of the places of English trade on the Guinea coast by the Liverpool Guinea merchant, Robert Norris, in May 1790:

From Gambia there is nothing to engage the attention until we get to the Isle de Los, a little to the Northward of Sierra Leone, where there is a British Factory, and generally several vessels; besides, many English traders reside on the Coast, in that neighbourhood, and possess a good many shallops and boats. . . . [At Sierra

---

[67] British Library, *Parliamentary Papers, Accounts & Papers*, 1790 Vol. 87, No. 698(8), pp. 500–512.

[68] British Library, *House of Commons Journals*, Vol. LIII, 25 May, 1798, Petition of John Anderson and Alexander Anderson, p. 624.

[69] British Library, *House of Commons Journals*, Vol. LIV, 10 April, 1799, Petition of Robert Seller, Merchant in Liverpool, p. 419.

[70] British Library, *House of Commons Journals*, Vol. LIV, 19 March, 1799, Petition of John Dawson of Liverpool. This and the other petitions were occasioned by a Bill in Parliament to abolish the slave trade in northwest Africa.

Leone] there is a Fort belonging to private merchants upon a small Island, about 6 leagues above the watering place, and there are generally some vessels lying there . . .[71]

All these resident merchants and agents employed a large number of small vessels permanently on the African coast, which were built in England. These wooden vessels employed continuously in tropical waters wore out quickly and were replaced with new purchases from England. The vessels employed permanently in Western Africa may be contrasted with ships in the East India country trade. Whereas the latter were built in India, the former were built in England and sent to Western Africa.[72]

As stated earlier in the chapter, and in greater detail in Chapter 5, a small number of vessels were employed in shipping African products directly from Western Africa to England. As we have seen, by the late eighteenth century about one-half of the African products arriving in England were shipped directly by traders specializing in the product trade and, therefore, not involved in the slave trade. The testimony of these specialized product traders shows that the vessels employed had a protracted stay on the Guinea Coast. Thomas Dean, who said he commanded a wood and ivory vessel for three years preceding 1788, told a government committee of enquiry that,

the collection of ivory requires some time; it is collected in different places on the coast, which makes it necessary to sail up and down. We took in our cargo of wood principally at Sierra Leone and the Island of Bananas, but the manner of carrying on our trade, as we are obliged to trust our goods to make purchases, and wait for return, occasions much delay, the goods are sent up into the country, and it is sometimes several months before the returns are made.[73]

Earlier in February, 1788, the Bristol slave trader, James Jones, had stated that the wood and ivory voyages "are very tedious from 12 to 16 months on the coast which is very destructive to the health of the seamen . . ."[74] Thus the wood and ivory voyage of the late eighteenth century must have taken an average of about two years to complete, round trip.

Apart from the pattern of employment, the other element that determined the level of demand for new ships and the cost of repairs and outfit in the trade with Western Africa was the high incidence of mishap among

[71] C.O.267/9, Robert Norris to Secretary of State, 29 May, 1790. The letter was about a proposed plan whereby intelligence of an impending enemy action against English property on the Guinea Coast could be communicated to the ships there.

[72] For the Country Trade in India, see C. N. Parkinson, "East India Trade," in C. N. Parkinson (ed.), *The Trade Winds*, pp. 141–156.

[73] PRO, BT.6/11, Evidence of Thomas Dean, 24 January, 1789.

[74] British Library, Add. MSS. 38,416, James Jones to Lord Hawkesbury, Bristol, 14 February, 1788.

the Guineamen, as shown in detail in Chapter 5. As can be seen in Table 5.2 of that chapter, known losses to British merchants in the African trade numbered 1,053 vessels between 1689 and 1807. These losses occurred in four of the major wars of the seventeenth and eighteenth centuries: 1703–10, 131; 1757–63, 140; 1776–83, 75; 1793–1807, 382. The total for these four war periods comes to 728, being 69 percent of the total. Yet most of the Guineamen lost between the Americas and Britain are not included for reasons explained in Chapter 5. The significance of the latter point may be inferred from the unwillingness of Dutch underwriters to provide insurance for vessels sailing from South America to England stated earlier in this chapter. As the evidence shows, the most trying period for the traders was during the French Revolutionary wars, 1793–1815. This is made clear in the "Memorial of the Merchants, Shipowners, Underwriters and others of the Town of Liverpool concerned in the trade to Africa, the West Indies and America, to the Lord Commissioners for executing the office of Lord High Admiral of Great Britain."[75] As the petitioners put it:

Since the commencement of the War the property of your Memorialists has been engaged in promoting objects of lawful commerce, in the confident hope that your Lordships would afford them that maritime protection to which from the magnitude of their undertakings and the large amount of Convoy Duty cheerfully paid by them they deem themselves entitled, and which the unparalleled success of the Enemy's Privateers has rendered necessary . . . The losses which your Memorialists have lately sustained furnish melancholy and incontrovertible evidence of the insufficiency of the protection afforded to them and that your Lordships may be able to appreciate the extent of these losses they beg to state that in the years 1803, 1804 and 1805 three hundred and thirty four ships cleared outwards from the port of Liverpool of the burthen of 78,900 tons navigated by 11,000 seamen, of these the enormous number of 54 have been taken by the Enemy: 47 of which have been carried into French ports and only seven retaken. Hence . . . nearly a sixth part of the ships which have sailed from Liverpool in the course of the last three years, have fallen into the hands of the Enemy; occasioning a loss of upwards of £600,000 . . . the enemy are not only encouraged by this success to increased enterprise but the ships so taken furnish them with the means of extensively and efficiently embarrassing the general commerce of the country; the greatest part of the said ships being fast sailing armed vessels and well calculated for privateers to which purpose the enemy commonly appropriate them.

The high incidence of mishap meant frequent replacements and high cost of repairs and outfit, the latter two elements being implied in the preceding quote. All the elements enumerated in the preceding paragraphs taken together point to some obvious implications – a generalized unusually high cost of outfit and repairs; a low average frequency of outward clearance per vessel for the ships employed in the African trade as recorded in the

---

[75]   T.70/1583.

customs books; a rather short span of life for the ships, on the average; a sustained demand by the African trade for new ships proportionately greater than the customs figures of yearly clearance would lead one to expect; and a much larger number of ships and shipping tonnage employed in the trade at any given moment than, again, the yearly clearance figures. The latter point is evident in the sources. It was noted by Gomer Williams when he wrote, "Owing to the length of the round voyage, which some-times occupied over a year, the returns of Guineamen that cleared annually for the coast from Liverpool do not represent all the vessels belonging to the port then actively engaged in the trade."[76] To substantiate, he referred to the returns of 1752 showing 58 vessels that cleared out from Liverpool for Western Africa, whereas "Williamson's Liverpool Memorandum Book," published in 1753, showed that in 1752 Liverpool possessed no less than 88 vessels employed in the African trade.[77] Consistent with the evidence of Gomer Williams, the annual clearance returns show that in 1749, 24 vessels cleared out of Bristol for Western Africa;[78] but a source showing a list of ships employed in the African trade from the port of Bristol in the same year (1749), with the names of the vessels, contains 47 vessels.[79] The adopted methods for quantifying the purchase of new ships and the cost of outfit which follow have been designed to take care of most of the problems arising from the peculiar nature of the pattern and circumstances under which the Guineamen operated.

The first step in the quantification is to ascertain the average length of a Guineaman's life, taking into consideration the high incidence of loss and the high rate of wear and tear, both of which were due to the factors enumerated earlier. In order to do this, a list of 137 Guineamen belonging to Liverpool was compiled from three sources showing the vessel's name, registry number, date of registration, tonnage, where built, year built, type of vessel, and the dimensions. This is shown in Appendix 6.2. Table 6.7 shows the age distribution of the vessels in this list. The age of each of the 12 vessels built in the last year of the period, 1788, is less than a year. Taking their date of registration, the average age comes to 6.5 months. This may be approximated to one year, making the total age of the 95 vessels for which information is available 648, and the average age per vessel 6.8 or approximately 7 years. With a generous allowance for error, the operational assumption is that the average age of the Guineamen at any given moment could not have exceeded 10 years.

From this assumption, the second step in the quantification is to determine the clearance frequency of vessels employed in the trade in a period of 10 years. For Liverpool the years 1789–98 are taken, and 1785–94 for

[76]   Williams, *Liverpool Privateers*, p. 472.   [77]   *Ibid.*   [78]   BT. 6/7.
[79]   C.O. 388/45 PART I.

Table 6.7. *Age Distribution of Guineamen in Liverpool (Prime) Registries, 1786, 1787, and 1788*

Year of Building	Number of Vessels	Age of Each Vessel	Age of All Vessels in Each Year of Building
1756	1	32	32
1759	1	29	29
1760	1	28	28
1765	1	23	23
1766	2	22	44
1769	2	19	38
1770	2	18	36
1771	1*	17	17
1772	2	16	32
1773	1	15	15
1775	2	13	26
1776	2	12	24
1777	3	11	33
1778	5	10	50
1779	2	9	18
1780	3	8	24
1781	4	7	28
1782	3	6	18
1783	10	5	50
1784	5	4	20
1785	3	3	9
1786	15	2	30
1787	12	1	12
1788	12	Less than a year	12 (Approx.)
	95		648

* This was completely rebuilt at Liverpool in 1788.
Source: See Appendix 6.1.

Bristol. In the case of London useful information is available for only 7 years, 1789–95. The choice of period has been imposed by the availability of data. Ships with their names and tonnage cleared outward from ports in England to Western Africa are available each year for various periods, but because of the irregular manner vessels' tonnages were declared before 1786 it is impossible to make accurate counts from the earlier data. The result of the exercise is presented in Table 6.8.

From the information in Table 6.8, the average number of clearance per vessel in Liverpool for the 10-year period 1789–98 is 2.01, for Bristol, 1785–94, it is 1.89, and for London, 1789–95, it is 1.59. Based on these

Table 6.8. *A List of Guineamen Cleared Outward from England
to Western Africa in Successive Years Analyzed to
Show Clearance Frequency*

No. of Clearances Per Vessel	Liverpool 1789–98 (10 yrs.)		Bristol 1785–94 (10 yrs.)		London 1789–95 (7 yrs.)	
	No. of Vessels	Total Clearances	No. of Vessels	Total Clearances	No. of Vessels	Total Clearances
1	237	237	61	61	97	97
2	99	198	37	74	21	42
3	58	174	16	48	11	33
4	34	136	10	40	8	32
5	27	135	3	15	4	20
6	7	42	1	6	—	—
7	2	14	—	—	—	—
Total	464	936	128	244	141	224

Sources and Notes: Liverpool, T.64/286; *Parliamentary Papers, Accounts & Papers,
1801–1802,* vol. IV, no. 449; Bristol, *Parliamentary Papers, Accounts & Papers
1789,* vol. 82, no. 631, pp. 6, 7; T.64/286; London, T.64/286. These sources show
the names of the vessels, their tonnage, dates of clearance and sometimes the names
of the owners. All this information has been used to identify each particular vessel
with relative ease in successive years of clearance. Eighty-four of the Liverpool
vessels and 12 of the London vessels made their first voyages in the last year of the
respective periods. In the case of Bristol, no vessel made her first voyage in 1794.

figures, two clearances per vessel per decade is estimated to be the average
for all vessels in the African trade from England. This low frequency, of
course, is accounted for by vessels clearing out from England only once and
spending the rest of their lives on the African coast, or being captured or
lost, and by the various other factors enumerated earlier. Given the average
clearance per decade and the 10-year average life span of each vessel, the
third step in the quantification is to apply the average clearance figure to
the total clearance tonnage for each decade to arrive at the total tonnage
of ships purchased and employed in the African trade each decade. This is
shown in Table 6.9.

Not all the vessels employed in the African trade were built in England.
Some were prizes taken in wartime and converted to British ships. Others
were imported from overseas, including the British colonies. To determine
the proportion supplied by each source, the information in Appendix 6.2
has been applied. This is shown in Table 6.10. As can be seen from the
table, 60 percent of the vessels were built in England, 3 percent in other

Table 6.9. *Number and Tonnage of Vessels Cleared Out from England to Western Africa Each Decade, with Estimates of Tonnage Purchased and Employed in the African Trade per Decade*

	Total Clearances		Purchased and Employed Per Decade	
Decade	Vessels	Tons	Vessels	Tons
1750–60	1,158	119,924	579	59,962
1761–70	1,506	168,268	753	84,132
1771–80	1,121	125,426	561	62,713
1781–90	1,255	190,023	628	95,012
1791–1800	1,637	320,005	819	160,003
1801–1807	1,145	259,039	573	129,520

Sources and Notes: For sources, see Table 6.12. The number and tonnage of vessels purchased and employed per decade are estimated by dividing the total number and tonnage cleared out every decade by 2, being the average clearance per vessel per decade.

parts of the United Kingdom, 30 percent were prizes, and 7 percent were imports from the British colonies.[80] Applying 60 percent to the estimated tonnage in Table 6.9 gives the tonnage built by shipyards in England for the African trade per decade as follows: 1750–60, 35,977; 1761–70, 50,479; 1771–80, 37,628; 1781–90, 57,007; 1791–1800, 96,001; 1801–07, 77,712.

As shown in Table 6.4, regular returns of ships built and registered in England each year are available from the 1780s. It is possible, therefore, to compare tonnage built in England for the African trade with the total tonnage built and registered in the late eighteenth and early nineteenth centuries. As can be seen in Table 6.4, the total tonnage built and registered in England in the periods 1791–1800 and 1801–07 is 652,064 tons and 505,702 tons, respectively. Tonnage destined for the African trade is thus 14.7 percent and 15.4 percent of the respective total tonnage.

As for the average price per ton of the vessels built in England for the African trade, Craig's estimates mentioned earlier in the chapter are quite close to the actual data available for a few vessels. The ship *True Blue*,

[80]   These percentages are somewhat different from those for the late 17th and early 18th centuries published by Walter E. Minchinton, "The British Slave Fleet, 1680–1775: The Evidence of the Naval Office Shipping Lists," in Serge Daget (ed.), *De La Traite à L'Esclavage: Actes du Colloque International sur la traite des Noires, Nantes 1985* (Nantes and Paris, 1988), Vol. 1, pp. 408–412.

Table 6.10. *Guineamen in Liverpool (Prime) Registries, 1786, 1787,*
and 1788, Analyzed to Show Place of Building

Place	Number	
Liverpool	71	
Lancaster	2	
Folkestone	2	
Hull, Yorks	1	
Workington, Cumbs.	1	
Parkgate, Cheshire	1	
Dublin	1	
Ringsend, Port of Dublin	1	
Isle of Man	1	
Bridport, Dorset	1	
Newport, Isle of Wight	1	
Creetown, Co. Galloway	1	
Portsmouth	1	
Cawsand, Devonshire	1	86
Rhode Island	1	
Bermuda	5	
St. Johns, Newfoundland	1	
Philadelphia, North America	1	
British Plantation or Colony	1*	
A British Settlement in the East Indies	1	10
Prizes		41+
		137

* The year of building for this vessel is stated to be unknown. Thus the age is not
known and therefore is not included in the age distribution list.
+ Only the years the prizes were taken and the date when condemned and made
free are stated. The actual years of building, and so their ages, are not known.
Sources: See Appendix 6.2 for sources.

measuring 180 tons, was built by Brechell & Charnley in 1770 for William
Davenport & Co. for £1,226:4s:0d, being approximately £6:16s. per ton;
the *Blayds*, 277^{49}/$_{95}$ tons, was built in 1782 by Grayson & Ross for Ingram
& Co. at £6 per ton; the *Earl of Liverpool*, 219 tons, was built by Quirk
& Baldwin of Liverpool in 1797 for Thomas Leyland & Co. for
£1,688:14s., being approximately £7:14s. per ton.[81] On the basis of these

[81] Davenport Papers in the Raymond Richards Collection, University of Keele Library;
380 TUO., David Tuohy Papers, Liverpool Record Office; AE 52, Midland Bank
Records, London, Photostat copy of Slave Ships' Books, Ships *Kitty* and *Earl of*
Liverpool.

Table 6.11. *Calculation of Outfit from Private Books of
Merchant Houses*

Year of Voyage	Number of Vessels	Total Tonnage	Total Amount of Outfit (in £ sterling)
1757–1760	4	400	3,668
1761–1770	27	2,890	23,052
1771–1780	42	4,270	42,082
1781–1790	8	1,333	18,525
1791–1800	4	1,242	12,479
1801–1807	5	1,213	17,648

Sources and Notes: Liverpool Museum, Account Book of Ships *Chesterfield*, *Calveley*, *Eadith* and *Aston*; Papers of William Davenport in the Raymond Richards Collection, University of Keele Library; Account Book of Ship *Hector*, in Lloyd's Corporation Archives, London; 380 TUO. David Tuohy Papers, Liverpool Record Office; Public Record Office, London, C.109/401 (Chancery Masters Exhibits) Wilson Vs. Sandys; Bristol Museum: Log Book of the Snow *Africa*; AE 52, Midland Bank Records, London, Photostat Copy of Slave ships' Books, Ships *Kitty* and *Earl of Liverpool*; C.107/1–15 and 59 Chancery Masters Exhibits, Papers of James Rogers & Co. of Bristol; 387 MD.40–44 Account Books of ships belonging to Messrs. Thomas Leyland & Co., Liverpool Record Office; C.114/1–3 and 154–158 Chancery Masters Exhibits, Papers of Thomas Lumley & Co. of London.

prices and Craig's estimates, the following average prices have been adopted for the Guineamen: 1750–70, £6 per ton; 1771–90, £6:10s. per ton; 1791–1800, £7:10s. per ton; 1801–07, £8 per ton. Applying these prices to the tonnage built in England for the African trade shown above gives the following values (in £ sterling, current prices):

1750–60	£215,862
1761–70	302,874
1771–80	244,582
1781–90	360,546
1791–1800	720,008
1801–07	621,696

As already stated, these figures are for the cost of building the hull of the vessels. The cost of outfit and annual repairs for the Guineamen was usually much greater for reasons already elaborated. Extant private accounts of Guinea merchants in England have been employed to estimate the average cost of outfit and repairs per ton. This is shown in Table 6.11.

Table 6.12. *Ships Cleared Out from England to Western Africa,*
1750–1807 (with Estimated Amount of Outfit)

Years	Number of Vessels	Total Tonnage	Estimated Amount of Outfit (in £ sterling)
1750–1760	1,158	119,924	1,079,316
1761–1770	1,506	168,268	1,346,144
1771–1780	1,121	125,426	1,254,290
1781–1790	1,255	190,023	2,654,322
1791–1800	1,637	320,005	3,200,050
1801–1807	1,145	259,039	3,885,585

Sources and Notes: 1750–53, BT 6/7; 1754–57, James Wallace, *A General and Descriptive History of the Ancient and present State of the Town of Liverpool* (Liverpool, 1795), p. 255. This gives figures for 1744–92 in 7-year averages (except for 1792). The average for 1752–58 (both inclusive) is 103 vessels, 10,038 tons. This has been taken for the four years 1754–57 in the absence of other figures. 1758–76, BT 6/3; 1777–1800, BT 6/185 (Compiled from Sir Whitworth, State of the Trade of England); 1801–7, Customs 17 and BT. 6/7. There seems to be an error in Customs 17 for 1786 that has gone into Whitworth's table, where it is shown that 152 vessels measuring 66,917 tons cleared out from England for Africa in 1786. The figure in BT. 6/7, 146 ships and 21,485 tons, is more convincing and is used here. The Estimated Amount of Outfit was arrived at by multiplying the yearly clearance tonnage in each decade by the amount of outfit per ton, decennial average, taken from Table 6.11.

The 90 vessels employed are arranged according to the decade in which the voyage occurred. This makes it possible to compute the mean cost of outfit per ton in each decade. As can be seen in the table, the decennial mean costs per ton are as follows: 1750–60, £9; 1761–70, £8; 1771–80, £10; 1781–90, £14; 1791–1800, £10; 1801–07, £15.

These decennial mean outfit costs per ton have been applied to the tonnage cleared out each year from England to Western Africa in the second half of the eighteenth century, for which period adequate evidence exists for the computation. The result is presented in Table 6.12. Adding the figures in the table to the decennial amounts for vessels built in England for the African trade shown earlier in the chapter gives the total decennial cost of ships and outfit in the African trade as follows:[82]

[82]   It should be noted that the amounts for outfit include some small sums for seamen's advanced wages and sometimes for seamen's provisions as well.

1750–60	£1,295,178
1761–70	1,649,018
1771–80	1,498,872
1781–90	3,014,868
1791–1800	3,920,058
1801–07	4,507,281

The activities in the shipyards connected with the building of hulls, outfit, and repairs were linked to the general industrialization process through the purchase of manufactures by the people employed (including the owners of the yards) and through the purchase of manufactured inputs by the ship-yards. With no detailed study of the English shipbuilding industry available precise measurement of these linkages is not possible. But some evidence in the merchants' private records can be used to show some order of magni-tude of the manufactured inputs employed in the shipyards.

Before the age of steel, timber seems to have been the most important material purchased by the shipyards. It was stated in November 1791 that, "A seventy Gun ship requires 3,000 loads of timber, each load containing 50 cubical feet . . . Three thousand loads of rough oak at 2 [shillings] per foot or £5 per load will cost £1,500 . . ."[83] Other materials employed in the shipyards in large quantities were iron, copper, and ropes. The evidence shows that a large amount of iron in one form or another was used in the building and outfit of vessels even before steel took over from timber. With the rapid expansion of copper sheathing of merchant ships in the last quarter of the eighteenth century, the amount of iron used appears to have been reduced somewhat. On this and other matters an advertisement in Liverpool in June 1789 is instructive:

Guineaman Building by Leather, Rogers & Elliots. . . . To compleat the said vessel with Iron work, joiners wk, plumbers, painters, Glaziers, Blockmakers (Bulk heads in the Hold & between Dks as customary) with masts & yards (with Block makers & Iron works to ditto) for the sum of nine hundred and fifty pounds.

N.B. The copper Bolts which are drawn in the stem, stern, Frame, Deadwood Keel & keelson will be included in the above price but whatever copper work is wanted hereafter is to be found by the purchasers, the builders allowing the weight of iron as customary in lieu of the copper (except what partains to the sheathing) . . .[84]

The available outfit data indicate, however, that large quantities of iron and copper were used side by side in the building and outfit of Guineamen throughout the last quarter of the eighteenth century. As a rough indica-tion of the order of magnitude of the materials used in the outfit of Guineamen evidence on four ships of the period is presented in some detail.

[83] 942 HOL., Holt and Gregson Papers, Vol. 10, pp. 287–296, Liverpool Record Office.
[84] PRO, C.107/5. This advertisement was sent to James Rogers of Bristol by William Roper.

The Guineaman, *Blayds*, measuring 277⁴⁹⁄₉₄ tons, mentioned earlier in the chapter, was built in 1782 at the cost of £1,665. The outfit in its first voyage in 1782, included in Table 6.11 above, was £5,258 (including £424 seamen's advance wages and £389 seamen's provisions). The main items in the outfit cost (to the nearest pound sterling) were the following:[85]

Iron work	£633
Guns, shots, etc.	368
Cordage	609
Copper Sheathing	232
Copper Nails and Braces	91
Sailmaker and Sailcloth	365
Timber	148
Carpenter's Work	380

The other Guineaman with information on building and outfit is the *Earl of Liverpool*, 219 tons, built for Thomas Leyland & Co. in 1797 at the cost of £1,688:14s. The total cost of its outfit for the first voyage in 1797 was £3,251, with the following as the main items:[86]

Iron work	£283
Guns	119
Copper	423
Ropes	438
Sailmaker	314
Carpenter's work	123
Copper pumps	35

The third Guineaman in the group, the *Enterprize*, 229 tons, was bought second-hand in 1803 for £2,100. The total outfit cost for its voyage to Western Africa in 1803 was £6,049, the main items of which were:[87]

Iron	£285
Carriage Guns, etc.	370
Copper and Gunpowder	438
Copper slag, braces, etc.	52
Sailmaker	468
Ropes	511
Carpenter's work	1,340

---

[85] 380 TUO. 5/9, David Tuohy Papers, Liverpool Record Office. Other items in the outfit cost include anchor, iron hoops, painting, and the like.

[86] Midland Bank Records, London, England, AE 52, Ship *Earl of Liverpool*. Other items include plumber's work, shipchanglers, painting, joiner, and the like.

[87] 387MD43, Liverpool Record Office.

The preceding three cases were all vessels outfitted in wartime. For a balanced view the last case is a vessel outfitted in peacetime. The *Ingram*, 160 tons, was sold by one Guinea firm to another in 1784 for £1,360. Its total outfit cost for the voyage of 1784 was £3,168, the main items being:[88]

Iron Work	£225
Copper Sheathing	210
Copper bolts, etc.	43
Cordage (ropes)	297
Sailmaker and Sailcloth	221
Carpenter's work	519

From the foregoing illustrative cases, it can be seen that the yearly outfit of Guineamen consumed large quantities of iron, copper, ropes, sailcloth, and timber, their combined cost being generally over one-half of the total outfit cost. The materials that went into the building of the hull are usually not stated in the merchants' records, and shipbuilders' records with such information, if they exist, have not been studied. As already mentioned, it is reasonable to assume that timber was the main material until the age of steel in the late nineteenth century. Next to timber, the evidence suggests that large quantities of iron and copper in the form of nails, bolts, and others were employed in the construction of the hulls. When the manufactured inputs employed in building the hulls are added to those employed in the yearly outfit and repair of the existing stock of shipping it becomes clear that the shipping and shipbuilding trades were important markets for some key industries of the period.

In this context, the very strong link between shipping employed in tropical waters and the copper industry deserves some special attention. The pattern of employment of Guineamen presented earlier in this chapter should help in understanding why merchants in the African trade were enthusiastic in adopting the technological innovation of sheathing merchant vessels with copper. This innovation protected the wooden vessels against the ravages of worms and other destructive elements in the tropical waters of Western Africa and the Caribbean;[89] hence it was more valuable to shippers doing business in those places, as well as the East Indies. There is some disagreement on when the practice of sheathing Guineamen with copper began. Arthur John had stated that ships in the Africa and East India trades

---

[88]   380 TUO. 4/10, David Tuohy Papers, Ship *Ingram*, 1784, Liverpool Record Office.
[89]   For more detail on this technological innovation, see J. R. Harris, "Copper and shipping in the Eighteenth Century," *Economic History Review*, 2nd ser., XIX, No. 3 (December, 1966), pp. 550–568; J. R. Harris, "The Copper Industry in Lancashire and North Wales, 1760–1815" (Ph.D. Thesis, University of Manchester, 1952); and Harris, *The Copper King*.

were copper-sheathed as early as the 1720s.[90] But J. R. Harris thinks this is a mistaken view.[91] According to Harris, the first merchant ship to be copper-sheathed in Liverpool was in 1778, and it was a Guineaman, the *Vulture*, belonging to William Boates, one of the largest slave traders in England.[92] This is consistent with the evidence in the Davenport papers. Among the many vessels of William Davenport & Co. none is mentioned as copper-sheathed until the late 1770s. The first vessel mentioned in the firm's records as being copper-sheathed was the *Hawke*, which was sheathed with copper in 1779. From this time to the last vessel of the firm which sailed in 1784, Davenport & Co. regularly sheathed their ships with copper.[93]

The importance of the African trade to the copper industry in England in this regard was clearly shown in the evidence of Thomas Williams before a House of Commons Committee on Copper Mines and Copper Trade in April 1799. Asked to state how the use of copper for merchant ships differed from that for the navy and the extent of the economies arising from the copper sheathing of merchant vessels, Thomas Williams, dubbed "Copper King" by his biographer because of his domination of the industry in the late eighteenth century,[94] elaborated:[95]

It consists in the merchant ships having more copper fastening in them than the ships of the navy. I mean, that copper nails are used in the merchant ships throughout their hulls, especially under the water's edge, and deck; nails of copper are almost universally adopted in merchant ships. I have an instance in my hand, which shows the advantage of copper bolting, fastening and sheathing a merchant man, in preference to the old mode of iron bolting and fastening, and wood sheathing in the Africa and West India trade. . . . I know a vessel belonging to Liverpool of 350 tons, that was copper bolted and sheathed in April 1785. She has within the last fortnight [statement made 22 April, 1799] or three weeks sailed from thence on her sixteenth voyage to Africa, the West Indies, and home; all the repairing expences upon this vessel, I am well informed, have not exceeded £55 in the whole time, except a few small repairs in her copper sheathing only, which her owner took no account of and she is so perfectly sound and tight at this time that she would sell

[90] Arthur H. John, "War and the English Economy 1700–1763," *Economic History Review*, 2nd ser. VII, No. 3 (April, 1955), p. 331.

[91] Harris, *The Copper King*, p. 45.

[92] Harris, "Copper and Shipping," p. 567. The vessel was copper-sheathed by the Warrington Copper Company.

[93] William Davenport Papers, University of Keele Library.

[94] Harris, *The Copper King*.

[95] British Library, *House of Commons Reports*, Vol. X (1785–1801), Report of a Committee on Copper Mines and Copper Trade, 7 May, 1799, Evidence of Thomas Williams (MP), 22 April, 1799, pp. 667–670. On the timing of the innovation, Williams told the Commons Committee that 30 or 40 years preceding the enquiry the custom of coppering ships was not in practice.

Table 6.13. *Ships Cleared Out from Liverpool to Western Africa with Estimated Amount of Outfit*

Years	Number of Vessels	Total Tonnage	Estimated Amount of Outfit (in £ sterling)	Liverpool's Share of Total for All England %
1751–1760	585	57,421	516,789	51.1
1761–1770	776	81,972	655,776	48.7
1771–1780	634	70,635	706,350	56.3
1781–1790	724	115,631	1,618,832	61.0
1791–1800	1,044	226,597	2,265,970	70.8
1801–1807	755	172,372	2,585,580	66.5

Sources and Notes: 1758–76, BT.6/3; 1751–57, 1777–93 and 1797–1807, Gomer Williams, *Liverpool Privateers*, p. 678; 1794–1796, T.70/1574. The estimated amount of outfit is arrived at by applying to the yearly clearance tonnage in each decade the decennial average outfit cost per ton computed from Table 6.11.

for as much if not more money than her building and fitting out cost in 1785. An iron-fastened and wooden-sheathed ship of the same tonnage, never was known to make more than eleven, or at the most twelve of those voyages in the same time, and each of these voyages at an extra expence of £2,000 and upwards, beyond that on the copper ship. A still more important saving is made by the use of copper on ships carrying slaves from Africa to the West Indies, in the number of lives saved by the shortness of its passage.

Thomas Williams added that his agent in Liverpool, "within the last 12 months, has sheathed 105 ships with copper, and repaired 33 more."

Because Liverpool overwhelmingly dominated the African trade in the last half of the eighteenth century, the activities connected with the shipping and shipbuilding trades outlined in the preceding paragraphs had their greatest impact concentrated in Lancashire and neighboring counties. As can be seen from Table 6.13, Liverpool's share of the total decennial outfit cost was between one-half and two-thirds in the second half of the eighteenth century. The building of ships for the trade was similarly concentrated. This concentration is reflected by the evidence on linkage to general manufacturing and other activities in the county and its main port city.

Roger Fisher, a well-known Liverpool shipbuilder of the period, wrote in 1763 that Liverpool "consumes more ship timber perhaps than any other, except the port of London." The main sources of supply were said to be "the south part of Lancashire, Cheshire, Shropshire, part of Staffordshire and Flintshire."[96] The transportation of the logs must have contributed to the mounting demand for transport services which attracted private capital to transport improvement in Lancashire and its neighboring counties in the second half of the eighteenth century. Responding to the demand for cordage, ropery firms were established in the port city. In 1792 it was estimated that they employed a total of 180 workers earning in wages 15 shillings to one guinea a week. Production was at 1,400 tons of cordage a year, of which only 60 tons were exported, the rest being employed in fitting the vessels belonging and trading to the port. The hemp used in the industry was imported from Prussia.[97] As can be inferred from the preceding account, the production and transportation of copper and iron in Lancashire and neighboring counties were also stimulated.

As a rough measure of the magnitude of the pressure exerted by these activities, the letter of a Liverpool merchant, who supported the abolition of the slave trade, to Lord Hawkesbury in 1788 offers some insight:

Liverpool possesses great advantages, in the spirit and diligence of her merchants, the vigour and industry with which the manufactures of Lancaster are carried on, the facility and light expence with which foreign products are conveyed by inland navigation and the coasting trade of the Port to a great distance in every direction. But the shipping of the Port is not supposed to bear that proportion to the shipping which resort to the harbour, nor the shipbuilding there to bear that proportion to the trade of the town which might be expected of both. And it has been alleged, that the expence bestowed on the outfits of African vessels, has tended to prevent the increase of shipping belonging to the Port in other branches of Trade.[98]

This statement has to be interpreted in the context of a decreasing capacity in the Liverpool shipbuilding industry from the late 1780s as the need to provide harbor and port facilities for the expanding trade of the port competed with the shipyards for space along the Mersey. As Stewart-Brown

[96] Roger Fisher, *Heart of Oak* (London, 1763), p. 32.
[97] Liverpool Record Office, 942 HOL., Holt & Gregson Papers, Vol. 10, pp. 297–299.
[98] This letter was written by Edgar Corrie of Liverpool to Lord Hawkesbury, but he asked the Lord to date the letter, London 27 Feb. 1788 and to sign it with the initial W. J. because, as he says in a letter accompanying this, "I think it necessary to avow the sheets which accompany this letter, and to explain to your Lordship the reasons why I must request my name to be concealed – I am a merchant of Liverpool, and it might be attended with irreparable prejudice to some branches of business in which I am engaged, that I stood forth with any opinion that would favour the abolition of the slave trade." British Library, Add. MSS. 38,416 fol. 35, Edgar Corrie to Lord Hawkesbury, 24 Feb., 1788. The letter signed W. J. is in the *Parl. Papers, Accts. & Papers*, 1789, Vol. 84 No. 646a. Edgar Corrie thought that a development of trade in African products could sufficiently replace the slave trade, and he suggested how this was to be done.

noted, "The digging of the docks had been the grave of the [shipbuilding] industry in Liverpool."[99] Gradually, the shipbuilding industry was pushed to the Birkenhead side of the Mersey.[100] Placed in this context the implication of the letter quoted above is that the available capacity was taken up by the repair and outfit of Guineamen and the building of new ones. The shipbuilding industry, nevertheless, continued to be one of the most important industries in the port city throughout the late eighteenth century. In 1792 it was stated that the building of ships and boats "may be called two of the leading occupations in Liverpool."[101]

As stated earlier, the foregoing detailed account concerning vessels employed in the Western African trade is intended to show more clearly elements in the link between English shipping employed in the slave-based Atlantic economy and the industrialization process in England which the customs clearance and entry statistics do not reveal. Clearly certain elements in the African trade were unique. The shipping of forced migrants from Western Africa across the Atlantic to the Americas was without doubt the first major seaborne passenger transport in world history. Yet this part of the African trade is not revealed by the clearance and entry statistics of the customs house in England, because it was part of the inter-port shipments overseas in which the customs offices in England played no role. The routes and pattern of employment outlined above were, to some degree, also peculiar. Following from these elements the African trade was the only branch of English trade in the seventeenth and eighteenth centuries in which the value of invisible exports was several times the value of merchandise exports. To illustrate, account of the annual value of Liverpool's African trade made by the traders in the first decade of the nineteenth century shows the following distribution:[102]

Shipping cost	£1,102,940
Insurance, Ships & Cargo, round	531,200
Goods Carried to Africa	750,000

---

[99]   Stewart-Brown, *Liverpool Ships*, p. 67.

[100]   The problems of the shipbuilding industry in Liverpool are outlined in the Report of a special Committee appointed by the Liverpool Town Council in 1850 to consider the state of the shipbuilding trade in the town. The report is reproduced in full in Steward-Brown, *Liverpool Ships*, pp. 62–67.

[101]   Liverpool Record Office, 942 HOL., Holt & Gregson Papers, Vol. 10, pp. 287–296.

[102]   PRO, T.70/1585, Brief Estimate of the Effect to the Town and Port of Liverpool from the Abolition of the African Trade. The account shows 147 ships, 34,976 tons, valued at £699,520 (£20 per ton); seamen's wages and provisions, and the cost of tradesmen and laborers employed in preparing the ships for their voyage amounted to £870,000. One-third of the value of the ships has been taken as part of the shipping cost, consistent with the 33% depreciation usually applied to the value of the ship by the merchants in their private accounts.

Adding merchants' profits, plus interest and other charges, to these figures would make the value of the invisible exports over three times that of merchandise export. This is why the amount of activities generated in the shipyards in England by the African trade was considerably out of proportion to the customs figures of shipping and exports.

It follows from this that the account of the Guineamen presented above cannot be directly applied to the shipping employed in the other components of England's Atlantic commerce. However, these other components shared a number of common elements with the African trade that distinguished all of them from the nearby trades in Europe – distance; exposure to the ravages of tropical waters, hurricanes, and greater risks of enemy attack in wartime; some amount of inter-port shipments overseas; etc. All of this would mean that outfit costs per ton per year and the rate of replacement were all significantly greater than among ships employed in the nearby trades in Europe and the coasting trade in Britain. Hence, the amount of activities generated in the shipyards in England per ton of shipping employed was also significantly greater. Thus, when the absolute weight of the shipping employed in the slave-based Atlantic economy, shown in Table 6.6, is interpreted in the light of the detailed African evidence, it becomes quite clear the extent to which activities in the shipyards in England depended on Atlantic commerce during the period of study. The African evidence also makes it easy to see the very strong link between the shipping trade and the industrialization process. And just as the activities generated by the African trade were concentrated in Lancashire and its main port, so too Liverpool and the rest of the county were among the main beneficiaries of the shipping and shipbuilding activities connected with the rest of England's Atlantic commerce. For example, of the 226,660 tons cleared out from Great Britain to the British Caribbean in 1804, and 188,916 tons in 1805, Liverpool alone had 39,861 tons, or 17.6 percent, and 36,516 tons, or 19.3 percent, respectively.[103] Although this is a much lower degree of concentration relative to that of the African trade, it is still a large concentration when account is taken of the number of ports in England and Scotland that shared Britain's Atlantic commerce during the period.

---

[103] PRO, T.70/1585, "Remarks on the Impolicy of Preventing Foreigners Carrying British Manufactures to Africa, as proposed by the Bill now before Parliament, brought in by His Majesty's Attorney General, for Preventing the Importation of Slaves into the Territories of Foreign Powers, and the Settlements in America and the West Indies Surrendered to His Majesty's Arms during the present War" (printed, pp. 4–5).

7

The Atlantic Slave Economy and the
Development of Financial Institutions

THE EVOLUTION OF FINANCIAL INSTITUTIONS – comprising banking houses, discount houses, the stock exchange, and insurance houses – constituted an important part of the development of the English economy between 1650 and 1850. The combined operation of these institutions structured the credit economy in England during and after the Industrial Revolution. Their importance in the development process can be viewed from different angles. Being part of the service sector of the economy, their independent contribution to the growth of national income and employment over time can be examined in its own right. Crafts has estimated that government and defense, and housing and services contributed 27 percent of British national output in the eighteenth century, and 26 percent in the period 1801–31.[1] C. H. Lee takes a broader view of the service sector to include trade, transport, insurance, banking, financial and business services, professional and scientific services, public administration, and defense – in short, the residual of the national income after taking out the contribution of agriculture, mining, industry, and construction. Under his broad conception of the service sector, Lee computes that the contribution of the respective sectors to the estimated overall employment growth rate of 1.73 percent per annum between 1755 and 1851 was 54.9 percent for industry (including manufacturing, mining, and construction), 22.0 percent for agriculture, 19.1 percent for services, and unclassified, 4.0 percent.[2] He further computes that agriculture, industry, and services contributed respectively 31.9 percent, 20.3 percent, and 47.8 percent to the total output growth rate of 0.69 percent per annum in 1700–60, 15.7 percent, 48.7 percent, and 35.5 percent to the 1.97 percent annual growth rate for 1801–31, and 14.4 percent, 38.8 percent, and 46.8 percent to the 2.50 percent annual growth

---

[1]   Crafts, *British Economic Growth*, pp. 34–35.
[2]   Lee, *The British Economy Since 1700*, Table 1.6, p. 14.

rate for 1831–60.[3] The uncertainty and disagreements concerning these estimates, mentioned in Chapter 2, notwithstanding, it can be said that the service sector made important contributions to the growth of national income and employment, especially after 1850. What is more, the export of financial and other services contributed immensely to the nineteenth-century export surplus that helped to pay for imports and build up over time British foreign investment.[4] Consistent with the latter point, it has been forcefully argued that the economic character of British imperialism in the nineteenth and twentieth centuries can only be understood properly when placed in the context of the growing predominance of financial and other services in the British economy after 1850.[5]

Another way of viewing the significance of the financial institutions in the development process is through their contribution in the provision of funds to finance industrial investment during and after the Industrial Revolution. It is generally agreed that the financial institutions made very little direct contribution to fixed capital investment in manufacturing during the decades of the Industrial Revolution, the fixed capital needs of manufacturing firms during the period being modest and easily met through the ploughing back of profits. But it is also generally agreed that the critical factor in the growth and maintenance of output in manufacturing and commerce during the period under consideration was not fixed capital. The critical factor was working capital (circulating capital). This has been documented for the principal industry of the Industrial Revolution – the cotton textile industry:

> The fixed capital of the northern and midland textile industries before 1815 has been shown to be modest, probably of the order that could readily be obtained by converting or adapting existing buildings and leaving the profits in the business, but the working capital requirements were already three times as much.[6]

On the basis of the evidence it is concluded that "The principal constraint on the growth of cotton firms, taking the century 1760–1860 as a whole, was clearly the difficulties and cost of marketing."[7]

A study of the woolen industry in the West Riding of Yorkshire shows the same importance of circulating capital. The circulating capital of one

[3]   *Ibid.*, Table 1.3, p. 10.
[4]   For the contribution of trade in services to British trade balance, 1851–1913, see Simon Kuznets, *Modern Economic Growth: Rate, Structure and Spread* (New Haven, CT: Yale University Press, 1966), Table 6.5B, pp. 322 and 323.
[5]   P. J. Cain and A. G. Hopkins, *British Imperialism: Innovation and Expansion, 1688–1914* (London: Longman, 1993); *idem, British Imperialism: Crisis and Deconstruction, 1914–1990* (London: Longman, 1993).
[6]   D. S. Chapman, "Financial Restraints on the Growth of Firms in the Cotton Industry, 1790–1850," *Economic History Review*, 2nd ser., vol. 32 (1979), p. 52.
[7]   *Ibid.*, p. 66.

of the largest firms in the industry was 88 percent of its average total capital (£275,534) in 1803–07, 92 percent of the total (£378,271) in 1808–16, and 95 percent of the total (£345,330) in 1817–20.[8] It is clearly reasonable to say that in the eighteenth and early nineteen centuries circulating capital was the overwhelmingly dominant element in the total capital investment of manufacturing firms, especially the larger ones involved in production for overseas markets. The funds for this circulating capital were provided by the financial institutions that developed in the decades preceding and during the Industrial Revolution. It has been suggested, and for good reason, that "The dominant factor explaining why the rate and scope of capital investment was capable of being stepped-up and enlarged as the occasions demanded is the rise of a credit economy prior to the Industrial Revolution."[9]

The main bottle-neck in the procurement of investible funds in the period 1650–1850 was not the absolute shortage of funds in England at the time. Postan argued several decades ago that at the opening of the eighteenth century, "there were enough rich people in the country [England] to finance an economic effort far in excess of the modest activities of the leaders of the Industrial Revolution."[10] The main problem, as Postan saw it, was that "the conduits to connect them with the wheels of industry were few and meager," for which reason the funds were largely hoarded and squandered: But in the last quarter of the eighteenth century, and the first quarter of the nineteenth, the country banks and the financial institutions of the City succeeded in mobilizing funds to finance the marketing of the new industrial products.[11] Although, as already stated, there is clear evidence that the financial institutions did not provide funds directly for fixed capital investment in manufacturing, it has been argued persuasively that by providing adequate funds for circulating capital the financial institutions freed the profits and other funds of manufacturing firms to finance fixed capital investment.[12] Hence, the financial institutions also made indirect contributions to the funding of fixed capital investment in manufacturing during the period. The direct funding of circulating capital and the indirect financing

---

[8]   Pat Hudson, *The Genesis of Industrial Capital: A Study of the West Riding Wool Textile Industry c. 1750–1850* (Cambridge: Cambridge University Press, 1986), Table 2.5, p. 51. The circulating capital of a smaller firm was 75 percent of the average total capital (£41,080) in 1812–1814 (*Ibid.*).

[9]   B. L. Anderson, "Aspects of Capital and Credit in Lancashire during the Eighteenth Century," (M.A. Thesis, University of Liverpool, 1966), p. 206.

[10] M. M. Postan, "Recent Trends in the Accumulation of Capital," *Economic History Review*, vol. VI, No. 1 (October, 1935), reprinted in François Crouzet (ed.), *Capital Formation in the Industrial Revolution* (London: Methuen, 1972), p. 71.

[11] *Ibid.*, pp. 71–72.

[12] Hudson, *The Genesis of Industrial Capital*, p. 9.

of fixed capital investment were clearly critical functions in the process of industrial development.

For a comprehensive study of the role of the financial institutions in the development of the English economy between 1650 and 1850 the analysis has to incorporate all the preceding considerations – their contribution to the growth of national income and employment and their support role in facilitating industrial development by mobilizing funds to finance industrial investment. Both roles, of course, intersected at some point. The initial growth of the financial institutions and the other components of the service sector, broadly defined, generated employment and income that contributed in creating a domestic market for manufactures leading subsequently to the growth of manufacturing through import substitution, as shown in Chapter 2. Incomes from the service sector continued to be an important part of the domestic market for manufactures during and after the Industrial Revolution. On the other hand, the continued growth of employment and income in the service sector from the later part of the eighteenth century onward was made possible by the Industrial Revolution through the technology, the cheapened mass consumer products and capital goods, and the sustained income growth it produced, again, as was argued in Chapter 2. Thus the significance of the financial institutions in the development process can be validly viewed from both angles. However, from the point of view of the focus of this study the more directly relevant function of the financial institutions is their contribution to industrial development. It is certainly not unreasonable to argue that the financial institutions performed one of the major functions without which an industrial revolution in the private enterprise English economy of the period would be inconceivable. As Arthur John pointed out some decades ago:

If the concept of a "take-off" into a "self-sustained economic growth" has any validity, then in the British case the development of a highly efficient set of financial institutions must be numbered among the important preconditions of that event.[13]

By focusing on the historical development of the financial institutions in England, it is proposed to shed a little more light from a little explored channel on the origin of the Industrial Revolution. The main objective of this chapter is to identify and analyze the central factors whose operation over time brought the financial institutions into being. The thesis whose details are worked out in the chapter is that the prime mover in the historical process, which produced the financial institutions in England in

[13] Arthur H. John, "The London Assurance Company and the Marine Insurance Market of the Eighteenth Century," *Economica*, new series, vol. 25 (May, 1958), p. 141.

the eighteenth and nineteenth centuries, was located in the Atlantic slave economy of the period. The expansion of the Atlantic slave economy in the seventeenth and eighteenth centuries caused a major shift in English foreign trade away from nearby Europe to Western Africa and the Americas. The peculiar risks and credit needs of British Atlantic commerce, and the economics of slave plantation agriculture in the Americas, generated considerable demand for credit and insurance cover that produced profitable opportunities for the creation of financial institutions – opportunities that were greater and more attractive than were ever offered by the pre-existing domestic trade and trade with Europe. Commercial wars over the control of the Atlantic slave economy also compelled public borrowing which, in England, further stimulated the development of financial institutions.

In contrast to Say's law that supply creates its own demand, the analysis in the chapter is premised on the logical assumption that the development of the credit economy in England depended on the growth of demand for credit and the availability of investible funds much of which had hitherto been squandered and hoarded. The growth of demand for credit is viewed in terms of the volume of credit instruments in circulation in which investors had sufficient confidence. The volume of such instruments in circulation at any given moment provided a measure of the extent of effective demand for credit to which hard calculating entrepreneurs responded by creating credit institutions that profited from the supply of credit. The financial institutions, whose historical evolution constitutes the focus of this chapter, include banking houses, discount houses, the stock exchange, and insurance houses. The first three are examined together in the first part of the chapter, while the fourth is taken up in the second part.

7.1 THE DEVELOPMENT OF BANKING, THE DISCOUNT MARKET, AND THE STOCK EXCHANGE

To explain the historical development of the credit economy in England, it is important to note the timing of the establishment of credit institutions in the country and what this timing suggests in terms of the key factors explaining the initial development of the institutions. Two of the best known early writers on the subject may be cited to establish the time line. In his classic on the Industrial Revolution, Paul Mantoux wrote:

It is surprising to note how late credit institutions developed in England. In the City of London, in the small area where today [1906] the most powerful financial associations in Europe are crowded together and where capital collects from the ends of the earth, there was not a single banking house until the middle of the seventeenth century. It was during the Civil War that merchants first began to entrust their capital to the goldsmiths of the Lombard Street. These men, from mere treasurers, soon came to fill the place of bankers, and their notes took the place of cash in ordinary City transactions. . . . It is to Italy and Holland that England owes the idea of a national bank.[14]

On the same subject Arnold Toynbee stated that in the England of 1760:

Ready cash was essential [for the home trade], for banking was very little developed. The Bank of England existed, but before 1759 issued no notes of less value than £20. By a law of 1709 no other bank of more than six partners was allowed; and in 1750, according to Burke, there were not more than "twelve bankers' shops out of London." The Clearing House was not established till 1775.[15]

Evidence showing huge sums hoarded in the house in the 1740s testifies to Toynbee's point that as late as 1760 "banking was very little developed" in England. Writing from the port town of Plymouth in 1743 to a friend and business partner about the fortune left by his late father, one Robert Hewer reported:

I wrote you last post the account of the loss of my Poor Dear Father, whose Will we have since open'd, and according to my expectations he hath given his whole fortune to my Brother, except a few Legacies to the value of about £500 to me & others. He died richer than I imagined. We found this evening in one corner £6,600 & upwards in money that hath lain there many a year untouched . . .[16]

Converted to present-day value of the pound sterling, this is clearly a very large sum to be hoarded in the house for "many a year untouched" by a rich family in a commercial town. As far as I am aware there is no systematic study of this phenomenon. Nevertheless, the evidence suggests that hoarding of this magnitude was not uncommon at this time in England.

That credit institutions took this long to be established in England must be seen as an important measure of the relative contribution of the home trade and overseas trade (in particular, extra-European trade) to the development of the credit economy of England. It must be noted that by the seventeenth century, the home trade and English trade with Europe had had several centuries of considerable growth. What the foregoing evidence demonstrates is that the growth of the home trade and that with Europe up to the second half of the seventeenth century did not generate sufficient demand pressure and a large enough market for credit to call forth a widespread establishment of credit institutions. Conversely, the evidence indicates that it was the extraordinary expansion of English trade to non-European territories from the second half of the seventeenth century[17] that

---

[14] Mantoux, *The Industrial Revolution*, p. 97.
[15] Toynbee, *Lectures on the Industrial Revolution*, p. 32.
[16] PRO, C.103/132, Robert Hewer to Thomas Hall, Plymouth, 3 June, 1743.
[17] See Davis, "English Foreign Trade, 1660–1700," and Davis, "English Foreign Trade, 1700–1774."

provided the spark. This is understandable, considering distance and the peculiarities of the non-European trade, a discussion of some of which is presented later in this chapter.

Evidence on the sources of stimulus for the development of credit institutions in England is provided by the origin of the instruments whose circulation created the market for credit. These instruments were bills of exchange, company bonds, and government securities. The contribution of these three instruments differed in the different parts of England. The circulation of company bonds and government securities made important contributions in London but not in the provinces. Country institutions owed their origin largely to the circulation of bills of exchange, which were also important in London. Now what were the sources of these instruments?

The Liverpool slave trader and banker, Benjamin Arthur Heywood, wrote in 1812 that as of 1636, foreign bills of exchange were the only bills in circulation in England.[18] And as late as 1761, according to the authority on country banking in the eighteenth century, L. S. Pressnell, inland bills were still very scarce, "too scarce for them to become regular investments on any scale for country people. There were instead bills that had arisen in the course of overseas trade."[19] Yet bill discounting constituted the bulk of the credit business in the provincial cities in the eighteenth century, providing a powerful stimulus for the growth of banking in those cities. In the major trading counties, the bills formed an important part of the means of exchange. In Lancashire in particular, "they for many years formed by far the greater part – in Lewis Lloyd's opinion, at least 90 percent – of the circulation, and such was the preference for them that local bankers refrained from issuing notes."[20]

Bill discounting was also an important part of the credit market in London. And the discount market there, like the rest of the country, was dependent on overseas trade. As W. T. C. King put it, "The discount market lived upon the international bill on London and it was its real *raison d'etre*."[21] In the capital city, however, the bonds of joint-stock companies and government securities provided important investment opportunities for credit institutions.

The joint-stock companies whose bonds dominated the market were the East India Company, the South Sea Company, and the Royal African

---

[18]   Benjamin Arthur Heywood, *Observations on the Circulation of Individual Credit and on the Banking System of England* (London, 1812), p. 27.

[19]   L. S. Pressnell, *Country Banking in the Industrial Revolution* (Oxford: Clarendon Press, 1956), p. 435.

[20]   W. T. C. King, *History of the London Discount Market* (London: Routledge, 1936), p. 31.

[21]   King, *History of the London Discount Market*, p. viii.

Company – all companies in non-European overseas trade. The Royal African Company made extensive use of bond-finance from the 1670s, while the bond-debt of the East India Company began well before 1688. The South Sea Company, which exported slaves to Spanish America, issued its first bonds in 1712. The combined bonds of the East India Company and the South Sea Company in the early 1720s was over £7 million.[22] By 1717, the total share capital of joint-stock companies was running at over £20 million; of this amount, the South Sea Company had £10 million, the Bank of England £5,559,995, and the East India Company £3,194,000,[23] the combined share capital of the South Sea Company and the East India Company being about two-thirds of the total. Thus, bond finance by overseas trading companies doing business outside Europe made immense contributions to the size of the market for credit in London in the early years of the development of credit institutions in England.

An equally important factor in the growth of the credit market in London in the eighteenth century is the establishment of the permanent national debt in the 1690s. The costly wars of the seventeenth and eighteenth centuries, provoked largely by the struggle over the acquisition of overseas colonies and the control of seaborne commerce, led to unprecedented government borrowing. The permanent national debt started with the loan of £1 million in 1693,[24] followed by the establishment of the Bank of England in 1694. By 1721, the national debt had risen to over £50 million; the War of Austrian Succession raised it to £71 million; the Seven Years War increased it to £128 million; the War of American Independence almost doubled it to £238 million; and by the end of the great war with revolutionary France, the national debt stood at over £700 million.[25] The seven wars fought by England between 1688 and 1815 cost the government

---

[22] P. G. M. Dickson, *The Financial Revolution in England: A Study in the Development of Public Credit, 1688–1756* (London, 1967), pp. 406–407. According to Dickson, the combined volume of the two companies' bonds at its peak in the early 1720s (over £7 m.) was equal to the combined volume of government short-term tallies, Exchequer bills, Navy and Victualling bills and the Bank of England note-issue. (*Ibid.*, p. 407.)

[23] E. V. Morgan & W. A. Thomas, *The Stock Exchange: Its History and Functions* (London, 1962), p. 30. For a further discussion on the history of financial institutions, see Larry Neal, *The Rise of Financial Capitalism* (Cambridge: Cambridge University Press, 1990); Larry Neal, "How the South Sea Bubble was blown up and Burst: A New Look at Old Evidence," Paper presented at the Salomon Center Conference on *Crashes and Panics in Historical Perspective*, New York, October 19, 1988.

[24] Morgan & Thomas, *The Stock Exchange*, p. 19.

[25] Morgan & Thomas, *The Stock Exchange*, p. 43.

approximately £1,143,000,000, 73 percent of which was accounted for by the war with revolutionary France, 1793–1815.[26]

The significance of public debt in the development of capitalist institutions was recognized by Karl Marx. Thus he wrote,

The system of public credit, i.e. of national debts, whose origin we discover in Genoa and Venice as early as the middle ages, took possession of Europe generally during the manufacturing period. The colonial system with its maritime trade and commercial wars served as a forcing-house for it. Thus it first took root in Holland. National debts, i.e., the alienation of the state – whether despotic, constitutional or republican – marked with its stamp the capitalistic era. . . . The national debt has given rise to joint stock companies, to dealings in negotiable effects of all kinds, and to agiotage, in a word to stock exchange gambling and the modern bankocracy.[27]

In England, government long-term borrowing was financed mainly by the mercantile bourgeoisie in London and its environs.[28] Hence, the operation of the national debt contributed, along with the bonds of the overseas trading joint-stock companies, to the development of the stock-exchange market in London.

The foregoing survey provides a general framework within which the contribution of the Atlantic slave economy to the development of credit institutions in England can be discussed. The elements to be considered in this discussion include the peculiar credit needs of British trade in Western Africa, those of planters in the Americas arising from the acquisition of African slave labor, the procurement of supplies from Europe, and the transportation and marketing of plantation produce in Europe. The main analytical task is to show how all these elements affected the extent and character of the credit market in England to call forth the creation of credit institutions.

What made credit an important requirement in British overseas trade in the seventeenth and eighteenth centuries was the expansion of British trade beyond Europe. The increased distance involved meant that remittance for the sale of goods outside Europe took a long time to reach the merchant exporters in Britain. This called for a large amount of capital investment in trade that was beyond the personal resources of the traders. To some extent, the need for credit in the African trade arose from a somewhat similar circumstance. But there were important elements peculiar to the African trade that made its credit needs relatively greater and more problematic than

[26] Computed from Stephen Dowell, *A History of Taxation and Taxes in England*, Volume II (London, 1884), p. 402.

[27] Karl Marx, *Capital: A Critique of Political Economy* (Vol. I, translated from the third German edition by Samuel Moore and Edward Aveling, and edited by Frederick Engels. Revised and amplified according to 4th German edition by Ernest Unterman, Chicago, 1926), p. 827.

[28] Dickson, *The Financial Revolution*, pp. 258–260 and 300–302.

those of other branches of British extra-European trade. These elements were connected with the conditions under which the trade was carried on in Africa and in the New World.

Only a tiny proportion of the British African trade in the eighteenth century was made up of direct trade between Britain and Africa. In the second half of the century when the trade reached its greatest volume, over 90 percent of it involved the purchase and shipment of people for enslavement in the New World. The collection of a shipload of slaves took several months to complete in Africa. The shipping of the slaves across the Atlantic and their sale in the New World took some months more. All this added to the time it took for the merchants to receive the returns on their investment and, therefore, to the amount of capital needed to keep the trade going. But, in Africa what further enlarged the amounts of capital invested in the trade by the merchants was the need to finance the building of extensive trading posts or "factories," and the extension of credit to traders resident on the African coast.

Not all the traders had fixed establishments on the coast. The large firms were the ones that made this kind of investment, and the sums involved were quite large. In 1799 John Dawson of Liverpool stated that his fixed investment in the vicinity of Sierra Leone was worth over £30,000.[29] John Anderson and Alexander Anderson, African traders in London, also indicated that their fixed investment in Bance Island and Sierra Leone was worth considerable sums. They stated that an invasion by American and French subjects in 1794 caused damages in these establishments to the tune of £20,000 sterling.[30] As these amounts were stated by the traders in their petitions against a proposed bill to abolish the slave trade in the northern parts of West Africa, one may suspect the possibility of some exaggeration. However, an oil painting of one of these private trading posts by a slave ship captain is available.[31] This is the trading post at Isles de Los, called Factory Point, owned by Messrs. John and Thomas Hodgson of Liverpool. The size of this establishment as indicated by this painting suggests that the amounts stated by the traders may not have seriously exaggerated what they actually invested in erecting those establishments. For the large-scale traders who found this kind of investment necessary, the amount involved was thus a significant addition to the capital requirements of the trade.

A further addition to the capital requirements of the trade, as far as the African end of it was concerned, was imposed by the need to extend fairly

[29] British Library, *House of Commons Journals*, Vol. LIV, 19 March, 1799, Petition of John Dawson of Liverpool.

[30] British Library, *House of Commons Journals*, Vol. LIII, 25 May, 1798, p. 624.

[31] See LOG/M/21, MS 53/035 (National Maritime Museum, Greenwich), Journal of a Voyage from London to Africa on board the *Sandown*, by Samuel Gamble, Commander, 1793–94. For more detail on the subject, see chapter 6 above.

long credits to European traders resident on the coast. To a lesser extent, credit was also extended to the African middlemen on the coast. The private records of the British traders suggest that the amounts involved were quite large and posed serious problems to the merchants. The private letters of Robert Bostock of Liverpool are particularly instructive. He traded mostly alone, and the credits he extended to traders in Africa strained his limited capital. In January 1790, he wrote to one of these resident European traders, "I hope you will take it into consideration how I am circumstanced in regard of having so much money lock'd up as it is in your power to relieve me."[32] A few months later he wrote again,

I am sorry to inform you I am much distressed for want of money at present that I can scarce keep my credit up, having so much property in your hands. I hope you will take it into consideration and relieve me from these difficulties as soon as possible as I know you have it in your power. The creditors will not be put off here. I often wish I was with you clear of these Philistines.[33]

The letter of June 1790 shows the extent of pressure on Robert Bostock. He wrote pathetically that he has been unhappy for several months, having no rest night and day, and pleaded:

Consider my situation, 5 small children and another a coming, and release me from these difficulties as I hope you are not without feeling, and it has always and shall be my study to do the best for your interest which I believe you will acknowledge, and you know I have no partners, if there was it would not be so heavy if there was three or four, but it lies a heavy burden upon one.[34]

His letter of September shows that he was finding it difficult to pay his debts to the tradesmen in England, as he says, "The tradesmen in this part will either have money or body."[35] At the time of James Cleveland's death on the coast in 1791 credit from Bostock still remaining in his hands amounted to £1,237:3/-(sterling).[36] Other letters show that another resident merchant, Charles Wilkinson, was also indebted to Robert Bostock.

Robert Bostock was not alone in this situation. In 1791, Captain William Roper wrote to James Rogers of Bristol that on his arrival on the Guinea

---

[32]   Liverpool Record Office, 387 MD 55, pp. 67–69, Robert Bostock to Cleveland, 20 Jan, 1790. James Cleveland was a British trader who resided on the Upper Guinea Coast where he had considerable trade with merchants from Britain. He died on the coast in 1791.

[33]   *Ibid.*, p. 88, Same to Same, 6 May, 1790.

[34]   *Ibid.*, pp. 91–92, Same to Same, 9 June, 1790.

[35]   *Ibid.*, p. 109, Same to Same, 6 September, 1790.

[36]   *Ibid.*, Bostock to Wm. Cleveland, 16 August, 1791. Apparently William Cleveland was the brother of James Cleveland, as the former is said to "have taken possession of all his effects." James Cleveland was also indebted to a number of other British traders at the time of his death.

coast he advanced some goods to a gentleman called John Ormond, "a man of large property," for 90 slaves, for which he could not be paid on account of the man's death.[37] There was a sizeable number of such resident European traders on the coast in the eighteenth century. The credits extended to them in this way, and occasionally to African middlemen as well, must have added a no mean amount to the capital requirements of the trade.

But by far the most important factor responsible for the extraordinary credit needs of the British African trade in the eighteenth century was the large amount of credit that the slave traders had to extend to the employers of slave labor in the New World. For all practical purposes, the purchase of a slave by a planter in the New World in the eighteenth century was like the purchase of modern capital goods by twentieth-century producers. Because modern capital goods cost a lot of money and yield a stream of income over many years, their purchasers frequently employ credit finance. It is not uncommon to find the exporter being forced to provide the needed credit. This was often the case in Britain in the twentieth century. Hence, the shift in British domestic exports from consumer goods to capital goods after 1944 precipitated export finance problems leading to the creation of the Export Credit Guarantee Department (E.C.G.D.).[38] The financial problems of the employers of slave labor in the New World in the eighteenth century were precisely the same. A lot of money was needed to pay for slaves employed in production, and these yielded streams of income to their purchasers over several years, about 15 on the average. And just as British exporters of capital goods in the twentieth century were forced to extend credit to their overseas customers, the British slave exporters of the eighteenth century were forced to grant large credits to the employers of slave labor in the New World.

The planters' inventories show clearly that investment in the purchase of slaves formed a large proportion of their total investments. For example, the total investment in a medium-sized sugar plantation in Jamaica in 1774 was £13,026, excluding the value of land. Of this amount the value of the slaves employed was £7,140, being 54.8 percent of the total. When the value of land is included (£6,001) the proportion comes to 37.5 percent.[39] In this way, the expansion of staple production in the Americas imposed considerable financial burden on the British slave suppliers.

This extension of credit to the planters was probably the most serious problem, which the slave traders had to contend with throughout the

[37] PRO, C.107/5, Capt. William Roper to James Rogers, Isles de Los, 22 September, 1791.
[38] See R. S. Sayers, *Modern Banking* (Oxford: Oxford University Press, 7th ed., 1967), pp. 192–195.
[39] R. B. Sheridan, "The Wealth of Jamaica in the Eighteenth Century", *Economic History Review*, 2nd Ser., XVIII (1965), Table 7, p. 302.

eighteenth century. Writing to Lord Hawkesbury in 1788, John Tarleton, one of the principal slave traders in Liverpool, enumerated the several risks to which the slave traders were "peculiarly exposed." What he considered the most serious of them all was that "the whole expectation of the enterprise, the whole security of the capital, and return of commerce, are in a great degree, at the mercy of the planter, to whom an unexampled credit is extended by the persons who are to be aggrieved by the depending Bill."[40]

Over the years much of the traders' capital came to be made up of revolving credits to the planters. Even with the meager business, which the Royal African Company had in slave trading during its existence, it still had large sums of money accumulated in the West Indies in this way. The company was the largest single creditor in the British West Indian colonies in the last quarter of the seventeenth century. Its credits in the colonies on various dates stood as follows:[41] 1681, £120,000 (sterling); 1685, £136,000; 1690, £170,000; 1694, £128,000; 1696, £140,000. In the first decade of the eighteenth century, during the trial period of semi-open trade, the separate traders submitted that of the total capital of about £500,000 employed by them in the African trade, accumulated credits granted to slave purchasers in the Americas amounted to £300,000.[42] The volume of the salve trade of the company in the seventeenth century and that of the separate traders in the early eighteenth century constituted a very small fraction of the considerably expanded volume of the British slave trade in the second half of the eighteenth century as can be seen in Chapter 5. Adding the much higher slave prices of the latter period, we can see why the sums involved must have been considerable in the last half of the century. Here, the account of the capital of John Dawson of Liverpool, the largest slave trader in all Europe in the late eighteenth century, may be used as an illustration. In April 1792, he stated the composition of his capital employed in the slave trade as follows:[43]

---

[40]   British Library, Add. MSS. 38,416, folios 103–106, John Tarleton to Lord Hawkesbury, 9 June, 1788. John Tarleton is here referring to the bill to regulate the number of slaves to be loaded per ton by British vessels in the slave trade. The persons to be aggrieved by the bill were, of course, the British slave traders.

[41]   K. G. Davies, "The Origins of the Commission system in the West India Trade," *Transactions of the Royal Historical Society*, 5th Ser. Vol. 2, (1952), p. 97. These figures were obtained by Davies from the annual statements of the assets of the Company, in P.R.O., T.70/101. Davies is of the view that "the floating debt must at times have made the total outstanding very much larger" (n. 1, p. 97).

[42]   P.R.O., C.O. 388/15 Part 1, folios 97 & 98, Representation of Separate Traders to the Board of Trade, with itemized computation of their total investment in the Slave Trade, c.1708.

[43]   British Library, *House of Commons Journals*, Vol. XLVII, 27 April, 1792, pp. 742–743.

Value of ships employed   £58,000

Value of warehouses, Floating Factories
and Factories and Goods contained therein   70,000

Value of Cargoes now on Float   89,000

Outstanding Property in the Spanish Islands,
viz. Trinidada, Carracas, Carthagena,
the Havannah and Mississippi   183,000

Outstanding Property in the British and
French Islands   45,000

India Goods and other property prepared
and now on hand intended to be exported
to Africa   64,000

From this account it can be seen that of the total capital of £509,000 employed in the slave trade by John Dawson in 1792, £228,000 was made up of accumulated debts in the New World, being approximately 45 percent of his total capital. The value of fixed establishments (part of the £70,000 in the account) also formed a sizeable proportion of the total. Dawson's account does not show the amount of credit extended to traders on the African coast. This is likely to form part of the £70,000 for fixed establishments and trade goods contained in them. The evidence thus makes it clear that the cost of fixed establishments on the African coast, together with the amount of credit extended to traders in Africa, and to the employers of slave labor in the New World, made up more than half of the total capital requirements of the trade. Hence, the total amount of capital employed in the trade by the merchants at any point in time was far in excess of the annual value of the trade as shown by the value of exports to Africa. In fact, if we regard the £89,000 shown against "Value of cargoes now on Float" in Dawson's account as representing approximately the value of goods exported to Africa in 1792 by the firm, the ratio of capital employed to the annual value of exports comes to 5.7 : 1. This means that the annual value of exports to Africa was about 17.5 percent of the amount of capital employed by the merchants. It is not clear whether the large-scale traders employed more capital per unit of export. The fact that the small traders did not own fixed establishments in Africa seems to point in that direction. But the evidence also suggests that the large-scale traders exported more goods per unit of shipping investment.[44] However, it is possible that the actual overall ratio of capital employed to the annual value

---

[44]   In general the large-scale traders employed larger ships and loaded far more slaves per ship, and in many cases, also more slaves per ton.

of exports to Africa was less than what Dawson's account suggests. Nevertheless the evidence makes it clear that the ratio must have been very high, much higher than what obtained in other branches of British overseas trade during the period. This conclusion is in general agreement with the view of the well-known authority on English foreign trade in the seventeenth and eighteenth centuries, Ralph Davis. Davis stated that during the period 1660–1701, although the total volume of English foreign trade did not grow exceptionally fast, yet English capital investment in commerce, when compared with investment in industry, "was abnormally high." According to him, this phenomenon was due to the revolutionary development of trade in re-exports, and the geographical re-orientation of English foreign trade away from Europe and the Mediterranean to Western Africa and the New World. As he put it,

Apart from the East India trade, with its own peculiar finances, nearly all trade early in the century [the seventeenth century] had been with Europe; and though voyages to the Mediterranean or the Baltic were longer than those to Holland or Hamburg, remittances for goods sold or freight earned could be, and were, sent by overland routes long before the ships carrying the goods returned home. After the Restoration [1660], trade with the Americas flourished; a trade at the end of long ocean routes, and in which, if exports were relatively small, imports were commonly given credit for in advance. The new long voyage had to be financed from its beginning to its end – and beyond – and investment was continuing in English trading stations abroad.[45]

In the "new long voyage" of English trade to the Americas, that portion directly connected with the trans-Atlantic slave trade and the slave economy of the Americas was by far the largest user of credit per unit of export. This was true of the slave plantations of Latin America and the Caribbean as well as those of mainland British America. Apart from the credit needed to purchase slaves imported from Africa, the planters also needed credit to secure supplies from Europe and to transport and market their produce in distant markets. As explained by the compilers of *The South in the Building of the Nation*, whereas farms in the northern states of the United States were largely self-sufficient in the eighteenth and early nineteenth centuries, for which reason they had very little need for credit, the plantations of the South were almost wholly devoted to the production of a single staple crop for sale in a distant market:

Through the proceeds of the sale of this crop were secured the slave laborers required on the plantation, the clothing, and, in large part, the food required for these laborers, the mules and plantation supplies, and the comfort and luxuries demanded by the planter and his family. The work of exchange was carried on for the most part by factors or commission merchants . . .[46]

[45]   Davis, "English Foreign Trade, 1660–1700," pp. 93 & 94.
[46]   *The South in the Building of the Nation*, Vol. 5, pp. 457–458.

Sheridan has shown the complex relationship which existed between the factors in the British Caribbean and Commission houses in Great Britain in the financing of plantation operations.[47] A similar relationship existed in the slave plantations of mainland British America, even after the political independence of the United States of America. As Mira Wilkins says, British merchants re-established pre-independence trading connections in the 1790s and opened new outlets in the United States, giving rise in 1792 to a letter by William Heth of Virginia to Alexander Hamilton, Secretary of the Treasury, complaining:

> The trade of this state is carried on chiefly with foreign [British] capital. Those engaged in it [the trade], hardly deserve the name of merchants, being factors, agents, and shop-keepers of the Merchants and Manufacturers of Great Britain – and their business to dispose of the goods of that, for the produce of this country, and remit it to the order of their principals with whom the profits of the trade of *course* centre.[48]

Through the factor and commission system, merchants in Great Britain granted large credits to finance the operations of the slave plantations in the British Caribbean and mainland British America. For the Caribbean, the evidence of one of the largest merchant houses in London in the late eighteenth century, the house of George Hibbert, is very revealing. This merchant house operated as a commission agent for planters in the Caribbean. It also had factors there doing business directly with the planters and the slave traders. In March 1790, George Hibbert told a House of Lords committee that on a rough estimate he believed the debts owed to merchants and other persons in Great Britain by the planters in the British Caribbean could not be less than £20 million.[49] He referred to the total market value of imports into Great Britain from the British Caribbean in 1788, which amounted to £6.8 million. Of this amount, £2,837,000 went to cover charges for customs duty, freight, insurance, commission agents' commissions (£232,000), and handling at the ports, leaving £3,963,000 credited to the accounts of the planters. Continuing, Hibbert stated that from this amount,

> must be further deducted what is paid to the manufacturers of this country for goods exported to the plantations, with the expenses of freight, insurance, commission, and port charges thereon; and also the sum paid to the African merchants annually

---

[47] R. B. Sheridan, "The Commercial and Financial Organisation of the British Slave Trade, 1750–1807," *Economic History Review*, 2nd ser., XI, 2 (December, 1958), pp. 219–263. See also Davies, "The Origins of the Commission System."

[48] Cited by Mira Wilkins, *The History of Foreign Investment in the United States to 1914* (Cambridge, Mass.: Harvard University Press, 1989), p. 40.

[49] House of Lords Record Office, London, House of Lords Main Paper, 3 May, 1792: Minutes of Evidence Touching the Slave Trade, Evidence of George Hibbert, Esquire, 20 March, 1790, p. 386.

for slaves; and when we add thereto the interest of the debt due from the British colonies to Great Britain, and the sums which some of the more opulent planters spend in the mother country, there cannot be a doubt but the whole £6,800,000 rested in and was applied to the use and benefit of Great Britain. In confirmation of the above I can assert that, in tracing the gross produce received from the West Indies through our house for many years back, in my own time and in that of my predecessors (which amounts to no inconsiderable sum) there is a very small portion of it indeed that I cannot follow home to one or other of the expenditures above stated.[50]

Similarly, the intricate web of the factor and commission system led to considerable indebtedness of the Southern planters to merchants in Great Britain. On the eve of the American War of Independence, the total debts owed by the thirteen colonies to merchants in England have been put at between £2 million and £6 million.[51] The debts claim presented to the British government in 1791 by the merchants shows a total of £4,984,655 still owed by all the American states by that time. Of this amount, Virginia alone owed £2,305,409, while the other four Southern states (Maryland, South Carolina, North Carolina, and Georgia) together owed £1,886,535. The five Southern states thus owed £4,191,944, being 84.1 percent of the total.[52]

The ability of the slave traders and the London commission agents to grant credits to the planters in the Americas depended on a further web of credit relationship that linked the slave traders and the commission agents to manufacturers and, ultimately, all three groups were linked to financial institutions (banking and discount houses) mostly through the mechanism of bill discounting. This is brought out by the evidence on the slave trade.

In the first instance the export suppliers were called upon to ease the credit problems of the British slave traders by allowing them some reasonable length of time for credit on the goods they exported to Africa. This export credit became an essential aspect of the slave trade. The evidence available for the last half of the eighteenth century makes this clear. The evidence, showing the amounts for credit and cash payments in the outward cost of 115 ventures made on various dates, has been employed to construct Table 7.1. The list is heavily weighted by the ventures of some medium-scale traders centered around William Davenport of Liverpool. As the individual ventures of this category of traders were usually much smaller

---

[50]   *Ibid.*, pp. 392–393.
[51]   Shepherd and Walton, *Shipping, Maritime Trade, and the Economic Development of Colonial North America*, p. 131.
[52]   *Ibid.*, fn. 2, pp. 131–132. For more on the credit situation in mainland British America, see Jacob M. Price, *Capital and Credit in British Overseas Trade: The View from the Chesapeake, 1700–1776* (Cambridge, MA: Harvard University Press, 1980); Jacob M. Price, "Credit in the Slave Trade and Plantation Economies," in Solow (ed.), *Slavery and the Rise of the Atlantic System*, pp. 293–339.

Table 7.1. *Outward Cost of Individual Ventures Analyzed to Show the Proportion of Cash and Credit Payments*

Period	Number of Ventures	Total Cost Outward (£s Sterling)	Credit (£s Sterling)	Percent
1757–63	7	26,684	17,838	66.8
1764–75	79	337,416	189,904	56.3
1776–83	19	105,988	54,196	51.0
1784–92	9	94,026	52,271	55.6
1793–1807	1	10,390	4,384	42.2
Total	115	574,504	318,593	55.5

Sources and Notes: Davenport Papers in the University of Keele Library, Keele; 387 MD 127 and 380 TUO 3/1, 3/6, 3/9, 3/12, 4/4, 4/7, 4/9, 4/10, Liverpool Record Office; Accounts of the ships, *Chesterfield, Calveley,* and *Eadith* in the Liverpool Museum; AE.52, Midland Bank Record, London; C.107/59, Public Record Office, Chancery Masters Exhibit. For the individual ventures, with the names of the vessels, see Inikori, "The Credit Needs of the African Trade," Appendix I, pp. 220–224.

than those of the larger firms that dominated the slave trade at this time, the ventures in the list are not representative of the typical ventures in the trade in terms of size. But the list may be sufficiently representative of the proportion of credit needed for the outward cost of African ventures during the period.

For the 115 ventures in the list, the total outward cost was £574,504. Of this amount, £318,593 was on credit, being 55.5 percent of the total, while £255,911 was paid cash. It is important to note that much of the cash payment was made for the cost of ship and outfit. The proportion of export goods purchased on credit is greater than the 55.5 percent for the whole outward cost. This may be illustrated with the venture of the ship, *Dobson,* in 1770. The total amount of the cargo for this venture was £4,820, of which £3,267 was on credit and £1,553 was paid cash. The cost of ship and outfit was £2,084. Of this amount, only £364 was on credit, £1,720 being paid cash. This means that 67.8 percent of the export goods was on credit, whereas only 52.6 percent of the total outward cost was on credit.[53]

[53] For a large number of the ventures in Table 7.1, the merchants' accounts show the cost of ship and outfit, and the cost of cargo separately. But this is not so for all of them.

A priori, it is to be expected that the planters' access to credit would depend on what creditors thought of the medium-term performance of the plantation economies. Increased demand and higher prices for slave-produced commodities led to increased demand and rising prices for slaves. In turn, increased demand and rising prices for slaves raised planters' need for credit at the same time that growing demand and increasing prices for slave-produced commodities improved creditors' perceptions about the medium-term performance of the plantation economies, making the creditors better disposed to grant credit. Because wartime conditions generally had adverse effects on the sale and prices of slave-produced commodities of the Americas, planters tended to face tight credit situations in wartime. The use of high discount rates by the export suppliers in England to induce cash purchases by the slave traders acted as the mechanism through which the conditions in the Atlantic slave economy were transmitted to the credit relations between the slave traders and the export suppliers in England. All this is more or less reflected in Table 7.1.

The extent to which Table 7.1 is indicative of the main operating forces in the credit relations of the Atlantic system is not altogether clear. In particular, the distribution of the ventures among the specified periods is extremely uneven: the first period has only seven ventures and the last, just one. However, changes in the level of credit shown in the table are basically consistent with logical expectation. The table shows that relatively less credit was involved in the trade of the Atlantic system during war years than in times of peace. The only exception to this is the period of the Seven Years' War: This itself is understandable. Unlike other war periods in the eighteenth century, the volume of British Atlantic commerce was not seriously affected by the war. On the whole, the general trend in Table 7.1 is supported generally by the evidence of the planters themselves. The Jamaican House of Assembly stated in 1792 that,

though the price of slaves, of lumber, salted beef, pork, and herrings, is considerably increased, and the taxes much higher, yet the neat [net] price of sugars to the planter having risen from 18s: 4½d to 32s: 2d per cwt., they have begun to pay their debts, and, in consequence of such payments, have got into better credit . . . This increase in the value of sugars has been occasioned, not so much by an increase of consumption in Great Britain and Ireland, as by a greater demand for foreign markets.[54]

---

[54]   Public Record Office, England, C.O. 137/91: Proceedings of the House of Assembly of Jamaica on the sugar and slave trade, in a session which began 23 October, 1792 (Printed). A somewhat similar view is presented in Jacob M. Price, "Credit in the slave trade and plantation economies." Price says that colonial laws in British America (including the Caribbean) favored the slave traders, relative to the planters, and encouraged the use of bills of exchange; on the other hand, colonial laws in French America favored the planters, and largely discouraged the use of bills of

The length of time for the credit granted by the export suppliers varied from industry to industry, and over time. In June, 1787, William and Samuel Rawlinson, a large cotton manufacturing firm in Manchester producing African goods, wrote to Messrs. Richard Fydell & Co. of Bristol:

The credit of this place is generally 12 months but the payment for African goods has been extended much longer even to 18 months by some Houses. We allow £10 per cent on an early remittance say in course of a month and a Bill agreeable to what you mention. No House whatever can serve you more to satisfaction than ours, dealing very extensively in that Branch, and being always acquainted with the patterns which have a preference at the different parts of the coast.[55]

The success of the British traders in capturing a large share of the slave trade in the eighteenth century was often attributed by the traders to this generous extension of credit by the export producers. Giving evidence before a Privy Council Committee in 1788, Robert Norris, who knew a lot about the trade, stated that Britain had a larger share of the African trade because of "the credit which the British merchant has with the manufacturers, which no other merchant in Europe enjoys. . . ."[56] James Penny also told the same committee that one of the main reasons for British success in the African trade was the longer credit which British merchants had from the manufacturers: "Our manufacturers give eighteen months credit, and the French only six."[57]

But the provision of this credit posed serious financial problems for the manufacturers. The firm of William and Samuel Rawlinson that had boasted of their ability to serve the African merchants to their satisfaction[58] soon ran into credit problems with these merchants. In December 1790, one of the Liverpool African traders, Joseph Caton, wrote to James Rogers of Bristol:

Rawlinson is a curious fellow as I have ever met with. He says he has wrote [sic] you that he would rather discount his bills as he can turn his money over to greater advantage, and that Mr. Taylor will take all his goods and allow 10 percent profit on them which is better than selling them to the merchant. Beside he said a man should never have too many eggs in one basquett. I told him I understand he was in cash in a month for the *Rodney*'s cargo last voyage, and if a man was to pay ready money for all his cargoes he must either have three capitals or let his ships

exchange. This must have acted to reduce the effects of the Atlantic system on the development of credit institutions in France.

[55] PRO, C.107/7, Part I, William & Samuel Rawlinson to Messrs. Richard Fydell & Co., Manchester, 11 June, 1787. Richard Fydell & Co. were slave traders in Bristol.
[56] PRO, BT.6/9, Evidence of Robert Norris, one of the delegates from Liverpool to the inquiry on the state of the African trade, 1788, p. 231.
[57] *Ibid.*, Evidence of James Penny, one of Liverpool's delegates, 8 March, 1788, pp. 356–357.
[58] See quotation above, fn. 55.

lay up two years out of three, for a ship was one year out and the Remittance Two years. This is just their ways and method of doing business.[59]

This letter spells out some of the problems in the granting of export credits in the slave trade in the late eighteenth century. The Rawlinsons seem to have been wise in their decision not to accumulate too large credits in the hands of Rogers & Co., for three years later, Rogers & Co. became bankrupt. Of the firm's various creditors, suppliers of export goods appear to have predominated. The petition of a London firm dealing in Indian piece goods shows that for five ventures by Rogers & Co. in 1792, the London firm supplied goods on credit to the tune of £15,356:7/-.[60]

The records of Farmer & Galton, a gun manufacturing firm in Birmingham that produced large quantities of firearms for the African trade, are particularly informative on the financial problems that manufacturers of African goods encountered in the eighteenth century. Writing to one of their agents in Liverpool in 1754, Samuel Galton wrote:

On revising the list of outstanding debts we find about £1,600 due more than 12 months or say since last July and before, all which we want and much more and had we not urgent reason for not being from home would have been at Liverpool ere now to insist on the immediate payment. Our stated credit is 8 months and when 12 months are taken there is no room for excuse of payment. As to Mr. Lownds beg you'l write to him not only for the former but last debt on Elijah and not wait his coming home. Pray be earnest with the rest that are due and not solicit orders unless can be better pay'd or ever take them when there is the least doubt of being punctually pay'd for when due, at whatever price....[61]

In September, 1755, Galton wrote again:

I am at times a good deal distressed for want of regular remittances and besides what is necessary for the circulation of my business I am obliged shortly to advance nigh £3,000, which obliges me to write in a more pressing manner than otherwise I should....[62]

The firm's inventory taken on March 31, 1772, shows the importance of export credit in its finances:[63] Unsold stock amounted to £17,653:14:10d;

[59] PRO, C.107/13, Joseph Caton to James Rogers, Liverpool, 2 December, 1790. Joseph Caton assisted Rogers of Bristol in fitting out some of the latter's vessels to Africa from Liverpool, and in purchasing needed goods from Manchester. The *Rodney* mentioned in the quote was one of James Rogers' slave ships. Mr. Taylor, also mentioned in the quote, is Samuel Taylor, one of the largest producers of African goods in Manchester in the late eighteenth century.

[60] PRO, C.107/4, Petition of Edmund Higginson, Daniel Barnard and Charles John Wheler, of New Court, Swithins Lane, London, Merchants, to the Lord High Chancellor of Great Britain (1795). There are other similar petitions.

[61] Birmingham Reference Library, Galt. 405/1, Samuel Galton to Mr. Parr, 13 July, 1754.

[62] Galt, 405/2, Samuel Galton to Mr. Parr, 27 September, 1755.   [63] Galt. 548.

debts due to the company totaled £22,228:6:7d, making a total asset of £39,882:1:5d. Debts owed by the company to sundry people was put at £905:9:10d. From the inventory it can be seen that debts due to the firm, evidently arising from credits to slave traders, formed a large proportion of its circulating capital. In fact, this item must have formed a large proportion of the firm's total capital at any point in time.

As the difficulties of the manufacturers increased they were forced to use high discount rates for cash payment to induce the merchants to make early payments. Whereas Samuel Galton could argue in 1752 that a discount of "7 percent for ready money and 3 percent for 6 months" was too much,[64] by 1771 the general discount for cash payment on guns for the slave trade was 17.5 percent.[65] The discount for cash payment on Manchester cottons for the African trade in the early nineteenth century was about 15 percent.[66] Thus, a banker manufacturer able to grant credit comfortably on the strength of the bank's resources must have made a handsome profit by retaining the discount.

The high discount rates for cash payment notwithstanding, the suppliers of African goods continued to be compelled to extend export credits to the traders throughout the century. It is clear from the evidence that this export credit created a major problem of circulating capital for the manufacturers. To finance the large amount of working capital which the export credit necessitated, the manufacturers themselves had to look for ways of raising capital. They resorted to bill finance. The manufacturers got bills of exchange from the slave traders. The former sent these bills to their bankers to be discounted, and got cash for their business. This may be illustrated with Samuel Galton's letter to one of his agents in Liverpool in 1755:

I shall be obliged to raise a large sum of money to discharge what Debts we owe as well as support my future trade with ready money. Now let me entreat you to send me as large a sum in Remittance as you possibly can. You know there's a large sum due and if you can't get bills at a short date do as well as you can by getting bills as I can then send them into my bankers hands and if accepted draw for the value.[67]

[64] Galt. 405/1, Samuel Galton to Mr. Farmer, 18 April, 1752.
[65] PRO, C.109/401. For the ventures made by Samuel Sandys & Co. of Liverpool in 1771, Thomas Falkner of Liverpool supplied guns to the tune of £2,657:18s.:4d. The total discount allowed for cash payment was £465. Farmer & Galton, Joseph Adams (both of Birmingham), and John Parr of Liverpool, also supplied Sandys & Co. with guns, all allowing a discount of 17.5 percent for cash payment.
[66] See the invoice of goods for Thomas Leyland's ventures in the Liverpool Record Office, 387 MD 42 & 43.
[67] Galt. 405/1, Samuel Galton to Mr. N. Atkinson, Birmingham, 22 March, 1755. On the same day a letter similarly worded was sent to John Parr, another agent of Farmer & Galton at Liverpool.

In using bill discounting as a way of raising credit, the manufacturers of African goods were, in fact, following the footsteps of the slave traders who had been using it as their main source of credit right from the early years of the century. The credit provided by the suppliers of export goods, generous as it was, fell far short of the credit needs of the traders. The discounting of bills of exchange received for the slaves sold in the New World was their main source of credit. This produced an immense amount of business in bill discounting activity in Liverpool, London, and Bristol. As the suppliers of African goods began to adopt this system of raising credit, the total amount of bill discounting business in the trading and manufacturing centers connected with the slave trade expanded considerably in the last half of the eighteenth century. The other British merchants involved in the Atlantic slave economy of the period, especially the commission agents of the planters and their export suppliers, were also extensively engaged in bill discounting. Although these other merchants and their export suppliers granted relatively less credit per unit of export, their much larger absolute volume of business increased considerably the overall amount of activity in bill discounting in England's major trading and manufacturing centers associated with the Atlantic slave economy.

The growth of banking in these trading and manufacturing centers connected with the slave economy was largely influenced by the opportunities that the expansion of bill discounting business offered. It is important to note that the banks that grew up in many of these centers in the second half of the eighteenth century, particularly in Lancashire, were primarily, if not entirely, bill discounting banks. The records of one of the most important of these banks, Arthur Heywood, Sons & Co., of Liverpool, show this clearly. Bill discounting occupied a dominant place in the intentions of the partners as declared in their agreement signed on August 26, 1776. The first article of the agreement states that the bank's business,

shall consist in exchanging cash for Bills or Notes, in Discounting Bills or notes, exchanging bills, advancing money on negotiable security, buying of gold or silver, Negotiations in money or Bills with the Kingdom of Ireland, receiving Lodgments or keeping the cash accounts of merchants or others in Liverpool or the places adjacent thereto, Hypothecation of goods, and such other legal transactions in cash, Bills or other Negotiations as can be undertaken with good and sufficient security, that is such security as may with ease be reconverted into cash. But it shall not be permitted to lend money on Mortgage, on Bond, or on any single personal security except in cases where there are running accounts and then only when exigencies require.[68]

---

[68]   Records of the Heywoods Bank of Liverpool in Barclays Bank, Heywoods Branch, Liverpool: Articles of Agreement for carrying on the bank with Joseph Denison & Co., dated in Liverpool, 26 August, 1776.

The balance books of the bank show that during its existence in the eighteenth century the primary business on which its revenue depended was bill discounting. This is made clear by the structure of the bank's assets and liabilities drawn up yearly from 1787 to 1790, and 1801 to 1807. This is presented in Appendix 7.1. As can be seen from these accounts, bills held in Liverpool and those sent to the partner bank of Joseph Denison & Co. in London regularly made up over 90 percent of the bank's income-yielding assets. Similarly, the main business of the bank of the Heywood brothers in Manchester at this time was the discounting of bills presented by the manufacturers of cotton goods in that city.[69] In the Bristol area, the bank of Cross, Baylys & Co., of Bath, had a good amount of business in discounting bills for the Bristol slave-trading firm of James Rogers & Co.[70]

On the whole, the evidence shows strongly that the growth of banking in Lancashire and other regions connected with the Atlantic slave economy was much influenced by the pressures and opportunities generated by the credit needs of the Atlantic merchants. Quite often when the growth of banking in some parts of England in the eighteenth century is related to the slave trade, the profits from the trade are what is stressed. This, of course, is quite important. Traders like the Heywood brothers who made fortunes in the slave trade were prominent among bankers in Lancashire. But an equally important, if not more important, relationship between the slave trade and the development of banking in the eighteenth century was the pressure and opportunities that its credit needs generated. The creative response of entrepreneurs to those pressures and opportunities forms an important aspect of the process through which banking facilities developed and expanded in the centers concerned. One of the reasons why many merchants who made fortunes in Atlantic commerce established banking houses in the eighteenth century could be that they were more aware than others of the pressures and opportunities, being themselves involved in the activities that generated them. The same thing is true of suppliers of goods for Atlantic commerce who became bankers. The opportunity of financing their credit to the traders from their customers' cash accounts must have been to them an attractive proposition. It is interesting to note that in 1804, Samuel Galton (Junior) established a banking firm that became the bank to his gun manufacturing firm.[71]

While the slave trade of London declined in the second half of the eighteenth century, the city continued to play a major role in the discounting

---

[69] Pressnell, *Country Banking*, p. 336. This bank was established by Benjamin Heywood and his sons. Benjamin Heywood was the brother of Arthur Heywood of the Heywoods bank in Liverpool.

[70] PRO, C.107/4, Extracts from the Account of Rogers, Blake & Co. with Cross, Baylys & Co.

[71] B. M. D. Smith, "The Galtons of Birmingham: Quaker Gun Merchants and Bankers, 1702–1831," *Business History*, IX, 2 (1967), pp. 146–147.

of bills connected directly or indirectly with the Atlantic slave economy.[72] London operated as a clearinghouse of a sort. The close connection between the factors in the New World and London financial houses meant that a large proportion of the slave bills were drawn on London houses. The bills were accepted by the London financial houses upon which they were drawn and endorsed by the slave traders who received the bills in payment for their slaves. London banks were thus in a good position to determine the financial soundness of the London houses upon which the bills were drawn and accepted. Where the London banks were not directly involved in the discounting they often offered advice to the provincial banks on the quality of the bills. This partly explains why the provincial banks often had branches in London or maintained special relationships with London banks. Joseph Denison & Co. of London operated in this way with the Heywoods Bank of Liverpool. Sheridan's analysis and that of Pressnell, taken together with the available evidence, suggest that the discounting of bills connected with Atlantic commerce made important contributions to the rise of the bill broker in London in the last years of the eighteenth century, and ultimately to the development of the London discount market.[73]

7.2 DEVELOPMENT OF MARINE INSURANCE

Marine insurance connected seaborne commerce directly to the financial market – it provided a mechanism for spreading the risk of floating considerable property by sea, while at the same time mobilizing funds for investment. In fact, in its earliest form marine insurance was little more than a loan granted to merchants trading overseas against the value of their ship and cargo. If the property got lost for reasons specified in the contract, the underwriters lost their money. But if the ship returned safely and the cargo got to its destination intact, the insurers got back their money plus a premium specified in the contract. This early form of marine insurance, going back to the Middle Ages, is called bottomry.[74] Even after the development of the modern form, whereby ship owners and merchants paid a specified premium on the stated value of their seaborne property, claiming from the underwriters the insured value in case of loss, underwriters and insurance brokers continued to be important operators on the financial

---

[72] The role of London in the discounting of slave bills has been masterly treated by Sheridan. See Sheridan, "The Commercial and Financial Organization of the British Slave Trade."

[73] Pressnell, *Country Banking*, pp. 94–101; Sheridan, "The Commercial and Financial Organization of the British Slave Trade," p. 261.

[74] Martin, *The history of Lloyd's*, pp. 2–5.

market, investing the premiums and the funds set aside against claims.[75] This section examines the contribution of the Atlantic slave economy to the development of marine insurance in the period 1650–1850.

Of the financial institutions whose historical development is the focus of this chapter, marine insurance was the earliest to reach England from the continental centers of seaborne commerce, Italy and Germany. From the early years of foreign trade in England to the end of the sixteenth century the merchants of the Steelyard on the Thames, who were the representatives of the Hanseatic League in England, and the Italian merchants in Lombard Street handled the limited business of insuring seaborne property in England. The Italians, who made money lending their main business, granted bottomry loans to overseas traders, which, as already stated, was the earliest form of marine insurance. The expulsion of the German and Italian merchants by Queen Elizabeth indigenized the business of marine insurance in England the same way that it helped indigenize England's foreign trade.[76]

It is thus clear that the practice of marine insurance was well established in England in the sixteenth century. However, it was as yet not a specialized business. It was undertaken as a sideline by merchants whose main business was something else. This remained the case up to the early eighteenth century. In the words of Wright and Fayle: "At the beginning of the eighteenth century the conditions of the insurance market seem to have been very much what they were under Elizabeth, prior to the creation of the Office of Assurances."[77] Attitude to marine insurance developed even more slowly. It has been argued that prior to the War of American Independence (1776–1783), the insurance of seaborne property was not regarded as absolutely necessary, and "there were a number of merchants who deemed it no more requisite to insure the vessels and cargoes they owned against loss, than to insure their houses against fire, and their lives against death."[78] Evidence of this attitude is revealed by a proposal to establish a marine insurance corporation in 1660 by some private entrepreneurs. These entrepreneurs estimated the total value of England's foreign trade at the time to be about £7 million, but thought only one-half of the amount would actually be insured at an average rate of 5 percent, yielding a premium income of £175,000; optimistically they hoped the whole amount would be insured. As a security against claims, the entrepreneurs proposed to raise a capital

---

[75] Arhtur H. John, "Insurance Investment and the London Money Market of the 18th Century." *Economica*, new series, vol. 20 (May 1953), pp. 137–158; Lucy Stuart Sutherland, *A London Merchant, 1695–1774* (London: Oxford University Press, 1933), pp. 55–65.

[76] Martin, *The History of Lloyd's*, pp. 2–33; Wright and Fayle, *A history of Lloyd's*, pp. 135–137; Sutherland, *A London Merchant*, p. 48.

[77] Wright and Fayle, *A History of Lloyd's*, pp. 35, 39.

[78] Martin, *The History of Lloyd's*, p. 161.

of £500,000, which would be invested in the East India Company or in some other form.[79] Nothing came out of the project, but the thinking of the entrepreneurs provides some window into the attitude of overseas traders to marine insurance at the time, and the probable size of the market.

Some further evidence of the irregularity of insurance cover by the overseas traders is available for the early eighteenth century. According to a contemporary guess, the total amount of insurable risks in English foreign trade in 1720 was £20.3 million, of which only £2.3 million were underwritten by the two joint stock insurance corporations, the London Assurance and the Royal Exchange Assurance, prompting Arthur John to say that this confirms what has long been known: "that a large part of coastal and foreign-bound shipping proceeded without cover."[80]

The slow development of marine insurance as a specialized business in England was due to the limited size of the market for marine insurance arising from the absolute volume of England's seaborne commerce as well as the attitude of the merchants to insurance. It was the phenomenal expansion of England's foreign trade from the second half of the seventeenth century – the "Commercial Revolution" – and the radical reorientation of that trade away from Europe to regions where the much greater risks compelled a more regular procurement of insurance cover that considerably increased the extent of the market and gave rise to the specialized underwriter and specialist insurance broker. These developments were aided by the success of England in wresting much of Atlantic commerce from rivals, particularly Holland and France, as shown in Chapter 6. Success begot further success: As increased market size gave rise to specialization and improved efficiency, London finally won the competition with Amsterdam and Rouen as the chief insuring center of the world, a competition stretching from the beginning to the mid-eighteenth century. According to Arthur John, "By the middle of the eighteenth century London had become the most important marine insurance centre of Western Europe."[81] Sutherland is even more time specific: "Before 1755 it was generally agreed that England had won the dominant position [in marine insurance], a position which she was never to lose."[82] The rest of the chapter is devoted to an assessment of the contribution of the Atlantic slave economy to the expansion of the market for marine insurance that was central to the emergence of England as the center of marine insurance in the world.

The Atlantic slave economy was linked to the marine insurance market in England through three distinct channels: (1) the British slave trade

---

[79]   Wright and Fayle, *A History of Lloyd's*, pp. 40–41.

[80]   John, "The London Assurance Company," p. 127. As John suggests, the private underwriters could not have done much more business than the two corporations in the early years of the century.

[81]   *Ibid.*, p. 127.   [82]   Sutherland, *A London Merchant*, p. 50.

providing premiums on ships and goods from England to Africa, on ships, slaves, and African products from Africa to the Americas, and on ships and African products from the Americas to England; (2) the trans-Atlantic trade in slave-produced commodities providing premiums on ships and goods from England to the Americas, on ships and goods from the Americas to England, and on ships and goods connected with the re-export trade in American produce between Great Britain and Europe; and (3) premiums on the American trade of European powers insured in England. Direct evidence on the third is too limited to permit quantification, but an attempt is made to demonstrate some order of magnitude for the first and second channels. Before doing so, however, it is important to offer some rough estimate of the over time size of the marine insurance market in Great Britain against which to measure the contribution of Atlantic commerce.

As we have seen, entrepreneurs with a reasonable knowledge of the market estimated the probable premium income for the whole market in 1660 to be about £175,000. Giving evidence before a select committee in 1810, 150 years later, the Chairman of Lloyd's, J. J. Angerstein, estimated that the total premium income from all the marine risks underwritten in 1809 was upwards of £10 million (£10,950,000).[83] No other reliable estimate of the size of the market between 1650 and 1809 is available. However, if it is accepted that the trend in the growth of premium income of the London Assurance Company from 1720 to 1820, shown graphically by Arthur John,[84] represents roughly the general trend in the growth of the market as a whole, then a tolerably reliable estimate of the volume of business in the period 1720–1807 can be made through a backward projection based on Angerstein's figure for 1809 and the premium income data of the London Assurance Company.[85]

---

[83] British Library, *British Parliamentary Papers*, 1810, IV, Select Committee on the means of effecting Marine Insurances in Great Britain, evidence of J. J. Angerstein, cited by John, "The London Assurance Company," p. 127. Angerstein stated that the total value of seaborne property insured was £146 million, of which £140 million was insured by individual private underwriters and £6 million by the two joint stock companies. Angerstein estimated the average premium to be 7.5 percent, yielding a total premium income of £11 million, approximately (£10,950,000). This is quite close to Colquhoun's estimate for 1811, put at £10,338,815. See Colquhoun, *Treatise*, p. 95.

[84] John, "The London Assurance Company," p. 130.

[85] A preponderant proportion of the marine business in the 18th century was in the hands of private underwriters doing business in their individual capacity. The London Assurance and the Royal Exchange Assurance Corporations were the only joint stock companies on the market. The act, which incorporated them in 1720, stipulated that no joint stock companies other than these two, and also no partnership firm, should insure ships and goods at sea. The two companies had only a small proportion of the total business throughout the eighteenth century, as can be seen from Angerstein's evidence (fn. 83 above). Arthur John thought the premium income trend of the London Assurance Company reflects the general trend of the market: "The years

The premium income of the London Assurance Company in 1809 was roughly three times its average annual premium income from about 1793–1807;[86] its annual average premium earnings for 1793–1807 were roughly twice those for 1750–92, and the latter were just a little more than those for 1720–50.[87] Applying this trend to Angerstein's figure for 1809 gives about £4 million as the annual average premium income for the market as a whole in 1793–1807, £2 million for 1750–92, and £1.8 million for 1720–50.[88] It must be noted that these are very rough computations. At best they represent an order of magnitude in terms of the size of the marine insurance market during the period, against which the contribution of the Atlantic slave economy can be measured.

As it is generally known that in the eighteenth century the average merchant in England did not regularly insure his property at sea, the first step in measuring the contribution of the Atlantic slave economy is to determine the degree of regularity of insurance cover in trans-Atlantic commerce. There is little doubt that even in peacetime the risks involved in trans-Atlantic trade in the eighteenth century were infinitely greater than those in the trade with nearby Europe. This was more so in wartime, because the wars of the period were fought largely over the control of trade and shipping with the Americas. As already shown in Chapters 5 and 6 above, the trans-Atlantic slave trade had the greatest amount of risk among all international trades of the period. The traders were very conscious of these risks and their private correspondence makes it clear. Some of these may be mentioned to illustrate. Writing from Rotterdam in July 1735, on his way to the African coast, a slave ship commander, Captain John Butler, stated anxiously:

1730–39 and 1763–76 were clearly associated with a fall in marine insurance activity, which there is reason to believe was not confined to the London Assurance. It is significant that these periods were characterized by modifications of the insurance policy – some temporary, some permanent – in favour of those who wished to insure" (*Ibid.*, pp. 131–132). John's evidence indicates that high premium income characterized the period 1739–63.

[86] Derived from the graph in John, "The London Assurance Company," p. 130. All subsequent measurements of the company's premium income are from the same source.

[87] The average income for 1750–1792 is about £38,000 and that for 1720–1750 is about £35,000.

[88] The figures for the whole market are obtained by applying the company's trend ratios to Angerstein's figure for 1809. Thus, because the company's annual average premium income for 1793–1807 is about 3 times its income for 1809, the annual average premium income for the entire market is put at approximately £4 million, the result of dividing by 3 Angerstein's figure for 1809; the company's premium earnings for 1793–1807 (annual average) are about twice those for 1750–1792, hence, those for the whole market for the latter period are put at about £2 million, annual average, being one-half of £4 million. The figure for 1720–1750 is a marginal adjustment arising from the closeness of the company's premium earnings in 1750–1792 and 1720–1750.

I wrote you by my last that I could make no Ensurance [sic] here and I beg of you that you would get insured for me two thousand pounds for it is too great a Risque for me to run with my little fortune without Insurance as times are so precarious.[89]

A senior manager of the already mentioned "Floating Factory" venture, Captain George Hamilton, frequently expressed similar anxiety concerning insurance cover for the venture's property at sea. One practice adopted by the venture, as stated in Chapter 5, was to ship gold and other African products in naval vessels, which made the insurance rate lower at the cost of a higher than normal freight charge. Hamilton was not sure whether the trade-off was to the venture's advantage, yet the expectation of war with Spain in the late 1730s appeared to leave little option. Writing from the Gold Coast to a member of the venture in England he stated:

It was my intention never to ship any more of our effects in King's ships [Naval ships] but by what we can reasonably imagine here, there are [sic] a war with the Spaniards, your last letters seemed to apprehend something from that quarter so that without dispute Insurance will amount to as much as the freight to the man of war; the principal to be feared is French vessels sailing with Spanish commissions; I apprehend the West Indies will be full of those craft . . .[90]

The venture thus continued to ship gold and African products in naval vessels, while using merchant ships to transport slaves to the Americas. He was subsequently told by a senior member of the syndicate, "you are quite right in shipping on the King's ship . . . we save more than the difference in insurance."[91] Earlier, however, Captain Hamilton had written with anxiety: "It is somewhat surprising you say none of the offices will underwrite on any of our vessels; there is Captain Southerland who departed from London the 24[th] August Insured at 5 p[e]rcent as he says; he is now at Cape Coast." Continuing, he promised to do his best to ensure that the venture succeeded, for "if it should prove otherwise (which God forbid) Poor More & self will have the worst of it, very possibly ruined; £74,000 is a large sum to be afloat, as the case now stands, which gives me great concern."[92]

When in 1742 the venture lost a chartered vessel that was not insured, Captain Hamilton charged: "it's well we had no greater interest on board her; however it's a neglect that insurance were [sic] not made seeing our effects on board King's ships are carefully insured at two guineas percent."[93]

---

[89] PRO, C.103/130, Capt. John Butler to "Brother Hall," Rotterdam, 15 July, 1735.
[90] C.103/130, George Hamilton to Richard Pinnell, Annamaboe, 24 December, 1738.
[91] *Ibid.*, Thomas Hall to George Hamilton, London, 28 August, 1742.
[92] *Ibid.*, Captain George Hamilton to Thomas Hall, Annamaboe Road, 2 December, 1739.
[93] *Ibid.*, George Hamilton to Thomas Hall, Annamaboe, 8 August, 1742. Hamilton had written to Hall on August 27, 1740, reporting the arrival of the vessel (commanded by Captain Clove Talbot) on July 4, 1740. He reported putting on board the vessel 990 oz gold dust, 506 elephant teeth weighing 28,348 lbs, 560 "screvilias" (small ivory) weighing 3,437 lbs, and 291 slaves. Captain More, another officer of

The extensive evidence in the highly valuable papers of Thomas Hall leaves the reader in no doubt that the British slave traders took the matter of insurance very seriously – so seriously that increases in premium rates were a matter of considerable concern for the community of British slave traders. Writing in September 1794, one of the traders reported:

The many captures by the French have raised the premium of Insurance to 20 Guineas per cent and the low price of sugars, and insecurity of West India property in the age of Equality, & Confiscation, has had such an effect on the price of slaves, that the average is fallen to £40 and bills lengthened to 30 and 36 months.[94]

The letters of the Tarleton brothers of Liverpool show that the business community there was very concerned about the high premium rates. As Clayton Tarleton wrote in January 1795:

We are rather gloomy about public affairs & not without cause – premiums out to Africa are 15, middle risks 15 to return 5 if [entered to] go to Jamaica, or 12 to return 2 for the very best ship, & best parts of the Coast, so that I think the trade is nearly knocked up.[95]

The extensive private records of slave-trading firms examined for this study show that unlike merchants in some other trades, who could afford to be more relaxed in matters of insurance, the slave traders were compelled by the unusual level of risk involved in their business to secure insurance cover regularly to help spread the risk. Of course, there were occasions when the insurance procured did not cover the full value of the property at sea.[96] However, because this was rare whenever it occurred it required specific instructions for the slave ship commanders. Two cases from the Liverpool firm of Thomas Leyland & Co. may be cited to illustrate. In 1797, having instructed Captain Whittle of his ship, the *Lottery*, to keep company

the venture commanding a stationed ship on the coast, was expected to add more slaves and more gold to complete the ship's cargo of 440 slaves and 2,000 oz of gold. It is not clear where the ship was lost. In all probability it was between the Americas and England, after the sale of the slaves and the gold and ivory shipped on board naval ships. This is the only reasonable explanation of Hamilton's statement, "it's well we had no greater interest on board her." Had all the slaves, ivory, and gold, estimated to return £17,000, been lost with the ship Hamilton could not have made that statement.

[94] PRO, T.70/1569, P. W. Brancker to Thomas Miles, Liverpool, 2 September, 1794.
[95] Liverpool Record Office, 920 TAR. 4/73, Clayton Tarleton to Thomas Tarleton, Liverpool, 8 January, 1795.
[96] It was usual for the slave traders to insure slaves across the Atlantic from Africa (the middle risk) below their market price in the Americas. Thus, between 1750 and 1790 slaves sold for between £35 and £50 in the Americas, while they were valued at £30 for insurance purposes; between 1791 and 1807 they were valued at £40 or £45 for insurance purposes, while they sold for £50 and above most of the time. This was a normal practice, different from what is referred to here in terms of coverage that was less than the full value of the property.

with Captain Bernard of his other ship, the *Earl of Liverpool,* the whole voyage, Liverpool to Bonny and from Bonny until arrival at Jamaica, Thomas Leyland stressed to Captain Bernard,

you are expressly required in like manner not to separate from the *Lottery*: your mutual safety against the enemy, the heavy sum of money which we shall risk on each ship without insurance, and a return of £2 percent which the underwriters have agreed to on what is insured in case you fulfil the afore-mentioned conditions, are points for your serious consideration and zeal, and in order that they may be carried into execution Captain Whittle (being the senior Captain in the employ and most likely in the fastest sailing ship) is to act as the commandore and you are to obey the signals which are arranged and delivered to each ship for this purpose.[97]

Again, in July 1803, Thomas Leyland told Captain Caesar Lawson of his ship, the *Enterprize*:

A considerable part of our property under your care will not be insured, and we earnestly desire you will keep a particular look out to avoid the Enemy's Cruisers, which are numerous and you may hourly expect to be attacked by some of them.[98]

The extraordinarily high premium rates of the French Revolutionary and Napoleonic War period (1793–1815) may have encouraged some of the larger firms like Leyland & Co. to carry part of their own risks. Their ships were heavily armed both for self-defense and for privateering. But the very careful and detailed instructions suggest that this was not a common practice even for the larger firms. However, some account must be taken of the practice in computing the amount of insurance involved in the British slave trade.

Appendix 7.2 shows the premiums paid on 60 individual ventures for which the private records of the merchants contain adequate relevant information. They are grouped chronologically according to periods of war and peace. This appendix, containing direct accounts from the merchants' private records, provides some firm basis for comparison with estimates that are computed subsequently. As can be seen from the appendix, the premiums paid outward for the ventures of the Seven Years' War period (1756–1762) constituted 19.2 percent of their outward cost; for the peace period 1763–75, 6.6 percent; for the peace period of the 1780s, 8.5 percent; and for the war period 1800–06, 16.2 percent. In some sense these percentages are misleading, because the amount of insurance information is not always the same for all ventures. In some cases the information covers

---

[97]   Midland Bank Records, London, AE 52, Ship *Earl of Liverpool*, Captain Geo. Bernard, Master: Instructions to the Captain by Thomas Leyland. The ship sailed from Liverpool on April 9, 1797, in company with the ship, *Lottery*.

[98]   Liverpool Record Office, 387 MD 43, Account Book of the ship *Enterprize* 1803–1804: Instructions to Captain Caesar Lawson, Liverpool, 8 July 1803. The ship sailed from Liverpool on July 20, 1803 and arrived Bonny on September 23, 1803.

the premiums paid for the ventures up to the Americas, but in other cases it is only up to the African coast. The premiums paid on the home journey from the Americas are not included in the appendix. These percentages do not, therefore, accurately reflect the premium rates for the periods, which are shown in a table below.

In fact, it is virtually impossible to obtain from the extant accounts of the traders information on all the insurance covers arising from each venture, except on a few occasions when legal proceedings compelled its presentation. Very often the slave ship commanders insured their own commissions, which did not form part of the ventures' accounts prepared for the owners.[99] On the other hand, the extant accounts used in constructing Appendix 7.2 do not include accounts of prizes captured and insured by the traders in wartime. This was big business in Liverpool. As an illustration, in 1793 the ship *Christopher* belonging to Thomas Leyland, took a prize, *Le Convention*. The total amount insured on the prize from Western Africa to the West Indies and from there to England amounted to £23,800, producing a total premium of £1,593:9s.[100]

To give some idea of how large the total insurance on a slaving venture could be, some ventures with more or less complete information may be cited. Due to a law suit between Captain Gilbert Wenman, Master of the *Bedford*, which traded on the coast in 1806, and Thomas Lumley & Co. of London, the owners of the venture, the captain submitted the following account of the venture:[101]

	£	S	D
To Cargo (Outward)	7,494	10	10
Insurance on Cargo (less Returns)	224	8	9
Ships and Stores	6,064	17	2
Insurance on ditto (less Returns)	1,427	8	=
Provisions	713	11	4
Insurance on Middle Risk (less Returns)	1,393	7	=
Charges of Shipping	1,740	10	7
Insurance on ship home & freight (less Returns)	708	=	=

[99]   For example, in 1807 Captain Hugh Crow sought to know from his insurance brokers in London at what rate of premium they would insure his commissions per *Kitty's Amelia*: Hugh Crow, *Memoirs of the late Captain Hugh Crow of Liverpool* (London, 1830), p. 135.

[100] Liverpool Record Office, 387 MD 40: Account Book of the Ship *Le Convention*, 1793–1795. At the time of capture the prize had on board 114 slaves, India piece goods, gunpowder, and some other articles.

[101] PRO, C.114/158. Papers of of Thomas Lumley & Co. of London, among the Chancery Masters' Exhibits. The case relates to the balance of Capt. Wenman's earnings from this voyage, which balance was £328:3s.:9d. Mr. Francis Const, of the Middle Temple, in his award, asked Thomas Lumley & Co. to pay Capt. Wenman this balance.

The total premium for this venture comes to £3,753:3s.:9d., which is 27.7 percent of the outward cost of ship, outfit and cargo, being £13,559:8s.:ød. The ventures of James Rogers & Co. of Bristol for 1792 and 1793 also show near complete information on insurance accounts:[102]

Insurance Made on African Ventures
by James Rogers & Co. in 1792

	£	S	D
On the *Rodney*, Bristol to Africa & the West Indies Ship & Goods, £9,000, at 6% & Policy 14/-	540	14	=
On the *African Queen*, Bristol to Old Calabar, Ship & Goods, £10,000, at 35/- percent. & Policy 14/-	175	14	=
On the *African Queen*, Africa to America, on Ship & Goods, Slaves valued at £30 per head, £10,000, at £3: 10. =d percent & Policy 14/-	350	15	=
On the *African Queen*, Bristol to Africa, Goods £400, at 35/- percent	6	10	=
On the *Ruby*, Africa to America, Ship & Goods, £7,000 at 4 guineas percent & Policy 14/-	294	14	=
On the *Ruby*, Jamaica to Bristol, on ship, £600 at 4 percent & Policy 9/-	24	9	=
On the *Ruby*, 20 Hhds Sugar, Jamaica to Bristol £800 at 4% & Policy 9/-	32	9	=
On the *Friendship*, Bristol to Africa & America Ship & Goods £3,500 at £6 percent & Policy 14/-	210	14	=
On the *Fame*, Bristol to Africa & America, Ship & Goods, £6,000 at £6 percent & Policy 14/-	360	14	=
On the *Triton*, Africa to England, Ship & Goods £6,000, 3 guineas percent & Policy 14/-	189	14	=
On the *Crescent*, Bristol to Africa & America, Ship & Goods, £10,000 at £6 percent & Policy 14/-	600	14	=

[102] Both the accounts for 1792 and 1793 can be found among the papers of James Rogers & Co., C.107/6, C.107/13, & C.107/15. Since the records of Rogers & Co. are very much scattered, these accounts may not exhaust all the insurance taken by the firm in the two years. None of these ventures is included in Appendix 7.2, because their total outward costs are not known. The accounts are exactly as they appear in the records. In some cases the arithmetic is not right; for example, £400 at 35/- percent (the *African Queen*, 1792) should be £7 instead of £6:10/-. Possibly there was a discount.

Insurance Made on African Ventures
by James Rogers & Co. in 1793

	£	S	D
On the *African Queen*, Jamaica to Bristol, on Ship, £2,000 at 15 Guineas percent & Policy 14/-	315	14	=
On the *Pearl*, Barbadoes to Bristol, on Ship £1,500 at 15 Guineas percent & Policy 12/-	236	17	=
On the *Crescent*, Jamaica to Bristol, Ship & Goods, £4,000	504	14	=
On the *Rodney*, Africa to the West Indies, Ship & Cargo, £3,200 at 10 guineas percent & Policy 14/-	336	14	=
On the *Rodney*, Jamaica to Bristol, on Ship, £2,000 at 12 guineas percent & Policy 14/-	252	14	=
On the *Recovery*, Africa to the West Indies, Ship & Cargo, Slaves valued at £40 per head £3,000 at 8 guineas percent & Policy 12/-	252	12	=
On the *Sarah*, Africa to the West Indies, Ship & Cargo, £5,000 at 10 guineas percent & Policy 14/-	525	14	=
On the *Sarah*, Africa to the West Indies, Ship & Cargo, £2,000	168	12	=
On the *Sarah*, Jamaica to Bristol, on Ship, £800 at 12 guineas percent & Policy 9/-	101	5	=
On the *Jupiter*, Africa to the West Indies, on Ship, Outfit & Cargo, £5,000 at 8 guineas percent & Policy 12/-	420	12	=
On the *Jupiter*, Jamaica to Bristol, Ship & Freight, £2,500	315	14	=

It is pertinent to note that £9,000 was insured on the *Rodney* outward, Bristol to Africa and the West Indies, in 1792, and in 1793 a further insurance of £3,200 was made on the venture for the "Middle Passage." So, the amount insured for the Middle Passage in this venture was £12,200, which is much more than the amount covered outward. Then £2,000 was insured on the ship from Jamaica to Bristol. These accounts give some idea of the amount of cover for the whole of a slaving venture. They also show that the cost of insurance formed a large part of the costs the slave traders had to meet. The records of other firms give the same message. For instance, the profit and loss account of Messrs. Tarleton & Backhouse of Liverpool in 1796 shows that for the insurance of their slave ships in this year they paid £5,407:11s.:6d.[103]

The foregoing direct evidence from the traders' private records serves to provide a firm basis for estimating the contribution of the Atlantic slave economy to the growth of the marine insurance market in England in the eighteenth century. The starting point for the estimate is the over time and route specific premium rates in trans-Atlantic commerce during the period. This is presented in Table 7.2. As can be seen in Appendix 6.1, not all the routes taken by the British slave ships are shown in Table 7.2. The rates shown in the table are for the more direct routes – England to Africa, Africa to British America (the West Indies and mainland America), and British America to England. Vessels going to European ports before heading to the African coast usually paid premiums half a percentage point more than those which went direct, England to Africa. Similarly, slave ships trading to non-British America paid higher premium rates. For example, the table shows that between 1717 and 1738 (a peace period), a round trip insurance – England to the African coast and from there to British America and then back to England – was at the rate of 11 percent. But in July 1735, round trip insurance on the *Hiscox*, Captain John Butler, Commander, Thomas Hall, owner, was at the rate of 14 guineas percent. The vessel was insured "at and from London to Holland and at and from thence to any ports and places where and whatsoever in Africa and at and from thence to Buenos Ayres and at and from thence back to London."[104] This example combines the additional insurance cost of sailing to Africa through ports in Europe and trading to Latin America rather than British America, all of which was quite common as evidence so far presented in the study shows. However, it is practically impossible to incorporate all the complex movements of the slave ships in the table. To that extent the rates in the table may be on the low side on the whole.

The premium rates in Table 7.2 have been applied to the evidence on ships, goods, and slaves moving between England, the African coast, the Americas, and back to England. The result is presented in Table 7.3. Again, this table is somewhat incomplete. It is clear from the evidence that gold and other African products transported along with the slaves to the Americas and, subsequently, from the Americas to England were insured regularly. Even when these products were shipped on naval vessels they

---

[103]   Liverpool Record Office, 920 TAR. 5/1–5/15. Annual Profit and Loss Accounts of Messrs. Tarleton & Backhouse, 31 Dec., 1796.

[104]   C.103/130, Policy of Insurance on the *Hiscox*, Captain John Butler, Master, 8 July 1735. The policy was on the ship, valued at £2,000, and it was effected on September 19, 1735, by 10 underwriters for a total premium of £294:4s:6d, including 4 shillings and 6 pence for the policy.

Table 7.2. *Period and Route Specific Insurance Rates in*
the Atlantic Slave Economy, 1701–1807 (percent)

	England to African Coast	African Coast to Americas	Americas to England
1701–13	4	8	10
1714–38	2	4.5	4.5
1739–48	4	8	10
1749–55	2	4.5	4.5
1756–62	6	10	10
1763–75	2	4.5	4.5
1776–82	5	10	10
1783–92	2	4.5	4.5
1793–1807	8	12	14

Sources and Notes: PRO, C.O. 388/15 Part 1, folios 97 and 98, Representation of Separate Traders to the Board of Trade, c.1708; PRO, T.70/1523, T.70/1527, and T.70/1529, insurance effected by the Committee of the Company of Merchants Trading to Africa; Essex Record Office, County Hall, Chelmsford, D/DRU/B7, William Braund Papers, Journals of Risks, 1759–73; PRO, C.103/130 and C.103/132, Thomas Hall's papers; C.107/13 and C.107/15, Papers of James Rogers & Co. of Bristol; C.114/158, Papers of Thomas Lumley & Co. of London; T.70/1569; Liverpool Record Office, 920 TAR.4/73, Tarleton Papers; Liverpool Record Office, 380 TUO.3/9 and 380 TUO.3/12, David Tuohy's Papers; Liverpool Record Office, 387 MD 40, Account Book of the Ship *Le Convention*, 1793–95; Carrington, *The British West Indies*, pp. 61–65; Watts, *The West Indies*, Table 6.5, p. 273; Davis, *The Rise of the English Shipping Industry*, p. 378 (Virginia–England rate was 5% in 1770). The rates stated in the table represent a rather conservative average view of the differing rates in the sources cited. The route, Americas to England, is limited to the British West Indies and North America (including the United States). The rates on the Latin American routes were much higher. The table does not include all the routes taken by vessels in the slave trade. This is discussed in the text.

were still insured, as preceding evidence in this chapter shows. Yet it was not practicable to include these products in the computations presented in Table 7.3. Everything considered, it is likely that the figures in the table understate the amount of premiums generated by the British slave trade during the period.

The latter point is confirmed by a comparison of the figures in the table with evidence produced by the merchants, planters, shipowners, ship-builders and manufacturers of Liverpool. The Liverpool account shows 147

Table 7.3. *Insurance Premiums in the British Slave Trade*

	Premiums on cargo, England to African coast (£000)	Premiums on slaves, Africa to Americas (£000)	Premiums on ship and outfit, England to Africa to Americas to England (£000)	Period Total (£000)
1750–60	127.4	514.3	230.8	872.5
1761–70	168.9	756.4	181.4	1,106.7
1771–80	205.6	433.4	164.9	803.9
1781–90	210.4	559.8	331.6	1,101.8
1791–1800	854.9	2,239.9	1,027.1	4,121.9
1801–1807	839.9	1,517.2	1,352.2	3,709.3

Sources and Notes: For exports from England to the African coast, see Inikori, "The Volume of the British Slave Trade," Table VI, p. 665; the official values of the exports have been converted to real (current) values by applying the ratio of 1.4:1, real to official values, the basis of which is demonstrated in Inikori, "West Africa's Seaborne Trade," pp. 61–62. For slave export figures, see Table 5.1. For the "middle passage" (Atlantic crossing from Africa to the Americas) insurance, the traders generally valued slaves at £30 each, 1750–90, and £40 or £45 between 1791 and 1807; £30 and £40 have been applied for 1750–90 and 1791–1807, respectively. These prices are below the actual prices in the Americas at the time, for which see Sheridan, *Sugar and Slavery*, Table 11.4, p. 252, and Inikori, "Market Structure and the Profits of the British African Trade," pp. 759–761. The periods for the premiums on slaves are somewhat different from the rest: They are 1750–59, 1760–69, 1770–79, 1780–89, 1790–1800, and 1801–07. The impact of this difference on the period totals is not large. Because of the way the periods are constructed for the slave exports, premiums on the slaves in the war years, 1776–82, have been computed on the peacetime rate of 4.5% instead of the wartime rate of 10%. This means that the premiums computed for this period, spread between 1770–79 and 1780–89, are too low. For the amount of ship and outfit, on which premiums have been computed, see Chapter 6, and for the premium rates in general, see Table 7.2.

ships, measuring 34,976 tons, cleared out from Liverpool to Africa for the slave trade in 1806. The total value of cargo was £750,000, and 36,000 slaves were shipped from Africa. The account shows a total premium of £531,200, including premiums paid between the Americas and England.[105]

[105]   PRO, T.70/1585: The Petition of the Merchants, Planters, Shipowners, Ship Builders and Manufacturers on behalf of themselves and others of the Town and Port of Liverpool interested in the Commerce with Africa and His Majesty's Settlements in America and the West Indies, to the Lords Spiritual and Temporal of the United

From the figures in Table 7.3, the annual average premium for all England in 1801–07 comes to £529,900, less than that for Liverpool alone. In some areas the calculations by the Liverpool group exaggerate. For example, insurance is computed on the ships and cargo "for 3 legs of the voyage"; only the ships covered the three legs of the voyage. Some African products were insured from the Americas to England, but their value was much less than that of the cargo shipped to Africa. In other important areas, however, the computations understate. The slaves were valued at £24 per head for purposes of insurance, contrary to the £40 to £45 generally applied by the traders at this time. Also the round trip premium rate of 20 percent employed is much lower than the prevailing rate of over 24 percent at the time. All told, the indication is that it is the estimates in Table 7.3 that are too low rather than the computations by the Liverpool group being too high. One of the several reasons for the low estimates in the table is the fact that the premiums are not included in the amounts of risks covered, which was the usual practice by the traders. This was properly done in the Liverpool calculations. The procedure may be illustrated with an actual account of a trader in 1732:[106]

Account of the *Argyle*, Captain George Hamilton, Master

Cargo taken on board in England:	£784.5
Cargo taken on board in Holland:	2,070.0
Total Cargo	£2,854.5
Ship	2,409.6
Outset of Ship and Cargo	£5,264.1
Insurance of £6,000 at 7%	420.0
Interest	315.9
Total Cost	**£6,000**

It can be seen that both the cost of insurance and the interest on the capital are included in the value insured. It was not practicable to make this kind of fine calculations in Table 7.3 and other tables that follow.

The next step in assessing the contribution of the Atlantic slave economy to the extent of the marine insurance market in eighteenth-century England is an examination of the over time level of insurance in the West Indian

Kingdom of Great Britain and Ireland in Parliament Assembled (not dated, but most likely some time in 1807). The document includes a list of the vessels, showing the names, tonnage, the number of seamen, and the date of clearance. Two separate calculations are shown, one shows the amount of insurance specifically, but the other has the insurance built into other calculations.

[106]   C.103/132, Senserf & Son to Thomas Hall, Rotterdam, 19 February, 1732.

Table 7.4. *Account Sales of a Jamaican Planter's Sugar in England 1792–1798 (in £ sterling and percent)*

	Gross Sale (1)	Less Duties and Charges (c.i.f. Value) (2)	Freight (3)	Insurance (4)	(4) as % of (2) (5)
1792	51,632	38,267	3,009	1,095	2.9
1793	42,604	30,221	4,199	3,175	10.5
1794	37,491	25,098	5,979	3,341	13.3
1795	51,588	39,534	5,970	4,995	12.6
1796	12,645	9,560	1,493	1,640	17.2
1797	42,360	31,538	4,613	5,069	16.1
1798	42,272	30,711	4,428	4,664	15.2

Source: Computed from Selwyn H. H. Carrington, *The Sugar Industry and the Abolition of the Slave Trade, 1775–1810* (forthcoming), Table 10.4, p. 579: Original Source, *Journal of the Assembly of Jamaica* (1799), vol. X, pp. 429–435. The planter is Simon Taylor.

trade. As shown in Chapter 4, the British Caribbean was the very center of the Atlantic system in the eighteenth century. The bulk of commodity production for export in British America, during that period, took place in the British Caribbean; much of the maritime business of New England derived from there as much as that of Old England, the mother country. And, apart from the absolute volume and value of goods shipped yearly, a number of factors ensured regular procurement of insurance cover. First, the West Indian trade shared many of the risks in the slave trade already discussed. The second factor was the tight control that the commission houses in England (especially those in London) had over the shipment and sale of the West Indian produce and the perennial indebtedness of the West Indian planters to these commission houses. To ensure payment of the debts, given the hazards, the commission houses could not risk shipping the goods without insurance. Hence, insurance cover in the West Indian trade was as regular as in the slave trade. This is shown consistently in the surviving sales accounts of the planters. One such account is presented in Table 7.4. It may be noted that the premium rates revealed by the planter's account are quite close to those shown in Table 7.2.

Based on the evidence from the planters' accounts and the rates presented in Table 7.2, insurance premiums on goods transported between Great Britain and the British West Indies, and between Great Britain and the

Table 7.5. *Insurance on Goods Transported Between Great Britain and the British West Indies, and Between Great Britain and the United States of America (Annual Average in £000)*

	1781–85	1786–90	1791–95	1796–1800
British West Indies:				
Exports (Real Value)	4,221.0	5,037.3	7,032.5	10,203.5
Insurance	189.9	226.7	632.9	1,428.4
Imports (Real Value)	1,513.7	1,672.0	3,405.8	5,999.2
Insurance	68.1	75.2	306.5	839.9
United States of America:				
Exports (Real Value)	556.8	1,260.1	1,619.3	2,915.1
Insurance	25.1	56.7	145.7	408.1
Imports (Real Value)	1,899.2	2,506.1	5,538.9	7,839.1
Insurance	85.5	112.8	498.5	1,097.5

Sources and Notes: The exports and imports figures are computed using the official values of Schumpeter, *English Overseas Trade Statistics*, Tables V and VI, pp. 17 and 18, and ratios of real to official values computed from Davis, *The Industrial Revolution*, Table 37, p. 86: for exports to Great Britain, the ratios are 1.45 for the 1780s and 1.73 for the 1790s; for imports from Great Britain, the ratios are 1.19 for the 1780s and 1.37 for the 1790s. For the insurance rates employed, see Table 7.2; for the period 1791–95, the premium rate applied is 9%, taking account of the non-war years.

United States of America have been computed and are shown in Table 7.5. There is some degree of uncertainty concerning the trade with the United States. From what Shepherd and Walton say, it would appear that insurance cover in the trade between Great Britain and mainland British America (United States) was not as regular as in the rest of British trans-Atlantic commerce:

It is probable that some portions of the goods shipped between the [mainland] colonies and the British Isles was not insured formally ... A customary practice in peacetime, for example, was to insure one-half the value of a shipment of goods to the colonies. ... We have assumed that colonial merchants purchased insurance in Great Britain on all their imports and one-half their exports on this route.[107]

On the other hand, Shepherd and Walton state that while underwriters in England "seldom insured colonists in the West Indies and coastal trades,

---

[107] Shepherd and Walton, *Shipping, Maritime Trade, and the Economic Development of Colonial North America*, p. 131.

Table 7.6. *Insurance Premiums on Shipping Transporting Goods
Between Great Britain and the West Indies*

	Total Inward and Outward Tonnage	Value of Ship and Outfit (£000)	Amount of Premium (£000)
1789	278,981	3,347.8	150.7
1790	267,323	3,207.9	144.4
1791	278,267	3,339.2	150.3
1792	274,044	3,288.5	148.0
1793	287,081	3,445.0	482.3
1794	354,281	4,251.4	595.2
1795	283,682	3,404.2	476.6
1796	314,509	3,774.1	528.4
1797	337,218	4,046.6	566.5
1798	381,418	4,577.0	640.8
1799	454,500	5,454.0	763.6
1800	424,068	5,088.8	712.4

Sources and Notes: For shipping tonnage, see David Macpherson, *Annals of Commerce, Manufactures, Fisheries and Navigation*, 4 Volumes, vol. 4 (London: Nichols, 1805), pp. 199, 215, 230, 261, 289, 333, 369, 400, 439, 467, 492, 535. The value of ship and outfit is computed at the cost of £12 per ton, derived from Davis, *The Rise of the English Shipping Industry*, p. 378, and Craig, "Capital Formation in Shipping," pp. 142–144. For the premium rates applied, 4.5 percent for 1789–92 and 14% for 1793–1800, see Table 7.2.

insurance in the trade with Great Britain and Ireland was usually purchased in London, even for colonial-owned ships."[108] The problem with the latter point is the extent to which the practice of purchasing all insurance for the trade on this route in London continued after independence in 1783. These are matters to take into account as the overall assessment of the contribution of the Atlantic slave economy to the size of the insurance market is conducted. The final part of the information needed for that exercise – insurance on shipping transporting goods between Great Britain and the West Indies, and between Great Britain and the United States – is presented in Table 7.6 and Table 7.7.

The last decade of the eighteenth century may be taken as the basis for some tentative generalization on the assessment. Taking together the figures in Tables 7.3, 7.5, 7.6, and 7.7, the annual average premiums in the 1790s for the British slave trade come to £412,200, for the West India trade, £2,110,000, and £1,313,300 for United States trade. If we apply the

[108]   *Ibid.*, p. 131.

Table 7.7. *Insurance Premiums on Shipping Transporting Goods Between Great Britain and the United States*

	British Shipping		U.S. Shipping	
	Value of Ship and Outfit (£000)	Amount of Premium (£000)	Value of Ship and Outfit (£000)	Amount of Premium (£000)
1789	1,361.4	61.3	760.4	34.2
1790	1,383.3	62.2	1,016.1	45.7
1791	1,301.2	58.6	1,416.7	63.8
1792	1,116.0	50.2	1,481.4	66.7
1793	452.4	63.3	1,586.9	222.2
1794	155.7	21.8	1,435.4	201.0
1795	59.5	8.3	2,049.9	287.0
1796	41.8	5.9	2,552.1	357.3
1797	84.9	11.9	2,014.4	282.0
1798	170.2	23.8	1,770.6	247.9
1799	288.8	40.4	1,846.9	258.6
1800	379.5	53.1	2,839.0	397.5

Sources and Notes: See Table 7.6.

assumption by Shepherd and Walton mentioned earlier – deduct one-half of the premiums on exports and on shipping carrying exports – the United States premiums come down to £1,117,200. What proportion of this amount went to underwriters in England is difficult to determine. The premiums for the slave trade and the West Indies trade together come to £2,522,000 per annum, on average, in the 1790s. This is 63 percent of the whole marine insurance market in Great Britain, put at about £4 million earlier in this chapter. In the light of the growing dominance of United States shipping in the trade with Great Britain during the period, as Table 7.7 shows, less than one-half of the United States insured risks may have been covered in Great Britain. Adding that amount may not, therefore, raise the total very much above 70 percent of the entire market.[109] Again, let it be said that all of these estimates should best be treated as representing an order of magnitude rather than specific figures. Given the necessary qualifications and caution stated earlier, the generalization that the estimates presented can reasonably support is that premiums on British trans-Atlantic commerce (including the slave trade), the re-export trade in slave-produced

[109] The estimates of marine insurance earnings by Elise S. Brezis are incomplete and are, therefore, not comparable. See Brezis, "Foreign capital flows."

American products, and on the trans-Atlantic commerce of other European powers constituted the bulk of the marine insurance market in England in the eighteenth century. This was the more so, because the East India Company that dominated the other major long distance trade of the period carried its own risks.[110]

Apart from this quantitative contribution to the extent of the marine insurance market, which facilitated the development of marine insurance as a specialized business, the peculiarly difficult problems of providing insurance cover for trans-Atlantic commerce, especially the trans-Atlantic slave trade, must have stretched the imagination of the practitioners, forcing them to devise ways and means of building efficiency into the business. One of the underwriters made the point unambiguously. Writing to his brother resident on the West African Gold Coast (now part of Ghana) he explained:

> I am an underwriter myself, and can from experience testify that the premium of Insurance on Guinea Risks is dearly earned; and also know that the risk of ivory home from Jamaica and the West Indies is not such a trifle as you Gentlemen on the Coast imagine. In times of the greatest tranquility the premium from the Coast was oftener 5 [guineas] than 4 [guineas] pct. and the Winter Premium home from Jamaica is oftener 10 Gs. than 8 Gs and 5 Gs. from the [other] Islands. You grudge that of 8 Gs. pct. on Marshall. Such a risk now would be 20 to 25 Gs. and from the Coast 7 to 8, 9 or 10 Gs. or in short whatever we can get it done for. Your supposing no risk of American privateers, clearly shows you know nothing of matters in these parts of the world.[111]

One way the underwriters dealt with the difficult problems of providing cover for trans-Atlantic commerce was to spread each coverage among many underwriters in and outside London, sometimes even beyond England into Scotland. A few examples will suffice. In May 1791, £12,000 was insured on the *Trelawney*, Captain King, Commander,

> at and from Bristol to the Coast of Africa during her stay and trade there, and at and from thence to her discharging Port in America, on Ship and Goods. Free from loss by trading in Boats. The assurers freed from any loss or damage that may happen from the Insurrection of Negroes, in case the same shall not exceed Ten Pounds percent, to be computed on the net amount of ship, outset and cargo. Negroes valued at £30 per head.[112]

---

[110]   Wright and Fayle, *A History of Lloyds*, pp. 188–189.

[111]   PRO, T.70/1534, J. Mill to his brother, David Mill, Camberwell, London, 20 August, 1776. At this time David Mill was Governor at Cape Coast Castle, Gold Coast (now part of Ghana).

[112]   C.107/6 Ship *Trelawney*, King, Master, May 1791. Rogers, Blake & Co. were the insurance Brokers. The list shows the underwriters and the amount underwritten by each. It is interesting to note that the largest single amount was underwritten by James Rogers, one of the owners of the venture. See also Carrington, *The British West Indies*, p. 64, for the spread of coverage on three vessels in the West Indian trade in 1778 and 1779.

The risk was spread among the underwriters as follows:

£400	Robert Hunter	£100	James Williams
300	H. K. Hunter	200	Thomas Cave
400	T. G. Vaughan	200	Robert Claxton
300	James Fowler	200	William Seyer
200	Edward Rogers	150	John Camplin
100	E. W. Viner	150	Samuel Munckley
200	Joseph Bonbonous	150	George Gibbs
200	John Gordon Jur.	150	James Richards
200	John McCullom	100	Henry Cooke
100	Francis Harris	200	Rd. Blake
400	Patrick Fitzhenry	200	John Purnell
100	Philip Crocker	200	John Marsh
300	Thomas Deane	2,000	James Rogers
300	James Lockier	600	Richard Fydell
400	William Gorden	600	James Laroche
500	Thomas Morton	400	John Fydell
200	Thomas Cole	300	Wm. Studley
400	Richard Blake	300	C. Jones
400	John Purnell	200	J. Rogers
200	Thomas Hobbs		

£12,000 at £6 percent: £720: =: =.
Policy   :   =: 14: =.
                                £720: 14: =d

This cover was provided by altogether 36 underwriters. Many of these may have been resident in Bristol. But it is quite likely that some of them were operating outside Bristol. For the spatial spread of the cover for Guinea risks (slave trade risks), the insurance of the *Lapwing* at the beginning of the nineteenth century provides a very good example. The vessel belonged to Charles Anderson, a Guinea merchant in Bristol. It was sent out to the Guinea Coast in 1801, for which an insurance of £26,500 was effected. This was spread as follows:[113]

---

[113]   T.70/1582. Petition of Charles Anderson, African merchant in Bristol (13 March, 1806) to the Lords of His Majesty's Treasury. This vessel was captured by a Spanish privateer on December 11, 1801, with 330 Gold Coast slaves on board, including 4,480 lbs of ivory, 215 oz of gold dust, and various articles of unsold outward cargo. Charles Anderson explained that the seizure was made subsequent to the cessation of hostilities. He therefore implored the government to help him obtain compensation from the Spanish government for this unlawful seizure. Charles Anderson computed the value of the ship and cargo, and interest for 4 years and 4 months on this, together with some other expenses, to be £57,511:15s.:6d. On the right hand side of the account, Anderson stated, "In consequence of so large a property being held,

Insurance effected in London	£10,000
Insurance effected in Liverpool	8,500
Insurance effected in Bristol	6,500
Insurance effected in Edinburgh	1,500

This shows that the cover for a Guinea risk was provided by the major commercial cities in Great Britain, not minding from where the venture commenced. The dominance of London is also clear. The same geographical spread is discernible in the covers provided the ventures of the Davenport slave-trading groups. The insurance brokers with whom they dealt included Messrs. French & Hobson, London; Joseph Denison, London; Geo. Warren Watts & Co., Liverpool; Messrs. Gregson, Case & Co., Liverpool; Messrs. Geo. Bowdon & Co., Liverpool; Thos. Hodgson (junior), Liverpool.[114]

On the whole London had the largest share of the business, and this was centered mainly among underwriters in Lloyd's. The physical representation of this can still be seen in Lloyd's today. In the Corporation's Library in London is displayed a policy dated September 3, 1794, issued to Fermin de Tastet & Co., on the ship *Guipuzcoa*, P. La Croix Du Fresne, Master, from Liverpool to the Coast of Africa, during her stay and trade there, and at and from thence to the island of Cuba, £10,000 at 20 guineas percent and policy £1: 4/-, being £2101: 4/-.[115]

More significantly, in 1804 Lloyd's presented a silver tea service to Captain Robert Hall, of the Liverpool Guineaman, *Fame*, for beating off a 24-gun French corvette in 1804, while sailing from the Guinea Coast to Demarara. This silver tea service is said to have been "recently acquired" by Lloyd's Corporation.[116] The secretary to the African Company, John Shoolbred, was one of the 79 insurance brokers and underwriters who met in 1771 and agreed to contribute £100 each for the construction of a new

---

and Mr. Anderson's difficulties increasing, he was compell'd thro' necessity to settle with the underwriters in the following way; for the amount of which he humbly conceives the Spanish government are not entitled to a reduction of his claim." This is then followed by the insurance account quoted above. See also T.70/1583, for Anderson's Memorial to Lord Hawkesbury, His Majesty's Principal Secretary of State for Foreign Affairs, on the same subject.

[114] Davenport Papers, University of Keele Library.
[115] Lloyd's Corporation Library, London. This vessel is shown in the Customs Books as belonging to Spanish nationals. See BT. 64/286. The letter of William Eden (English Ambassador to Spain at this time) to the Marquis of Carmarthen, dated Aranjuez, June 10, 1788, shows that Mr. De Tastet was the agent of a Spanish Company known as the Philippine Company. He resided in London where he fitted the company's ships to the Guinea Coast to purchase slaves that were shipped to South America and the West Indies. British Library, Add. MSS. 38,416 fols. 114–117.
[116] Wright & Fayle, *A History of Lloyd's*, p. 212; the plate opposite p. 212 of this book contains the *Fame* Tea Service at Lloyd's, made up of 3 beautiful pieces.

home for the New Lloyd's at the Royal Exchange.[117] What is more, one of the two acknowledged leaders of Lloyd's in the late eighteenth and early nineteenth centuries, Sir Francis Baring, was a member of the Company of Merchants Trading to Africa. All this is testimony to the role of trans-Atlantic commerce in the development of Lloyd's and marine insurance in England.

7.3 CONCLUSION

The historical developments narrated and analyzed in this chapter may now be pulled together. It is clear from the preliminary survey of the literature that by the late nineteenth century shipping, banking, marine insurance, and other commercial services had become major contributors to employment and income in England as the growth rate of manufacturing output and employment slowed under fierce competition from newly industrialized nations, such as Germany. In particular, the high income levels of London and the home counties came to depend very much on these services, which helped to sustain in these regions a level of consumption above the national average. What is more, the large export surplus generated by the export of these services contributed immensely to finance the import of much needed food and raw materials and fund the growth of British foreign investment that was a key element in the British economy in the twentieth century. Earlier in the period 1650–1850, the development of the English merchant marine and the evolution of financial institutions provided in part the necessary conditions for the development of industrial production, leading to the Industrial Revolution. The latter subject has been particularly emphasized in the chapter, consistent with the central focus of the study.

Given such important contributions by these services, it is rather surprising that the circumstances of their historical development have not been an important part of studies focused on the origins of the Industrial Revolution in particular, and the development of the English economy in the very long run in general. This chapter has attempted to shed some further light on the origins of the Industrial Revolution by focusing on the little explored question of the main factors behind the development of financial institutions in England between 1650 and 1850, following a similar treatment of the merchant marine in Chapter 6.

The evidence marshaled in the chapter shows that banking houses, discount houses, and the stock exchange evolved in response to the growth of the market for credit. The provincial credit market that provided business for these credit institutions was dominated in the eighteenth century by bills of exchange originating from overseas trade. Similar bills also dominated

---

[117]   Martin, *The History of Lloyd's*, p. 148.

the discount market in London. The credit market in London, however, received an additional boost from two sources – the bonds of joint-stock overseas trading companies doing business outside Europe and government securities. As public borrowing was financed almost entirely by the bourgeoisie (largely the merchants) in London and its environs, the contribution of government securities was limited virtually to the London credit market. As large as wartime government borrowing was, it would appear that, on the average, annual dealings in mercantile instruments (bills of exchange and company bonds) by the credit institutions in London were greater than their dealings in government securities during the period. The bulk of the bills of exchange that circulated in the provincial trading and manufacturing centers and in London, as well as the company bonds, originated directly and indirectly from the trans-Atlantic slave trade and the trade centered on slave-produced American products. Profits accumulated from trans-Atlantic commerce also went a long way in funding the establishment of the credit institutions, as the well-known activities of the London merchants demonstrate in this regard.

Similarly, the qualitative and quantitative evidence assembled in the chapter shows clearly that marine insurance in England developed in the eighteenth century largely on the basis of the market for marine insurance provided by the Atlantic slave economy. Not only was trans-Atlantic commerce the main engine of growth for British seaborne trade during the period, but also the peculiar risks of transporting slaves and goods across the Atlantic, exacerbated by the struggles among the European powers to gain control of the trade, compelled regular procurement of insurance cover in contrast to trade with nearby Europe. Rough estimates of the size of the entire market and annual premiums generated by trans-Atlantic commerce indicate that premiums from the slave trade, trade with the Americas, the re-export trade in American products, and from the cover provided for the American trade of other European powers could not have constituted less than two-thirds of the total premiums earned by marine underwriters in Great Britain in the late eighteenth century.

It can thus be concluded on the basis of the evidence that the Atlantic slave economy was a critical factor in the evolution of financial institutions in England in the decades preceding and during the Industrial Revolution. To the extent that those institutions played a significant role in the development of industrial production during the period, this should be considered some additional measure of the contribution of trans-Atlantic commerce to the origin of the Industrial Revolution.

8

African-Produced Raw Materials and Industrial Production in England

AS IS WELL KNOWN, THE PRODUCTION of woollen cloth overwhelmingly dominated industrial production in England for several centuries. It was stated in Chapter 2 that raw wool export was to medieval England what crude oil export has been to Saudi Arabia in the modern world. The woollen industry thus developed initially as an import substitution industry on the basis of a domestically produced raw material. For as long as industrial production in England remained dominated by one product – woollen cloth – imported raw material was marginal to the growth and development of manufacturing in the country. Hence, English overseas trade in the early decades of the modern era was not seriously concerned with the supply of raw materials for industrial production in England. Manufactures for domestic consumption and tropical and Oriental products for re-export and domestic use dominated imports into England for many decades. This was to change gradually following the establishment of a wide range of import substitution industries in the late seventeenth and early eighteenth centuries, as mentioned in Chapter 2.

The growing importance of imported raw materials for the development of industrial production in England is reflected by the over time change in the structure of England's imports between 1699 and 1846:[1]

	1699–1701	1784–86	1804–06	1844–46
	%	%	%	%
Raw Materials	34.7	43.6	50.1	62.3
Foodstuffs	33.6	42.2	43.1	33.4
Manufactures	31.7	14.2	6.8	4.3
	100	100	100	100

[1] Davis, "English Foreign Trade, 1700–1774," p. 109; Davis, *The Industrial Revolution*, pp. 110–123.

As these figures show, raw materials and foodstuffs were already about one-third of total imports, respectively, at the beginning of the eighteenth century, the remaining one-third being made up of manufactures. Practically speaking, some of the products included among the foodstuffs, such as sugar and tobacco, should be treated as raw materials since they were further processed in England and contributed to value added in manufacturing, as will be shown later. When this is done the share of raw materials at the beginning of the eighteenth century increases significantly. Even with sugar and tobacco treated simply as foodstuffs the share of raw materials in total imports increased from about one-third in 1699–1701 to about two-thirds in 1844–46, while that of manufactures declined from about one-third to less than 5 percent in the same period. These figures indicate the progress of import substitution industrialization in England during the period and the role played by imported raw materials and foodstuffs in the process.

The main thrust of the analysis and discussion in this chapter is directed at the contribution of African-produced raw materials to the overall supply of raw materials for the industrialization process in England from the eighteenth to the mid-nineteenth century. It is argued that while the absolute shares are important considerations, the assessment must go beyond quantitative magnitudes and consider as well strategic values of individual raw materials in the industrialization process. For purposes of the main focus of the chapter, African-produced raw material is defined as production by African peoples and their descendants in the Americas and by Africans on the African continent.

8.1 IMPORTED RAW MATERIALS AND INDUSTRIAL PRODUCTION

The importance of imported raw materials in England's industrialization process may be assessed in the first instance in purely quantitative terms. Using the estimates by Crafts, under his assumption of gross industrial output being equal to 1.52 times value-added, it is possible to compute roughly the total value of raw materials employed yearly in industrial production in Britain from 1700 to 1851:[2]

	Gross Industrial Output	Value-Added	Raw Materials
1700	£15.6 million	£10.3 million	£5.3 million
1760	23.6	15.5	8.1
1780	39.9	26.3	13.6
1801	82.5	54.3	28.2
1831	178.0	117.1	60.9
1851	272.8	179.5	93.3

[2] Crafts, *British Economic Growth*, Table 6.7, p. 132.

These figures may be compared with the three-year average value of raw material imports into Britain in the period 1784–1856, compiled from the customs records by Ralph Davis:[3]

	Raw Material Imported (£000)	Raw Material Re-exported (£000)	Retained Raw Material (£000)
1784–86	9,917	810	9,107
1794–96	15,655	1,494	14,161
1804–06	27,809	2,129	25,680
1814–16	37,016	5,937	31,079
1824–26	36,130	5,333	30,797
1834–36	47,659	5,373	42,286
1844–46	51,033	5,893	45,140
1854–56	89,432	13,378	76,054

The years do not match exactly. However, as an approximate comparison, the average of the figures for 1794–96 and 1804–06 may be taken for 1801, 1824–26 and 1834–36 for 1831, and 1844–46 and 1854–56 for 1851. This gives £19,920,500 for 1801, £36,541,500 for 1831, and £60,597,000 for 1851. By these figures, retained imported raw materials constituted 70.6 percent of the total value of raw materials employed in industrial production in Britain in 1801, 60 percent in 1831, and 64.9 percent in 1851. Thus, in purely quantitative terms overseas trade was already the main source of raw materials for British industries in 1794–1856.

Clearly a more dynamic way of viewing the importance of imported raw materials in the Industrial Revolution is by examining the individual industrial sectors. As was seen in Chapter 2, developments in certain industrial sectors were critical to the rise of the factory and mechanized system of industrial production, which characterized the Industrial Revolution. Examining the individual sectors captures the strategic importance of raw material supply for the leading industries in the leading regions. Again, using the estimates by Crafts and his assumption, mentioned earlier in this chapter, we can compute the gross value of output and the value of raw materials employed for cotton, iron, linen, silk, and woollen industries in the years 1770, 1801, and 1831:[4]

---

[3] Davis, *The Industrial Revolution*, pp. 102–125.
[4] Crafts, *British Economic Growth*, Table 2.3, p. 22. The assumption is that gross value of output is equal to 1.52 times value-added.

	1770 (£000)	1801 (£000)	1831 (£000)
Cotton:			
Value Added	600	9,200	25,300
Gross Output	912	13,984	38,456
Raw Materials	312	4,784	13,156
Iron:			
Value Added	1,500	4,000	7,600
Gross Output	2,280	6,080	11,552
Raw Materials	780	2,080	3,952
Linen:			
Value Added	1,900	2,600	5,000
Gross Output	2,888	3,952	7,600
Raw Materials	988	1,352	2,600
Silk:			
Value Added	1,000	2,000	5,800
Gross Output	1,520	3,040	8,816
Raw Materials	520	1,040	3,016
Woollen:			
Value Added	7,000	10,100	15,900
Gross Output	10,640	15,352	24,168
Raw Materials	3,640	5,252	8,268

Cotton, linen, silk, and iron-using industries were the main import substitution industries of the seventeenth and eighteenth centuries. Their growth and development triggered the technological and organizational changes of the Industrial Revolution. Taken together their contribution to value added in manufacturing in Britain increased from 24.4 percent in 1770 to 50.5 percent in 1831.[5] Of course, of all the new industries it was the revolutionary changes in the cotton industry that were at the center of the Industrial Revolution. The cotton industry led in technological and organizational change as well as in quantitative contribution to value-added in manufactring, increasing from 2.9 percent in 1770 to 29.2 percent in 1831. The value of raw materials employed in the industry increased from £312,000 in 1770 to £13,156,000 in 1831. For linen, silk, and the iron-using industries, the total value of raw materials employed grew from

[5] Computed from Crafts, *British Economic Growth*, Table 2.3, p. 22. Table 2.3 of Crafts includes 13 Sectors: Cotton, Wool, Linen, Silk, Building, Iron, Copper, Beer, Leather, Soap, Candles, Coal, and Paper. Value added in manufacturing is taken to include all but building, which gives £20.5 million for 1770, £44.8 million for 1801, and £86.5 million for 1831.

£2,288,000 in 1770 to £9,568,000 in 1831. Taking the four industries together, the value of raw materials employed in production increased from £2,600,000 in 1770 to £22,724,000 in 1831.

For the supply of the raw materials of these four industries, overseas trade was critically important. The raw materials for the cotton, linen and silk industries were supplied entirely by overseas trade. As was shown in Chapter 2, domestic production of pig iron in England in 1720 was only 48.5 percent of the total supply (17,350 tons out of a total supply of 35,800 tons). And while the figures presented above show that the value of raw materials employed in the iron industry was £780,000 in 1770, the customs records show a total iron import of £476,000 in 1770,[6] being 61 percent of the total. Thus, of the £2.6 million total value of raw materials employed in the main growth industries in Britain in 1770, imported raw materials amounted to £2,296,000, being 88.3 percent of the total. With the revolutionary developments in the production of bar iron shown in Chapter 2, domestic production increasingly replaced iron imports, which averaged only £336,000 in 1824–26 and £314,000 in 1834–36,[7] while raw materials employed in the iron-using industries amounted to £3,952,000 in 1831. For the other three growth industries, however, overseas trade continued to be the only source of raw materials to the end of the period of study.

As for woollen textile, the old industry, while its absolute weight in the manufacturing sector remained considerable over the period, its share of value added in manufacturing decreased from 34.1 percent in 1770 to 18.4 percent in 1831. Consistent with the slow growth of output, the industry's raw material needs expanded in no way comparable to those of the cotton industry. Even so overseas trade increasingly became a major source of supply. The three-year average values of retained imported raw wool for 1794–96 and for 1804–06, taken together, average out to £1,186,500, and those for 1824–26 and 1834–36 come to £5,324,500 on average.[8] The value of raw materials employed in the industry, computed on the basis of Crafts's assumption, was £5,252,000 in 1801, and £8,268,000 in 1831. This would mean that the value of retained imported raw wool was about one-fifth of the value of raw materials employed in 1801 and about six-tenths in 1831.[9]

---

[6] Schumpeter, *English Overseas Trade Statistics*, Table XV, p. 51.

[7] Davis, *The Industrial Revolution*, pp. 119, 121.

[8] *Ibid.*, pp. 102–121

[9] Ralph Davis cites K. G. Ponting to the effect that in the 1850's "raw material accounted for nearly two-thirds of the direct cost of woollen cloth, and some three-quarters of that of worsted," and that in 1858 Baines estimated that nearly half of the value of the wool used by British industry was imported: Davis, *The Industrial Revolution*, p. 50; K. G. Ponting, *Baines Account of the Woollen Manufacture of England* (1970), p. 78, cited by Davis. The share of raw material in the gross value of output cited by Davis is much greater than the ratio employed by Crafts, which in turn is greater than the one employed by Deane, "British Woolen Industry," p. 215.

Thus from the late eighteenth century through the first half of the nineteenth overseas trade was a critical source of raw materials both for the new growth industries and for the old industry, woollen textile. The only major growth industry with a contrary trend during the period was the iron industry, which was largely dependent on imported raw material for much of the eighteenth century, but became increasingly dependent on domestic supply from the late eighteenth century.

For the textile industries the discussion so far has been limited to the basic raw materials – raw cotton, raw wool, raw silk, and flax. In addition to these, however, other raw materials were employed in the finishing processes. Among these were gums, indigo, and other dyestuffs. They were all imported. Their total value each year was a small fraction of the value of raw materials employed annually in manufacturing. The three-year average value of retained import of dyestuffs (including indigo) in 1794–96 was £1,325,000; in 1804–06, £1,936,000; in 1824–26, £3,127,000; and in 1834–36, £1,878,000.[10] The figures for 1794–96 and 1804–06 average out to £1,630,500, and those for 1824–26 and 1834–36 average out to £2,502,500. The average for the late eighteenth and early nineteenth centuries comes to 5.8 percent of the total value of the raw materials employed in industrial production in 1801, while the average for 1824–36 is only 4.1 percent of those employed in 1831. Their share of the value of raw materials employed in the textile industries was greater, of course – 13.1 percent in 1801 and 9.3 percent in 1831. Because gums and dyestuffs were crucial in the finishing processes of the textile industries, the importance of these raw materials in the Industrial Revolution was much greater than their quantitative weight would indicate. This is reflected in the kind of effort made to secure the supply of some of them, as will be shown later in the chapter.

One important way of measuring the importance of imported raw materials in the Industrial Revolution is to compute what the cost of industrial production would have been had Britain been forced to devote domestic resources to the production of all the raw materials employed and all the food consumed by workers and capitalists. It can be argued a priori that production cost would have been so high that only a few people would have been able to afford the products. Besides, some of the raw materials would have been totally unavailable, and much of the textile industries, including the entire cotton textile industry and some of the finishing processes in the other textile industries, would have been non-existent. Such an experiment is, however, beyond the scope of this chapter. Nevertheless, it is pertinent to show that falling prices of imported raw materials contributed significantly to the reduction of production costs in the leading industry of the Industrial Revolution, the cotton industry. The average

[10] Davis, *The Industrial Revolution*, pp. 102–125.

Liverpool price of raw cotton fell from 16.21 pence per pound (weight) in 1796–1800 to 5.85 pence per pound in 1826–30 and to 5.19 pence per pound in 1846–50.[11] This represents a fall in price of 63.9 percent between 1796–1800 and 1826–30, the average price for the latter period being 36.1 percent of that of the former. Under Crafts's assumption of raw materials being equal to about 34.2 percent of the gross value of industrial output, this fall in the Liverpool price of raw cotton would translate to approximately 22 percent reduction in the production cost of cotton textile. When compared with the sectoral price relatives computed by Crafts, the indication is that falling prices of raw cotton contributed almost one-half of the reduction in cotton textile prices between 1801 and 1831.[12]

The evidence thus shows that imported raw materials were crucially important in the Industrial Revolution, both in quantitative and qualitative terms. It may be recalled at this point the regional view of the Industrial Revolution argued in Chapter 2. Placed in that regional context, the importance of imported raw materials looms even larger, since the industrial revolution in Lancashire, a function of the cotton textile industry, derived from imported raw materials. In the sections that follow an attempt is made to assess the contribution of African-produced raw materials to the overall supply of imported raw materials just examined.

8.2 REGIONAL DISTRIBUTION OF BRITISH RAW MATERIAL IMPORTS

For purposes of isolating the historical forces behind the developing international division of labor in the late eighteenth and early nineteenth centuries, the overseas sources of raw materials for British industries at the time may be grouped as follows: Africa and the Americas, northern Europe, northwest Europe, southern Europe, the Near East, and Asia. The contribution of these regional groups to British raw material imports in the years 1784–1856 is shown in Table 8.1. The imports from Northern Europe came largely from the Baltic region. The repeal of the Navigation Acts in 1849 made it possible for Baltic products to be legally re-exported to Britain from Hamburg and Amsterdam. This may partly explain the great increase in imports from northwest Europe in 1854–56. If sugar and tobacco are treated as foodstuffs instead of raw materials, as Ralph Davis does, the Baltic region would feature as the largest source of raw material imports up to 1804–06, as can be seen from Table 8.1. In 1784–86, 32.8 percent of the value of all raw materials imported into Britain came from northern

---

[11]   *The South in the Building of the Nation,* Vol. V, p. 434.
[12]   The price index for cotton textile constructed by Crafts (1770 = 100) shows the movement of prices from 123.6 in 1801 to 66.2 in 1831. See Crafts, *British Economics Growth,* Table 2.5, p. 25.

Table 8.1. *Regional Distribution of British Raw Material Imports, 1784–1856*
(in £000 sterling)

	Africa and The Americas	Northern Europe	Northwest Europe	Southern Europe	Near East	Asia	Total
1784–86	2,890	3,254	1,086	1,563	265	859	9,917
1794–96	4,159	5,406	1,634	2,009	362	2,085	15,655
1804–06	9,261	10,668	2,027	3,089	175	2,589	27,809
1814–16	15,116	8,044	4,030	4,884	287	4,655	37,016
1824–26	12,480	6,604	7,237	3,195	1,069	5,545	36,130
1834–36	20,371	7,091	8,779	2,838	1,188	7,392	47,659
1844–46	22,839	7,360	7,357	2,485	1,508	9,284	51,033
1854–56	38,702	7,581	15,860	4,033	3,846	19,410	89,432

Source and Notes: Compiled from Davis, *Industrial Revolution*, pp. 110–125. Davis makes it clear that all the raw cotton imported was produced outside Europe (*Ibid.*, p. 39). But his import table shows some small quantities imported from places in Europe. These quantities have been treated as re-exports from Europe imported originally from the Americas. They have, therefore, been subtracted from the European regional totals and added to the totals for Africa and the Americas. Imports from Ireland are entered under northwest Europe. The figures for Asia include imports from China and Australia. The Australian figures were extremely small until 1834–36 when they began to increase very rapidly. The Near East figures include imports from North Africa, especially Egypt. As mentioned earlier in the chapter, Davis treats sugar and tobacco as food and not as raw material.

Europe. This rose to 38.4 percent in 1804–06. Thereafter the share declined continuously, dropping to 8.8 percent in 1854–56.

The over-time decline in the share of the Baltic region and the rest of Northern Europe was due in part to a rapid growth of supplies from other regions, especially the regional grouping of Africa and the Americas. If tobacco and sugar are treated as raw materials, as they should, the latter regional grouping would clearly feature as the largest source of raw material imports into Britain from the seventeenth century through the eighteenth.[13] When sugar and tobacco are excluded, the group still remains a major source, second to the Baltic in the eighteenth century. In 1784–86 it contributed 29.1 percent of the value of all raw material imports (excluding sugar and tobacco), as compared to 32.8 percent by northern Europe mentioned earlier. By 1814–16, with 40.8 percent of the value of all raw materials imported into Britain, Africa and the Americas had become the main source of imported raw materials even without tobacco and sugar.

[13] See Davis, "English Foreign Trade, 1660–1700," pp. 96–97, 119.

This position was maintained to the end of the period of study, the contribution rising to 43.3 percent in 1854–56, having reached 44.8 percent earlier in 1844–46.

The contribution of southern Europe to the import of raw materials into Britain ranged from a low of 4.5 percent in 1854–56 to a high of 15.8 percent in 1784–86, while that of northwest Europe ranged from a low of 7.3 percent in 1804–06 to a high of 20.0 percent in 1824–26. From 1784 to 1816 the share of southern Europe was greater than that of northwest Europe, but from 1824 to 1856 the latter contributed much more than the former. The other sources of supply were rather marginal for much of the period. The contribution of the Near East, which came largely from Egypt, was less than 3 percent for most of the period covered in Table 8.1, the highest being 4.3 percent in 1854–56. From 1784 to 1846 imports from Asia were between 8.7 percent and 18.2 percent of the total. A rapid expansion thereafter, both from Asia proper and from Australia, raised the contribution to 21.7 percent in 1854–56.

While the absolute magnitude of the contributions by the regional groupings already shown is important, the dynamic role of imports from the different regions can be gauged by examining the makeup of the imports,[14] as this will show which industries were being served by imports from different regions. From the Baltic region, represented by imports from northern Europe in Table 8.1, the main products by value were naval stores, made up of timber and hemp and jute. These products taken together constituted about one-third of the total value of raw material imports from northern Europe during the period covered by Table 8.1. Northern Europe (Baltic) produced virtually the entire supply of hemp and jute imported into Britain up to the 1830s. Supply from Asia grew rapidly from the 1840s, reaching 30.1 percent of total imports in 1854–56. The imports of hemp and jute from northwest Europe were clearly re-exports of Baltic products, which explains the sudden expansion in 1854–56 to 35.7 percent of the total imports from less than 1 percent in previous years. Timber imports were also largely from northern Europe (Baltic) up to the early nineteenth century. From the second decade of the nineteenth century Canada became a major supplier, and by the 1820s had become the main supplier. Again, timber imports from northwest Europe, which grew from 11 percent of the total in 1834–36 to 16.2 percent in 1854–56, were re-exports of Baltic products. Some quantities came from the Caribbean throughout the period. Thus, the import of raw materials that supported the shipbuilding industry in England came largely from the Baltic.

The other imported raw materials produced largely in the Baltic at some points during the period were flax (for the linen industry), iron, and tallow

---

[14]   For the composition of raw material imports from the regions specified in Table 8.1, see the source for the table.

(for the candle industry). From the 1780s to the 1840s, between 67 percent and 88 percent of the total value of flax imported into Britain came from northern Europe (Baltic). The lower figure is in fact misleading, because it is due to a growing re-export of Baltic flax from northwest Europe, with a sudden jump in 1854–56, which made the latter region the largest source of flax import into Britain in the latter period. Since the linen industry depended entirely on imported flax, the industry can be said to have been supported largely by the Baltic. Tallow imports for the whole period covered in Table 8.1 came almost entirely from northern Europe, except in 1854–56 when 13.6 percent of the total came from Latin America. Again, the sudden increase of imports from northwest Europe in 1854–56 represents the re-export of Baltic produce. The candle industry seems to have been largely dependent on imported raw materials, for which reason northern Europe can be seen as the main source of support. As was shown earlier, more than one-half of the iron employed in the iron-using industries in the first three-quarters of the eighteenth century was imported. This import came almost entirely from northern Europe (Baltic). Hence, for much of the eighteenth century iron imports from the Baltic region played a very important role in the development of the iron-using industries. However, that role diminished considerably from the last quarter of the century as those industries became increasingly dependent on domestic raw materials as earlier stated. Thus, raw materials imported from northern Europe (mainly the Baltic) were vital for the shipbuilding industry, without being the main support, which came from domestic timber; but they provided virtually the entire support for the linen and candle industries, and the main support for the iron-using industries in the first three-quarters of the eighteenth century.

Examining the composition of imports from the regions specified in Table 8.1 helps to make clear that a substantial proportion of raw material imports from Northwest Europe from 1830–56, especially in 1854–56, were re-exports of Baltic products. If the value of the more obvious products, such as flax, hemp and jute, timber, and tallow, is deducted from the 1854–56 total for northwest Europe and added to that for northern Europe, the total for the latter increases to £14,563,000, being 16.3 percent of the total annual average value of raw material imports for the period, while that of the former decreases to £8,948,000, or 10.0 percent of the total annual average. It can thus be said that, in general, northwest Europe was not a major source of raw material production for the industrialization process in England. However, the region did become briefly the main source of raw wool and raw silk imports (1814–16 for silk, and 1824–36 for wool) before Asia became the main source of imports for raw silk and Australia for raw wool. Apart from raw silk, Asia also became the largest source of indigo imports from the 1790s, supplying virtually the entire imports from 1804–56. Significant imports of raw cotton from Asia began in 1814–16, being 3.6 percent of the total annual average value of imports during the period. This rose to between 6 percent and 7 percent in 1824–46, and 11 percent in 1854–56. Thus, raw materials from Asia provided a major support for the silk industry from 1814 to 1856, a significant support for the cotton industry from 1824 to 1856, and a major support for the dyeing processes in all the textile industries from 1794 to 1856.

Both in quantitative and strategic terms, southern Europe and the Near East were marginal in the supply of raw materials for the industrialization process in England. The one important raw material produced and exported to England by southern Europe was raw wool. Up to 1816, southern Europe was the main source of imported raw wool. However, by this time the woollen industry was still largely dependent on domestic raw wool and the annual average value of imports remained small. For example, the annual average value of imports from southern Europe in the years 1794–1806 was £1,132,500 (virtually the total imports from all parts), being about one-fifth of the estimated total value of raw materials employed in the industry in 1801, as stated earlier in this chapter. By the time imported raw wool became the main source of supply for the industry from the 1820s and 1830s, southern Europe had lost ground, first to northwest Europe and later to Australia. From 1824 to 1856 the proportion of total imports supplied by southern Europe decreased from 15.7 to 2.2 percent. The other raw materials supplied in some significant quantities by southern Europe include raw silk (increasingly taken over by Asia in the nineteenth century), dyestuffs, and vegetable oil. The Near East supplied some significant quantities of raw cotton, raw silk, and dyestuffs from 1824 to 1856. But the supply was a very small fraction of the total value of each of these products imported into Britain, except in 1854–56, when the share was 20.2 percent for raw silk, 17.8 percent for dyestuffs, and 3.6 percent for raw cotton (the highest share for cotton was in 1824–26, 7.6 percent).

Finally, the composition of raw material imports from Africa and the Americas may now be examined. Excluding sugar and tobacco, raw material imports from the region were dominated by five products for much of the period 1784–1856 – cotton, dyestuffs, indigo, timber, and hides and skins. The value of these five products (shown in Table 8.2) taken together made up between 70 percent and 90 percent of the total value of imports from the regional grouping between 1784 and 1856. As Table 8.2 shows, imports from the group were dominated overwhelmingly by raw cotton imports, whose value was more than half of the total value of imports from the group for most of the years from 1784 to 1856. The region completely dominated the import of raw cotton into Britain from the eighteenth to the mid-nineteenth century. Between 1784 and 1856 the proportion of the total value of raw cotton annually imported into Britain that came from Africa and the Americas ranged from 85 to 98 percent. The region lost ground to Asia in the supply of indigo in the nineteenth century but continued to be a major supplier of other dyestuffs, supplying yearly between 30 and 48

Table 8.2. *Three-year Annual Average Value of the Principal Raw Material Imports from Africa and the Americas (in £000)*

	Cotton	Dyestuffs	Indigo	Timber	Hides and Skins	Vegetable Oil
1784–86	1,617 (56.0)	329	130	221	258	6
1794–96	2,474 (59.5)	196	126	274	395	1
1804–06	5,538 (59.8)	823	48	825	841	6
1814–16	8,276 (54.7)	728	30	1,942	2,532	29
1824–26	6,410 (51.4)	835	117	2,586	885	93
1834–36	13,063 (64.1)	762	52	2,905	1,173	311
1844–46	10,374 (45.4)	1,070	24	4,546	2,118	535
1854–56	19,160 (49.5)	913	97	5,167	1,794	1791

Sources and Notes: Compiled from Davis, *Industrial Revolution*, pp. 110–125. The figures in parentheses show the percentage of all imports from Africa and the Americas. All imports of raw cotton from regions in Europe are regarded as re-export of cotton from the Americas and are deducted from those regions and added to imports from Africa and the Americas.

percent of the total value of the latter products imported into Britain from 1804 to 1856. Hides and skins and timber are other products whose imports into Britain were dominated by the region. For hides and skins, the proportion of the total imports contributed by the region in the period 1784–1856 was about two-thirds and above half of the time, and between 44 and 59 percent for the other half. Between 1814 and 1856 the region supplied from one-half to three-quarters of the total value of timber imported into Britain. From the 1830s the region also became the main source of supply for vegetable oil (mainly palm oil), supplying 43.7 percent of the total in 1834–36; 48.4 percent in 1844–46; and 54.9 percent in 1854–56. In the 1840s and 1850s, two products dominated by the region became important imports in Britain. Guano, seabird dung used as fertilizers in agriculture, was imported in 1844–46 to the tune of £1,214,000 per annum and in 1854–56, £2,580,000 yearly, virtually all of which came from Africa and the Americas. Similarly, the import of copper and copper ore, which expanded rapidly from the 1840s, was dominated by the region – 94.1 percent of the total (£337,000) in 1844–46 and 73.4 percent of the total (£1,986,000) in 1854–56.

From the foregoing figures, it is clear that the cotton textile industry in England was almost entirely dependent on raw material produced in Africa and the Americas in the eighteenth through the mid-nineteenth century. The shipbuilding and other industries employing timber also became largely dependent on timber produced in Africa and the Americas in the second quarter of the nineteenth century. Similarly, soap making, leather, and copper industries – even fertilizers for agriculture – were heavily supported by raw materials produced in Africa and the Americas from the 1830s. In fact, two other industries in England had been dependent totally on raw materials produced in the Americas from the seventeenth century to the nineteenth – sugar and tobacco. The first sugar refinery in England had been established in London in about 1544, but the expansion of sugar refining began in the second half of the seventeenth century. In 1695 there were about 30 sugar refining houses in England, and in 1753 there were roughly 120 in England and Scotland. Of the latter number, 80 were in London and 20 in Bristol. In 1753 about 1,800 people were employed directly in the industry.[15] In 1812, Patrick Colquhoun estimated value-added in the sugar refining industry to be £250,000, and £300,000 in the tobacco manufacturing industry.[16] Taking sugar and tobacco as industrial raw materials the regional grouping, Africa and the Americas, was always the leading producer of raw materials for British industries from the seventeenth to the mid-nineteenth century, quantitatively speaking. The Baltic region came second. Interestingly, as shown in Chapter 4, the imports from the Baltic were paid for largely with the re-export of produce from British America. Thus, quantitatively speaking, the industrialization process in England from the seventeenth to the mid-nineteenth century depended heavily on raw material imports from Africa and the Americas. However, what clearly is even more important is the dynamic role of the raw materials from the region. As earlier mentioned in this discussion, it is hard to overstate the dynamic role of the cotton industry in the Industrial Revolution. The fact that the industry's raw materials came almost entirely from Africa and the Americas is a critical measure of the dynamic role of raw materials from the region in the Industrial Revolution.

8.3 ENGLAND'S INDUSTRIAL RAW MATERIALS PRODUCED BY AFRICANS IN THE AMERICAS

Of the total value of raw materials imported into Great Britain from Africa and the Americas in the period 1784–1856, as shown in Table 8.1, an annual average of between 92.2 and 96.6 percent came from the Americas.[17] The imports came largely from British America – the British Caribbean and mainland British America – especially in the eighteenth century. Some imports from non-British America came as re-exports from

---

[15] Sheridan, *Sugar and Slavery*, pp. 29–30.
[16] Colquhoun, *Treatise*, p. 94.
[17] For the value of imports from Africa, see Davis, *Industrial Revolution*, pp. 110–125.

Table 8.3. *Total Value (in £000 sterling) and Percentage Distribution of Raw Material Imports into Great Britain from the North American Colonies, 1768–1772*

	Total Value	Northern Colonies	New England	Middle Colonies	Upper South	Lower South	Florida, Bahama, Bermuda
1768	223,103	0.4	4.4	13.5	30.7	50.8	0.3
1769	278,579	4.1	3.5	11.2	20.9	55.4	4.9
1770	309,270	4.8	3.9	14.4	17.9	54.1	4.9
1771	353,868	6.4	3.2	10.5	17.2	52.4	10.2
1772	408,681	3.0	3.3	6.4	14.1	65.0	8.2

Sources and Notes: Computed from Shepherd and Walton, *Shipping, Maritime Trade*, Table 2, pp. 211–216. To be consistent with the data of Ralph Davis employed in the chapter, tobacco is not included. The commodities included are deerskins, iron, naval stores, wood products, beeswax, cotton, indigo, and hemp.

other European countries. With the political independence of the Latin American countries early in the nineeenth century, direct import from those countries expanded, particularly imports from Brazil. This section focuses on the proportion of the imports from the Americas produced by African peoples and their descendants in the Americas, both British and non-British.

A combination of the commodity composition and the regional distribution of the imports from the Americas helps to show the African contribution. As shown in Chapter 4, the main commodities produced for export in British America in the eighteenth century were sugar, tobacco, rice, and fish. If sugar and tobacco are not treated as raw materials, the absolute value of raw material imports into Great Britain from British America in the eighteenth century is reduced considerably. Table 8.3 shows the imports from the mainland colonies in 1768–72. The commodities included are indigo, deerskins, iron, naval stores, beeswax, cotton, wood products, and hemp. Indigo, produced mainly in the lower South, was by far the largest in value of the commodities included. As the table shows, the proportion of the imports produced in the lower South ranged between 50.8 and 65 percent during the period. The upper South and lower South together produced between 69.6 and 81.5 percent of the total. Very few raw material imports came from New England and the northern colonies. To be conservative, indigo from the lower South may be taken as the only raw material produced by Africans in mainland British America at this time.

As for the British Caribbean during the same period, the main raw material import, apart from sugar, was raw cotton. As Table 8.4 shows, raw

Table 8.4. *Quantity of Raw Cotton (in 1000 lbs) Imported into England, 1768–1783*

	Total Import from all Parts	Import from British Caribbean
1768	4,276	3,409
1769	4,527	3,354
1770	3,679	2,945
1771	2,512	2,264
1772	5,290	5,290
1773	3,000	3,000
1774	5,668	5,668
1775	6,688	6,688
1776	6,283	6,283
1777	7,156	7,156
1778	7,172	7,172
1779	4,528	4,528
1780	7,169	7,169
1781	4,958	4,958
1782	11,531	11,531
1783	9,503	9,503

Sources and Notes: Import from all parts taken from Schumpeter, *English Overseas Trade Statistics*, p. 62; imports from the British Caribbean are taken from Selwyn H. H. Carrington, *The British West Indies During the American Revolution* (Dordrecht, Holland: Foris Publications, 1988), pp. 31 and 59. The Caribbean figures are stated as imports into Great Britain. It is somewhat curious that the two sets of figures are exactly the same from 1772 to 1783.

cotton imports into England in the eighteenth century came almost entirely from the British Caribbean. The Caribbean cotton was produced by African peoples. For the whole period 1768–72, the value of indigo imported from the lower South and of cotton from the Caribbean taken together was 56.3 percent of the total value of raw material imports from the mainland colonies (Table 8.3) plus Caribbean cotton.[18] Thus, in the third quarter of

[18]   The value of cotton was computed by applying the prices for cotton from the lower South derived from the quantities and values in Shepherd and Walton, *Shipping, Maritime Trade*, p. 215, to the quantities imported from the Caribbean in Carrington, *British West Indies*, p. 31. The values are as follows: 1768, £175,574; 1769, £151,279; 1770, £126,629; 1771, £84,902; 1772, £211,071. The values of indigo from the lower South included in the total values in Table 8.3 are as follows: 1768, £78,113; 1769, £75,375; 1770, £103,285; 1771, £106,285; 1772, £196,118. Adding the value of Caribbean cotton to the values in Table 8.3 gives a total of

Table 8.5. *Regional Distribution of British Raw Material Imports from
the Americas, 1784–1856 (3-year average in £000)*

	United States	Canada	British Caribbean	Latin America	Total
1784–86	408	342	1,268	730	2,748
1794–96	679	479	1,563	1,281	4,002
1804–06	3,235	802	2,683	2,168	8,888
1814–16	3,108	2,173	2,609	6,620	14,510
1824–26	5,238	2,916	939	2,966	12,059
1834–36	12,346	3,204	647	3,128	19,325
1844–46	10,891	4,580	1,331	4,137	20,939
1854–56	20,844	5,188	1,303	8,347	35,682

Source and Note: Compiled from Davis, *Industrial Revolution*, pp. 110–125. The
Latin American figures include cotton imported from Europe treated as Latin
American produce re-exported from Europe, as already explained.

the eighteenth century Africans in British America produced at least 56
percent of the raw materials imported into Great Britain from the British
American colonies. Of course, when sugar and tobacco are added the proportion rises considerably. What is more important, however, in these formative years of England's cotton textile industry, the raw material for this
technological leader of the Industrial Revolution was produced almost
wholly by Africans in the Americas.

For the period 1784–1856, Table 8.5 shows the regional distribution of
British raw material imports from the Americas. As can be seen from the
table, in the last decades of the eighteenth century the British Caribbean
was the main source of the imports, contributing about two-fifths of the
total. The United States took over in the nineteenth century and by 1854–56
was supplying about 54 percent of the total. Imports from Canada and
Latin America that had remained very small in the eighteenth century also
expanded considerably in the nineteenth century. By examining the commodity composition and the regional origins of these imports it is possible
to estimate roughly the proportion produced by African peoples in the
Americas.

The imports from the United States were overwhelmingly dominated by
raw cotton. At the beginning of the nineteenth century, cotton contributed
about two-thirds of the U.S. total, and from 1814 to 1856 the contribution

£2,322,956 for the whole period, and adding the values of indigo from the lower
South and Caribbean cotton gives a total of £1,308,774 for the same period, being
56.3 percent of the former figure.

was between 84 and 92 percent. As shown in Chapter 4, cotton was produced in the southern slave states by African peoples. Other plantation crops in the U.S. supply produced in the southern states by Africans were dyestuffs. In the nineteenth century their amounts were very small as Asia took over much of the supply of dyestuffs, especially indigo which was mentioned earlier. The imports from the British Caribbean included in Table 8.5 were also dominated by raw cotton up to the second decade of the nineteenth century, contributing between about 70 and 80 percent of the British Caribbean total from 1784 to 1816. The British Caribbean had remained the main source of raw cotton imports in the eighteenth century. But in 1804–06 imports from the United States and from the British Caribbean were almost equal, £2,098,000 and £1,919,000, respectively.[19] Thereafter, imports from the British Caribbean declined fast as those from the U.S. grew rapidly. In fact, the sharp decline of the overall value of raw material imports from the British Caribbean observable in Table 8.5 was due to the movement of raw cotton production from the British Caribbean to the United States and, subsequently, to other tropical regions as well. Because of the overwhelming dominance of the population of African peoples in the British Caribbean during the period, the total raw material supply from the region may be taken as the product of African peoples.

For the other American regions in Table 8.5, Canada and Latin America, imports from Canada, which expanded rapidly from 1814–16, were made up largely of timber, with some contribution from hides and skins. It is assumed that Africans made no contribution to the production of the Canadian products. As for Latin America, initially raw cotton was the main product, especially when the amount re-exported from European countries, mentioned earlier in the chapter, is included. The share of cotton in the imports from Latin America, including Latin American cotton re-expoted to Great Britain from Europe, is as follows:

1784–86	98.9%
1794–96	78.5%
1804–06	70.0%
1814–16	56.0%
1824–26	49.1%
1834–36	45.5%
1844–46	13.5%
1854–56	8.4%

The share of cotton decreased as the import of other raw materials from Latin America grew. First was hides and skins, whose value was more than that of cotton for the first time in 1844–46. Then in 1854–56, the import

[19] Davis, *Industrial Revolution*, p. 115.

of guano from Latin America expanded suddenly to £2,503,000, being by far the largest single product in these years. Copper and copper ore, imported in very small amounts previously, also exceeded cotton by value in 1854–56. It is assumed, to a certain degree unrealistically, that African peoples in Latin America did not contribute to the production of hides and skins, guano, and copper and copper ore. As for Latin American cotton, this came largely from Brazil, and to a lesser extent from non-British Caribbean. According to José Arruda, the total value of Brazilian cotton re-exported from Lisbon in the period 1796–1811 amounted to £11,788,338.[20] This cotton re-export must have gone largely to England. Figures for direct import from the Americas in 1835 and 1836 show that in the respective years 284.5 million lbs and 289.6 million lbs were imported from the United States, 25.0 million lbs and 27.5 million lbs from Brazil, 0.3 million lbs and 0.4 million lbs from non-British Caribbean, and 1.5 million lbs and 1.3 million lbs from the British Caribbean.[21] Based on the evidence presented in Chapter 4, cotton imports from Latin America, coming from Brazil as shown, may be taken as the product of African peoples in Latin America. Other raw material imports from Latin America that can be taken as the product of African peoples amounted to very small sums during the period – the dyestuffs.

On the basis of the foregoing evidence, the contribution of African peoples to the production of the raw materials included in Table 8.5 is limited to cotton and dyestuffs, which are wholly assigned to them. The estimate arising from this is presented in Table 8.6. As can be seen from the table, African peoples and their descendants produced the bulk of the raw materials imported into Great Britain from the Americas between 1784 and 1856. The share of total imports from the Americas produced by African peoples during the period ranged from 58 percent to 77 percent. For half of the time it was 70 percent and above. It is important to note, as mentioned earlier, that sugar and tobacco are not included in these computations. Again, what is more important than the absolute share is the specific raw material produced by African peoples in the Americas from the point of view of the dynamics of the industrialization process in England.

[20] José Jobson de Andrade Arruda, "Colonies as mercantile investments: The Luso-Brazilian empire, 1500–1808," in James D. Tracy (ed.), *The Political Economy of Merchant Empires: State Power and World Trade, 1350–1750* (Cambridge: Cambridge University Press, 1991), Table 10.8, p. 416. I have added Arruda's export value (value of the product as exported from Brazil) and profit achieved when re-exported (re-export value minus export value) to obtain 41,966,485 milreis, converted to pound sterling at 3.560 milreis to the pound. The conversion rate is derived from Arruda, *O Brasil no Comércio Colonial*, p. 625 and fn. 58, p. 625.

[21] Porter, *Progress of the Nation*, Vol. 2, p. 128. See also Platt, *Latin America and British Trade*, p. 257, where annual average Brazilian cotton supply for European and North American manufacturing is stated to be 25.3 million lbs in 1836–40, 18.9 million lbs in 1841–45, and 23.8 million lbs in 1846–50.

Table 8.6. *British Raw Material Imports Produced by Africans in the Americas (3-year average in £000)*

	United States	British Caribbean	Latin America	Total	% of Total Imports from the Americas
1784–86	119	1,268	723	2,110	76.8
1794–96	228	1,563	1,027	2,823	70.5
1804–06	2,274	2,683	1,560	6,517	73.3
1814–16	2,622	2,609	3,882	9,113	62.8
1824–26	4,807	939	1,769	7,515	62.3
1834–36	11,457	647	1,821	13,925	72.1
1844–46	9,839	1,331	982	12,152	58.0
1854–56	18,553	1,303	1,149	21,005	58.9

Sources and Notes: See the sources cited for the preceding discussion in the text and for Table 8.5. As stated in the text in several places, sugar and tobacco are not included. The raw materials included are cotton, indigo, and other dyestuffs, except for the British Caribbean where all the raw materials but sugar and tobacco are included. Again, the Latin American figures include cotton imported from Europe treated as Latin American produce re-exported from Europe. Total imports from the Americas, stated in the last column, refers to all raw materials imported from the Americas (Table 8.5).

The major raw materials imported from the Americas, to which African peoples made little contribution during the period, were timber, hides and skins, and copper. These served important industries – shipbuilding, leather, and copper – but they were not leading industries in the industrialization process. The really dynamic industry in the process, as already stated, was the cotton industry. The share of raw material imports from the Americas produced by African peoples was made up almost entirely of raw cotton. Of the total value of raw material imports from the Americas produced by African peoples shown in Table 8.6, the percentage for raw cotton is as follows:

1784–86	76.5%
1794–96	84.1%
1804–06	84.9%
1814–16	90.8%
1824–26	85.3%
1834–36	93.2%
1844–46	85.4%
1854–56	91.1%

It follows from the evidence presented thus far in the chapter that the cotton textile industry in England depended for its raw material almost totally on African peoples in the Americas from its formative years in the eighteenth century to its maturity in the middle of the nineteenth.

8.4 EXPORT PRODUCTION OF RAW MATERIALS IN AFRICA IN THE SLAVE TRADE ERA C.1650–C.1850

It is well known that what attracted West European entrepreneurs to Western Africa initially was the produce of Africa's natural resources, especially gold. Ivory, dyestuffs (redwood and cam-wood in particular), pepper, and copper were additional attractions after gold. These products overwhelmingly dominated the export trade of Western Africa by way of the Atlantic in the second half of the fifteenth century.[22] Portuguese trade in West-Central Africa was centered on copper in the early sixteenth century.[23] In the formative years of the slave trade in the fifteenth and early sixteenth centuries, the main focus was the islands off the coast of Western Africa, where the sugar economy of the Atlantic first took roots, especially Sao Tomé, as mentioned in Chapter 4. However, the development of the sociopolitical and economic infrastructure for the expanding production of these and other commodities in Western Africa was seriously challenged and then arrested by the competing use of Africans to produce similar commodities in the Americas.[24] The first known English man to enter the trade, John Hawkins, did so by transporting to the Americas Africans he had captured on the coast. Later English traders bought gold and other African products as a supplement to the slave trade. As the transportation of Africans to the Americas increased and the production of commodities for Atlantic commerce in the Americas expanded, export production of commodities in Western Africa declined. Reliable statistics concerning the trade in African products in the early decades are hard to come by. Nevertheless, estimates by researchers show that by the first decades of the seventeenth century, the value in Europe of products imported from Western Africa was 36 percent and the value of Africans imported and sold in the Americas was 64 percent of the combined total; the proportions changed further to 32 and 68 percent, respectively, in 1680–90.[25] In the second half of the eighteenth

---

[22] John W. Blake, *West Africa, Quest for God and Gold, 1454–1578: A Survey of the first Century of White Enterprise in West Africa, With Particular Reference to the Achievement of the Portuguese and their Rivalries with Other European Powers* (London: Curzon Press, 1977; first edition, 1937).

[23] Anne Hilton, *The Kingdom of Kongo* (Oxford: Clarendon, 1985), pp. 51–55.

[24] Inikori, *The Chaining of a Continent*, pp. 44–52.

[25] Ernst van den Boogaart, "The Trade Between Western Africa and the Atlantic World, 1600–90: Estimates of Trends in Composition and Value," *Journal of African History*, 33 (1992), p. 378.

century, up to the time of British abolition in 1807, the proportions changed radically – the produce trade was now only about 9 percent of the total value of Western Africa's exports via the Atlantic, as stated in Chapter 5. This section examines, in the first instance, the restrictive impact of the Atlantic slave trade on the export production of raw materials in Western Africa and proceeds to show in some detail the strategic importance of the quantitatively limited raw materials exported to England from the region during the period.

In 1730 officers of the Dutch West India Company resident on the Gold Coast offered a rather comprehensive insight for the reasons why export production of commodities in Western Africa had stagnated:

In the first place it should be observed that that part of Africa which as of old is known as the "Gold Coast" because of the great quantity of gold which was at one time purchased there by the Company as well as by Dutch private ships, has now virtually changed into a pure Slave Coast; the great quantity of guns and powder which the Europeans have from time to time brought there has given cause to terrible wars among the Kings, Princes and Caboceers of those lands, who made their prisoners of war slaves; these slaves were immediately bought up by the Europeans at steadily increasing prices, which in its turn animated again and again those people to renew their hostilities, and their hope for big and easy profits made them forget all labour, using all sorts of pretexts to attack each other, or reviving old disputes. Consequently, there is now very little trade among the coast Negros except in slaves . . .[26]

This testimony, though conceptually innocent in economic and political logic, provides, together with other similar evidence, some empirical basis upon which that logic can be reasonably constructed. The factual statement dealt directly with one side of the equation on the production of commodities in Western Africa for the European markets – that concerning African political and economic entrepreneurs – and only indirectly with the other side – that relating to the determinant of the changing demand of the European traders in Western Africa. For the historian seeking to understand the causal sequence of events, the statement provides the empirical evidence for the politico-economic consequences of relative price change, although understandably the Dutch trader who observed the events (with no training in political economy) did not fully comprehend the economic and political logic in every respect. The evidence in the statement is clear that growing demand for captives to be shipped to the Americas as slaves by the European traders led to rising prices offered for them by the latter traders. Increasing demand and rising prices for captives, while demand and prices for African products stagnated, altered relative prices over time in favor of captives and against African produce. African economic and political entrepeneurs, made up initially in several instances of bandits and

[26] Cited by Inikori, "Africa in World History," pp. 106–107.

warlords, responded to the demand pressure by expanding the taking of captives. In other words, the nature of the relative price change favored this type of people and their activities and discouraged the evolution of capitalists investing capital in the peaceful production of raw materials and other products for export and for internal sale. Unlike the peaceful production of raw materials and other products, the taking of captives and the socio-political conflicts it engendered called for the instruments of violence – firearms. The European traders flooded Western Africa with firearms to meet the demand and the rising prices for captives provided the wherewithal. Easy access to firearms by bandits and warlords through the Atlantic slave trade, in turn, provoked more social and political conflict that generated more captives, creating a vicious circle. The evolution of socio-political institutions, social classes, and the distribution of political power among the classes were all strongly adapted during the period to the violent production of captives rather than the peaceful production of raw materials and other products.[27]

What is not mentioned explicitly in the quoted statement is the reason why the European traders shifted their growing demand from African products to African captives. The reason appears simple on the surface – it was because expanded demand for African workers in the Americas made the trade in captives more profitable to the European traders than the earlier trade in African produce. But the issue ceases to look simple and becomes quite complex when one seeks to explain why European economic and political entrepreneurs considered it more economically advantageous to them to transport Africans to the Americas to produce commodities for Atlantic commerce there, instead of encouraging the employment of the same Africans to produce similar commodities for Atlantic commerce in Africa. As we have seen, the main commodities produced in the Americas by Africans were gold, sugar, tobacco, rice, cotton, indigo, and coffee. These products could all be produced in different parts of Africa and at some points, during the period of study, some attempts were made by the European traders to get them produced. As to be expected, the efforts centered around the production of raw cotton, sugar, and gold, although other products, such as indigo, were frequently mentioned. Information coming from these efforts may help to produce a comprehensive explanation, which includes factors on the European side of the equation.

It would seem the Dutch were the first to contemplate a serious program of plantation agriculture in mainland Western Africa. In June 1702, the director of the Dutch West India Company on the Gold Coast, W. De la Palma, wrote to the board of directors of the company in Holland:

In view of the general poor condition of the Trade [the slave trade], we have taken into consideration the planting of cotton and sugar cane. Concerning the cotton,

[27] For more detail see Inikori, *The Chaining of a Continent*, pp. 25–39.

with which our predecessor has started more than a year ago, we may say that it is reasonably successful, but, in order to continue this work with vigour we would need a very great number of slaves, which is absolutely lacking on this Coast [the Gold Coast]. We have therefore resolved to send the yacht Anna Jacoba to Fida [Whydah] ... to buy there 250 Ps slaves, so as to make use of them for the cultivation of cotton, on the banks of the river of Chama, as well as at Boutry and Axem. We may convince the natives, by our example, that the planting of cotton is profitable, and induce them to grow those plants to their own profit, because this work can only be profitable when done on a large scale; we will require an instrument like the mills which are in use on Curaçao and other places, in order to purify the cotton.[28]

In October 1703, De la Palma informed the board of directors that he had shipped a sample of cotton, which they had collected: "During the last heavy rains we made a start with the planting of cotton on the hills to the North and Northeast of the St. Jago Hill, in the same way as it is being done at Boutry, Chama and Saccondee."[29] A year later he wrote to the board:

Y.Hs. may have perceived from our successive letters, that we regard the slave trade as the unique cornerstone of Y. Hs' interest, and Y.Hs. may now be persuaded that apart from that (trade) nothing could be found which may render the Noble Company happy. But since the years 1700–01 the price of the slaves has gone up by more than a half.[30]

De la Palma died in 1705 and late that year Pieter Nuyts became the provisional director general of the Dutch company in Western Africa, resident in Elmina.[31] Over a year later, the company's officers on the coast wrote to the board of directors:

Concerning the sugar, cotton and indigo plantations, that we would be quite able to continue that work, if only the required tools, slaves and other materials were sent, and especially if we were to be allowed to buy as many slaves as President Nuyts proposed in his letter of 24th April 1706.[32]

---

[28]   W. De la Palma to Assembly of Ten, Elmina, 26 June, 1702, in A. Van Dantzig, *The Dutch and the Guinea Coast, 1674–1742: A Collection of Documents from the General State Archive at the Hague* (Accra: Ghana Academy of Arts and Sciences, 1978), p. 84. De la Palma adds that "We are of the opinion that it might be profitable to take an experiment in planting sugar (cane) on the riverbanks near Chama, Boutry and Axem."

[29]   W. De la Palma to Assembly of Ten, Elmina, 10 October, 1703, in Dantzig, *The Dutch and the Guinea Coast*, p. 92.

[30]   Same to Same, 31 August, 1704, *Ibid.*, p. 104.

[31]   *Ibid.*, p. 119. De la Palma wrote a "Circular Letter" to the Chamber of Amsterdam on June 22, 1705, and on November 13, 1705, Pieter Nuyts wrote to the Assembly of Ten, the board of directors in Holland, as the Povisional Director-General. Another document, dated November 13, 1705 (*Ibid.*, pp. 122–123), mentions the company's property in possession of De la Palma at the time of his death.

[32]   Officers on the coast to the Assembly of Ten, 14 March, 1707, *Ibid.*, p. 130.

The evidence suggests that the Dutch continued to believe that it was commercially possible to produce cotton, sugar, indigo, and other products on a large scale in Western Africa, but never seriously committed themselves to doing it. The Dutch West India Company and its officers on the coast remained committed to the slave trade. Nor does the evidence show that the Dutch made any serious effort to encourage governments and peoples in Western Africa to develop the production of these commodities. Having conceived the idea probably as early as the late seventeenth century, very little was actually done for several decades, and in 1720 the company was still repeating earlier instructions to the officers on the coast:

In previous letters we recommended Y. H. several times to promote with force the cultivation of certain crops on the Coast and to send us the fruits of it. We make use of this opportunity to tell Y. H. . . . that we are informed that the bush on the sides of the Gallows Mountain was burnt, and that during the rainy season some cotton-seeds had fallen on that land, which had grown into little cotton-trees. We think therefore that cotton could easily be cultivated on that hill, and as it is covered by the guns of the forts, and the Negroes do not show much attachment to that land, we recommend to Y. H. to plant cotton-seeds in a regular fashion on mentioned mountain, and to continue its cultivation there with force . . .[33]

The idea of plantation agriculture and gold mining in Western Africa was also conceived by the English traders about the same period. In July 1708, about 10 years after Parliament declared the African trade legally open to private British traders, the director of the English Royal African Company, Sir Dalby Thomas, who was resident on the Gold Coast, recommended to the company that a settlement be established at Fetue on the Gold Coast for the purpose of developing plantations. Such a settlement, he argued,

Will be an inlet to all manner of Plantations and I would not question but in a few years after it's known that your people live here in plenty and you have a mind to go on with plantations, that you will have people enough make application [to] you to come and settle here upon such terms as you may think convenient to permit them to settle on and I should not question but that in a few years after a plenty is here, that you will have plantations all along the River side to as near the seaside as it is reasonable for them to be.[34]

The proposed settlement was to have a large house with a wall around it to accommodate the company's workers and its cattle, with a place for all traders to lodge. The company would need 100 men and 70 women

---

[33]   Secret papers of the Assembly of Ten, 20 November, 1720, *Ibid.*, p. 216. During the same period the Dutch Company also made unsuccessful attempts to mine gold on the Gold Coast.

[34]   PRO, C.113/273 Part 1, Copy of a letter sent to the Royal African Company about Forts and Factories, 30 July, 1708 (folio 27).

slaves to start with, all of whom should be bought in Gambia and Whydah, and to work under the supervision of the Africans already employed by the company. They were to be "armed, trained, exercised and do duty by turns . . . a party of them should attend with their arms on all traders going and coming and they should look after your cattle, plant corn, sugar canes, indigo & cotton which we now have here of & ginger, when we can get any fit for planting . . . "[35] In September 1708, Sir Dalby Thomas wrote that if he had enough slaves from Gambia and Sherbrow to employ on the Gold Coast he could develop as much plantations for cotton, sugar, indigo, ginger, and provisions as the company thought fit.[36] He wrote again in October 1709, informing the company that "The Natives have had Indigo growing among them time out of mind and make as good Dye with it as any that comes from the East Indies."[37] Then in his letter of November 29, 1709, reference is made to an intended bill in Parliament to prohibit the cultivation of indigo, sugar, and cotton on the Gold Coast. Expressing disappointment, Dalby Thomas wrote:

Cotton grows common there and the natives make good profit by cotton cloths, ye profit of which if we had, could be no damage to ye nation. Indigo is a common weed in that country and is used by the natives. If indigo were cheaper it would be the more advantage to the woollen manufactory.[38]

It is unclear what became of the bill. What is clear is that nothing tangible came out of the proposal by Dalby Thomas. The company had to make a fresh start in the 1720s, apparently in reaction to the declining profitability of its slave trade. As the company instructed its officers on the coast:

We have already in diverse letters acquainted you with our thoughts concerning the carrying on of our Trade, and as the negroe branch of it grows every day less and less profitable it is from the article of the home returns we see our chief advantage must arise, and therefore we direct you very strictly to turn your thoughts principally that way; to which end, and for our better satisfaction, we desire you in Council consider as soon as possible and draw out a state of what trade may be expected annually on the Gold Coast, as well in regard to slaves for the plantations, as Gold, Teeth, Cotton and all other commoditys proper for home trade . . . One species of goods proper for the home Returns you cannever want sufficient quantitys of, vizt the cotton, which is very good, cheap and in great plenty all about you . . .[39]

---

[35]   *Ibid.*
[36]   PRO, T70/5, Folio 48, Sir Dalby Thomas to the Royal African Company, Cape Coast Castle, 24 September, 1708.
[37]   *Ibid.*, folio 63, Same to Same, 22 October, 1709.
[38]   *Ibid.*, folio 64, Same to Same, 29 November, 1709.
[39]   PRO, C. 113/272, Part 2, folio 235, Court of Assistants to James Phipps and others, African House, London, 13 March, 1721/22. The date should read 1722.

Earlier in 1721, the company's board of directors in London (the Court of Assistants) had written to its officers on the coast,

You are to use your utmost endeavours to improve the planting of cotton, Indigo and pepper, & to encourage the natives in doing the same . . . we desire and direct you in order to the greater improvement thereof, to take such an additional number of slaves into the company's service, as you shall judge necessary for that purpose.[40]

In September 1721, the company tried to revive the project proposed by Sir Dalby Thomas early in the century. The officers on the coast were asked to consider

Whether that large country of Fetue, being the entire property of the company, is not capable of being improved very advantageously to the Company's service, either by planting it in general yourselves for the Company's accounts with sugar canes, Indigo, cotton, corn or what else may produce Trade, or by apportioning out such & such divisions to any who will take it on their own accts and sell at rates fixt prices to the company the product thereof, which the company shall oblige themselves to take off from them . . .[41]

The reply of the company's officers on the coast to these instructions and directives from London points to some of the factors responsible for the failure of export production of commodities to develop in Western Africa during the era of the Atlantic slave trade. First, the officers dealt with some problems on the side of the European traders:

As to what your [honours] recommends in the 6th paragraph relating to the apportioning out divisions for the planting of sugar canes, Indigo, Cotton, Corn, etc., we only think there's a number of industrious husbandmen wanting to improve such manufactories, there being Extent of ground enough that we can secure your [Honours] the property of but we have found no encouragement from among the small numbers of white people that we are commonly furnished with under their small abilitys to believe their thoughts are turned to that sort of husbandry otherwise we should not be wanting in our assistance to promote such a cultivation . . .[42]

On the side of the African entrepreneurs, the officers noted that the "Free Natives" had no need for land being allotted to them, for each state official or community leader had access to as much land "as he cares for and has people to manure." However, they noted that, "their husbandry consists only in the planting of corn and other vegetables the former of which they make their advantage of by selling it to your [Honours'] and other shipping Trading to this coast as they have occasion." This is an indication

---

[40] PRO, C.113/272 Part 1, folio 77, Court of Assistants to Phipps and others, London, 27 February, 1720/21 (read, 1721).

[41] *Ibid.*, folio 127, Same to Same, London, 7 September, 1721.

[42] PRO. C. 113/274, Part 3, fols. 209–210, Officers on the coast to the Royal African Company, Cape Coast Castle, 2 July, 1722.

that market opportunity was a problem for African producers on the Gold Coast. The officers added that they had written to their subordinate officers in the company's trading posts in different parts of Western Africa asking them to promote the production of cotton and that to encourage African producers they had offered to pay them $2\frac{1}{2}$ pence per lb for uncleaned cotton (that is, cotton with the seeds in it).[43]

They concluded by expressing surprise that the company had built up high hopes that large quantities of cotton would be shipped home from its plantations on the coast:

the whole year's produce at all your settlements on the Gold Coast was it to have been collected would not amount to two thousand [pounds] weight the greatest produce of which will be at this place. We are improving of it the best we can and hope double the quantity may be gathered next year and with the assistance of hands we doubt not it may be improved in time to what quantity you please.[44]

To stress their problem of labor shortage, they added that the company's soldiers on the coast had no inclination for agricultural work, and "the inclemency of the air proving fatal to Europeans is the chief reason we suppose why improvements of that nature have not been hitherto managed to better purpose."[45]

The evidence shows a number of common elements in the early eighteenth-century Dutch and English efforts to develop export production of commodities in Western Africa. Both efforts were by companies whose main business in Western Africa, the Atlantic slave trade, had at the time become increasingly less profitable as a result of the fierce competition from private traders in England and Holland, as well as from the growing slave trade of France and other European countries and their American colonies. The private traders, particularly the English, were singlemindedly committed to the slave trade at this time and showed no interest in committing their time and resources to the development of commodity production for export in Western Africa. Together with the relative price situation, the resultant politico-military environment in Western Africa gave rise to political economies more favorable to the violent generation of captives than the peaceful production of commodities for export. It is significant that the proposal by the director of the English company, Sir Dalby Thomas, included a private army of African slaves to be "armed, trained, exercised," who would "attend with their arms on all traders going and coming." Both the unfavorable relative prices and the associated politico-miliary conditions may partly explain why both projects concentrated efforts on direct company production and very little on African peoples and their communities to develop the structures for export production of commodities. There is evidence that several of the commodities mentioned in both projects, espe-

[43]   *Ibid.*   [44]   *Ibid.*, folio 237.   [45]   *Ibid.*, folio 237.

cially cotton, were produced throughout the period for local use. But the scale and technique of production, and other cost factors appear to have made their prices relatively high. An officer of the Dutch company, who traveled overland from Whydah to Accra between December 1717 and February 1718, reported going through "a road of about half a mile, regularly planted with cotton-trees."[46] In April 1718, the same officer reported finding at Keta (on the Anlo coast just to the east of the Volta estuary),

a large number of children and men constantly busy spinning cotton on little sticks of about a foot length. I wanted to buy some, as they said that they collected this cotton in order to maintain their children. They were prepared to sell, but they asked no less than three strings of cowries for one ball of cotton which does not weigh more than about half a pound, which would mean paying about as much as at home [Holland]. When I proposed to buy a big quantity of about hundred pounds for 20 Angels, they just laughed at me . . . I am sure that if the Negroes did their best to make cotton-plantations, they could gain a lot from it; but these people think only in a day-to-day manner, and never think of tomorrow.[47]

The Dutch trader clearly misinterpreted the result of limited market opportunity for capitalistic investment as a cultural trait. But this and other similar evidence do suggest that inadequate development of commodity production in Western Africa was making it difficult for African products to compete with similar ones produced with African slave labor in the Americas. The evidence that the British Parliament thought it necessary to prohibit efforts by British traders to develop in Western Africa the production of commodities that could compete with those being produced in the British Caribbean at this time indicates both the growing political power of the West Indian interest in England as well as the recognition by the American planters that their superior competitiveness depended on the regular supply of cheap African slave labor, a supply which would be negatively affected by an extensive development of commercial agriculture in Western Africa. Such a development would offer market opportunities in Western Africa for the competing profitable employment of African labor, slave or free, in large-scale commodity production.

This point is made even clearer by the more detailed evidence on the reaction of the British government to similar efforts repeated in the early 1750s. In 1750, the Royal African Company went out of business as the British government reorganized the African trade and placed it under the control of a regulating company, the Company of Merchants Trading to

---

[46] Oral Report by Bookkeeper-General Ph. Eytzen about his return overland from Fida, in Dantzig, *The Dutch and the Guinea Coast*, p. 201.

[47] Diary kept by Ph. Eytzen on board of the barque *Utregt* and in the lodge at Fida, April–May 1718, in Dantzig, *The Dutch and the Guinea Coast*, p. 206. See also pp. 208–209, where it is said that cotton-yarn on the Whydah market was "exceptionally expensive."

Africa, with no legal authority to trade as a corporate body. British African trade was now entirely the business of private British traders, the company's responsibility being limited to coordination and management of the British forts or trading posts in Western Africa. The evidence shows that in 1752 or thereabout, some of the private British traders – including Melvil, Roberts, and Stockwell – informed the managing committee of the company in London that they were carrying out the production of cotton and indigo in Western Africa and needed the committee's approval. These traders also wrote two letters to the British Board of Trade, charged with the management of all matters relating to international trade and the British colonies. The company's committee gave its approval. But when all the documents reached the Board of Trade the members expressed their indignation that the company's committee "had signifyed their approbation in the most positive manner of Mr. Melvil's having introduced the culture of cotton & Indigo upon that Coast." The members of the company's committee, comprising Messrs. Touchit (Touchet), Poole, Briscoe, and Scott, were summoned to appear before the Board of Trade. They did so on Friday, February 14, 1752, and were told by the board in no uncertain terms:

That the introducing of Culture and Industry amongst the Negroes was contrary to the known establish'd Policy of this Trade [the African trade] – that there was no saying where this might stop and that it might extend to Tobacco, Sugar & every other Commodity which we now take from our Colonies – and thereby the Africans who now support themselves by war would become Planters & their slaves be employed in the Culture of these articles in Africa, which they are now employed in in America. That our Possessions in America were firmly secured to us, whereas those in Africa were more open to the Invasions of an Enemy, and besides that in Africa we were only tenants in the Soil which we held at the good will of the Natives.[48]

Mr. Touchet, himself a cotton textile manufacturer, informed the Board of Trade "that the Committee did consider the introducing the Culture of cotton in Africa might give some umbrage [offence] to the West Indies," but as for indigo, "there was none produced in any of the colonies except Carolina," and that "the encouragement lately given by the Parliament had not answered the end proposed, the Carolina Indigo being bad and but a small quantity produced," for which reason England had to import indigo from France and Spain.[49] The other member of the committee, Mr. Briscoe, explained that the ongoing project by Mr. Melvil and others "was only intended to teach the art of cultivating indigo & cotton to the negroes about the Forts." A third member of the committee, Mr. Poole, argued that if

[48]   PRO, C.O. 391/60, folios 66–71, Minutes of the Board of Trade relating to the African trade. At this time the Board of Trade was made up of the Earl of Halifax, Mr. Pitt, Lord Dupplin, Mr. Townshend, Mr. Grenville, Mr. Fane, and Mr. Oswald.
[49]   *Ibid.*

necessity called for it there was no reason why British policy on trade with Africa could not be altered: If indigo was not produced in British America and the production of cotton there should decrease, these commodities should be produced in Africa; the production of sugar in Africa would also help to distress French shipping, for "formerly the French sugars passed through our colonies by which means we were the carriers of all the produce of America but . . . now the French had their own shipping to export their produce."[50] Summing up the committee's understanding of the issue, Mr. Touchet noted that,

> the whole of the question rested upon the point whether our property and posses-sions in Africa were established & secured with respect to the natives, for if our possession was dependant upon the natives, and we were only tenants at will, it was clear that the introducing of culture and produce might prove of bad consequence.[51]

The Board of Trade thus concluded that since the effort to develop in Western Africa the production of such commodities as were produced in "our colonies" was contrary to what had hitherto been the policy of "this country," the "Board could not give countenance to it without having the sense of Parliament," and directed the committee to write to Mr. Melvil asking him to "suspend any further proceedings in this scheme until the sense of Parliament be known."[52]

Direct evidence on what Parliament decided is yet to be uncovered. However, indirect evidence indicates that Parliament ruled against the devel-opment in Western Africa of export production of commodities then pro-duced in British America for Atlantic commerce with African slave labor. The indirect evidence comes from a letter by the committee of the Company of Merchants Trading to Africa to the British Treasury in April, 1812. The Treasury had sought to know the views of the committee on closing some of the British trading posts on the Gold Coast following the British aboli-tion of the slave trade to British nationals. The committee argued in response that the Atlantic slave trade had negated the original intention of British traders to develop trade in African products, and with the abolition of the slave trade rapid progress was being made in that direction, imports of African products into England having reached half a million pounds ster-ling in value in 1810, exclusive of the value of gold which was being imported "in far greater quantities than during the slave trade."[53] The com-mittee added:

[50] *Ibid.* [51] *Ibid.* [52] *Ibid.*
[53] PRO, T. 70/73, pp. 137–150, The Committee of the Company of Merchants Trading to Africa to the Treasury, 9 April, 1812. As the Committee put it: "By the abolition of the slave trade the commerce of Africa was rendered so insignificant that it may have appeared scarcely worth the maintenance of the settlements on the coast, but it must be recollected that those settlements which are supported at so trifling an

It is a lementable but certain fact, that Africa has hitherto been sacrificed to our West India Colonies. Her commerce has been confined to a trade which seemed to preclude all advancement in civilization. Her cultivators have been sold to labor on lands not their own, while all endeavours to promote cultivation and improvement in agriculture have been discouraged by the Government of this country, lest her products should interfere with those of our more favoured colonies. With better views, and a more liberal Policy, we are now returned to our original object, and returned to it in possession of a large proportion of the forts long established on the coast, and with an opportunity singularly favourable of subjecting the whole of them to our dominion.[54]

Taking together all the preceding evidence it can now, in summary, be concluded that several factors combined to retard the development of commodity production for export in Western Africa during the Atlantic slave-trade era. By far the most important of these factors was the colonization of the Americas, the destruction of the indigenous populations and polities, and appropriation of the vast natural resources by the economic and political entrepreneurs of Western Europe. Faced with the choice, under these circumstances, of helping to develop in Western Africa the production of tropical and other commodities for Atlantic commerce or transporting African labor to the Americas to exploit the natural resources there for the same purpose, their secure possession of the resources of the Americas made the latter the preferred choice of the West European entrepreneurs. It should be stressed that this was purely a rational choice determined strictly by economic and political considerations. Being in complete possession of the Americas meant that the European entrepreneurs could ensure that the colonial state in the Americas would make rules and regulations that both enhanced and secured for them the private benefits of their entrepreneurial efforts. They could not trust the African states to do the same. In particular, they could not be sure the independent African states would prevent the nationals of competing European nations from reaping the benefits of their efforts, a consideration that was especially important for the mercantilist states of Western Europe at this time.

Conditions in Western Africa contributed to facilitate the process of forced migration of Africans to the Americas. As rising demand for captives by European traders altered relative prices for captives and African products in favor of the former, political fragmentation and the existence of weakly organized communities made it relatively easy, initially, for bandits, warlords, and stronger states to take captives at very little cost to

---

expence, were originally formed with no view to the slave trade, which was then neither in existence nor in contemplation" (p. 139). The evidence presented by the committee shows that the value of imports into England from Western Africa was £224,747 in 1807, the last year of the British slave trade. It increased to £374,306 in 1808, £383,926 in 1809, and £535,577 in 1810.

[54]   *Ibid.*, pp. 139–140.

themselves. The large quantity of firearms brought by the European traders helped to make the process of captive taking by small groups of persons much easier still.[55] Once the process had begun and European demand and prices for captives continued to grow exponentially, a self-reproducing vicious circle emerged, as stated earlier. At the same time, limited market opportunities for capitalistic investment in large-scale commercial agriculture by African entrepreneurs seriously weakened competing domestic demand for captives that could raise their price to a point where it was uneconomic to transport them to the Americas.[56] The socio-political conflicts engendered by the violent procurement of captives, the retarding impact on population growth, and the stagnation of the produce export trade all combined to put a lid on the growth of market opportunities for capitalistic investment in agriculture by African entrepreneurs, thereby ensuring a sustained flow of captives at prices that made their employment in the Americas profitable for the European entrepreneurs. And so, as the politico-military conditions occasioned by the slave trade interacted with the operation of the relative price merchanism to make the procurement of captives more privately rewarding for a few well-placed individuals in Africa, the availability of cheap African labor made the Americas by far the more competitive producers of tropical and mineral products for Atlantic commerce. European traders unable to compete in the Atlantic slave trade tried halfheartedly from time to time to alter the equation. But economic and political factors conspired to ensure that the odds were heavily stacked against them.[57]

[55] See Joseph E. Inikori, "The Import of Firearms into West Africa, 1750–1807: A Quantitative Analysis," *Journal of African History*, XVIII, 3 (1977), pp. 339–368; H. A. Gemery and J. S. Hogendorn, "Technological Change, Slavery, and the Slave Trade," in Clive Dewey and A. G. Hopkins (eds.), *The Imperial Impact: Studies in the Economic History of Africa and India* (London: Athlone Press, 1978), pp. 243–258.

[56] Joseph E. Inikori, "Export Versus Domestic Demand: The Determinants of Sex Ratios in the Transatlantic Slave Trade," *Research in Economic History*, Vol. 14 (1992), pp. 117–166.

[57] For additional information and analysis, see Joseph E. Inikori, "West Africa's Seaborne Trade, 1750–1850: Volume, Structure and Implications," in G. Liesegang, H. Pasch, and A. Jones (eds.), *Figuring African Trade* (Berlin: Dietrich Reimer Verlag, 1986), pp. 66–70; Inikori, *The Chaining of a Continent*, pp. 44–52. Gemery and Hogendorn have argued that West Africa had a "comparative disadvantage" in the production of sugar relative to the Americas, and, therefore, sugar could not have been produced in West Africa in the absence of the Atlantic slave trade. The error in this counterfactual argument is that the comparative analysis is conducted with the Americas retaining African slave labor, African labor that ought to be removed from the Americas and placed on West Africa's side of the equation for the counterfactual analysis to make sense. Thus, the analysis is not focused on what would have happened if the Americas did not have African slave labor. See H. A. Gemery and J. S. Hogendorn, "Comparative disadvantage: the case of sugar cultivation in

As will be shown later, things changed somewhat after the British government abolished the slave trade for its nationals, who then frantically struggled to find alternative employment for their mercantile capital. Even so, for as long as that trade remained very large under the control of traders from Europe and the Americas, it continued to limit the growth of other forms of trade in Western Africa. Thus, a nineteenth-century writer, who noted the phenomenal expansion of raw material import into Britain from Western Africa between 1808 and 1836, still observed the retarding impact of the trans-Atlantic slave trade:

In 1808 the whole quantity of palm oil imported [into Britain from Western Africa] did not exceed 200 tons; in 1836 it amounted to 13,850 tons. Twenty years ago African timber was unknown to us, and now our annual importations amount to 15,000 loads. This increase has taken place, too, under the most unfavourable circumstances. The whole country is disorganised, and except in the immediate vicinity of the towns, the land lies waste and uncultivated, the wretched natives living under constant dread of being carried off into slavery. . . . The legitimate trade of our vessels when on the African coast is continually impeded by the appearance of slave traders, on the arrival of which, the natives quit all other occupations and proceed on marauding expeditions, to seize the members of some neighbouring tribe, and sell them as slaves. Until a sufficient number of these poor creatures is collected to crowd the vessel of the slave trader, all other occupations are stopped, and it is not merely the loss of time and consequent expense thus occasioned that are to be deplored, but the great waste of life among the crews of the English traders while uselessly detained upon an unhealthy coast. Everywhere are to be seen the baleful effects of this traffic, producing desolation where nature has been prodigal of her gifts.[58]

Thus, quantitatively speaking, the production of raw materials for British industries by Africans during the slave trade era, c.1650–c.1850, was carried out mainly in the Americas rather than in Africa. From the point of view of commodity production for Atlantic commerce by Africans during

West Africa," *Journal of Interdisciplinary History*, Vol. IX, no. 3 (Winter, 1979), pp. 429–449. What should be stressed, however, is that commodity production in Western Africa in the absence of the Atlantic slave trade did not have to be limited to sugar, as can be seen from the evidence of British African trade in the years immediately following British abolition and the general growth of commodity production for Atlantic commerce in Western Africa from the mid-nineteenth century onward.

[58]   Porter, *Progress of the Nation*, Vol. 2, pp. 111–112. One of the sources cited by Porter is Mr. Laird, "one of the most recent travellers in that region" (p. 112). Porter observed that "Among the objects to which the industry of Africans could be profitably applied, perhaps the most important is the article of cotton. . . . the market for it is continually being extended; and as regards this country [England], it is a matter of very high importance that the million of persons who are dependent for their daily subsistence upon the regular supply of that material should have the chances of disappointment lessened, as far as possible, by extending the number of the producers, and multiplying the regions in which they are found" (p. 113).

the period, Brazil, the Caribbean, and the Southern slave colonies/states of the United States were all part of Africa, even though continental Africa bore the cost without sharing the benefits. Yet some raw materials were produced by Africans on the African continent during the slave trade period. The sterling amount of what was imported into England constituted a very small percentage of the total amount of raw materials imported. Nevertheless, the strategic importance of these raw materials for manufacturing industries in England far exceeded their sterling amount. Evidence is presented in the discussion that follows to make this clear.

In relation to the development process in England between 1650 and 1850, two sets of commodities produced in Western Africa and imported into England were strategically important. These are gold and raw materials for the finishing processes in the textile industries – redwoods, gum, and palm oil (used as a lubricant for the expanding machines and by wool-combers in Yorkshire and soap boilers). In the seventeenth and eighteenth centuries, Western Africa was the only gold-producing region to which England had direct access.[59] Much of the gold imported during the period was sent to the government mint for coinage. Existing evidence shows only the amount coined for the Royal African Company. Gold imported by the company from Western Africa was minted into guinea coins bearing the company's elephant stamp and circulated as part of the English currency.[60] The re-coinages of 1696–98 established the gold guinea as the British standard coinage, with a fixed value in 1717 of 21 shillings.[61] Between 1673 and 1713, 548,327 guineas were coined for the company, which is approximately £575,743. From 1677 to 1689, the Royal African Company accounted for 7 percent of the total gold coined by the mint.[62] When imports by private traders are included the proportion for African gold may be no less than 10 percent.

Even more important strategically than gold were the raw materials for the textile industries. Redwoods were used in the dyeing process and gums were employed as fixatives also in the dyeing process by calico printers, silk dyers, and hatters. In terms of the overall production cost of textile products, the dyeing process may represent a small proportion. Yet, ultimately, the extent of demand for the product depends to a large degree on the quality of the colors:

Few people can estimate the intrinsic value of manufactured woollens, silks or cottons, but men, women and children can judge of their colours, on the beauty of which therefore the first sale of a new manufacure must depend; and the continuance of that sale will also depend more on the permanency of the colours than

[59] Davies, *The Royal African Company*, p. 166.   [60] *Ibid.*, p. 181.
[61] B. L. Anderson, "Money and the Structure of Credit in the eighteenth century," *Business History*, Vol. XII, No. 2 (July, 1970), p. 87.
[62] Davies, *The Royal African Company*, p. 181.

Table 8.7. *Quantity of Redwoods, Gum Senegal, and Gum Arabic Imported into England from Western Africa, 1750–1807 (6-year totals in tons)*

	Redwood	Gum Senegal	Gum Arabic
1750–55 (7 years)	2,884	477	
1756–61	1,734	1,670	
1762–67	3,517	1,651	5*
1768–73	3,239	4,001	113
1774–79	4,671	2,102	45
1780–85	5,005	195	429
1786–91	6,005	1,166	1,125
1792–97	3,198	543	943
1798–1803	6,406	720	348
1804–07 (4 years)	5,343	1,853	396

* The quantity is for 1765–67 only.
Sources and Notes: 1750–80, Customs 3/50–80; 1781–1807, Customs 17/7–29.

on the strength of the stuff; a faded gown is given to Mrs. Betty long before it is worn out.[63]

Because there was no domestic production of any of the dyestuffs in England textile manufacturers depended entirely on imports from overseas. Western Africa supplied redwoods, which produced red colors. The other two main sources of red colors for textiles were cochineal and madder. The customs records indicate that redwoods were supplied almost exclusively by Western Africa during the period of study. For example, in 1781 the customs records show a total import of redwoods into England amounting in quantity to 393 tons (rounded to the nearest ton), all of which came from Western Africa. In 1782 and 1783, total imports were 1,385 tons and 590 tons, respectively, of which 1,374 tons and 588 tons, respectively, were imported from Western Africa.[64] Table 8.7 shows six-year totals of the quantity of redwoods, gum Senegal, and gum arabic imported into England from Western Africa in the period 1750–1807.

The redwoods came mainly from Gambia and Sierra Leone, with some from Gabon and Angola. In the late seventeenth century, the Royal African Company held a royal monopoly over British trade with Gambia and Sierra Leone, which enabled it to monopolize the import of redwoods from the

[63] Translator's Preface to Hellot, *The Art of Dyeing Wool, Silk and Cotton* (1789), quoted by Susan Fairlie, "Dyestuffs in the Eighteenth Century," *Economic History Review*, Vol. XVII, No. 3 (April, 1965), p. 488.

[64] PRO, Customs 17/7 & 8.

region. When the company tried to preserve this monopoly in the late seventeenth and early eighteenth centuries, clothiers in England mounted a strong opposition, arguing that the company's monopoly of redwood imports, which came almost exclusively from the Gambia and Sherboro (Sierra Leone) had led to increases in the price from £20 to as much as £70 or £90 a ton.[65] After the company lost its monopoly in the second half of the eighteenth century, the price fell to as low as £25 a ton in the late eighteenth century.[66]

Of all the raw materials needed in the textile industries gum from Senegal, regularly referred to in the records as gum Senegal, was probably the most localized in production. At a time when textile manufacturing was expanding in Western Europe, the market for good quality gum was geographically extensive, but the supply was limited to Senegal, with some quantity of inferior quality, called gum arabick, coming from the Barbary States to the north of Senegal. The importance of this commodity to manufacturers in Western Europe in the eighteenth century can be gauged from the cut-throat struggle over the possession of Senegal on the one hand, and speculation by merchants over its distribution in Europe, on the other. Monopoly efforts punctuated the history of the gum trade in the eighteenth century.

The French led the way. In the early eighteenth century, when the French Company of Senegal had possession of the gum-producing region, the members endeavored to monopolize the sale of gum in Europe.[67] The annual consumption of gum in Europe was estimated to be 1,000,000 lbs, and it was thought to be growing yearly. The Rouen merchants calculated that the supply was seriously short of the demand. The French company came to the conclusion that if it monopolized the sale of gum in Europe it could do anything with its price without reducing the quantity consumed, because the company's directors were convinced that the manufacturers could not afford to do without gum Senegal. They ruled out the possibility of the manufacturers finding a useful substitute for gum Senegal, pointing out that the Dutch had tried this before and failed.

In 1718, the company bought all the available quantities of gum Senegal that could be found in Holland, England, Germany, and France, amounting in all to 30,700 quintals, valued by the company at 890,000 florins (about £85,791).[68] The success of the company brought hardship to the manufacturers in Europe, particularly those of Hamburg. At first they

---

[65] J. M. Gray, *A History of the Gambia* (London and Edinburgh, 1940), p. 121.

[66] PRO, T. 70/1545, Sergent Chambers & Co. to Richard Miles, London, 27 November, 1782.

[67] Andre Delcourt, *La France et les Etablissements francaises au Senegal entre 1713 et 1763* (Dakar: I.F.A.N., Memoires, No. 17, 1952), pp. 180–184. This work gives an excellent account of the struggle over the gum trade in the first half of the 18th century.

[68] Conversion based on McCusker, *Money and Exchange*, p. 309.

resisted the company's prices but were soon forced by necessity to yield. The French Company of India, which succeeded the Senegal Company, continued the policy of monopoly. For this to be effective at this time the company tried to prevent the sale of gum at Senegal to anyone but the company. This led to a serious confrontation between the company on the one hand, and Dutch and English traders on the other. After three armed confrontations in 1721, 1722, and 1724, the Dutch were driven out from the gum producing region of Senegal, and on January 13, 1727, they renounced all claims to any part of the region.

The English, who were often protected by naval escorts, could not be so easily dislodged. A compromise was, therefore, reached in 1740, whereby the Royal African Company of England was to supply the French Company of India with 300 slaves every year in return for 360,000 lbs of Senegal gum.[69] This arrangement provided some peace for a while. But when the expansion of manufacturing in Western Europe after the Peace of Aix-la-Chappelle produced a very strong demand for Senegal gum, the manufacturers in France protested the export of gum Senegal from France to foreign countries. Consequently, an *arret* of November 2, 1751, prohibited the export of gum from France to foreign countries.[70] Manufacturers in England were hard hit. They petitioned parliament on January 28, 1752 to allow them to import gum Senegal from any part of Europe. By the Act of Parliament, 25 Geo. II, gum Senegal was allowed to be imported from any part of Europe.[71] However, the restrictive measures imposed on the import and re-export of gum Senegal by the French government meant that the supply reaching England did so clandestinely, for which reason the prices were very high, from £130 to £140 per ton, instead of the normal price of between £35 and £40 per ton.[72] This caused much hardship for the manufacturers, who did all they could to find ways to import gum Senegal directly from Senegal.

The opportunity came during the Seven Years' War (1756–1763). Samuel Touchet, a prominent cotton manufacturer in Manchester, and also a merchant in the African trade, collaborated with Thomas Cumming and some other English traders to dislodge the French from Saint Louis and Gorée in Senegal, with the assistance of the British navy. In his effort to secure the

---

[69] Delcourt, *Les Etablissements Francaises*, p. 342.

[70] *Ibid.*, p. 184.

[71] Adam Smith, *The Wealth of Nations*, J. R. McCulloch edition (London, 1838), p. 520.

[72] Shelburne Papers, Vol. 72, pp. 415–426, Sir Francis Baring to the Earl of Shelburne, 24 September, 1782, William L. Clements Library, The University of Michigan, Ann Arbor, U.S.A. Sir Baring stated that before the Seven Years' War (1756–1763) when Senegal was in the hands of the French, the gum trade was a monopoly and gum Senegal "sold here [England] for £130–140 per ton," instead of the implied normal price of £35 to £40 (pp. 416–417).

benefits of his investment, Samuel Touchet wrote in a petition to the Lord Commissioners of the Treasury in 1764,

> that he had fitted out at his own expense five vessels of a particular construction completely armed and adapted for the purpose of an intended conquest of Senegal, which armament was so conducted, that your memorialist's vessels assisted by His Majesty's ships of war had conquered Senegal.[73]

The evidence shows that Secretary Pitt had promised Thomas Cumming and Samuel Touchet that he would help them secure an exclusive charter, for a limited term of years, over the trade "which your industry and risk shall have opened to your country."[74] After the capture of Saint Louis and Gorée from the French in 1758, Samuel Touchet and Thomas Cumming struggled in vain to secure an exclusive trade to Senegal.

The importance of gum Senegal to both England and France was made manifest during the peace negotiations which ended the Seven Years' War. The French Controller General, Bertin, wrote on September 27, 1762, to the French representative at the peace negotiations, the duc de Nivernais, to ensure that Senegal was returned to France, stressing: "La traite de la gomme est l'objet le plus pressant qui fait cherir aux Anglais la possession du Senegal et qui rend sa restitution d'autant plus instante."[75] In the end, the French failed to get back Senegal. By the Peace of Paris, 1763, Senegal came into the possession of Great Britain.

Soon after the treaty, English manufacturers secured from parliament an act confining to Great Britain the export of gum Senegal from His Majesty's dominions in Africa. It was subjected to the same regulations as the enumerated commodities in British America. Its import was subjected to a token duty of 10 shillings a ton, but a prohibitive duty of £30 a ton was imposed on its re-export.[76] An officer of the customs was appointed in Senegal by the Treasury Warrant of December 30, 1765, to give account of gum exported from Senegal.[77] Great Britain kept possession of Senegal up

---

[73] PRO, C.O. 388/51, The Memorial of Samuel Touchet of London, Merchant, to the Lord Commissioners of the Treasury. The petition is not dated, but internal evidence indicates it should be dated 1764. See also C.O. 388/48, letter from Mr. Wood, by order of Mr. Secretary Pitt, to the Board of Trade, 10 April, 1759, in which it is stated that Mr. Thomas Cumming took part in "the late Expedition against Fort Louis in the River Senegal"; and the Memorial of Thomas Cummings to the Lord of the Treasury, 8 July, 1759, among the Shelburn Papers, Vol. 81, p. 45, William L. Clements Library, The University of Michigan.

[74] Shelburne Papers, Vol. 81, pp. 37–38, Secretary Pitt to Mr. Cumming, 9 February, 1757.

[75] Cited by Delcourt, *Les Etablissements Francaises*, p. 84: "The gum trade is the most pressing object which makes the English desire the possession of Senegal and which renders its restoration as much immediate" (translation).

[76] Smith, *The Wealth of Nations*, p. 520.

[77] PRO, T. 64/276.B.346. Figures collected in Senegal exist for only 3 years: 1773, 1,013 tons; 1774, 613 tons; 1775, 318 tons. The corresponding imports recorded in

to 1783, when it was returned to France under the Peace Treaty of 1783, which ended the War of American Independence.

Between 1758 and 1778, when the trade of Senegal was under British control, large quantities of gum Senegal were imported into England. This can be seen in Table 8.7. British traders took charge of the distribution of gum Senegal in Europe and manufacturers in England were able to procure that commodity more readily. However, like the French traders before them, merchants in England attempted a monopoly of the gum trade. The private papers of Miles Nightingale, a London drysalter, who tried hard between 1768 and 1771 to corner gum Senegal, are very revealing on the subject.[78] The foreign correspondence between Nightingale and his agents in Europe, Rocquette, Elsevier & Co. of Rotterdam, gives account of a considerable smuggling trade in gum Senegal and a high level of speculation in the commodity. Nightingale attempted to buy up all the gum Senegal available in England and arranged with his agents in Europe to do the same. When he and his agents thought they had bought up the bulk of the commodity available, they waited for the price to skyrocket before unloading their stock on the market. As Nightingale continued to insist on not selling his stock until the prices were much higher, his Rotterdam agents advised him to sell, for "You know when any article grows dear, its consumption lessens, and is supplied thro' industry with other sorts answering then the same purposes."[79]

His Rotterdam agents were later surprised to learn that other merchants in England, apart from Nightingale and his associates, were also speculating in gum Senegal at the same time, and these seem to have released their stock onto the market, thus arresting the upward movement of gum prices. From what they heard it would appear that "there is in England besides your stock and your clubs 400 to 450 tons of gum and we have all along been telling there was not in England 150 to 180 tons to be found."[80] Their letters of January 29, and April 5, 1771, show that as prices of gum Senegal rose efforts were made by some manufacturers to substitute gum arabic, as mentioned earlier. The evidence suggests they were not particularly successful. What ultimately brought misfortune to Nightingale's venture was famine that broke out on the continent in 1771, reducing the demand for all manufactured goods and, consequently, the demand for gum Senegal. As Nightingale's Rotterdam agents put it:

England are as follows: 1773, 844.5 tons; 1774, 566.6 tons; 1775, 341.6 tons. Because of the very high re-export duties, British traders smuggled the gum from Senegal direct to Europe to avoid the duty.

[78]   The private papers of Miles Nightingale are among the Chancery Masters Exhibits in the Public Record Office, C.109/1–14. C.109/3, 4, 7 & 9 were consulted.

[79]   C.109/9, Rocquette, Elsevier & Co. to Miles Nightingale, Rotterdam, 9 October, 1770.

[80]   C.109/9, Same to Same, Rotterdam, 13 November, 1770.

The misery in Germany and France and Suisse affect this and many other articles above common expance [sic]. These countries are afflicted with want of food, and other unlucky events which lay a great stress on all fabricks . . . We don't remember such a dismal time for almost all articles except eating and drinking commodities since 12 years forwards.[81]

As already mentioned, during the American War of Independence, France seized the opportunity to recapture Senegal. At the time of the preliminary peace negotiations in 1782, the Earl of Shelburne desired to be informed on the importance of Senegal.[82] One of his principal advisers mentioned earlier, Francis Baring, a prominent London financier and member of the Company of Merchants Trading to Africa, wrote to him that:

The real importance of Senegal arises almost wholly from its gum trade. There was imported in one year about 700 tons, and the average annual imports may be computed at about 400 tons. The price is now £270 to £280 per ton . . . There is more speculation or rather gaming in this article than in any other.[83]

The Prime Minister, Shelburne, was further advised by Benjamin Vaughan that if a choice were to be made between Senegal and Gambia,

I am more and more inclined to wish for the Gambia river, if the trade can be reserved at Port Anderic on the Gum Coast. If the French monopolize the gums, they may raise the price. But in an age of chemical discoveries, a gum may be a very short lived article of trade, and the Senegal has a barren country to the north, whereas the Gambia is good on both sides.[84]

It became clear subsequently, as will be shown later, that chemical discoveries would not find it easy to produce a good substitute for gum Senegal. In the Peace Treaty of 1783, in exchange for returning Senegal to France, Great Britain was allowed to trade for gum Senegal at Port Anderic on the gum coast, north of Senegal. This enabled English traders to procure some quantity of gum Senegal for British manufacturers. But it would appear that the quantity fell short of the demand, so that gum arabic, which was previously imported in very small quantities, began to be imported in

---

[81] C.109/9, Same to Same, Rotterdam, 30 April, 1771.

[82] William, Earl of Shelburne, afterwards Marquis of Landsdowne, had refused the Prime Ministership on the fall of Lord North's Ministry in March 1782; but he accepted the appointment of Home Secretary under Rockingham and when the latter died in July he was selected to form a cabinet. His Ministry negotiated the Preliminary Treaty of Peace with the American Commissioners. See Howard H. Peckham, *Guide to Manuscript Collections in the William L. Clements Library, University of Michigan* (Ann Arbor: University of Michigan Press, 1942), p. 220.

[83] Francis Baring's autograph notes on Senegal and the African Gum trade, 18 September, 1782, sent to the Earl of Shelburne, Shelburne Papers, Vol. 72, in William L. Clements Library, University of Michigan, Ann Arbor.

[84] Lady Lucas Collection, Bedfordshire Record Office, L.29/336, Benj. Vaughan to the Earl of Shelburne, 19 September, 1782.

relatively larger quantities, as can be seen from Table 8.7.[85] Manufacturers in England also tried other substitutes. Cashew gum from Jamaica was tried. In April 1790, the Society for the Encouragement of Arts, Manufactures, and Commerce wrote to the Council for Trade and Foreign Plantations that,

> by letters from Messrs. Newton and Leach, Callicoe printers at Merton Abbey, Surrey, to whom a quantity [of cashew gum] was sent for trial, that the cashew gum does not answer the purposes of Gum Senegal in Callicoe printing. That by letters from Mr. Desormeaux, Black Silk Dyer in Spital Fields it appears that the cashew gum answers the purpose of Gum Senegal in dyeing Black Silk ... That by a letter from Mr. Kilpin, Black Silk Dresser in Prince's Street, Spital Fields, it appears that Mr. Kilpin had made trial of the Cashew Gum and finds it will answer his purposes nearly as well as Gum Senegal.[86]

The Society for the Encouragement of Arts, Manufactures, and Commerce recommended to the Council for Trade and Foreign Plantations that,

> although from the above letters it appears that Cashew Gum does not answer the purpose of the Callicoe printer, yet as it supplies the place of gum Senegal in dyeing and dressing Black Silk in which businesses there are great quantities of gum used ... the importation from any of the colonies subject to the Crown of Great Britain of Cashew gum or any other gums useful in callicoe printing, Dyeing, etc., is an object well worthy [of] attention as it will tend to lessen the price of these gums and consequently promote the manufactures of the Kingdom.[87]

It is clear from the foregoing evidence that gum from Western Africa was a strategically important raw material for textile manufacturers in England in the eighteenth century. Taken together with the redwoods, it can be said that although the trans-Atlantic slave trade seriously retarded the development of commodity production for export in Western Africa, yet raw materials produced by Africans on the continent were critically important for manufacturers in England during the period. As stated earlier, the value of produce imported into England from Western Africa increased dramatically after the British government abolished the slave trade for its nationals in 1807. This is examined briefly to conclude the chapter.

---

[85]   Susan Fairlie was clearly in error when she said, "of the gums 'gum arabic' from Alexandria, Morocco, Tripoli, etc., was the staple, with inferior varieties from the East Indies. 'Gum Senegal' or 'Senecca' was a slightly inferior substitute, though the two were often mixed." See Fairlie, "Dyestuffs," p. 499. As the preceding evidence makes clear, gum Senegal was the staple in all Europe, including England, gum arabic being used in large quantities only when the former was scarce. She contradicted herself when she said later that efforts were sometimes made to substitute Barbary and arabia gum for gum Senegal (*Ibid.*, p. 506).

[86]   BT. 6/244, pp. 41–42, Samuel More to Council for Trade and Foreign Plantations, 29 April, 1790. Samuel More was the Secretary to the Society.

[87]   *Ibid.*

The abolition of the slave trade for British nationals presented incentives for British traders to make determined efforts to develop produce exports from Western Africa. Some of the Liverpool slave traders had complained to their friends in 1807 that with the impending abolition of the slave trade they were at a loss "how to employ either our time or capital to advantage."[88] The evidence indicates that they quickly moved their capital and energy into the produce trade, especially palm produce and timber. The maximum quantity of palm oil imported into Britain from Western Africa in any single year during the era of the British slave trade was 489 tons. Barely three years after the abolition the quantity jumped to 1,288 tons in 1810.[89] From 1827 to 1850 (with no entry for 1836 and 1837) the official value of palm oil imported into Britain from Western Africa amounted in total to £7,070,874, being 44.5 percent of all imports into Britain from Western Africa during the period.[90] In quantity terms, an annual average of 16,070 tons of palm oil were imported in the years 1827–1850.[91]

In the 1840s a new product entered the import list. This was guano, the dung of seabirds used as fertilizer. This product appears to have been imported into Britain from Western Africa for the first time in 1843. It was produced almost entirely in southwest Africa (Namibia).[92] In 1844 and 1845, the import figures rose suddenly to 76,898 tons (valued at £768,979) and 206,629 tons (valued at £2,066,293), respectively.[93] Thereafter the imports declined also suddenly: £53,087 in 1846 and £29,529 in 1850. Apart from the sudden growth and decline of guano exports from Western Africa, gum Senegal remained a major export product in the first half of the nineteenth century, second only to palm produce, which came largely from Nigeria. At this time, however, gum Senegal went largely to France. For example, in the 1830s the annual average value of gum exported from Senegal was £245,741, of which £227,863 went to France and £17,905 went to Britain.[94]

It is clear from the evidence that the determined efforts of the Liverpool traders following the abolition of the British slave trade in 1807 had begun to lay, between 1808 and 1850, the foundation for the transformation of Western Africa into a quantitatively important producer of raw materials for the United Kingdom, the continuing adverse impact of the Atlantic slave trade by Spain and Portugal and their American territories, notwithstanding. Palm oil led the way. In 1842 over 20,000 tons were imported, and over 30,000 tons in 1851. By this time Western Africa's palm oil had

---

[88] PRO, T.70/1568(1), John Bridge Aspinall to Simon Cock, Liverpool, 4 July, 1807.
[89] Inikori, "West Africa's Seaborne Trade," p. 69.
[90] PRO, Customs 4/11 – Customs 4/45.   [91] *Ibid.*
[92] Inikori, "West Africa's Seaborne Trade," fn. 12, p. 73.
[93] PRO, Customs 4/39 & 40.
[94] Inikori, "West Africa's Seaborne Trade," fn. 21, p. 74.

become an important raw material for the new machines in Lancashire, Yorkshire, and the Western Midlands. Ground-nuts, cotton, rubber, cocoa, tin, coal, and timber were to become major export products from Western Africa. Gold also soon became a major export product from the Gold Coast, now Ghana, after the introduction of scientific mining in the late nineteenth century. All these developments were to give rise to the important transformations in Western Africa's international trade appropriately described by McPhee as "The economic revolution in British West Africa."[95]

However, the fact remains that during the era of the trans-Atlantic slave trade, even though Africans were the most important overseas producers of raw materials for manufacturers in England, they did the bulk of it in the Americas rather than in continental Africa. Raw materials produced by Africans on the continent during the period were strategically important for textile manufacturers in England but not quantitatively. For the industrialization process in England, though, it mattered very little where Africans produced the raw materials – Africa or the Americas. What mattered was that the raw materials were produced by Africans where the cost for British manufacturers was lowest. This was to come back to hurt the competitiveness of African economies on the world market in the late nineteenth and twentieth centuries, a subject that is beyond the scope of the present study.

[95] Allan McPhee, *The Economic Revolution in British West Africa* (2nd ed., London: Frank Cass, 1971; first published in 1926), pp. 28–105. In spite of large-scale employment of raw cotton in domestic manufacturing, southern Nigeria and northern Nigeria exported annually to the U.K. 4,000,000 lbs. and 2,000,000 lbs. of cotton on average, respectively, in the 10 years, 1913–1922 (*Ibid.*, pp. 49–50). The Gambia also became an important producer of raw cotton.

9

Atlantic Markets and the Development of the Major Manufacturing Sectors in England's Industrialization

THE CRITICAL ROLE OF AFRICAN PEOPLES in the evolution and operation of Atlantic markets and commerce from the sixteenth to the nineteenth century has been demonstrated in multiple ways in several of the preceding chapters. It has also been shown that the growth of English manufactured exports to Atlantic markets in the eighteenth and early nineteenth centuries was largely responsible for increments in the sale of industrial products in England during the period and that the consequent expansion in the scale of industrial production provided the main source of pressure and opportunity for sustained technological and organizational development in manufacturing. This chapter continues the analysis by focusing on the specific mechanisms and channels through which access to Atlantic markets impacted the industrialization process in England from the mid-seventeenth to the mid-nineteenth century. To demonstrate the extent to which the process was trade driven – in particular, trade centered in the Atlantic basin – the specifics of the import substitution cum re-export substitution industrialization (ISI plus RSI), mentioned in Chapter 2 are examined in detail, both in industry-wide terms and in terms of the major manufacturing sectors. For purposes of the issues central to the analysis in this study, made clear in the preceding chapters, included among the Atlantic markets to which England's manufacturers had access during the period are Western Africa, the Americas, and the Iberian peninsula (Portugal and Spain). As evidence presented in Chapter 4 shows, English manufactured exports to Portugal and Spain during the period depended largely on purchases derived directly and indirectly from the Brazilian and Spanish American economies, respectively. This explains the inclusion of Portugal and Spain among the Atlantic markets accessible to English manufacturers. Specifically the evidence presented and analyzed in the chapter shows the central role of Atlantic markets in the English industrialization process; but, in addition, the analysis also unveils in a sharper relief than hitherto the general pattern of the process. However, the main thrust of the analysis is on the link between Atlantic markets and the development of the major manufacturing sectors during the process.

9.1 CHANGING STRUCTURE OF ENGLAND'S EXPORTS TO THE ATLANTIC MARKETS

As stated in Chapter 2, the growth and development of manufacturing in England followed a path charted by trade. In the Middle Ages the export trade in raw wool helped to create in England a market for manufactured goods produced by European manufacturers. From the fourteenth century, the manufacturing of woollen cloth developed as an import substitution industry to take over the domestic market previously supplied with imported woollen textile. Over time the industry also developed an export market that was even larger than the domestic one. The second stage of the trade-led manufacturing development was more wide-ranging. It followed the growth of English entrepôt overseas trade in the seventeenth and early eighteenth centuries. During the latter period, apart from the products provided by the woollen textile industry, which had been developing since the fourteenth century, English products sold overseas were mainly agricultural. The rest of the goods shipped abroad and sold by English merchants were made up of produce from the Americas and manufactured goods from Europe and East India. Earnings from the growth of entrepôt overseas trade, together with the proceeds from the export of woollen textile and agricultural products, considerably increased effective demand for a wide range of imported manufactures in England, which helped to extend the domestic market for manufactures during the period. At the same time, by transporting and selling European and East Indian manufactured goods in various parts of the Atlantic basin the English traders opened up Atlantic markets for these manufactures, markets whose character they came to know thoroughly over time. For this reason the development of manufacturing, which started in the late seventeenth and gathered momentum from the mid-eighteenth century, followed the path of import substitution at two levels: the domestic production of manufactures as substitutes for foreign products previously imported for the domestic market, and the domestic production of manufactured exports as substitutes for foreign products previously re-exported to various Atlantic markets.

The production of substitute manufactures for re-exports was a very important mechanism in the transformation of the technology and organization of the import substitution industries in the late eighteenth and early nineteenth centuries. The details of this are presented in later sections of the chapter. In this section focus is on the changing structure of exports from England to Atlantic markets. The over time changes in the export structure provide a clear view of the strategic role of the preceding entre-pôt trade in the early development of the export sector in the new manu-facturing industries in England.

Given the central role of Western Africa in the development of Atlantic commerce as shown in Chapter 4, it is appropriate to begin the analysis with English trade to Africa. The data showing the percentage shares of English and foreign manufactures in the total value of merchandise shipped to Western Africa by English traders are presented in Appendix 9.1. As stated in Chapter 5, the beginning of English trade to Western Africa can be traced to the sixteenth century. However, the earliest available invoices of goods transported to Western Africa by English traders are for the late 1650s. From what is known about the growth of English foreign trade in the seventeenth and eighteenth centuries, the middle of the seventeenth century is certainly not a bad point to start the analysis.

It is pertinent to comment briefly on the data at the onset. Ultimately the evidence comes from two sources. For the years 1658–93, the private records of two English companies, the East India Company and the Royal African Company, provide invoices of goods shipped to Western Africa by their vessels. Because the information available does not cover all the ship-ments made during the period, the data presented may be treated as a random sample. The British customs ledgers of exports and imports are the source for the data covering the period 1701–1856. For our present purpose, the customs data are very valuable, because they cover much of the merchandise shipped to Western Africa from ports in England even when allowance is made for the shortcomings discussed in earlier chapters. However, for the issue at hand, these records contain a major weakness that cannot be remedied. They show only goods shipped from ports in England; they do not show goods shipped by English traders directly to Western Africa from ports overseas. As can be seen from the evidence presented in Chapter 6, a large proportion of the European and East Indian manufac-tures transported to Western Africa by English traders in the seventeenth and early eighteenth centuries went directly from ports in Europe. This would mean that the computations in Appendix 9.1 significantly understate the actual share of foreign manufactures shipped to Western Africa in the first half of the eighteenth century. The appendix has to be read with this point in view.

It is clear from Appendix 9.1 that from the 1650s to the 1670s English trade to Western Africa depended almost entirely on the re-export of foreign manufactures, averaging between 70 and 86 percent of the total value of merchandise exported. The proportion dropped continuously from the 1680s to the middle of the second decade of the eighteenth century, being about one-third of the total in 1713–15. In the second half of this decade the proportion began to rise again, over 47 percent in 1716–18; and be-tween 1719 and 1748, the share was almost three-fifths of the total. By the mid-eighteenth century the proportion was still over 50 percent. Thereafter it declined to between one-third and one-quarter in the years 1752–93, rising somewhat in the last seven years or so of the century, before falling continuously in the nineteenth century, being about 14 percent in 1854–56, roughly the same position occupied by English manufactures in the 1650s.

Unlike Western Africa, the available data for English trade with the Americas do not go back beyond the eighteenth century. These are presented in Appendix 9.2. Not having the shares for the seventeenth century creates a major gap in the analysis. As Ralph Davis observed, the demand of British America for manufactured goods in the seventeenth century was small; yet it could not all be met by English manufacturers. Prevented by British colonial laws from importing these goods directly from the suppliers abroad, the colonies bought them from British traders as re-exports from England.[1] The percentage share of these foreign manufactures (mainly European) in the total value of merchandise exported to the Americas by English traders in the seventeenth century cannot be precisely determined. However, from what is known of the general trend, it may be reasonable to say that it was significantly larger than that of the first half of the eighteenth century. In the first three decades of the latter century, the proportion of foreign manufactures sold by English traders in the Americas was over one-third of the total value of merchandise exported. By mid-century the proportion had decreased to 27 percent. Thereafter it declined rapidly; it was less than 10 percent in the last years of the eighteenth century and less than 5 percent in 1856.

As for the trade with Portugal and Spain, which depended largely on the American colonies of these countries, re-exports played a very limited role throughout the period of the study. This can be seen in the data presented in Appendix 9.3. The reason for this is simple. First, as independent maritime powers Portugal and Spain imported directly from Europe manufactures that England could not produce competitively in the seventeenth and eighteenth centuries. Second, because Spain and Portugal had direct access to American produce from their own colonies they did not form part of the European market for English re-export of American products. As will be shown later, the products of the English woollen textile industry dominated exports to Portugal and Spain throughout the eighteenth century.

Examining the commodity composition of the foreign manufactures re-exported by English traders to the Atlantic markets in the seventeenth and eighteenth centuries constitutes an important first step in showing the complex relationship between domestic import substitution and re-export replacement in the industrialization process. Appendix 9.4 shows the makeup of the foreign merchandise, which English traders exported to Western Africa in the second half of the seventeenth century. As the ap-

---

[1]   Davis, *A Commercial Revolution*, pp. 12–13.

pendix makes clear, East Indian cottons and European linens were over-whelmingly dominant, followed by European bar iron (mainly from Sweden and to a lesser extent from Russia). In the 1650s European linens made up about one-half of the total, and East Indian cottons about one-third; both products made up together between 77 and 88 percent of the total at this time. The share of woollen textile was rather small, except for 1668 and 1684. The share of linens declined from the 1660s but that of East Indian cottons held steady. This general pattern in the last half of the seventeenth century applied generally to all the regions of Western Africa except two – the Dahomean coast and the Calabar trading area of southeastern Nigeria. In the seventeenth and early eighteenth centuries these regions imported very little textiles. Their imports were overwhelmingly dominated by com-modity currencies; cowries in the case of the Dahomean ports (Whydah and Ardra), and copper rods and iron rods in the case of Calabar. This is re-flected in the dominance of iron and cowries in the 1681 and 1682 data derived entirely from invoices of cargoes destined for the two regions.

The structure of foreign merchandise shipped to Western Africa by English traders changed considerably in the one and a half centuries from 1700 to 1856. This is shown in Appendix 9.5. Between 1699 and 1806 East Indian cottons became completely dominant. For the greater part of the period its share of the total was over 60 percent; the lowest was 33.9 percent in 1709–18, and the highest was 75.1 percent in 1789–98. The pro-portion fell off quickly in the nineteenth century; by 1854–56 it was only 15.4 percent. Linens and metals began their decline much earlier in the eighteenth century; they disappeared altogether in the nineteenth, by which time spirits (mainly rum), wine, tobacco, and some unspecified products had become the main foreign merchandise exported to Western Africa by English traders.

Like Western Africa, foreign products exported to the Americas in the eighteenth century by English traders were dominated by European linens and East Indian cottons and silks, as Appendix 9.6 shows. In the first half of the century the share of linens was between 46 percent and 50 percent, and that of cottons and silks was between 17 percent and 33 percent. The share of linens declined rapidly in the nineteenth century, disappearing alto-gether in 1854–56. The share of silks and cottons also declined from the 1780s, but remained at about 10 percent in the first half of the nineteenth century. By the latter period, processed foodstuffs and raw materials had become overwhelmingly dominant.

In the case of Portugal and Spain, represented in Appendix 9.7, the strictly limited amount of foreign goods traded by English merchants was dominated by foodstuffs and raw materials, which together made up be-tween 61 and 96 percent of the total during the whole period. The share of cottons and silks was between 12 and 31 percent in the first three-quarters of the eighteenth century but declined from the 1780s and was only 3.6 percent in 1854–56. Linens and other manufactures remained insignificant throughout the period.

Analyzing the changing structure of English domestic exports to the Atlantic markets is the second step in showing the interaction between import substitution in England and re-export substitution in the Atlantic markets. Appendix 9.8 shows the structure for Western Africa in the last half of the seventeenth century. As can be seen from the appendix, copper, brass, and other metals were dominant in the 1650s. However, as stated in the notes to the appendix, the sources seem to suggest that most metals, especially copper and brass, exported to Western Africa in the seventeenth and early eighteenth centuries by English traders were European products (German and Dutch). Undoubtedly, European metals dominated English metal exports to Western Africa in the early decades of the trade. The problem is to ascertain the point in time when domestic substitutes replaced the re-exports. It is beyond doubt, nevertheless, that the growth of domestic metal exports from England to Western Africa followed the path charted by the re-export of European metals by English traders.

Appendix 9.8 also shows that woollen textile did not become an important product in English domestic exports to Western Africa until the late seventeenth century. This is consistent with information from other sources that will be discussed later in the chapter. For now it should be noted that, although the woollen textile industry had existed in England for several centuries, its extensive export sector had depended on demand from northern and northwestern Europe for heavy cloth unsuitable for regions with warm climate. Consequently, in the early decades of English trade to Western Africa the lighter types of woollen textile appropriate for warm climate were imported from the Low Countries and re-exported to Western Africa. Hence, the subsequent growth of domestic woollen textile exports from England to Western Africa from the late seventeenth century still took the form of domestic substitutes for re-exports. More will be said on this later in this chapter.

Further important changes in the structure of English domestic exports to Western Africa are shown in Appendix 9.9. The Appendix shows the continuing dominance of woollens in the first four decades of the eighteenth century. Between 1699 and 1738 the share of woollens in the total value of English domestic exports to Western Africa ranged between 47 and 69.6 percent, which is a measure of the success achieved in producing domestic substitutes for previously re-exported foreign woollens. Metals were next to woollens in percentage share at this time, varying between 17.9 percent and 34.8 percent. Domestic cotton textile exports made little contribution at this time.[2] From the middle of the eighteenth century the share of cotton

---

[2]   In fact, the cottons entered for 1699–1708 in the appendix may not be cotton textile at all. It would seem they are a class of woollens referred to in the customs ledgers

exports jumped from 2.2 percent in 1739–48 to 28.3 percent in 1750–59; by 1790–99 it was 40.2 percent, and in 1800–07 it rose further to 49 percent. Again, this reflects a considerable success achieved in producing domestic substitutes for previously re-exported foreign products, which in this case were East Indian cottons. The details of the protracted struggle between them over the Western African market in the second half of the eighteenth and the early nineteenth centuries will come later in the chapter. As the table shows, English cottons did not only compete with East Indian cottons for the Western African market, but also with English woollens, whose share of English domestic exports to Western Africa fell as that of cottons rose. The share of linens also increased from the fourth decade of the eighteenth century, from less than 1 percent in the first three decades to 8.2 percent in 1739–48 and 15.4 percent in 1760–69. From this high point the share fell continuously for the rest of the eighteenth century down to the nineteenth, being a mere 1.4 percent in 1854–56. The share of metals held steady for much of the second half of the eighteenth century; it began to rise in the nineteenth. The main increases in the nineteenth century, however, were in the share of several unspecified manufactures, from about 12 percent in the first half of the eighteenth century to between 28 and 40 percent in the first half of the nineteenth.

The changing structure of English domestic exports to the Americas, shown in Appendix 9.10, is similar to that of Western Africa in several important respects. Again, because the data do not cover the seventeenth century the starting point in the analysis is not exactly the same as that for Western Africa. However, the figures for the eighteenth and early nineteenth centuries are comparable. Like Western Africa, domestic woollen exports were dominant in the first half of the eighteenth century. Metals were next in their shares as cottons, linens, and silks remained relatively marginal. The share of linens increased substantially in the years 1752–86 as the production of domestic substitutes for European linens re-exported to the Americas progressed. From the 1790s the main change came from the rapid growth of domestic cotton exports, again, a reflection of the continuing development in the production of domestic substitutes for East Indian cottons earlier re-exported. Similar to Western Africa, the share of woollens declined as that of cottons rose. Still like Western Africa, the share of metals held steady in the late eighteenth century after rising from 13.9 percent in 1699–1701 to 19.7 percent in 1752–54; it began to rise again from the 1830s, reaching 26 percent in 1854–56. For the entire first half of the nineteenth century, cottons and metals together were over 50 percent

as "cottons, Welch plain," "cottons, Kendal," "cottons, Northern," etc. As will be shown later, of the voluminous petitions in 1707 and 1708 by manufacturers producing goods for the African trade none came from cotton textile producers.

of the total value of British domestic exports to the Americas most of the time.

For the years 1783–1856, for which the available information allows a separate treatment of the West Indies, as shown in Appendix 9.11, the structural changes are different from those of the Americas as a whole in some important areas. As the appendix shows, linens remained by far the largest single domestic product by value exported from Britain to the West Indian islands up to 1787. It was only in the 1790s that metals and cottons, in that order, became greater in value than linens. Even so, the value of domestic linen exports remained large from the late eighteenth century to the 1850s. Of course, like the rest of the Atlantic markets, cottons were by far the largest single domestic export by value in the first half of the nineteenth century.

Coming to Portugal and Spain, Appendix 9.12 shows virtually a single product market for English manufactures for almost the entire eighteenth century. Metal exports began to make some significant contribution from the 1780s, and cottons from the 1790s. But it was not until the early nineteenth century that cottons became dominant, and as that happened the value of woollen exports to the Iberian Peninsula declined in absolute terms. The other important change at this time was the growth of the value of several unspecified manufactured exports, increasing from £338,000 in 1804–06 to £1,893,000 in 1854–56, annual average.

The over-time changes in the structure of exports from England to the Atlantic markets, shown in the statistical appendixes, provide clear evidence that the initial development of the export sector in English manufacturing from the eighteenth century followed the path laid out by the growth of entrepôt overseas trade in the seventeenth and early eighteenth centuries. The evidence also indicates a protracted competition between the domestic substitutes and the re-exports in Atlantic markets during the period. As already mentioned, the growth of manufacturing for the domestic market from the late seventeenth century was also trade driven through import substitution. The details of the interaction between domestic import substitution and re-export substitution in England's industrialization process are worked out in the following sections that are centered on specific manufacturing sectors.

9.2 ATLANTIC MARKETS AND THE WOOLLEN INDUSTRY

From the high Middle Ages to early Tudor England, woollens production was virtually the only major manufacturing industry in England. The situation changed little in the sixteenth and early seventeenth centuries. As several new industries sprang up from the late seventeenth century, however, its share of output in the manufacturing sector of the English economy declined over time. But even at the beginning of the nineteenth century it was still the largest single manufacturing industry in Great Britain.[3] Of course, within the first few decades of the century, the cotton industry in its continuing explosive growth quickly overtook it. Thus, even though the woollen industry did not provide leadership in technology and industrial organization, it can still be said that over the centuries the industry contributed significantly in laying the basic social and manufacturing infrastructure for the subsequent socio-economic and technological transformations of the Industrial Revolution.

In this long history of slow and steady development the woollen industry depended heavily on overseas markets. In the sixteenth century the export market absorbed about two-thirds of the industry's total output.[4] As stated in Chapter 2, the evidence indicates that this level of export dominance continued in the early seventeenth century. It seems to have decreased considerably in the middle decades of the century, as estimates derived from Gregory King indicate an export share of only 40 percent in the 1680s.[5] Over the eighteenth century the share of exports rose again to the levels prior to the seventeenth-century decline; at the end of the century, the declared value of woollens exported from England and Wales exceeded two-thirds of total output.[6]

The renewed expansion of exports in the eighteenth century, after the deceleration of the seventeenth, was due entirely to the expansion of exports to the Atlantic markets. This can be seen in Table 9.1. Between 1699 and 1806 exports to the Americas and Western Africa increased from 6.1 percent of total exports to 50.2 percent. For the greater part of this period exports to Western Africa, the Americas, and southern Europe taken together were 60 percent or more of total exports. The exports to southern Europe were largely for Portugal and Spain. As Appendix 9.13 shows, between 1701 and 1760, the boom years of the Brazilian gold-driven economy, English exports (domestic exports plus re-exports) to southern Europe went largely to Portugal. In fact, Portuguese share of total exports to southern Europe, as shown in Appendix 9.13, matches very well Portugal's share of English woollen exports to southern Europe for the one period comparable figures are available. Average annual export of all English woollen goods to Portugal in 1750–55, according to Board of Trade

---

[3] Crafts, *British Economic Growth*, Table 2.3, p. 22.
[4] Inikori, "Slavery and the Development of Industrial Capitalism," pp. 776–777; Bowden, *The Wool Trade*, pp. 37–38.
[5] Deane, "Output of the British Woolen Industry," pp. 220–221. The seventeenth-century deceleration is indicated by the estimated export figures of £1,540,000 in 1606/14 and £1,452,000 in 1640. See Coleman, *Economy of England*, Table 6, p. 64.
[6] Deane, "Output of the British Woolen Industry," p. 221.

Table 9.1. *Export of English Woollens to Atlantic Markets, 1699–1856*

	All Parts of the World £000	Americas and Western Africa		Southern Europe	
		£000	%	£000	%
1699–1701	3,045	185	6.1	1,201	39.4
1722–1724	2,986	303	10.1	1,606	53.8
1752–1754	3,930	374	9.5	1,954	49.7
1772–1774	4,186	1,148	27.4	1,667	39.8
1784–1786	3,882	1,013	26.1	1,662	42.8
1794–1796	5,764	2,597	45.1	1,047	18.1
1804–1806	6,800	3,413	50.2	744	10.9
1814–1816	8,722	3,914	44.9	1,636	18.8
1824–1826	6,882	2,894	42.1	763	11.1
1834–1836	7,321	3,894	53.2	652	8.9
1844–1846	9,534	3,722	39.0	926	9.7
1854–1856	12,720	5,177	40.7	1,141	9.0

Sources and Notes: Compiled from Davis, "English Foreign Trade, 1700–74," p. 120, and Davis, *The Industrial Revolution*, pp. 94–101. For the eighteenth century Schumpeter's overall export figures are much greater than those of Davis. They are as follows (in £000):

1699–1701	3,045
1722–24	3,636
1752–54	4,827
1772–74	5,241
1784–86	4,479
1794–96	6,150

Schumpeter, *English Overseas Trade Statistics*, Table XII, pp. 35–38, and Table XIII, pp. 39–43. The figures are 3-year annual average as in the table. Davis's figures have been used, because Schumpeter gives no regional distribution.

figures, was £778,930. This is approximately 40 percent of the £1,954,000 shown in Table 9.1 as the annual average value of English woollens exported to southern Europe in 1752–54. As shown in Appendix 9.13, 35 percent of all English exports (exports plus re-exports) to southern Europe went to Portugal; the share of woollens is thus five percentage points higher, but they are both close. The Board of Trade figures show further a considerable increase in the annual average value of woollens exported to Portugal in 1755–60, being £1,123,036. As Brazilian gold production and export began to decline from the 1760s, English woollen exports to

Portugal in 1760–65 fell to £709,310.[7] The general indication is that the share of Portugal and Spain in English woollen exports to southern Europe was a little greater than their share of all English exports to southern Europe shown in Appendix 9.13.

The importance of the Atlantic markets for the woollen industry in the eighteenth and early nineteenth centuries becomes even greater when viewed against developments in northern Europe (Norway, Denmark, Iceland, Greenland, and the Baltic) and northwest Europe (Germany, Holland, Flanders, and France). Between 1699/1701 and 1752/54, English woollen export to northwest Europe and northern Europe declined absolutely by 13 and 22 percent, respectively; over the whole of the first three-quarters of the century, from 1699/1701 to 1772/74, it decreased by 37.4 and 38.9 percent, respectively; for the rest of the century, 1772/74–1804/06, export to northwest Europe declined further by £647,000 (about 76 percent decrease), more or less made up by a £686,000 increase in exports to northern Europe. Thus, between 1701 and 1806, English woollen exports to northwest and northern Europe together fell from £1,544,000 to £1,002,000. In spite of this decrease, however, overall exports increased during the period – by £1,141,000 in 1699/1701–1772/74, and £2,614,000 in 1772/74–1804/06. During these two periods, exports to the Americas and Western Africa increased by £963,000 and £2,265,000, respectively. Exports to southern Europe increased by £753,000 in 1699/1701–1752/54 and by £466,000 in 1699/1701–1772/74. Declining exports to Portugal, as Brazilian gold exports fell after 1760, contributed largely to produce an absolute decline of £923,000 in English woollen exports to southern Europe between 1772/74 and 1804/06.[8] From these figures it can be seen that increases in exports to the Americas and Western Africa accounted for the bulk of increments in English woollen exports in the eighteenth and early nineteenth centuries. The percentage increases further when account is taken of exports to Portugal and Spain induced by the American colonies of these countries.

Falling exports to northwest and northern Europe and growing exports to the Atlantic markets led to important structural changes in the industry.

---

[7] For the Board of Trade figures presented, see PRO, CO 390/5 Part 3, "Averages of Exports from England to Portugal from the year 1750 to the year 1784." No figures are shown for the years 1765–84. The figures presented include hats (beaver and castor), worsted hose, bays of different sorts, long and short cloths, stuffs, and "other species of woolens." Fisher's figures for six principal English woollen manufactures exported to Portugal in 1756–1760 averaged £1.034 million per annum. See Fisher, *The Portugal Trade*, Table XIII, p. 128; also p. 127.

[8] All the figures in this paragraph have been computed from Davis, "English Foreign Trade, 1700–1774," p. 120, and Davis, *The Industrial Revolution*, pp. 94–96. For the role of Brazil in Anglo-Portuguese trade, see Fisher, *The Portugal Trade*, especially pp. 13–40, 53–63, 125–139.

Products demanded in the two groups of regions were very different. Demand in northwest and northern Europe was for the heavy and very expensive cloths, while the Atlantic markets demanded the lighter and cheaper fabrics. It follows from this that as exports to the former regions declined absolutely in the eighteenth century, and those to the latter increased, the two sets of products were affected differently – the production and export of the heavier and more expensive cloths decreased and that of the lighter and cheaper fabrics expanded. These two sets of products were manufactured largely in different regions of England – the heavy and costly products largely in the south and the lighter and cheaper woollens mainly in the north, especially Lancashire and the West Riding of Yorkshire. For this reason the structural changes also had a regional component.

Evidence concerning exports to Western Africa suggests the course of these developments. As mentioned earlier, it is clear from the evidence that woollen manufactures produced in England up to the third quarter of the seventeenth century were not suitable for the markets in Western Africa. It was continental producers, particularly the Dutch, who produced woollen goods appropriate for those markets at the time. Consequently, in the early decades of the British African trade, English traders procured these woollen manufactures in Europe for shipment to Western Africa. The evidence shows that it was during the time of the Royal African Company, whose charter began in 1672, that conscious efforts were made, through the company's encouragement, to produce substitutes for these re-exports in England. As the company's account shows, in the four years 1657, 1658, 1660, and 1661, the quantity of English woollen manufactures exported to Western Africa totaled only 669 pieces of says and 484 pieces of perpets.[9] But in the four years 1683–86, about a decade and a half after it began business, the company exported 8,208 pieces of says, 15,595 pieces of perpets, 2,801 pieces of boysados, 1,776 pieces Welch plains, 250.5 pieces bays, 165.5 pieces broadcloth, 1,520 pieces blankets, 600 yards flannels, 1,170 pieces carpets, 104 pieces crapes, 2,067 fine annabas cloths, and 69,388 ordinary annabas cloths, all English woollens appropriate for the markets in Western Africa.[10] From these figures the company noted,

[it is] made evident that the Company by their Industry & great charge in building of forts & castles & in setting up of sundry new Manufactures in England and sending staple comodities [sic] well manufactured and well dyed, have gained this Trade from the Dutch, who were before the Company in a manner the sole Traders to Guiney from whence the Company was at first forced to buy the greatest part of

---

9   PRO, T70/175, An Account of the Improvement of the Woollen Manufactures by the Royal African Company of England, signed Richd. Beaumont, African House, 9 December, 1707. The company stated that these figures were taken from the records in the Custom House, London, and that "the Register of 1659 was Burnt."
10   *Ibid.*

the cargoes vitz Leyden Sayes, scarlett cloth, fustians, knives, muskets, Boysados, Annabasses and for many years past they [have] manufactured all these comodities in England, and have sent several Woollen & other Manufactures that were sent to Guiney before they were a Company . . .[11]

The company's claim is supported by the testimony of several manufacturers. For example, in March 1710, "the President, Wardens, and others, concerned in the Woollen Manufactory in and about Kidderminster," stated in a petition to the House of Commons that,

the petitioners, with many hundreds of others, had a great encouragement from the Royal African Company who were the first that introduced the making of divers of our manufactures, and constantly for many years, while they enjoyed that trade uninterrupted, did carry on a very considerable and regular trade.[12]

It is clear from the numerous petitions of the early eighteenth century that after the African trade was made open to all British nationals by an Act of Parliament in 1698, the production of light, coarse, and cheap woollens for Western Africa increased considerably, although some producers seem to have been adversely affected by the impact of competition on the company's business. Producers who petitioned Parliament in favor of keeping the trade free to all English merchants were far more numerous than those who petitioned in favour of a monopoly by the Royal African Company. One of the petitions among the former group is of particular interest. In April 1711, the dealers in wool, serge-makers, wool-combers, and weavers, in and about the town of Totnes in Devonshire stated in their petition to the House of Commons that,

as of late years the trade on fine serges has been lessened, we have been employed in making coarse serges, commonly called Perpetuanas, for the coast of Africa, which of late has been much increased; the petitioners have thereby increased the manufacture of coarse wool, and what is more, many aged poor people are thereby employed in spinning for those coarse goods. If a monopoly of the trade be restored to the Royal African Company the quantities made will be lessened.[13]

The expanded production of coarse woollens for Western Africa, following the Act of 1698, was also noted by Bristol merchants, who wrote in March 1710, that "the trade of this city to Africa since the Act of Parliament in 1698, is become so considerable that there has been exported from this port to Africa between 29 September 1709 and 1 February 1710, in 24 ships, 16,897 pieces of Perpetuanoes, besides other woollen goods . . ."[14]

[11]   *Ibid.*
[12]   British Library, *House of Commons Journals*, Vol. XVI, 15 March, 1710, p. 551.
[13]   British Library, *House of Commons Journals*, Vol. XVI, p. 589. The petition of woollen manufacturers in Ashburton in Devonshire also in April 1711, made similar points.
[14]   British Library, *House of Commons Journals*, Vol. XVI, 15 March, 1710, p. 551.

English woollen manufacturers made considerable advances in the production of light and cheap woollens for Western Africa in the first half of the eighteenth century. Judging from the list of tenders made to the Company of Merchants Trading to Africa, a regulating company that took over from the Royal African Company in 1750, the number of the manufacturers was large and competition was keen. Considerable finishing business was carried on in London, but the actual production of the cloth was at first centered in the West Country, as appears from the early eighteenth century petitions.[15] In due course, the concentration of the African trade in the northwestern port of Liverpool in Lancashire was matched by the shift in the production of the coarse, light, and cheap woollens to the West Riding of Yorkshire. Thus, a manufacturer in the finishing side of the trade, carrying on his business in Halifax in the West Riding, could boast in 1780 that,

as I reside amongst the makers [of light woollens for Western Africa] where alone they are made I can always buy the best fabric on the very lowest terms & using none other than the very best indigo, 't is impossible that any house whatever can deliver goods of equal quality for less . . .[16]

From the keen competition among the firms one of them established such a high reputation in Western Africa that its brand name became synonymous with high quality. The history of this firm is of twofold importance: First, it shows the progress made in the manufacture of light woollens for the African trade; and, second, it reveals the fastidious character of the Western African market. For these two reasons, some detailed account of the firm is pertinent.

The firm seems to have been founded by a Mr. William Knipe. In December 1750, his widow wrote to the Committee of the Company of Merchants Trading to Africa:

As the Deceas'd Mr. Willm. Knipe, whose business is now carried on by his widow Mrs. Martha Knipe & Jos. Partridge, have had the honour to serve the gentlemen of London, Bristol and Liverpool, and the old African Company with woollen goods proper for the coast of Africa, & that without having had any complaints, we earnestly beg your favours, & if we are so happy to be the persons appointed to serve you with the woollens, you may be assured that we will sell them on as low terms as anyone whatsoever shall, agreeable to the quality of the goods, & those of the best as you will be able to judge by samples we have already with us in our Warehouses.[17]

[15] For these petitions, see *House of Commons Journals*, British Library, especially Vol. XVI.
[16] PRO, T70/1540, James Kershaw of Halifax to Thomas Rutherfoord of African Office, London, 14 October, 1780.
[17] PRO, T70/1516, Martha Knipe & Co. to Committee of the Company of Merchants Trading to Africa, London, 11 December, 1750.

By 1740 the products of the firm were already commanding sale in Western Africa, relative to those of other firms. George Hamilton, the resident manager of the "Floating Factory" joint venture of Thomas Hall and others discussed in Chapter 6, writing from the Gold Coast in August 1740, told his business partner,

[I] am in hopes shall be able to put off all our perpetts and Long Ells. Boothly has used the concerned in a most vilanous manner. I can make it appear to the loss of £4,000 sterling. Boxton the Packer served us within a trifle as bad. I must do Mr. Knipe that justice to say his woollen goods that he made up for the concern'd were extraordinary good, not a piece of them refused.[18]

In 1755, an officer of the African Company of Merchants, complaining about the high prices of Knipe & Partridge's woollens, remarked that "Partridge surely makes you pay for the attachment which the negroes have for the word, Knipe . . ."[19]

The popularity of the firm's products continued to the late eighteenth century, especially on the Gold Coast. In the last quarter of the century it appears some firms were forging the firm's brand name on their products to facilitate their sale. Thus, in December 1782, Knipe & Partridge complained that the Liverpool slave-trading firm of Thos. & John Backhouse fitting out a ship, the *Tom*, from Liverpool to the Gold Coast, desired to be informed about the assortment of goods suitable for that trade, which the firm did. It was later learned that Backhouse & Co. gave their order to another manufacturer who,

has put our names on the Half Ell & half Says Tillots in order to pass them off for our goods which will greatly hurt our reputation on the coast and deceive the buyers. We well know them to be far inferior in quality to ours as they are such goods as we would not on any account manufacture and are what we always refused when we have been obliged to buy at the warehouses.[20]

The available evidence covers the firm's business from 1740 to the early nineteenth century. But it is not known when it began operation. The fact that it had already achieved a reputation for high quality products by 1740 could mean that it was one of the firms established in the early years when the Royal African Company was encouraging domestic production of woollen goods as substitutes for foreign manufactures previously reexported to Western Africa, or at least not long after. What is clear from the evidence, however, is that beginning in the last quarter of the seventeenth century, English woollen producers achieved considerable success in the

---

[18] PRO, C. 103/130, George Hamilton to Thomas Hall, Annamaboe, 16 August, 1740.
[19] PRO, T.70/1523, Thomas Melvil to Committee, Cape Coast Castle, 17 March, 1755.
[20] PRO, T.70/1545, Knipe & Partridge to Richard Miles, London, 28 December, 1782. Richard Miles was a British trader resident on the Gold Coast. He traded privately but was also a Senior Officer of the Company of Merchants Trading to Africa.

production of coarse, light, and cheap woollen manufactures suitable for the Western African market in the eighteenth century. The issue now is how this development related to the growth of English woollen exports to the other Atlantic markets in the eighteenth century.

The lighter types of woollens were generically called by contemporaries the "new draperies." Some of them were already being produced and exported in the late sixteenth and early seventeenth centuries. Coleman believes this early development was due mainly to the changing character of demand and the migration to England of craftsmen under religious persecution in Europe. The main centers of production at the time were northern Essex, Devon, western Somerset, and Norwich in Norfolk.[21] As was mentioned earlier, some of these places were also the ones that developed in the late seventeenth century the production of a new set of coarse, light, and cheap woollen manufactures that met the demand of consumers in Western Africa. The fact that the early "new draperies" produced in these places were unsuitable for Western Africa and the more suitable ones had to be procured initially from Holland, as shown earlier, would suggest that the early products were not particularly suitable for warm climates. It is, therefore, likely that the light woollens whose exports were responsible for the growth discussed above were different from the "new draperies" of the late sixteenth and early seventeenth centuries. Put differently, they were part of a new development which started with the production of light woollens suitable for markets in Western Africa in the late seventeenth century. To that extent it may not be unreasonable to deduce that the latter development made a contribution to the growth of English woollen exports to the other Atlantic markets in the eighteenth century.

In the context of the foregoing point, it is significant to note that Africans in the Americas constituted an important part of the market for English woollen manufactures in the Americas at this time. As an eighteenth-century writer pointed out, "a great part of the Woollens sold in Portugal is for the Brazils, and the great Consumption of Woollens in Brazils is by the Negroes."[22] Did the "Negroes" in the Americas demand woollen manufactures similar to those sold in Western Africa at the time? That is a possibility one may not be able to prove. The point being argued is also consistent with the fact that the old centers of the "new draperies" in the West Country, East Anglia, and southern England in general declined in the eighteenth century[23] and the manufactures that spurred the export growth of the eighteenth century were produced largely in the West Riding of Yorkshire. The West Riding owed its success not only to its ability to

---

[21]   Coleman, *The Economy of England*, pp. 63–64, 80–81.

[22]   Mathew Decker, *An Essay on the Causes of the Decline of the Foreign Trade* (1744), p. 107, cited by Fisher, *The Portugal Trade*, fn. 1, p. 53.

[23]   Coleman, *The Economy of England*, p. 161; Coleman, "Growth and Decay," p. 117.

produce at lower cost than its rivals, but also to its ability to adapt its production to the changing character of overseas demand.[24]

While a precise connection between the production of coarse woollens for Western Africa and the growth of English woollen exports to the other Atlantic markets may be hard to demonstrate, the evidence presented in this chapter thus far shows beyond doubt that the growth and development of the English woollen industry in the eighteenth century depended largely on the Atlantic markets as defined here. The capture of these markets by West Riding producers was responsible for the concentration of the industry in that region in the course of the century, away from its traditional centers in southern England, especially the West Country and East Anglia. The relatively greater technological dynamism of the industry in the region and its more rapid adoption of the factory system, all of which was shown in Chapter 2, were all a product of this same factor. The export data show a protracted competition between the light woollens and cottons on the Atlantic markets. Ultimately cotton manufactures won. As their sale on those markets exploded woollen exports continued to grow, but less impressively. Finally, the evidence presented does show unambiguously that the development of the industry in the eighteenth and early nineteenth centuries was trade driven.

9.3 ATLANTIC MARKETS AND THE LINEN INDUSTRY

Linens production was one of the import substitution industries that developed in England from the late seventeenth century. Its early source of growth and development was the taking over of a domestic market previously supplied with imports from Europe. The progress of the industry from this period is relatively well documented. It is clear from the evidence that very little progress was made in the seventeenth century. The 1697 Board of Trade Report, mentioned in Chapter 2, reporting on the industry, stated:

We do not find that the Linen Manufacture in this Kingdom hath made any great progress of late, the Stock subscribed for that purpose was soon diverted by a Stock-jobbing Trade, and thereby the Corporation disabled to promote it, & tho' that Corporation do still subsist, yet they have not any Looms; But what Linens they sell at their Sales are only such as they buy of Weavers in Yorkshire, Durham and Lancashire. But we find not only those but other Countrys [Counties] are capable of to afford great quantities of Hemp and Flax, and therefore as good Linen for all ordinary uses may be made in England as any that comes from abroad, and that it is a manufacture that would be of great use for the employment of both sexes, from 5 years old & upwasrds, and that in remote Countries [Counties] wages are cheap and the people inclined to carry on the said manufacture which if it could be increased it would give a great employment to the poor & prevent the importation

---

[24]   Wilson, "Supremacy of the Yorkshire Cloth Industry," pp. 235–244.

of great quantities of Linens now imported on us from France & other foreign Countrys. Wherefore We are humbly of opinion that encouragement be given to the said manufacture by keeping on a considerable duty on all Linens imported except from Ireland, and by such other ways as may be thought convenient.[25]

Some of the available import figures may be used to measure the probable size of the domestic market for linens in England in the late seventeenth century. According to the Board of Trade Report just mentioned, a report submitted to the Lords of the Privy Council for Trade by Sir George Downing, then one of the Commissioners of the Customs, dated 9 March, 1675, put linen imports from France alone in one year at £500,700.[26] The Board, in its preoccupation with the balance of trade, overlooked linen imports from Germany and the Low Countries, because England's trade with those countries had a favorable balance, thanks to large re-exports of produce from British America. Other evidence suggests that imports from Germany and the Low Countries at this time could not have been less than those from France. This would mean that the annual consumption of linen products in England in the late seventeenth century was in the order of a million pounds sterling.

To this domestic market must be added the re-export market overseas to which English traders transported European linen manufactures in the entrepôt trade of the seventeenth and early eighteenth centuries. As can be seen in Table 9.2, the re-export market grew from £182,000 per annum in 1699–1701 to £331,000 in 1752–54. As will be shown later, the re-export market was almost entirely in the Americas, Western Africa taking much of the rest, especially in the seventeenth century. The indication is that the market for imported linens in the Americas in the first half of the eighteenth century was considerably larger than the re-exports from England suggest. It appears that Irish linen producers were able to export directly to British America at this time, Ireland being a quasi British colony in Europe. This view rests on evidence presented to a House of Commons Committee by the Inspector to the Trustees of the Linen Manufacture of Ireland, Mr. Robert Stephenson. The export account he presented was taken from the Custom Books of Ireland. This shows figures averaging £284,669 a year in 1722–24 (£194,627 cloth and £90,042 yarn) and £845,739 in 1752–54

---

[25]   PRO, C.O. 390/12, A Report Concerning the General Trade of England made by the Board of Trade, December 23, 1697, pp. 161–163 (also pp. 129–131, a second set of pagination). The linen weavers in Yorkshire and Lancashire mentioned in the report may be noted. These, according to Coleman, were small-scale independent weavers – small-holding peasants who carried on linen manufacture as a supplementary by-employment. They had been in existence in Lancashire and Yorkshire since the sixteenth century, using mostly linen yarn imported from Ireland. See Coleman, *The Economy of England*, p. 81.

[26]   C.O. 390/12, Board of Trade Report, p. 137 (also p. 105).

Table 9.2. *Linens Imported into England,*
Re-exported and Retained, 1699–1856 (in £000)

	Total Imported	Re-exported	Retained
1699–1701	903	182	721
1722–24	1,036	232	804
1752–54	1,185	331	854
1772–74	1,246	322	924
1784–86	1,753	182	1,571
1794–96	2,269	477	1,792
1804–06	2,789	562	2,227
1814–16	2,111	106	2,005
1824–26	2,577	15	2,520
1834–36	91	59	32
1844–46	58	20	38
1854–56	95		95

Sources and Notes: Computed from Davis, "English Foreign Trade 1700–74," p. 119, and Davis, *The Industrial Revolution*, pp. 94–125. The figures are 3-year annual averages.

(£707,260 cloth and £138,479 yarn).[27] As would be expected, Robert Stephenson stated that Irish linen exports at this time depended on Great Britain and its colonies.[28] Yet linen imports into England from Ireland in both periods averaged £114,000 and £332,000 a year, respectively.[29] This must mean that the bulk of the remaining Irish exports (£170,669 in 1722–24 and £513,739 in 1752–54) went directly to British America. In fact, a textile manufacturer in Manchester, Samuel Touchet, told a House of Commons Committee in 1751 that the rising price of Irish linen yarn was due to the bounties given in Ireland on coarse brown linens and that "the narrow Irish linens are used by Negroes in the Plantations, which in some measure interferes with our Trade." Touchet noted that the bounties enabled the Irish to undersell the Germans.[30]

[27] British Library, *House of Commons Sessional Papers of the 18th Century, Reports & Papers*, Vol. 25, 1763–1774, Report from the Committee Appointed to Enquire into the Present State of the Linen Trade in Great Britain and Ireland, pp. 404–409 and Appendix No. 9, pp. 423–424.

[28] *Ibid.*, p. 407.

[29] Davis, "English Foreign Trade, 1700–1774," p. 119.

[30] British Library, *House of Commons Reports*, Vol. II, Miscellaneous Subjects, 1738–65, Report from the Committee Appointed to Examine and State to the House,

Touchet's evidence suggests that up to the first decade of the eighteenth century the home market for linen manufactures in England still depended on imports from Europe. As he put it, "forty years ago [that is, 1710 or 1711] the Dutch supplied our Home Consumption..."[31] Imports from Europe increased from an annual average of £846,000 in 1699–1701 to £922,000 in 1722–24 (excluding imports from Ireland, being £57,000 in the first period and £114,000 in the second). Thereafter, imports from Europe fell continuously, down to £853,000 a year in 1752–54 and £594,000 in 1772–74. From the mid-eighteenth century, Ireland became the principal source of imports into Great Britain. Hence, while imports from Europe became a small proportion of linen manufactures sold for home consumption in Great Britain from the last quarter of the century, retained imports continued to grow, as Table 9.2 shows. This means that European imports were replaced with substitutes produced in England and with imports from Ireland.[32] Between the 1670s and 1770s, the consumption of linen manufactures in England appears to have almost tripled, with a retained import of £924,000 per year in 1772–74 and a gross domestic output value of £2.5 million in 1770. Gross output value for Ireland and Scotland in the same year (1770) was £2,525,000 and £634,000, respectively.[33] Linen output growth in England in the eighteenth century peaked at this time, when its contribution to England's national product in terms of net value added may have been as much as 1.5 percent[34] and was third in value added among the manufacturing industries in Great Britain, behind woollen and leather.[35]

Output in England stagnated for the rest of the eighteenth century, while it grew in Ireland and Scotland. In 1806 gross output value in England was £2,100,000, £4,600,000 in Ireland, and £900,000 in Scotland.[36] The linen industry in England grew rapidly again in the early decades of the nineteenth century, during which time spinning was mechanized. Evaluation of the evidence by Deane and Cole suggests that gross output value of the English industry was about £4.2 million in 1823, out of a total of £12.5 million for the United Kingdom.[37] For Scotland, the value of linen

---

the Matters of Fact in the Several Petitions of the Manufacturers of, and Traders and Dealers in, The Linen Manufactory, Reported by Lord Strange, 26 April, 1751, pp. 290–293, Evidence of Samuel Touchet.

[31]   *Ibid.*

[32]   For the import figures, see Davis, "English Foreign Trade, 1700–1774," p. 119. Davis's figures for British Islands (Ireland and Channel Islands) are taken as coming from Ireland alone.

[33]   For the gross output values, see Deane and Cole, *British Economic Growth*, p. 202.

[34]   *Ibid.*

[35]   Crafts, *British Economic Growth*, Table 2.3, p. 22.

[36]   Deane and Cole, *British Economic Growth*, p. 203.

[37]   *Ibid.*, p. 204. Deane and Cole state that the value of the English output was over a third of the U.K. total at the end of the first quarter of the nineteenth century. Apply-

manufactures stamped for sale in 1822 was £1,396,000.[38] This would mean that gross output value for Ireland was £6,904,000 in 1823. Ellison's figure for the United Kingdom in 1856, adopted by Deane and Cole, is £15,100,000.[39] Figures showing the distribution of this amount among the three countries are not available. However, judging from the trend in the first half of the nineteenth century, £7 million for Great Britain and £8.1 million for Ireland may not be far from the mark. By this time the linen industry in England employed 27,421 workers.[40]

The initial efforts of the industry in England were devoted to the taking over of the domestic market from imported European linens. But it was not long before similar efforts were made to take over overseas markets to which English traders had previously re-exported European linen manufactures. And this was done with some help from Parliament. As reported by a House of Commons Committee in 1751, 1742, and 1743, Parliament allowed a bounty of 1d. per yard for all British and Irish linens made of hemp or flax, of the value of 6d. and not exceeding 12d. per yard, and a bounty of a half penny per yard on those under 6d. per yard, "exported from Great Britain to Africa, America, or Portugal, or Spain," effective from March 25, 1743, for seven years. Similar Acts were passed in 1745 and 1749 either modifying or extending the period for the bounties.[41]

The efforts appear to have paid off; a relatively large export sector developed in the third quarter of the eighteenth century as British and Irish linen manufactures were substituted for the European re-exports. The years for which output figures are available do not exactly match the export time series shown in Table 9.3. But they can be compared roughly. The gross output value for the English industry in 1770 (£2.5 million) may be compared with the three-year mean value of English linen manufactures exported from England in 1772–74 (£740,000). From these figures, it can be seen that roughly 30 percent of the total output was exported at this time. The output figures for Great Britain in 1806 and 1856, stated earlier, were £3 million and £7 million, respectively. Comparing these with the relevant three-year average export figures for 1804–06 and 1854–56 gives 25 and 60 percent, respectively, as the proportion of the total output of the British industry exported in 1806 and 1856. Thus the export sector that developed was very important for the industry.

As can be seen from Table 9.3, the exports went almost entirely to the Americas and Western Africa during the entire period of the study. The little

ing this statement to their figure of £12.5 million for the U.K. in 1823 (Table 49, p. 204) gives £4.2 million, approximately.

[38] Mitchell, *Abstract of British Historical Statistics*, Table 18, p. 200.
[39] Thomas Ellison, *The Cotton Trade of Great Britain* (London: Frank Cass, 1968; first published in 1886), p. 124.
[40] Deane and Cole, *British Economic Growth*, p. 205. The figure is for 1851.
[41] British Library, *House of Commons Reports*, Vol. II, 1738–65, pp. 289–290.

Table 9.3. *Domestic and Foreign Linens Exported from England,*
1699–1856 (in £000)

	DOMESTIC EXPORTS			RE-EXPORTS		
		Americas and Western Africa			Americas and Western Africa	
	Total			Total		
	£000	£000	%	£000	£000	%
1699–1701				182	157	86
1722–24	25	22	88	232	222	96
1752–54	211	189	90	331	301	91
1772–74	740	681	92	322	285	89
1784–86	743	619	83	182	173	95
1794–96	895	799	89	477	430	90
1804–06	756	719	95	562	543	97
1814–16	1,675	1,370	82	106	88	83
1824–26	1,879	1,498	80	15	13	87
1834–36	2,212	1,773	80	59	46	78
1844–46	2,765	2,010	73	20	16	80
1854–56	4,225	3,182	75			

Sources and Notes: Computed from Davis, 1969, p. 120; Davis, 1979, pp. 94–125.
The figures are 3-year annual averages. Figures for 1699–1774 are for England and
Wales, those for 1784–1856 are for Great Britain.

that was left went largely to Portugal and Spain. The European linens
re-exported by British traders had also gone almost exclusively to the
Americas and Western Africa. Naturally the development of the export
sector, which produced substitutes for the re-exports, followed the path
charted by the preceding entrepôt trade. As Table 9.3 shows, there was an
inverse relationship between domestic exports and re-exports; as domestic
exports increased, re-exports stagnated at first, then fell off continuously
and finally disappeared – re-export substitution was complete.

Further evidence indicates that the linens exported went largely to
Africans in the Americas. Table 9.4 shows this clearly. Between 1725
and 1775 the West Indies received by far the largest share of British linens
exported from England and Scotland, more than one-half in several years
and over one-third most of the time. In North America the linens went
mostly to the slave-holding colonies (states) during the period, especially
Virginia. The West Indies and the slave colonies of North America taken
together received 70 percent or more of the British linens exported from
Great Britain in most of the years between 1725 and 1775, for which there
is information.

Table 9.4. *Shares of American Regions in the Export of British Linen Textile from England and from Scotland, 1725–1736, 1772–1775*

	Exports to all Parts of the World	The West Indies	North American Slave Colonies	Rest of North America
	Pieces	%	%	%
1725	19,195	37.3	31.5	22.6
1726	16,414	41.7	27.1	19.6
1727	18,067	38.4	26.0	21.7
1728	21,211	50.4	23.0	15.5
1729	23,291	54.1	16.7	10.1
1730	21,163	51.5	22.2	16.2
1731	21,372	37.6	28.0	16.1
1732	19,200	45.7	26.8	16.9
1733	17,496	45.2	31.5	12.4
1734	18,438	38.8	38.2	14.7
1735	27,232	44.7	34.6	11.4
1736	29,714	39.0	31.0	15.8
	Yards			
1772	2,534,608	28.1	53.7	13.3
1773	2,300,969	33.9	44.6	14.9
1774	2,556,767	29.8	43.9	22.6
1775	1,433,136	67.7	3.5	11.9

Sources and Notes: Computed from T64/275, "An Account of the quantity of British Linens Exported from that part of Great Britain called England from Christmas 1724 to Christmas 1736," Custom House, London, 14 March, 1737, and T64/252, "An Account of the quantity of British, Irish and Foreign Linens Exported from Scotland from 1772 to 1775." For 1725–36, the main markets in the West Indies were Jamaica, Barbados, and Antigua. The North American slave colonies comprised Maryland, Virginia, North Carolina, South Carolina, and Georgia; only a total of 33 pieces were exported to Georgia in the first period (1725–36). New England, New York, and Pennsylvania made up the rest of North America in 1725–36, but Canada and New Foundland were included in 1772–1775.

9.4 ATLANTIC MARKETS AND THE COTTON INDUSTRY

Very few will disagree that the development of the cotton textile industry in England between the 1780s and 1850s was revolutionary by all account. The industry was established in the early eighteenth century as a peasant craft. It remained so for several decades. But between the 1780s and 1850s, its pace of development accelerated and by the 1850s its organization and technology of production were almost totally transformed. Of the total workforce of 374,000 employed in the industry in 1850, only 43,000 were employed outside the factory system of organization. The industry's technology was virtually mechanized by this time: There were 20,977,000 spindles and 250,000 powerlooms in the industry in 1850.

What is more, steam had become the dominant form of power used in the industry – 71,000 horsepower supplied by steam as opposed to 11,000 supplied by water.[42] Value added in the industry by this time exceeded by about 50 percent that in the woollen textile industry, the dominant industry in England for over four centuries. Both in quantum and quality, this pace of development was something that had never been experienced in any industry in the pre-industrial world. Undoubtedly, the Industrial Revolution in England, in the strict sense of the phrase, is little more than a revolution in cotton textile production. The analytical task in this section of the chapter is to demonstrate the contribution of the Atlantic markets to these revolutionary developments.

The argument to be elaborated is that the cotton textile industry developed in England in the eighteenth and early nineteenth centuries as an import and re-export substitution industry (ISI plus RSI), like the other new industries of the period as earlier stated. For this reason, the industry grew quickly in the first few decades, behind protective tariffs, on the basis of pre-existing domestic demand. As the early expansion reached the limits of the protected pre-existing domestic market, stagnation set in. The crisis of stagnation was resolved through the exploitation of export opportunities in the Atlantic basin earlier created by the trade in re-exports, first in Western Africa and later in the slave-based economy of the Atlantic system. The early export opportunities were crucial to the subsequent transformation of the industry for several reasons. First, the larger market made possible by export demand helped to enlarge the total number of firms in the industry at an early stage, which contributed to the development of its competitiveness. Second, the operation of the export producers outside the protected domestic market exposed them to stiff competition with cheap- and high-quality products traded in Western Africa during the period, a competition that induced them to adopt cost-reducing and quality-raising innovations. These eighteenth-century developments enabled the industry to successfully invade major European markets from the 1780s, and those of Asia from the 1820s. The rapid expansion of exports that resulted, together with the multiplier effects on the domestic market for cottons and other manufactures, provided the favorable environment for the rapid transformation of the industry's technology and organization between the late eighteenth and mid-nineteenth centuries. The empirical and logical details of the argument now follow.

---

[42]   Mitchell, *Abstract of British Historical Statistics*, pp. 185, 187.

It is impossible to give a precise date for the establishment of a cotton textile industry in England. Nevertheless, the evidence suggests, and writers generally agree, that while cotton manufacture of a sort existed in England in the seventeenth century, the development of the industry was an eighteenth-century phenomenon. As P. J. Thomas wrote:

> It is now really difficult for us to realize that 200 years ago [writing in 1926] hardly any genuine cotton cloth was made in England. It is true that "cottons" were spoken of even in the sixteenth century; and in the seventeenth we have definite records mentioning the manufacture of cloth from cotton wool imported from the Levant, but these were not genuine cotton cloth but the hybrid fustians made of linen warp and cotton weft. English artisans did not know in those days how to make cotton strong enough to serve for warp.[43]

The growth of the industry in England in the eighteenth century followed a pattern of industrialization working its way through import substitution in the sense of Albert Hirschman's postulate that "import fulfils the very important function of demand formation and demand reconnaissance for the country's entrepreneurs."[44] In this particular instance, the role of imports was performed by East India cotton goods. The usual role of the state in the control of imports was also crucial.

The English East India Company began test imports of East India cotton goods into England in 1613. Before then, the company had been involved in the sale of these products in Indonesia in exchange for pepper and other spices which were later taken to England. At first only a few thousand pieces were imported. The company's sales in 1613 amounted to 5,000 pieces. They increased to 12,500 pieces in 1614. The company seems to have met with early success in the trial sales, as the imports increased considerably in the 1620s: 100,000 pieces in 1620, 123,000 pieces in 1621, and 221,500 pieces in 1625. The imports declined in the 1630s but began to rise again towards the end of the decade.[45]

---

[43]   P. J. Thomas, *Mercantilism and the East India Trade: An Early Phase of the Protection v. Free Trade Controversy* (London: P. S. King, 1926), p. 121. For the early history of the cotton textile industry in England, see also Wadsworth and Mann, *The Cotton Trade*. Thomas Ellison's view is similar to that of P. J. Thomas. Writing in 1886 he said, "the first recorded import of cotton into England took place in 1298. It was used for the manufacture of candle-wicks. . . . Mention is made of 'Manchester cottons' as early as 1352 and at various dates down to 1641; but these were really not cotton goods but fabrics composed of wool and cotton or linen and cotton." Thomas Ellison, *The Cotton Trade of Great Britain* (London: Frank Cass, 1968, first edition, 1886), p. 3.

[44]   Albert O. Hirschman, *The Strategy of Economic Development*, (New Haven, CT: Yale University Press, 1958), p. 123.

[45]   K. N. Chaudhuri, *The English East India Company: The Study of an Early Joint-Stock Company 1600–1640* (London: Frank Cass, 1965), pp. 191–193.

Table 9.5. *East India Textiles Ordered by the*
English East India Company, 1661–1694
(quantity in pieces, annual average)

1661–64 (4 years)	174,000
1669–73 (5 years)	365,100
1674/75–1680/81 (7 years)	781,800
1681–83 (3 years)	2,445,700
1684/85–1687/88 (3 years)	711,700
1688–94 (3 years)	1,417,300

Sources and Notes: Computed from Bal Krishna, *Commercial Relations between India and England, 1601–1757* (London: G. Routledge, 1924), Appendix A, p. 301. The combined orders for 1696 and 1697 amounted to 2,571,000 pieces (*Ibid.*, p. 141). The number of years in brackets indicates the number of years for which figures are available for each period.

From the middle decades of the seventeenth century, the East India cotton goods built up considerable popularity among English consumers of all classes because of their cheapness, the high quality of the texture, and the sheer beauty and fastness of their colors. Contemporary observers wrote about high-class English ladies appearing "all the morning in muslin night-rails," visiting and receiving visitors in that dress. Even the queen and the court ladies regularly wore Indian muslins and calicoes.[46]

The Indian cottons created in England new demand for cotton textile among the poorer classes, who previously could not afford the expensive woollen and silk goods produced in England. However, an important part of the demand for East India piece goods by English consumers in the seventeenth and early eighteenth centuries represented a shift in demand from English woollen and silk goods. All this culminated in a phenomenal growth of East India cotton imports into England in the second half of the seventeenth century as Table 9.5 shows.

The East India cottons imported by the English East India Company were not all sold for domestic consumption in England. A large part of them was sold for re-export to Europe, Western Africa, and the Americas. Evidence presented to the House of Commons in 1703 shows that during the years 1699–1702, East India textiles re-exported from England were valued at £1,589,935, using the sales prices in London. Of this total, cottons

---

[46] Thomas, *Mercantilism and the East India Trade*, p. 29.

amounted to £1,053,725 and £536,210 was for silk goods.[47] For these four years the annual average value of East India cottons re-exported from England comes to £263,431. Another source[48] shows the quantity (in pieces) of East India cottons imported into England and the quantity re-exported for six years, from which the quantity retained for domestic consumption (3-year annual average) has been computed as follows: 369,964 pieces a year for 1699–1701 and 328,338 for 1713–15; comparable figures for re-exports are 507,825 and 612,455, respectively. Annual average imports for the two 3-year periods are thus 877,789 and 940,793, respectively. Applying to these figures the average price of 13.6 shillings per piece computed from the merchants' records[49] gives, for re-exports, £345,321 (1699–1701) and £416,469 (1713–15), annual average. The comparable figures for retained imports are £251,576 (1699–1701) and £223,270 (1713–15). The re-export figure for 1699–1701, £345,321, is directly comparable with Ralph Davis's re-export figure for the same period, being £340,000.[50] The closeness of the two figures indicates the reliability of the average price computed from the merchants' records.

These figures provide a reasonably reliable basis for measuring the size of the domestic market for cotton goods in England by the end of the seventeenth century. Judging from the value of retained imports in 1699–1701, it may be concluded that effective demand for cottons in England at this time was about £252,000 per annum, assuming the prices at which East India cottons were sold in London at the time.

As already noted, the imports of East India textiles for the domestic market and for re-exports had adverse effects on the demand for woollen and silk goods produced in England. This provoked noisy agitation by the woollen and silk manufacturers in the late seventeenth century. With their political clout, the latter secured a protective act early in the eighteenth century. The law stipulated that from September 29, 1701, all silk goods and painted, dyed, printed, or stained calicoes imported into England from China or the East Indies could not be worn in England or Wales. The law allowed the prohibited goods to be imported and warehoused for re-exportation; it also allowed white calicoes from India to be imported and printed in England for the domestic market and for export. Muslins were

---

[47] Krishna, *Commercial Relations*, p. 138.

[48] PRO, CO 390/5 Part I, folio 59, signed Custom House, Inspector General's Office, October 13, 1718, Exam Jn Oxenford.

[49] PRO, T 70/917 and T 70/921. These are records of the Royal African Company of England showing six invoices of cargoes shipped to Western Africa from London between 1693 and 1720, two cargoes each for the Gold Coast, Whydah, and Angola. Altogether 9,932 pieces of a wide variety of East India cottons were shipped, amounting to 134,758.67 shillings according to the purchase costs in London. This works out to approximately 13.6 shillings per piece.

[50] Davis, "English Foreign Trade, 1700–1774," p. 120.

not affected by the law and were therefore free to be imported and sold for domestic consumption in England.[51]

The prohibition of printed East India calicoes stimulated the growth of calico printing in England in the first two decades of the eighteenth century. Calico printing is said to have started in England in 1676 with methods copied from India; the goods were sold as East India products. But it was not until after the prohibition act that the cotton-printing industry expanded and developed to provide the foundation for the cotton textile industry in England. This expansion was so great that a contemporary observer wrote in 1706 that "greater quantities of calicoes had been printed and worn in England annually since the importing of it was prohibited than ever was brought from India."[52] The growth of the industry is reflected in the following import figures for white calicoes: 1717, 676,082 pieces; 1718, 1,220,324 pieces; 1719, 2,088,451 pieces.[53]

Once again, the silk and woollen manufacturers called upon Parliament for more protection. Bowing to the pressure, Parliament first imposed import duties on the white calicoes and excise duties on the calicoes printed in England from the imported plain ones, on which import duties had already been paid. The printers calculated that all the duties put together amounted to 82 percent ad valorem.[54] Not satisfied with the effects of these duties, Parliament then enacted a law, effective from December 25, 1722, prohibiting the consumption in England of calicoes printed, painted, stained, and dyed from plain East India calicoes.[55] Muslins, neckcloths, fustians, and calicoes dyed all blue were excepted. Printed East India calicoes could still be imported for re-export, and plain calicoes were allowed to be imported and printed for export. But the home market was closed for these goods.

Although this extreme protectionism was intended to favor the woollen and silk industries, it was the cotton textile industry that reaped the benefits. The prohibition stimulated the domestic production of cotton goods for the printing industry, which had relied on imported white calicoes in the first decades of the eighteenth century.[56] This is somewhat reflected in

---

[51]   Thomas, *Mercantilism and the East India Trade*, pp. 114–115.

[52]   *Ibid.*, p. 125.

[53]   *Ibid.*, pp. 125 and 162. The growth of cotton printing in the first two decades of the eighteenth century, employing imported plain East India cottons, means that raw cotton imports do not give an accurate indication of the quantity of cotton goods available for domestic consumption and for export. Nor do they give a proper picture of the infant cotton industry at this time. Thus, while cotton printing was expanding, retained imports of raw cotton stagnated between 1695 and 1714 (see Deane and Cole, *British Economic Growth*, Table 15, p. 51).

[54]   Thomas, *Mercantilism and the East India Trade*, pp. 125–126.

[55]   *Ibid.*, p. 160.

[56]   Wadsworth and Mann, *The Cotton Trade*, p. 144.

the sudden expansion of retained raw cotton imports between 1715 and 1724.[57] From this point we can begin to observe the development of cotton textile production in England as an import substitution industry, with all the expected characteristics.

There are no reliable figures of total output for the industry in the first half of the eighteenth century. What is available is the indirect evidence of retained raw cotton imports. The decennial averages for the period 1711–60, in pounds, are as follows: 1711–20, 1.48 million; 1721–30, 1.51 million; 1731–40, 1.72 million; 1741–50, 2.14 million; 1751–60, 2.76 million.[58] The retained raw cotton import figures indicate that after the rapid expansion of the first two years following the promulgation of the new law (retained imports were over 2 million pounds in 1722 and 1723), there was stagnation for the rest of the decade. Hence, the average for the 1720s exceeded that for the preceding decade by only 2.0 percent. It is not quite clear whether this means that production was expanded to the limit of the pre-existing domestic demand within a few years following the prohibition act. Other evidence seems to point in that direction. The existing estimates of total output in the industry indicate that the home market for cotton textiles in England grew very little, if at all, in the first half of the eighteenth century. According to the estimate by Postlethwayte, the gross value of output in the industry in 1766 was £600,000, of which £379,241 represented domestic consumption and £220,759 export.[59] If we recall the size of the domestic market for cotton textiles before the prohibitions of the early eighteenth century, we see that not much growth took place in the first half of the century. Of course, it is true that some classes of Indian cotton goods, such as muslins, were still allowed into the domestic market. And some smuggling of the prohibited ones may have occurred.[60] Hence, domestic sales of English cotton textiles would not represent the size of the entire domestic market for cotton goods during the period. Even so, the evidence suggests that the growth of domestic demand for English cotton textiles after the completion of first-stage import substitution in the industry was decidedly slow.

This seems to be borne out by the timing of the export drive by the cotton textile manufacturers. As has been suggested, "the international market is highly competitive and considerable effort is required to be successful. Few sensible entrepreneurs would choose to operate in that market if their

---

[57] Deane and Cole, *British Economic Growth*, Table 15, p. 51.
[58] Computed from Mitchell, *Abstract of British Historical Statistics*, p. 177.
[59] Hobson, *The Evolution of Modern Capitalism*, p. 44.
[60] The calicoe printers stated in 1719 that "The clandestine running of East India, French, Dutch and all other foreign wrought silks do in all probability far exceed the clandestine running of printed calicoes..." (C O 388/21 Part 2, p. 243, Representation of the Printers of Calicoes and Linens, Recd 24 Nov, Read 25 December, 1719.) See also Thomas, *Mercantilism and the East India Trade*, p. 162.

alternative was a comfortable, sheltered domestic market."[61] The manufacturers must have been forced to look for markets abroad in the third and fourth decades of the eighteenth century, as the expansion of output reached the limit of the pre-existing domestic demand. This is suggested by the evidence of the manufacturers presented to a House of Commons committee in 1751. Samuel Touchet of Manchester, owner of one of the largest firms in the industry at this time, stated that production of cottons mixed with linen had begun in England about "forty years ago" (that is, about 1711), and none of the products had been exported "till about 25 years since" (about 1736?).[62] Other export producers who testified gave the 1730s for their entry into export production. For example, James Johnson of Spitalfields, a very large export producer at the time, said he had been in the business for "16 or 18 years" (that is, since 1735 or 1733).[63] Another export producer, Thomas Tipping, who held that export was "the most advantageous" trade, stated that he had been in it for "15 or 16 years" (that is, since 1736 or 1735).[64]

It took some time for the English cottons to establish a reputation in the export markets. This is why the progress of the industry remained unimpressive throughout the first half of the eighteenth century. During this period, it has been observed, the industry "was a minor trade, little more than a subsidiary occupation for a few thousand agriculturalists."[65] Through persistent effort by the manufacturers, however, overseas demand began to grow from the middle of the eighteenth century. In due course the

[61]   Anne O. Krueger, *The Benefits and Costs of Import Substitution in India: A Microeconomic Study* (Minneapolis: University of Minnesota Press, 1975), p. 114.

[62]   British Library, *House of Commons Reports*, Vol. II, 1738–65, pp. 290–293. 25 years after production began will make it about 1736.

[63]   *Ibid.*, pp. 294–295.

[64]   *Ibid.*, pp. 293–294. As will be shown later, Western Africa was the first important export market for the English cotton manufacturers. There is clear, though indirect, evidence that English cotton manufacturers were not yet much interested in that market in the first two decades of the eighteenth century. This is suggested by the total absence of petitions from cotton manufacturers during the great struggles between the Royal African Company and the private traders over the African trade in the late seventeenth and early eighteenth centuries. A large number of petitions came from woollen manufacturers, some supporting the company and others supporting the case of the private traders. But there were none from cotton textile producers. (For these petitions, see *House of Commons Journals*, Vol. XVI, British Library.) This indirectly confirms that in the first two decades or so of the eighteenth century, the cotton manufacturers concentrated their efforts on the protected domestic market. Some limited quantity of fustians had been exported since the late seventeenth century. But they did not command much external demand. The export market developed around cotton checks, the type produced by Samuel Touchet from about the third or fourth decade of the eighteenth century.

[65]   Deane and Cole, *British Economic Growth*, p. 183.

export market became the main dynamic force behind the industry's development. This can be seen in Table 9.6.

Output figures, with which to follow the progress of exports relative to domestic sales, are not available for the early decades from the late 1720s to the 1750s. The available estimates for the second half of the century show that as early as 1760 the industry was exporting as much as one-third of its gross output. The export proportion increased to near two-fifths in the first half of the 1770s. Then the War of American Independence (1776–83) disrupted British overseas trade. But from the 1780s exports grew rapidly to reach almost two-thirds of the gross output value in the last years of the century. From then to the 1850s exports were regularly between one-half and two-thirds of the industry's gross output.

Quantitative and qualitative evidence make it possible to trace stage by stage the historical development of the all-important export sector. The evidence shows that it evolved from the production of cotton and linen checks as substitutes for the re-export of East India cottons to Western Africa. The cotton and linen checks branch of the industry provided a preponderant share of English cottons exported between 1750 and 1774, ranging between 48 and 86 percent during the period.[66]

The check manufacturers produced mainly for export, although a small quantity of their products was sold on the home market. Throughout the third quarter of the eighteenth century, cotton checks were the most important branch of the English cotton textile industry. The largest of the mercantile and manufacturing houses at this time were in the check branch. These men employed a large number of the weavers of Ashton, Oldham, and Royton. In 1758, one of them claimed to have five hundred weavers in his employ.[67]

The important point to note is that the manufacture of cotton checks for export was almost entirely a function of the British slave trade from Africa and the employment of enslaved Africans on plantations and in mines in the Americas. The cotton check branch specialized in the production of goods in imitation of Indian piece goods for the markets of Western Africa. These goods also became very important as clothing material for the enslaved Africans in the New World. For example, in 1739 the total export of English cotton checks amounted to £5,279. Of this, export to Western Africa was £4,339, or 82.2 percent, and the rest went to the New World slave plantations. The figures in Table 9.7 illustrate the pattern up to the American War of Independence, specifically, that as the population of enslaved Africans on the plantations increased in the eighteenth century,

---

[66] See Inikori, "Slavery and the Revolution in Cotton Textile Production," Appendix 1, pp. 371–372; also in Inikori and Engerman (eds.), *The Atlantic Slave Trade*, Appendix 1, pp. 173–174.

[67] Wadsworth and Mann, *The Cotton Trade*, pp. 173, 211, 243.

Table 9.6. *Distribution of Gross Output Value of British Cottons Between Exports and Domestic Consumption, 1760–1856*

	Gross Value Cotton Output (£ million)	Exports at Current Prices		Domestic Consumption	
		(£ million)	%)	(£ million)	%)
1760	0.6	0.2	33.3	0.4	66.7
1772–74	0.8	0.3	37.5	0.5	62.5
1781–83	3.0	0.6	20.0	2.4	80.0
1784–86	5.4	1.1	20.4	4.3	79.6
1787–89	7.0	1.5	21.4	5.5	78.6
1795–97	10.0	3.5	35.0	6.5	65.0
1798–1800	11.1	6.8	61.3	4.3	38.7
1801–03	15.0	9.3	62.0	5.7	38.0
1805–07	18.9	12.5	66.1	6.4	33.9
1811–13	28.3	17.4	61.5	10.9	38.5
1815–17	30.0	17.4	58.0	12.6	42.0
1824–26	33.1	17.4	52.6	15.7	47.4
1834–36	44.6	22.4	50.2	22.2	49.8
1844–46	46.7	25.8	55.2	20.9	44.8
1854–56	56.9	34.9	61.3	22.0	38.7

Sources and Notes: Deane and Cole, *British Economic Growth*, Tables 42, 43, pp. 185, 187 (for output figures and for exports 1801–17); Schumpeter, *English Overseas Trade Statistics*, Tables X, XI, pp. 29–34 (for exports, 1760–1800, converted to current values using formula by Deane and Cole); Davis, *The Industrial Revolution*, pp. 98–101 (for exports, 1824–56). Deane and Cole computed gross output value by adding the value of retained imported cotton to the total cost of transforming the raw cotton into cotton manufactures. This transformation cost, which includes the value of other raw materials such as coal and purchased services, is treated by them as value added. However, for 1772–74 and 1781–83 their gross value figures are larger than the sum of their retained import values and value added. The gross value figures in the table for these two periods have been computed, in the manner described, from the original table of Deane and Cole. Also, to eliminate some errors detected in the exports shown by Deane and Cole in their table, their method of converting official values to current values has been applied to figures taken from Schumpeter, *English Overseas Trade Statistics*, pp. 29–34, for 1760–1800, while incorporating their figures for 1801–17. The available output estimates used in the table are for Great Britain, 1760–1817, and for the United Kingdom, 1824–56. Since the English industry exported a larger proportion of its output than the Scottish and Irish industries did, the table may have understated the importance of exports in the revolution in cotton textile production that occurred in England in the first instance.

Table 9.7. *Distribution of English Cotton Check Exports in Selected Years*

Year	Total Export of Cotton Checks	Western Africa		New World Plantations	
1750	£9,743	£7,839	80.5%	£1,904	19.5%
1759	80,605	39,090	48.5	40,850	50.7
1769	142,302	97,972	68.8	40,597	28.5

Source: Wadsworth and Mann, *The Cotton Trade*, Table 2, p. 146.

the export of English cotton checks to the New World colonies also increased. However, Western Africa remained the main market for the cotton checks, except during a few years. Between 1750 and 1802 the export of English cotton checks to Western Africa was less than 50 percent of the total only in 16 years, and for most of these 16 years the African share was above 40 percent. For the rest of this period of 53 years, the African share varied between 50 and 94 percent and often was 70 percent or more. When this variety of English cotton goods lost its popularity in Western Africa, its exports gradually became insignificant.[68]

The evidence thus makes it clear that the check branch of the English cotton textile industry owed its growth and development in the eighteenth century to purchases by Africans in Western Africa and in the Americas. Since it was demonstrated above that the export sector of the cotton industry was founded upon the export of cotton checks, the inference can be drawn that the initial development of the export sector was a function of demand by Africans. It was when the check makers found their markets in Western Africa and on the New World plantations interrupted by the American War of Independence that they turned their eyes to Europe.

Many check makers had manufactured some other varieties of cotton goods as a sideline to the production of checks for the slave trade, when the check branch was the most important branch of the industry. When the check makers moved to Europe, it was natural that some of these varieties should be tried in the European markets. The discovery that "Manchester cottons and velverets" were popular among European consumers must have been the outcome of trial-and-error searching for a product suitable for a new market in the face of problems in the old ones. This variety was developed from the fustian branch,[69] which was closely related to the check

[68] Inikori, "Slavery and the Revolution in Cotton Textile Production," pp. 371–372.
[69] Wadsworth and Mann, *The Cotton Trade*, pp. 174, 175.

branch. Thus there was a relatively easy transfer from checks to the new leading branch.

The Manchester firm of William and Samuel Rawlinson, for example, which for a long time was a considerable producer of checks for the slave trade, had at the same time produced fustians as a sideline. When Samuel Rawlinson decided to give up the check branch, he concentrated on articles in the fustian branch. In his letter of November 26, 1789 to James Rogers, a Bristol slave trader, after reporting that he had given up the "check business," Rawlinson added, "P/S The cotton branch, say all kinds of fustians, muslinetts, dimitty, jeans, jeanett, cords, velitts [velverets?], etc., etc., is carried on as usual by W. & S. R. [William and Samuel Rawlinson] who will be glad to receive your favours in that line."[70] His brother, William, continued with the check business, and in April 1790 he complained to James Rogers of being short of capital, "for to be open I find myself at present so very poor on acct. of the large sums I have paid my brother since his relinquishing the African concern that it has caused such a diminution of capital that to up an old phrase, I am enabled to have half the number of eggs in the same basket as formerly."[71]

Even Samuel Taylor, one of the largest producers of cotton checks for the slave trade in the last quarter of the eighteenth century, who boasted of specializing in the few products he could best manufacture, still combined checks with articles in the fustian branch. He wrote in April 1785 to inform James Rogers that,

the order you send us for 100 ps. of printed linen & calicoes with bordering is not an article that we manufacture and print, & it is not the practice of our house (Haberdasherlike) to clap on a profit upon everything we can lay our fingers on; we are anxious to both give satisfaction to our customers & get something by them too. Therefore we supply only our own manufacture & what we are masters of – those are the various articles in the CK [check] & stripes way for Africa, the West Indies & America.

But he added, "Likewise the various articles in the Fustian Branch for any part."[72]

It was the production of articles in the fustian branch as a sideline to checks that made the shift to Europe by check makers easy and successful. The evidence suggests that check manufacturers led the way in the development of cotton exports to Europe from 1775 onwards. It is particularly important that by the time the check makers turned to Europe, they had acquired much competitiveness from their long-drawn-out battle with East

[70] PRO, C. 107/9, Samuel Rawlinson to James Rogers & Co., Manchester, 26 November, 1789.
[71] PRO, C. 107/9, William Rawlinson to James Rogers & Co., Manchester, 2 April, 1790.
[72] PRO, C. 107/8, Samuel Taylor to James Rogers & Co., Manchester, 29 April, 1785.

India piece goods in Western Africa. In fact, it can be argued that the success of the English cotton textile industry in expanding the sale of its products in European markets in the last quarter of the eighteenth century resulted from the beneficial effects of protracted competition with Indian cottons in Western Africa. This subject is very important for our analysis. It is, therefore, necessary to pursue it at some length.

As an import substitution industry, cotton textile production grew in England in the early eighteenth century in a protected domestic market. Although the import restriction and prohibition laws were not specifically designed for the cotton industry, naturally the domestic market for cotton goods created in England by the East India cottons was inherited by the English cotton industry. Under these circumstances, the industry had little or no opportunity for competition in the domestic market. Only those manufacturers who were compelled by the limited size of the home market to produce for export faced stiff competition with the Indian cottons that had been kept away from the English market by law. This competition occurred mainly in Western Africa.

From the early years of English trade to Western Africa, when the Royal African Company had a monopoly of it under a royal charter, East India cotton goods formed a large proportion of the exports, as was shown earlier. As the limited size of the domestic market forced some of the English cotton producers to move into the markets of Western Africa, they came face to face with the Indian cottons. Here there was no question of the British government providing any protection, as all the European nations were entirely free to trade in Western Africa and carry there whatever commodities they thought would sell. Under these conditions, English producers of cotton textiles in imitation of Indian piece goods for the Western African markets had to stretch their ingenuity to be equal to the fight, which to some seemed futile; pamphleteers in England had begun to complain in the late seventeenth century of the impossibility of the English competing with Indian labor at a half penny a day.[73] The English producers employed a simple method of advertisement. They requested officials of English companies resident on the African coast to promote among the inhabitants of the coastal states a comparison of English imitations with the Indian originals, noting the reaction of the African consumers.

To illustrate, in February 1750 the Committee of the English Company of Merchants Trading to Africa bought from Thomas Norris and Company of Chorley some cotton bafts of 18 yards per piece at 18 shillings each. In the letter accompanying the goods, Thomas Norris stated that he,

should be extremely glad to have them [his own bafts] compared with Indian bafts at the same price & if the committee of Company of Merchants trading to Africa

[73] Davis, "English Foreign Trade, 1660–1700," p. 82.

would make further tryal by sending a few pieces in different ships to different parts of the Coast, that would be the readyest way to find out which goods have the preference, at the same time giving orders to their factors to take notice how such goods was [*sic*] approved of by the Negroes.[74]

In 1751, this firm claimed that the prices of its goods were already lower than those of their Indian equivalents. In a letter of May 7, 1751, the firm pointed out that though the goods sent to the English Company of Merchants were "charged higher than the price you there limit to us I make not the least doubt but they will be very agreeable if compared with India bafts that are 2 to 3s per piece higher & I should be greatly obliged to you to promote their being compared if [when] they are opened."[75] Norris seems to have become so confident of the quality of the firm's products that he could ask the company to,

write upon them Chorley Superfine Cotton Bafts which I forgot than after they were packed. I here inclose you two partons [patterns] & Beg You'll shew them to some of the knowing ones. We are making a large quantity of them for the Liverpool merchants and are rather too Backwards with our orders or would have sent a piece of each sort by way of sample.[76]

English imitations of East India cotton goods seem to have established some reputation on the African coast by the 1750s. Thomas Melvil, governor of the English Company of Merchants Trading to Africa, who was resident on the Gold Coast (Ghana), wrote to the company's committee in London in July 1751 that "to Windward Manchester checks and Grass green long Ells are greatly in demand," and reported that Manchester goods were as popular as Indian goods on the coast.[77] In 1753, he specifically asked for "large quantities of checks cross barred & Manchester" in "our supply."[78] Then, in August 1754, Melvil reported, "If the Ashantee paths open, the goods wanted will be guns, Gunpowder, Pewter basons [basins], Brass pans, Knives, Iron, Cowries, Silks, The Bejutapauts will go out. Of these Touchet's are preferred to India."[79]

[74]   PRO, T. 70/1516, Thomas Norris & Co. to Committee of the English Company of Merchants Trading to Africa, 25 February, 1750.

[75]   PRO, T. 70/1516, Thomas Norris to William Hollier (secretary to the African Company), Chorley, 7 May, 1751.

[76]   *Ibid.* The patterns referred to by Norris were still in the letter at the time of research.

[77]   PRO, T.70/1520, Thomas Melvil to Committee, 23 July, 1751.

[78]   PRO, T.70/1520, Thomas Melvil to Committee, Cape Coast Castle, 24 April, 1753. The salaries of the Company's officials resident on the African coast were paid in goods supplied from England. These goods were sold by the officials to the African consumers on the coast. As the popularity of the goods among the African consumers determined the purchasing power of their salaries, the Company's governors on the coast took pains to ensure that only goods in popular demand were sent down from England.

[79]   PRO, T. 70/1523, Thomas Melvil to Committee, 10 August, 1754. As mentioned earlier in the text, Samuel Touchet was a wealthy Manchester cotton manufacturer

These reports give the impression that English cotton manufacturers had ousted Indian cottons from Western Africa by the 1750s. This was by no means the case. Subsequent decades saw further intense competition. What made the competition particularly difficult for the English producers was that English merchants trading to Western Africa were confronted in the slave trade with merchants from other European nations. Since the slave trade from Africa was completely open to all nations, and the African middlemen on the coast bought freely from whoever sold goods of the best quality and at the lowest price, what determined one's success in the trade was the ability to sell goods in demand and at the lowest possible prices. English merchants, though they wished, from national attachment, to export homemade goods, were compelled by the conditions of the Western African markets to export other goods that would not place them at a disadvantage with their European rivals. This fact is spelled out clearly in a memorial addressed to His Majesty's Treasury by the Merchants of Liverpool Trading to Africa in March 1765:

The trade to Africa being free and open to all the Nations of Europe, it becomes necessary for your Memorialists, not only to carry such goods as are in demand, but also to be able to purchase them as cheap as other Nations, otherwise they can't long support the Rivalship, & this so valuable a branch of Commerce must inevitably languish and decay. That the East Indian Company for many years past, have not had a sufficient quantity of sundry sorts of Goods proper for the African Trade, denominated Prohibited Piece Goods etc. which has obliged your memorialists to send several ships to Holland for the same, the consequence of which is, a great sum of money is laid out there, in buying other goods for assortments, as also, in the equipments of the ships, which wou'd otherwise have centred amongst the Manufacturers & others of this Kingdom. That the manufactures of this Kingdom exported to Africa are woollens, arms & other ironware, hats, gunpowder, brass and copper wares commonly called battery, Pewter, lead etc. as also checks & other goods made at Manchester in imitation of East India Goods, when the latter are at high prices, or not to be got, but some they cannot imitate & their imitation of many kinds is but indifferent. That the trade on the coast of Africa differs from the trade in civiliz'd Nations, & is carried on chiefly by Barter, the certain consequence of which is, if a ship there wants a commanding article brought by one of another Nation, the first must wait till the latter is dispatched, which is often fatal to the lives of the seamen & Negroes, & renders the success of the voyage very precarious. That your memorialists bound both by ties of inclination & interest, do always give the preference to the manufactures of their own country, & several branches of them, they can with pleasure say, have the preeminence, & it is with great reluctance they are forced to purchase any part of their cargoes elsewhere, but in so

who produced large quantities of cotton checks for the African trade. The "Bejutapauts" were a variety of East India cottons. Their English imitations went by the same name.

precarious a Trade as this, they must either have proper assortments of goods, or not adventure to those parts.[80]

These Liverpool merchants requested permission to go to the different markets in Europe and bring the required goods directly to their own port, "on payment of half the old subsidy, & to be kept in warehouses, under the locks of His Majesty's officers, for exportation to Africa only."[81]

It was this peculiar character of the slave trade from Africa that imposed extra strains on the English check manufacturers in their struggle to take over the Western African market from Oriental textiles. The evidence shows that they made an impressive effort, one aspect of which was their ready adoption of the available technology. Of all the English cotton manufacturers, they led the way in applying the textile inventions which transformed the cotton industry. The first of the series of inventions which revolutionized cotton textile production in England was Paul's spinning machine, patented on June 24, 1738. The first manufacturers who encouraged Paul with their patronage were check manufacturers supplying the markets in Western Africa:

Of the three men engaged in the cotton trade who took up the machine two – Johnson and Touchet – were intimately connected with the manufacture of checks for Africa, and their interest in cheap yarn of a quality comparable with that from India was evidently great enough to encourage them to take considerable risks in the hope of obtaining it.[82]

James Johnson purchased 150 spindles and Samuel Touchet 300.[83] The spinning machine had to wait for later improvements before it became fully productive. However, the evidence shows the dynamic attitude of the check producers supplying the African markets to available technology.

The Liverpool merchants, in their memorial, were unfair in some way to the English cotton manufacturers. It may be assumed that by 1765 English imitations of Indian cottons still had some way to go to achieve perfection. But no doubt considerable progress had been made before the American War of Independence disrupted English cotton exports to Western Africa. When the war was over, some producers who had switched their products

---

[80] PRO, T. 1/447/LA17, Memorial of the Merchants of Liverpool Trading to Africa to the Commissioners of His Majesty's Treasury, Read 16 March, 1765.

[81] *Ibid.*

[82] Wadsworth and Mann, *The Cotton Trade*, p. 447. The authors had earlier stated that "the first manufacturer to be associated with him [Paul] was James Johnson the younger, of Spitalfields, who had begun to make goods for the African trade in 1735 and had carried on business on a large scale. It will be remembered that by 1740 imitations of Indian cottons for Africa had had a considerable success. Good and cheap yarn was essential for them, and London was dependent on imported yarn, which there must have been a shortage in 1738–40" (*Ibid.*, p. 425).

[83] *Ibid.*, pp. 427, 444–445.

to Europe may have failed to resume production for the slave trade, some may have combined both, but others did resume full-scale production of African goods. It is not correct to say that Manchester manufacturers failed in their competition with Indian cottons on the African coast in the eighteenth century.[84]

Table 9.8 shows the official figures of East India and English cottons exported from England to Western Africa from 1751 to 1850. English cottons seem to have made great progress; from £14,573 in 1751, they had reached £125,343 by 1767. Further progress was hampered by the political upheavals in the American colonies, which affected the slave trade. Indian goods were higher in value than English cottons in the early 1780s, but from 1783 to 1794 the competition was fairly even. From 1794 to 1801 Indian cottons again were significantly higher in value than English cottons; from 1802 to 1807 English cottons were back in full force.

The achievements of the English cottons were quite impressive, given that Indian cottons had completely dominated the Western African market at the beginning of the eighteenth century. What is more important, however, is that the ceiling on English cotton exports to Western Africa in the late eighteenth century seems to have been fixed not by the greater popularity of Indian cottons on the coast, but by the inability of the producers to expand production adequately to meet growing African demand. A combination of the quantitative and qualitative evidence for the years 1790 to 1792 points strongly to this conclusion.

On the basis of the statistics in Table 9.8, it is clear that English cottons lost ground to East India cottons from 1789 to 1792, except for the sudden swell of English cottons in 1792. Export of East India cottons rose significantly in 1790, 1791, and 1792. When we turn to the qualitative evidence, however, we discover that, at least in 1790, 1791, and 1792, English cotton manufacturers producing African goods had more orders than they could supply. For example, in January 1790, Captain William Woodville wrote to James Rogers of Bristol, a slave trader:

---

[84] *Ibid.*, p. 164. This view may be due to the fact that Wadsworth and Mann end their study with 1780. Furthermore, they are wrong to say that by 1780 checks had ceased to be an important branch of the cotton industry (*Ibid.*, p. 166). The share of checks in total cotton exports fell during the war but rose again afterwards, reaching 30 percent by 1786; see Inikori, "Slavery and the Revolution in Cotton Textile Production," Appendix 1, pp. 371–372. Though it then continued to decline, it remained over 10 percent up to 1792, after which it fell off and became less than 1 percent by 1803 and after. Ralph Davis has been misled by these empirically wrong views of Wadsworth and Mann into believing that the markets of Western Africa and the West Indies for English cottons "were lost when Indian supply became plentiful again in the mid-1760s; the trade had caused only temporary acceleration of growth, which died away" (Davis, *The Industrial Revolution*, p. 65).

Table 9.8. *Competing Exports of East India and English Cotton Goods from England to Western Africa, 1751–1850*

	East India Cottons (£ sterling)	English Cottons (£ sterling)		East India Cottons (£ sterling)	English Cottons (£ sterling)
1751	59,083	14,573	1794	213,275	206,511
1752	49,170	35,752	1795	159,024	69,231
1753	30,860	67,328	1796	214,560	134,786
1754	44,860	49,740	1797	289,332	133,980
1755	37,048	28,503	1798	437,852	204,645
1756	36,214	35,486	1799	464,952	317,381
1757	20,014	35,918	1800	402,729	166,259
1758	24,483	47,565	1801	408,769	187,163
1759	64,150	39,125	1802	306,561	336,306
1760	70,920	52,264	1803	235,491	288,246
1761	50,855	59,672	1804	389,479	352,304
1762	39,447	52,413	1805	322,666	282,834
1763	61,629	119,402	1806	364,315	418,982
1764	87,327	100,438	1807	175,119	270,274
1765	61,889	119,925			
1766	66,925	85,784			
1767	79,362	125,343		East India Cottons (Yards)	British Cottons (Yards)
1768	104,179	64,568			
1769	116,683	98,674			
1770	130,659	72,702			
1771	143,987	118,486	1827	643,670	1,025,942
1772	166,103	123,711	1828	726,190	1,535,493
1773	116,015	72,190	1829	929,120	1,910,940
1774	156,432	95,544	1830	536,520	2,443,202
1775	159,206	76,132	1831	416,160	2,361,090
1776	77,876	91,480	1832	409,750	3,364,360
1777	47,153	31,368	1833	621,970	4,988,400
1778	29,457	14,148	1834	577,570	4,975,636
1779	43,439	8,402	1835	303,790	3,905,729
1780	53,583	4,995	1836	276,460	7,706,901
1781	72,622	17,304	1837	500,420	4,973,412
1782	71,244	48,777	1838	463,630	7,370,755
1783	153,212	162,724	1839	478,050	9,160,022
1784	122,545	141,735	1840	488,400	10,489,550
1785	116,390	147,898	1841	503,210	8,389,266
1786	175,778	279,864	1842	388,810	12,021,627
1787	186,258	111,666	1843	610,880	16,571,981
1788	165,744	175,137	1844	521,010	n.a.
1789	171,454	121,501	1846	873,830	9,463,310
1790	222,051	200,977	1847	665,590	12,465,956
1791	241,674	188,535	1848	347,710	14,595,528
1792	348,809	437,370	1849	407,970	17,275,824
1793	93,133	128,867	1850	457,580	16,891,599

Sources and Notes: Public Record Office, Customs 3/51–80; Customs 17/7–29; Customs 8/25–71; Customs 10/18–41. From 1827 to 1850 the British cottons are shown in yards in the customs ledgers, while the East India cottons are shown in pieces. The conversion of the Indian cottons to yards is based on information taken from the records of Thomas Lumley & Co. of London, slave merchants and dealers in East India goods (C. 114/154). The computation from this source gives 10 yards per piece, average. Figures for British cottons are not available for 1844.

I arrived this morning in Manchester & applied to the different gentlemen here who deal in African goods & found everything bought up by the Liverpool people except a very small quantity & Mr. Rawlinson who had but few goods by him except the Romals you ordered some time since, advised me to look amongst the different manufacturers – but very kindly took that trouble upon himself & by using very great exertions he has procured a sufficient quantity for us.[85]

A bill for 1,000 pounds (sterling) had to be drawn on Rogers for immediate payment for these goods, as Mr. Rawlinson was obliged to pay cash for them; "otherwise it had been impossible to procure a single piece."[86]

The letter of Joseph Caton, a Liverpool merchant who undertook to prepare for the slave trade one of Rogers's vessels, is even more revealing. In December 1790, he wrote:

Sir I received your letter at Mr. Robinsons and Heywoods and had at last engaged your two small cargoes but the Tradesmen at this time is rather full of orders as they say which I believe to be the case, and the short time allowed to have them ready makes it more difficult to get what you want, particularly windward Coast goods as they cannot get weavers to work that article. . . . I must beg leave to tell you the cunning and art of these Old Tradesmen. In the first place, they are all combined together and you cannot do one thing with any of them but all the rest knows it before you get to the second House. . . . the Old Tradesmen is [*sic*] grown so arrogant that they compel one to do as they please. They keepd [kept] me running from one house to another for two days desiring I would try to get what I could at other houses. . . . I would advise you to divide your future orders equally amongst these people then you are sure of being served, for when you employ one man in general and goods much wanted as is often the case then your friend cannot supply you in your time, then you go to another, then he immediately says how do you expect me to supply you if you could get them at another House.[87]

The letter of a manufacturing firm may serve to show some of the factors responsible for the supply problems. In May 1791 Robinson and Heywood wrote to James Rogers, "We have in hand engagements for more goods than we can manufacture in the next six weeks which must be sent as they come from the looms; and our workpeople are so much our masters at present that we cannot this spring add to our manufacture."[88] Finally, we may cite a letter from 1792, also from a manufacturer of African goods. William Green, writing to James Rogers and Company in November 1792, acknowledged receipt of their letter of "the 19th current" but complained that "Mr. Parke is not yet returned from Lpool and I don't know what

[85] PRO, C. 107/13, Captain William Woodville to James Rogers, Manchester, 29 January, 1790.

[86] *Ibid.*

[87] PRO, C. 107/13, Joseph Caton to James Rogers, Liverpool, 2 December, 1790.

[88] PRO, C.107/8, Robinson & Heywood to James Rogers & Co., Manchester, 13 May, 1791.

engagements he may make during his absence, but from what I am acquainted with I am confident it will not be in his power to supply your order of the 1ˢᵗ inst. [instant] under five or six months."[89]

It is sufficiently evident from the foregoing that the ceiling for English cotton exports to Western Africa in the late eighteenth century was not fixed by a limited demand for them on the African coast. On the contrary, the demand from merchants trading to Western Africa was pressing exceedingly hard on limited production capacity. As some of the above letters show, the supply of labor seems to have been one of the crucial bottlenecks for cotton manufacturers producing African goods in the late eighteenth century. In regard to popularity, Manchester manufacturers can be said to have achieved remarkable success in their competition with Indian cottons in Western Africa. In fact, they were so successful that even before Manchester cottons had really established their supremacy in Europe, manufacturers producing African goods had begun to supply them to continental merchants trading to Africa.

The success achieved by English producers in the manufacture of cotton textiles for the slave trade was the first development in the cotton industry to catch the eye of continental merchants; it served to popularize the industry's products with continental consumers. Samuel Taylor told a Privy Council committee in 1788 that,

about twelve months after the Peace, various French African Merchants from Bourdeaux, Nantes, but particularly from Havre, came over here, and examined the species of goods destined for Africa in several warehouses, but particularly in my own, and expressed their surprise at the quality and Price of these goods, the expedition with which they can be furnished, and the credit at which they were sold, and they told me that if I or any other capital manufacturer would establish a House of the same extent, and upon the same plan at Rouen, they should be ready to give me, or such manufacturer every encouragement from Government.[90]

In answer to a question, Taylor told the committee that before the Anglo-French Commercial Treaty of 1786, "all Manchester goods destined for the African trade were . . . by a special Edict, allowed to be imported into France free of Duty, and warehoused for that purpose."[91] If France, of all

---

[89] PRO, C. 107/10, William Green to James Rogers & Co., Manchester, 23 November, 1792.

[90] PRO, BT. 6/9, Evidence taken before the Committee of Privy Council appointed by an Order in Council, 11 February, 1788, to consider the State of the African Trade; Evidence of Samuel Taylor, 8 March, 1788 (pp. 309–317). Samuel Taylor told the Committee he had been producing cotton goods for the African trade for 27 years previous to the time of the enquiry and had raised and supported by it a family of ten children.

[91] *Ibid.*

countries, depended on Manchester cottons for her slave trade, it can be safely said that no slave trader on the continent could do without Manchester cottons in the late eighteenth century.

In the first decade of the nineteenth century, again as shown in Table 9.8, British cottons and East India piece goods shared almost equally British export of cotton goods to Western Africa: British cottons totaled £2,136,109 in 1801–07, and East India cottons totaled £2,202,400 during the same period. But the trend from 1806 (second half of the decade) is clear; British cottons were decisively taking over the Western African market. In the 1820s (1827–30), East India cottons were 29 percent of the total quantity of cottons (measured in yards) exported to Western Africa by British traders, while British cottons were 71 percent. In the 1830s the shares were 7 and 93 percent, respectively; and in the 1840s, East India cottons were a mere 4 percent and British cottons 96 percent.[92] Thus, British cottons won a decisive victory over East India cottons in Western Africa very early in the nineteenth century.

The evidence shows that British cottons decisively took over the markets in the Americas earlier than they did in Western Africa. In 1784–86, British cottons exported to the Americas amounted to £292,000 annual average, while East India cottons averaged £40,000, being 12 percent of the total amount of cottons exported to the Americas by British traders in these years, with 88 percent for British cottons. The share of East India cottons continued to decline: 4 percent in 1794–96; 1 percent in 1804–06; and for the rest of the first half of the nineteenth century it was 2 percent, except the years 1824–26 when it was 3 percent.[93]

In consequence the Atlantic markets were by far the most important overseas markets for the British cotton textile industry for the whole of the eighteenth century, as can be seen in Table 9.9. The Americas and Western Africa together absorbed between 57 and 94 percent of total British cotton exports in the eighteenth century. In the first decade of the nineteenth century the share was still over one-half even though exports to Europe had begun to grow. For the rest of the first half of the century exports to the Americas and Western Africa were about one-third of the total, except in the one period 1844–46 when they were about a quarter. Actually, the share in the nineteenth century would be much larger if consideration is limited to cotton cloth export, leaving out yarn export. Cotton cloth exports to the Americas and Western Africa were 61.2 percent of the total in 1804–06, 42.9 percent in 1814–16, 47.1 percent in 1824–26, 47.2 percent in 1834–36, 35.1 percent in 1844–46, and 39.7 percent in 1854–56.[94] When

---

[92] Computed from Table 9.8 above.
[93] Computed from Davis, *The Industrial Revolution*, pp. 94–109.
[94] Computed from Davis, *The Industrial Revolution*, pp. 96–101.

Table 9.9. *Regional Distribution of British Cottons Exported,*
1699–1856 (in percentages)

	Americas Western Africa	Southern Europe	Ireland	Rest of Europe	Asia	Middle East
1699–1701	80.0	5.0		15.0		
1722–24	83.3		16.7			
1752–54	94.0		4.8	1.2		
1772–74	79.6	2.7	16.7	0.9		
1784–86	57.2	11.4	3.9	27.5		
1794–96	69.2	7.2	10.8	12.9		
1804–06	52.3	10.1	2.9	34.2	0.3	0.2
1814–16	37.3	21.8	1.3	38.2	0.7	0.6
1824–26	37.6	17.1	2.9	32.8	6.4	2.8
1834–36	35.5	16.3		31.0	11.7	4.6
1844–46	25.4	12.2		27.1	24.7	9.8
1854–56	31.6	10.2		19.2	24.7	12.4

Sources and Notes: Computed from Davis, "English Foreign Trade, 1700–74," p. 120, and Davis, *The Industrial Revolution*, pp. 94–101. The only region left out is Australia, whose imports were less than 1 percent except in 1854–56 when it was 1.7% of the total. Percentages may not add up to exactly 100 because of rounding.

southern Europe is excluded, the rest of Europe (Table 9.9) imported mostly cotton yarn. From 1834 to 1856, yarn exports to the rest of Europe were between 62 and 72 percent of the total value of cotton manufactures exported to the region. The large cotton cloth exports to the region in 1804–06 and 1814–16 fell by almost 50 percent between 1824 and 1856.[95] Thus, exports to the rest of Europe did not contribute much to the demand pressure that culminated in the mechanization of weaving in the 1830s. This came from the Atlantic markets, to which was added the fast-growing markets of Asia from the 1830s (Table 9.9). When southern Europe is added to the Americas and Western Africa, the Atlantic markets, as they were defined earlier, took regularly two-thirds to nine-tenths of total British export of cotton manufactures between 1699 and 1806, and over one-half between the first decade of the nineteenth century and the 1830s.

In summary, cotton textile production in England developed from the early eighteenth century to the first half of the nineteenth as an import substitution industry. Undoubtedly, the industry displayed the usual charac-

[95] *Ibid.*

teristics of import substitution industries – initial rapid growth behind tariff protection on the basis of a pre-existing domestic demand; then stagnation as the expansion of output reaches the limit of the protected domestic market. Like the more recent cases of successful import substitution industrialization in Asia, the industry overcame the limitations of the protected narrow domestic market of eighteenth-century England through an early development of an export sector, facilitated by the preceding re-export trade in East India cotton textile by British merchants: The export sector developed initially from the production of substitutes for re-exports that British merchants had traded in the Atlantic basin since the seventeenth century.

Western Africa was the first major export market for the industry. Its growth was associated with the success achieved by British traders in the export of Africans for enslavement in the Americas in the eighteenth century. The protracted competition with East India cottons in Western Africa was important in the development of the industry's competitiveness over time. Subsequently, the Americas were added, and when the French Revolutionary and Napoleonic wars (1793–1815) left all of the Americas open to British commercial domination, exports to the Americas grew enormously. But Western Africa remained important in the late eighteenth century. The phenomenal expansion of exports to the Americas, from £292,000 annual average in 1784–86 to £7,949,000 in 1804–06[96] expanded the industry's scale of operation to a new level, which encouraged the mechanization process of the first half of the nineteenth century. The addition of substantial cloth exports to Europe from the early nineteenth century and the rapid expansion of exports to Asia from the 1830s contributed to the sustained growth of exports, on the basis of which the pace of mechanization increased from the 1830s.[97] Even so, the Atlantic markets remained the largest overseas markets for British cotton cloths up to the early 1850s.

Ralph Davis has suggested that the growth of exports was driven by technological development in cotton production, stimulated by growing domestic demand.[98] This view is clearly contrary to the evidence. The application of the conceptual framework of ISI to the evidence helps considerably to clarify the issues. Had the industry been limited to production for the protected narrow domestic market of eighteenth-century England, as many unsuccessful import substitution industries in the Third World did in the more recent past, there would have been little incentive or market opportunity to profitably adopt new technology. Contrary to Davis's

[96] Computed from Davis, *The Industrial Revolution*, pp. 94–96.
[97] Timmins, *The Last Shift*, pp. 20–21.
[98] Davis, *The Industrial Revolution*, pp. 65, 84–85.

argument,[99] a larger proportion of increments in the gross output of the British cotton industry was already going to overseas markets from 1784–86. According to the evidence of Deane and Cole, which has been used by virtually all historians, the gross value of output increased from £5.4 million in 1784–86 to £10.0 million in 1795–97, while exports (current value) increased from £0.9 million to £3.7 million during the same period. This means that increases in exports accounted for 60.9 percent of the increments in gross output, and growth in home consumption accounted for 39.1 percent.[100]

That growing exports were responsible largely for the transformation of the industry's organization and technology between the 1780s and 1850s is reflected in the fact that, like the woollen industry, it was the region which produced largely for export (mainly to the Atlantic markets), Lancashire, which adopted more rapidly the new technologies and the factory system. In 1787 Lancashire, Derbyshire, and Nottinghamshire had among them 50 percent of the estimated £500,000 capital value of all cotton mills in Great Britain.[101] By 1835, 56.5 percent of all the powerlooms in Great Britain were in Lancashire alone; and in 1850 that proportion had increased to 70.9 percent.[102] There are no precise figures for Lancashire exports, but the evidence of a large-scale producer in Manchester in the late 1780s offers some glimpse. Samuel Taylor, who was commissioned by the Manchester cotton manufacturers to present their case to a committee of the Privy Council in 1788, stated:

The value of goods annually supplied from Manchester and the Neighbourhood for Africa, is about £200,000, from which, if I deduct the small value which is taken for the purchase of wood, Ivory, etc. which cannot amount to £20,000,

---

[99] *Ibid.*, p. 65. As Davis put it, "All British exports were rising fast in the 1780s and 1790s; cotton goods accounted for less than a third of the increase in manufactured exports between 1784–6 and 1794–6. In the following decade, ending in 1804–6, however, cotton goods were going increasingly to export markets . . ." (p. 65).

[100] Computed from Deane and Cole, *British Economic Growth*, Table 42, p. 185. If the calculations are based on the corrected figures of Deane and Cole in Table 9.6, the proportions change slightly. The contribution of exports to the increment in gross output becomes 52.2 percent and home consumption 47.8 percent.

[101] Ian Inkster, *Science and Technology in History: An Approach to Industrial Development* (New Brunswick, NJ: Rutgers University Press, 1991), p. 65.

[102] Timmins, *The Last Shift*, Table 1.1, p. 20. This concentration of the new technology and the factory system was accompanied by the concentration of employment: nearly 60 percent of UK cotton operatives in 1838 resided in Lancashire; by the end of the century the proportion was 76 percent. See Geoffrey Timmins, *Made in Lancashire: A History of Regional Industrialisation* (Manchester and New York: Manchester University Press, 1998), p. 181. The Midlands and Scotland were other major cottons centers in Great Britain in the eighteenth century.

there remains upwards of £180,000, for the purchase of Negroes only. This value of manufactures employs immediately about 18,000 of His Majesty's subjects, men, women and children. . . . This manufacture employs a capital of at least £300,000 including that part of the capital which belongs to the Dealers in the materials who sell them to the manufacturer. The coarse kinds of goods serve for a School or means of improvement to Workmen to enable them in time to work finer goods. Besides the manufactures which are directly furnished by the manu-facturers of Manchester for the African trade, they equally furnish for the West India Trade, which is intimately connected with the former, upwards of £300,000 a year worth of manufactures, in the making of which a still greater number of hands are employed.[103]

By this evidence, annual export of Lancashire cottons to the West Indies and Western Africa alone amounted to £500,000 in the 1780s. Since total annual cotton exports from Britain were valued at £797,000 in 1784–86,[104] the bulk of the exports in the 1780s must have come from Lancashire and the Lancashire exports must have represented the bulk of the county's gross output. Of course, this is consistent with the general views of historians. The evidence is thus clear that technological development in the British cotton industry was driven by overseas trade, in particular Atlantic com-merce, and not the other way round.

9.5 ATLANTIC MARKETS AND THE METAL INDUSTRIES

Like the textile industries just examined, the growth of English overseas trade in the seventeenth and eighteenth centuries was very important for the development of the various industries in the metal group – mainly iron, copper, brass, and the manufacturing industries using these materials. As already mentioned, these industries developed in England from the seven-teenth century along the pattern of ISI. A wide range of metal products sold in England for domestic consumption and traded overseas by British mer-chants had been supplied by producers in Germany and the Low Countries. From the late seventeenth century, the production of domestic substitutes grew to replace imports for domestic use and for re-export. Over the eighteenth century these industries, especially the iron and iron-using trades, developed to become major pillars in the Industrial Revolution. This section

---

[103] PRO, BT. 6/12, Evidence Taken before the Committee of Privy Council appointed by an Order in Council, 11 February, 1788, to consider the state of the African Trade; Evidence of Samuel Taylor, 6 March, 1788. On 8 March, 1788, Samuel Taylor further informed the committee that he had "been concerned in this Trade [the manufacture of cottons] for 27 years; about three fourths of my trade is in goods for Africa, and the rest for the West Indies. . . ."

[104] Davis, *The Industrial Revolution*, p. 94.

examines the contribution of the Atlantic markets to this development. Because the metal industries produced both intermediate and final products, overseas trade exercised demand pressure on them through indirect and direct channels. This presents a serious measurement problem. Export overseas exercised direct demand pressure and this can be measured on the basis of the export statistics. But, as will be shown, there are hardly any statistics with which to measure precisely the magnitude of the indirect demand. To deal with this problem, pertinent evidence is examined and discussed to offer some impressionistic measurement.

In his controversial "take-off" analysis, Rostow stated that

The British cotton-textile industry was large in relation to the total size of the economy. From its modern beginnings, but notably from the 1780s forward, a very high proportion of cotton-textile output was directed abroad, reaching 60% by the 1820s. The evolution of this industry was a more massive fact, with wider secondary repercussions, than if it were simply supplying the domestic market. Industrial enterprise on this scale had secondary reactions on the development of urban areas, the demand for coal, iron and machinery, the demand for working capital and ultimately the demand for cheap transport, which powerfully stimulated industrial development in other directions.[105]

This is a broad illustration of the backward and forward linkage effects of given economic activities in the development process conceptualized by development economists. The indirect demand pressure exerted on the metal industries by overseas trade is to be viewed through these linkage effects: Overseas trading activities stimulated the growth of the shipbuilding and repairing industry that employed annually large quantities of materials from the metal industries as shown in Chapter 6; apart from the cotton industry mentioned by Rostow above, the other export industries had strong linkage effects on the metal industries in the form of demand for machinery, the building of factories and workmen's housing, and in some other forms; overseas trading stimulated the growth of population in the port towns and manufacturing centers – London, Liverpool, Bristol, Manchester, Birmingham, etc. – and thereby induced the building of urban housing and other urban constructions, all of which employed large amounts of materials produced by the metal industries; similar materials

---

[105]   W. W. Rostow, *The Process of Economic Growth* (2nd ed., Oxford: at the Clarendon Press, 1961; 1st ed., 1953; first published by W. W. Norton, New York, 1952), pp. 54–55. On purely national aggregate income growth basis, Deane and Habakkuk questioned whether the cotton industry was large enough to have forced the pace of growth to quicken. Phyllis Deane and H. J. Habakkuk, "The Take-off in Britain," in W. W. Rostow, *The Economics of Take-off into Sustained Growth* (London: Macmillan, 1963), p. 72. In the context of the analysis in this study, it is more relevant to apply Rostow's statement to the economy of Lancashire in the first instance.

were employed in the building of docks, harbors, and warehousing facilities to meet the needs of expanding foreign trade; and, lastly, investment in internal transport improvement – roads, bridges, canals, and railways – directly and indirectly induced by the transportation needs of foreign trade, the export-producing industries, and the large populations of the port towns and manufacturing centers employed large quantities of metal materials. If statistics of annual purchases of metal materials employed in these activities were available one could devise some method of quantification that would allow a measurement of the contribution of foreign trade. In the absence of such statistics, some other evidence may be presented to offer an impression.

As was shown in Chapter 6, the building, fitting, and repairing of the wooden vessels employed in Atlantic commerce, especially the slave-trade branch, was unusually expensive, relative to trade with Europe, and consumed a large amount of iron and copper. If the building of many wooden houses in America consumed large quantities of iron nails,[106] the construction, fitting, and repairing of many wooden ships consumed equally prodigious quantities of iron and copper nails, in addition to other iron and copper materials. What is more, because of the unusual risk to which these vessels were exposed, as documented in Chapter 6, they had to be heavily armed for self-defense and other purposes, particularly during the several trade wars. The heavy guns used in arming the ships consumed a lot of iron in their making. The evidence suggests demand for them was particularly high during the French revolutionary and Napoleonic wars. Thus, in 1793 the Carron Company wrote with a sense of urgency asking its agents at Greenock to seek permission to allow the shipping of 32 guns to Liverpool:

The merchants in Liverpool are daily writing to us in the most pressing manner for the guns in order to enable them to arm their vessels for the defence of their private property, and we are anxious to give them the most speedy assistance in our power.[107]

The making of naval and marine stores – anchors, chains, shackles, bolts, ballast, etc. – was a major industry in the ports of Liverpool, Bristol, and London. It has been said that "large quantities of bar iron were sent by

---

[106]   A nail producer, giving evidence before a House of Commons Committee in 1812, said any person "who knew the quantity of nails required in America would be surprised, unless he saw the immense number of houses built of wood in that country, and then he would rather be surprised where the nails were made that were necessary for the erection of so many wooden houses. . . ." (Cited by Court, *The Rise of the Midland Industries*, pp. 206–207.)

[107]   Carron MSS, James & Co., Greenock, 18 February, 1793, cited by Birch, *British Iron and Steel Industry*, p. 49. The Carron Company is one of four concerns mentioned by Ashton as typical representatives of the factory system (Ashton, *Iron and Steel*, p. 40.)

water to furnish the thriving shipbuilding industry of Liverpool with material for chains and anchors."[108]

The cotton industry, already mentioned, may be used to illustrate the backward linkage effects of the manufacturing export industries on the metal trades. As the industry expanded rapidly from the 1780s, and with the growing adoption of the steam engine, iron foundries and machine-making firms developed all over Lancashire in the late eighteenth and nineteenth centuries. In 1825 there were about 24 iron foundries and 37 machine-making firms in Manchester, besides numerous roller-makers and spindle-makers. In the same year, Oldham had 10 iron foundries and 21 establishments making machinery, besides five producing rollers and spindles.[109] The export industries in the West Riding of Yorkshire, the West Midlands, the Bristol area, and London had similar backward linkage effects on the metal trades.

The one industry whose growth was particularly tied up with the backward, forward, and lateral linkage effects of overseas trading in the 200 years from 1650 to 1850 is building, defined to include investment in dwellings, public building and works, industrial and commercial buildings, railways, roads and bridges, canals and waterways, docks and harbors, and one-half of agricultural investments.[110] All of these construction activities, with the possible exception of agriculture, were largely influenced by the impact of overseas trade, and they all employed to varying degrees large amounts of metal materials. The building of dwellings was very much connected with the growth of urban populations in the port towns and manufacturing centers, to which overseas trading made considerable contribution. The construction of internal transportation facilities – roads and bridges, canals, waterways, railways – carried out during the period by private enterprise and directed by market forces, was largely influenced by the direct and indirect impact of overseas trade – the transportation of exports and imports; the transportation of domestically produced materials to export industries, including shipbuilding and repairing; the transportation of coal, food, and other needs of the urban populations brought into being largely by the impact of foreign trade; and so forth. Variations in the level of investment in internal transport improvement during the period correlated strongly with fluctuations in the volume of overseas trade.[111] The growth of value added in the building industry may, therefore,

---

[108]   G. H. Tupling, "The early metal Trades and the beginning of Engineering in Lancashire," *Transactions of the Lancashire and Cheshire Antiquarian Society*, Vol. LXI (1949), p. 10.

[109]   *Ibid.*, p. 26.

[110]   Crafts, *British Economic Growth*, p. 22, notes to Table 2.3.

[111]   Deane, *The First Industrial Revolution*, pp. 71 & 75. The evidence presented by Phyllis Deane shows that in the first half of the eighteenth century an annual average of 8 road acts authorizing turnpikes went through Parliament; the number increased

be viewed as some measure, albeit rough, of the linkage effects of overseas trading on the metal industries: £2.4 million in 1770; £9.3 million in 1801; £26.5 million in 1831.[112]

The indication from the foregoing impressionistic evidence is that the demand pressure exerted on the metal industries, especially iron, by the backward, forward, and lateral linkage effects of overseas trading was probably greater than that of the direct export of metal and metal products. This should be kept in mind as we proceed to examine the export figures. As Alan Birch has observed, the demand for iron in England in the second half of the eighteenth century was determined by the general level of investment in housing, shipping, mining, and transport, as well as by a steadily growing export trade.[113]

According to the figures of Deane and Cole, the estimated annual average value of the gross product of the British iron and steel industry between 1805 and 1854 is as follows: 1804–06, £16.21 million; 1817–19, £9.15 million; 1820–24, £11.01 million; 1825–29, £17.89 million; 1830–34, £13.78 million; 1835–39, £22.72 million; 1840–44, £19.06 million; 1845–49, £34.44 million; 1850–54, £35.72 million. During the respective periods the percentage shares of exports are 23.6, 29.6, 21.4, 16.5, 22.7, 21.5, 28.5, 24.1, and 38.7.[114] When the indirect demand discussed earlier is added, it is clear that overseas trade was of critical importance to the development of the iron and iron-using industries. The fact that much of the overseas demand was concentrated in the West Midlands, as shown in Chapter 2, would mean that overseas trade was the main motive force for the industrial development of the region.

We turn now to the geographical origin of the overseas trade that was so critical for the development of the metal and metal using industries. The evidence presented in the preceding chapters makes it obvious that the bulk of the indirect demand discussed above must be assigned to Atlantic commerce, quantitatively the main source of growth of British overseas trade

---

fivefold in 1750–1770; it decreased to 37 a year the following two decades, and reached a peak of 55 acts per annum in 1791–1810 (p. 71). For canal construction, there were two hectic bursts: The first was in the 1760s and early 1770s, halted by the trade recession resulting from the American War of Independence (1776–1783); the second started in the 1780s after the war was well over, and became a national mania in the 1790s (p. 75). The page references and manner of presentation in the first and second editions of the book differ. The references made here are to the first edition. For the general treatment of the role of overseas trade in the development of internal transportation in the second edition, see pp. 70–71 and Chapter 5.

[112] Crafts, *British Economic Growth*, Table 2.3, p. 22.
[113] Birch, *British Iron and Steel Industry*, p. 16.
[114] Deane and Cole, *British Economic Growth*, Table 56, p. 225. These figures are for both iron and ironwares. Crafts's figures are apparently for iron alone and are, therefore, much smaller: £1.5 million for 1770; £4.0 million for 1801; £7.6 million for 1831 (Crafts, *British Economic Growth*, Table 2.3, p. 22).

Table 9.10. *Share of Atlantic Markets in the Export of*
British Metal Products, 1699–1856

	Total Exports £000	Americas and W. Africa		Southern Europe	
		£000	%	£000	%
1699–1701	114	73	64	7	6
1722–24	181	107	59	35	19
1752–54	587	331	56	76	13
1772–74	1,198	755	63	6	1
1784–86	1,691	892	53	158	9
1794–96	3,798	1,941	51	347	9
1804–06	4,959	2,691	54	479	10
1814–16	4,400	2,418	55	488	11
1824–26	4,455	2,055	46	387	9
1834–36	5,432	3,322	61	476	9
1844–46	8,848	3,822	43	1,361	15
1854–56	20,903	9,906	47	1,761	8

Sources and Notes: Computed from Davis, "English Foreign Trade, 1700–74," p. 120, and Davis, *The Industrial Revolution*, pp. 94–101. The metal products include all iron and ironwares, but exclude lead, tin, and other metals described by Ralph Davis as raw materials. The percentages are computed to the nearest decimal. The figures are 3-year annual averages.

during the period. The regional distribution of the metal exports, presented in Table 9.10, also shows that the bulk of the metal products went to the Atlantic markets between 1699 and 1856. In the first three quarters of the eighteenth century exports to the Americas and Western Africa ranged between 56 and 64 percent of the total; from the late eighteenth century to the middle of the nineteenth, the proportion was 50 percent and above most of the time and above 40 percent for the remainder. When southern Europe is included, by our definition of Atlantic markets, the proportion rises to two-thirds and above most of the time and more than one-half the entire period.

Table 9.11 focuses exclusively on iron. It shows the total quantity of British wrought iron and nails exported per year (annual average for specified periods) in the eighteenth century and the percentage shares of specified regional markets of the Atlantic basin. The West Indies took about one-quarter of the total during the entire period; British North America (U.S.A. and Canada) took about one-third. The West Indies and British North America thus took between 51 and 63 percent of the total British

Table 9.11. *Share of Atlantic Markets in Total Quantity of British Wrought Iron and Nails Exported, 1700–1800*

	Total Exports (Tons)	Western Africa (%)	West Indies (%)	North America (U.S., Canada) (%)	Southern Europe (%)
1700–20	1,639	n.a.	28	34	14
1725–45	3,666	n.a.	23	34	15
1750–70	9,594	4	29	34	9
1775–1800	15,201	4	27	24	12

Sources and Notes: Computed from Schumpeter, *English Overseas Trade Statistics*, Tables XXV and XXVI, p. 64. Africa and East Indies are put together in Schumpeter's tables, making it impossible to show the share of Western Africa separately using those tables. For 1750–70 and 1775–1800, the share of Western Africa is computed from Customs 3/50–80 and Customs 17/7–29. The figures in Schumpeter's two tables are collapsed into one, and annual averages are computed from her selected years representing each period.

wrought iron and nails exported in the eighteenth century. The data for Western Africa are not complete. The evidence for the second half of the century suggests that about two-thirds of British wrought iron and nails exported in the eighteenth century went to the Americas and Western Africa.

Ralph Davis got it right when he wrote:

[T]he expansion of the American market for iron- and brass-ware was on so great a scale that it must have contributed very significantly to the eighteenth-century development of those industries in England, and so to the process of rationalisation, of division of labour, of search for new machines and new methods which helped so much towards the Industrial Revolution.[115]

There is one industry, gun manufacturing, whose history very much illustrates the influence of Atlantic markets on the development of the metal-using trades in the West Midlands. It was one of the new industries that developed in the region from the second half of the seventeenth century; by the end of the eighteenth century it had become one of the staple industries in the region, especially in Birmingham and its neighborhood. It employed a large number of competent mechanics to perform the skilled work of gun making. In the early nineteenth century about 1,000 workers were engaged in the arms industry in Wednesbury and upwards of 600 were employed in

[115]   Davis, *A Commercial Revolution*, p. 20.

Darlaston.[116] In Birmingham itself, a large-scale gun manufacturer testified in 1788 that the making of small arms employed between four and five thousand persons in the late eighteenth century.[117] The growth of the population of the region was considerably influenced by the gun manufacturing industry, which played an important part in its industrial development. The history of the industry illuminates several of the issues central to the arguments of this study. It is pertinent, therefore, to devote some space to it.

Unlike several of the industries examined in this chapter, gun making was supported by private demand and state purchases. There are no estimates of the value of the industry's gross output in the eighteenth century. It is, therefore, not possible to compare exports with domestic sales. However, contemporary observations and those of the industry's operatives provide some basis for assessing the relative importance of the different markets for the industry.

The comparative importance of exports and government purchases for the industry comes out in the account given by John Whately, a leading gun manufacturer in Birmingham, to the Council of Trade in March, 1788:

According to the best calculation I have been able to make on the subject, the gun trade, in which I am considerably engaged, affords subsistence to between four and five thousand persons, who, in time of peace, are almost entirely supported by the African trade, a business so very different to any other, that their whole existence may be said to depend on it.[118]

Whately added that in time of war the best of the artisans were collected from every part of the industry and employed by government or its agents and were capable of making from sixty to eighty thousand guns annually,

which are indisputably superior in quality, supplied on lower terms, and much more expeditiously manufactured than they could possibly be, but for the regular support of this business by means of the African Trade. These artificers thus selected are well known to excel all others in Europe for good, sound, and serviceable, workmanship.[119]

The whole document shows the subordinate role of state purchases in the development of the industry over time. This was the more so, because

---

[116]   D. W. Young, "History of the Birmingham Gun Trade" (M. Com. Thesis, University of Birmingham, 1936), pp. 23, 65.

[117]   See John Whately's evidence below.

[118]   PRO, BT. 6/10, pp. 354–357: "Representation of Mr. John Whately dated Birmingham 27 March, 1788 on the importance of the Manufacture of guns carried on there, which in times of peace is chiefly supported by the African Trade, to the Lords of the Committee of the Council of Trade." This was during an enquiry into the state of the African trade by a committee of the Privy Council on Trade.

[119]   *Ibid.* In all likelihood, the production capacity stated by Whately was for artisans selected from the Birmingham area alone.

in the eighteenth century the Ordnance Department gave orders for firearms only when England was actually engaged in war.[120] The private records of the manufacturers suggest that even the large-scale producers, who enjoyed government patronage, were still more interested in the export markets than in the windfall wartime state demand. For example, during the War of American Independence a managing director of one of the largest firms wrote to an employee:

J. Whately returned Sunday. Times change and we change with them. The very different aspect after today's news is truly afflicting. Before then ships [were] fitting for Africa and mostly the Gold Coast and a prospect of returning peace seem'd to announce the probability of a large number likely to be wanted.[121]

This indicates that the firm relied more on production for export than on wartime government purchase. As this was one of the major firms said to have supplied a large proportion of the government's wartime purchases in the eighteenth century,[122] this statement gives some measure of the comparative importance of exports and government purchases for the industry.

John Whately, earlier mentioned, stated an additional value of the African market: "A market is also presented by the African Trade for all the arms deemed by Government unservice-able, which would not otherwise produce one fourth if one sixth of their present value."[123] The latter point was echoed by Samuel Galton on June 17, 1806, when he complained to the Board of Ordnance that the abolition of the slave trade in that year had taken away the market that had enabled his firm to dispose of the barrels rejected by the Ordnance. The government was convinced by the argument and compensated the firm by raising the price of the Indian pattern guns it was producing for the government.[124]

Although gross output figures for the industry are not available for the eighteenth and early nineteenth centuries, some figures for total exports and the geographical distribution are available for the late eighteenth and early nineteenth centuries. This is contained in an account of all English iron exports for 10 years (1796–1805) prepared for the House of Commons in 1806 by the Inspector General for Imports and Exports of Great Britain,

[120]   Birmingham Reference Library, L.65.52, *Observations on the Manufacture of Firearms for Military Purposes, on the number supplied from Birmingham to British Government* (1829), p. 5.

[121]   Galton Papers, Birmingham Reference Library, Galton 421/5, Samuel Galton to William Bird, Birmingham, 24 August, 1780. William Bird was an employee of Samuel Galton & Son, one of the largest gun manufacturing firms in Birmingham in the 18th century.

[122]   Barbara M. D. Smith, "The Galtons of Birmingham: Quaker Gun Merchants and Bankers, 1702–1831," *Business History*, Vol. 9, No. 2 (1967), p. 135.

[123]   BT. 6/10, Representation of Mr. John Whately.

[124]   Smith, "The Galtons of Birmingham," p. 138.

William Irving. The regional distribution of the annual average exports for the 10-year period is as follows:[125]

Africa	£107,865	44.0%
U.S.A. and Foreign Settlements in America	26,372	10.8
British West Indies & Northern Colonies	13,564	5.5
British Possessions in the East Indies	79,094	32.2
Foreign Countries in Europe	11,401	4.6
Ireland	7,012	2.9

The average for Western Africa is 44 percent of the total, and that of the East Indies is 32 percent. The average for Western Africa and the Americas taken together is 60 percent of the total. The African share is consistent with the importance of the Western African market stressed in the private records of the manufacturers as earlier presented.

Apart from direct exports from England to Western Africa, gun manufacturers in England also supplied continental merchants with guns designed for the African market. In fact, they seem to have aimed their production at the purchases made by both English and continental merchants trading to Western Africa. This comes out from the correspondence between James Farmer and Samuel Galton who were copartners in a gun manufacturing firm, which later became the Galton & Son earlier mentioned. In 1748 and 1749 James Farmer toured the major trading towns of northwestern Europe in connection with the sale of his firm's products. In October 1748 he wrote to Samuel Galton from Dunkirk mentioning "a prodigious quantity of all sorts of toys of Birmingham make" sold there. He reported having been "recommended to the Principal Houses and if I had a proper set of patterns could have order for any quantity. . . . There are two ships going for Africa from this place one for Angola the other for the Gold Coast. The cargoes are not fixed but when they are fixed I shall have the order." He further stated that he had been given the names "of all the principal merchants in all the ports of France and there are a number of ships fitting out for Mertinico and St. Domingo which carry great quantities of iron mongory which I am to send samples of and [I] shall have large orders . . ."[126] In January 1749 James Farmer wrote again from Rouen asking Samuel Galton to curtail the firm's production,

. . . for our Africa business will never support them, I am afraid, according to the prospects I see here, and accounts from Liverpool and Bristol. What is of the utmost prejudice here is the account from African Coasts that the English arms are bad.

[125]　British Library, *Parliamentry Papers, Accts. & Papers*, 1806, Vol. XII, No. 399, p. 4 and No. 443.

[126]　Galton papers, Birmingham Reference Library, Galton 408/3, James Farmer to Samuel Galton, Dunkirk, 14 October, 1748.

I shall be glad when our stocks [are] reduced and desire you could bring up with you as particular account of all the stock on hand as possible with also the stock at Liverpool and Bristol that we may see where about we are. . . .[127]

This letter suggests that at this time the reputation of English-made guns on the African coast was still shaky. This is true of several English products in Western Africa at this time. But in the course of the second half of the eighteenth century English-made guns became popular on the African coast, along with other English products. The document also indicates that the gun makers were hit by the unsettledness of the African trade in the late 1740s, which ended with the establishment of a new company (the Company of Merchants Trading to Africa) in 1750 for a better management of the trade. However, in November 1749, Farmer wrote another letter, this time from Bordeaux, advising Galton to withhold reducing the output of guns. On the other hand, Galton was asked to "make no more Angola musqts. as there are a good many at Nantes unsold. . . ."[128] Samuel Galton's letter of July 27, 1754, gives further information about the firm's guns stocked in Europe for sale to the African merchants there. He wrote:

I have your favours of 23 and 24 and as I have no knowledge of customs in French Ports I can't pretend to say. But you have used your utmost endeavours to get them back, but really it seems very hard as well as uncustomary that goods imported may not be exported again and I think by some means or other our guns may be got of and not left there to be entirely spoiled, it's now several years they have been there and it's likely impair'd by rust etc., but to have £1,100 worth of guns, valued very moderately, sold for a trifle is preposterous and the largeness of the value as well as the readiness of their being disposed of claims some attention and if after all can't be brought of to have them disposed of there. I have never had any advice of sales of those at Lisbon which if not disposed of will it not be better to have them returned than lye there to be spoiled? You mentioned having enclosed an order from Holland but omitted it.[129]

There is clear evidence here of active sale of English-made guns to continental merchants trading to Western Africa. The difficulties encountered at this time are also shown. This is understandable as English manufactures generally were struggling at this time to have a footing on the African coast. But we can infer from the evidence that by the time English-made guns became popular on the African coast, some time after 1750, continental African merchants must have bought a fairly large quantity of the English made arms as to make a significant addition to the size of the African market for English made arms.

The importance of guns in the African trade meant that periods of high activity in the trade produced strong demand pressure on the gun-making

[127]   Galt. 408/4, James Farmer to Samuel Galton, Rouen, 3 January, 1749.
[128]   Galt. 408/5, James Farmer to Samuel Galton, Bordeaux, 17 November, 1749.
[129]   Galt. 405/1, Samuel Galton to Mr. Farmer, Birmingham, 27 July, 1754.

industry. The nature of this can be gleaned from two periods for which such evidence is available. The records of Galton and Farmer (also Galton & Son) mentioned earlier show the pressure of demand from British African traders in the period just before the Seven Years' War; while the private papers of James Rogers & Co., an extensive African trading firm in Bristol, show the demand pressure mounted on the arms manufacturing industry by the African trade, and the way supply responded in the period just before the outbreak of the French revolutionary wars.

In September 1754, Samuel Galton wrote to Mr. Farmer:

I have your favour of 20 and by mine of 19 you'l find how much we are pressed on every hand and that some orders will be disappointed we must expect and I fear my best endeavours will be short of the expectation everyone had of being supplied in time and that I shall be severely reproached for neglect and every new and pressing order will put the preceding ones further of.[130]

His letter of December 9, 1754, shows one of the major factors that influenced the response of supply to the mounting demand. He reported receiving letters from Mr. Atkinson and John Parr (both of Liverpool), the former requiring 1,400 guns for two vessels, to be in Liverpool soon after Christmas; the latter ordered 450 round musquets that must be in Liverpool in a month. Galton informed Farmer that the firm could not supply all the orders received.

I am really at a loss how to improve by additional hands for I have generally found new ones introduced into the warehouse have rather confused than assisted us nor do I know of a proper person to apply to. I think there is very little affinity in the Gun Trade and Manchester [cotton textile industry], as the manufacturers in those goods keep severally a stock on hand and can readily supply another whereas at this time each manufacturer in Guns hath orders for more than [he] can supply and at this time Hadley [is] endeavouring to get our workmen....[131]

The letter shows the labor problem the manufacturers had to cope with in the face of increasing demand. The same situation is revealed by the correspondence of James Rogers & Co. of Bristol in the 1790's. In June, 1792, Henry Whately wrote to the firm:

We are favoured with your Mr. Bower's letter on the 25th instant and [we] are sorry to have no alternative but to refer you to ours of the 22nd in which we speak very sincerely of our concern at being unable to execute the *Hornet's* order. To undertake any part of it would be equally unjustifiable in us, as we are already under more engagements for guns than we expect to be able to supply. Therefore to

---

[130]   Galt. 405/1, Samuel Galton to Mr. Farmer, 22 September, 1754.

[131]   Galt. 405/1, Samuel Galton to Mr. Farmer, Birmingham, 9 December, 1754. Thomas Hadley was one of the gun manufacturers in Birmingham producing arms for the African market. See text that follows for rivalry between him and the Galton firm.

bind ourselves by another promise to you would be more injurious to you than serviceable . . .[132]

Again, on June 30, 1792, Galton & Son wrote to James Rogers & Co. regretting their inability to complete the firm's orders for guns although they had had to send them every single gun they had made, and in doing which,

We have disobliged some Liverpool friends. We have offered to buy musquets of Gun makers at the price we charge to serve you but cannot get one which we have before noticed. We lament the present hurry and shall hope when it is once over to serve you better in future.[133]

Labor was again a major problem. Pointing to this in a letter to James Rogers & Co., Galton & Son said,

if you know how we are controlled by our workmen and harrassed on everyside you would make great allowances for us . . . We sent to Mr. Whately agreeable to our promise to Capn. Simmons to give him half the order of the Pearl but he like us could not effect it. We intreat you not to wait, for our difficulties accumulate upon us and we are every day declining orders.[134]

Further information on this labor problem is provided by Henry Whately's letter of January 11, 1793, in which he apologized for not being able,

to send the guns which we are providing for your ship *Flora* by the last spring as we intended. At this season our workmen are accustomed to treat themselves with a holiday of some continuance and our having occasion for them in the shops is but little regarded by them, I might say not at all. This has caused the delay of your guns.[135]

It would seem that growing demand for labor induced by expanded orders of British merchants trading overseas encouraged the workmen in the gun industry to organize themselves for purposes of securing higher wages. This created a labor management problem for the larger firms. The workmen's riots of 1772 is a case in point.

From the evidence of the witnesses in the case, which resulted from the riots, it is gathered that in the curse of January 1772, the orders in the books of Farmer and Galton for guns were 15,900 and upwards. These

---

[132]   PRO, C.107/10, Henry P. Whately to James Rogers & Co., Birmingham, 27 June, 1792. Henry Whately was the son of John Whately, a large manufacturer of guns for the African market (see above). The *Hornet* mentioned here was one of the Guinea vessels of James Rogers & Co.

[133]   PRO, C. 107/5, Galton & Son to Rogers & Co., Birmingham, 30 June, 1792.

[134]   PRO, C. 107/10, Galton & Son to James Rogers & Co., Birmingham, 27 June, 1792. The order involved here is for guns stated in indent of goods sent by John Simmons to James Rogers & Co. on January 9, 1792. See C. 107/10, John Simmons to James Rogers, Liverpool, 9 January, 1792.

[135]   PRO, C. 107/7 Pt. 1, Henry Whately to James Rogers & Co., Birmingham, 11 January, 1793.

were guns for the Western African market. One order from Liverpool was for 6,410 guns. The firm could not make up these orders on account of its workmen being enticed away by a rival maker, Thomas Hadley. It is further shown that the workmen in the gun-making industry in Birmingham formed a society on June 17, 1772, "to regulate the wages the masters in general should pay" them. The activities of this society, influenced by Thomas Hadley, led to the riots of the gunworkers on November 28, 1772, during which upwards of 70 workmen rioted in the streets of Birmingham, "with a Blue flag and cockades in their hats," before the premises of Farmer and Galton for allegedly reducing the workmen's wages.[136]

It is not important to go into the details of the cause or causes of these riots. What is important to note is that the pressure of demand in the gun-making industry was creating a labor problem whose effects must have gone beyond the gun trade itself to affect other industries in this area.[137] Furthermore, the demand pressure documented so far in this section of the chapter illustrates in some important way the kind of pressure and opportunity which overseas demand presented to the export industries. It will be recalled that the section on the cotton textile industry above showed similar pressure and opportunity. For the export industries in general, these pressures and opportunities must have contributed immensely in precipitating the processes that led to the adoption of new technologies and new forms of organization.

The available Wills of the manufacturers, who produced guns for the African trade, offer a window into the profits that were made and the way they were applied, apart from what was used in expanding gun manufacturing. Possibly the most successful of these manufacturers was the Galton family concern in Birmingham. The members of the concern, in addition to producing large quantities of guns for the African trade, also participated occasionally in African trading ventures. Among the Galton papers, there is an account of the ship *Perseverance* in a voyage to Western Africa, selling 527 slaves in the West Indies and returning to Liverpool with a net profit of £6,430.[138] When Samuel Galton died in 1832, he owned a considerable amount of landed property in several parts of England. His non-landed assets included 38 shares in the Birmingham Canal Navigations at £250 each; 20 shares in the Warwick and Birmingham Canal Navigations; 15

---

[136]   A detailed account of these riots can be found in Galt. 549–Galt. 552.

[137]   1772 was one of the peak years for English domestic exports to the African coast from 1750 to 1807, so that demand for guns in this year must have been very high. This explains the occasion for the foundation of the gun workers society in the middle of this year.

[138]   Galton 564. There is further evidence in the firm's records of their occasional participation in the African trade. They also sent some guns directly to the African coast to be sold there on their behalf by some agents. See Galton 405/1, Samuel Galton to Mr. Farmer, 11 January, 1752, and Galton 405/2.

shares in Warwick and Napton Canal Navigations; and many shares and stocks of the East India Company and the Bank of England.[139] The firm had founded a bank in 1804 which came to serve the gun business. The total fortune left by Samuel Galton has been put at £300,000.[140]

The gun-making firm of John Whately was another concern in Birmingham, which made large quantities of arms for the African market in the period of this study. The firm was founded by John Whately senior and in May 1766 an article of assignment between him and his son, John Whately the younger, shows that the two "are jointly possessed and entitled unto a considerable stock in the Gun Trade now and for sometime past under a verbal agreement carried on by them in partnership and of debts owing to them in the said trade" in equal proportion. Following the marriage of John Whately the younger in this year, the father assigned his own half of the business to him.[141] After the father's death John Whately carried on the production of arms for the African trade on a large scale. The size of the firm's business may be gauged from the fact that on October 24, 1791, it had upwards of 50,000 guns in the warehouse in Birmingham.[142] His Will and codicil dated March 10, 1792, and July 20, 1794, respectively, show that he made large fortunes out of the manufacture of arms for the African trade. He had a very large number of estates spread all over the Midland. He bequeathed a legacy of £28,000 to his five daughters and two sons, excluding Henry Whately, his senior son, to whom the real estate went. An annual income of £800 was to be paid to his wife until her death. These legacies, together with his just debts, were to be paid out of his personal estate "not here specifically bequeathed in and towards the payment thereof." But if his personal estate should be inadequate, the balance was to be made up from his real estates bequeathed to his son, Henry Piddock Whately. All rights to the future prosecution of his gun-manufacturing business were given to his two sons, Henry P. Whately and John Whately.[143] In 1801 the firm was still heavily engaged in gun making. In this year it was said that "the population of the hamlet of Smethwick had much increased of late years by the Canal passing through it to Birmingham . . . on which canal a Mr. Whately had established a large Manufactory of gun barrels, which were forged and bored by the aid of a steam engine."[144]

[139] Galton 198/2, Will of Samuel Galton, Esquire.
[140] Smith, "The Galtons of Birmingham," p. 150.
[141] Birmingham Reference Library, j 257, Assignment: Mr. John Whately Senior to Mr. John Whately Junior, 8 May, 1766. John Whately Senior seems to have died shortly after this assignment, as the codicil to his Will is dated 5 November, 1766. See j 408, Will of John Whately the elder.
[142] PRO, C. 107/7 Pt. I, John Whately to James Rogers & Co., Birmingham, 24 October, 1791.
[143] Birmingham Reference Library, j 276, Will of John Whately the younger.
[144] Shaw, *History of Staffordshire*, 1801, Vol. 2, p. 126, cited by Young, "The Birmingham Gun Trade," p. 30.

The importance of Liverpool in the African trade attracted the gun-making industry to the port, and the Wills of two large makers there show that they made large fortunes out of the business. One of these was John Parr who was mentioned earlier in this chapter. He started as an agent in Liverpool to the Galton gun-making firm in Birmingham. He later became a large manufacturer of guns for the African market, while participating occasionally in African trading ventures. His will, dated June 19, 1794, shows that his business was very profitable. The extent of his gun-making business comes out from the will. It shows that he had been,

largely concerned in the Gun Trade for a great number of years and for the greater convenience and more extensively carrying on the same [I] have erected very large and commodious workshops and warehouses adjoining and contiguous to my messuage or Dwelling house in Argyle Street and extending also to Pitt Street upon ground held by me under lease from the Corporation of Liverpool for three lives and twenty-one years which workshops and warehouses with the messuage and Appurtenances I compute and value at three thousand pounds.[145]

The will shows that John Parr made a considerable investment in landed property in Liverpool, Saint Helens, and other places, including,

a large and commodious Building by me lately erected in and near Suffolk Street and Greetham Street in Liverpool for carrying on a Cotton Manufactory with a steam Engine and suitable Reservoirs and Pumps and all proper wheels and Machinery with Houses for the workmen and all other reasonable conveniencies.[146]

Later in the will, John Parr stated that the cotton buildings referred to above had been "built for the purpose of and have been lately used and occupied as a Cotton Manufactory with a proportionate part of the power of the said steam Engine." He mentioned "my share of the stock [of the Cotton Manufactory]."[147] John Parr's children continued with the gun-making business along with African trading. The ship *Parr* of 566 tons burden, reported blown up on the African coast in 1798, belonged to one of them, Thomas Parr.[148]

The other important gun maker in Liverpool, about whom information is available, is Thomas Falkner. In 1771, a single Guinea trading firm, that of Samuel Sandys, James Kendall, Andrew Whyte, and Robert Macmillan, bought from him for the cargoes of five of their Guinea ships, 4,991 guns and 1,250 cutlasses, all amounting to £2,348:5:3d.[149] His will, dated April 23, 1785, shows that he made considerable fortunes from his business. He bequeathed £8,500 to his two daughters and 5,000 stock "part of my stock

---

[145]   Lancashire Record Office, Preston, Will of John Parr of Liverpool, Gunsmith. Will dated 19 June, 1794. Probate issued, 30 September, 1799.

[146]   *Ibid.*   [147]   *Ibid.*   [148]   See Chapter 6.

[149]   See C. 109/401 for the cargoes of the five vessels and the manufacturers from whom they were bought.

in the three pounds percent. Consolidated annual Funds" to his executors upon trust, interest from which was to be given to his son, Thomas Falkner. The will refers to messuages, lands, tenements, and hereditaments "whatsoever and wheresoever," to "all my lease hold Estates and chattels, real shares in the bod [board] of the Sankey Navigation and the tolls and profits therefrom arising, seats or pews in Saint Peter's and Saint Paul's Churches in Liverpool," to "all other my real estates whatsoever," and to the remainder of "my personal estate," all this was to go to his eldest son, Edward Falkner.[150]

These surviving wills show that the manufacture of cheap, common guns for the Western African market was a profitable enterprise for the gun makers in England. This must have had a positive influence on the development of the arms industry in the country during the period of study. On the other hand, the Wills show that fortunes made from this business made some contributions to capital formation in other sectors of the economy. Of course, the direct impact of gun making was on the iron industry. Through the backward linkage effects of gun manufacturing and the iron industry, exports to Western Africa and the Americas also stimulated investment in coal mining. Early in the nineteenth century, a German engineer noted in Birmingham the enormous quantities of coal that the repeated heatings of the gun makers required.[151]

It is appropriate to end this section of the chapter with a brief discussion of the evidence illustrating the role of Atlantic markets in the growth and development of the copper and brass industries in England. To this end, it should be noted that the two main authorities on these industries agree that Atlantic markets were central to their initial development.[152] "Before the time when British manufacturers were able to flood the continent with their products," wrote Dr. Harris, "they had made advances in the African market." Elaborating, he stated:

Indeed the rise of the copper industry after 1690 corresponds very closely in time with the expansion of the slave trade, and the geographical connection between copper works sites and slave trade ports is very remarkable. Of the four important markets for copper in the eighteenth century, three, London, Bristol and Liverpool had adjacent copper works, while in the fourth, Birmingham, articles for the Africa trade were manufactured. Moreover it was the case that an increasing proportion of the works were established in the Bristol and Liverpool orbits as London lost its slave trade predominance to these ports, and towards the

---

[150]   Lancashire Record Office, Preston, Will of Thomas Falkner of Liverpool, Esquire, 23 April, 1785. The 3% Consolidated Annual Fund mentioned here was a government security.

[151]   Court, *The Rise of the Midland Industries*, p. 142.

[152]   Harris, "The Copper Industry" and *The Copper King*; Henry Hamilton, *The English Brass and Copper Indutries to 1800* (London: Frank Cass, 1967).

end of the century only one important works, Temple Mills, existed in the London region.[153]

There is not much evidence on the development of the industry in the London area, but ample evidence exists in the case of Bristol and Liverpool. In 1713 it was stated that the trade to Western Africa was giving employment to a large number of people in the brass and copper industries in Bristol, among other trades.[154] Then in 1722, a correspondent of Lord Sundon wrote: "I have been pretty much employed of late in examining the whole process of making copper, brass, lead, which are the main branches of the trade of this city [Bristol] to Africa."[155] The brass and copper industry in the Bristol region grew rapidly soon after the opening of the African trade to all English merchants by an act of Parliament in 1698. By the opening of the eighteenth century, Bristol had already developed an active trade to Western Africa. In 1725 the merchants there boasted of having 63 vessels regularly employed in the trade with a carrying capacity for 16,950 slaves a year.[156] It was this development that induced the establishment of the first brassworks in England, the Bristol Brass Wire Company, at the Baptist Mills in Bristol, in 1702. It was largely engaged in the production of brass and copper goods for the African trade. Various changes occurred in the Company's title. The last was the Harfords and Bristol Bras and Copper Company.[157]

The extent of the company's sales of African products may be viewed from the purchases of James Rogers & Co. of Bristol. In 1788, it sold to the latter 820 "Guinea pans" and 640 "Guinea Kettles," for the *Ruby's* cargo, all weighing 30 cwt. 2 qr. [quarter of cwt.] 24 lb, for £228:5s:6d.[158] In 1789, Rogers & Co. bought from the company 14 boxes brass rods and 58 boxes copper rods all weighing 54 cwt. 0 qr. 11 lb, for the *Pearl's* cargo.[159] In 1791, they bought from it 300 neptunes, 5,100 copper rods, 900 brass rods, and 16 casks manillas, weighing altogether 133 cwt. 2 qr. 12 lb, for the cargos of the *Trelawney* and the *African Queen*, amounting to £811:

[153]   Harris, "The Copper Industry," pp. 13–14.

[154]   British Library, *House of Commons Journal*, 23 April, 1713.

[155]   *Memoirs of Viscountess Sundon*, by Mrs. Thompson, 2 vols. (London, 1847) vol. II, p. 99, Dr. A. Clarke to Mr. Clayton; quoted by Harris, "The Copper Industry," p. 22.

[156]   C.O. 388/25/S 37. Bristol Merchants Trading to Africa to the Lords of Trade, 17 March, 1725. A list of these ships, together with the Masters' names, was enclosed in this letter.

[157]   R. A. Buchanan & Neil Cossons, *Industrial Archaeology of the Bristol Region* (Newton Abbot: David & Charles, 1969), p. 121.

[158]   C. 107/14, *Ruby's* Cargo Notes. The *Ruby* was one of Rogers & Co.'s Guinea vessels.

[159]   C. 107/12, *Pearl's* Cargo Notes.

9s.: 8d.[160] And in 1792 Rogers & Co. bought from the company 1,805 "Guinea pans," 1,115 "Guinea kettles," 38 neptunes, and 8 boxes copper rods, all weighing 73 cwt. 3 qrs. 27 lb.[161]

These are only chance pieces of information from the badly sorted records of Rogers & Co. They by no means represent the total purchases of Rogers & Co. from the company in any of these years. But because this was just one among the many firms trading to Africa in Bristol at this time, the information does indicate that the company was producing considerable quantities of brass and copper goods for the African trade. The company extended its activities throughout the eighteenth century and had factories in other parts of England in addition to those in Bristol. It was considered as the most considerable brass house in all Europe. Some of the branches were still operating in the early years of the twentieth century. It has been shown that the final liquidation of the company's activities was due to "the fact that foreign competitors took their Portuguese and West African markets for rolled-rim brass pans," and that "several of these vessels can still be found in houses in and around Kaynsham, and have such names as 'Lisbon pans' and 'Guinea Kettles.'"[162] Other smaller brass and copper firms also grew up around the African trade in the Bristol region and the records of Rogers & Co. show that they purchased brass and copper goods from many other firms.

With the rapid growth of Liverpool's African trade in the eighteenth century, considerable investment in the brass and copper industry was induced in and around Liverpool, with many firms springing up to take advantage of the high demand for brass and copper goods opened up by the expansion of this trade. In 1725, Liverpool was said to have made much progress in expanding its trade to Western Africa, owning 21 vessels regularly employed in the trade. In this year it was stated that,

the manufactures of cotton, woollen, copper, pewter, etc. spread particularly all over the county of Lancashire, and parts adjacent, so much influenced by this trade [the African trade] are now put into the most flourishing circumstances, whereby the numerous inhabitants (far too numerous to be supported upon the small farms into which those parts are divided) are furnished with means sufficient to enable them to pay their rents, and a handsome subsistence for their families.[163]

The important point about the development of the brass and copper industry in this region is that the investment decisions of all the firms established were to a very large extent influenced by the opportunities offered

[160] C. 107/13. Cargo Notes, Ship *Trelawny* and ship *African Queen*.
[161] C. 107/1 & C. 107/3.
[162] Buchanan & Cossons, *Industrial Archaeology of the Bristol Region*, p. 121.
[163] CO 388/25/S44. Memorial of Samuel Ogden and Charles Pole of Liverpool, Merchants, on behalf of themselves and the merchants of Liverpool Trading to Africa to the Lord Commissioners of Trade and Plantations, 22 March, 1725/26.

by the rapid expansion of Liverpool's African trade. When the Warrington Company was established on July 12, 1755, by Thomas and Robert Patten, together with Thomas Watkins and William Dumbell, one of the main aims of the partners was to make copper fit "for the making and finishing copper rods such as are usually sold to Guinea merchants."[164] The firm of Charles Roe & Co., which established a copper smelting works at Liverpool in 1767, was also largely interested in manufacturing goods for the African trade and the company is said to have dealt extensively in "slave trade copper" and it was among the pioneers in copper sheathing.[165] Again, the agreement made in 1780 by the partners of the reorganized Cheadle Company showed that the partners were to manufacture at Warrington "or in such other place or places the . . . parties hereto shall think fit certain goods made of mixt metal called manillas for the Africa trade."[166] The great copper works built at the Holywell stream in Flintshire by the company of Thomas Williams was wholly induced by the desire to profit from the production of African goods. The buildings which have been described as "stupendous in extent, expense and ingenuity of contrivance"[167] were opened in 1780; "to begin with, production was largely for the African slave trade of Liverpool, but by the mid-1780s naval copper was of great importance. . . ."[168] In July, 1788, Thomas Williams himself wrote a petition to the House of Commons on behalf of his partners that,

the petitioner and his partner have laid out a capital of £70,000, and upwards, to establish themselves in the aforesaid manufactories, which are entirely for the African market, and not saleable for any other; and that the petitioner has lately been informed, that a Bill is now depending in the House, for the purpose of regulating, for a limited time, the shipping and carrying slaves, in British vessels, from the coast of Africa, which the petitioner is informed, and believes, will greatly hurt, if not entirely ruin, the British trade to Africa in the Manufactures aforesaid, whereby the petitioner and his partners would lose the greatest part of the aforesaid capital . . .[169]

The firm of Thomas Williams did produce goods for other purposes as well in the course of its development. But there is no doubt that the

---

164   Quoted by Harris, "The Copper Industry," p. 44.
165   *Ibid.*, pp. 52 & 56. Copper sheathing of the wooden ships mentioned in Chapter 6.
166   *Ibid.*, quoted on p. 39.   167   *Ibid.*, p. 39.   168   *Ibid.*, p. 39.
169   *House of Commons Journals*, Vol. XLIII, Nov. 1787–Sept. 25, 1788. Petition of Thomas Williams, Esquire, on behalf of himself and his partners in the Manufacture of Brass Battery, and other copper, Brass and mixed metal goods, for the African Trade, at Holywell, in the County of Flint, Penclawdd, in the County of Glamorgan, and Temple Mills, in the County of Berks. Presented to the House and read, 8 July, 1788, p. 651.

decision to invest this huge sum in the building of the firm's works was largely influenced initially by the opportunities offered by the African trade. And even in the production of copper for the sheathing of ships, which was the major development in the firm's operations in later years, the sheathing of vessels trading to Western Africa and the Americas at Liverpool and elsewhere formed a large proportion of the firm's business in this sphere, as is shown by the evidence of Thomas Williams before a House of Commons Committee in 1799, fully treated in Chapter 6. Other firms in the brass and copper industry in this region whose investment decisions were significantly influenced by the African trade can be cited. But the examples given here sufficiently show that investments in the brass and copper industry in Lancashire and its neighboring counties were largely induced by the opportunities offered by the expanding African and American trade of Liverpool. These firms, established with the aim of profiting from Liverpool's Atlantic commerce, did, in the course of their operation, produce goods for other markets, home and foreign. But the problem of making the initial decision to go into production was facilitated by the profit possibilities held out by the trade to Western Africa and the Americas, which was a critical factor in the development of this industry in this area. This, in a way, is the sort of thing Minchinton had in mind when he wrote: "the growth of foreign trade brought about shifts in the disposition of factors of production at the margin which were crucial to the whole industrial process."[170]

It is important to note that at the time when the export trade in brass and copper goods to Western Africa was being built up, the brass and copper industry in England was still struggling to find its feet. As earlier mentioned, the home market was still being supplied with the products of brass and copper manufacturers on the continent, particularly Nuremberg and other parts of Germany; "even brass pans for the purposes of the dairies of our country could not be procured but of the German make. So late as 1745, 1746, and 1750, copper tea kettles, saucepans, and pots of all sizes, were imported here in large quantities from Hamburgh and Holland."[171] The quality of English brass products was still in doubt among the home consumers, and often kettles made of English brass were said to be returned to the makers.[172] Thus the African trade provided a profitable outlet for the products of the industry at a critical state of its development and helped to ensure its survival and growth to maturity. Other relatively more important foreign markets, such as those in the East Indies, grew up later in the

---

[170]   Minchinton (ed.), *English Overseas Trade*, Editor's Introduction, p. 51.
[171]   *House of Commons Reports*, vol. X (1785–1801). Report on Copper Mines and Copper Trade, 7 May, 1799. Evidence of Thomas Williams (MP.), p. 666.
[172]   Hamilton, *English Brass and Copper Industries*, p. 291.

eighteenth century. But the formative influence of the African trade was a critical factor in the development of the brass and copper industries in England in the eighteenth century. And throughout the century direct export to Western Africa and the Americas, and the copper employed in the building and fitting of vessels in the triangular trade, remained important to these industries.

10

Conclusion

In the mid-1950s Simon Kuznets, the Nobel prize economist, was requested by the United Nations to compare "the present situation in underdeveloped countries with the earlier situation of the more developed countries, with special reference to the factors that seem . . . to be critical in respect of potentialities of development."[1] Kuznets started his task with a rather long statement of the difficulty in chronologically identifying periods in the history of the economically advanced countries of the West during which their situation was comparable with that of the then underdeveloped countries. The difficulty was partly self-imposed by the initially chosen criterion for the comparison – a period in history during which the industrialized Western countries,

were underdeveloped, i.e. lagged behind the then leading economies; when their backwardness relative to the leaders was as marked as that of the underdeveloped countries of today; when their *per capita* incomes were as low and material deprivation and misery were as widespread as in the latter. If so and if such an earlier situation were found, could we discern the strategic factors that produced the economic leadership of today?[2]

Kuznets recognized that for several centuries up to the fifteenth the Western economies "lagged behind most of the economies of the Near and Far East," but considered the period too distant for him to handle competently.[3] Ultimately, he settled for relative levels of industrial development, measured in terms of the ratios of the labor force employed in agriculture and industry, to determine the comparable situation for his task. As he put

---

[1] Simon Kuznets, "Underdeveloped Countries and the Pre-Industrial Phase in the Advanced Countries: An Attempt at Comparison," in A. N. Agarwala and S. P. Singh (eds.), *The Economics of Underdevelopment* (Oxford: Oxford University Press, 1958; Published as a Galaxy Book, 1963), p. 135.
[2] Kuznets, "Underdeveloped Countries," p. 138. [3] *Ibid.*, p. 139.

it, "the substance of modern economic development lies in the adoption of the industrial system – a term denoting widespread application of empirical science to the problems of economic production."[4]

Having identified the comparable situation conceptually and chronologically, Kuznets proceeded to show the factors that were critical in the successful industrialization of the Western economies. The central factor identified was population size and the pattern of its movement. For the economically advanced Western countries the size of their population in the decades preceding the initiation of industrialization was small and the rate of growth was low. What is more, the extra population produced in the course of industrialization was removed by massive migrations to semi-empty lands overseas – the Americas, Australia, New Zealand, and so forth. As Kuznets saw it, the problem for the underdeveloped countries of the 1950s was that the absolute size of the national populations was too large, its rate of growth was too high, and there was no opportunity for massive migrations comparable with those available to the Western European countries as their industrialization matured.[5]

Consistent with the dominant view of mainstream economists between post-World War II and the 1970s, as shown in this study, Kuznets completely ignored the role of international trade in explaining the successful industrialization of the leading Western economies, especially those of Britain and the United States. This was a missed opportunity for policy makers in the Third World, the mid-1950s being the period when serious industrialization strategies were initiated in several Third World countries. Had the authoritative and highly respected voice of Simon Kuznets demonstrated the critical role of international trade in the first industrial revolution in the world – the Industrial Revolution in England – his execution of the assignment given to him by the United Nations might probably have mitigated the serious errors in the policies pursued by most developing countries from the 1950s to the 1970s. The emphasis of Kuznets on population size and growth pattern drew the attention of policy makers away from the truly critical factor – international trade – and made the lessons of the Industrial Revolution in England inaccessible to developing countries.

But the fault does not rest with Simon Kuznets; it rests with historians. Had historians followed the lead provided by the "Commercial Revolution" thesis of the pre-World War II historiography of the Industrial Revolution by providing empirical and logical details, Kuznets would have had unambiguous help in executing his task. Instead they abandoned the outward-looking explanations of the pre-war period and focused on inward-looking analysis. The Industrial Revolution was explained mainly in terms of population growth, progressive agrarian structure and social

[4]   *Ibid.*, pp. 141–142.   [5]   *Ibid.*, pp. 147–153.

institutions, and changes in science and technology derived from these factors, or very boldly in terms of accidental technological development. These arguments that dominated the historiography of the Industrial Revolution between the 1950s and the early 1980s have failed to stand up in the face of detailed empirical and logical scrutiny.

In the first place, progressive agrarian structures and social institutions similar to those that existed in England in the seventeenth and eighteenth centuries existed in Italy and Holland much earlier, but neither of those countries succeeded in launching the first industrial revolution in history. Within England itself, the southern counties, particularly those in East Anglia and the West Country, which dominated agricultural and proto-industrial development for several centuries and had virtually all the progressive agrarian structure and social institutions in pre-industrial England, were not the leading regions in the Industrial Revolution. In the course of the eighteenth century they suffered deceleration and decay. It was the northern counties, especially Lancashire and the West Riding of Yorkshire, with the most backward agrarian structure and social institutions in pre-industrial England, which led the Industrial Revolution and eventually pulled the lagging southern counties along after the railways created a strongly integrated national economy.

Research by historical geographers, whose evidence is presented in this study, sheds a new light on the course and character of England's industrialization. What the evidence shows is a process of industrialization that was highly regional. Up to the peak of the railway age in the nineteenth century, the internal transportation facilities that were developed, especially the canals that were the most important of all, created regional economies within which there was keen competition but between them there was very little competition because of the structure of internal transportation costs. These facilities considerably reduced transportation costs within the regional economies and permitted competitive allocation of resources within them. But, because of the way the facilities were constructed, transportation costs rose quickly as the regional boundaries imposed by them were crossed. This created regional markets in which local producers were protected by inter-regional transportation costs. Arising from this, the main arena for competition among producers located in the different regions of England was in overseas markets rather than inter-regional domestic sales. Hence, over time regional concentration of the leading industries was determined by success or failure in the promotion of overseas sales.

This character of the industrialization process places a large discount on factors such as population growth and agricultural improvement. Much of the agricultural improvement occurred in the southern counties, while the leading counties in the Industrial Revolution were in the north. And the evidence of the historical geographers makes it clear that the agricultural south did not provide major markets for the manufactures of the leading northern counties. The successful northern counties sold the greater part of their manufactures overseas. What is equally important, these industrializing northern counties appear to have generated the bulk of the labor for their growing industries themselves. Naturally increasing population in response to expanding employment opportunities in manufacturing and commerce is shown by county historians as the main source of long-term labor supply. Inter-regional migration was a minor source. All this places considerable discount on earlier arguments connecting agriculture and population to England's industrialization. The shape of the connection now has to be redrawn.

The pieces of the puzzle in the home market versus overseas sales debate fall into place when the foregoing points are placed within the conceptual framework of import substitution industrialization that informs the organization and analysis of the data presented in the study. The evidence showing the import substitution character of England's industrialization from the late seventeenth century is unambiguous. The growth of the domestic market for manufactures, upon which the import substitution industries were initially established, owed much to centuries of England's involvement in overseas trade, particularly during the commercial revolution period (seventeenth and early eighteenth century). The domestic versus overseas market arguments are often not well informed on factors that determine success or failure in ISI. The argument, that the home market was initially more important than overseas demand, therefore, the home market was the main factor explaining England's successful industrialization, misses the point by a wide margin. By definition, all ISI processes start on the basis of a pre-existing domestic demand. For this reason the protected domestic market remains the main source of demand for some decades. The discovery that the home market was initially more important for England's manufacturers is more or less a non-issue. What should be noted is that success or failure does not depend very much on what happens during this early home-based period. Whether industrialization based on ISI strategy is successfully completed or not depends on what happens after the growth of manufacturing output reaches the limit of the pre-existing domestic market. At this point, the analytical task is to explain what accounts for further expansion of output to a point where the production and adoption of new technology is a rewarding proposition for industrial entrepreneurs. What needs to be measured here is increments in sales at home and overseas in relation to increments in industrial output, taking manufacturing industry as a whole and by sectors, nationally and, more important, regionally. The contribution of export production to the growth of the domestic market should also be considered, especially the domestic market for intermediate and capital goods.

Measured in this manner the central role of overseas markets in the successful completion of the industrialization process in England is unmistakable. Increases in overseas sales accounted for more than half of the increments in British industrial output between 1700 and 1760, and between 1780 and 1800, respectively. Yet this does not include the contribution of export and import activities to the growth of the domestic market. It must be stressed that this measurement based on industrial output as a whole still minimizes the contribution of exports to England's industrialization process. As already mentioned, it is clear from the evidence that the process was led by a few industries – textiles and metals – and a few regions – Lancashire, the West Riding of Yorkshire, and the West Midlands. Increases in overseas sales were concentrated in the leading industrial sectors and in the leading regions. The textile industries in Lancashire and the West Riding produced mainly for export and increases in overseas sales of textiles occurred mainly in that part of the textile industries located in those two northern regions. Similarly, the metal industries in the West Midlands produced largely for export and increases in overseas sales of metal products occurred mainly in the industries located in that region. Judging from the proportion of the textile and metal industries initially located in these regions, the contribution of increases in overseas sales to increments in regional output in these industries must have been considerably greater than the national and industry-wide measurement stated earlier. It was this concentrated contribution of increases in overseas sales that was responsible for the concentration of these industries in these regions over time. Conversely, the inability of the southern counties – several of which (especially in East Anglia and the West Country) had dominated proto-industrial expansion – to secure growing overseas markets, as output reached the limits of their regional home markets, was the cause of their stagnation.

The consequences of success or failure in export sales for the domestic market should also be noted. The evidence points to the fact that the domestic market expanded much more in the industrializing northern counties than in the southern counties in the eighteenth and early nineteenth century. There was much greater population growth in the north (in response to growing employment opportunities) than in the south. Yet, because of the explosive growth of export industries wages increased more in the north than in the south during the period. Thus, more rapidly growing population and faster rising wages, all due largely to phenomenal increases in overseas sales, combined to bring about a more rapid expansion of the domestic market in the north than that of the south during the period.

The conceptual framework of ISI also helps to explain the course of technological change and the regional pattern. The pressure and opportunities generated by the concentrated increases in overseas sales in the northern industries help to explain the regional location of inventions and technological innovations. Measurements based on national aggregate and industry-wide data conceal the magnitude of the problems and

opportunities which provided the environment for the inventions, the technological innovations, and the reorganization of industrial production.
When the evidence is disaggregated, and regional and sectoral analysis is
conducted, the real situation becomes more clearly visible; it becomes easy
to see how technological change was trade driven. In the first place, regional
analysis makes it easy to see that the northern counties became leaders in
overseas sales before they became leaders in technological innovation.
Hence, it was their leadership in overseas sales that led to their leadership
in technological innovation. Conversely, the failure of the proto-industrial
regions of the south to secure growing overseas markets was responsible
for their lag in technological innovation *vis-a-vis* the northern counties. On
the other hand, regional analysis makes it difficult to argue that technological change was accidental and that the causal connection flowed from
technological development to trade – that is, trade did not cause technological change, but rather, autonomous technological development gave rise
to trade. To establish the proof for the latter claim, it has to be explained
why technological change occurred in socially and agriculturally backward
northern counties where export sales were growing rapidly and not in the
south where social structures and agriculture had initially been more progressive. What is more, the claim, that technological development, whether
autonomous or derived from home demand, caused the growth of overseas
sales instead of the other way round, is contrary to the clear evidence from
the northern counties that led the technological change in cottons, woollens, and metals.

That the industrialization process in England was trade driven is also
supported by evidence showing what is described in this study as re-export
substitution industrialization (RSI). The industrialization drive which gathered momentum from the mid-eighteenth century had been preceded by
the growth of entrepôt trade conducted by British traders for more than a
century. It was during this period that imported manufactures created the
domestic market that subsequently supported import substitution industrial
development. During the same period, the re-export of foreign manufactures by British traders helped to create overseas markets for manufactures.
The evidence presented in the study shows that the import substitution
industries followed the lead provided by the British traders to substitute
British manufactures for the re-exports largely before the widespread adoption of new technologies in industrial production.

The contribution of international trade to the industrialization process
in England went beyond the procurement of export markets for British
manufactures. Imported raw materials also played a major role. In particular, the falling cost of imported raw cotton was as important as new
technologies and new forms of industrial organization in bringing down
production costs in the cotton textile industry in the eighteenth and early
nineteenth century. Similarly, the development of financial institutions in

England – a *sine qua non* for the establishment of a modern industrial economy – and the growth of the English shipping industry, all of which became major income earners in the nineteenth century and beyond, were products of overseas trade expansion. When all of these contributions documented in the study are taken together it can be reasonably said that the study provides sufficient proof that the Industrial Revolution in England was a product of overseas trade – the first case of export-led industrialization in history. This is not to say that the internal factors, such as agricultural improvement and progressive social institutions, were unimportant. The development of these elements in the South of England was clearly important in the rapid transmission of the growth forces from the North, once the railways established a strongly integrated national economy in the nineteenth century. This is why it is held in this study that it is not altogether accurate to argue, as Wrigley and others do, that the centuries of socio-economic development which preceded the more immediate developments leading to the Industrial Revolution – the development of the organic economy versus that of the inorganic, mineral-based energy, economy, to use Wrigley's terms – were causally unconnected.[6]

If international trade was a critical factor in the successful completion of the industrialization process in England, what was the role of Africans in the growth of England's international trade? This study's answer to the question is based on the central position of trans-Atlantic commerce in England's overseas trade during the period under consideration. During the period the Atlantic basin became by far the most important center of international trade in the world. The production of commodities in the Americas for trans-Atlantic commerce grew from £1.286 million per annum in 1501–50 to £7.970 million in 1651–70, £21.903 million in 1761–80, and £89.204 million in 1848–50. Based on these products, the total annual average value of Atlantic commerce grew from £3.241 million in 1501–50 to £57.696 million in 1761–80, and £231.046 million in 1848–50.

Within the first few decades of the sixteenth century, the volume and value of Atlantic commerce had completely overshadowed that of the international trade centered on the Mediterranean. The evolving international economy became totally centered in the Atlantic basin. Whatever trade Western Europe had with Asia in the seventeenth and eighteenth centuries depended largely on Atlantic commerce – the trade was heavily dependent on American bullion that paid for European imports from Asia; a large proportion of the Asian products, particularly the textiles, were intended as re-exports in Atlantic commerce. What is more, the international exchange of goods within Western and northern Europe during the period was, for all practical purposes, an extension of Atlantic commerce. The bulk of the

---

[6] Wrigley, *Continuity, Chance and Change*. Wrigley's argument and those based on the notion of accidental development of technology belong together, logically.

goods traded in Europe by Portugal and Spain came from their American colonies; and the bulk of the goods they imported in exchange, for internal consumption and for re-export to the American colonies, were paid for largely with American resources. The same thing was true of British and Dutch trade in Europe, and that of France before the French Revolution (1789). On the west of the Atlantic, the tripartite division of labor that evolved in the U.S. economy from the late eighteenth century, which was central to that economy's development between 1790 and 1860, derived largely from the growth of Atlantic commerce dating from the colonial period.

England successfully employed its naval power to wrest from the other Atlantic powers (Spain, Portugal, Holland, and France) a disproportionate share of the expanded Atlantic commerce of the period. Thus, commodity production in British America for Atlantic commerce increased from 5 percent of the total for all the Americas in 1651–70 to 50 percent in 1781–1800, and 61 percent in 1848–50. Because of the unique position of British America in the intra-American commerce of the New World economies, and the American-derived trade between England and the Iberian peninsula (especially the trade with Portugal), the place of Atlantic commerce in England's international trade during the period is not fully revealed by the direct statistics on English Atlantic commerce. Yet the direct figures show the centrality of Atlantic commerce to the development process in England. Between 1699/1701 and 1772/1774 increases in the sale of English manufactures in Western Africa and the Americas accounted for 71.5 percent of the increment in overseas sales of English manufactures; Europe (including Ireland) accounted for 16.7 percent. Much of the increase in Europe came from southern Europe (largely Portugal and Spain). Sales in northern and northwest Europe declined absolutely during the period. Between the late eighteenth and early nineteenth century (1784/86–1804/06), the critical period for the development of the new technologies of the Industrial Revolution, increments in the sale of British manufactures in Western Africa and the Americas accounted for 60 percent of the increment in British manufactures exported overseas. When exports to Portugal and Spain, which depended largely on the American colonies of these countries, are taken into account these percentages increase significantly.

When the figures are disaggregated and the analysis is focused on the leading manufacturing sectors the contribution of Atlantic commerce looms even larger. The growth of woollen, linen, cotton, and metal exports during the period was virtually a function of exports to Atlantic markets. Because Lancashire, the West Riding, and the West Midlands dominated exports to these markets, Atlantic commerce was far more dominant in the economies of these regions than was the case for the rest of England at the time. The growth of British imports and British shipping during the period depended similarly on Atlantic commerce.

This centrality of Atlantic commerce to the development process in England is the real measure of the contribution of Africans to the British Industrial Revolution. Apart from the forced labor of American Indians employed in the production of silver in Spanish America, enslaved Africans and their descendants were the only specialized producers of commodities in the Americas for Atlantic commerce during the period. Abundance of agricultural land in the Americas and easy access to it by independent cultivators encouraged free migrants from Europe to engage largely in subsistence agriculture. Even the indentured servants imported from Europe were motivated by the idea of setting themselves up as independent subsistence cultivators at the expiration of their contract. Given this situation, legally free labor could not form the basis of large-scale commodity production in the Americas for Atlantic commerce. Hence, enslaved Africans became the specialized large-scale producers of commodities for Atlantic commerce in the Americas, because they did not have the choice available to legally free European migrants at the time. The gold, sugar, cotton, coffee, and other plantation crops produced in Brazil and the Caribbean were produced entirely by Africans and their descendants. The rice, tobacco, and, above all, the cotton produced in the South of the United States were produced by Africans. Even in Spanish America where the forced labor of American Indians was important in silver production, Spanish American gold was produced by Africans; and African labor was not insignificant in silver production.

The labor of enslaved Africans did not only make possible large-scale commodity production for Atlantic commerce in the Americas. It also made possible the expansion of European consumption of these products. A combination of the economies of scale and the below subsistence cost of the labor of enslaved Africans brought down the cost of production and the consumer price of these products. Following from this, the American products changed over time from being luxury products for the European aristocracy and the upper middle class to necessities even for the lower classes. This explains the phenomenal expansion of Atlantic commerce during the period.

The fall in the prices of these commodities over time was particularly important for the expansion of British commerce, especially as England also came to dominate the supply of African slave labor to the economies of the Americas. Between 1650 and 1807 the shipping of African slave labor to all of the Americas, British and non-British, constituted an important element in the growth of England's Atlantic commerce. Equally important, the cheap raw materials produced by Africans, especially raw cotton, were critical to England's industrialization. While the Atlantic slave trade retarded the development of commodity production in Western Africa, continental Africans still managed to produce some strategic raw materials, such as gum Senegal and palm oil, for British industries during the period. Taking together all the commodities produced for Atlantic commerce in the Americas, the proportion produced by Africans and their descendants grew from approximately 54 percent in 1501–50 to 69 percent in 1651–70, reaching a peak of 83 percent in 1761–80, before falling somewhat to 80 percent in 1781–1800 and 69 percent in 1848–50.

Thus, to the extent that Atlantic commerce was central to the successful completion of England's industrialization, as elaborately demonstrated in this study, the conclusion can be drawn on the basis of the evidence that the contribution of Africans was central to the origin of the Industrial Revolution in England – defining the Industrial Revolution broadly as we have done in the study.

Comparative studies of European and Chinese economic history from the sixteenth to the nineteenth century, and the more recent cases of ISI in Asia and Latin America, help to place the arguments in this study in a broader perspective. As already mentioned, Simon Kuznets had noted the leadership of the main economies in the Near and Far East for several centuries up to the fifteenth, but did not explain why those economies were overtaken by the West between the sixteenth and nineteenth century. At about the same time, the mid-1950s, Joseph Needham pioneered a detailed study of Chinese science and technology that showed more clearly the extent of Chinese leadership over the West in science and technology.[7] This prompted efforts by Immanuel Wallerstein to search for explanations why the Chinese lagged while the West industrialized.

Wallerstein employed a political economy analysis centered on Atlantic commerce. The argument is that European expansion to the Americas gave rise to a world economy (what has been described in the literature as the Atlantic economic order)[8] on the basis of which the West developed industrial capitalism. China had the technology and the resources to expand the way Western Europe did. The Chinese actually embarked on the process and could have made the achievement earlier than the West did, but they stopped it abruptly. Why China could not sustain expansion politically and the West did is explained by Wallerstein in terms of the social basis of power, the sources of state revenue, and the degree and character of inter-state

---

[7] Joseph Needham, *Science and Civilization in China* (London and New York: Cambridge University Press, 1954).

[8] Inikori, "Africa in World History." The term, Atlantic economic order, is more appropriate in describing the international economic arrangement which evolved in the Atlantic basin between the sixteenth century and the nineteenth. By definition, it is inaccurate to talk of a world economy in the sixteenth century, as Wallerstein does. The extension of the Atlantic economic order to the rest of the world from the nineteenth century ultimately produced what has come to be known as the world economic order. Wallerstein's data and analysis are actually consistent with this view. Why he chose to speak of a world economy as early as the sixteenth century is difficult to explain. Abu-Lughod, *Before European Hegemony*, has followed his lead to talk about a world economy of the thirteenth and fourteenth centuries.

power competition in China and in Western Europe during the relevant period.[9]

It is not necessary to present the details of Wallerstein's argument. What is important to note is that it makes the several centuries of socio-economic change preceding the Industrial Revolution relevant to the analysis, as this study has done. More important, the growth of Atlantic commerce occupies the center stage in the explanation of Western leadership.

The Wallerstein argument has been further extended in a more detailed comparative study of China and Europe in the context of the historical development of the hierarchically structured World Economy. In his recently published book, Kenneth Pomeranz has pushed the leadership of northwest Europe over China to a much later period. Employing a regional analysis of the development process in China, Pomeranz compares the history of England and the Yangzi Delta, the leading economies in the development process in northwest Europe and China, respectively. Up to 1750, according to Pomeranz, per capita incomes in China and the operation of market institutions compared favorably with those of Europe. The Yangzi Delta, with a population roughly 31 million in 1750, produced in that year between 12 and 15 pounds (weight) of cotton cloth per head, as compared with roughly 13 pounds of cotton, linen, and woollen cloth produced altogether per capita in the United Kingdom in 1800. It was between 1750 and 1900 that China fell behind, while northwest Europe pulled ahead.

Pomeranz explains that the Yangzi Delta, China's leading economy, lost its export markets and sources of imports as proto-industrialization spread to all Chinese regions that had earlier acted as the hinterlands of the leading region, the Yangzi Delta. Not having overseas markets and sources of raw material similar to those of the Atlantic basin, industrial development in the Yangzi Delta stagnated; its population remained stationary between 1750 and 1850. Without access to growing export markets and sources of raw material imports, none of the other proto-industrial regions succeeded in taking over leadership. Hence, industrial development in China as a whole failed to advance.

Pomeranz identified two advantages that made success possible in northwest Europe: 1) advantageous location of the latter's coal resources; 2) the constitution of the economies and societies of the Americas in a manner that made them to play a supporting role to the development process in northwest Europe – the employment of slaves to produce export commodities in contrast to the settlement of the Chinese frontiers with freehold farmers. Ultimately the critical factor in the explanation is, again, the Atlantic basin and its slave economy. Without this factor, as Pomeranz puts

---

[9] Wallerstein, *The Modern World System I.*

it, "domestic forces alone could easily have made England produce another Yangzi Delta (or another Flanders)."[10]

Comparative studies of the more recent industrialization processes in Asia and Latin America offer similar insights on the critical role of access to overseas markets. A combination of factors had encouraged inward-looking policies in most Third World countries, particularly in Latin America, in the 1950s and 1960s – the collective memory of disappointment with the export production of primary commodities following the disastrous collapse of the international economy brought about by the two world wars and the Great Depression; the influence of the closed economy models of mainstream growth economists; and the successes achieved by the command economy of the Soviet Union. Given this environment, all the ISI strategies in Latin America from the 1930s to the 1960s were directed exclusively at the home market. Starting its ISI strategy in the 1930s, by 1960 Brazil exported only 1.7 percent of its industrial output. As late as 1970 the proportion was still only 5.3 percent. In spite of the early rapid rate of growth, and the promise shown by many (especially Argentina, Brazil, and Mexico), none of the processes in Latin America was successfully completed by the opening of the 1990s. The failure of inward-looking industrialization strategy compelled some to change course and pursue export promotion. To the extent that they had access to export markets, the performance of those economies improved thereafter, despite the burden of external debts arising from past policy errors.

On the other hand, a few Asian countries – South Korea, Taiwan, Singapore, and Hong Kong – due to their peculiar circumstances pursued ISI in a manner very similar to that of England. They moved quickly to encourage manufactured exports in the import substitution industries as output reached the limits of the pre-existing home demand. For example, the proportion of industrial output exported by South Korea in 1960 was similar to that of Brazil, 1.9 percent. But by 1970 South Korea was exporting 37.9 percent of its industrial output. The success achieved in expanding overseas sales of labor-intensive manufactured goods helped to sustain a high rate of industrial growth, which created jobs and expanded the

---

[10]   Pomeranz, *The Great Divergence*. The information presented comes from a summary of the book placed on the internet. I am grateful to my graduate student, Michael Easterly, who brought it to my attention. The detailed argument in the later published book is fully captured by the internet summary. However, the emphasis in the book is on the supply of raw materials by the slave economy of the Atlantic; the importance of the Atlantic markets for manufactures is de-emphasized. The latter is in error, because the failed transition of the Yangzi Delta, on Pomeranz's own evidence, was a function of the loss of export markets as its previous hinterland regions in China took to proto-industrialization of their own, similar to what happened to England in northern and northwest Europe in the eighteenth century (which Pomeranz does not seem to take into account).

domestic market for both consumer goods and intermediate and capital goods. Consequently, these economies were able to extend their import substitution to the competitive production of intermediate and capital goods, and at the same time upgrade their manufactured exports. The contribution of overseas markets was critical in the successful completion of the industrialization process in these countries by the beginning of the 1990s. So far these are the only Third World economies to record this achievement. Yet no economist or economic historian in the 1950s and 1960s counted any of these economies among those likely to make it. The favorites were India, Argentina, Brazil, and Mexico.

The industrialization process in these Asian countries is similar to that of England in more ways than one. Like England in the late seventeenth and early eighteenth centuries, Singapore and Hong Kong were engaged in entrepôt trade before they embarked on industrialization. Hence, like England, their import substitution industrialization included re-export substitution (RSI). Their entrepôt trade in manufactures was transformed into domestically produced manufactured exports. A similarity that is probably more important, for both England and the Asian countries, access to overseas markets did not depend solely, or even mainly, on purely economic elements. The struggle by West European powers for the acquisition of export markets and sources of cheap imports in the Atlantic basin was decided not by economic efficiency. Had the latter been the case, the contest would have been won by the Dutch. The winning card in the contest was naval power, and the socio-economic and political power structure that determined the way it was applied.

Similarly, access to overseas markets for manufactured exports by the Asian countries had a large political dose. In a detailed study of the role of the United States in the rise of East Asia since 1945, Jacques Hersh has shown the geo-political considerations that informed the opening of the U.S. market to these Asian countries. It was a policy of selective admission of Third World manufactured exports into the markets of the industrial nations of the West. In fact, even the aggressive policy of export promotion in South Korea was imposed by the United States, Hersh points out.[11] The leaders of the industrial nations did this in the 1960s and 1970s at very little political cost to themselves, because world trade was growing at a compound rate of 8 percent per annum at the time. This kept at bay pressure from organized labor to protect their jobs through domestic market protection.

Thus, the industrialization process in England has a lot of lessons that can inform policy and scholarship. It was trade driven with a considerable political input. This, among other things, makes the long history of socio-economic change that preceded the Industrial Revolution relevant to the

---

[11]   Hersh, *The USA and the Rise of East Asia.*

story. There can be little doubt, however, that ultimately the growth of Atlantic commerce was the central element which permitted the successful completion of the industrialization process in England. Similarly, there can be little doubt that the labor of Africans and their descendants was what made possible the growth of Atlantic commerce during the period. It is, therefore, reasonable to conclude that Africans made an invaluable contribution to the Industrial Revolution in England.

Appendixes

Appendix 4.1. *Average Annual Estimates of Bullion Import into Europe from the Americas, 1501–1800*

	Tons	Kilograms	Pesos	£ (sterling)
1501–1525	40	41,216	1,612,456	362,803
1526–1550	105	108,192	4,232,698	952,357
1551–1575	205	211,232	8,263,839	1,859,364
1576–1600	205	211,232	8,263,839	1,859,364
1601–1625	245	252,448	9,876,296	2,222,166
1626–1650	290	298,816	11,690,309	2,630,319
1651–1675	330	340,032	13,302,765	2,993,122
1676–1700	370	381,248	14,915,222	3,355,925
1701–1725	415	427,616	16,729,235	3,764,078
1726–1750	500	515,200	20,766,657	4,672,498
1751–1775	590	607,936	24,504,655	5,513,547
1776–1800	600	618,240	24,919,988	5,606,997

Sources and Notes: Barrett, "World bullion flows," Table 7.3, pp. 442 and 443. Barrett's quantities in tons have been converted to kilograms and pesos using the conversion ratios of Tepaske, "New World Silver," pp. 440 and 441: 1500–1730, 0.025561 kilogram of silver = 1 peso; 1731–70, 0.024809 kilogram of silver = 1 peso; 1771–90, 0.024433 kilogram of silver = 1 peso; 1791–1800, 0.024245 kilogram of silver = 1 peso. The ton is taken to be 1030.4 kilograms, 25 lbs. being 11.5 kilograms (Phillips, "The growth and composition of trade in the Iberian empires," p. 39). The peso has been converted to pound sterling at the rate of 1 peso to £0.225 (or 54d. sterling), McCusker, *Money and Exchange*, pp. 99–100. The figures in the last column of the table, when converted to period totals, add up to £894,813,500 as the total value of bullion exported to Europe from the Americas during the entire period 1501–1800. This may be compared with the estimate attributed to Humboldt by Roberto Simonsen. The latter estimate shows that

Notes to Appendix 4.1 *(cont.)*

total production of silver and gold in Portuguese Brazil and Spanish America between 1493 and 1803 was £1,300,000,000, of which £1 billion was silver and £300 million was gold. Registered production in Spanish America was £920 million and £186 million was by contraband; in colonial Brazil, registered production was £155 million, plus the royal fifth (quinto) of £39 million, totaling £194 million. See Roberto C. Simonsen, *Historia Economica do Brasil, 1500–1820* (6th edition, Sao Paulo: Companhia Editora Nacional, 1969), pp. 24–25. These are much larger figures. Given the magnitude of illegal exports, one may be inclined to accept the larger figures. However, the figures in the table are preferred, because they appear more soundly founded as discussed in the text.

Appendix 4.2. *Brazilian Sugar Export, 1536–1822 (£000 sterling)*

Period	Number of Years	Annual Average	Period Total
1536–1570	35	300	10,500
1571–1580	10	450	4,500
1581–1600	20	1,500	30,000
1601–1630	30	2,400	72,000
1631–1641	11	3,100	34,100
1642–1650	8	3,600	28,800
1651–1670	20	3,000	60,000
1671–1710	40	2,000	80,000
1711–1760	50	2,000	100,000
1761–1776	16	1,900	30,400
1777–1783	7	1,600	11,200
1784–1795	12	1,300	15,600
1796–1814	19	1,200	22,800
1815–1820	6	1,800	10,800
1821–1822	2	2,300	4,600

Source: Buescu, *Historia Economica do Brasil*, p. 197.

Appendix 4.3. *Average Annual Value and Commodity Composition of Exports from British America to Britain*

Product	Average Annual Value (£000)						
	1663–69	1752–54	1794–96	1804–06	1814–16	1824–26	1854–56
Sugar	256	1,302	5,567	6,664	10,641	6,102	5,853
Tobacco	69	560	368	585	746	594	1,242
Cotton		56	1,367	4,017	4,499	4,953	18,440
Coffee		3	1,228	2,402	2,076	803	98
Dyestuffs	3	97	133	508	406	426	478
Rice		167	176	166	77	117	62
Corn			72	114	61	40	6,005
Spirits		70	703	506	1,028	475	1,074
Timber		90	206	460	221	277	774
Hides and Skins		46	157	379	87	91	235
Metals and Ores		5	1	4	2		439
Indigo			120	44	30	85	27
Drugs		55					
Oils		43	2	8			381
Wine		11	27	60	66	68	2
Miscellaneous Foods	22	82	154	157	220	224	2,174
Miscellaneous Raw Materials	71	97	256	498	472	345	1,373
Others						38	334
Total	421	2,684	10,537	16,572	20,632	14,638	38,991

Sources and Notes: Compiled from Davis, "English Foreign Trade, 1660–1700," p. 96; Davis, "English Foreign Trade, 1700–74," p. 119; Davis, *The Industrial Revolution and British Overseas Trade*, pp. 112–125. The spirits are from the West Indies and, therefore, must be rum, a sugar by-product; cotton also belonged to the West Indies until the nineteenth century when it was shared more or less equally with the Southern plantations of the United States between 1800 and 1816, after which it became predominantly the latter's export from the second quarter of the century. Imports from Canada remained extremely small for most of the period; they became relatively large only in the nineteenth century, with timber accounting for about three-quarters of the total. Imports from Canada are not included in the table.

Appendix 5.1. *Mean Slave Loading by Ships Cleared Out to Africa from Ports in England*

Years	No. of Cargoes	Slaves Imported	Mean (Per Ship)
1698/99–1707	113	27,229	241
1710–19	205	52,338	255
1720–29	294	72,649	247
1730–39	333	77,989	234
1740–49	245	69,097	282
1750–59	321	72,197	225
1760–69	299	72,556	243
1770–76	231	53,701	233
1777–89	211	71,471	339
1790–1800	344	107,249	312
1801–07	250	69,082	276

Sources: 1698/99–1776, PRO, CO 137/38, fo. 5; 1777–89, CO 142/19–22, CO 33/18&20, CO 76/4–5, CO 243/1; 1790–1800, House of Lords List, Order date, 28 July, 1800. The Cuban data (comprising 20 cargoes for 1790–1800 and 50 cargoes for 1801–1807) were kindly made available to me by Herbert S. Klein. For the Cuban data, we have followed Klein's practice of treating only ships landing 200 slaves and above as those from Africa. (See Herbert S. Klein, "African Women in the Atlantic Slave Trade," in Claire C. Robertson and Martin A. Klein (eds.), *Women and Slavery in Africa* (Madison: University of Wisconsin Press, 1983), p. 32.) The estimate for 1790–1800 is for export loading, later converted to imports, using middle passage mortality rate of 5 percent. 1801–1807, CO 142/21–25, CO 33/18, CO 76/5, and the Cuban data. For details concerning the problem of computing mean slave loading per unit of shipping, see Inikori, "The Volume of the British Slave Trade," pp. 652–656.

Appendix 5.2. *Vessels Reported Lost but not Found on the Lists of Vessels Cleared Out to Africa from Ports in England, 1796–1805*

Vessel's Name	Commander's Name	Port Belonging	Where Lost	Date of Report
Accomplished Quaker	Walker	Liverpool	Outward	1796
Will	Quay	Liverpool	Africa-Americas	1796
Friends Goodwill	Pigot	Liverpool	Homeward	1796
Endeavour	Wyatt	London	Homeward	1796
Dispatch	Jackson		Africa-Americas	1796
Maria	Watson		Africa-Americas	1796
Nymph	Robson		African Coast	1796
Middleton	Graham		African Coast	1796
Stag	Murdock		Africa-Americas	1796
Eliza	Lang		Africa-Americas	1796
Atlantic	Rae		African Coast	1797
Ocean	Macaulay		African Coast	1797
Roebuck	Delano		African Coast	1797
Sugar	Marman		Africa-Americas	1797
Onslow	Giles	Liverpool	Outward	1797
Britannia	Prince	Liverpool	Outward	1797
Betsey and Ann	Bellas		African Coast	1797
Harmony	Walker		Homeward	1797
Abby	Webb	London	Outward	1797
Isabella	Rogers	Liverpool	Outward	1797
Calypso	Cole		African Coast	1798
Favourite	Crosby	Liverpool	African Coast	1798
Betsey	Hayward	Liverpool	African Coast	1798
Oxholme	Fowle		African Coast	1798
Eliza	M'Gaulay	London	African Coast	1799
Triton	Lilburn	London	Outward	1799
Frederick	Clark		Homeward	1799
Tartar	Hewitt		African Coast	1800
Pilgrim	Scott		African Coast	1800
Lively	Crawford		Africa-Americas	1800
Young Jonah	Corbett	Martinico	African Coast	1800
St. George Packet	Bell		Africa-Americas	1800
Fame	Carr	London	Homeward	1800
Dolly		Liverpool	Africa-Americas	1801
James & George	Bailey	London	Outward	1801
Cotterel	Martin		Africa-Americas	1801
Sally	Hanson	London	Outward	1801
Edward	McCornish	Liverpool	Outward	1801
King Bell	Little		Africa-Americas	1803
Flying Fish			Homeward	1804
Emerald	Eccles	Liverpool	Outward	1804
Imperial	Price		Africa-Americas	1804
Eagle	Ramsay	London	African Coast	1804
Anna Maria	Leydon	Bristol	Africa-Americas	1804
Nelly	Sedden		African Coast	1805
Thomas	Welsh	London	Africa-Americas	1805

Vessel's Name	Commander's Name	Port Belonging	Where Lost	Date of Report
William	Christie	Liverpool	African Coast	1805
Mars	Mitchell	Liverpool	African Coast	1805
Mermaid	Horsley	Liverpool	Outward	1797
Lively	Bell		Africa-Americas	1797
General Marian			Africa-Americas	1797
Heral			Africa-Americas	1798
Nymyh	Macaulay	London	Outward	1799
Mairton Hall	Dixon	London	Outward	1800
Crescent	Cuite	Liverpool	Africa-Americas	1801
Swallow	Dolby	London	Homeward	1801
Hoffnung	Waben	Hambro	Outward	1801
Mary	Fiddis	Rotterdam	Outward	1802
George	Anderson		Homeward	1803
Mercury	Dixon		Africa-Americas	1805
Sally	Neale	Liverpool	Africa-Americas	1805
Connecticut	Harman	Liverpool	African Coast	1796
Friends	Estil		African Coast	1798
Pilgrim	Schwindy		African Coast	1800
Bestemodern	Northorp		African Coast	1801
Good Intent	Inch	W. Indies	African Coast	1801
Diana	Ward	Liverpool	African Coast	1801
Anna Maria	Wolffen	Hambro	African Coast	1801
Stranger	Mariner		African Coast	1802
Eloisa	Davis	London	African Coast	1802
Diligence		Trinidad	African Coast	1803
Washinton	Homer	Philadelphia	African Coast	1805
Spy	Clark	Damerara	Outward	1797
Maria		Boston	Africa-Americas	1797
Express	Steele	St. Vincent	African Coast	1798
Mary	Farrel	Guernsey	Outward	1799
Juno		Barbadoes	African Coast	1800
Concord		America	African Coast	1800
Plumper		Martinico	African Coast	1800
Martilda		Martinico	African Coast	1800

Sources and Notes: Compiled from Lloyd's List, National Maritime Museum, Greenwich, London; clearance information is from British Library, Parliamentary Papers, Accounts and Papers, 1806, Volume XII, pp. 783–796, An Account of Vessels which cleared out annually from Liverpool, London, and Bristol for the coast of Africa, 1795–1804 (January 1795–April 1805, for Liverpool). Only vessels reported lost in 1796–1805 have been examined, because many of the vessels reported lost in 1795 must have cleared out from England to the African coast in 1794, which is outside the clearance list employed. To confirm whether or not a vessel reported lost is on the clearance lists, both the name of the vessel and that of the commander must be used, because many vessels had the same name. Where the name of the commander is not stated, absence from the clearance lists is confirmed only when no vessel bearing the name is found on the clearance lists of the current and preceding two years.

Appendix 6.1. *Routes of Vessels Insured to Africa by
William Braund, 1759–1772*

Year	Vessel	Master	Owners	Route to Africa
1759	*Woodford*	Hale	G. Mathias Gale	London to Holland to Guinea & to Leeward Islands
1759	*Crown Prince*	Christ. Anker	B. Oswald & Co.	St. Croix to Guinea and to St. Croix
1760	*Bon Tesus de Navigater*	Marquez	G. Mayne & Co.	Lisbon to Angola
1760	*Jolly Batchelor*	Buchanan	S. Oswald & Co.	Cadiz to Cape de Verdes to Antigua
1760	*George*	Stirling	B. Oswald & Co.	Rotterdam to Sierra Leone
1761	*Jane*	Brown	B. Hutchinson & Mure	London to Rotterdam to Guinea and to Jamaica
1761	*Garland*	Fleming	G. M. Gate	Whitehaven to Isle of Man to Guinea
1761	*Four Brothers*	Kennedy	B. Mat. Gate	Whitehaven to Isle of Man to Africa
1761	*Catherine*	Kenny	G. Oswald & Co.	Rotterdam to Bance Island
1762	*Experiment*	Johnson	G. Samuel Touchet	London to Guernsey to Guinea to America
1762	*Knight*	Jenkinson	S. Cha. Pole	Liverpool to Isle of Man to Whydah
1763	*Charming Kitty*	Conolly	B. Oswald & Co.	St. Eusta. to Guinea to St. Eusta.
1764	*Betsey*	Patterson	G. Malcomb & Co.	London to Holland to Guinea
1764	*Industrious Friends*	Todd	B. Wm. Todd	London to Holland to Guinea to West Indies
1764	*Elizabeth*	McNeal	S. Alex. Grant	Holland to Guinea to West India
1764	*Grenada*	Gray	B.	St. Croix to Guinea to West India
1765	*Speedwell*	Twist	S. Gamportz & Co.	London to Helvoet to Senegal

Appendix 6.1 *(cont.)*

Year	Vessel	Master	Owners	Route to Africa
1765	*Hope*	Munford	G. Champion	Rhode Island to Guinea to West India
1765	*St. Ann*	Viera	Gideon Arbonin	Lisbon to Angola & Bueguella
1765	*Frederick*	Davidson	G.	London to Holland to Guernsey & Bance Island
1765	*Minerva*	Michael	B. F. Wishart	Nantes to Guinea to St. Domingo
1765	*D. de Pratton*	Morratteu	B. F. Wishart	Nantes to Guinea to St. Domingo
1766	*Peacock*	Robinson	B. Bindley & Co.	London to Cork to Canary to Africa
1766	*Negrillan*	Gaspard	S. Fonblanque & Co.	London to Dunkirk to Senegal & to St. Domingo
1766	*Count D'Estang*	De Beaumount	B. Tussier	Nantes to Angola to West India
1766	*Margs. de Chateau Beuvid*	Du Bois	B. Tussier	Nantes to Angola to West India
1766	*Jupiter*	Bossetye	S. D. Andre	Dunkirk to Guinea to St. Domingo
1766	Fanny	Bragg	B. Larcells	Demerary to Guinea to West India
1766	*Beckmont*	Murry	B. Oswald, Grant & Co.	London to Holland to Bance Island
1766	*Africa*	All	B. Wm. Stead	Rhode Island to Guinea to West India
1767	*Juno*	Lothain	S. Oswald, Grant & Co.	London to Holland to Africa
1767	*Dudley*	Chandler	B. Boddam	Bombay to Africa to Bombay
1768	*Liberty*	Crapy	B.	Antigua to Guinea to West India

Source: D/DRU/B7, Journals of Risks, William Braund Papers, Essex Record Office, County Hall, Chelmsford, England.

Appendix 6.2. *Guineamen Identified in Liverpool (Prime) Registries, 1786, 1787, 1788*

Registry Number	Date of Registry	Vessel's Name	Tons	Where Built	Year Built	Type of Vessel	Dimensions
62	20 Sept. 1786	*Brooks*	297	Liverpool	1781	Ship	99.8 × 26.7a × 5.6
37	12 Sept. 1786	*Mosley Hill*	376	Liverpool	1782	Ship	104.8 × 29.3a × 6
156	13 Nov. 1786	*Eliza*	90	Liverpool	1785	Ship	61.8 × 19.5a × 4.6
7	4 Sept. 1786	*Sir Robert Curtis*	181	A Br. Settlement in the E. Indies	1778	Ship	85.8 × 22.3a × 5.1½
8	4 Sept. 1786	*Gainsborough*	49	Hull, Yorks	1784	Schooner	45.9 × 16.6 1/2a × 8.3¼
94	6 Oct. 1786	*Christopher*	170	Prize from Americans in 1780		Ship	82.0 × 22.0a × 4.5
127	25 Oct. 1786	*Peggy*	81	Folkestone	1783	Schooner	59.10 × 18.2a × 7.4
58	19 Sept. 1786	*Mary*	75	Liverpool	1785	Brigantine	60.4 × 17.6a × 7.6
20	7 Sept. 1786	*Elliot*	334	Liverpool	1783	Ship	102 × 27.0a × 6
154	13 Nov. 1786	*Tarleton*	342	Prize taken in 1778, French built		Ship	97.3 × 28.6a × 5.7
153	10 Nov. 1786	*Lady Penrhyn*	183	Prize taken in 1782, American built		Ship	80.4 × 23.4a × 5.10
107	13 Oct. 1786	*Hinde*	126	Liverpool	1769	Ship	69.0 × 21.2a × 4.2
50	15 Sept. 1786	*Vale*	208	Dublin	1765	Ship	86.3 × 23.10a × 5.6
113	19 Oct. 1786	*Bud*	97	Liverpool	1783	Ship	65.0 × 19.4a × 4.2

Appendix 6.2 *(cont.)*

Registry Number	Date of Registry	Vessel's Name	Tons	Where Built	Year Built	Type of Vessel	Dimensions
48	15 Sept. 1786	*Little Joe*	127	Liverpool	1784	Ship	70.0 × 21.0a × 3.8
14	6 Sept. 1786	*John*	166	Liverpool	1784	Ship	81.0 × 22.0a × 4.10
51	16 Sept. 1786	*Mary Ann*	174	Bermuda	1781	Ship	89.3 × 22.2a × 4.5
109	14 Oct. 1786	*Chambres*	233	Prize taken in 1783, American built		Ship	94.10 × 23.9a × 3.8
176	2 Dec. 1786	*Europe*	257	Prize from the French in 1782		Ship	88.8 × 26.6a × 5.5
1	12 Aug. 1786	*Renown*	195.6	Prize from Americans, Foreign built		Ship	80.9 × 23.9a × 5.4
2	12 Aug. 1786	*Crescent*	64.49	Liverpool	1786	Schooner	51.5 × 17.9a × 9.1
6	2 Sept. 1786	*Dick*	37	Liverpool	1786	Schooner	42.3 × 15.3a × 7.7½
29	9 Sept. 1786	*Molly*	239	Liverpool	1778	Ship	98.0 × 25.0a × 5.6
21	7 Sept. 1786	*Three Brothers*	428	Prize, condemned 21 Jan. 1783		Ship	96.0 × 33.6a × 3.6
55	16 Sept. 1786	*Searle*	137	Newport, Isle of Wight	1756	Snow	71.0 × 21.8a × 3.9½

No.	Date	Name	Tons	Origin	Year	Type	Dimensions
59	19 Sept. 1786	*King Grey*	145	Prize from the French, cond. 1782		Ship	71.0 × 22.4a × 4.0
42	13 Sept. 1786	*Mercer*	54	Liverpool	1766	Sloop	52.0 × 16.5a × 8.1
53	16 Sept. 1786	*Juno*	75	Prize from Americans in 1780, Foreign built		Brigantine	59.5 × 19.3a × 8.2
47	14 Sept. 1786	*James*	78	Prize from Americans in 1781 Am. built		Brigantine	62.2 × 18.2a × 3.8
65	23 Sept. 1786	*Sisters*	252	Liverpool	1786	Ship	90.10 × 25.8a × 6.0
131	27 Oct. 1786	*King Jos*	201	Prize from Spain in 1782		Snow	73.10 × 26.9a × 4.1
146	7 Nov. 1786	*Ormond*	80	Cawsand, Devonshire	1780	Brigantine	63.0 × 17.8a × 6.2
159	14 Nov. 1786	*Othello*	122	Liverpool	1786	Ship	68.0 × 21.1a × 4.11
41	13 Sept. 1786	*Heart of Oak*	153	Prize from the French, cond. 1779		Ship	72.1 × 22.10a × 4.6
151	9 Nov. 1786	*Swallow*	231	Prize from Americans in 1772		Ship	90.2 × 24.7a × 5.10
178	7 Dec. 1786	*Perseverance*	157	Prize taken in 1781		Ship	83.3 × 21.0a × 9.0
196	30 Dec. 1786	*Fisher*	186	Liverpool	1786	Ship	80.9 × 23.9a × 5.2

Registry Number	Date of Registry	Vessel's Name	Tons	Where Built	Year Built	Type of Vessel	Dimensions
167	20 Nov. 1786	*Philip Stevens*	114	Liverpool	1786	Ship	67.7 × 20.3a × 4.1
191	20 Dec. 1786	*Betsey*	55	Isle of Man	1776	Cutter	45.4 × 17.11a × 9.2
88	6 Oct. 1786	*Kite*	50	Liverpool	1780	Cutter	49.0 × 16.10a × 8.5
4	31 Aug. 1786	*Mary*	278	Liverpool	1782	Ship	94.6 × 26.6a × 5.4
179	6 Aug. 1787	*Gregson*	258	Liverpool	1769	Ship	93.0 × 26.0a × 5.5
32	20 Jan. 1787	*Gascoyne*	294	Liverpool	1772	Ship	96.5 × 27.0a × 5.6
96	24 Mar. 1787	*Princess Royal*	596	Liverpool	1783	Frigate built ship	127.0 × 33.6a × 6.0
145	18 June 1787	*Madam Pookata*	110	Prize taken from the Americans in 1782		Brigantine	69.0 × 19.5a × 8.2
125	12 May 1787	*Blayds*	306	Liverpool	1782	Ship	99.0 × 27.0a × 5.3
167	23 July 1787	*Little Ben*	45	Liverpool	1786	Schooner	49.4 × 15.8a × 8
253	3 Nov. 1787	*Bloom*	154	Prize taken from Americans in 1782		Ship	80.2 × 21.4a × 4.6
88	21 Mar. 1787	*President*	254	Philadelphia, North America	1773	Ship	93.6 × 25.6a × 4.7
163	18 July 1787	*Thomas*	232	Prize taken from the French in 1783		Ship	81.9 × 26.0a × 4.3

	Date	Ship	Tons	Where built	Year	Type	Dimensions
117	4 May 1787	*Benson*	169	Liverpool	1776	Ship	77.0 × 23.0a × 5.6
54	9 Feb. 1787	*Garland*	525	Portsmouth	1778	Ship	118.6 × 32.6a × 6.0
134	31 May 1787	*Venus*	146	Prize taken from the Americans in 1781		Ship	81.6at × 21.6a × 4.2
104	11 April 1787	*King Pepple*	323	Liverpool	1785	Frigate built ship	110.0 × 27.3a × 5.6
121	8 May 1787	*Mary*	118	Bermuda	1781	Ship	70.0 × 20.6a × 4.4
181	7 Aug. 1787	*Fanny*	100	Bermuda	1780	Ship	70.0at × 20.0a × 4.1
5	3 Jan. 1787	*Fly*	93	Creetown, Co. Galloway	1784	Cutter	54.0 × 21.4a × 9.4
203	3 Sept. 1787	*Tartar*	190	Liverpool	1772	Ship	90.0 × 22.10a × 4.8
33	24 Jan. 1787	*Darnall*	233	Liverpool	1777	Ship	88.9 × 25.2a × 5.3
114	24 April 1787	*Hero*	365	Prize taken from the Americans in 1782		Ship	108.0 × 28.6a × 5.8
182	7 Aug. 1787	*Mary*	164	Built in some Br. Plantation or Colony	not known	Ship	80.6asp × 22.6a × 4.1
53	7 Feb. 1787	*Rose*	147	Lancaster	1783	Ship	74.7 × 21.9a × 5.0
98	29 Mar. 1787	*Eliza*	216	Prize taken from the Americans in 1782		Ship	83.3 × 25.0a × 5.0
17	12 Jan. 1787	*Louisa*	117	Prize from French in 1782		Ship	78.0 × 18.6a × 7.7

Registry Number	Date of Registry	Vessel's Name	Tons	Where Built	Year Built	Type of Vessel	Dimensions
64	1 Mar. 1787	*Young Hero*	80	Liverpool	1786	Brigantine	64.6 × 17.6a × 3.0
154	27 June 1787	*Hornett*	142	Prize taken from the Americans in 1781		Ship	72.0 × 22.0a × 4.3
138	7 June 1787	*Fancy*	183	Prize taken from the Americans in 1781		Ship	87.0 × 22.9a × 4.6
92	23 Mar. 1787	*Prince*	52	Liverpool	1786	Schooner	52.0 × 16.0a × 3.2
214	15 Sept. 1787	*Assistance*	37	Liverpool	1786	Schooner	42.6 × 15.5a × 6.10
222	24 Sept. 1787	*Lord Stanley*	240	Liverpool	1775	Ship	92.4 × 24.4a × 5.6
142	9 June 1787	*Jemmy*	83	Liverpool	1786	Ship	58.6 × 18.6a × 4.1
239	28 Sept. 1787	*Ingram*	207	Prize taken in 1782		Ship	82.0 × 24.9a × 4.5
208	8 Sept. 1787	*George*	229	Prize taken in 1781		Ship	83.0 × 26.2a × 5.3
116	2 May 1787	*Jane*	242	Liverpool	1766	Ship	102.0t × 24.6a × 5.4
221	24 Sept. 1787	*Colonel*	119	Prize taken from Americans		Ship	71.0 × 20.0a × 4.4

136	6 June 1787	*Golden Age*	377	Prize taken from the Spaniards in 1783		Ship	108.0 × 28.6a × 5.0
235	27 Sept. 1787	*Hannah*	192	Liverpool	1786	Ship	84.3 × 23.2a × 5.4
173	28 July 1787	*Will*	128	Liverpool	1777	Ship	70.2 × 21.0a × 4.4
28	17 Jan. 1787	*Union*	129	Liverpool	1770	Ship	69.0 × 21.6a × 5.3
43	31 Jan. 1787	*Kitty*	333	Liverpool	1784	Ship	98.3 × 22.6a × 6.0
30	19 Jan. 1787	*Clemison*	247	Bridport, Dorset	1779	Ship	82.5 × 27.4a × 4.6
63	27 Feb. 1787	*Hope*	93	Prize taken in 1781		Brigantine	77.2 1/2 × 20.6 × 7.9
38	29 Jan. 1787	*Iris*	268	Liverpool	1783	Ship	93.6 × 26.0a × 5.8
71	8 Mar. 1787	*Chance*	39	St. Johns, Newfoundland	1786	Schooner	48.10 × 13.10a × 8.0
77	12 Mar. 1787	*Banastre*	93	Ringsend, port of Dublin	1759	Ship	64.8 × 18.6a × 4.9
89	21 Mar. 1787	*Ferrett*	24	Parkgate, Cheshire	1787	Schooner	41.4 × 12.0a × 6.0
84	17 Mar. 1787	*Comet*	263	Folkestone	1781	Clinker built ship	91.0 × 29.0a × 4.4
81	15 Mar. 1787	*Viper*	258	Prize from French in 1779		Ship	90.8 × 26.2a × 5.8

Registry Number	Date of Registry	Vessel's Name	Tons	Where Built	Year Built	Type of Vessel	Dimensions
106	12 Apr. 1787	*Alert*	31	Liverpool	1787	Schooner	39.5 × 14.4a × 7.5
94	24 Mar. 1787	*Ally*	186	Liverpool	1786	Ship	81.9 × 23.6a × 5.4
110	19 April 1787	*Albion*	158	Liverpool	1783	Ship	76.4 × 22.6a × 4.10
109	16 April 1787	*Mars*	147	Prize taken from the Americans in 1782		Ship	78.0 × 21.2a × 4.8
119	7 May 1787	*Eliza*	346	Liverpool	1787	Frigate built ship	113.0t × 27.9a × 5.6
113	20 April 1787	*Ned*	193	Prize taken from the Americans in 1781		Ship	91.0 × 22.1a × 4.5
128	15 May 1787	*Hammond*	84	Liverpool	1787	Snow	58.1 × 19.0a × 8.4
118	7 May 1787	*Ann*	222	Liverpool	1787	Frigate built ship	92.6 × 23.9a × 5.6
139	7 June 1787	*Johanna*	19	Liverpool	1787	Schooner	32.11 × 12.8a × 5.11

130	Alice	24 May 1787	205	Liverpool	1787	Ship	90.10 × 24.4a × 4.9
123	Henrietta	10 May 1787	76	Liverpool	1783	Schooner	56.0 × 18.2 1/2 × 10.10
143	Brothers	14 June 1787	325	Liverpool	1787	Frigate built ship	106.0at × 28.6a × 6.0
141	Fanny	9 June 1787	96	Prize taken in 1782, French built		Brigantine	66.8 × 18.6a × 3.11
160	Hazard	13 July 1787	126	Bermuda	1779	Brigantine	69.8 × 21.0a × 3.10
168	Toms	24 July 1787	270	Prize taken from the Americans 1781		Ship	94.0 × 26.6a × 5.3
185	Betsey	9 Aug. 1787	23	Liverpool	1787	Schooner	39.9 × 12.0a × 6.0
199	Shirburn Castle	28 Aug. 1787	130	Prize taken from the Americans in 1782		Ship	72.4 × 20.6a × 11.6
215	Nancy	17 Sept. 1787	106	Bermuda	1777	Ship	70.3 × 19.4a × 3.10
55	Fisher	14 Feb. 1787	411	Workington, Cumbs.	1778	Ship	105.8 × 30.7b × 5.6
261	Peggy	15 Dec. 1787	42	Liverpool	1787	Schooner	44.8 × 15.6a × 9.0

Appendix 6.2 (cont.)

Registry Number	Date of Registry	Vessel's Name	Tons	Where Built	Year Built	Type of Vessel	Dimensions
236	27 Sept. 1787	*Robust*	313	Prize taken from the French in 1781		Ship	98.6 × 27.9a × 4.7
47	22 May 1788	*James*	100	Liverpool	1788	Ship	62.0 × 20.0 × 4.2
42	5 May 1788	*Vulture*	315	Prize from French 1778		Ship	117.0at × 26.3a × 5.6
70	18 Aug. 1788	*Brothers*	119	Liverpool	1783	Ship	70.3 × 20.3a × 5.6
35	19 April 1788	*Ann*	76	Liverpool	1775	Snow	57.8 × 18.0a × 4.8
32	1 April 1788	*Joseph*	130	Liverpool	1786	Ship	70.0 × 21.3a × 5.0
2	4 Jan. 1788	*Mary*	130	Prize from Americans		Brigantine	75.6 × 20.6a × 8.10
5	9 Jan. 1788	*Crescent*	150	Liverpool	1787	Ship	81.6at × 22.0a × 4.6
3	9 Jan. 1788	*Aeolus*	159	Liverpool	1787	Ship	76.0 × 22.6a × 4.10
13	15 Feb. 1788	*Martha*	141	Liverpool	1788	Ship	72.6 × 21.9a × 4.6
9	7 Feb. 1788	*Squirrel*	180	Liverpool	1788	Ship	89.6at × 22.6 × 4.10
28	17 Mar. 1788	*Stag*	159	Liverpool	1788	Ship	76.8 × 22.4a × 4.8
38	28 April 1788	*Diana*	248	Liverpool	1788	Ship	92.0 × 25.4a × 5.8
41	3 May 1788	*Amacree*	205	Liverpool	1788	Ship	88.0 × 23.8a × 5.5

No.	Date	Name	Tonnage	Notes	Year	Type	Dimensions
52	16 June 1788	Gipsy	147	Prize from Americans, cond. 1782		Ship	78.0 × 21.3a × 3.3
46	19 May 1788	Sally	367	Rhode Island	1770	Ship	102.9 × 29.8a × 6.0
57	27 June 1788	Sally	19	Liverpool	1788	Schooner	33.7 × 12.0a × 6.0
61	5 July 1788	Ellen	89	Liverpool	1788	Schooner	62.6 × 18.3a × 9.3
69	15 Aug. 1788	Anne	148	Liverpool	1788	Ship	76.6 × 21.10a × 5.0
68	7 Aug. 1788	Rose	164	Lancaster	1783	Ship	74.9 × 23.1b × 5.0
71	20 Aug. 1788	Bridget	295	Liverpool	1760	Ship	97.10 × 26.6a × 5.2
87	17 Nov. 1788	Bell	148	Liverpool	1788	Ship	76.0 × 22.0a × 5.2
91	26 Nov. 1788	Edgar	159.50	Liverpool (Completely rebuilt at Liverpool in 1788)	1771	Ship	76.10 × 22.2a × 5.1
83	30 Oct. 1788	Molly	279.64	Liverpool	1778	Ship	98.0 × 25.9a × 5.9
44	10 May 1788	Joshua	125	Prize taken from Americans in 1782		Barque	70.0 × 20.8a × 4.4
55	26 June 1788	Liverpool Hero	211	Prize from French in 1780		Ship	82.3 × 25.1a × 5.6

Appendix 6.2 (cont.)

Registry Number	Date of Registry	Vessel's Name	Tons	Where Built	Year Built	Type of Vessel	Dimensions
59	3 July 1788	*Beatrice*	147	Prize in 1782, Spanish built		Polacre Kerch	65.9 × 24.0a × 3.3
64	16 July 1788	*Trinidada Packet*	43	Liverpool	1788	Schooner	50.10at × 15.6a × 8.0
98	29 Dec. 1788	*Margaret*	112	Liverpool	1788	Ship	68.0 × 20.0a × 4.0

Sources and Notes: R. Craig and R. Jarvis, *Liverpool Registry of Merchant Ships* (Manchester, Printed for the Chetham Society, 1967). This shows the vessels' names, Date of Registration, Registry Number, Tonnage, where built or whether Prize, year of building (or year condemned and made free if Prize), physical description of the vessels, all the owners or owner, and the Masters. This covers the three years immediately following the Registration Act of 1786. *British Parliamentary Papers, Accounts and Papers*, 1789, Vol. 82, No. 631, pp. 1–6. This shows vessels cleared out from Liverpool for Africa in 1785, 1786, 1787 and 1788, showing their names, dates of clearance, Tonnage, Dates of Registry, and Places of Registry. Using this information, the vessels in this list were easily identified in the Registry transcribed by Craig and Jarvis, above. T.64/286. This shows vessels cleared out from Liverpool for Africa in 1789–1795, showing their names, their owners' names, tonnage, and dates of clearance. Using the information here, a handful of vessels for 1789 were identified in the Registry.

Appendix 7.1. *Transcripts from the Balance Books of Arthur Heywood, Sons & Co., of Liverpool, Showing the Structure of the Bank's Assets and Liabilities, 1787–1790 and 1801–1807*

1787	Assets	£	s	d
	Cash	10,040	15	5
	Bills Receivable	112,896	19	2
	Four Percent	3,800	=	=
	Joseph Denison & Co.	70,800	=	7
		197,537	15	2

1788	Assets	£	s	d
	Cash	9,808	5	10
	Bills Receivable	86,576	14	=
	Four Per Cent	3,800	=	=
	Error 31 December '86.	=	6	=
		100,185	5	10

1789	Assets	£	s	d
	Cash	8,139	18	5
	Bills Receivable	148,136	1	10
	Four Per Cent	3,800	=	=
	Joseph Denison & Co.	37,509	15	9
		197,585	16	=

1790	Assets	£	s	d
	Cash	2,697	16	9
	Bills	145,638	1	10
	India Stock	3,125	5	=
	Ditto	339	5	=
	Three Per Cent	2,028	7	6
	Four Per Cent	3,800	=	=
	Joseph Denison & Co.	21,236	18	10
		188,865	14	11

31 December, 1801

Assets	£	s	d	Liabilities	£	s	d
Amount from Balance Book	431,354	12	9	Amount from Balance Book	1,071,288	=	3
Cash	10,449	15	6	Bills Payable	297,090	12	3
Bills on Hand	616,023	10	8	Bills Outstanding	447	2	8
Bills Remitted	260,065	7	2	Interest	15,000	=	=
Denison & Co.	130,386	5	8	Stock	64,453	16	7
	1,448,279	11	9		1,448,279	11	9

Appendix 7.1 *(cont.)*

31 December, 1802

Assets	£	s	d	Liabilities	£	s	d
Amount from				Amount from			
Balance Book	452,811	9	2	Balance Book	993,053	19	10
Cash	6,722	5	5	Bills Payable	301,197	9	11
Bills on Hand	626,626	3	4	Bills Outstanding	336	17	8
Bills Remitted	263,406	13	=	Interest	18,000	=	=
Denison & Co.	16,654	12	10	Stock	53,632	16	4
	1,366,221	3	9		1,366,221	3	9

31 December, 1803

Assets	£	s	d	Liabilities	£	s	d
Amount from				Amount from			
Balance Book	336,392	11	5	Balance Book	850,311	13	4
Cash	10,497	4	4	Bills Payable	209,553	12	5
Bills on Hand	571,631	13	7	Bills Outstanding	313	16	8
Bills Remitted	210,062	4	11	Interest	15,000	=	=
Denison & Co.	22,653	16	1	Stock	76,057	7	11
				Error	1	=	=
	1,151,237	10	4		1,151,237	10	4

31 December, 1804

Assets	£	s	d	Liabilities	£	s	d
Amount from				Amount from			
Balance Book	410,292	2	11	Balance Book	1,179,753	2	9
Cash	7,255	18	6	Bills Payable	29,173	14	9
Bills on Hand	1,000,629	7	=	Bills Outstanding	314	10	5
Bills Remitted	186,084	19	4	Denison & Co.	293,236	5	2
	1,604,260	7	9	Interest	15,000	=	=
				Stock	86,781	4	8
				Error	1	10	=
					1,604,260	7	9

31 December, 1805

Assets	£	s	d	Liabilities	£	s	d
Amount from				Amount from			
Balance Book	368,674	8	6	Balance Book	1,045,778	4	1
Cash	20,460	11	1	Bills Payable	234,642	15	1
Bills on Hand	851,107	=	9	Bills Outstanding	335	16	8
Bills Remitted	248,455	3	6	Denison & Co.	73,715	3	5
	1,488,697	3	10	Interest	15,000	=	=
				Stock	119,223	14	7
				Errors	1	10	=
					1,488,697	3	10

31 December, 1806

Assets	£	s	d	Liabilities	£	s	d
Amount from				Amount from			
Balance Book	389,749	4	8	Balance Book	1,094,562	15	11
Cash	9,232	5	6	Bills Payable	257,382	1	=
Bills on Hand	933,354	17	2	Bills Outstanding	545	2	2
Bills Remitted				Denison & Co.	80,607	14	=
Denison & Co.	269,618	10	4	Interest	15,000	=	=
Error 31 Dec.				Stock Old Concern	119,223	14	7
1802 £2 Notes				Stock New Concern	34,684	18	4
£50:8:4	52	8	4	Error in Balance			
				31 December, 1803	1	=	=
	1,602,007	6	=		1,602,007	6	=

31 December, 1807

Assets	£	s	d	Liabilities	£	s	d
Amount from				Amount from			
Balance Book	348,872	14	10	Balance Book	1,217,195	15	1
Cash in Hand	21,419	11	1	Bills Payable	237,893	15	3
Bills on Hand	1,098,035	19	6	Bills Outstanding	522	8	8
Bills Remitted				Denison & Co.	96,905	18	3
Denison & Co.	251,615	19	9	Interest	15,000	=	=
Error 31 Dec.				Ar. Heywood &			
1806 £2: =:				Sam Thompson	108,549	13	2
=Dr.				Stock	43,877	14	11
31 Dec.1807							
=: =: 2 Dr.	1	=	2				
31 Dec. 1803							
1: =: = Cr.							
	1,719,945	5	4		1,719,945	5	4

Source: Records of the Heywoods Bank of Liverpool in Barclays Bank, Heywoods Branch, Liverpool.

Appendix 7.2. *Insurance Premiums Paid on African Ventures*

Year of Venture	Vessel's Name	Total £	Cost S	Outward D	Of £	Which S	Insurance D
1757	Chesterfield	6,948:	8:	=	1,502:	16:	=
1758	Calveley	2,119:	13:	6	527:	11:	=
1759	Chesterfield	7,058:	6:	8	1,078:	16:	=
1760	Eadith	4,101:	12:	=	892:	7:	=
1761	Eadith	4,058:	4:	=	966:	12:	=
1761	Tyrrell	8,283:	8:	=	1,038:	17:	4
1762	Union	6,149:	11:	10.5	1,172:	8:	=
1762	Dalrymple	3,425:	10:	=	511:	16:	=
1762	Plumper	6,278:	4:	=	1,589:	12:	8
		48,422:	18:	1	9,280:	16:	=
1763	Dalrymple	3,524:	9:	$9\frac{1}{2}$	384:	8:	=
1763	Delight	3,201:	6:	=	271:	6:	=
1763	Friendship	4,971:	17:	6	579:	11:	=
1764	Union	4,056:	=:	6	415:	2:	=
1764	Dalrymple	5,953:	8:	4	403:	15:	=
1764	Delight	3,900:	12:	8	321:	=:	=
1764	William	2,458:	=:	$7\frac{1}{2}$	257:	10:	$7\frac{1}{2}$
1765	Union	4,338:	2:	6	245:	=:	6
1765	Friendship	5,577:	17:	=	393:	12:	=
1765	Active	8,623:	19:	4	658:	4:	=
1765	Henry	3,000:	12:	8	308:	4:	=
1766	Dalrymple	6,923:	7:	$8\frac{4}{5}$	457:	18:	$11\frac{1}{5}$
1766	Friendship	4,697:	12:	9	159:	6:	=
1766	William	2,340:	3:	=	341:	18:	6
1767	New Union	5,507:	14:	=	311:	3:	=
1767	Dobson	8,167:	14:	$6\frac{2}{5}$	423:	1:	$7\frac{1}{2}$
1767	Henry	2,111:	14:	8	111:	12:	=
1767	King of Prussia	3,843:	18:	8	234:	4:	8
1768	Plumper	6,450:	5:	4	617:	3:	4
1768	William	2,319:	13:	6	170:	=:	10
1768	Dalrymple	7,161:	10:	=	589:	16:	=
1768	New Union	6,208:	18:	=	271:	=:	=
1769	Plumper	7,476:	14:	4	947:	16:	=
1769	William	2,286:	=:	5	144:	=:	8
1769	Dobson & Fox	8,606:	17:	6	517:	19:	6
1769	Hector & Andromache	7,168:	5:	2	536:	8:	=
1770	New Dobson & Fox	9,813:	4:	6	796:	16:	=
1770	Dalrymple	6,930:	10:	4	471:	18:	$2\frac{2}{3}$
1770	New Union	5,818:	17:	4	399:	6:	=

Appendix 7.2 *(cont.)*

Year of Venture	Vessel's Name	Total £	Cost S	Outward D	Of £	Which S	Insurance D
1770	*Knight*	6,595:	12:	2	354:	2:	=
1770	*Austin*	6,815:	12:	2	276:	18:	2
1771	*Lively*	4,223:	7:	$9\frac{1}{3}$	243:	11:	$1\frac{1}{3}$
1771	*Nanny*	8,121:	1:	$7\frac{1}{2}$	347:	19:	6
1771	*Austin*	5,748:	13:	6	303:	8:	=
1771	*King of Prussia*	4,169:	9:	8	267:	4:	=
1771	*Hector & Andromache*	7,915:	18:	$4\frac{4}{5}$	612:	19:	$2\frac{2}{5}$
1771	*Dalrymple & Swift*	9,455:	18:	$2\frac{2}{3}$	458:	18:	$10\frac{2}{3}$
1771	*Fox*	3,499:	9:	2	248:	14:	8
1772	*King of Prussia*	4,083:	6:	8	253:	=:	=
1772	*May*	4,674:	14:	8	85:	8:	=
1772	*Badger & Fox*	8,009:	17:	8	489:	6:	=
1772	*Patty*	4,629:	11:	8	193:	18:	4
1772	*Nanny*	8,553:	15:	$10\frac{1}{2}$	388:	15:	=
1773	*Hector & Andromache*	11,887:	11:	$7\frac{1}{5}$	749:	6:	$4\frac{4}{5}$
1773	*Dalrymple*	14,798:	19:	8	671:	10:	8
1774	*Fox*	3,808:	9:	$9\frac{3}{4}$	230:	1:	3
1774	*Badger*	4,960:	1:	9	300:	17:	3
		275,391:	=:	10	18,215:	1:	=
1785	*Elliot*	26,041:	17:	2	2,210:	6:	8
1800	*Perseverance*	22,920:	=:	=	2,520:	=:	=
1805	*Frederick*	24,004:	13:	10	4,212:	12:	9
1806	*Frederick*	23,964:	16:	9	4,753:	5:	11
		70,889:	10:	7	11,485:	18:	8

Sources and Notes: Liverpool Museum, Account Book of ships *Chesterfield*, *Calveley*, & *Eadith*; Papers of William Davenport in the Raymond Richards Collection, University of Keele Library; 387MD127, Account Book of John Tomlinson & John Knight 1757–1777, Liverpool Record Office; 380Tuo.3/12, David Tuohy's papers, Liverpool Record Office; Galton 564, Galton Papers, Birmingham Reference Library; C.114/155, Chancery Masters' Exhibit, Papers of Thomas Lumley & Co. of London. In some cases the accounts from which this table was compiled belonged to one member of a partnership in a venture. In such cases the accounts show only his proportion of the venture. The total accounts for such ventures have been calculated using the member's proportion.

Appendix 9.1. *Shares of English and Foreign Products in Manufactures Exported from England to Western Africa, 1658–1856*

	Three-year Total Exports £	English Manufactures %	Foreign Manufactures %
1658, 1659, 1660	71,905(10)	14.2	85.8
1661, 1662, 1668	51,211(9)	14.2	85.8
1680, 1681, 1682	27,111(29)	29.8	70.2
1684, 1685, 1693	82,441(33)	49.5	50.5
1701–03	334,191	60.5	39.5
1704–06	143,124	59.0	41.0
1707–09	208,762	63.6	36.4
1710–12	133,263	62.4	37.6
1713–15	227,135	64.9	35.1
1716–18	303,649	52.6	47.4
1719–21	322,849	43.1	56.9
1722–24	541,432	42.1	57.9
1725–27	571,326	43.9	56.1
1728–30	698,414	40.3	59.7
1731–33	538,726	44.3	55.7
1734–36	461,765	43.3	56.7
1737–39	726,009	42.9	57.1
1740–42	373,620	42.5	57.5
1743–45	385,541	42.1	57.9
1746–48	537,545	44.0	56.0
1749–51	576,740	49.9	50.1
1752–54	746,480	68.0	32.0
1755–57	516,750	67.9	32.1
1758–60	741,906	65.4	34.6
1761–63	1,062,252	75.6	24.4
1764–66	1,430,701	71.5	28.5
1767–69	1,775,634	67.7	32.3
1770–72	2,149,938	63.3	36.7
1773–75	2,294,804	62.0	38.0
1776–78	864,083	62.1	37.9
1779–81	667,947	64.2	35.8
1782–84	1,665,285	71.4	28.6
1785–87	2,203,570	65.7	34.3
1788–90	2,334,256	65.7	34.3
1791–93	2,608,590	64.1	35.9
1794–96	1,778,944	52.9	47.1
1797–99	3,261,595	55.6	44.4
1800–02	3,223,224	53.9	46.1
1803–05	2,985,449	58.7	41.3

Appendix 9.1 *(cont.)*

	Three-year Total Exports £	English Manufactures %	Foreign Manufactures %
1806–07 (2 years)	1,945,131	61.9	38.1
1814–16	1,299,000	81.5	18.5
1824–26	1,515,000	73.7	26.3
1834–36	3,723,000	77.9	22.1
1844–46	5,079,000	80.8	19.2
1854–56	9,096,000	86.5	13.5

Sources and Notes: T70/309, T70/635, T70/910–T70/917: Invoices of cargoes shipped to Western Africa by the Company of Royal Adventurers Trading to Africa, and by the Royal African Company of England, 1662–93; T64/273/55 and T64/273/57 (Domestic Exports and Re-exports from England to Western Africa compiled by the Custom House in London); Customs 3/50–Customs 3/80 (1750–1780); Customs 17/7–Customs 17/29 (1781–1807); Margaret Makepeace, "English Traders on the Guinea Coast, 1657–1668: An Analysis of the East India Company Archive," *History in Africa*, 16 (1989), pp. 237–284 (1658–61); Marion Johnson, *Anglo-African Trade in the Eighteenth-Century: English Statistics on African Trade 1699–1808*, Edited by J. Thomas Lindblad and Robert Ross (Leiden: Intercontinenta No. 15, Centre for the History of European Expansion, 1990), p. 64 (1701–15 and 1725–39); Davis, *The Industrial Revolution*, pp. 97–101, 105–109 (1814–56). It should be noted that the seventeenth-century figures are not total exports for the years specified. They represent available invoices of cargoes carried by vessels to Western Africa; in a manner, they are sample figures. The figures in parenthesis indicate the number of cargoes in each case. For the years 1701–1856, the figures are three-year total exports, as stated in the table, and they are all derived ultimately from the Customs records in the Public Record Office, London, England.

Appendix 9.2. *Shares of English and Foreign Products in Manufactures Exported from England to the Americas, 1701–1856*

	All Exports £000	Domestic Products %	Foreign Products %
1700–01	698	66.0	34.0
1730–31	1,116	65.0	35.0
1750–51	1,944	73.0	27.0
1772–73	4,319	84.0	16.0
1780–81	3,290	80.7	19.3
1789–90	5,655	88.2	11.8
1797–98	11,165	92.4	7.6
1804–06	20,981	94.1	5.9
1814–16	21,238	94.1	5.9
1824–26	17,595	93.8	6.2
1834–36	22,580	91.8	8.2
1844–46	21,727	91.8	8.2
1854–56	39,000	95.7	4.3

Sources and Notes: Computed from B. R. Mitchell, *Abstract of British historical statistics* (Cambridge: Cambridge University Press, 1962), Table 11, p. 312 (1701–1798); Davis, *The Industrial Revolution*, pp. 96–101 and 104–109 (1804–56). The figures for 1701–1798 represent exports to the West Indies and North America; those for 1804–56 are for the West Indies, North America, and Latin America. The 1804–56 figures are three-year averages; the others are yearly figures.

Appendix 9.3. *Shares of English and Foreign Products in Manufactures Exported from England to Southern Europe, 1699–1856*

	All Exports £000	Domestic Products %	Foreign Products %
1699–1701	1,708	86.9	13.1
1722–24	2,317	92.4	7.6
1752–54	3,164	91.0	9.0
1772–74	2,664	83.0	17.0
1784–86	2,671	92.8	7.2
1794–96	2,873	87.0	13.0
1804–06	4,032	87.4	12.6
1814–16	9,471	84.0	16.0
1824–26	6,125	84.0	16.0
1834–36	7,609	78.4	21.6
1844–46	6,978	84.7	15.3
1854–56	9,799	83.6	16.4

Sources and Notes: Computed from Davis, "English Foreign Trade, 1700–74," p. 120, and Davis, *The Industrial Revolution*, pp. 94–109. The values are 3-year annual averages.

Appendix 9.4. *Commodity Composition of Foreign Products Exported from England to Western Africa, 1658–1693 (in percentages)*

Year	Indian Cotton Textile	European Linens	Woollen Textile	Bar Iron	Beads	Cowries	Others
1658	33.5	54.3	2.6	8.6			4
1659	41.3	42.5	5.6	6.6		1.1	2.9
1660	27.6	49.7	9.1	10.3			3.3
1661	50.3	21.0	2.0	26.4			0.3
1662	15.6	18.1	5.4	27.3	9.8		23.8
1668	21.6	41.7	26.3	6.0			4.4
1681	7.8	5.5		47.6	7.4	28.1	3.6
1682	23.6	4.3		8.7	5.2	53.8	4.4
1684	33.4	14.4	18.3	10.9	6.4	15.6	1.0
1685	44.1	10.1	9.6	12.8	8.2	13.6	1.6
1693	32.5	20.5	3.7	16.1	8.6	14.1	4.5

Sources and Notes: For the sources to the table, see *Appendix 9.1.* Almost in every case the sub-region in Western Africa for which the cargo was intended is specified in the records. During the period covered by the table, the composition of cargoes going to Ardra (in Dahomey) and Calabar (in southeastern Nigeria) was clearly different from all the others. The Calabar cargoes were overwhelmingly dominated by copper bars and bar iron, while those for Ardra were similarly dominated by cowries. There are 11 cargoes each for 1681 and 1682 in the table. Both of them are entirely for Calabar and Ardra; hence, the unusually large share of iron bars in 1681, and cowries in 1681 and 1682.

Appendix 9.5. *Commodity Composition of Foreign Products Exported from England to Western Africa, 1699–1856 (in percentages)*

Period	Indian Cottons	European Linens	Iron	Copper Brass	Beads Cowries	Spirits Wine	Tobacco
1699–1708	34.9	15.6	14.6	9.9	18.7	0.1	1.3
1709–1718	33.9	23.3	12.3	6.2	17.6	0.3	1.2
1719–1728	53.2	11.8	5.2	6.1	20.2	0.4	0.5
1729–1738	67.3	6.8	7.3	2.7	9.6	0.4	0.6
1739–1748	72.0	4.7	7.3	1.1	7.1	0.3	0.7
1749–1758	64.6	3.9	11.4	1.8	7.1	0.5	2.1
1759–1768	62.0	2.1	7.9	0.8	9.5	5.6	3.8
1769–1778	57.8	2.5	5.7	0.4	12.5	12.1	3.7
1779–1788	68.3	3.3	4.0		7.3	9.0	2.5
1789–1798	75.1	4.1	2.3		4.0	7.5	2.6
1804–1806	75.0	1.9	0.2		1.0	14.0	1.9
1814–1816	18.8	1.3				50.0	5.0
1824–1826	33.8					27.1	8.3
1834–1836	9.1					27.4	9.5
1844–1846	14.8					32.0	11.7
1854–1856	15.4					28.9	24.2

Sources and Notes: For the sources to the table, see *Appendix 9.1*. The figures do not add up to 100, because not all products are included. The products left out include processed foods and drinks other than wine, spirits, and tobacco. Up to 1806 the products left out accounted for less than 7 percent of the total, except for the period 1749–68, when they accounted for over 8 percent. From 1814, however, the share of these products increased significantly, reaching 54 percent in 1834–36. Processed foods and drinks remained dominant in the category.

Appendix 9.6. *Commodity Composition of Foreign Products Exported from England to the Americas, 1699–1856 (in percentages)*

	Linens	Cottons Silks	Other Manufactures	Processed Foodstuffs	Raw Materials
1699–1701	50.3	18.9	11.5	10.9	8.3
1722–24	45.6	33.3	7.4	5.7	8.0
1752–54	48.0	17.2	3.7	23.6	7.5
1772–74	29.3	30.3	1.6	28.1	10.6
1784–86	29.2	7.0	8.8	50.0	4.9
1794–96	42.8	11.2	2.8	40.2	3.0
1804–06	43.3	7.2	1.8	45.1	2.6
1814–16	6.9	9.2	0.9	70.0	13.0
1824–26	1.2	15.3	2.9	50.5	30.1
1834–36	2.4	8.4	2.3	49.6	37.3
1844–46	0.9	8.3	5.6	42.1	43.0
1854–56	0.0	11.8	7.4	33.7	47.1

Sources and Notes: Computed from Davis, "English Foreign Trade, 1700–74," p. 120, and Davis, *The Industrial Revolution*, pp. 102–109. The figures for 1699–1774 are for North America, British and Foreign West Indies, Spanish America, and West Africa, according to Ralph Davis; those for 1784–1856 are for North America, the West Indies, and Latin America. The percentages may not add up to 100 because of rounding to the nearest decimal.

Appendix 9.7. *Commodity Composition of Foreign Products Exported from England to Southern Europe, 1699–1856 (in percentages)*

	Cottons Silks	Linens	Other Manufactures	Foodstuffs	Raw Materials
1699–1701	18.3	5.8	4.5	54.0	17.4
1722–24	20.5	4.5	2.3	39.2	33.5
1752–54	11.9	5.3	0.7	55.8	26.3
1772–74	30.9	7.3	0.7	44.4	16.8
1784–86	6.2	3.1	1.6	47.2	42.0
1794–96	11.8	8.0	1.9	58.2	20.1
1804–06	2.8	2.2	0.8	88.8	5.5
1814–16	8.8	1.1	0.1	59.6	30.4
1824–26	14.7	0.2	0.8	47.3	36.9
1834–36	4.4	0.5	0.5	54.0	40.6
1844–46	3.6	0.1	0.7	43.1	52.4
1854–56	3.6		1.4	47.1	47.9

Sources and Notes: Computed from Davis, "English Foreign Trade, 1700–74," p. 120, and Davis, *The Industrial Revolution*, pp. 102–109. Percentages may not add up to 100 because of rounding.

Appendix 9.8. *Commodity Composition of British Products Exported from England to Western Africa, 1658–1693 (in percentages)*

Year	Woollen Textile	Copper Brass	Pewter Ware	Guns Powder	Other Metals	Others
1658		25.5	8.5	47.7	11.0	7.3
1659	16.1	28.5	9.0	21.4	8.5	16.5
1660	6.5	35.4	35.8	3.8	7.2	11.3
1661			61.6	17.7	12.9	7.8
1662	9.8	48.2	1.0	12.2	5.7	23.1
1668	38.1	7.9	2.4	9.4	21.9	20.3
1681		85.5	5.7		8.9	0.0
1682		88.0	3.8	2.7	5.5	0.0
1684	42.7	10.6	8.1	18.3	5.3	15.0
1685	31.8	36.4	4.6	11.3	7.9	8.0
1693	64.9	12.1	5.7	3.5	2.1	11.7

Sources and Notes: For the sources to the table, see *Appendix 9.1*. It is likely that most of the copper and brass products in the table are European products (Dutch and German) re-exported from England. The evidence given to a House of Commons Committee in 1799 by Thomas Williams, who dominated the industry in the late eighteenth century, states that most copper and brass products sold in England in the early decades of the eighteenth century were imported from Germany and Holland. See British Library, *House of Commons Reports*, Vol. X (1785–1801), p. 666. As stated in *Appendix 9.4*, the unusually large share of copper and brass for 1681 and 1682 is due to the dominance of Calabar cargoes in the sample for these years, which is an unavoidable distortion.

Appendix 9.9. *Commodity Composition of British Products Exported from England to Western Africa, 1699–1856 (in percentages)*

	Woollen Textile	Cotton Textile	Linen Textile	Metals	Other Manufactures	Other Products
1699–1708	56.7	15.5	0.1	17.9	6.0	3.7
1709–1718	69.6	2.2	0.5	18.9	6.3	2.5
1719–1728	47.1	10.9	0.4	30.9	7.5	3.2
1729–1738	47.0	4.7	3.4	34.8	7.3	2.8
1739–1748	36.7	2.2	8.2	38.7	10.4	3.7
1750–1759	15.1	28.3	9.4	21.6	14.2	11.4
1760–1769	18.8	26.9	15.4	16.5	11.5	10.9
1770–1779	30.7	20.6	12.5	16.1	12.1	8.0
1780–1789	30.8	31.2	5.8	13.5	12.3	6.4
1790–1799	20.2	40.2	1.9	13.6	11.8	12.3
1800–1807	13.1	49.0	0.6	14.4	8.5	14.4
1814–1816	11.9	25.2	2.0	14.7	36.5	9.6
1824–1826	8.1	23.9	3.2	18.3	40.1	6.5
1834–1836	6.3	40.8	2.9	17.9	28.0	4.0
1844–1846	6.4	33.6	2.0	18.9	30.4	8.5
1854–1856	5.2	33.2	1.4	20.0	32.0	8.0

Sources and Notes: Computed from Customs 3/50–Customs 3/80 and Customs 17/7–Customs 17/29, for 1750–1807; Johnson, *Anglo-African Trade*, pp. 53–59, for 1699–1748; Davis, *The Industrial Revolution*, pp. 97–101, for 1814–56. For the period 1750–1807, "other manufactures" are made up entirely of gunpowder and spirits. And for the years 1699–1748, the figures for metals include military stores which are mixed up with gunpowder. The percentages may not add up to 100 because of rounding.

Appendix 9.10. *Commodity Composition of British Products Exported from England to the Americas, 1699–1856 (in percentages)*

	Woollen Textile	Cotton Textile	Linen Textile	Silk Textile	Garments Hats, etc.	Metal Products	Other Manufactures	Other Products
1699–1701	34.3	3.0	0.0	6.7	4.5	13.9	26.2	11.5
1722–24	40.0	2.0	2.9	5.0	5.0	14.4	20.6	10.2
1752–54	21.9	4.6	11.1	3.5	3.5	19.7	28.1	7.7
1772–74	27.5	4.2	16.3	3.2	2.2	18.2	23.8	4.5
1784–86	18.4	5.9	11.9	5.3	4.9	16.7	30.3	6.7
1794–96	20.8	20.0	6.5	4.1	5.7	15.8	19.7	7.4
1804–06	17.1	40.2	3.6	1.9	6.4	13.6	14.4	3.0
1814–16	19.4	35.1	6.8	1.7	5.0	12.4	12.4	7.3
1824–26	17.4	39.1	9.0	1.2	4.8	12.5	11.8	4.3
1834–36	18.5	36.5	8.4	3.0	4.0	15.6	10.3	3.3
1844–46	18.2	30.5	9.9	2.1	5.0	18.4	10.6	4.8
1854–56	13.4	27.2	8.4	1.7	7.0	26.0	9.2	6.8

Sources and Notes: Computed from Davis, "English Foreign Trade, 1700–74," p. 120, and Davis, *The Industrial Revolution*, pp. 94–101. The figures for 1699–1774 include exports to Western Africa, as stated by Ralph Davis. Most of the cottons went to Western Africa during the period. For 1784–1856, the figures are for North America, the West Indies, and Latin America. Exports to Latin America included in the table were very small before 1804; they increased rapidly from the latter date. 1699–1774 exports are for England and Wales, and those of 1784–1856 are for Great Britain. The percentages may not add up to 100 because of rounding.

Appendix 9.11. *Commodity Composition of British Products Exported to the British West Indies, 1783–1856 (in £000)*

	Linen Textile	Cotton Textile	Woollen Textile	Haberdashery, Hats, etc.	Metals	Other Manufactures	Other Products
1783	443	111	74	69	161	478	110
1784	269	82	77	46	154	363	94
1785	250	59	56	52	186	384	95
1786	283	59	61	49	189	373	94
1787	422	127	100	58	211	446	116
1794–96	521	754	291	365	951	1,325	283
1804–06	444	2,568	306	678	1,361	1,568	335
1814–16	871	2,498	351	512	680	1,204	790
1824–26	542	1,498	174	343	444	753	369
1834–36	437	1,641	203	340	482	749	265
1844–46	550	1,315	152	310	511	721	307
1854–56	545	1,313	133	255	666	663	372

Sources and Notes: Compiled from House of Lords Records, *Parliamentary Papers, Accounts and Papers*, Vol. XXVI, No. 646a, Part IV (1789): "An Account of the quantity and Value of British Manufacture and Produce Annually exported from Great Britain to the British West India Islands, between the 5th of January 1783 and the 5th of January 1788 . . ." (for 1783–87), and Davis, *The Industrial Revolution*, pp. 95–101 (for 1794–1856). For 1794–1856, the figures include exports to non-British West India Islands.

Appendix 9.12. *Commodity Composition of British Products Exported from England to Southern Europe, 1699–1856 (in £000)*

	Woollen Textile	Cotton Textile	Garments, Hats, etc.	Metal Products	Other Manufactures	Other Products
1699–1701	1,201	1	12	7	123	140
1722–24	1,606		81	35	166	253
1752–54	1,954		154	76	237	458
1772–74	1,667	6	128	6	294	110
1784–86	1,662	91	4	278	161	282
1794–96	1,047	269	33	447	281	423
1804–06	744	1,629	100	520	338	193
1814–16	1,636	4,079	179	570	789	702
1824–26	763	2,660	73	440	845	364
1834–36	645	3,074	59	507	1,035	648
1844–46	700	2,503	64	930	1,280	430
1854–56	680	2,730	119	1,814	1,893	955

Sources and Notes: Computed from Davis, "English Foreign Trade, 1700–74," p. 120, and Davis, *The Industrial Revolution*, pp. 94–101. "Other Manufactures" are made up mainly of linens, cotton yarns, woollen yarns, silks, and unspecified products. "Other Products" are mainly foodstuffs, plus coal and some unspecified products.

Appendix 9.13. *Shares of Portugal and Spain in Total Exports (Domestic and Re-exports) from England to Southern Europe, 1701–1800*

	Southern Europe £000	Portugal %	Spain %	Spain and Portugal %
1701–05	1,329	45.9	9.0	54.9
1706–10	1,462	44.6	11.4	56.0
1711–15	1,833	34.8	22.1	56.9
1716–20	1,987	35.0	21.5	56.5
1721–25	2,247	36.1	25.9	62.0
1726–30	2,400	38.1	26.3	64.4
1731–35	2,861	35.8	27.3	63.1
1736–40	2,868	40.6	24.5	65.1
1741–45	1,920	58.1	4.5	62.6
1746–50	2,748	40.5	25.5	66.0
1751–55	3,136	35.0	33.1	68.1
1756–60	3,380	38.5	37.7	76.2
1761–65	2,831	34.1	36.1	70.2
1766–70	2,572	23.1	39.0	62.1
1771–75	2,790	22.0	36.2	58.2
1776–80	2,002	26.2	36.1	62.3
1781–85	1,728	36.0	25.1	61.1
1786–90	2,411	25.8	26.3	52.1
1791–95	2,298	25.8	25.6	51.4
1796–1800	1,663	48.8	6.6	55.4

Sources and Notes: Computed from Schumpeter, *English Overseas Trade Statistics*, p. 17. Southern Europe grouped together from Schumpeter's table includes Portugal, Spain, The Straits, Italy, Turkey, and Venice. The figures are 5-year annual averages. Southern Europe is being used as a proxy for Portugal and Spain, because the relevant information available does not show Portugal and Spain separately.

Bibliography

Manuscript Sources

Public Record Office, London

Records of the Board of Customs and Excise:

Customs 3:	Ledgers of Imports and Exports.
Customs 17:	States of Navigation, Commerce and Revenue.
Customs 8/25–71:	Customs 10/18–41.

Shipping Returns:

T 64/47–50:	Ships Entered and Cleared Barbados, 1710–1829.
T 64/273–289:	Colonies (including Shipping and Trade Returns), 1680–1867.
HO 76/1–2:	Naval Officers Returns, 1791–97.
T 1/512:	Naval Office Shipping Returns for Antigua, St. Christopher, Nevis and Montserrat, 1774–75.
CO 157/1:	Naval Office Shipping Returns for Antigua & Montserrat, 1704–20; Nevis, 1683–1715; St. Christopher, 1685–1787; Leeward Islands, 1683–1787.
CO 27/12–15:	Bahamas, 1721–1815.
CO 33/13–26:	Barbados, 1678–1819.
CO 41/6–12:	Bermuda, 1715–1820.
CO 142/13–29:	Jamaica, 1680–1818.
CO 76/4–8:	Dominica, 1763–1819.
CO 106/1–8:	Grenada, 1764–1816.
CO 243/1:	St. Christopher, 1704–87.
CO 265/1–2:	St. Vincent, 1763–1812.
CO 278/7–9:	Surinam, 1804–16.
CO 317/1:	Virgin Islands, 1784–86.
BT 6/186:	Jamaica, 1784–88.

Records of the English African Companies:

These records cover the years 1660 to 1823, and amount to 1,693 volumes and bundles. They have been well described by Hilary Jenkinson, "The Records of the English African

Companies," *Royal Hist. Soc. Transactions*, 3rd. Ser. VI (1912) pp. 185–220. They are made up of the records of three companies: The Company of Royal Adventurers of England trading with Africa (1663–72); The Royal African Company of England (1672–1750); The Company of Merchants Trading to Africa (1750–1821). The Records of the last company that have been most helpful for this study are the 73 or so bundles of detached papers, T.70/1515–T.70/1587. Being loose papers, without any index, and in a somewhat poor condition, research into them presents a very tedious task. Some of the papers of the Royal African Company are among the Chancery Masters Exhibits that follow.

Treasury Papers:

T.1/447; T.64. In particular, T.64/276 and T.64/286.

Board of Trade Papers:

In the Colonial Office List: C.O. 268/1; C.O. 388; C.O. 389; C.O. 390; C.O. 391. Board of Trade Miscellanea: BT.6/1; BT.6/2; BT.6/3; BT.6/4; BT.6/5; BT.6/6; BT.6/7; BT.6/9–BT.6/12: Minutes of Evidence taken before a committee of the Privy Council appointed to inquire into the state of the African Trade, 1788–89; BT.6/17; BT.6/14; BT.6/185; BT.6/240; BT.6/241; BT.6/244; BT.6/262. BT.1/1: Board of Trade Papers, 1791 (The Annamaboe Palaver).

Chancery Masters Exhibits:

C.107/1–C.107/15 and C.107/59: Papers of James Rogers & Co. of Bristol. These are made up of over 16 boxes of unbound papers, covering the years 1771–93. They are badly sorted, but they have been very helpful for this study.

C. 109/401: contains accounts of five Guinea ventures by Samuel Sandys & Co., of Liverpool, made in 1771–72.

C.114/1–C.114/3 & C.114/154–C.114/158: Records of Thomas Lumley & Co., of London, Guinea merchants and dealers in East India Goods, 1801–07.

C.103/130–C.103/133: Papers of Thomas Hall & Co., of London, Guinea merchants, 1730–43.

C.104/151: A box of Coral and Glass Beads, belonging to Robert Ross.

C.108/212–C.108/214: Records of John Leigh & Co., of Liverpool, Guinea merchants, 1803–11.

C.109/1–C.109/14: Papers of Miles Nightingale of London, relating to gum Senegal.

C.113/261–C.113/295: Papers of the Royal African Company of England.

Correspondence of the Principal Secretaries of State (Plantation Department):

C.O.267/1–C.O.267/22. Original Correspondence, 1750–1804.

Probate Records, Prerogative Court of Canterbury Wills:

Prob. 11/996	Folio Number 101.
Prob. 6/155	Folio Number 1779.
Prob. 11/1263	Folio Number 431.
Prob. 11/1269	Folio Number 694.
Prob. 11/1259	Folio Number 260.
Prob. 11/1292	Folio Number 393.

House of Lords Record Office, London

House of Lords Main Paper, Order date, 18 February, 1790.
House of Lords Main Paper, Order date, 3 May, 1792.
House of Lords Main Paper, Order date, 31 May, 1793.

House of Lords Main Paper, Order date, 24 March, 1794.
House of Lords Main Paper, "1794 Undated: Certificates of Slaves, etc."
House of Lords Main Paper, Order date, 21 June, 1799.
House of Lords Main Paper, Order date, 25 June, 1799.
House of Lords Main Paper, Order date, 28 July, 1800.

British Library, London, Department of Manuscripts

Add. MSS. 1162A & 1162B. Papers relating to the commerce of Africa.
Add. MSS. 14,035. Papers of the Board of Trade and Plantation, 1710–81.
Add. MSS. 22,676. Papers relating to the Trade of Africa in the eighteenth century.
Add. MSS. 38,350. African Company's Papers relating to 1791.
Add. MSS. 38,354. African Company's Papers relating to 1796.
Add. MSS. 38,392. Minutes of Committee of Trade relating to the African Company, 1787–92.
Add. MSS. 38,393. Minutes of the Committee of Trade relating to the African Company 1787–92.
Add. MSS. 38,416. Liverpool Papers relating to the slave trade, 1787–1823.
Add. MSS. 42,074. Papers of C. F. Grenville relating to British African Trade, 1765–78.

National Maritime Museum, Greenwich, London

Log/M/21. MS.53/035. Journal of a voyage from London to Africa on board the *Sandown* by Samuel Gamble, slave merchant, London, 1793–94.
Log/M/46. MS.66/103. Journal of three voyages from Liverpool to Africa, 1750–54, kept by John Newton, Master and slave trader. Two voyages in the *African*, and one in the *Duke of Argyle*.
Log/M/23. Two voyages to Old Calabar from Liverpool, 1840–41, and 1847.
Log/M/22. One voyage from Liverpool to Africa, 1838.
REC/19/MS 66/069. Case of the Ship *Zong* in the King's Bench, Wednesday, May 21, 1783.
AMS/4/MS 35/024. Ship *Castle*'s Day Book, Second Voyage to Africa, 1727, John Malcolme, Master.

Lloyd's Corporation Library, London

Account Book of the ship *Hector*, belonging to John Chilcott and Co., of Bristol. This contains accounts of three Guinea ventures made from 1770 to 1776.
Insurance Policy of the Ship *Guipuzcoa*, on a voyage from Liverpool to Africa and Cuba, 1794.

Midland Bank, London

Records of the Liverpool banking firm of Leyland and Bullins.
These are:
AE10 to AE12. Profit and loss items ledgers from 1807–60.
AE14. Bills sent for acceptance book 1815 to 1817.
AE17 to AE19. Bills sent for acceptance 1807 to 1809; 1817 to 1819; 1821 to 1824.
AE37 to AE40. Bills sent for acceptance 1809 to 1811; 1813 to 1814; 1819 to 1822.
AE49. Sundry letters and receipts around 1845.
AE52. Photostat of slave ships' books, *Kitty*, 1789 and *Earl of Liverpool*, 1797, belonging to Thomas Leyland.

Guildhall Library, London

Papers of Edward Grace & Co., brokers and merchants, London (MSS. 12,048–12,052).

Liverpool Record Office, Liverpool

The Tarleton Papers (920 TAR.)
There are also microfilm copies of the Tarleton family papers not available in manuscript.

Papers and correspondence of David Tuohy of Liverpool, Merchant (380TUO.)
Holt and Gregson Papers (942HOL., in particular, volume 10).
Account Books of Guineamen belonging to Thomas Leyland & Co., of Liverpool (387MD40–387MD44).
Account Book of John Tomlinson and John Knight 1757–77 (387MD 127).
Letter Book etc. of Robert Bostock of Liverpool 1779–92 (387MD 54 &387MD 55).
Gregson Correspondence (920 GRE.)
Account Books of Messrs. Case & Southworth, 1754–69, 380MD33–380MD36.
Log of the Brig *Ranger*, 1789–90 (387MD56).
Petition of the Corporation of Liverpool to the House of Lords against the Abolition of the slave trade (942 MD 37).
Petition of Liverpool Merchants against the abolition of the slave trade (942 MD 36).

Liverpool City Museum, Liverpool

Account Books of ship *Chesterfield*, Brig *Calveley*, Brig *Eadith*, Snow *Aston*, 1757–73.

Barclays Bank, Heywoods Branch (formerly Martins Bank, Heywoods Branch), Liverpool

Records of the Heywoods Bank, of Liverpool.

Lancashire Record Office, Preston

Wills of Liverpool Guinea Merchants.

John Rylands Library, Manchester

Miscellaneous Papers relating to the slave trade, 1751–87 (English MS.517).

Bristol Reference Library, Bristol

Committee Book of the Copper Company (B.4771).
The Bristol Presentments (in microfilm. There are also printed copies).

Bristol City Museum, Bristol

Log of the Snow *Africa*, 1774–76.

Merchants' Hall, The Promenade, Clifton, Bristol

Papers relating to Bristol's Guinea trade; Petitions, etc. Some are for Liverpool Guinea merchants.

Birmingham Reference Library, Birmingham

The Galton Papers.
Papers relating to John Whately, gun manufacturer (j257, j258, j262, j273, j276, j280, j285, j408), 1766–96.
Clarke, *History of Birmingham*, MSS. (7 volumes) vol. III.

University of Keele Library, Keele

The Davenport Papers in the Raymond Richards Collection. These number several volumes.

Essex Record Office, Chelmsford

William Braund's Papers.

Bedfordshire Record Office, Bedford

Lady Lucas Collection (L.29/333–L.29/337 and L.29/339–L.29/341).

William L. Clements Library, The University of Michigan Ann Arbor, 48104, U.S.A.

Shelburne Papers, Vols. 72 and 81.

Newspapers
Lloyd's List, National Maritime Museum, Greenwich, London.
Liverpool Directory, Liverpool Record Office, Liverpool.

Official Publications

Public Record Office, London

C.O.137/88: Reports by the Committee of the House of Assembly of Jamaica on The Slave Trade. First Report 16 Oct., 1788. Second Report 12 Nov., 1788.
C.O.137/91: Proceedings of the House of Assembly of Jamaica on the Sugar and Slave Trade, 1792.
C.O.137/104: Report from the Committee of the House of Assembly, Dominica, 22 December, 1799.

British Library, London: State Paper Room

British Parliamentary Papers, *Accounts and Papers*:

    1789 Vol. 81
    1789 Vol. 82
    1789 Vol. 83
    1789 Vol. 84
    1789 Vol. 87
    1790 Vol. 88
    1790 Vol. 89
    1790–91 Vol. 92
    1792 Vol. 93
    1798–99 Vol. 104
    1798–99 Vol. 106
    1799–1800 Vol. 107
    1801–02 Vol. IV
    1802–03 Vol. VII
    1806 Vol. XII

House of Commons Journals

Vols. XVI, XLIII, XLVI, XLVII, XLVIII, XLIX, LIII, LIV, LX, LXI.

House of Commons Reports

Vols. II, VII (2), X.

House of Commons Sessional Papers of the 18th Century, Reports & Papers

Vol. 25, 1763–74; Vol. 67; Vol. 70, 1789; Vol. 82, 1791 & 1792.

Public General Acts:

    28 Geo. 3 Cap. 54
    29 Geo. 3 Cap 66
    30 Geo. 3 Cap 33
    31 Geo. 3 Cap 54
    32 Geo. 3 Cap 52
    33 Geo. 3 Cap 73
    34 Geo. 3 Cap 80
    35 Geo. 3 Cap 90
    37 Geo. 3 Cap 118
    38 Geo. 3 Cap 88
    39 Geo. 3 Cap 80

House of Lords Record Office, London

British Parliamentary Papers, *Accounts and Papers*:

Volume XXIV, 1789
Volume XXVI, 1789

Pamphlets

Observations on the Manufacture of Firearms for Military Purposes, on the Number Supplied from Birmingham to the British Government (1829). Birmingham Reference Library, L 65.52.

B. A. Heywood, *Observations on the Circulation of Individual Credit and on the Banking System of England* (London, 1812).

Secondary Sources

Abu-Lughod, Janet L. *Before European Hegemony: The World System A. D. 1250–1350* (New York: Oxford University Press, 1989).

Ahmad, Jaleel. *Import Substitution, Trade and Development* (Greenwich, CT: JAI, 1978).

Alden, Dauril. "Late Colonial Brazil, 1750–1808," in Leslie Bethell (ed.), *The Cambridge History of Latin America*, Vol. II: *Colonial Latin America* (Cambridge: Cambridge University Press, 1984).

Allen, Robert. "Agriculture during the industrial revolution," in Roderick Floud and Donald McCloskey (eds.), *The Economic History of Britain Since 1700, Volume 1: 1700–1860* (2nd edition, Cambridge: Cambridge University Press, 1994).

Allen, Robert C. *Enclosure and the Yeoman: The Agricultural Development of the South Midlands, 1450–1850* (Oxford: Clarendon Press, 1992).

Anderson, B. L. "Aspects of Capital and Credit in Lancashire during the Eighteenth Century," (M.A. Thesis, University of Liverpool, 1966).

"Money and the Structure of Credit in the eighteenth century," *Business History*, Vol. XII, No. 2 (July, 1970).

Anstey, Roger T. "Capitalism and Slavery: A Critique," *Economic History Review*, 2d ser. 21 (August, 1968).

The Atlantic Slave Trade and British Abolition, 1760–1810 (London: Macmillan, 1975).

"The Volume of the North American Slave-Carrying Trade from Africa, 1761–1810," *Revue française D'Histoire D'Outre-Mer*, LXII, Nos. 226–227 (1975).

"The Volume and Profitability of the British Slave Trade, 1761–1807," in Stanley L. Engerman and E. D. Genovese (eds.), *Race and Slavery in the Western Hemisphere: Quantitative Studies* (Princeton, NJ: Princeton University Press, 1975)."

Appleby, John C. "A Guinea Venture, c.1657: A Note on the Early English Slave Trade," *The Mariner's Mirror*, Vol. 79, No. 1 (February, 1993).

"English Settlement in the Lesser Antilles during War and Peace, 1603–1660," in Robert L. Paquette and Stanley L. Engerman (eds.), *The Lesser Antilles in the Age of European Expansion* (Gainesville, Florida: University Press of Florida, 1996).

Arruda, José Jobson de Andrade. *O Brasil No Comércio Colonial* (Sao Paulo: Editora Atica, 1980).

"Colonies as mercantile investments: The Luso-Brazilian empire, 1500–1808," in James D. Tracy (ed.), *The Political Economy of Merchant Empires: State Power and World Trade, 1350–1750* (Cambridge: Cambridge University Press, 1991).

Ashton, Thomas Southcliffe. *Iron and Steel in the Industrial Revolution* (2nd Edition, Manchester: Manchester University Press, 1951).

Ashton, T. S. *The Industrial Revolution: A Study in Bibliography* (London: Published for the Economic History Society by A. & C. Black, 1937).

The Industrial Revolution, 1760–1830 (London: Oxford University Press, 1948).

An Economic History of England: The 18th Century (London: Methuen, 1955).

Aston, T. H. and C. H. E. Philpin (eds.), *The Brenner Debate: Agrarian Class Structure and Economic Development in Pre-Industrial Europe* (Cambridge: Cambridge University Press, 1985).

Aston, Trevor (ed.), *Crisis in Europe, 1560–1660: Essays from Past and Present* (London: Routledge & Kegan Paul, 1965).

Attman, Artur. "Precious Metals and the Balance of Payments in International Trade, 1500–1800," in Wolfram Fischer, R. Marvin McInnis, and Jurgen Schneider (eds.), *The Emergence of a World Economy, 1500–1914: Papers of the IX International Congress of Economic History* (Stuttgart: Steiner Verlag Wiesbaden, 1986).

Austen, Ralph A. and Woodruff D. Smith, "Private Tooth Decay as Public Economic Virtue: The Slave-Sugar Triangle, Consumerism, and European Industrialization," in Inikori and Engerman (eds.), *The Atlantic Slave Trade.*

Austen, Ralph A. "Marginalization, stagnation, and growth: The Trans-Saharan caravan trade in the era of European expansion, 1500–1900," in James D. Tracy (ed.), *The Rise of Merchant Empires: Long-Distance Trade in the Early Modern World, 1350–1750* (Cambridge: Cambridge University Press, 1990).

Baer, Werner and Andrea Maneschi, "Import Substitution, Stagnation and Structural Change: An Interpretation of the Brazilian Case," *Journal of Developing Areas*, 5 (1971).

Bailey, Ronald W. "Africa, the Slave Trade, and the Rise of Industrial Capitalism in Europe and the United States: A Historiographic Review," *American History: A Bibliographic Review*, Vol. II, 1986.

Bakewell, Peter. "Mining in Colonial Spanish America," in Leslie Bethell (ed.), *Cambridge History of Latin America*, Vol. II (Cambridge: Cambridge University Press, 1984).

Balassa, Bela. *The Process of Industrial Development and Alternative Development Strategies* (Princeton, NJ: Princeton University, Department of Economics, International Finance Section, 1981).

Bank, World. *World Development Report: Workers in an Integrating World* (New York: Oxford University Press, 1995).

Barnes, Harry Elmer. *An Economic History of the Western World* (New York: Harcourt, Brace & Co., 1937).

Barrett, Ward. "World bullion flows, 1450–1800," in James D. Tracy (ed.), *The Rise of Merchant Empires* (Cambridge: Cambridge University Press, 1990).

Bath, B. H. Slicher Van. "The absence of white contract labour in Spanish America during the colonial period," in P. C. Emmer (ed.), *Colonialism and Migration: Indentured Labour Before and After Slavery* (Dordrecht: Martinus Nijhoff, 1986).

Bauer, P. T. *Equality, the Third World and Economic Delusion* (London: George Weidenfeld and Nicolson, 1981).

Bean, Richard. "A Note on the Relative Importance of Slaves and Gold in Western African Exports," *Journal of African History*, XV (1974).

Beckles, Hilary McD. " 'The Williams Effect': Eric Williams's Capitalism and Slavery and the Growth of West Indian Political Economy," in Solow and Engerman (eds.), *British Capitalism and Caribbean Slavery.*

Berg, Maxine and Pat Hudson, "Rehabilitating the industrial revolution," *Economic History Review*, XLV, 1 (1992).

Bernstein, Henry (ed.), *Underdevelopment and Development: The Third World Today* (New York: Penguin Books, 1973).

Berrill, K. "International Trade and the Rate of Economic Growth," *Economic History Review*, 2nd series, Vol. XII, No. 3 (1960).

Birch, Alan. *The Economic History of the British Iron and Steel Industry, 1784–1879: Essays in Industrial and Economic History with Special Reference to the Development of Technology* (London: Cass, 1967).

Birmingham, David and Phyllis M. Martin (eds.), *History of Central Africa*, Vol. I (London: Longman, 1983).

Birmingham, David. "Central Africa from Cameroun to the Zambezi," in Roland Oliver (ed.), *The Cambridge History of Africa, Volume 3, From c. 1050 to c. 1600* (Cambridge: Cambridge University Press, 1977).

Blake, John W. *West Africa, Quest for God and Gold, 1454–1578: A Survey of the First Century of White Enterprise in West Africa, With Particular Reference to the Achievement of the Portuguese and their Rivalries with Other European Powers* (London: Curzon Press, 1977; first edition, 1937).

Blanchard, Peter. *Slavery and Abolition in Early Republican Peru* (Wilmington, DE: Scholarly Resources, 1992).

Boogaart, Ernst van den and Pieter C. Emmer, "The Dutch Participation in the Atlantic Slave Trade, 1596–1650," in Henry A. Gemery and Jan S. Hogendorn (eds.), *The Uncommon Market: Essays on the Economic History of the Transatlantic Slave Trade* (New York: Academic Press, 1979).

Boogaart, Ernst van den. "The Trade Between Western Africa and the Atlantic World, 1600–1690: Estimates of Trends in Composition and Value," *Journal of African History*, 33 (1992).

Borah, W. and S. F. Cook, "The Aboriginal population of Central Mexico on the eve of Spanish conquest," in Lewis Hanke (ed.), *History of Latin American Civilization: Sources and Interpretation* (2 Vols., Vol. 1, London: Methuen, 1967).

Bowden, Peter J. *The Wool Trade in Tudor and Stuart England* (London: Macmillan, 1962).

Brading, D. A. "Bourbon Spain and its American Empire," in Leslie Bethell (ed.), *The Cambridge History of Latin America, Volume I: Colonial Latin America* (Cambridge: Cambridge University Press, 1984).

Brenner, Robert. *Merchants and Revolution: Commercial Change, Political Conflict, and London's Overseas Traders, 1550–1653* (Princeton, NJ: Princeton University Press, 1993).

"Agrarian Class Structure and Economic Development in Pre-Industrial Europe," *Past and Present*, No. 70 (1976).

"The Origins of Capitalist Development: A Critique of Neo-Smithian Marxism," *New Left Review*, No. 104 (July–August, 1977).

"England, Eastern Europe, and France: Socio-Historical Versus 'Economic' Interpretation," in Frederick Krantz and Paul M. Hohenberg (eds.), *Failed Transitions to Modern Industrial Society: Renaissance Italy and Seventeenth Century Holland* (Montreal: Interuniversity Centre for European Studies, 1975).

"Agrarian Class Structure and Economic Development in Pre-Industrial Europe," *Past and Present*, No. 70 (1976).

"The Agrarian Roots of European Capitalism," *Past and Present*, No. 97 (1982).

Brewer, John. *The Sinews of Power: War, Money and the English State, 1688–1783* (New York: Alfred A. Knopf, 1989).

Brezis, Elise S. "Foreign Capital Flows in the century of Britain's industrial revolution: new estimates, controlled conjectures," *Economic History Review*, XLVIII, 1 (1995), pp. 46–67.

"Did foreign capital flows finance the industrial revolution? A reply," *Economic History Review*, L, 1 (1997), pp. 129–132.

Bridbury, A. R. *Economic Growth: England in the Later Middle Ages* (London: Allen and Unwin, 1962).

Bruijn, Jaap R. "Productivity and costs of private and corporate Dutch ship owning in the seventeenth and eighteenth centuries," in Tracy (ed.), *The Rise of Merchant Empires*.

Bruton, Henry J. "The Import Substitution Strategy of Economic Development: A Survey," *Pakistan Development Review*, 10 (1970).

Buchanan, R. A. and Neil Cossons, *Industrial Archaeology of the Bristol Region* (Newton Abbot: David & Charles, 1969).

Buckatzsch, E. J. "The Geographical Distribution of Wealth in England, 1086–1843: An Experimental Study of Certain Tax Assessments," *Economic History Review*, 2nd series, Vol. III, No. 2 (1950).

Buescu, Mircea. *Historia Economica do Brasil: Pesquisas e Analises* (Rio de Janeiro: Apec, 1970).

Bulmer-Thomas, Victor. *The Economic History of Latin America Since Independence* (Cambridge: Cambridge University Press, 1994).

Butel, Paul. "France, the Antilles, and Europe in the seventeenth and eighteenth centuries: renewals of foreign trade," in Tracy (ed.), *The Rise of Merchant Empires*.

Cain, P. J. and A. G. Hopkins, *British Imperialism: Innovation and Expansion, 1688–1914* (London: Longman, 1993).

British Imperialism: Crisis and Deconstruction, 1914–1990 (London: Longman, 1993).

Caldwell, John C. "The Social Repercussions of Colonial Rule: Demographic Aspects," in A. Adu Boahen (ed.), *UNESCO General History of Africa, Volume VII, Africa Under Colonial Domination 1880–1935* (Berkeley: California, Heinemann, UNESCO, 1985).

Cameron, Rondo. "The Industrial Revolution: Fact or Fiction?", *Contention*, Vol. 4, No. 1 (Fall, 1994).

Campbell, Bruce M. S. "Measuring the commercialisation of seigneurial agriculture c.1300," in Richard H. Britnell and Bruce M. S. Campbell (eds.), *A Commercialising Economy: England 1086 to c. 1300* (Manchester: Manchester University Press, 1995).

Cannadine, David. "The Present and the Past in the English Industrial Revolution 1880–1980," *Past and Present*, No. 103 (May, 1984).

Carrington, Selwyn H. H. *The British West Indies During the American Revolution* (Dordrecht, Holland: Foris Publications, 1988).

The Sugar Industry and the Abolition of the Slave Trade, 1775–1810 (forthcoming).

Carus-Wilson, E. M. "Trends in the export of English woollens in the fourteenth century," *Economic History Review*, 2nd series, Vol. III, No. 2 (1950).

Carus-Wilson, E. M. and Olive Coleman, *England's Export Trade, 1275–1547* (Oxford: Clarendon Press, 1963).

Chambers, J. D. and G. E. Mingay, *The Agricultural Revolution, 1750–1880* (London: Batsford, 1966).

Chapman, D. S. "Financial Restraints on the Growth of Firms in the Cotton Industry, 1790–1850," *Economic History Review*, 2nd ser., Vol. 32 (1979).

Chartres, J. A. *Internal Trade in England, 1500–1700* (London: Macmillan, 1977).

Chaudhuri, K. N. *The English East India Company: The Study of an Early Joint-Stock Company 1600–1640* (London: Frank Cass, 1965).

Chenery, Hollis B. "Patterns of Industrial Growth," *American Economic Review*, Vol. 50 (1960).

Chenery, Hollis, Sherman Robinson, and Moshe Syrquin, *Industrialization and Growth* (New York: Oxford University Press, 1986).

Clapham, J. H. "The Growth of An Agrarian Proletariat, 1688–1832: A Statistical Note," *Cambridge Historical Journal*, Vol. I (1923).

Clark, G. N. *Guide to English Commercial Statistics 1696–1782* (London: Royal Historical Society, 1938).

Clark, Gregory. "Agriculture and the Industrial Revolution: 1700–1850," in Mokyr (ed.), *The British Industrial Revolution*.

Cole, W. A. "Factors in demand, 1700–1780," in Roderick Floud and Donald McCloskey (eds.), *The Economic History of Britain since 1700, Volume 1: 1700–1860* (New York: Cambridge University Press, 1981).

"Eighteenth-Century Economic Growth Revisited," *Explorations in Economic History*, Vol. 10, No. 4 (1973).

Coleman, D. C. *The Economy of England, 1450–1750* (Oxford: Oxford University Press, 1977).

"Growth and Decay During the Industrial Revolution: The Case of East Anglia," *The Scandinavian Economic History Review*, Vol. X, Nos. 1 and 2 (1962).

"Proto-Industrialization: A Concept Too Many," *Economic History Review*, 36 (1983).

Colquhoun, Patrick. *Treatise on the Wealth, Power and Resources of the British Empire* (2nd edition, London, 1815).

Coughtry, Jay. *The Notorious Triangle: Rhode Island and the African Slave Trade, 1700–1807* (Philadelphia: Temple University Press, 1981).

Court, W. H. B. *The Rise of the Midlands Industries, 1600–1838* (Oxford: Oxford University Press, 1938).

"Industrial Organisation and Economic Progress in the Eighteenth-Century Midlands," *Transactions of the Royal Historical Society*, 4th Series, XXVIII, 1946.

Crafts, N. F. R. and T. C. Mills, "The industrial revolution as a macroeconomic epoch: an alternative view," *Economic History Review*, XLVII, 4 (1994).

Crafts, N. F. R. *British Economic Growth during the Industrial Revolution* (Oxford: Clarendon Press, 1985).

"British Economic Growth: 1700–1831: A Review of the Evidence," *Economic History Review*, 2nd series, XXXVI, No. 2 (1983).

Crafts, N. F. R. and C. K. Harley, "Output Growth and the British Industrial Revolution: A Restatement of the Crafts-Harley view," *Economic History Review*, XLV, 4 (1992).

Crafts, Nick. "The industrial revolution," in Floud and McCloskey (eds.), *The Economic History of Britain*, 2nd edition.

Crafts, N. F. R. "British Industrialization in an International Context," *Journal of Interdisciplinary History*, XIX, 3 (1989).

"Exogenous or Endogenous Growth? The Industrial Revolution Reconsidered," *Journal of Economic History*, Vol. 55, No. 4 (December, 1995).

Craig, R. "Capital Formation in Shipping," in J. P. P. Higgins and Sidney Pollard (eds.), *Aspects of Capital Investment in Great Britain, 1750–1850: A Preliminary Survey* (London: Methuen, 1971).

Craig, R. and R. Jarvis, *Liverpool Registry of Merchant Ships* (Manchester: Printed for the Chetham Society, 1967).

Crosby, A. W. *Ecological Imperialism: The Biological Expansion of Europe, 900–1900* (Cambridge: Cambridge University Press, 1986).

Cross, Harry E. "South American bullion production and export, 1550–1750," in J. F. Richards (ed.), *Precious Metals in the Later Medieval and Early Modern Worlds* (Durham: Carolina Academic Press, 1983).

Crouzet, Francois. *The First Industrialists: The Problem of Origins* (New York: Cambridge University Press, 1985).

Crouzet, François. "Wars, Blockade, and Economic Change in Europe, 1792–1815," *Journal of Economic History*, Vol. XXIV, No. 4 (December, 1964).

Britain ascendant: comparative studies in Franco-British economic history (Cambridge: Cambridge University Press, 1990; translated version of the 1985 French edition by Martin Thom).

Cunningham, William. *The Growth of English Industry and Commerce in Modern Times*, 3 Vols. (Cambridge: Cambridge University Press, 1882).

Dantzig, A. Van. *The Dutch and the Guinea Coast, 1674–1742: A Collection of Documents from the General State Archive at the Hague* (Accra: Ghana Academy of Arts and Sciences, 1978).

Darity, Jr., William A. "A General Equilibrium Model of the Eighteenth-Century Atlantic Slave Trade: A Least-Likely Test For the Caribbean School," *Research in Economic History*, Vol. 7 (1982).

Davies, K. G. "Essays in Bibliography and Criticism, XLIV: Empire and Capital," *Economic History Review*, 2nd ser. 13 (1960).

The Royal African Company (London: Longmans, 1857).

"The Origins of the Commission System in the West India Trade," *Transactions of the Royal Historical Society*, 5th Ser. Vol. 2, (1952).

Davis, Lance E. " 'And it will never be literature,' The New Economic History: A Critique," in Ralph L. Andreano (ed.), *The New Economic History: Recent Papers on Methodology* (New York: John Wiley and Sons, 1970).

Davis, Ralph. *The Industrial Revolution and British Overseas Trade* (Leicester: Leicester University Press, 1979).

The Rise of the English Shipping Industry in the Seventeenth and Eighteenth Centuries (London: Macmillan, 1962).

"English Foreign Trade, 1660–1700," *Economic History Review*, 2nd series, VI (1954).

"English Foreign Trade, 1700–1774," *Economic History Review*, 2nd series, XV (1962).

A Commercial Revolution: English Overseas Trade in the Seventeenth and Eighteenth Centuries (London: Historical Association, 1967).

English Overseas Trade, 1500–1700 (London: Macmillan, 1973).

The Rise of the Atlantic Economies (London: Weidenfeld and Nicolson, 1973).

"The Rise of Protection in England, 1689–1786," *Economic History Review*, XIX, No. 2 (August, 1966).

Day, Clive. *A History of Commerce* (New York: Longmans, 4th ed., 1938; first published, 1907).

Deane, Phyllis and W. A. Cole, *British Economic Growth, 1688–1959: Trends and Structure* (Cambridge: Cambridge University Press, 1962).

Deane, Phyllis. "The Output of the British Woolen Industry in the Eighteenth Century," *Journal of Economic History*, XVII (1957).

The Evolution of Economic Ideas (Cambridge: Cambridge University Press, 1978).

The First Industrial Revolution (Cambridge: Cambridge University Press, 1965; 2nd edition, 1979).

Deane, Phyllis and H. J. Habbakkuk, "The Take-Off in Britain," in W. W. Rostow (ed.), *The Economics of Take-Off into Sustained Growth: Proceedings of a Conference held by the International Economic Association* (London: Macmillan, 1963).

Decker, Mathew. *An Essay on the Causes of the Decline of the Foreign Trade* (London, 1744).

Delcourt, Andre. *La France et les Etablissements françaises au Senegal entre 1713 et 1763* (Dakar: I.F.A.N., Memoires, No. 17, 1952).

Devisse, J. and S. Labib, "Africa in inter-continental relations," in Niane (ed.), UNESCO *General History*.

Dickson, P. G. M. *The Financial Revolution in England: A Study in the Development of Public Credit, 1688–1756* (London: Macmillan, 1967).

Dixin, Xu and Wu Chengming (eds.), *Chinese Capitalism, 1522–1840* (London: Macmillan; New York: St. Martins, 2000).

Dowell, S. *A History of Taxation and Taxes in England, from the Earliest Times to the Present Day*, 2 Vols, Vol. 2 (London: Frank Cass, 1965; first published by Longmans Green in 1884).

Duignan, Peter and L. H. Gann, "Economic Achievements of the Colonizers: An Assessment," in Peter Duignan and L. H. Gann (eds.), *Colonialism in Africa, 1870–1960: Volume IV, The Economics of Colonialism* (Cambridge: Cambridge University Press, 1975)

Dyer, C. C. "The Occupation of the land: The West Midlands," in Miller (ed.), *Agrarian History*.

Ellison, Thomas. *The Cotton Trade of Great Britain* (London: Frank Cass, 1968; first published in 1886).

Eltis, David. "Free and Coerced Transatlantic Migrations: Some Comparisons," *American Historical Review*, Vol. 88, No. 2 (1983).

"The Volume and African Origins of the British Slave Trade before 1714," *Cahiers d' Études africaines*, 138–139, XXXV (2–3), 1995.

The Rise of African Slavery in the Americas (Cambridge: Cambridge University Press, 2000).

Emmer, P. C. "The Dutch and the making of the second Atlantic system," in Solow (ed.), *Slavery and the Rise of the Atlantic System.*

Engerman, Stanley L. "The Slave Trade and British Capital Formation in the Eighteenth Century: A Comment on the Williams Thesis," *The Business History Review*, 46 (Winter, 1972).

"Comments on Richardson and Boulle and the 'Williams Thesis'," *Revue francaise d'histoire d'outre-mer*, 62, Nos. 226–227 (1975).

Engerman, Stanley L. and Barry W. Higman, "The Demographic Structure of the Caribbean Slave Societies in the eighteenth and nineteenth centuries," in Franklin W. Knight (ed.), *General History of the Caribbean, Volume III: The Slave Societies of the Caribbean* (London and Basingstoke: UNESCO Publishing/Macmillan Education Ltd, 1997).

Esteban, Javier Cuenca. "The United States balance of payments with Spanish America and the Philippine Islands, 1790–1819: Estimates and Analysis of Principal Components," in Jacques A. Barbier and Allan J. Kuethe (eds.), *The North American Role in the Spanish Imperial Economy, 1760–1819* (Manchester: Manchester University Press, 1984).

Eversley, D. E. C. "The Home Market and Economic Growth in England, 1750–1780," in E. L. Jones and G. E. Mingay (eds.), *Land, Labour and Population in the Industrial Revolution: Essays Presented to J. D. Chambers* (London: Edward Arnold, 1967).

Fairlie, Susan. "Dyestuffs in the Eighteenth Century," *Economic History Review*, Vol. XVII, No. 3 (April, 1965).

Farnie, D. A. *The English Cotton Industry and the World Market, 1815–1896* (Oxford: Clarendon Press, 1979).

Faulkner, Harold Underwood. *American Economic History* (eighth edition, New York: Harper & Brothers, 1954; first published, 1924).

Feinstein, C. H. "Capital Accumulation and the Industrial Revolution," in Roderick Floud and Donald McCloskey (eds.), *The Economic History of Britain since 1700: Volume I, 1700–1860* (Cambridge: Cambridge University Press, 1981).

Felix, David. "The Dilemma of Import Substitution – Argentina," in Gustav F. Papanek (ed.), *Development Policy – Theory and Practice* (Cambridge, Mass.: Harvard University Press, 1968).

Findlay, Ronald. "Trade and Growth in the Industrial Revolution," in Charles P. Kindleberger and Guido di Tella (eds.), *Economics in the Long View: Essays in Honour of W. W. Rostow: Volume I, Models and Methodology* (New York: New York University Press, 1982).

The "Triangular Trade" and the Atlantic Economy of the Eighteenth Century: A Simple General-Equilibrium Model (Princeton, NJ: International Finance Section, Department of Economics, Princeton University, 1990).

"The Roots of Divergence: Western Economic History in Comparative Perspective," *American Economic Review*, Vol. 82, No. 2 (1992).

Fisher, H. E. S. *The Portugal Trade: A Study of Anglo-Portuguese Commerce 1700–1770* (London: Methuen, 1971).

Fisher, Roger. *Heart of Oak* (London, 1763).

Flinn, M. W. *Origins of the Industrial Revolution* (London: Longman, 1966).

Floud, Roderick and Donald McCloskey (eds.), *The Economic History of Britain since 1700: Volume I: 1700–1860* (New York: Cambridge University Press, 1981).

The Economic History of Britain Since 1700, Volume 1: 1700–1860 (2nd edition, Cambridge: Cambridge University Press, 1994).

Fogel, Robert W. and Stanley L. Engerman, *Time on the cross: The economics of American Negro Slavery* (Boston: Little, Brown and Company, 1974).

Frank, André Gunder. *Capitalism and Underdevelopment in Latin America* (New York: Monthly Review Press, 1967).

 ReOrient: Global Economy in the Asian Age (Berkeley: University of California Press, 1998).

Freeman, Michael. "The Industrial revolution and the regional geography of England: a comment," *Transactions of the Institute of British Geographers*, New Series, Vol. 9 (1984).

 "Introduction," in Derek H. Aldcroft and Michael J. Freeman (eds.), *Transport in the Industrial Revolution* (Manchester: Manchester University Press, 1983).

Gale, W. K. V. *The Black Country Iron Industry: A Technical History* (London, 1966).

Gemery, H. A., Jan Hogendorn, and Marion Johnson, "Evidence on English/African Terms of Trade in the Eighteenth Century," *Explorations in Economic History*, 27 (1990).

Gemery, H. A. and J. S. Hogendorn, "Technological Change, Slavery, and the Slave Trade," in Clive Dewey and A. G. Hopkins (eds.), *The Imperial Impact: Studies in the Economic History of Africa and India* (London: Athlone Press, 1978).

 "Comparative disadvantage: the case of sugar cultivation in West Africa," *Journal of Interdisciplinary History*, Vol. IX, No. 3 (Winter, 1979), pp. 429–449.

Gilboy, Elizabeth Waterman. "Demand as a factor in the Industrial Revolution," in Arthur H. Cole, A. L. Dunham, and N. S. B. Gras (eds.), *Facts and Factors in Economic History: Articles by former Students of Edwin Francis Gay* (Cambridge, Mass.: Harvard University Press, 1932).

Gillespie, James E. *The Influence of Overseas Expansion on England to 1700* (New York: Longmans, 1920).

Glass, D. V. and D. E. C. Eversley (eds.), *Population in History: Essays in Historical Demography* (London: Edward Arnold, 1965).

Goldenberg, Joseph A. "An Analysis of Shipbuilding Sites in Lloyd's Register of 1776," *The Mariner's Mirror*, Vol. 59, No. 4 (November 1973).

Goody, Jack. *The East in the West* (Cambridge: Cambridge University Press, 1998).

Gould, J. D. "The Price Revolution Reconsidered," *Economic History Review*, 2nd series, 17 (December, 1964).

Gragg, Larry. " 'To Procure Negroes': The English Slave Trade to Barbados, 1627–1660," *Slavery and Abolition*, Vol. 16, No. 1 (April, 1995).

Gray, J. M. *A History of the Gambia* (London and Edinburgh, 1940).

Gregory, Derek. *Regional Transformation and Industrial Revolution: A Geography of the Yorkshire Woollen Industry* (Minneapolis: University of Minnesota Press, 1982).

Gregory, Derek and John Langton, "Discussion," *Journal of Historical Geography*, 14, 1 (1988), pp. 50–58, and 14, 2 (1988), pp. 170–176.

Grossman, Gene M. and Elhanan Helpman, "Trade, Innovation, and Growth," *American Economic Review*, Vol. 80, No. 2 (May, 1990).

 Innovation and Growth in the Global Economy (Cambridge, Mass.: MIT Press, 1991).

Habakkuk, J. H. "English Landownership, 1680–1740," *Economic History Review*, X (1939–40).

Haggard, Stephan. *Pathways from the Periphery: The Politics of Growth in the Newly Industrializing Countries* (Ithaca, NY: Cornell University Press, 1990).

Hallam, H. E. "England Before the Norman Conquest," in H. E. Hallam (ed.), *The Agrarian History of England and Wales: Volume II, 1042–1350* (Cambridge: Cambridge University Press, 1988).

Hamilton, Earl J. *American Treasure and the Price Revolution in Spain, 1501–1650* (Cambridge, Mass.: Harvard Economic Studies, Vol. 43, 1934).

Hamilton, E. J. "American Treasure and the Rise of Capitalism," *Economica*, 9 (November, 1929).

Hamilton, Henry. *The English Brass and Copper Industries to 1800* (London: Frank Cass, 1967).

Harley, C. Knick. "British Industrialization Before 1841: Evidence of Slower Growth During the Industrial Revolution, " *Journal of Economic History*, Vol. XLII, 2 (1982).

Harris, Abram L. *The Negro as Capitalist: A Study of Banking and Business Among American Negroes* (Philadelphia: Published for the American Academy of Political and Social Science by the Rumford Press, 1936).

Harris, J. R. "Copper and shipping in the Eighteenth Century," *Economic History Review*, 2nd ser., XIX, No. 3 (December, 1966).

"The Copper Industry in Lancashire and North Wales, 1760–1815" (Ph.D. Thesis, University of Manchester, 1952).

The copper king; a biography of Thomas Williams of Llanidan (Toronto: University of Toronto Press, 1964).

Hartwell, R. M. "Economic Growth in England before the Industrial Revolution," in R. M. Hartwell, *The Industrial Revolution and Economic Growth* (London: Methuen, 1971), first published in *Journal of Economic History*, Vol. 29 (1969), pp. 13–31.

"The Causes of the Industrial Revolution: II An Essay on Process," in R. M. Hartwell (ed.), *The Industrial Revolution and Economic Growth* (London: Methuen, 1971).

"Interpretations of the Industrial Revolution in England," *Journal of Economic History*, Vol. XIX, No. 2 (June, 1959), reprinted in Hartwell, *Industrial Revolution and Economic Growth*.

"The Causes of the Industrial Revolution: An Essay in Methodology," in R. M. Hartwell (ed.), *The Causes of the Industrial Revolution in England* (London: Methuen, 1967), first published in *Economic History Review*, Vol. XVIII, No. 1, 1965.

Harvey, Sally. "Domesday England," in H. E. Hallam (ed.), *The Agrarian History of England and Wales: Volume II, 1042–1350* (Cambridge: Cambridge University Press, 1988).

Harvey, Barbara F. "Introduction: the 'crisis' of the early fourteenth century," in Bruce M. S. Campbell (ed.), *Before the Black Death: Studies in the 'crisis' of the early fourteenth century* (Manchester: Manchester University Press, 1991).

Hatcher, John. *Plague, Population and the English Economy, 1348–1530* (London: Macmillan, 1977).

Hatton, T. J., John S. Lyons, and S. E. Satchell, "Eighteenth-Century British Trade: Homespun or Empire Made?" *Explorations in Economic History*, Vol. 20 (1983).

Hawke, Gary. "Reinterpretations of the Industrial Revolution," in O'Brien and Quinault (eds.), *Industrial Revolution*.

Heckscher, Eli F. *The Continental System: An Economic Interpretation* (Oxford: Clarendon, 1922).

Hersh, Jacques. *The USA and the Rise of East Asia since 1945: Dilemmas of the Postwar International Political Economy* (London: Macmillan, 1993).

Hicks, George. "Explaining The Success of the Four Little Dragons: A Survey," in Seiji Naya and Akira Takayama (eds.), *Economic Development in East and Southeast Asia: Essays in Honor of Professor Shinichi Ichimura* (Pasir Panjan, Singapore, and Honolulu, Hawaii: Institute of Southeast Asian Studies and East-West Center, 1990).

Higman, Barry W. *Slave Populations of the British Caribbean, 1807–1834* (Baltimore: Johns Hopkins University Press, 1984).

Hilton, R. H. *The Decline of Serfdom in Medieval England* (London: Macmillan, 1969).

Hilton, Anne. *The Kingdom of Kongo* (Oxford: Clarendon, 1985).

Hirschman, Albert O. *The Strategy of Economic Development* (New Haven, CT: Yale University Press, 1958).

Hoberman, Louisa S. *Mexico's Merchant Elite, 1590–1660: Silver, State, and Society* (Durham, NC and London: Duke University Press, 1991).

Hobsbawm, Eric J. "The General Crisis of the European Economy in the 17th Century," *Past and Present*, 5 (1954), pp. 33–53; 6 (1954), pp. 44–65.

Industry and Empire (London: Pelican Books, 1969).

Hobson, John A. *The Evolution of Modern Capitalism: A Study of Machine Production* (London: Allen & Unwin, 1894, revised edition, 1926).

Hogendorn, Jan S. and Henry A. Gemery, "Anglo-African Trade in the Eighteenth Century: The significance of the Marion Johnson Data Set," in Johnson, *Anglo-African Trade.*

Holloway, Thomas H. "The coffee colono of Sao Paulo, Brazil: migration and mobility, 1880–1930," in Kenneth Duncan and Ian Rutledge (eds.), *Land and Labour in Latin America: Essays on the development of agrarian capitalism in the nineteenth and twentieth centuries* (Cambridge: Cambridge University Press, 1977).

Hopkins, A. G. *An Economic History of West Africa* (London: Longman, 1973).

Hoppit, Julian. "Counting the Industrial Revolution," *Economic History Review*, 2nd series, XLIII, 2 (1990).

Howell, Cicely. "Stability and Change 1300–1700: The Socio-Economic Context of the Self-Perpetuating Family Farm in England," *Journal of Peasant Studies*, Vol. 2, No. 4 (1975).

Hudson, Pat (ed.), *Regions and Industries: A Perspective on the Industrial Revolution in Britain* (Cambridge: Cambridge University Press, 1989).

  The Genesis of Industrial Capital: A Study of the West Riding Wool Textile Industry c. 1750–1850 (Cambridge: Cambridge University Press, 1986).

Hueckel, G. "Agriculture during industrialization," in Floud and McCloskey (eds.), *Economic History of Britain.*

Hughes, J. R. T. "Fact and Theory in Economic History," in Andreano (ed.), *New Economic History.*

Hunt, E. H. "Industrialization and Regional Inequality: Wages in Britain, 1760–1914," *Journal of Economic History*, XLVI, 4 (December, 1986).

Hunter, Henry C. *How England Got its Merchant Marine, 1066–1776* (New York: National Council of American Shipbuilders, 1935).

Hyde, Charles K. *Technological Change and the British Irone Industry 1700–1870* (Princeton, NJ.: Princeton University Press, 1977).

Hyde, F. E., B. B. Parkinson, and S. Marriner, "The Nature and Profitability of the Liverpool Slave Trade," *Economic History Review*, 2d ser. 5, No. 3 (1953), 368–377.

Hyde, Francis E. "The Growth of Liverpool's Trade, 1700–1950," in *Scientific Survey of Merseyside* (Liverpool: Published for the British Association for the Advancement of Science by the University of Liverpool Press, 1953).

Imlah, Albert H. *Economic Elements in the Pax Britannica: Studies in British Foreign Trade in the Nineteenth Century* (Cambridge, Mass.: Harvard University Press, 1958).

Inikori, Joseph E. and Stanley L. Engerman (eds.), *The Atlantic Slave Trade: Effects on Economies, Societies and Peoples in Africa, the Americas, and Europe* (Durham, NC and London: Duke University Press, 1992).

  "Introduction: Gainers and Losers in the Atlantic Slave Trade," in Inikori and Engerman (eds.), *The Atlantic Slave Trade.*

Inikori, J. E. "Market Structure and the Profits of the British African Trade in the Late Eighteenth Century," *Journal of Economic History*, Vol. XLI, No. 4 (Dec. 1981).

  Slavery and the Rise of Capitalism: The 1993 Elsa Goveia Memorial Lecture (Mona, Jamaica: The University of the West Indies, 1993).

  "The Credit Needs of the African Trade and the Development of the Credit Economy in England," *Explorations in Economic History*, 27 (1990).

  "The Import of Firearms into West Africa, 1750–1807: A Quantitative Analysis," *Journal of African History*, XVIII, 3 (1977).

  "The slave trade and the Atlantic economies, 1451–1870," in *The African slave trade from the fifteenth to the nineteenth century* (Paris: UNESCO, 1979).

  "Slavery and the Development of Industrial Capitalism in England," *Journal of Interdisciplinary History*, Vol. XVII, No. 4 (Spring 1987).

  "Slavery and the Revolution in Cotton Textile Production in England," *Social Science History*, Vol. XIII, No. 4 (1989).

"Slavery and Atlantic Commerce, 1650–1800," *American Economic Review*, Vol. 82, No. 2 (1992).

"Africa in World History: The Export Slave Trade and the Emergence of the Atlantic Economic Order," in B. A. Ogot (ed.), *The UNESCO General History of Africa. V. Africa from the Sixteenth to the Eighteenth Century* (Paris and Berkeley, California: Heinemann, UNESCO, and University of California Press, 1992).

"Measuring the Atlantic Slave Trade: An Assessment of Curtin and Anstey," *Journal of African History*, XVII, 2 (1976).

"The Volume of the British Slave Trade, 1655–1807," *Cahiers d' Études africaines*, 128, XXXII (4), (1992).

The Chaining of a Continent: Export Demand for Captives and the History of Africa South of the Sahara, 1450–1870 (UNESCO Project Published by the Institute of Social and Economic Research, University of the West Indies, Mona, Jamaica, 1992).

"Measuring the Atlantic Slave Trade: A Rejoinder," *Journal of African History*, XVII, 4 (1976).

"Measuring the unmeasured hazards of the Atlantic slave trade: documents relating to the British trade," *Revue Française D'Histoire D'Outre-Mer*, 83, No. 312 (1996).

"Export Versus Domestic Demand: The Determinants of Sex Ratios in the Transatlantic Slave Trade," *Research in Economic History*, Vol. 14 (1992).

"West Africa's Seaborne Trade, 1750–1850: Volume, Structure and Implications," in G. Liesegang, H. Pasch, and A. Jones (eds.), *Figuring African Trade* (Berlin: Dietrich Reimer Verlag, 1986).

"Slavery in Africa and the Transatlantic Slave Trade," in Alusine Jalloh and Stephen E. Maizlish (eds.), *The African Diaspora* (College Station: Texas A & M University Press, 1996), pp. 39–72.

"International Trade and the Eighteenth-Century Industrialisation Process in England: An Essay in Criticism," Unpublished Paper Presented at the Institute of Historical Research Seminar, University of London, 7 February, 1975.

Inkster, Ian. *Science and Technology in History: An Approach to Industrial Development* (New Brunswick, NJ: Rutgers University Press, 1991).

Jack, Sybil M. *Trade and Industry in Tudor and Stuart England* (London: Allen and Unwin, 1977).

Jackson, R. V. "Growth and Deceleration in English Agriculture, 1660–1790," *Economic History Review*, 2nd series, XXXVIII, No. 3 (August, 1985).

"Rates of Industrial Growth during the Industrial Revolution," *Economic History Review*, XLV, 1 (1992).

James, C. L. R. *The Black Jacobins: Toussaint L'Ouverture and the San Domingo Revolution* (New York: Vintage Books, Random House, 1963; first published, New York: Dial Press, 1938).

Johansen, Hans C. "How to pay for Baltic products?" in Wolfram Fischer, R. Marvin McInnis, and Jurgen Schneider (eds.), *The Emergence of a World Economy, 1500–1914: Papers of the IX International Congress of Economic History* (Stuttgart: Steiner Verlag Wiesbaden, 1986).

John, A. H. "English Agricultural Improvement and Grain Exports, 1660–1765," in D. C. Coleman and A. H. John (eds.), *Trade, Government and Economy in Pre-Industrial England: Essays Presented to F. J. Fisher* (London, 1976).

"Aspects of English Economic Growth in the First Half of the Eighteenth Century," *Economica*, No. 28 (1961), reprinted in Minchinton (ed.), *The Growth of English Overseas Trade*.

"War and the English Economy 1700–1763," *Economic History Review*, 2nd ser. VII, No. 3 (April, 1955).

"The London Assurance Company and the Marine Insurance Market of the Eighteenth Century," *Economica*, new series, Vol. 25 (May, 1958).

"Insurance Investment and the London Money Market of the 18th Century," *Economica*, new series, Vol. 20 (May 1953).

Johnson, Marion. *Anglo-African Trade in the Eighteenth Century: English Statistics on African Trade 1699–1808*, Edited by J. Thomas Lindblad and Robert Ross (Leiden: Intercontinenta No. 15, Centre for the History of European Expansion, 1990).

Jones, S. R. H. "Transaction Costs, Institutional Change, and the Emergence of a Market Economy in later Anglo-Saxon England," *Economic History Review*, XLVI, 4 (1993).

Jones, E. L. "Agriculture and Economic Growth in England 1660–1750: Agricultural Change," *Journal of Economic History*, 25 (1965).

"Agricultural Origins of Industry," *Past and Present*, 40 (1968).

Kindleberger, Charles P. *A Financial History of Western Europe* (2nd edition, New York: Oxford University Press, 1993).

King, Edmund. "The Occupation of the Land: The East Midlands," in Miller (ed.), *Agrarian History*.

King, W. T. C. *History of the London Discount Market* (London: Routledge, 1936).

Klein, Herbert S. *African Slavery in Latin America and the Caribbean* (Oxford: Oxford University Press, 1986).

The Middle Passage: Comparative Studies in the Atlantic Slave Trade (Princeton, NJ: Princeton University Press, 1978).

Krantz, Frederick and Paul M. Hohenberg (eds.), *Failed Transitions to Modern Industrial Society: Renaissance Italy and Seventeenth Century Holland* (Montreal: Interuniversity Centre for European Studies, 1975).

Krishna, Bal. *Commercial Relations between India and England, 1601–1757* (London: G. Routledge, 1924).

Krueger, Anne O. *The Benefits and Costs of Import Substitution in India: A Microeconomic Study* (Minneapolis: University of Minnesota Press, 1975).

Kup, P. *A History of Sierra Leone, 1400–1787* (Cambridge: Cambridge University Press, 1961).

Kuznets, Simon. *Modern Economic Growth: Rate, Structure and Spread* (New Haven, CT: Yale University Press, 1966).

"Underdeveloped Countries and the Pre-Industrial Phase in the Advanced Countries: An Attempt at Comparison," in A. N. Agarwala and S. P. Singh (eds.), *The Economics of Underdevelopment* (Oxford: Oxford University Press, 1958; Published as a Galaxy Book, 1963).

Landes, David S. *The Unbound Prometheus: Technological Change and Industrial Development in Western Europe from 1750 to the Present* (Cambridge: Cambridge University Press, 1969).

"The Fable of the Dead Horse; or, The Industrial Revolution Revisited," in Mokyr (ed.), *The British Industrial Revolution*.

The Wealth and Poverty of Nations: Why Some Are So Rich and Some Are So Poor (New York: W. W. Norton, 1998).

Langton, John., "The Industrial Revolution and the Regional Geography of England," *Transactions of the Institute of British Geographers*, New Series, Vol. 9 (1984).

Langton, John. and R. J. Morris, "Introduction," in John Langton and R. J. Morris (eds.), *Atlas of Industrializing Britain, 1784–1914* (London and New York: Methuen, 1986).

Law, Robin. "The Slave Trade in Seventeenth-Century Allada: A Revision," *African Economic History*, 22 (1994).

The Slave Coast of West Africa, 1550–1750: The Impact of the Atlantic Slave Trade on an African Society (Oxford: Clarendon Press, 1991).

Lee, C. H. *The British Economy since 1700: A macroeconomic perspective* (Cambridge: Cambridge University Press, 1986).

"Regional Growth and Structural Change in Victorian Britain," *Economic History Review*, 2nd ser., XXXIV, 3 (1981).

Lemire, Beverly. *Fashions Favourite: The Cotton Trade and the Consumer in Britain, 1660–1800* (Oxford and New York: Oxford University Press, 1991).

Leonard, E. M. "Inclosure of Common Fields in the Seventeenth Century," *Transactions of the Royal Historical Society*, new series, XIX (1905), reprinted in E. M. Carus-Wilson (ed.), *Essays in Economic History*, Vol. II (London: E. Arnold, 1962).

Lewis, W. Arthur. *The Theory of Economic Growth* (London: George Allen & Unwin, 1955).
"The Slowing Down of the Engine of Growth," *American Economic Review*, LXX (September, 1980), pp. 555–564, reprinted in Lal (ed.), *Development Economics*, Vol. III, pp. 73–74.
"Economic Development with Unlimited Supplies of Labour," *Manchester School of Economic and Social Studies*, XXII (May, 1954), pp. 139–191, reprinted in Lal (ed.), *Development Economics*, Vol. I, pp. 117–169.
The Evolution of the International Economic Order (Princeton, NJ: Princeton University Press, 1978).

Lindert, Peter H. "English Occupations, 1670–1811," *Journal of Economic History*, Vol. XL, No. 4 (1980).

Lindert, Peter H. and Jeffrey G. Williamson, "Revising England's Social Tables, 1688–1812," *Explorations in Economic History*, 19 (1982).

Lindsay, W. S. *History of Marchant Shipping and Ancient Commerce*, 4 Vols, Vol. 3 (London: Samson Low, Marston, Low and Searle, 1876).

Lloyd, T. H. *The English Wool Trade in the Middle Ages* (Cambridge: Cambridge University Press, 1977).

Lockhart, James. and Stuart B. Schwartz, *Early Latin America: A History of Colonial Spanish America and Brazil* (Cambridge: Cambridge University Press, 1983).

Mabogunje, Akin. "The Land and Peoples of West Africa," in J. F. Ade Ajayi and Michael Crowder (eds.), *History of West Africa*, Vol. I (London: Longman, 1971).

Macleod, Murdo J. "Spain and America: The Atlantic Trade, 1492–1720," in Bethell (ed.), *The Cambridge History of Latin America*, Vol. I.

Macpherson, David. *Annals of Commerce, Manufactures, Fisheries and Navigation*, 4 volumes, volume 4 (London: Nichols, 1805).

Makepeace, Margaret. "English Traders on the Guinea Coast, 1657–1668: An Analysis of the East India Company Archive," *History in Africa*, 16 (1989).

Manchester, Alan K. *British Preeminence in Brazil, Its Rise and Decline: A Study in European Expansion* (New York: Octagon Books, 1964).

Mann, Julian de Lucy. *The Cloth Industry in the West of England from 1640 to 1880* (Oxford: Clarendon Press, 1971).

Manning, Patrick. "The Impact of Slave Trade Exports on the Population of the Western Coast of Africa, 1700–1850," in Serge Daget (ed.), *De La Traite à L'Esclavage: Actes du Colloque International sur la traite des Noirs*, Nantes 1985, Vol. II (Paris: Societé Française D' Histoire D'Outre-Mer, 1988).
Slavery and African Life: Occidental, Oriental, and African Slave Trades (Cambridge: Cambridge University Press, 1990).

Mantoux, Paul. *The Industrial Revolution in the Eighteenth Century: An Outline of the Beginnings of the Modern Factory System in England* (New York: Harper Torchbooks, 1928; original French edition, 1906).

Marx, Karl. *Capital: A Critique of Political Economy* (Vol. I, translated from the third German edition by Samuel Moore and Edward Aveling, and edited by Frederick Engels. Revised and amplified according to 4th German edition by Ernest Unterman, Chicago, 1926).

Massarella, Derek. "'A World Elsewhere': Aspects of the Overseas Expansionist Mood of the 1650s," in Colin Jones, Malyn Newitt, and Stephen Roberts (eds.), *Politics and People in Revolutionary England: Essays in Honour of Ivan Roots* (Oxford: Basil Blackwell, 1986).

Mathias, Peter. *The First Industrial Nation: An Economic History of Britain 1700–1914* (London: Methuen, 1969).

Mauro, Frédéric. "Structure de l'économic interne et marche international dans une epoque de transition: le cas du Bresil, 1750–1850," in Wolfram Fischer, R. Marvin McInnis, and Jurgen Schneider (eds.), *The Emergence of a World Economy 1500–1914: Papers of the IX. International Congress of Economic History*, part I (Stuttgart: Steiner-Verlag-Wiesbaden, 1986).

"Portugal and Brazil: political and economic structures of empire, 1580–1750," in Bethell (ed.), *Cambridge History of Latin America*, Volume I.

Mayhew, Nicholas. "Modelling medieval monetisation," in Richard H. Britnell and Bruce M. S. Campbell (eds.), *A Commercialising Economy: England 1086 to c. 1300* (Manchester: Manchester University Press, 1995).

McCloskey, D. N. "The Economics of Enclosure: A Market Analysis," in W. N. Parker and E. L. Jones (eds.), *European Peasants and Their Markets* (Princeton, NJ: Princeton University Press, 1975).

McCusker, John J. *Money and Exchange in Europe and America, 1600–1775* (Chapel Hill: University of North Carolina Press, 1978).

McCusker, John J. and Russell R. Menard, *The Economy of British America, 1607–1789* (Chapel Hill: University of North Carolina Press, 1985).

McDaniel, Antonio and Carlos Grushka, "Did Africans Live Longer in the Antebellum United States? The Sensitivity of Mortality Estimates of Enslaved Africans," *Historical Methods*, Vol. 28, No. 2 (Spring, 1995).

McDonald, John and G. D. Snooks, *Domesday Economy: A New Approach to Anglo-Norman History* (Oxford: Clarendon Press, 1986).

McLachlan, Jean O. *Trade and Peace with Old Spain, 1667–1750: A Study of the Influence of Commerce on Anglo-Spanish Diplomacy in the First Half of the Eighteenth Century* (Cambridge: Cambridge University Press, 1940).

McPhee, Allan. *The Economic Revolution in British West Africa* (2nd ed., London: Frank Cass, 1971; first published in 1926).

Mennell, Stephen. "Bringing the very Long Term Back In," in Johan Goudsblom, Eric Jones, and Stephen Mennell (eds.), *The Course of Human History: Economic Growth, Social Process, and Civilization* (New York: M. E. Sharpe, 1996), pp. 3–13.

Merrick, Thomas W. and Douglass H. Graham, *Population and Economic Development in Brazil, 1800 to the Present* (Baltimore: Johns Hopkins University Press, 1979).

Miller, Edward. "Introduction: Land and People," in Edward Miller (ed.), *The Agrarian History of England and Wales: Volume III, 1348–1500* (Cambridge: Cambridge University Press, 1991).

"The Occupation of the Land: Yorkshire and Lancashire," in Miller (ed.), *Agrarian History*.

Minchinton, W. E. (ed.), *The Growth of English Overseas Trade in the Seventeenth and Eighteenth Centuries* (London: Methuen, 1969).

"Introduction," in Minchinton (ed.), *The Growth of English Overseas Trade*.

"The British Slave Fleet, 1680–1775: The Evidence of the Naval Office Shipping Lists," in Serge Daget (ed.), *De La Traite à L'Esclavage: Actes du Colloque International sur la traite des Noires, Nantes 1985* (Nantes and Paris, 1988), Vol. 1.

Mingay, G. E. *Enclosure and the Small Farmer in the Age of the Industrial Revolution* (London: Macmillan, 1968).

"The Land Tax Assessments and the Small Landowner," *Economic History Review*, 2nd series, XVII (1964–65).

Mitchell, Brian R. *International Historical Statistics: The Americas, 1750–1988* (2nd ed., New York: Stockton, 1993).

Abstract of British Historical Statistics (Cambridge: Cambridge University Press, 1962).

Mokyr, Joel (ed.), *The Economics of the Industrial Revolution* (Totowa, NJ: Rowman and Littlefield, 1985).

The British Industrial Revolution: An Economic Perspective (Boulder, Colorado: Westview Press, 1993).

"Introduction: The New Economic History and the Industrial Revolution," in Joel Mokyr (ed.), *The British Industrial Revolution: An Economic Perspective* (Boulder, CO: Westview Press, 1993).

"Demand vs. Supply in the Industrial Revolution," in Joel Mokyr (ed.), *The Economics of the Industrial Revolution* (Savage, MD: Roman and Littlefield, 1985).

"Evolutionary Biology, Technological Change and Economic History," *Bulletin of Economic Research*, 43:2 (1991).

Morawetz, David. "Employment Implications of Industrialization in Developing Countries: A Survey," *Economic Journal*, 84 (1974).

Morgan, E. V. and W. A. Thomas, *The Stock Exchange: Its History and Functions* (London, 1962).

Morris, Arthur. *Latin America: Economic Development and Regional Differentiation* (London: Hutchinson, 1981).

Morrison, Donald G. *Understanding Black Africa: Data and Analysis of Social Change and Nation Building* (New York: Paragon, Irvington, 1989).

Moulder, Frances V. *Japan, China, and the modern world economy: Toward a reinterpretation of East Asian development, ca. 1600 to ca. 1918* (Cambridge: Cambridge University Press, 1977).

Musson, A. E. *The Growth of British Industry* (New York: Holmes and Meier, 1978).

Musson, A. E. and E. Robinson, *Science and Technology in the Industrial Revolution* (Manchester: Manchester University Press, 1969).

Musson, A. E. "Introduction," in A. E. Musson (ed.), *Science, Technology and Economic Growth in the Eighteenth Century* (London: Methuen, 1972).

Myint, H. "The 'Classical Theory' of International Trade and the underdeveloped Countries," *The Economic Journal*, Vol. LXVIII (June, 1958), reprinted in Deepak Lal (ed.), *Development Economics*, Vol. III (Aldershot: Edward Elgar, 1992).

Nash, R. C. "The balance of payments and foreign capital flows in eighteenth-century England: a comment," *Economic History Review*, L, 1 (1997), pp. 110–128.

Neal, Larry. *The Rise of Financial Capitalism* (Cambridge: Cambridge University Press, 1990).

"How the South Sea Bubble was blown up and Burst: A New Look at Old Evidence," Paper presented at the Salomon Center Conference on Crashes and Panics in Historical Perspective, New York, October 19, 1988.

Needham, Joseph. *Science and Civilization in China* (London and New York: Cambridge University Press, 1954).

Nef, John U. "The Progress of Technology and the Growth of Large Scale Industry, 1540–1640," *Economic History Review*, original series, V (1934–1935).

"A Comparison of Industrial Growth in France and England from 1540 to 1640," *Journal of Political Economy*, XLIV (1936).

Niane, D. T. "Mali and the Second Mandingo expansion," in D. T. Niane (ed.), *UNESCO General History of Africa. IV, Africa from the twelfth to the sixteenth century* (Berkeley: California, Heinemann, UNESCO, 1984).

"Conclusion," in D. T. Niane (ed.), *UNESCO General History of Africa. IV, Africa from the twelfth to the sixteenth century* (Berkeley: California, Heinemann, UNESCO, 1984).

"Relationships and exchanges among the different regions," in Niane (ed.), *UNESCO General History*.

Norris, Robert. *A Short Account of the African Slave Trade* (London, 1789).

North, Douglass C. and Robert P. Thomas, "An Economic Theory of the Growth of the Western World," *Economic History Review*, 2nd series, Vol. 22, No. 1 (1970).

The Rise of the Western World: A New Economic History (New York and London: Cambridge University Press, 1973).

North, Douglass C. *Structure and Change in Economic History* (New York and London: W. W. Norton, 1981).

   Institutions, Institutional Change and Economic Performance (New York: Cambridge University Press, 1990).

   The Economic Growth of the United States, 1790–1860 (New York: W. W. Norton, 1966).

   "The United States Balance of Payments, 1790–1860," in *Trends in the American Economy in the Nineteenth Century: Studies in Income and Wealth, Volume Twenty-Four, By the Conference on Research in Income and Wealth* (Princeton, NJ: Princeton University Press, 1960).

O'Brien, Patrick and Caglar Keyder, *Economic Growth in Britain and France 1780–1914: Two Paths to the Twentieth Century* (London: 1978).

O'Brien, Patrick K. "Political Preconditions for the Industrial Revolution," in Patrick K. O'Brien and Roland Quinault (eds.), *The Industrial Revolution and British Society* (Cambridge: Cambridge University Press, 1993).

   "Central Government and the Economy, 1688–1815," in Floud and McCloskey (eds.), *Economic History of Britain*, 2nd ed., Vol. 1.

O'Brien, Patrick, Trevor Griffiths, and Philip Hunt, "Political components of the industrial revolution: Parliament and the English cotton textile industry, 1660–1774," *Economic History Review*, XLIV, 3 (1991).

O'Brien, Patrick K. "Introduction: Modern conceptions of the Industrial Revolution," in Patrick K. O'Brien and Roland Quinault (eds.), *The Industrial Revolution and British Society* (Cambridge: Cambridge University Press, 1993).

O'Brien, Patrick K. and Stanley L. Engerman, "Exports and the growth of the British economy from the Glorious Revolution to the Peace of Amiens," in Solow (ed.), *Slavery and the Rise of the Atlantic System*.

O'Brien, Patrick K. "Agriculture and the Home Market for English Industry, 1660–1820," *English Historical Review*, Vol. 91 (1985).

   "European Economic Development: The Contribution of the Periphery," *Economic History Review*, 2nd series, Vol. XXXV, No. 1 (1982).

Oppenheim, M. (ed.), *The Naval Tracts of Sir William Monson*, 5 vols. (Navy Records Society, 1902–1914).

Outhwaite, R. B. "Progress and Backwardness in English Agriculture, 1500–1650," *Economic History Review*, 2nd ser., XXXIX, 1 (1986).

Packenham, Robert A. *The Dependency Movement: Scholarship and Politics in Development Studies* (Cambridge, Mass.: Harvard University Press, 1992).

Palmer, Colin A. *Slaves of the White God: Blacks in Mexico, 1570–1650* (Cambridge, Mass.: Harvard University Press, 1976).

   Human Cargoes: The British Slave Trade to Spanish America, 1700–1739 (Urbana: University of Illinois Press, 1981).

Parkinson, C. N. "East India Trade," in C. N. Parkinson (ed.), *The Trade Winds*.

   (ed.), *The Trade Winds: A Study of British Overseas Trade during the French Wars, 1793–1815* (London: George Allen and Unwin, 1948).

Peckham, Howard H. *Guide to Manuscript Collections in the William L. Clements Library, University of Michigan* (Ann Arbor: University of Michigan Press, 1942).

Pelling, H. *A History of British Trade Unionism* (London, 1963).

Phillips, Carla Rahn. "The growth and composition of trade in the Iberian empires, 1450–1750," in Tracy (ed.), *The Rise of Merchant Empires*.

Pitkin, Timothy. *A Statistical View of the commerce of the United States of America: Including also an Account of Banks, Manufactures and Internal Trade and Improvements: Together with that of the Revenues and Expenditures of the General Government: Accompanied with numerous Tables* (New Haven, CT: Durrie & Peck, 1835).

Platt, Desmond C. M. *Latin America and British Trade, 1806–1914* (London: Adam & Charles Black, 1972).

Pollard, Sidney and David W. Crossley, *The Wealth of Britain, 1085–1966* (London: B. T. Batsford, 1968).

Pollard, Sidney. *Peaceful Conquest: The Industrialization of Europe 1760–1970* (Oxford: Oxford University Press, 1981).

Pomeranz, Kenneth. *The Great Divergence: China, Europe, and the Making of the Modern World Economy* (Princeton, NJ: Princeton University Press, 2000).

Poos, L. R. *A Rural Society after the Black Death: Essex, 1350–1525* (Cambridge: Cambridge University Press, 1991).

Porter, R. "The Crispe Family and the African Trade in the Seventeenth Century," *Journal of African History*, IX, No. 1 (1968).

"European Activity on the Gold Coast, 1620–1667" (Ph.D. thesis, University of South Africa, 1974).

Porter, G. R. *The Progress of the Nation in its various Social and Economical Relations from the Beginning of the Nineteenth century to the Present Time*, 3 volumes (London: Charles Knight, 1836–1843).

Postan, M. M. *The Famulus: The Estate Labourer in the XIIth and XIIIth Centuries* (*Economic History Review*, Supplements 2, 1954).

"Recent Trends in the Accumulation of Capital," *Economic History Review*, Vol. VI, No. 1 (October, 1935), reprinted in François Crouzet (ed.), *Capital Formation in the Industrial Revolution* (London: Methuen, 1972).

Postma, Johannes M. *The Dutch in the Atlantic Slave Trade, 1600–1815* (Cambridge: Cambridge University Press, 1990).

Power, Eileen. *The Wool Trade in English Medieval History: Being the Ford Lectures* (Oxford: Oxford University Press, 1941).

Pressnell, L. S. *Country Banking in the Industrial Revolution* (Oxford: Clarendon Press, 1956).

Price, Jacob M. *Capital and Credit in British Overseas Trade: The View from the Chesapeake, 1700–1776* (Cambridge, MA: 1980).

"Credit in the Slave Trade and Plantation Economies," in Solow (ed.), *Slavery and the Rise of the Atlantic System.*

Randall, Adrian J. "Work, culture and resistance to machinery in the West of England woollen industry," in Hudson (ed.), *Regions and Industries.*

Richardson, David. "Profits in the Liverpool Slave Trade: The Accounts of William Davenport, 1757–1784," in Roger Anstey and P. E. H. Hair (eds.), *Liverpool, the African Slave Trade, and Abolition: Essays to Illustrate Current Knowledge and Research* (Historic Society of Lancashire and Cheshire Occasional Series, Vol. 2, 1976).

"Profitability in the Bristol-Liverpool Slave Trade," *Revue francaise d'histoire d'outre-mer*, 62, Nos. 226–227 (1975).

"The Slave Trade, Sugar, and British Economic Growth, 1748–1776," in Barbara L. Solow and Stanley L. Engerman (eds.), *British Capitalism and Caribbean Slavery: The Legacy of Eric Williams* (Cambridge and New York: Cambridge University Press, 1987).

"Cape Verde, Madeira and Britain's Trade to Africa, 1698–1740," *Journal of Imperial and Commonwealth History*, Vol. 22, No. 1 (1994).

"Slave Exports from West and West-Central Africa: New Estimates of Volume and Distribution," *Journal of African History*, 30 (1989).

Rodney, Walter. *How Europe Underdeveloped Africa* (London: Bogle-L'Ouverture, 1972; revised edition, Washington: Howard University Press, 1981).

A History of the Upper Guinea Coast, 1545–1800 (Oxford: Clarendon Press, 1970).

Romer, Paul M. "Increasing Returns and Long-Run Growth," *Journal of Political Economy*, Vol. 94, No. 5 (1986).

"The Origins of Endogenous Growth," *Journal of Economic Perspectives*, Volume 8, Number 1 (1994).

Rosenberg, Nathan and L. E. Birdzell, Jr., *How the West Grew Rich: The Economic Transformation of the Industrial World* (New York: Basic Books, 1986).

Rostow, Walt W. *How it all began: Origins of the Modern Economy* (London: Methuen, 1975).

Theorists of Economic Growth from David Hume to the Present, With a Perspective on the Next Century (New York: Oxford University Press, 1990).

The Process of Economic Growth (2nd ed., Oxford: at the Clarendon Press, 1961; 1st ed., 1953; first published by W. W. Norton, New York, 1952).

Rothstein, Morton. "The Antebellum South as a Dual Economy: A Tentative Hypothesis," in Eugene D. Genovese (ed.), *The Slave Economies: Volume II, Slavery in the International Economy* (New York: John Wiley, 1973).

Rowlands, Marie B. "Continuity and Change in an industrialising society: the case of the West Midlands industries," in Hudson (ed.), *Regions and Industries.*

Russell-Wood, A. J. R. "Colonial Brazil: The Gold Cycle, c. 1690–1750," in Leslie Bethell (ed.), *The Cambridge History of Latin America, Volume II: Colonial Latin America* (Cambridge: Cambridge University Press, 1984).

Ryder, A. F. C. *Benin and the Europeans 1485–1897* (London: Longman, 1969).

Sayers, R. S. *Modern Banking* (Oxford, 7th ed., 1967).

Schumpeter, Elizabeth B. *English Overseas Trade Statistics, 1697–1808* (Oxford: At the Clarendon Press, 1960).

Shepherd, William R. "The Expansion of Europe," *Political Science Quarterly*, Vol. 34, 1919.

Shepherd, James F. and Gary M. Walton, *Shipping, Maritime Trade, and the Economic Development of Colonial North America* (Cambridge: Cambridge University Press, 1972).

Sheridan, R. B. "The Wealth of Jamaica in the Eighteenth Century," *Economic History Review*, 2d ser. 18 (Aug. 1965).

"The Wealth of Jamaica in the Eighteenth Century: A Rejoinder," *Economic History Review*, 2d ser. 21 (April 1968).

"Eric Williams and Capitalism and Slavery: A Biographical and Historiographical Essay," in Barbara L. Solow and Stanley L. Engerman (eds.), *British Capitalism and Caribbean Slavery: The Legacy of Eric Williams* (Cambridge: Cambridge University Press, 1987).

Sugar and Slavery: An Economic History of the British West Indies, 1623–1775 (Baltimore: Johns Hopkins University Press, 1973).

"The Commercial and Financial Organisation of the British Slave Trade, 1750–1807," *Economic History Review*, 2nd ser., XI, 2 (December, 1958).

Short, Brian. "The de-industrialisation process: a case study of the Weald, 1600–1850," in Pat Hudson (ed.), *Regions and Industries: A Perspective on the Industrial Revolution in Britain* (Cambridge: Cambridge University Press, 1989).

Sideri, S. *Trade and Power: Informal Colonialism in Anglo-Portuguese Relations* (Rotterdam: Rotterdam University Press, 1970).

Simonsen, Roberto C. *Historia Economica do Brasil, 1500–1820* (6th edition, Sao Paulo: Companhia Editora Nacional, 1969).

Smith, Adam. *The Wealth of Nations*, J. R. McCulloch edition (London, 1838).

Smith, Barbara M. D. "The Galtons of Birmingham: Quaker Gun Merchants and Bankers, 1702–1831," *Business History*, Vol. 9, No. 2 (1967).

Snooks, Graeme Donald. *Economics Without Time: A Science Blind to the Forces of Historical Change* (London: Macmillan, 1993).

"Great Waves of Economic Change: The Industrial Revolution in Historical Perspective, 1000 to 2000," in Graeme Donald Snooks (ed.), *Was the Industrial Revolution Necessary?* (London and New York: Routledge, 1994).

Solow, Barbara L. "Caribbean Slavery and British Growth: The Eric Williams Hypothesis," *Journal of Development Economics*, 17 (1985).

Solow, Barbara L. (ed.), *Slavery and the Rise of the Atlantic System* (Cambridge: Cambridge University Press, 1991).

Solow, Barbara L. and Stanley L. Engerman (eds.), *British Capitalism and Caribbean Slavery: The Legacy of Eric Williams* (Cambridge: Cambridge University Press, 1987).

Soon, Cho. *The Dynamics of Korean Economic Development* (Washington, DC: Institute of International Economics, 1994).

Steensgaard, Niels. "The growth and composition of the long-distance trade of England and the Dutch Republic before 1750," in Tracy (ed.), *The Rise of Merchant Empires.*

Stewart-Brown, R. *Liverpool Ships in the Eighteenth Century* (London: University of Liverpool Press, 1932).

Sutherland, Lucy Stuart. *A London Merchant, 1695–1774* (London: Oxford University Press, 1933).

Szostak, Rick. *The Role of Transportation in the Industrial Revolution: A Comparison of England and France* (Montreal & Kingston: McGill-Queen's University Press, 1991).

Tai, Hung-chao (ed.), *Confucianism and Economic Development: An Oriental Alternative?* (Washington, D.C.: The Washington Institute Press, 1989).

Tepaske, John J. "New World Silver, Castile and the Philippines, 1590–1800," in J. F. Richards (ed.), *Precious Metals in the Later Medieval and Early Modern Worlds* (Durham, NC: Carolina Academic Press, 1983).

The South in the Building of the Nation, 12 volumes, Vol. 5 (Richmond, Virginia: The Southern Historical Publication Society, 1909).

Thirsk, Joan. "Introduction," in Joan Thirsk (ed.), *The Agrarian History of England and Wales: Volume IV, 1500–1640* (Cambridge: Cambridge University Press, 1967).

   Economic Policy and Projects: The Development of a Consumer Society in Early Modern England (Oxford: Clarendon Press, 1978).

Thomas, Robert Paul. "The Sugar Colonies of the Old Empire: Profit or Loss for Great Britain?" *Economic History Review*, 2d ser. 21 (April 1968).

Thomas, Robert Paul and Richard Nelson Bean, "The Fishers of Men: The Profits of the Slave Trade," *Journal of Economic History*, 34 (Dec. 1974).

Thomas, P. J. *Mercantilism and the East India Trade: An Early Phase of the Protection v. Free Trade Controversy* (London: P. S. King, 1926).

Thornton, John. *Africa and Africans in the making of the Atlantic World, 1400–1680* (New York: Cambridge University Press, 1992).

Timmins, Geoffrey. *The Last Shift: The Decline of Handloom Weaving in Nineteenth-Century Lancashire* (Manchester: Manchester University Press, 1993).

   Made in Lancashire: A History of Regional Industrialisation (Manchester and New York: Manchester University Press, 1998).

Toynbee, Arnold. *Lectures on the Industrial Revolution of the Eighteenth Century in England: Popular Addresses, Notes, and other Fragments* (London: Longmans, 1884).

Trevor-Roper, H. R. *Religion, the Reformation and Social Change, and Other Essays* (second edition, London: Macmillan, 1972).

Tuck, J. A. "The Occupation of the Land: The Northern Borders," in Miller (ed.), *Agrarian History.*

Tupling, G. H. "The early metal Trades and the beginning of Engineering in Lancashire," *Transactions of the Lancashire and Cheshire Antiquarian Society*, Vol. LXI (1949).

Turnbull, Gerard. "Canals, coal and regional growth during the industrial revolution," *Economic History Review*, 2nd ser., XL, 4 (1987).

Vansina, Jan. *Paths in the Rainforests: Toward A History of Political Tradition in Equatorial Africa* (London: James Currey, 1990).

Verger, Pierre. *Trade Relations between the Bight of Benin and Bahia from the 17th to 19th Century* (Translation by Evelyn Crawford; Ibadan: University of Ibadan Press, 1976).

Vila, Enriqueta. "The Large-scale Introduction of Africans into Veracruz and Cartagena," in Vera Rubin and Arthur Tuden (eds.), *Comparative Perspectives on Slavery in New World Plantation Societies* (New York: New York Academy of Sciences, 1977).

Wadsworth, A. P. and J. de L. Mann, *The Cotton Trade and Industrial Lancashire* (Manchester: Manchester University Press, 1931).

Wallerstein, Immanuel. *The Modern World System I: Capitalist Agriculture and the Origins of the European World Economy in the Sixteenth Century* (New York: Academic Press, 1974).

"Failed Transitions or Inevitable Decline of the Leader?: The Workings of the Capitalist World-Economy: General Comments," in Krantz and Hohenberg (eds.), *Failed Transitions*.

The Modern World System II: Mercantilism and the Consolidation of the European World-Economy, 1600–1750 (New York: Academic Press, 1980).

The Modern World System III: The Second Era of Great Expansion of the Capitalist World-Economy, 1734–1840s (New York: Academic Press, 1989).

Walton, Gary M. and James F. Shepherd, *The economic rise of early America* (Cambridge: Cambridge University, 1979).

Walton, John K. *Lancashire: A Social History, 1558–1939* (Manchester: Manchester University Press, 1987).

"Proto-industrialisation and the first industrial revolution: the case of Lancashire," in Hudson (ed.), *Regions and Industries*.

Ward, J. R. "The Profitability of Sugar Planting in the British West Indies, 1650–1834," *Economic History Review*, 2d ser. 31 (May, 1978).

Poverty and Progress in the Caribbean, 1800–1960 (London: Macmillan, 1985).

Warren, Bill. *Imperialism: Pioneer of Capitalism*, Edited by John Sender (London: Verso, 1980).

Watts, David. *The West Indies: Patterns of Development, Culture and Environmental Change since 1492* (Cambridge: Cambridge University Press, 1987).

West, Robert C. *Colonial Placer Mining in Colombia* (Baton Rouge: Louisiana State University Press, 1952).

The Pacific Lowlands of Colombia: A Negroid Area of the American Tropics (Baton Rouge: Louisiana State University Press, 1957).

Wilkins, Mira. *The History of Foreign Investment in the United States to 1914* (Cambridge, Mass.: Harvard University Press, 1989).

Williams, Wilson E. "Africa and the Rise of Capitalism" (Master's thesis, Howard University, 1936).

Williams, Eric. *Capitalism and Slavery* (Chapel Hill: University of North Carolina Press, 1944).

Williams, John H. "The Theory of International Trade Reconsidered," *The Economic Journal*, Vol. XXXIX (June, 1929).

Williams, Gomer. *History of the Liverpool Privateers and Letters of Marque with an account of the Liverpool Slave Trade* (London, 1897).

Wilson, R. G. "The Supremacy of the Yorkshire Cloth Industry in the Eighteenth Century," in N. B. Hart and K. G. Ponting (eds.), *Textile History and Economic History: Essays in Honour of Miss Julia de Lacy Mann* (Manchester: Manchester University Press, 1973).

Wilson, Charles. *Profit and Power: A Study of England and the Dutch Wars* (London: Martinus Nijhoff, 1978).

"Trade, Society and the State," in E. E. Rich and C. H. Wilson (eds.), *The Cambridge Economic History of Europe, Volume IV: The Economy of Expanding Europe in the sixteenth and seventeenth centuries* (Cambridge: Cambridge University Press, 1967).

Wordie, J. R. "The Chronology of English Enclosure, 1500–1914," *Economic History Review*, 2nd series, XXXVI, No. 4 (1983).

Wrigley, E. A. "The Growth of Population in eighteenth-century England: A Conundrum Resolved," *Past and Present*, No. 98, February, 1983.

Wrigley, E. A. and R. S. Schofield, *The Population History of England, 1541–1871: A Recon-struction* (Cambridge: Cambridge University Press, 1986).

Wrigley, E. A. *Continuity, Chance and Change: The Character of the Industrial Revolution in England* (Cambridge: Cambridge University Press, 1988).

Yelling, J. A. *Common Field and Enclosure in England, 1450–1850* (London: Macmillan, 1977).

Zook, George F. "The Company of Royal Adventurers of England Trading into Africa, 1660–1672," *Journal of Negro History*, Vol. IV, No. 1 (January, 1919).

Index

Printed in the United Kingdom
by Lightning Source UK Ltd.
131868UK00001B/95/A